A FREE NATION DEEP IN DEBT

A FREE NATION DEEP IN DEBT

THE FINANCIAL ROOTS OF DEMOCRACY

JAMES MACDONALD

PRINCETON UNIVERSITY PRESS

PRINCETON AND OXFORD

Published by Princeton University Press, 41 William Street, Princeton, New Jersey 08540

First published in hardcover by Farrar, Straus and Giroux, 19 Union Square West, New York, New York 10003

First Princeton edition, 2006

Library of Congress Cataloging-in-Publication Data

Macdonald, James.
A free nation deep in debt : the financial roots of democracy / James Macdonald.
p. cm.
Originally published: New York : Farrar, Straus & Giroux, 2003.
Includes bibliographical references and index.
ISBN-13: 978-0-691-12632-6 (pb : alk. paper)
ISBN-10: 0-691-12632-1 (pb : alk. paper)
1. Debts, Public—History. 2. Democracy—Economic aspects. 3. Political science—Economic aspects. I. Title.
HJ8011.M27 2006
336.3′4—dc22
2005058699

British Library Cataloging-in-Publication Data is available

This book has been composed in Bodoni

Printed on acid-free paper. ∞

pup.princeton.edu

Printed in the United States of America

1 3 5 7 9 10 8 6 4 2

For Mollie, Robbie, and Claire

CONTENTS

A FREE NATION DEEP IN DEBT

INTRODUCTION: THE FINANCIAL ROOTS OF DEMOCRACY

> No Man whatever having lent his Money to the Government on the Credit of a Parliamentary Fund has been Defrauded of his Property. . . . The Goodness of the Publick Credit in England, is the reason why we shall never be out of Debt. . . . Let us be, say I, a free Nation deep in Debt, rather than a Nation of Slaves owing Nothing.[1]

The author of these words, an anonymous English pamphleteer writing in 1719, was expressing an idea that was just starting to take hold—that there was a connection between political freedom and public debt. The idea gained ground in the following decades, and one hundred years later it had become almost a commonplace. In 1815, a French Minister of Finance could state simply that "liberty and credit are always united."[2] By that time, France had suffered a century of military defeats, political revolutions, and counterrevolutions as it attempted to come to grips with this political insight.

Nowadays the idea of a link between public debt and democracy comes as an initial surprise to almost everyone to whom I have expressed it. The connection has been lost for reasons that will become apparent by the end of the book. However, the thread has been taken up by some recent historians seeking to explain the very questions that challenged eighteenth-century thinkers: Was the necessity of borrowing vast sums of money to finance the ever-increasing cost of war altering the political landscape? Was it perhaps England's parliamentary government that explained the country's astonishing ability to outborrow and outspend France in spite of having a population less than half the size? One high-ranking French official, writing in 1774, worried that this was indeed the case: "If people believe [Louis XVI] to be a despot it will be impossible to open loans, or, if that route is taken, they will be so costly that England will always finish by having the last *écu* in any war."[3]

That the rise of the bond market had irrevocably changed the political arithmetic was dramatically demonstrated in August 1788, when the Bourbon government of France was forced to declare bankruptcy, and then found itself obliged to summon the Estates General as the only way to escape from its financial predicament. The bankruptcy of August 1788 ushered in the Revolution of 1789. The history of public finance therefore provides a crucial perspective on one of the most important questions of our times—the rise of democracy.

In recent decades this rise has started to appear almost unstoppable. However, it was not always so. Indeed, for most of recorded history it would have appeared absurd to predict the long-term success of democratic government at all. The history of the world showed that the most sophisticated and advanced societies had invariably been headed by emperors, not elected officials. Apart from a few brief historical moments, such as Athens in the fourth and fifth centuries B.C., civilization and autocratic rule appeared to go hand in hand. Furthermore, it seemed that democratic government could only be practiced in small, intimate societies, such as city-states, whose existence was always threatened by larger and more powerful empires. Even if a city-state managed, like the Roman Republic, to circumvent the risk of being conquered by conquering others, this would lead to insurmountable political tensions that could only be resolved by one-man rule. Only a lunatic or a clairvoyant would have forecast that the day would come when the world's most advanced and most powerful states would be democracies.

The inevitable question is, Why is democracy taking on the appearance of an unstoppable force now, when it appeared doomed to the margins of the civilized world for so long? The standard explanation centers on the Industrial Revolution and the dramatic increase in economic development that has occurred in its wake. High levels of technology require an educated workforce, and a high-output economy requires wealthy consumers. These parallel forces push inexorably toward mass participation in politics; and it seems that above a certain level of income per capita it is hard to prevent democracy from taking root even in autocratic societies. Conversely, societies that insist on retaining rigid state control are unable to advance economically beyond a certain point.

I do not seek to challenge or dismiss this line of reasoning, which is undoubtedly valid as far as it goes. However, such arguments can only address the modern world. The requirements of an advanced economy cannot explain the English, American, or French Revolutions—the three seminal events of the rise of modern democracy. After all, these countries were still at "Third World" levels of development.

This is where the history of war finance enters the picture. Once wars could only be financed by borrowing, the outlook for autocracy dimmed. But even the rise of the bond market in eighteenth-century Europe leaves two crucial questions unanswered. First, where did public borrowing and bond markets come from? Are they a purely fortuitous development, a *deus ex machina* in the political life of the planet? Is it merely a coincidence that they first emerged in Europe, the same continent that gave birth to the democratic revolutions of the seventeenth and eighteenth centuries?

Second, what about earlier examples of democratic government, such as the republics of the ancient world? Their existence certainly cannot be ascribed to high levels of income per capita, nor can it be attributed to the workings of sophisticated financial markets. Are they, therefore, entirely unconnected to modern democratic states? This was not the view of seventeenth- and eighteenth-century political philosophers. They looked back to ancient liberties that had been enjoyed not only by the city-states of classical Greece, but by primitive peoples everywhere before the rise of the state. Political freedom, in their view, was a primeval birthright that had been usurped by kings and emperors (an argument most memorably expressed by Jean-Jacques Rousseau: "Man was born free, but is everywhere in chains"). Countries where liberty reigned, such as England and Holland, had merely fought back against royal usurpations more successfully; and it was up to other nations to do the same if they wished to recover their freedom.

These ideas have fallen out of favor. Although anthropologists may agree that tribal life is indeed characterized by an absence of autocratic state power, few, if any, political theorists or historians are willing to see a direct chain of descent from such primitive freedom to modern democratic constitutions.* Moreover, if the rise of modern democracy is attributable to economic development, then it makes little sense to delve into the ancient world.

This book, however, takes a different path. It looks back centuries, even millennia, before the events of the eighteenth century and comes up with some surprising conclusions.

First, the origins of public debt. Nowadays the bond market is seen as an impersonal, almost superhuman force that responds only to the laws of economics and that passes harsh judgment on the shortcomings of human

---

*Semantically, however, the chain still exists—an inheritance from the eighteenth century. It is enshrined in the word *Senate*—taken from the venerable Roman institution that started out as the council of elders of the Roman tribe, and whose root is the word *senex*, or "old."

politics—favoring those forms of government that are most likely to ensure that debts are paid promptly, without any special preference for one system or another. However, a study of history reveals a different story. Public borrowing is not politically neutral, but has a particularly intimate relationship with democracy. It is no coincidence that public borrowing and parliamentary government both originated in Europe. For the bond market was not a *deus ex machina*; it was the product of the quest for political freedom.

The second conclusion is equally surprising. The financial origins of democracy are not to be found in the seventeenth and eighteenth centuries. They can be traced to the earliest recesses of human history.

In order to understand this conclusion, it is necessary to look at the origins of the state. When one does so, it soon becomes clear why the laws of economic efficiency seemed to suggest that the future lay with autocracy, not democracy. It was autocracies who could best concentrate power and wealth in the hands of the state and then use that concentration both for military expansion and for economic development.

There was, however, a potential chink in the economic armor of the great empires. Few states have found it easy to deal with emergencies (especially warfare) merely by raising taxes, because of the economic disruption and political unrest that this can cause. Until quite recently, the solution to this problem was to store up treasure; and states with the greatest ability to accumulate were assumed to have an inherent advantage in the struggle for survival. But the "treasury" solution contained an in-built economic inefficiency. Societies mined precious metals to act as currency at enormous economic cost. They then proceeded to hoard these same metals for a rainy day in a process that was tantamount to mining in reverse. (The Persian Empire, possibly the greatest hoarder of the ancient world, actually melted down its gold again before burial underground, making the analogy quite literal.) It is not difficult to see the superiority of a system that allowed this hard-earned wealth to circulate in the general economy, to be tapped only insofar as necessary. Hence the economic utility of public debt.

To state that public borrowing is a superior method of dealing with emergencies is not sufficient to explain its existence. With the benefit of hindsight, public borrowing may have the appearance of inevitability; but from a historical perspective, it was not an obvious development. Where did the idea come from? The great states of the ancient world were conspicuous for their ability to store up surpluses (take the story of Joseph in Egypt, for example), but public borrowing was an entirely alien concept. Why would a pharaoh, a god in human form with the power to compel his subjects to build veritable mountains of stone to house his mortal remains, think of borrowing? Whatever he needed was his by right.

What was required was an alternative form of government in which public borrowing was an organic growth. Only then was it conceivable that public debt might flower into a force sufficiently powerful to change the world. The thesis of this book is that the alternative form of government was democracy. Not the democracy that has become familiar since the political revolutions of the eighteenth century, but precisely those earlier forms of democracy whose existence cannot be explained by high levels of income per capita.*

What was the crucial element that made public borrowing natural in democracies, but unnatural in autocracies? The standard explanation for the superior creditworthiness of constitutional governments is that they are limited by law and therefore make more trustworthy counterparts for the private individuals who lend them money. However, this explanation does not answer the question of whether public borrowing is in some way *indigenous* to democracy. The true answer lies in the identity of borrowers and lenders. Divine, or semidivine, autocrats are unlikely to perceive lenders as their equals. In democracies, the opposite is true. As long as the state borrows from its citizens, there is no divergence of interest between borrower and lenders, for the two are one and the same. This is a far more powerful reason for the inherent creditworthiness of democracies than mere constitutional constraint. But it is important to note that the argument holds good only for domestic borrowing—when the lenders are citizens. The argument does not apply to external borrowing. A democracy may have a natural inclination to respect the rules of credit when dealing with foreign creditors, because democracies are, on the whole, readier than autocracies to adapt to the purely economic logic of credit markets. But it was not the ability to borrow abroad that counted in the struggle between rival forms of government. It was above all the symbiosis of borrowers and lenders inherent in domestic borrowing that turned public debt into a powerful weapon capable of upsetting the long-term advantage of autocratic government.

While, on one level, then, this book deals with the hard facts of money and credit markets, its underlying motif is the relationship of the state with

---

*It is often argued that nothing short of universal adult suffrage qualifies as true democracy. By this standard, most forms of government before the twentieth century fall short. For the purposes of this book, however, governments are allowed to be essentially democratic as long as they are controlled and run by their citizens through a process of voting, even if the citizens form only part of the population. For it is the element of citizen control that separates such governments most crucially from autocratic rule.

its citizens. Its hero is the citizen creditor—a subspecies of *Homo sapiens* not hitherto recognized or given his due. Indeed the role of the citizen creditor in history did not end in 1789. In many ways, his greatest days were in the twentieth century, not the eighteenth.

But there remains a further mystery. Public borrowing may be a form of public finance naturally suited to democratic government; but where did the idea first come from? The answer is that it always existed in nascent form within the simple customs of primitive tribes. These customs may seem very distant from the complex paraphernalia of modern government, but they contain within them the financial roots of political freedom. This book uncovers a chain of descent that links tribal financial practices to modern public debts; and this leads to an intriguing reflection. The political philosophers of the seventeenth and eighteenth centuries sought the roots of democracy in the political customs of their tribal ancestors. Their views have often been dismissed as unhistorical wishful thinking. But it now seems that the ideas of the old philosophers may have contained an element of truth. Political liberty may have descended from tribal customs—but for hitherto unsuspected reasons.

The first chapter of the book traces the story of public finance and political freedom from the end of the Bronze Age to the end of the Dark Ages. The outer boundaries of this field of vision are not chosen by chance. For the possibility of a challenge of any sort to the apparently unstoppable tide of autocracy lay in a cyclical pattern of world history in which great civilizations were slowly built up, and then disrupted by waves of "barbarian" invasion. These invasions allowed the periodic reintroduction of tribal customs into the historical mix before the tide resumed its advance. The story starts with the first of these great waves, which marked the end of the Bronze Age, and which introduced into the historical landscape many of the peoples who later dominated the era of classical antiquity. It ends with the second of these waves, which heralded the end of that era, and which, crucially, had effects that were more profound and lasting in Western Europe than elsewhere.

The book then moves to medieval Europe. Although the roots of democratic public finance can be traced to the ancient world, the examples of public borrowing to be found there amounted to no more than tantalizing experiments that came to an end with the rise of the Roman Empire. It was the role of the city-states of medieval Italy to resurrect the idea and transform it into a viable financial strategy. The system that they created, although in one way fatally flawed, set off a chain of events with results that no one could have predicted.

The following several chapters of the book describe the attempts of the states of Europe to come to terms with the implications of the Italian invention. On one level, the question they faced appeared to be purely technical: How could the exhilarating freedom of borrowing be reconciled with the dull constraints of solvency? But there was a second question of equal importance, without which there could be no defininitive answer to the first: Were the benefits of public borrowing available to states that did not enjoy the symbiosis between borrowers and lenders of the Italian cities? The answer to this question was finally delivered in August 1788 when the Bourbon monarchy threw in the towel, admitting bankruptcy and agreeing to recall the Estates General, the parliamentary institution that it thought it had consigned to the history books nearly two hundred years earlier.

The final section of the book looks at the events that followed the French Revolution. The outcome of the Napoleonic Wars demonstrated the superiority of a political system based on the alliance of parliamentary government and public debt, but now there was a new question: Would a system created in a world where participation in politics was confined to those with property prove compatible with universal suffrage? For the story of public debt and political freedom is interwoven with a parallel theme: the story of public debt and class warfare. Public borrowing may have represented political freedom—but whose freedom? Only that of the wealthy who had money to lend? It was the role of the nineteenth century to find a solution to this problem. In the devastating wars of the first half of the twentieth century, this solution was put to the test. The First World War was the apotheosis of "democratic" public finance, the Second its swan song.

One final introductory comment: Although the book is, on one level, about politics, it necessarily deals with the other side of public credit: the logic of the market. The lay reader can rest assured, however, that the financial jargon has been kept to a minimum, and the critical terms (none of which are very complicated) are explained as they occur. A glossary is also provided at the end of the book. Inevitably, in covering several millennia of history, I refer to a number of different currencies. A detailed appendix describes them and sets out their relationships in historical context.

ONE

TRIBES AND EMPIRES

And the Children of Israel took all the women of Midian captives, and their little ones, and took the spoil of all their cattle, and all their flocks, and all their goods. . . . And the LORD spake unto Moses, saying, Take the prey that was taken, both of man and beast, thou and Eleazar the priest, and the chief fathers of the congregation: and divide the prey into two parts; between them that took the war upon them, who went out to battle, and between all the congregation.

—Numbers 31:9, 25–27

RAGS TO RICHES

It can never be wrong to start a book with a quotation from the Bible; and yet the reader might reasonably ask what, if anything, this passage has to do with the relationship between public debt and democracy. The Israelites had progressed beyond the stage of an extended family and had reached the relative political maturity of a network of related clans requiring at least a minimal form of government. Yet they had no money, no trade, no public revenue, and most certainly no central bank or financial markets. Still, in the books that separate Moses from Solomon, the Israelites can be seen progressing from a tribe of nomads to an established kingdom with significant, if short-lived, regional power in a transformation that can teach us much about the process of state formation.

The destruction of the Midianites was a small act in this drawn-out, and often agonizing, drama. But in this episode, the Bible gives explicit detail about one of the most important aspects of primitive public finance: the division of spoils. God's instructions covered not only the division between combatants and noncombatants, but also the portion due as a sacrifice, and the portion due to the priestly caste of Levites. God was to receive 0.2% of the warriors' half: "one soul of five hundred both of the persons, and of the beeves [cattle] and of the asses, and of the sheep." The Levites were to receive 2% of the remainder: "one portion of fifty, of the persons, of the beeves, of the asses, and of the flocks." This was, therefore, an egalitarian apportionment, with only minimal amounts set aside for religious purposes. No booty was retained by "the state" for the simple reason that the Israelites did not yet have one.

Thus far the division covered only the "productive" assets—the livestock and virgins. The men and boys had been slaughtered wholesale, as had the women "who had known men by lying with them." The unproductive assets—precious metals and ornaments—had been taken directly by the warriors, mostly stripped from the bodies of the dead Midianites. These were now brought to Moses by the officers of the host:

> We have therefore brought an oblation for the LORD, what every man hath gotten, of jewels of gold, chains, and bracelets, rings, earrings and tablets, to make an atonement for our souls before the LORD. . . . And Moses and Eleazar the priest took the gold of the captains of thousands and of hundreds, and brought it unto the tabernacle of the congregation, for a memorial for the children of Israel before the LORD.*

In theory, these spoils, too, were offered to God. But unlike his share of the livestock, they were not to be burned as a sacrifice, but to be stored as a permanent public treasure. Here, then, is the first sign of the fiscal dichotomy at the heart of this book. Are the interests of the group best served by creating a store of surplus assets against a rainy day, or by leaving all assets in the hands of the people? The Israelites here took one of the seminal steps in state formation: the establishment of a treasury. But, significantly, they resolved the dichotomy by leaving the productive assets in the hands of the people, and by placing only the unproductive ones (in a premonetary age) in the relative safety of a central store.

The road from nomadism to statehood involves far more than the establishment of a treasury. The main thrust of the process involves the gradual transformation of the minimal institutions of tribal society into an organiza-

---

*The Bible is remarkably exact about quantities. The gold taken weighed 139 kilograms (306 pounds), worth about $2 million at $400 per ounce (but far more in terms of its purchasing power in the second millennium B.C.). The live spoil consisted of 675,000 sheep, 72,000 cattle, 70,000 donkeys, and 32,000 virgins. The scale of the "ethnic cleansing" implied by the number of the female survivors is hard to contemplate with equanimity—even if the figures are exaggerated.

tion with sufficient power to direct the life of a larger and more articulated society. The surviving evidence from ancient, preliterate societies is scanty, but the story told in the Bible can be fleshed out by historical records and by the research of anthropologists.

Primitive societies appear to operate with forms of government so minimal that they are sometimes referred to, rather alarmingly to laymens' ears, as "acephalous" (headless). Such societies may have leaders with religious, judicial, or military roles, but these leaders have very little coercive power. Communal decisions are most often taken by a council of elders, sometimes with the participation of the whole adult male population in a general assembly. In the society of the Lapps of northern Scandinavia, for instance, "Internal affairs are managed by what some writers have called a council. Since this includes in its body the heads of every family, the term 'council' is in fact somewhat misleading in its connotation of formal organization and delegation of power. Group decisions are actually the collective responsibility of the adult male population as a whole."[1]

In certain African societies the tacit acceptance of unofficial, but powerless, leaders allows the tribesmen to avoid accepting even the authority of a general assembly. One such people are the Nuer:

> What the "bull" [unofficial leader] gets out of his position is another question. No Nuer will let another address an order to him. The leadership of the "bull" is recognized only in the sense that people wait for him to give a lead. . . . The people in a Nuer camp do not discuss and reach a decision. They wait till the leading man moves and then follow when it suits them.[2]

Apart from the "bulls," the Nuer have a "leopard-skin chief," whose role is to assist in the resolution of blood feuds. The role of judicial arbiter is found in so many primitive societies that as a general rule, it may be said that "judging is thought of as the first duty of a ruler."*[3] The apparent anarchy displayed by a lack of formal political structure does not imply lawlessness. Obedience by all (including tribal leaders) to a commonly accepted body of immutable law is, on the contrary, one of the greatest protections of primitive peoples from the dangers of a state with legislative autonomy.

---

*Very often it was the only duty, as is delightfully shown by the weekly schedule of an Irish chieftain of the eighth century A.D. as set out in a surviving legal text: Monday was for settling disputes between villages; Tuesday for board games; Wednesday for following hounds; Thursday for marital intercourse; Friday for horse racing; Saturday for judging individual cases; and Sunday for beer drinking. (A. J. Duggan, ed., *Kings and Kingship in Medieval Europe*, London, 1993, p. 101)

The Israelites at the time of their arrival in the Promised Land were not quite as anarchic as the Nuer (although their persistent disobedience is one of the main themes of the Bible). The authority of the elders and of the whole congregation was shared informally with religious/judicial figures, such as Moses and Samuel, and ad hoc military commanders, such as Joshua and Gideon. The power of these leaders was circumscribed and limited by immutable religious law. When the Israelites offered the throne to Gideon, he rebuked them for blasphemy: "I will not rule over you, nor shall my son rule over you; the LORD shall rule over you."[4]

The Israelites arrived in the Promised Land around the thirteenth century B.C. But there is evidence that similar types of tribal organization may have preceded the very earliest civilizations on record. In the Sumerian city-states of the third millennium B.C., there is sufficient evidence of government by elected kings, in tandem with councils of elders and assemblies, to suggest "that prehistoric Mesopotamia was organized politically along democratic lines, not, as was historic Mesopotamia, along autocratic [ones]."[5]

Apart from their appealing lack of coercive political structures, another characteristic of primitive societies that has often excited the wistful envy of the civilized is their failure to produce an economic surplus. If the society is not living in a particularly inhospitable climate, this absence is not generally the result of inadequate technological development. The tribal members simply prefer to work fewer hours per day—as few as three to four under ideal conditions—and to enjoy the rest of their time. The wearisome exhortations of politicians and economists to increase savings and reduce consumption have no place in their counsels. Some anthropologists have accordingly referred to primitive peoples as the "first leisure societies." Not surprisingly, then, the first act of statehood is to build up a disposable, or storable, surplus. The principle means by which this is achieved is only too familiar to modern readers: taxation.

Yet the transition to taxation is not as simple as it might seem. Why would these happy, leisured tribesmen wish to create a state that will force them to work harder in order to create a taxable surplus? In many cases they do not. Such a state is forced upon them by conquest.[6] That this is certainly the case will be amply demonstrated throughout this book; but force cannot account for all instances of state formation. A large number of societies have moved toward a more powerful form of government without coercion.

In unconquered societies, taxation evolves out of a primitive mode of exchange in the form of gifts. Such gift exchange predates, and is the parent of, every other form of exchange, whether it is barter and credit, or taxation and expenditure. Chiefs of primitive societies generally receive gifts* from the members of the tribe, but they come with strings attached. As the French anthropoligist Marcel Mauss wrote in his seminal 1925 study, *The Gift*: "In theory such gifts are voluntary, but in practice they are given and repaid under obligation."[7] The chief must somehow redistribute his wealth to the people. The Caraja of South America, like many polygamous tribes, grant extra wives to their chief; but this "most unreciprocal acquisition of multiple wives puts him in a condition of perpetual indebtedness to his people, so that he must become their servant."[8] The chief is obliged to give regular feasts at which he must entertain the people with his oratory. Chiefs may appear wealthy, but the obligation to reciprocate makes their riches illusory.

The rise to power of kings is aided, therefore, by the fact that they already receive regular gifts. The challenge is to transform their gift revenues, with their implicit reciprocity, into tax revenues with no, or at least fewer, strings attached. They must also lay claim to an ever greater portion of irregular surpluses such as war booty. The emerging Hebrew state did both. When the people clamored for a king, Samuel warned them of the implications of their decision:

> This will be the manner of the king that will reign over you. . . . He will take a tenth of your seed, and of your vineyards, and give them to his officers, and to his servants. . . . He will take a tenth of your flocks: and you shall be his servants. And you shall cry out in that day because of your king which ye shall have chosen you; and the LORD will not answer you in that day.[9]

It is thus not surprising to find that when the question of division of the spoils next crops up in the Bible, David takes a rather different line from Moses. During his reign, the Amalekites made a major cattle and slave raid on both the Israelites and the Philistines. David pursued them, put them to flight, and "took all the flocks and the herds which they drove before those other cattle, and said, This is David's spoil."[10]

The passage is not entirely clear, but since David insisted that the spoils taken from Hebrew households be returned to their owners, it is likely that he was laying claim to all the plunder originally taken from the

*Before they become taxes, these gifts are usually referred to as *tribute*—a term of profound ambivalence, its meaning hovering between "gift" and "forcible exaction."

Philistines. And while it is true that David subsequently made a number of gifts to the elders of Judah, the story is a measure of the political changes that had occurred since the exodus from Egypt. It is simply not conceivable that Moses would have said, "This is Moses' spoil."

Why would the Israelites have wished to abandon their old tribal constitution? The Bible gives us three reasons.

> But the people refused to hearken unto the voice of Samuel; and they said, Nay: but we will have a king over us; so that we may be like all the nations; and that our king may judge us, and go out before us, and fight our battles.[11]

The Israelites were aware of being surrounded by more politically advanced nations, and they wished to imitate them as a reflection of their growing regional power. More significantly, perhaps, they wished to unite the roles of judge and general into one supreme hereditary office. Earlier they had already offered the kingdom to Gideon in gratitude for his generalship, but he had turned them down. Now there was a new incentive: a vacuum in the system of justice. Samuel was old, and his sons "turned aside after lucre, and took bribes, and perverted judgement." It was on a law-and-order issue that the political revolution was finally effected.

The Bible is not the only source that recounts such transitions. Herodotus, the "father of history," writing several centuries later, tells a remarkably similar story about the Medes:

> Deïoces was already a person of some standing in his village (the Medes used to live in village communities). . . . There was, at the time, considerable lawlessness throughout Media. . . . The Medes from his village . . . appointed him a judge, and . . . his conduct earned him a great deal of praise from his fellow citizens. . . .
>
> [Deïoces then craftily refused to judge any more, and lawlessness returned] . . . The Medes considered what action to take under the circumstances. I suspect that Deïoces' supporters played a major part in this debate. "The country is ungovernable," they said, "on our current system, so let us make one of us king. . . ." They were immediately faced with the question of whom to appoint as king. Everyone was full of praise for Deïoces and wholeheartedly supported his nomination, until at length they agreed that he should be their king.[12]

The consequences of these actions could have been predicted by Samuel. Deïoces immediately ordered the Medes to build him "a palace fit for a king, and to assign him personal guards for his protection." The palace was then surrounded by seven circles of walls to protect the king and, significantly, the royal treasuries. Deïoces then withdrew into regal isolation and instituted a complex protocol of behavior to dignify his position.

The transition from tribal to monarchic rule, then, is partly the result of a yearning for law and order; but it is also a necessary passage in the development of military muscle. For both the Israelites and the Medes, it was the precursor of the establishment of regional empires. The king collects taxes that he can use to pay his armies and can store up in his treasury as emergency finance. The equation of political centralization and military power was clearly visible to European explorers of nineteenth-century Africa and Polynesia. The tax-gathering Tutsi kingdoms in Uganda and Rwanda clearly had greater military resources than the "primitive" tribal structures of Kenya. The Polynesian kingdoms in Tonga, Hawaii, and Fiji offered more serious resistance to the European advance than the more simple and egalitarian tribes of Melanesia. In her study of the Tutsi kingdoms of Africa, Lucy Mair concluded (she could equally well have been discussing the Israelites, Medes, Tongans, or any other society):

> We begin to see already how important it is for the building up of kingship that the society should have some surplus of wealth which can be concentrated in the hands of the ruler and used for the purposes of state.[13]

Power, therefore, lies in disposable surplus. But the process of state building did not stop at mere military sufficiency. The redistributive cycle implicit in the chiefly practice of gift exchange could be, and was, extended into far-reaching powers of economic management in the most sophisticated and evolved civilizations. The public storehouses of the early empires contained not only "financial assets" such as precious metals, ornaments, and jewels, but grain and other consumption goods. They were filled by taxes on agricultural production that ranged from 10% to as high as 50%. Their contents served as a mechanism of supply regulation, as a buffer against famine, and as a food store for the substantial portion of the population that lived directly off state rations. Among the recipients of these rations were those conscripted into the annual labor levies that amplified the public revenues by allowing large-scale construction projects such as the irrigation works that characterized the most advanced and populous civilizations—not to mention the awe-inspiring funerary monuments of their rulers.

All the great Bronze Age civilizations depended on a system of state granaries. The story of Joseph has made us familiar with the workings and scale of the pharaoh's grain stores. Similar storehouses existed in Mesopotamia, Minoa, Mycenae, and China. In the Indus valley civilizations of Mohenjo-daro and Harappa, "the granaries were replenished by a system of state-tribute, and in some measure they fulfilled in the state economy the function of the modern state-bank or treasury. In a moneyless age, their condition at any given moment must have reflected, however partially, the national credit and the efficiency or good fortune of the administration."[14]

It is here that we get to the nub of the issue. If the public storehouses "reflected the national credit," it was not in the way that we now understand, for the state was not a borrower. It was a lender.

At first glance, it might seem that credit could not develop in the absence of money. In fact, the opposite is true. Recorded credit transactions preceded coined money by around two thousand years, and the evidence suggests that the history of debt must be coterminous with that of civilization. The formalization of lending and repaying probably evolved out of the reciprocity implicit in gift exchange. The adjunct of interest seems to have occurred as a natural outgrowth of settled agriculture. The earliest interest-bearing loans were probably of livestock and later, with the development of cereal farming, of grain. The concept of interest would have suggested itself naturally as part of the reproductive processes of nature. The loan of livestock would be repaid by the return of the animals together with a portion of their offspring born in the intervening period. This concept is shown most vividly by the Sumerian word for interest—*mas*—which means "calves." The ancient Mesopotamians had no trouble extending this principle of reproduction of borrowed capital, first to grain, where the repayment with interest would come from the harvest, and then to precious metals. The medieval condemnation of usury on the grounds of the infertility of inanimate objects would have been rejected as mere pedantry and lack of imagination by the Mesopotamians.

The state granaries did not merely distribute food in time of famine but also acted as seed banks for the annual growing cycle. The earliest records of interest rates that have come down to us are those of seed loans from the state and temple granaries of Mesopotamia, repayable out of the following harvest. The first thing that impresses us is that these rates were, by modern standards, extremely high. The norm in the Sumerian period appears to have been 33.3% per year, a rate that was then codified as a legal maximum by the Babylonian ruler Hammurabi. In Assyria, the rates were, if anything, higher, and 50% per year would not have been unusual.[15]

Ancient Egypt was almost entirely without money or credit, but a series of interest rates for state lending extending over two millennia has survived from China, with rates ranging from 26% for silver to 150% for grain. The longevity of the practice is demonstrated by the fact that in 1933 China's Central Bureau of Agricultural Experimentation was still charging 34% for money and 85.2% for grain.[16]

Interest rates at these levels were in part a reflection of the lack of credit in financially undeveloped societies. It is obvious that there could be no long-term debt at such rates. If loans were not repaid out of the next reproductive cycle, the only plausible outcome was default. But the significance of these rates goes beyond this. The portion of the harvest that they represented was so high that they have to be considered a form of ancillary taxation—an addition to the already substantial revenues available to the state. They have to be seen in the context of a process of state formation that seemed to lead inexorably toward ever more powerful forms of government.

Compared to tribal societies and their primitive democratic egalitarianism, the big empires seemed to hold all the trumps. Their rulers were legitimized by divine, or semidivine, status. Their powers of economic management encouraged increased agricultural production via irrigation and thereby permitted greater population density. The size of these empires and the ample revenues of their rulers allowed them to maintain armies that no primitive tribe could rival. The extensive public treasuries and storehouses not only mitigated the vicissitudes of the weather but also provided ample reserves for military emergencies. It seemed that there were only two paths open to the surrounding tribes: to emulate or to be conquered. In either case, the end result would be a form of state that would have no place for public borrowing.

BARBARIANS AT THE GATE

And yet, it was not so simple. The great empires were not invulnerable to destabilizing pressures. Few states could withstand a succession of inept rulers, however divine their status. The unchecked ambitions of local magnates could lead to political fragmentation; and the population at large might even prove to be less than ideally quiescent. Beyond the frontiers, the primitive tribes were often far from the pushovers that they seemed. A period of internal weakness might open the gates to these unwelcome visitors; but just as often, it was large-scale demographic movements quite beyond the control of the civilized empires that created pressure on their frontiers. Toward the end of the Bronze Age, from around 1600 B.C., the ancient world was increasingly disrupted by waves of tribal migrations similar to those that would herald the end of the classical world after A.D. 200. Most of these new arrivals were of Indo-European descent, such as the Aryans, who occupied northern India; the Medes and Persians, who occupied what is now Iran and Afghanistan; the Hittites and later the Lydians in Turkey; the Dorians and Ionians in Greece; and the Etruscans and Latins in Italy. Others were of Semitic origin, such as the Hyksos, who invaded and temporarily ruled Egypt; the Israelites; and the Philistines.

These new arrivals brought with them the institutions (or lack thereof) typical of tribal life. Yet, once established, they seemed inevitably to start down the political path taken by the states they had so rudely disrupted. The early Hittite kingdom had a council of elders that participated in government with the king. There is no mention of such an institution in the later Hittite empire. In Israel the relatively primitive form of kingship represented by Saul and David was followed by the Egyptophilia of Solomon. Not for nothing did he choose to marry the daughter of the pharaoh. The Bible leaves us in no doubt as to the nature of his rule. His horses numbered forty thousand, his chariots twelve thousand. His building projects were so grandiose that they required labor levies to complete. His riches were legendary, and his palace was decorated with gold.

The Persians, who established the largest empire that the world had yet seen, started out on their road to imperial grandeur quite uneducated in the principles of government. Herodotus tells a wonderful tale about Cyrus the Great's education on the principles of treasure formation at the hands of King Croesus of Lydia, the contents of whose treasuries were already the stuff of legend. After the fall of the Lydian capital, Sardis, to the Persian armies, Croesus was dragged before Cyrus—who was surprised when the deposed ruler dared to ask him a question:

> "Should I tell you, my lord, what I have in mind, or must I now keep silent?"
>
> Cyrus replied that he might say what he pleased without fear, so Croesus put another question: "What is it," Croesus asked, "that all those men of yours are so intent upon doing?"
>
> "They are plundering your city and carrying off your treasures."
>
> "Not my city or my treasures," Croesus answered. "Nothing there any longer belongs to me. It is you who they are robbing."
>
> Cyrus thought this over carefully; then he sent away all the company that was present, and asked Croesus what advice he saw fit to give him in the matter.
>
> "Since the gods have made me your slave," Croesus said, "I think it is my

duty, if I have advice worth giving you, not to withhold it. The Persians are proud—too proud; and they are poor. They are ransacking the town, and if you let them get possession of all that wealth you may be sure that which ever of them gets the most will rebel against you. So do what I advise—if you like the advice: put men from your guard on watch at every gate, and when anyone brings out anything of value, let the sentries take it and say that a tenth part of the spoil must be given to Zeus. If you do that, they will not hate you, as they certainly would if you confiscated the things by mere authority."[17]

An apocryphal tale, perhaps; yet once again Herodotus' version of events parallels the political wisdom of the Bible. It is reverence for the gods, whether instinctively felt, or cynically exploited, that first persuades the tribesmen to confer a portion of their hard-earned spoils of victory to a central treasure chest.

Herodotus' tale also illustrates another aspect, hitherto left to one side, of state building. The Persian Empire was not only the largest political unit that the world had yet seen but was also assembled in a mere twenty-five years. State formation of such magnitude and velocity could be accomplished in no other way than by conquest. The empires of the Bronze Age, too, had been formed in the fire of war, especially those of Mesopotamia. The wave of barbarian migrations gave new impetus to the phenomenon. It was now possible, and indeed increasingly normal, to see empires whose rulers were far less civilized, at least at first, than those they ruled.

The laws of ancient warfare were simple: The winner takes all. Not only did the goods and possessions of the defeated pass to the victors; so, too, did their lives. If the vanquished were not actually put to the sword en masse, as was quite often the case, it was purely because such slaughter was not in the victors' interest. Very often only the men might be massacred; the women were spared for breeding purposes, as was the fate of the Midianites. Sometimes the whole people might be taken off into slavery, like the Hebrews to Babylon. If they were surplus to the labor needs of the victors, they might be sold off in the slave markets or, if they were especially lucky, ransomed by some unconquered residue of their conationals. Even if they were allowed to continue living in their native city, their freedom and property were forfeit. When Croesus prefaced his advice to Cyrus with the words "since the gods have made me your slave," he was not using a rhetorical metaphor but simply stating a fact.

The defeated people left in situ were now expected to work for their conquerors. Their surplus production was simply extracted by taxation, which was, in the ancient view of things, slavery by another name. Herodotus makes the connection quite clear:

> Croesus was the first non-Greek of which we know to have subjected Greeks to the payment of tribute, though he made alliances with some of them. . . . Before Croesus's reign, all Greeks were free.[18]

An empire created by conquest was by definition a "despotism," from the Greek word *despotes*, denoting the "master" in the master-slave dyad. And the concept of *freedom* originally meant not a complex series of civil rights, but the easily comprehended state of being unconquered, and therefore not enslaved. Yet, in a world of conquest states of ever-increasing size and vigor, it seemed that the room for this simple freedom was shrinking. If one wished to be truly free, the best solution might be to conquer others. This was certainly the solution of the Spartans, a Dorian tribe that conquered and enslaved the indigenous population of the Peloponnese in the eighth century B.C. It was also the choice that Cyrus put to the Persians when he wished to persuade them to rebel against the Medes. He first ordered the assembled tribesmen to spend a day clearing an area with particularly thorny undergrowth. The following day he invited them to a sumptuous feast. Cyrus then asked the Persians which way they preferred to live, and on receiving the obvious reply, he pointed out that if they conquered the Medes they would be able to live at the expense of others: "So do as I suggest: free yourselves from slavery."[19]

Armed with this clearheaded vision of the ways of the world, the Persians set off and conquered not only the Medes but also the rest of the Middle East, including both the venerable civilizations of Babylonia and Egypt and such relative newcomers as Lydia. Their subjects now paid them tribute as a sign of subjugation. And the Persians, until the time of their own conquest by Alexander, enjoyed the freedom from taxes that was understood to be the privilege of conquerors.

Like other barbarian invaders, the Persians did not need to create an elaborate tax-gathering regime in order to enjoy the fruits of their victories. They were taking over societies—in some cases very ancient and sophisticated societies—that already had the necessary structures in place. Their assertion of the rights of conquest merely removed any residue of primitive reciprocity in the old taxes and completed their transformation into unreciprocal exactions backed up by force. And in addition to the preexisting rights of the displaced indigenous rulers, the new despots could lay claim to ownership of the whole land by right of conquest. In Egypt the pharaohs had already exercised a monopoly of land distribution, and the later Persian and Hellenic regimes merely continued this tradition. The same principle operated in Han China and Mauryan India, and it was taken up by the great Islamic empires from the Abbasid caliphate to the Ottomans and the Moghuls.

Armed with the necessary muscle, both military and juridical, the rulers of the new empires were able to collect revenues by a considerable variety of means; but ultimately it was direct taxes that underlay their wealth and power. The twin progenitors of all direct taxes were the levies that functioned effectively within a moneyless society: crop and livestock taxes payable in kind, and labor levees (the latter an integral part of societies dependent on complex irrigation systems). The advent of coinage in the seventh century B.C. merely created new variations of these ancient themes.*

The monetization of government finances led to a second generation of direct taxes that included poll, income, and wealth taxes. These were largely directed at those parts of the economy that the old taxes could not reach; but the balance varied from empire to empire. In Mauryan India (c. 320–220 B.C.)—as in all later Indian states—heavy crop taxes remained at the center of government finance. The basic rate was one-sixth of production but could go over one half for irrigated land. The Greek ambassador Megasthenes reported that a tax rate of one-fourth was the norm.[20] There were poll taxes and income taxes to cover those not involved in agriculture, including even lowly providers of entertainment like singers, dancers, and prostitutes. In Han China (c. 200 B.C. to A.D. 200), crop taxes were generally a modest one-fifteenth to one-thirtieth of production, and the peasants' main burden was the poll tax—not to mention compulsory unpaid labor of one month per year. The state's fiscal armory also included a comprehensive range of property taxes on all sectors of the population.[21]

The ubiquitous direct taxes by no means exhausted the resources of the great empires. There were extensive revenues from crown lands and from state monopolies, which might include mining, forests, foreign trade, minting, and salt distribution. There was also the revenue from indirect taxes

*Before the advent of coins, societies used precious metals by weight, sometimes cast in ingots. Coins were, in essence, precious metals cut into small standardized sizes (usually disk-shaped), and stamped with a seal of authenticity. The advent of monetary units in multiple demoninations allowed for easy calculation and encouraged the monetization of sectors of the economy that could not be reached by the heavy ingots. These smaller units allowed farmers to sell their wares for silver, rather than on the basis of barter, and encouraged agriculture to move beyond the bounds of self-sufficiency. They encouraged the growth of city life, international trade, and the availability of credit. The first known coins were created in Lydia by Croesus' predecessor, Gyges, in the seventh century B.C. (although there is some evidence that coins may have been invented more or less simultaneously in India). Within one hundred years, coins had spread across the ancient world and were to be found in all major trading cities.

and fines, and of course from lending from the royal treasury. In Ptolemaic Egypt, in particular, there was no sector of the economy in which the state was not heavily involved, and the range of taxes was awe-inspiring.

The advent of coined money meant that the treasuries of the new empires were more often full of coins than full of grain. But they were certainly no less full. The Persians may have started out as simple warriors, but under the tuition of such veteran hoarders as Croesus, they proved rapid learners. Cyrus and Cambyses were more interested in conquest than in administration and were content merely to cream off the excess from the existing tax base by collecting tribute. Their successor, Darius I, the Great King, however, set about the process of accumulation in earnest.

The jewels in the crown of the Persian Empire were undoubtedly the provinces that had been at the center of the great Bronze Age states. Under Darius I's tax regime, Babylonia was the most lucrative of the twenty imperial provinces, contributing 1,000 talents of silver per year ("and 500 child eunuchs").* Egypt was the second highest contributor at 700 talents.[22] Impressive as they are, these figures represented only the surplus: Herodotus states that the governor of Babylonia disposed of total revenues more than eight times the amount that was sent to the imperial treasury in Persepolis.[23] In such a sprawling empire, local conditions varied considerably, and it was inconceivable that a semipastoral tribe on the periphery could be taxed in the same way, or to the same extent, as the well-drilled cultivators of the great river basins.

Since all local government costs, including military garrisons, were paid for by local taxes, the vast revenue received at the central treasuries had to pay for only the, admittedly extravagant, requirements of the imperial court and the cost of military campaigns (such as those against the troublesome Greeks). The majority of the coins received by the central government were simply melted down and stored. Over two hundred years of relative peace, the amounts accumulated became one of the wonders of the ancient world. Alexander's conquest of the great empire in 332 B.C. was so rapid that he was able to capture the contents of these treasure troves almost intact, apart from the 8,000 talents that Darius II took with him on his ignominious flight. Alexander's haul amounted to no less than 180,000 talents.[24] The total Persian treasure amounted to over 400 tons of gold, worth around $6 billion at $400 per ounce. This is already an impressive-sounding

*The talent was a unit of weight that varied from place to place between 25 and 40 kilograms. Herodotus was using the Attic talent of 25.8 kilograms, which is the value used throughout this chapter.

figure; and given the modest size of the population (some fifteen to seventeen million) and the low price levels prevailing, its true value was far higher. It almost undoubtedly represents the high-water mark of ancient treasure accumulation.

In the ancient world (and for long after), a well-stocked treasury was seen as the only reliable means of providing for emergency military expenditures. The prime theorist of ancient Indian public finance, Kautilya, writing around 300 B.C., had no doubt that that under peacetime conditions revenues should be as much as four times expenses. He describes the ideal treasury in these terms: "Justly obtained by inheritance or by self-acquisition, rich in gold and silver, filled with an abundance of big gems of various colours and of gold coins, and capable to withstand calamities of long duration, is the best treasury."[25] Sukra, following in the same tradition, asserted that revenues should be twice expenses. According to Sukra, the ideal treasury should be equivalent to twenty years' expenses, twelve years' being "low," sixteen years' "middling," and thirty years' "very good." The early Hindu empires had treasuries that were, by repute, easily able to rival those of the Persian emperors, but no evidence of their contents has survived. The Persians, however, did begin to meet the criteria of Indian statecraft. Darius II probably had an annual surplus of at least 10,000 talents out if his 27,000-talent income—not 50%, but close enough.[26] The Persian treasury would therefore have represented around eleven years' expenses.

THE FREE MEN FIGHT BACK

So the primitive freedom of tribal life was first whittled away by the self-aggrandizement of chiefs and kings and was then annihilated by conquest. The vanquished became slaves to the conquerors. But this was not the only form of slavery known in the ancient world. There was a third threat to primitive freedom that operated even within those societies that had not started down this slippery slope. The obligation to reciprocate a gift made its receipt a potential snare for its recipient. According to Marcel Mauss:

> Potlatch must normally be returned with interest like all other gifts. . . . If a subject receives a blanket from his chief for a service rendered he will return two on the occasion of a marriage in the chief's family or on the initiation of the chief's son. . . . The sanction for the obligation to repay is enslavement for debt.[27]

Unlike the chattel slaves taken in war, debt slaves were free men who had (temporarily) lost their freedom through debt. Theirs was a lesser form of servitude that was always understood to require more humane treatment. The Laws of Hammurabi already distinguished between the two and limited the period of debt bondage to three years. Later Assyrian and Babylonian codes allowed it to continue until the debt was repaid. All forbade the selling of the enslaved debtor. The Hebrews limited the period of bondage to six years—or at most until the arrival of the "jubilee" every fifty years, when all unpaid debts were canceled. Debt slaves were members of the same nation, the same tribe, and therefore not to be treated as mere chattel: "And if your brother becomes poor beside you, and sells himself to you, you shall not make him serve as a slave; he shall be with you as a hired servant and as a sojourner. . . . You may buy male and female slaves from among the nations that are around you. . . . They may be your property [and] you may bequeath them to your sons after you."[28] The same racial distinction between forms of unpaid labor was still visible in eighteenth-century America. Indentured servants imported from Europe were entitled to work off the cost their transatlantic voyage over a period of years. Chattel slaves imported from Africa had no such privilege.

Even if he were better treated than a chattel slave, the lot of the debt slave was not enviable. The practice had its roots deep in prehistory, but the advancing commercialization of social relations could only make it more prevalent. The advent of interest, and especially of compound interest, risked the progressive enslavement of one part of society to the other—a process made more likely by the high prevailing interest rates. Term limits of the sort imposed by Hammurabi might not suffice. Already in ancient Babylonia the emperor Ammisaduqa (c. 1646–1626 B.C.) had cancelled all debt and ransomed those who had been sold into slavery. As the post–Bronze Age societies evolved, they confronted similar problems. Their solutions, however, were quite distinct.

The Hebrews simply eliminated the problem of interest by banning it in toto. The statement in Deuteronomy on the subject is quite straightforward: "Unto a stranger thou mayest lend upon usury; but unto thy brother thou shalt not lend upon usury." As in the provisions of Leviticus on chattel slavery, a sharp distinction is made between tribal members and outsiders. Foreigners were specifically excluded from the Hebrew usury law; thus, ironically, they found themselves in the same position as the Jews in medieval Europe, as the only legal lenders.

The Greeks took a different route. By the seventh century B.C., whatever sanctions may have limited debt bondage in earlier times appear no longer to have applied. The fate of the Athenian peasantry aroused the wrathful eloquence of Friedrich Engels:

> All the fields of Attica were thick with mortgage columns bearing inscriptions stating that the land on which they stood was mortgaged to such and such for so and so much. The fields not so marked had for the most part already been sold on account of unpaid mortgages or interest and had passed into the ownership of the noble usurer. The peasant could count himself lucky if he was allowed to remain on the land as a tenant and live on *one sixth* of the produce of his labour while he paid *five sixths* to his new master as rent. And this was not all. If the sale of the land did not cover the debt, . . . the debtor, in order to meet his creditor's claims, had to sell his children into slavery abroad. Children sold by their father—such was the first fruit of father-right and monogamy! And if the bloodsucker was still not satisfied, he could sell the debtor himself as a slave. Thus the pleasant dawn of civilization began for the Athenian people![29]

The great lawgiver Solon (c. 594 B.C.) eventually banned debt bondage outright and limited the size of landholdings. As a result there was no need for any limitations on interest taking—even on the practice of compounding. The result, not surprisingly to believers in the free market, was that interest rates fell to levels that for the first time came within the spectrum of affordability: 10–12% by the fifth century B.C. However, the Greeks never quite overcame their distaste for interest. It was Aristotle who first put about the canard that while livestock and grain were naturally reproductive, coin was not, and that interest was therefore contrary to the laws of nature.

A third alternative was pursued in Rome. The early republic (established around 509 B.C.) was dominated by the patrician class, and the status of poorer citizens was threatened by growing agricultural debt. The Twelve Tables, drawn up in 451–450 B.C., reversed Athenian practice by allowing debt bondage while limiting interest. The maximum interest rate was to be 1 ounce per Roman pound. Since the Roman pound contained 12 ounces, this translated into an annual rate of 8.33%, lower than other prevailing rates in the ancient world. Interest costs had indeed fallen dramatically since the introduction of coins, but even in Athens the best credit risks could borrow only at 10%. In 347 B.C., as a result of a new debt crisis, the maximum rate was halved to 4.167%, and in 342 B.C., interest was banned altogether. But such Hebraic extremism inevitably led to a severe credit shortage, and later the 8.33% interest maximum was reintroduced. The intelligent Roman solution of interest rate maxima was to last until the adoption of Christianity introduced the precepts of the Bible into the later empire. It was to take over one thousand years for the economic damage to be undone.

That debt bondage could be successfully resisted suggests that the loss of primitive tribal freedoms may not have been quite so foredoomed as it appeared. At least in some quarters, the free men were able to fight back against the inroads of the superstate and of the aristocrats.

Solomon was undoubtedly a wise judge, and the Israelites may have rejoiced in the splendors of the new temple. Naturally, the most oppressive burdens of his regime were laid on the conquered:

> As for all the people that were left of the Amorites, Hittites, Peruzzites, Hivites, and Jebusites . . . whom the children of Israel were not able utterly to destroy, of them did Solomon raise a levy of bondservants unto this day. But of the children of Israel did Solomon make no bondservants: but they were his men of war, and his servants, and his princes, and his captains.[30]

But Solomon's projects were so grandiose (and perhaps the survivors of the conquered tribes so few) that the Israelites, too, felt the yoke of his rule. It was apparent to many by the end of his reign that Samuel's warning had been all too apposite. When Solomon's son Rehoboam succeeded to the throne, he was faced by a taxpayers' revolt. To his subjects' petitions he responded, memorably but rashly, that whereas his father had chastised them with whips, he would chastise them with scorpions. To this the taxpayers cried out, "What portion have we in David? Neither have we inheritance in the son of Jesse: To your tents, O Israel." In the resulting upheaval the unity of the kingdom was destroyed. This tale of tensions between the Hebrews and their kings continued in the northern successor kingdom of Israel.

After the fateful day when they ignored Samuel's warning, the Israelites never really succeeded in creating stable constitutional arrangements. Other societies enjoyed greater success in limiting the powers of their rulers. From the evidence of the *Mahabharata*, it seems that the kingdoms set up by Aryan invaders of northern India had popular assemblies: the *sabha*, probably a council of elders, and the *samiti*, a general assembly. Subsequently two divergent tendencies were played out, one leading to ever more powerful kings, the other to republics. By the sixth century B.C. there are records of sixteen great states along the Ganges and Indus basins, of which several were republics. The greatest of these was Vrijji, with its splendid capital, Vaisali. The founder of Jainism, Mahavira, was a Vrijjian, and the Buddha was an admirer and a regular visitor.

The nemesis of the republican tribes was not their rulers, but the superior military force of the absolute monarchies. By the end of the fourth century B.C., the entire Ganges basin had been conquered by the rising kingdom of Magadha, which became the home of three Hindu empires: the Nanda, the Maurya, and the Gupta. The Indus valley had its own republics, and the invading army of Alexander recognized the similarities to Greece immediately. According to Diadorus, "At last after many generations had come and gone, the sovereignty, it is said, was dissolved and democratic governments were set up in the cities." In fact the whole panoply of Greek forms of government could find equivalents in India. The state of Patala had a "constitution drawn up on the same lines as the Spartan; for in this community the command in war is vested in two hereditary kings . . . while a council of elders rules the whole state with paramount authority."[31] The Indus valley republics fared no better than those of the Ganges. Alexander conquered them all, and in the wake of the rapid fragmentation of his empire after his death, the Maurya established hegemony over the whole of northern India.

The history of the Phoenicians shows some of the same features. Their city-states were monarchies rather than republics, but the power of the kings was limited to a greater or lesser extent by councils of elders and popular assemblies. Carthage, for instance, had a constitution that was much admired by Aristotle as an example of balance of powers—a balance that he found sorely lacking in Greece. If anything the trend was toward a more democratic form of government rather than less. After the defeat of the First Punic War, the powers of the kings was taken over by two annually elected *suffetes* similar to the consuls of Rome. Looking back on the final demise of the great city, the Greek historian Polybius gave the following evaluation:

> Regarding the Carthaginian state, it seems to me that its institutions . . . were well thought out. There were kings. The council of the elders, of aristocratic nature, for its part had certain powers at its disposal; and the people were sovereign in matters within their jurisdiction. Taken as a whole the organization of power in Carthage resembled what it was in Rome or Sparta. But at the time when Hannibal's war commenced, the Carthaginian constitution had deteriorated and that of the Romans was superior. . . . In Carthage the choice of the people had become predominant in deliberations, whereas in Rome the senate was at the full height of its powers. For the Carthaginians, it was the opinion of the greatest number that prevailed; for the Romans, that of the elite of its citizens.[32]

The Phoenician cities suffered fates even worse than the republics of India. Sidon was captured by the Persians in 351 B.C. Its citizens self-immolated in order to avoid the inevitable slaughter and slavery that awaited them. The fabled treasures of the citizens were melted in the heat of the conflagration. Undaunted, the Persian emperor Artaxerxes Ochus sold the right of scavenging for a large sum, which he added to the imperial reserves. In 332 it was the turn of Tyre. Alexander captured it after a seven-month siege. Ten thousand citizens were massacred, and the remaining thirty thousand were sold in the slave markets. In 146 B.C. the final chapter closed on the bitter struggle between Rome and Carthage. Carthage was razed to the ground, salt was poured on the surrounding earth to render it infertile, and the surviving citizens were sold, like those of Tyre, into slavery.

The Greeks and Romans also succeeded in limiting the ambitions of their rulers. Their kings were replaced by republics; and subsequently the original aristocratic monopoly of republican office was weakened by an increase in popular participation in government. But the path to democratic rule was not straightforward. It was interrupted, sometimes terminally, by the rise of tyrants—classified by Aristotle as "unconstitutional" monarchs. They generally rose out of the ranks of the oligarchy by playing on popular discontent. It was the tyrants who were most often responsible for the freeing of debt slaves, and for the abolition of debt bondage. The only reason that Solon is not classified as a tyrant is that he refused to attempt to perpetuate his rule and went into self-imposed exile. Other tyrants, such as Periander in Corinth and Peisistratus in Athens, had dynastic pretensions. Had the tyrants succeeded in their ambitions, the Greek flirtation with republicanism would have passed almost unnoticed in the annals of history.

Given the threats from within and without, how can one account for the flowering of democracy in the ancient world? The best explanation remains the one put forward by Aristotle. He based his argument on advances in military technique:

> The earliest government which existed among the Greeks, after the overthrow of the kingly power, grew up out of the warrior class, and was originally taken from the knights (for strength and superiority in war at that time depended heavily on cavalry; indeed, without discipline, infantry are useless, and in ancient times there was no military knowledge or tactics, and therefore the strength of armies lay in their cavalry). But when cities increased and the heavy-armed [infantry] grew in strength, more had a share in government; and this is the reason that states which we call constitutional governments have hitherto been called democracies.[33]

By the "heavy-armed" Aristotle meant the formations of phalanxes and legions that were to dominate the later centuries of the classical world. The light cavalry that had replaced the great era of chariot warfare around 1000 B.C. was no match for these highly disciplined infantry regiments. It is necessary only to contemplate the kind of sociopolitical organization that coexisted with the heavy cavalry of medieval Europe to see that Aristotle's analysis was correct. The hoplites had armor that was heavy enough to withstand light cavalry attacks but simple enough to be within the financial capacities of the free peasants. In a world in which membership in a tribe was still synonymous with military service, the implications were enormous. The growing importance of heavy infantry to the military capacity of the Greek cities meant that it was possible—although not easy—for the perennial struggles between nobles and free peasants to be resolved without resort to autocratic rule.

The intimacy of the connection between warfare, politics, and finance is shown by the constitutions of both Athens and Rome. Citizenship conferred military obligations that depended on relative wealth. In Athens, Solon's reforms instituted four classes. The first class (*pentacosiomedimnoi*) was liable to the cost of manning triremes. The second (*hippeis*) formed the cavalry. The third (*zeugites*) consisted of hoplites, and the fourth (*thetes*) of light infantry. In Rome the classes were defined by specified monetary hurdles. Military service was viewed as much as a privilege as an obligation, and those with assets of less than 11,000 asses (the as was the principal monetary unit, originally one pound of copper) were excluded from the army. As the strains of ruling a growing empire challenged the social and military basis of republican society in Rome, one of the first symptoms of its decay was the proletarianization of the army. During the second century, the property qualification was lowered to 4,000 asses and then to 1,500 asses before being ended entirely under Marius around 100 B.C.

The city-states of Greece and Rome were "military" democracies. And increasingly their democratic credentials came to depend on military successes that generated ever larger numbers of chattel slaves. Slaves rendered the agricultural labor of the free peasants unnecessary and simultaneously gave them more time to concentrate on war and politics. Democracy, as understood in the ancient world, meant the rule of the free-born citizens, as opposed to the rule of an aristocracy, or of one man. It did not mean the rule of the general population. The success of the "heavy-armed" made them increasingly an elite supported by a disenfranchised underclass. Sparta was undoubtedly the most extreme case, but in Periclean Athens, the demos (the trueborn Athenians) constituted no more than half the total population. No wonder that it was the citizens' exclusive right to bear arms.

Little is known about the public finances of the Phoenician city-states or the Indian republics. The public revenues of the Phoenicians may have derived from the participation of the state in the trade for which their cities were so famous. Even less is known about the finances of the Indian republics. The information available comes almost entirely from writers in the great empires. It is in Greece and Rome that the financial implications of democratic rule can be seen in operation.

GREEKS AND THEIR "GIFTS"

> From Ionion the wind drove me along and brought me to Isamros, the land of the Ciconians. There I sacked the city and put the men to death. We captured from the city their wives and much treasure, and divided it all among us, in such a way that no one went away deprived of his fair share through me.
>
> —Homer, *Odyssey* 9.39–42

This passage in the *Odyssey* forms a striking parallel to the division of the spoils of the Midianites. The men were slaughtered, the women and treasure divided among the victors. More important for our purpose is the equitable nature of the operation. Odysseus was a tribal leader on the archaic model. His position among his men was no more than primus inter pares, and he made no special claims on the booty. Throughout the enormous political and social changes that convulsed ancient Greek society through the following centuries, the principle of the fair (although not necessarily equal) distribution of surplus assets never quite disappeared. In Athens it can be seen in full flower right up to the final assertion of Macedonian hegemony over Greece in 336 B.C.

The early Greek city-states appear to have continued the archaic practice of automatic distribution of surpluses to their citizens. Such surpluses came mainly from warfare, which was for a long time virtually indistinguishable from cattle raids and piracy. Indeed, Solon's laws recognized piracy as a legitimate occupation.

The exact principles that underlay the division of spoils are not recorded in detail. Every soldier participated, but usually with gradations according to rank and to valor. Whether some of the spoils were originally reserved for noncombatants is not clear. In the early period the army and the citizen body were virtually identical, so it would have made little difference. When pay for military service was introduced in the fifth century B.C., the picture changed. Pay was seen not only as a compensation for lost time on the farm, but also as an advance against participation in the profits of war. Distributions of booty were often made simply to make up arrears. In Athens, at least, the assembly insisted on a full and proper accounting for the spoils, and Athenian expeditionary forces were accompanied by official accountants—*tamiai*—to ensure that the full haul returned home. Generals who assumed that they had some automatic right to a generous helping of the fruits of victory could find themselves liable to prosecution.

Like the Israelites, the Greeks also expected to honor their tribal deities by a contribution to their temples. These offerings do not appear to have represented a very high percentage of the total, to judge by the surviving records. But over time some temples came to hold substantial sums—especially since they started to lend their money at interest, and since they also acted as depositaries for private funds.

As societies grew more sophisticated, a new source of possible surpluses offered itself: gold and silver mines. It was commonly understood that such mines were communal property. Like booty and plunder, the profits from the mines were also distributed among the people rather than stored. (Indeed, since the mines were worked by captured slaves, their revenues represented the profitable utilization of the booty of previous wars.) As with other surpluses, a portion might be allocated to the gods. The temple treasury of Apollo at Delphi owed its establishment to the partial diversion of revenue from the mines of Siphnos:

> Siphnos was at that time at the height of its prosperity; its gold and silver mines had made it the richest of the Aegean islands. The mines were so productive that from a mere tenth of the wealth generated from them a treasury at Delphi was established, which was one of the richest there, and every year they used to distribute the revenue from the mines among the citizen body.[34]

Athens, too, owed a good portion of its revenues to its mines. Until 483 B.C. the silver was automatically divided among the citizens. In that year, however, an almost shocking proposal was put before the assembly:

> The Athenians being wont to divide up the revenue from the silver mines at Laureion, [Themistocles] alone dared to come before the people and say that they should forgo this division and should build with this money triremes for the war against Aigina.[35]

One source of potential surpluses was notably absent. If the inhabitants of the Asiatic empires accepted powers of direct taxation as a matter of course, the Greeks rejected them entirely. They were an offense to the dignity of the citizen. State revenues from publicly owned property were acceptable, as were taxes on foreigners and limited indirect taxes. But the citizen would not have his money taken from him at the behest of some leviathan. As was commonly stated, citizens should freely "offer service with their bodies and their money." In return they would be repaid out of the city surpluses, if any. It was therefore entirely illogical that a surplus should be created out of taxation. As Mauss noted, the semiobligatory gifts made by the Greek citizens to their polis were no more than the continuation of the principles of primitive gift exchange into a more complex monetary age.

The most important of these quasi-obligatory gifts were the liturgies. They were offered by individual citizens to fund specific expenses such as religious festivals, public building works, and military expenditure. In Athens the most costly of the liturgies was the trierarchy, which provided for the maintenance of the triremes on which the city's military strength was based. In prosperous times the wealthy competed to display their wealth and public spirit by volunteering for liturgies—especially those which supported public festivals, and especially close to election time. Apart from the liturgies the cities could also raise *epidoseis*—donations subscribed by the general public in a fund-raising drive. Donations were "voluntary," but not to have participated according to one's means would have been to risk public disdain or worse.

These distinctive fiscal arrangements were, tellingly, confined to the democracies. The tyrants attempted, insofar as they were able, to emulate the rulers of Asia. Peisistratus was able to enforce a land tax in Athens in the seventh century amounting to some 5% of production. Not surprisingly it was abolished as soon as his family was expelled. Dionysius of Syracuse was able to collect a tithe on agricultural production in the fourth century. But generally the tyrants were unable to establish regular direct taxes on a secure footing, and they were forced to resort to the varied forms of improvised fiscal extortion for which they became notorious.

The decision of the Athenians to build up a fleet rather than distribute their fiscal surplus was of more significance than they could have imagined. The Athenian thassalocracy—the "empire of the sea"—can perhaps be dated from this moment. Unlike other ancient empires, it was disguised initially as a voluntary alliance against the Persian threat. Under this guise the allies were persuaded to contribute into the largest recorded treasury of classical Greece. At its height the reserves of the Delian League amounted to 9,700 talents—an insignificant amount compared to that of the Persian Empire, perhaps, but accumulated from a population base unlikely to have greatly exceeded one million persons.

Treasure on this scale would seem to contradict the idea that the Greeks preferred distribution to accumulation. But the exceptional circumstances of the Delian treasure have to be borne in mind. It was the product of coercion, at first unstated, but in the end quite naked. The Athenians set the scale of tribute paid by the "allies." They themselves did not contribute. At first the treasury was stored at Delos. Later it was moved to Athens for reasons of "security." It was not possible simply to distribute it among the Athenians if the pretense of voluntary alliance was to be maintained. But there seems little doubt that that the scale of public spending in Periclean Athens was not supportable out of Athenian domestic revenues alone. Internal revenues amounted to some 400–500 talents per year. Public spending, however, was running at around 700 talents, and the remainder could come only out of the annual tribute from the allies.[36] The buildings that still excite the awe of modern visitors were only part of that expense. The Athenian citizens increasingly expected to be paid as a reward for their membership in the greatest demos of all Greece. By the time of Pericles, not only military service but participation in the assembly and the juries (open to all citizens) were paid. In the end, the fortunate Athenians were paid even to attend public festivals. Aristotle (no great admirer of the extreme democracy prevailing in the city) made the connection between empire and public pay quite clear:

> For from the allied tribute and indirect levies more than 20,000 persons were supported. For there were 6,000 judges, 1,600 bowmen plus 1,200 cavalrymen, 500 Councilmen, 500 guards of the dockyards plus 50 guards on the Akropolis, and about 700 State officials at home plus about 700 abroad. In addition, when they later engaged in war, there were 2,500 hoplites, and 20 guardships plus other ships carrying the guardians, that is, 2,000 men chosen by lot. Still more there were the Prytaneion and the orphans and the jailkeepers. Indeed, all these people made a living from the public funds.[37]

Historians have objected that Aristotle's total of twenty thousand persons represented the large majority of the adult male citizenry, and that he was a biased observer. But other sources tend to confirm that the intention, at least, was as Aristotle suggested. In *The Knights* Aristophanes portrays the demagogue Cleon (the most hawkish of the Athenian imperialists) as stating that his true aim is "to make the people rulers of all the Greeks; for the oracles foretell that the *demos* shall have jury service at 5 obols per day in Arcadia, if they persevere."[38] (This would have represented a 60% increase over existing pay scales.)

The Peloponnesian War consumed the accumulated wealth of the Delian League. Athens, of course, merely "borrowed" the funds in the treasury; but even if the military outcome had been less disastrous, it is unlikely that they would have been repaid. The war destroyed the Athenian empire. The second Athenian league of 377 B.C. specifically prohibited the imperialistic practices of its predecessor. But the city could never quite adapt to its reduced status. Like Great Britain after the Second World War (but arguably with even less justification), Athens felt entitled to live off the vanished riches of its past glory. There was no tribute, and no treasury, but the distributions continued. In 352 B.C. Eubulus made a vain attempt to restore some sense of the original connection between distributions and surpluses. The most politically emblematic (but financially specious) of the doles—the *theorikon*, payable for attendance at public festivals—was to be limited to the budget surplus, if any. But this measure only increased popular militarism. The level of soldiers' pay meant that it was more profitable for the poorer citizen to fight than to cultivate his fields. Given the system of liturgies to pay for extraordinary expenses, the financial burden of war fell heavily on the rich. The result was a decline in civic spirit among the wealthy and an increasing dislike of democracy. In 354 B.C. the orator Isocrates bemoaned the new attitudes:

> When I was a boy, being rich was considered so secure and respectable that almost anyone pretended he owned more property than was the case, because he wanted to share in the prestige it gave. Now, on the other hand, one has to defend oneself against being rich as if it were the worst of crimes.[39]

The unity of democratic cities was increasingly divided into popular war parties and patrician peace parties. This was perhaps the inevitable consequence of a revenue system that has been described as regressive in peacetime and highly progressive in wartime. The attempt to compensate for the increasing inadequacy of voluntary donations led to the institution of the *eisphora*, an emergency wealth tax levied for the first time in 428 B.C. in Athens. This was designed to raise the substantial amount of 200 talents per levy and was repeated periodically throughout the war. The introduction of the offensive principle of direct taxation, however, was bound to undermine the level of civic spirit required for the principle of public giving to flourish.

The gradual waning of the spirit of donation was allied to the increasing monetization of economic relations within society. By the fourth century B.C. lending by individuals, and occasionally by temples, was augmented by the arrival of professional bankers. The increasing acceptability of credit relations encouraged, and was in turn encouraged by, the gradual fall in interest rates. The availability of money accelerated after Alexander's capture of the Persian treasury in 330 B.C. Neither Alexander nor his successors displayed quite the fixation on hoarding that had been the hallmark of Persian rule.

The scene was set for the birth of public credit.

CIVIC DEBT

From the end of the fifth century until the middle of the first century B.C., more than one hundred records of civic borrowing exist.[40] The picture that emerges is not of a regular system of public finance, but of a series of improvised reactions to fiscal emergencies. Yet in this period the Greeks can be seen groping, often reluctantly, toward principles and practices that are recognizable today as the precursors of modern public credit.

And yet the transition to a system of domestic debt was not obvious. The Greeks had two of the necessary ingredients: the principle of voluntary contribution to the public funds and the principle of distribution of surplus assets. What was needed was the explicit connection of these two processes so that distributions were explicitly tied to contributions, and the result was expressed as a loan. The step was not simple. Debts were understood to be an economic relationship between distinct individuals, whereas the state and the citizens were seen as essentially identical. Indeed the Greeks rarely spoke of cities by name, usually referring to the whole people. Athens was *ὁi Atheniaoi* ("the Athenians").

It is not surprising, therefore, that the first public loan of which there is record was external. At the end of the Peloponnesian War in 404 B.C. the defeated Athenian democrats fled to Piraeus, while the victorious Spartans installed a subservient oligarchy in the city. The new government's first act was to borrow 100 talents from the victors to fund a fruitless campaign to oust the democrats from their residual stronghold. One of the most interesting aspects of the loan is its repayment. When the democrats subsequently returned to power in Athens, there was a public debate as to whether the city as a whole should repay the loan—the first recorded discussion of the duty of successor (most often revolutionary) governments to honor the debts of their ousted predecessors. In the event the assembly voted to honor the obligation even though it meant levying another of the unpopular *eisphorai.*

Athenians never tired of boasting of this fine example of civic responsibility, although one might validly suspect that fear of antagonizing the then-dominant Sparta played a major part in the decision-making process. Indeed the Boeotian allies of the Spartans were threatening to seize individual Athenians who came within their power and to confiscate their goods in order to obtain repayment (a logical corollary of the equation of citizens and city).

In the following century there were a considerable number of similar, politically driven public loans. Athens lent to its allies on several occasions, as when it made a loan of triremes to Calcis in 334 B.C. Its famous orator Demosthenes lent one talent to Oreos in 340 B.C. as part of his struggle against the growing power of Philip of Macedon. The following year Tenedos lent money to Athens during its siege by the Macedonian king. During the years 394–340 B.C., the temple of Delos, at that stage under Athenian control, made a number of loans to allied cities at an unvarying interest rate of 10%.

The most interesting external loan for which records have survived occurred in 283 B.C. The city of Miletus, on the Ionian coast of modern-day Turkey, borrowed 12 talents from the neighboring city of Cnidus in what can be described as the first foreign bond issue. Cnidus ran a public offering to find subscribers for the money requested. Miletus ran a parallel public drive to find seventy-five guarantors. The loan was obviously something of a sweetheart deal, since a portion was interest-free for one year, and the rest was for three years at the below-market rate of 6%.

The Miletan search for guarantors was not unique. The Athenian loan to Calcis had been guaranteed by fifteen citizens. The important point here is that the guarantors were, in effect, lending their credit to the city, and this suggests the possibility of domestic public borrowing. In fact, the first such loans had already taken place in the mid-fourth century. In 350 B.C. the city of Clazomenae (also on the Ionian coast—the Ionians seem to have been the financial pioneers of the Greek world) requisitioned the olive oil reserves of its citizens and sold them abroad in exchange for wheat. The profits on the transaction were to suffice to pay interest on the value of the oil. Around the same time the mainland city of Mende, which was then at war with Olynthus, required its citizens to sell all their slaves except two, and to lend the proceeds to the city. Perhaps the most interesting of all the recorded forced loans of the fourth century is another example from Clazomenae, noted by Aristotle in his *Economics*. In 360 B.C. the city faced a debt of 20 talents to its mercenary captains, which was costing so much interest (some 4 talents, or 20%, per annum) that it was beyond the means of the city to reduce the principal. The city resolved its dilemma by minting drachmas of iron instead of silver, and by forcing its wealthier citizens to lend it 20 talents of silver, allocated "in proportion to their wealth," in exchange for these intrinsically worthless coins.* The interest saved by paying off the mercenaries was then used to redeem the fiat currency over a period of five years.[41]

These loans are significant for a number of reasons. The last two, in particular, point to the possibility of a new method of war finance. Since the Mendian loan served to finance Mende's conflict with Olynthus, it would have been a simple matter to repay the loan in kind out of the slaves captured in battle (assuming, of course, that the campaign was successful). The Clazomenian loan of 360 B.C. was not directly related to the distribution of the spoils of war—for obviously there were none, or they would have been used to pay off the mercenaries. But it, too, can be seen as a sort of repayable *eisphora*—a wartime levy that would have been repaid out of the booty had there been any. This was not an idea that would have gone down well in populist Athens. The distribution of the spoils of war there was in no way connected to the payment of liturgies and *eisphorai*, just as it was no longer an automatic privilege of military rank.

Equally significant is the fact that the loans were raised by methods that, however informally, related the amounts lent to the wealth of the contributor. The last two even introduced an element of progressivity into the process. The practice of debt raised on the basis of assessed wealth was to be of the utmost importance when public borrowing reemerged in medieval Europe after a hiatus of nearly fifteen hundred years.

By the third century there is some evidence of loans raised by voluntary subscription. These loans were related to the *epidoseis*, the public fundraising events frequently held in the cities during later antiquity. In 275 B.C., for instance, the city of Helicarnassus raised money by public subscription to rebuild its public gymnasium. Subscribers were given the choice of an outright gift of 500 drachmas or a 3,000-drachma interest-free loan. (Unless the loan was relatively short-term, an opportunity-cost analysis would surely have suggested the former option.)

The most significant voluntary loan was another loan raised by the city

*The drachma was the most common currency of the Greek cities. It was a silver coin containing around 4.3 grams of silver. It was minted in various denominations, most frequently as a tetradrachm (4 drachmas). There were 6,000 drachmas in a talent.

of Miletus in 205 B.C. A total of 140,400 drachmas (23.4 talents) was raised to repay accumulated obligations and debts. The lenders were to receive an annuity equal to 10% of their subscriptions for life. Since there was no further provision for repayment of capital, this was the first instance ever recorded of a life-annuity loan of the type that would become of great importance in seventeenth- and eighteenth-century Europe. Given that the annual payments represented both interest and principal, it is not possible to calculate the effective interest cost to the city in the absence of information about the life spans of the subscribers. It was in any case under 10% and would therefore be among the very lowest on record (just under 6.5% if the lenders died at an even rate over the following forty years, for instance). It would have been lower if the lenders had not been allowed to nominate third parties as the beneficiaries. The inevitable result was that twenty-five of the thirty-nine subscriptions were in the name of minors. In this, the Miletans showed themselves no less canny than their successors in London, Paris, and Geneva. In addition, the lenders insisted on obtaining severe legal sanctions to protect their position. The mere proposal to cancel or reduce the agreed-on payments would be punished by a fine of nearly 20,000 drachmas. Although life annuities are no longer a normal part of public finance, the Miletan loan had three critical features that separate it from other ancient debts and relate it to modern practices: it was long-term, it was raised by voluntary subscription, and it had a low interest cost.

Loans raised from the general public were not the most frequent instances of public borrowing in the Greek world, however. Most surviving records are of loans by private individuals—especially in the Macedonian period. Such loans were often without interest and are generally known from inscriptions honoring the lenders for their public spirit. Very often, statues were raised to them, especially if they forwent interest or part of the principle. Ultimately, it is hard to separate many private loans from acts of individual generosity. On the other hand, sometimes lenders settled for something of more obvious commercial use than a statue, as in the case of a certain Philiston who renegotiated his loan to Delphi for tax exemptions in the early second century B.C. Around 228 B.C. the city of Orchomenus was able to renegotiate its debt to Eubolos for pasturage rights.

Insofar as the surviving evidence reveals the relevant details, the credit record of the Greek cities does not appear to be very good. But then civic debts were very rarely seen as normal commercial transactions. Loans without interest outnumbered those with interest throughout the Macedonian period, especially if those loans where interest was subsequently forgone are included. Loans with repayment difficulties clearly outnumber those repaid on time. Of the thirteen state loans made by the Temple of Delos, for example, only two were repaid in full; and after regaining its independence from Athenian influence, the temple preferred to return to its more traditional role of banker to the private sector. On the other hand, this dubious credit record may be partly a reflection of the way in which the details have come down to us:

> Repayments *in extremis,* enforcement of pledges, seizures or pressures of all sorts, compromises, renegotiations and remittance of debt, these were the most frequent outcomes of public debts. Without doubt this large number of examples is a reflection of reality. One should not deceive oneself, however: when they were made without problems, repayments left no traces except in the public accounts and were in general neither engraved in stone nor commented on by authors.[42]

If one seeks to evaluate Greek public credit, one is forced to say that it did not amount to a system. It was too sporadic and improvised in nature. In many cases it was distinguished only with difficulty from acts of generosity by wealthy citizens or foreigners looking for secondary gains. Of all the reasons that may be advanced, the most important lies in the realm of the underlying political beliefs of the Greeks. The idea that citizens should freely offer their resources to their city remained an article of faith. It was therefore hard to accept the payment of interest to those who might otherwise be offering liturgies. Hence the prevalence of interest-free loans, or loans converted into gifts. It was also true that

> however much the Greek city-state might profess to leave undisturbed the property of its citizens, it had no hesitation in times of stress in treating their property as its own. It might hypothecate their individual property as well as that of the city, or its creditors might demand and obtain the collateral guarantee of one or more specifically named citizens.[43]

Equal problems stood in the way of a reliable system of foreign borrowing. The identification of citizens with city allowed the forcible distraint of any citizen and his goods to answer for the debts of the whole city; and this possibility made the mercantile class (i.e., those who traveled abroad with their wares) view the contracting of external debt with grave suspicion. A further problem was the limited sense of universal or international law. Outside the city itself there prevailed only the law of the jungle. Listen to the Athenian ambassadors to Melos in 416 B.C., as quoted by Thucydides:

> We Athenians will use no fine words. . . . You and we should say what we really think, and aim only at what is possible, for we both alike know that into the discussion of human affairs the question of justice only enters where the pressure of necessity is equal, and that the most powerful exact what they can, and the weak grant what they must.[44]

Here, at least, the situation may be said to have improved in the later classical period, and especially after the conquests of Alexander. According to Plutarch, Alexander encouraged men to regard themselves "as inhabiting one fatherland whose acropolis and fortress was his camp, and regard as fellow citizens those men who were good and as foreigners those who were bad."[45] As against the original Greek concept of citizenship of a tribal group represented by the city, Zeno and the Stoics proposed the concept of citizenship of the world. Claimants were sometimes able to take their cases to neutral but allied cities for adjudication. An event of this sort is recorded in 300 B.C., when the city of Kalymnos was sued (unsuccessfully) by various creditors in the neutral city of Cnidus. Perhaps it was for these reasons that loans become more frequent in the later period.

However, for all its limitations, the evolution of Greek philosophy provided a base on which the concept of a limited and responsible state could develop. Although their cities may have had virtually unlimited powers over their citizens, the Greeks saw themselves as radically different from the inhabitants east of the Hellespont. Aristotle was reflecting the accepted Greek view when he wrote, "Barbarians are more servile by nature than Greeks, and Asians are more servile than Europeans; hence they endure despotic rule without protest."[46] Under the analysis of the philosophers, the state came to be seen as based on a compact between citizens. The pivotal moment came during the Peloponnesian War, when the Sophists, whose belief in moral relativism would generally appear to lend support to the realpolitik of the statements of the Athenian ambassadors to Melos, developed a startling new analysis of the origins and purpose of society:

> So, when men do wrong and are wronged by one another and taste of both, those who lack the power to avoid the one and to take the other, determine that it is for their profit to make a compact with one another neither to commit nor to suffer injustice; and this is the beginning of legislation and covenants between men.[47]

Here we have the distant ancestor of the Enlightenment theories of the social contract. And in spite of the originally symbiotic relationship of

Greeks and their cities, their philosophers slowly paved the way for the idea of a limited state responsible to its citizens. Without such a theory there was no room for growth of the parallel idea of the value of public credit standing. Demosthenes was certainly not an advocate of public borrowing, but he expressed the concept of public credit in a passage that would have done credit to a nineteenth-century orator:

> Apart from this, there being two good things that the city possesses, wealth and the confidence of all, the greater of the two is the possession by us of this credit; for if any one thinks that because we lack money there is no need of our having good repute, he is wrong. For I pray heaven that we may, to be sure, have plenty of money, but if not this, that we may continue to have the reputation of being reliable.[48]

What was not yet understood, either in Greek times or for a very, very long time thereafter, was the connection between public credit and economic efficiency. Yet Aristotle, at least, came close to seeing the tie. Plato famously advocated communal property for his ideal republic; but Aristotle was less of an abstract dreamer and took a more pragmatic view of human affairs that was undoubtedly closer to that of his contemporaries. "Property," in Aristotle's view, "should be in a certain sense common, but as a general rule private; for when everyone has a distinct interest, men will make more progress, because everyone will be attending to his own business."[49] In other words, private property is justified on the grounds of Adam Smith's "invisible hand." Laissez-faire economics start at this point. It was Aristotle, too, who first glimpsed, if only in passing, why returning surplus wealth to citizens might, in the long term, be better than storing it in vaults. In his criticism of the treasures that the tyrants sought so avidly to stash away (ensuring, like modern Third World dictators, against the moment of their downfall), Aristotle objected that not only was such treasure a temptation to rivals, but also as long as he retained the support of his subjects, the ruler would always be able to tap their wealth in time of need.

KINGS AND TYRANTS

Although some pages have been spent in describing the evolution of public debt in terms of city finances, it is not true that the Greek cities were the only early borrowers on record. Another class of loans can be identified through the fragmentary information that survives from the period of late antiquity, namely, loans to kings and despots. One might legitimately ask why kings, if supported by the kind of ample tax structure described earlier, would have any need of borrowing. The answer is that the new kingdoms and empires were not static; they were in an irregular process of formation, destruction, and re-creation. Under these conditions the aspiring new contenders for power could find themselves short of the wherewithal to fund their ambitions. Similarly the established but challenged rulers might find their revenues depleted and their treasuries consumed or, worse, captured. Just such a fate, after all, had befallen the great treasure of Solomon after his death. The ancient empires and dynasties rose and fell, and their treasuries followed their fortunes. They were empty as often as they were full. The process of monetization of all aspects of life, including warfare, affected them as much as it did the Greek cities. The same processes also increased the availability of credit and enabled the rulers of these kingdoms and empires to turn in time of need to whatever sources of finance were available. For the lenders, these loans, whose repayment generally depended on the outcome of a military campaign, were highly risky and may almost be termed venture capital.

The most significant of these debts, at least in relation to subsequent world history, must be those of Alexander the Great. Although his father, Philip, enjoyed great military successes and controlled profitable state-owned silver and gold mines, his son inherited a mere 60 talents in the treasury, against unpaid debts of 500 talents. Alexander promptly pawned his lands to his nobles in exchange for a further 800 talents so as to equip his Persian expedition. "But what have you left for yourself?" Perdiccas asked him. "My hopes," replied Alexander. Given the 180,000 talents captured during the subsequent campaign, one can be sure that both Alexander and his backers had reason to be satisfied.

A similar type of borrowing (albeit for purposes of defense rather than conquest) occurs in the twelfth book of the *Mahabharata*, where the king addresses his subjects as follows: "To meet this calamity and dreadful danger, I seek your wealth for concerting measures for your protection. When the danger passes away I will repay you what I now take. Our foes will not return what they take from you by force." In this instance there is no mention of interest, and the incentive to lend is provided by the risk of loss of property to an invading army. The *Mahabharata* describes the heroic era of tribal kingship, but the great empires, too, may have accepted the idea of borrowing in exceptional circumstances. Kautylia, the chief financial minister and political theorist of the Mauryan empire, suggested the idea of borrowing if the strategic odds looked favorable but warned against making such operations a habit.[50]

The risk attached to lending to such borrowers went beyond that of an uncertain military outcome. The value of a good credit record was slowly dawning on the Greek cities; but it is unlikely that kings and tyrants saw matters in the same light. Borrowing was only one of the many emergency financial measures available to these rulers. Others included extra taxes and levies, confiscations, and extortions. Kautylia, who has been described as the Indian Machiavelli, was a particular advocate of such extortionate measures:

> The enemies of the State, above all, are to be singled out as victims of this shameless policy of spoliation of the king's subjects: [Kautylia] shows by concrete examples how they are to be hauled up, on trumped-up charges of assault on chaste women, murder, theft, manufacture of counterfeit coins, and treason against the king. . . . The fundamental principle underlying the above criteria is that the necessity of the king (or the State) justifies the application of force and fraud in varying degrees for raising revenue in a grave emergency. This is subject only to the limitation imposed by sound policy in the shape of avoiding public discontent.[51]

Kings, then, when confronted by an emergency, could not be relied upon to follow normal rules of commercial honesty. The Greek tyrants would have been even worse. Not only were their regimes perceived by the Greeks to be intrinsically unconstitutional, but their accepted sources of revenues were those typical of Greek cities, not of oriental kingdoms. Their ambitions were thus constantly running up against their limited incomes, and they were notorious for their illegal exactions and confiscations. One of the most colorful of these rulers was Dionysius of Syracuse. A military commander who rose to power in the wake of the ill-fated Athenian siege of 413 B.C., he made the Syracuse one of the most powerful cities in the Greek world, and the chief rival to Carthage in the central Mediterranean before the rise of Rome. In the annals of finance he goes down as the first to use the weapon of debasement as a means of reducing debt. When his subjects requested the repayment of sums that they had advanced to him, he responded by forcing them, on pain of death, to hand over all their money for reminting. He then simply restamped the coins at twice their old value, gave back half as the new official currency, and used the remainder to "repay" his debts.[52] His behavior is more remarkable in light of the very good track record of the Greeks in maintaining sound currencies. The Athenian drachma remained unaltered for six hundred years and was the international standard currency for most of that time, until its replacement by the Roman denarius.*

THE CARTHAGINIAN WARS

The cost of fighting the Carthaginians was as hard for Rome to finance in the third century B.C. as it had been for Syracuse in the fourth. It has been regularly stated that ancient Rome did not borrow, and in general terms, this is true. There is certainly no recorded instance of Rome borrowing at interest. The Punic Wars, however, provide the most significant example we have of tribal public finance adapted to a monetary age.

It should come as no surprise that the early Romans were accustomed to divide the spoils of war among them; and, as they were possibly the greatest plunderers of the ancient world, there was much to divide. But how to divide it? In one sense it was easy. If any state qualified as a military democracy, it was the Roman Republic. Since the constitution conferred military obligations based on wealth, it was straightforward enough to divide the spoil according to military rank. The centurions generally received double, and the cavalry triple, the amount allocated to legionaries. But the Senate also had to take into account the claims of the noncombatant population and the state of the public finances. If the captured city was within reach of Rome, noncombatants expected to take part in the plunder. To attempt the accumulation of a treasury was to risk political upheaval. This is vividly shown in the senatorial debate after the fall of Veii in 400 B.C.:

> The Senate was divided. It is reported that the aged P. Licinius, who was the first to be asked his opinion by his son, urged that the people should receive public notice that whoever wanted to share in the spoils should go to the camp at Veii. Appius Claudius took the opposite line. He stigmatised the proposed largesse as unprecedented, wasteful, unfair, reckless. If, he said, they thought it sinful for the money taken from the enemy to lie in the treasury, drained as it had been by the wars, he would advise that the pay of the soldiers be supplied from that source, so that the plebs might have so much less tax to pay. "The homes of all would feel alike the benefit of a common boon, the rewards won by brave warriors would not be filched by the hands of city loafers, ever greedy for the plunder, for it so constantly happens that those who usually seek the foremost place in toil and danger are the least active in appropriating the spoils."

*The denarius was first minted at the end of the third century B.C., and was similar in size and weight to the Greek drachma. It became the standard silver coin of the late republic and early empire.

> Licinius, on the other hand, said that this money would always be regarded with suspicion and aversion, and would supply material for indictments before the plebs, and consequently bring about disturbances and revolutionary measures. It was better, therefore, that the plebs should be conciliated by this gift, that those who had been crushed and exhausted by so many years of taxation should be relieved and get some enjoyment from the spoils of a war in which they had almost become old men. "When anyone brings home what he has taken from the enemy with his own hand, it affords him more pleasure and gratification that if he were to receive many times its value at the bidding of another."[53]

It is quite likely that before the war with Veii the financial needs of the state had been met by means of voluntary contributions on the Greek model. The war with Veii had been so long that it had become necessary to pay stipends to the soldiers to compensate for time away from their farms, and these had been financed by levies on the citizens (the *tributum*—based, like military rank, on relative wealth). But if voluntary contributions fell into abeyance after 400 B.C., they would need to be revived for Rome to cope with the costs of the Punic Wars—wars that were as destructive as any in the twentieth century. From surviving census figures it has been calculated that Rome lost a third of its adult male population in the course of the first two wars (264–241 and 218–201 B.C.), and economic losses must have been commensurate. To cope with the financial strain Rome reversed Athenian practice. In the Peloponnesian War Athens had depended on voluntary contributions and, when these proved inadequate, had resorted to a compulsory wealth tax. Rome depended first on its wealth tax and, when this could no longer bear the strain, resorted to voluntary contributions reminiscent of the Athenian trierarchy to finance the last, decisive campaign of the first war in 242 B.C.

> The Romans . . . now determined for the third time to make trial of their fortune in naval warfare. . . . The treasury was empty, and would not supply the funds necessary for the undertaking, which were, however, obtained by the patriotism and generosity of the leading citizens. They undertook singly, or by two or three combining, according to their means, to supply a quinquereme fully fitted out, *on the understanding that they were to be repaid if the expeditions were successful* [italics added]. By these means a fleet of 200 quinqueremes was quickly prepared.[54]

Here, at last, we have the missing link in the chain that connects the spoils of war, gifts, and public debt. The Roman elite "donated" money to equip the fleet on the specific understanding that the spoils of war would be used to repay their donations. They had created a repayable liturgy. Such a step was probably conceivable only in a constitution that "balanced" the Aristotelian principles of "aristocracy" and "democracy." Athens—whose constitution had no such balance—never allowed the providers of liturgies a first claim on the booty.

The Second Punic War created even greater strains on the Roman finances. The war started disastrously for Rome, which was caught by surprise by Hannibal's bold invasion. With the loss of two armies in succession at Lake Trasimene and Cannae, the city faced economic and military collapse by 216 B.C. It was from that time that a continuous stream of extraordinary contributions was recorded. In 215 the army in Spain was supplied on credit. In 214 ships were built by liturgy, and slaves were lent for the armed forces. In the same year widows' and orphans' trust funds were offered to the state. The most famous of these contributions was the very public donation of family treasures in 210 B.C.—the Roman equivalent of the Greek *epidoseis*:

> Let us senators, bring into the treasury tomorrow all our gold, silver, and coined bronze, [various minimum quantities excepted]. All the rest . . . let us immediately carry to the triumviri for banking affairs, no decree of the Senate having been previously made, so that our voluntary contributions, and our action in assisting the state, may excite the minds, first, of the equestrian order to emulate us, and after them of the rest of the community. . . . The Senate was adjourned, and every member brought his gold, silver, and bronze into the treasury, each vying with the other to have his name appear among the first on the public tables. . . . The unanimity displayed by the Senate was imitated by the equestrian order, and that of the equestrian order by the commons. Thus without any edict, or coercion of the magistrates, the state neither lacked rowers to make up the numbers, nor money to pay them.[55]

The stream of voluntary contributions lasted until 205 B.C., when a further round helped finance Scipio's victorious expedition to Africa. The significant feature of these contributions to the war effort is that, like the liturgy of the First Punic War, they took the form of a contingent loan—contingent, that is, on a Roman victory. As that victory loomed into sight in 204 B.C., and the booty started to roll in, a formal repayment structure was established, at least for the amounts contributed in 210. One-third was made payable in 204 B.C., with two further equal installments to be paid in 202 and 200 B.C.

It was not merely the voluntary contributions that were repaid from the fruits of victory. In 187 B.C. the arrival of new shipments of booty from

Greece allowed the repayment of all the supplementary levies of *tributum* that had been raised during the second war. It is quite possible that such repayments of taxation had occurred before, unrecorded by later historians; but in the absence of such records, the repayment of taxes in 187 B.C. must be considered an event quite as seminal in the history of public finance as the repayment of the liturgy of 242 B.C. One and a half millennia later, the citizens of the city-states of medieval Italy were to take up the principle of repayable taxation and develop it into the centerpiece of their public finances, quite unconscious (it seems) of any ancient precedent. And yet, however portentous it may appear in retrospect, there is nothing that should be so very surprising in the action of the Romans. They were simply operating on the principle that all monetary contributions from the citizens, whether voluntary, semivoluntary, or compulsory, should be considered repayable if the fortunes of war allowed. In no case was there any mention of interest. The repayment of the citizens' war contributions was just a method of adapting the primitive division of spoils among the members of the tribe to the requirements of monetized public finance.

The exact amounts raised by these contributions is not known, but some estimate of their magnitude can be made. For the first war, the historian Tenney Frank[56] suggested a figure of 3 million denarii. In the second war, loans took on a far more important role. The only way to estimate them is that the booty taken at the end of the war was barely sufficient to repay the debts still outstanding. By 200 B.C. any remaining funds were required for the Macedonian War, and the final debt payment had to be made via grants of public land. Livy valued the booty taken from Carthage at just over 11 million denarii. If that was the case, then, the outstanding public debt may have come to around 15 million denarii. The tax repayments of 187 B.C. came to a further 22.5 million. The total of all types of repayable contributions would have been in the region of 40 million denarii.

The implication of these figures is extraordinary. Forty million denarii is the equivalent of 6,000 talents—a figure far greater than any other instance of public debt yet encountered in the ancient world. The national income of third-century Rome can be estimated in only the most tentative way, but given the importance of the events involved, it is worth the attempt. One possibility is to use the assessed national wealth implicit in the *tributum* payments. This sum has been calculated at 887 million denarii.[57] If the Romans estimated capital values by multiplying incomes by a fixed multiple, the multiple would most likely have been based on the current legal interest rate of 8.33%. In this case, national income would have been around 75 million denarii. Another estimate is possible on the basis of the pay of the legionaries. If the basic foot soldier's stipend of ⅓ denarius per day bore a reasonable relationship to national income per capita (a tolerable assumption given that the entire citizen body was liable for military service), then national income would be more like 50 million denarii. In either case the Roman public debt would have been more than 50% of GNP and would probably have placed the republic over the 60% threshold of fiscal prudence laid down by the sages who framed the Maastricht Treaty. On the other hand Rome's debt was interest-free, and its repayment was only a contingent obligation. Its management was therefore a simple affair.

The "loans" described above were not the only responses of Rome to the financial crises of the Punic Wars. Like Dionysius of Syracuse, the Roman Republic has gone down in history as settling its debts by means of currency debasement. The third-century coinage of Rome consisted of large cast-bronze pieces centered around the as, an unwieldy affair weighing 10 Roman ounces. (The original as had weighed a full Roman pound of 12 ounces, or 327.5 grams, and had evolved out of a more primitive system depending entirely on payment by weight). This bronze coinage circulated internally in parallel with an unrelated silver currency based on the drachma, which was used for external trade with the Greeks of southern Italy. This idiosyncratic dual currency managed to survive the ravages of the First Punic War more or less unscathed. The second war was another matter. Under the stress of Hannibal's invasion the whole system collapsed. Only in 211 was the military and financial situation sufficiently restored to permit the creation of a new bimetallic system based on a 2-ounce as and a new 4.55-gram silver coin very similar to a drachma, but known as the denarius ("10 asses") to express its new fixed relationship with copper. The old as had lost no less than 80% of its weight in the process.

The implications of such a loss of value are significant enough, but under a series of interpretations and misinterpretations handed down from Pliny to Adam Smith, a devaluation of four-fifths swelled into a cumulative devaluation of twenty-three twenty-fourths (96%) over a period of a century. *The Wealth of Nations* is acerbic on the causes and effects of such monetary policies:

> The raising of denomination of the coin has been the most usual expedient by which a real public bankruptcy has been disguised under the appearance of a pretended payment. . . . By combining the three Roman operations into one, a debt of a hundred and twenty-eight millions of our present money, might in this

> manner be reduced all at once to a debt of £5,333,333 6s 8d. Even the enormous debt of Great Britain might in this manner soon be paid.[58]

Such strictures make sense only in the light of eighteenth-century financial practice. Rome did not have a public debt of the type familiar to Adam Smith. The "debt" described above was totally contingent on military success and was therefore not subject to such legalistic niceties as debasement of the currency. The most likely reason for the minting of lower-weight coins was to relieve an acute shortage of bronze money within the city. Bronze was still an important metal for military uses—such as shields, wagons, and harnesses—and therefore tended to become scarce during protracted military campaigns. This problem was exacerbated in the second war by Hannibal's conquest of Etruria, which shut off Rome's supply of the metal. A severe credit crisis at all levels was the inevitable result. In the circumstances, the move toward a silver-based currency with reduced-weight subsidiary bronze coins was an intelligent solution. It is almost certainly true that the currency reform was intended to provide debt relief as well as to create a more functional monetary system, but private, not public, debts were its main target. This, in any case, is the implication of the Roman historian whose version of events most closely conforms to the surviving numismatic evidence:

> Sextantal [2-ounce] asses came into use when because of the Hannibalic War the Senate decreed that instead of being libral [i.e., 1 pound] asses should be sextantal; their intention was that when the latter were used for discharging obligations the Roman people would be relieved of its indebtedness and private individuals to whom the state owed money would not suffer serious loss.[59]

By far the biggest public expense during the war was military pay, and it seems that this was restated in terms of the new silver-based currency at ⅓ denarius per day. Amounts payable to suppliers outside the city can scarcely have been affected since such payments were already made in silver rather than bronze, and if anything the new silver currency was heavier than the old. It is possible (although not certain) that some domestic suppliers suffered in the reform, but only in the context of generalized sacrifices made by all citizens in those desperate years.

Whatever the nature of the events surrounding the monetary reform of 211 B.C., the new silver denarius was to become the monetary foundation of the late republic and the empire. Its initial weight of 4.55 grams fell to around 3.9 grams by the end of the war. At this level it stabilized, surviving the chaos of the late republic, and remaining essentially unaltered until the reign of Nero (A.D. 54–68). From his reign to that of Marcus Aurelius (A.D. 161–180), it was subjected to modest periodic devaluations, so that by the end of the golden age of the empire, it contained just over 2.5 grams of silver. During this period the denarius fully justified its acceptance as the international currency standard, in essence continuing the role of the Greek drachma on which it had originally been modeled.

IMPERIUM ROMANUM

The Second Punic War marked the turning point in Rome's rise to power. After 200 B.C., it went forward to a series of victories that, far from threatening its survival or solvency, brought it a continuing stream of booty paraded through its streets in ever more extravagant triumphal processions. With the supplementary tax assessments of the Second Punic War refunded in 187 B.C., the next step was obvious. In 167 B.C. the Senate decided that the profits from imperial expansion were sufficient to allow the *tributum* to be entirely abolished. The Romans thereafter enjoyed a half-millennium tax holiday. The subjects would have been amazed if the Senate had done otherwise. Not surprisingly, there is no more evidence of the emergency fiscal measures that so strangely anticipated the financial practices of medieval Italy.

Yet the thirteen hundred years that separate the ancient and medieval city-states cannot merely be passed over in silence. When the states of medieval Europe rediscovered the art of public borrowing, they were operating in a vacuum. There were no contemporary examples to follow. This aspect of the finances of European states would have surprised—and certainly not impressed—an informed visitor from the more sophisticated cultures of the East. It is inconceivable that there were any useful memories or records from the ancient world to act as a guide. And yet clearly something occurred in the dissolution of the classical world that can explain, or at least shed some light on, the origins of societies that, however dynamic, seemed to be almost congenitally incapable of running balanced budgets. The first place to look is the transition from the Roman Republic to the Roman Empire.

From the point of view of classical republican virtue, the road to imperial glory was a poisoned chalice. To rule an population of fifty million was not possible using a constitution that depended on cosanguineal tribal relationships within one city. There were not enough Romans to go around, and, like empire builders before them, the Romans needed to co-opt the services of their defeated opponents. One of the most historic innovations of the Romans, as early as the fourth century B.C., was the offer of citizenship, or partial citizenship, to non-Romans as a method of imperial expansion.[60] Taken in tandem with the equally remarkable habit of regularly freeing their slaves, the Romans can claim to be the first people in history to establish a concept of political liberty that extended beyond the immediate tribe. But the dilution of tribal freedom came at a cost, and ultimately it proved impossible to reconcile the forms of republican life with the ineluctable facts of empire. To cope with the astonishing sweep of his conquests, Alexander the Great had assumed the role of divine ruler, declaring that all were equal who accepted his authority. The Romans were forced down a similar route, which led toward oriental divinity and global citizenship. In the end, the old Roman families would suffer the indignity of finding their empire run by an oriental despot surrounded by freed slaves.

And yet the process by which this occurred was remarkably slow. Alexander had entered into his new imperial role with positive gusto. He was doing little more than following the example of the Persians before him.[61] Of course neither the Macedonians nor the Persians had evolved the sophisticated republican constitution of the Romans. The Greeks considered the Macedonians untutored barbarians, still living in the age of tribal chieftaincy. The Persians were little different. The Romans, by contrast, let go of their republic only with the greatest reluctance.

The best-known product of this reluctance is the constitutional facade erected by Augustus. This "crafty tyrant" had no desire to suffer the fate of his uncle, who had so rashly toyed with the title of "king." The first emperor therefore accepted no powers that had not at one time or another been granted to his predecessors. He merely held a very large number of "republican" offices for life. Within Rome this allowed the illusion that the ancient constitution was still alive. In the distant provinces such legal niceties were meaningless, and the subject population merely welcomed their release from a century of republican exploitation by a benevolent despot.

Nor did the Romans rush to adopt the financial practices of earlier empires. As long as they could, they continued their traditional pattern of surplus distribution. The citizen army was financed out of the spoils of war. In addition to their regular pay, soldiers were paid generous bonuses at the conclusion of each campaign. As a result the treasury never contained more than a portion of the booty, indemnities, and tribute that were extracted from the vanquished kingdoms and cities of the ancient world. Indemnities and booty collected from 200 to 157 B.C. amounted to around 260 million denarii (about 40,000 talents), but only 26 million denarii remained in the treasury by that date, a small sum when compared to the extent of the empire by that time.[62]

This relatively small treasury probably represented the high point of the republic's finances, and thereafter the booty stream was not always sufficient to pay for the costs of virtually unceasing warfare. The conquest of the east brought in vast sums, but much fell into the hands of the generals. Julius Caesar found the state treasury empty and only 12 million denarii in the sacred treasury when he entered Rome after crossing the Rubicon. In his quadruple triumph of 46 B.C. he displayed booty worth no less than 400 million denarii. Of this, 200 million were distributed in acts of extravagant largesse, including payments of 6,000 denarii each to his legionaries—the equivalent of more than twenty-six years' basic pay! At the Ides of March of 44 B.C. there were still 175 million denarii to be found in the treasury; but this sum was rapidly consumed in the civil war that followed.

The situation was rectified by Augustus, into whose capable hands the empire and its accumulated plunder fell. His personal fortune must have been immense by the time of his victory over his rival, Mark Antony, at the battle of Actium, but he had the wit to use it for public purposes and to die a relatively poor man. In the *Res Gesta* he claimed to have given away the vast sum of 600 million denarii to disbanded soldiers, the plebs, and the public treasury, apart from other sums spent on public building programs. These gestures of political largesse did much to restore social tranquillity, but rather less to rebuild the public treasury, which contained 25 million denarii (4,000 talents) at the time of his death in A.D. 14, no more than in 157 B.C. This was an astonishingly low sum for the greatest empire the world had yet seen. Not only does it pale into insignificance when compared to the 180,000 talents of Darius II, but even the 9,700-talent treasury of the diminutive fifth-century Athenian empire was twice as large, while in A.D. 23 the Chinese emperor Wang Mang had over forty times as much in his reserves.[63]*

The fiscal system of the Augustan state was scarcely more extensive than its treasury. As conqueror of the ancient world, Rome was, of course,

*The corollary of such governmental openhandedness was an abundance of money within the economy. The Augustan period witnessed the lowest recorded interest rates of the ancient world, with commercial loans for good credit recorded as low as 4%. This can be compared to interest rates of 36% in China at the same time, and to minimum rates of 15% for secured credit and 24% for unsecured in India in the late centuries B.C.

entitled to collect taxes as it thought fit. But the tax burden that Augustus thought fit to impose was evidently not very great. Two records of the revenues of his empire survive, giving a total income of 150 and 200 million denarii (23,000 and 32,000 talents). These are certainly impressive sums in absolute terms, but not in relative ones—by one calculation they represented no more than 3.33–4.0% of GNP.[64] Darius II had enjoyed a similar income in an empire with a population one-third as large.

Perhaps equally significant is the nature of the taxes collected. No more than one-third of the total came from direct taxes—the main prop of all empires past. One-quarter of the revenues came from customs duties, 15–18% from the imperial estates, 12–13% from the emancipation tax on freed slaves, and the rest from various lesser dues. None of these taxes impinged heavily on the economy. In contrast to the Ptolemaic policy of state taxation and regulation of every aspect of economic life, the Romans pursued a policy of almost complete laissez-faire. In this they followed the example of the Greek city-states. Even within Egypt, which was administered as an imperial estate, the state monopolies were relaxed, and much land was returned to the private sector. The Ptolemaic import duties of 25–50% were lowered to the negligible 2–2.5% that was the standard throughout the empire.

Even the direct taxes of the empire were not what they seemed. The *tributum*, abolished in Rome, now took on a second life as the direct tax paid by its subjects. Under the republic its collection was handed over to Roman tax farmers,* in whose hands it became truly an instrument of imperial oppression. One of the principle measures of pacification undertaken by Augustus was the removal of these hated figures. Thereafter the central government fixed the amount to be paid by each province but left collection to the local city elites. The result was a renewed emphasis on the semivoluntary civic finance that had characterized the Greek world:

> The solution appears to have been to eschew taxation of property as such and to set in its place a body of public-spirited contributors to communal finances. . . .
>
> One accumulated riches and otherwise exploited fellow citizens in the way of private business, but in public matters open-handedness was the rule. Far from evading taxes or trying to pass the burden down to lower social levels, one gloried in one's scale of contributions and paid heavily for the privilege of a

*Tax farming is a system in which the government subcontracts the collection of a tax to a group of private investors. The tax farmers agree to pay the government a fixed sum and take the risk of how much they will eventually collect from the taxpayers.

> public memorial. Nothing quite like it has happened again in the history of public finance; it was one of the traditions of Antiquity that fell once and for all with the end of the Roman Empire.[65]

The municipalization of the empire was evident in places as different as Gaul and Egypt. Where there were no cities, the Romans built them. Where they already existed, their autonomy was encouraged. In A.D. 132 Hadrian founded the Panhellenion in evocation of the Achaean League. Citizenship was granted freely to co-opt the local elites, and they were generally happy to be co-opted. In A.D. 143 the Greek orator Aelius Aristides waxed lyrical about this novel concept of empire:

> [Prior to the Roman Empire] government and slave management were not yet differentiated, but king and master were equivalent terms. . . . For all who have ever gained empire, you alone rule over men who are free . . . nor is the country said to be enslaved. . . . [Thanks to] your magnificent citizenship, with its grand conception, [unparalleled] in the records of mankind, . . . there is no need of garrisons to hold their citadels, but the men of greatest standing and influence in every city guard their own fatherlands for you.[66]

Aelius did not specifically praise the paucity of direct taxation within the empire in his lengthy eulogy. But as a right-minded Greek, he would scarcely have considered his country "free" had it been subject to heavy direct taxes.

The tax base of the early empire was so low, and collection so decentralized, that one can reasonably wonder how it survived. One of Augustus' most important reforms was a dramatic reduction in military costs. Half the army was disbanded, and the emphasis on imperial expansion gave way to a more defensive strategy. The residual standing army of under 300,000 was not a large force in relation to a population of fifty million, let alone to the length of the border. (By way of comparison, Chandragupta Maurya, the founder of the Mauryan empire, is reputed to have maintained a standing army of around 650,000 in a population of no more than twenty million.) For the system to work, twenty-five legions had to be adequate for any military contingency, and the tax base had to permit a modest peacetime surplus so that a reasonable treasury could be built up. For the following two hundred years, the size of the imperial treasury fluctuated, but only three emperors left it full (Tiberius in A.D. 36, Antoninus Pius in 143, and Septimius Severus in 211), and many left it empty.[67]

The modest central tax-gathering system of the early empire may help to explain the severe fiscal problems of its later history. In the third century

A.D. a series of foreign invasions led to a doubling in the size of the army. Yet it seems to have been virtually impossible to increase the existing taxes in order to cope with this additional expense. The cities had become too used to their fiscal autonomy. Instead the emperors resorted to debasement of the currency. By the time of Claudius II (A.D. 267–270) the currency had lost 98.4% of its value of one hundred years earlier. The cash economy was in disarray, and the only way to restore the public finances was a move to taxation in kind. Since silver had been the core of the Greco-Roman monetary system since the invention of coins, its disappearance from circulation was shocking. In A.D. 301 Diocletian attempted to retrieve the situation by issuing a new silver coin with the same weight as the old denarius, but his silver supplies were too limited to give the coin wide circulation. After his voluntary retirement from office in 305, the process of devaluation recommenced and accelerated. By 320 the new coin had lost 70% of its value.

The classical world had come full circle. Its flowering was encapsulated by the life span of the drachma-denarius currency standard. The Roman Empire would continue in existence for another millennium within an increasingly restricted area, but only by a process of evolution and transformation that would leave it almost unrecognizable.

BREAKDOWN

From the end of the second century A.D. a wave of tribal movements, in some ways comparable to those at the end of the Bronze Age, disrupted and finally overthrew the classical world. The history of the period until the end of the first millennium is a litany of Scythians, Huns, Goths, Vandals, Saxons, Franks, Avars, Bulgars, Bedouin, Danes, Vikings, Normans, and Magyars—the list could easily be extended. No civilization was immune. For each, the process continued until such time as a new, reinvigorated society, formed either by internal reform or out of some synthesis of conquerors and conquered, proved strong enough to withstand the next wave. But it was in western Europe that the collapse of central power was longest and most complete.

The first victim of the process was the empire established by Augustus. The internal struggles of rival pretenders to the imperial throne sucked the treasury dry and removed the legions from their border posts, thus opening up the frontiers to dangers from abroad. After the disasters of the third century A.D. Diocletian managed to restore order; but a very different kind of order from that of the early empire. State finances were reorganized around a newly created poll tax and a land tax based on a percentage of crop production and payable in kind. These were exactly the kind of taxes that had been absent from the early empire, with the exception of the imperial province of Egypt. The state bureaucracy was enlarged, and a harsher penal code was enforced. The powers of the Senate were reduced to virtual insignificance, while Diocletian removed the seat of government from Rome, divided the empire into two halves, and established himself in the eastern half as a remote and increasingly theocratic figure.

Diocletian's successor, Constantine the Great (306–337) temporarily reunited the empire after nearly twenty years of struggle but confirmed the new trend by the foundation of Constantinople as his capital. Whereas Augustan Rome had no city walls, both the new capital and its predecessor now boasted the strongest fortifications that the imperial engineers could devise. The easygoing religious pluralism of the old pagan pantheon was replaced by a new monolithic state religion. Although Constantine was, in theory, a believer in religious tolerance, his conversion to Christianity gave him justification to replenish the imperial treasury by confiscating the wealth of the old pagan temples. The gold thus acquired helped him to establish a new currency standard based on a new gold coin, reassuringly named the solidus,* that now served as the main vehicle of taxation, spending and treasure accumulation.

In the eastern half of the empire the new political and fiscal arrangements established lasting roots, especially after the administrative reforms of Theodosius II in the early fifth century. That the Eastern Empire managed to survive while the West did not owed a great deal to this. Theodosius was in a position to buy off Attila by payments totalling 1.28 million solidi between 433 and 450, and thus to deflect his attention further west.[68] By the sixth century the Byzantine emperors had revenues of around 5–6 million solidi (12,000–15,000 talents), or by some accounts considerably more, and in 518 Anastasius I left a treasury of more than 23 million solidi (60,000 silver talents or 105 tons of gold).[69]

The opposite occurred in the West. It would take hundreds of years for the process of disintegration work its way through. Each time a respite

*The solidus contained 4.55 grams of gold. It proved to be as good as its name and remained unaltered for seven hundred years as the official coin of the Byzantine Empire. It also provided the model for the gold dinar of the Islamic caliphate and for the gold florins and ducats of late medieval Europe.

seemed at hand, it proved to be temporary. In the early fifth century the Germanic tribes, which could no longer be kept at bay, established kingdoms throughout the Western Empire. Under the most romanized of them, the Ostrogoths, who controlled Italy and Illyria, it seemed briefly that a new period of stability and recovery might emerge. But then a reconquest by the Byzantine emperor Justinian in the sixth century inflicted even more destruction than the previous barbarian invasion. In the seventh century Justinian's work was undone by the Arabs in the south, and by the Lombards in the north. In the eighth century the Lombards fell to the Franks under Charlemagne, who appeared for a short moment around 800 to be capable of reestablishing a new stable imperial structure under which Western Christendom might recover. It was not to be. His empire was divided three ways on his death, and its fragmentation coincided with—and possibly allowed—the incursions of the Norsemen and Magyars in the ninth and tenth centuries.

One result of the arrival of the barbarian kingdoms was the intrusion of tribal customs. The most controversial aspect is political. The Germanic tribes brought with them the tradition of seasonal assemblies at which communal matters were decided. Two hundred years ago, it was taken almost for granted that the parliamentary bodies of western Europe were the linear descendants of these assemblies. Perhaps not surprisingly, the events of the twentieth century have caused such ideas to fall into disrepute. Teutonic tribalism has produced too many unattractive offspring to make it a desirable ancestor. Modern research has also contradicted the simplistic visions of the writers of the seventeenth and eighteenth centuries. The role of tribal assemblies in the Dark Age kingdoms is, nowadays, played down, and the autonomy of their kings is emphasized.

Undoubtedly the act of conquest produced the same tensions within Germanic society as it had in other tribal conquerors. The leaders of the Goths and Franks, like so many before them, sought to increase their power and authority not only by assuming the mantle of the overthrown empire, but by enveloping themselves in the aura of divine sanctification. The position of the council of elders was undermined by the infiltration of retinues of warriors owing direct allegiance to their chief. The need to co-opt the services of the defeated elites led to a weakening of the tribal bonds. The sheer distances involved hindered the convening of regular meetings. Yet, for all this, assemblies of some sort continued to meet, even if less frequently, and important business was still transacted. Visigothic and Lombard assemblies appear to have retained the power to elect kings. The

Merovingian kings managed to establish the hereditary principle, but even in France the principle of elected kingship did not entirely disappear. In 987 the replacement of the decaying Carolingian dynasty by the Capetian was accomplished by the formal election of Hugh Capet at an assembly of nobles and clergy. The endurance of the ideal of popular assent to legislation is shown in the Edict of Pitres of 864, enacted "by the consent of the people and royal decree."[70]

For the purposes of this book, however, the most important aspect of the breakdown of the state was financial. Here, too, the intrusion of tribal customs had their part to play. The assemblies were occasions for quasi-fiscal gift exchange. Hincmar, the court historian of the Carolingians, described the *annua dona,* or *dona militum*—gifts to the king to display loyalty or to help fund his campaigns. Conversely the king gave regular gifts to his followers so as to ensure their continued loyalty. Even the most powerful ruler of the Dark Ages, Charlemagne, was not exempt from these rules:

> [In 792] King Charles held an assembly at Regensburg; and when he saw his faithful men, bishops, abbots and counts, who were with him there, and the rest of the faithful people, who had not joined with Pippin [his son] in that terrible conspiracy, he rewarded them many-fold with gold and silver and other gifts.[71]

The survival of old customs in financial matters went beyond gift exchange. When direct taxation made a precocious reappearance in England to pay the Danegeld (tribute paid to the Danes following the well-understood principle that tax exemption for the conquerors means tax subjection for the vanquished), seven out of nine levies were recorded as being formally approved by the Witenagemot, the descendant of the old tribal council of elders.[72]

Together with gifts there appeared those other perennial favorites of tribal finance: plunder and tribute. Each wave of barbarian invasion was accompanied by the usual pillage. But the practice did not disappear even in the more established and advanced kingdoms. The Frankish writers complained bitterly of destructive effects of the Viking raids on the Carolingian "renaissance," but the Franks lived almost equally on a stream of plunder and tribute. When Charles III was forced to pay tribute to the Vikings in 882, he was roundly condemned by the chronicler: "He did not blush to pay tribute, against the custom of his ancestors, the kings of the Franks, . . . to a man from whom he ought to have exacted tribute and hostages."[73] The crucial point here is not the allure of the spoils of war per se, but their substitution for taxation and expenditure. An eighth-century writer was only slightly exaggerating when he asserted that "nowadays no-one leads fighting-men at his own expense, but instead maintains them through violence and theft."[74]

The reappearance of more primitive forms of public finance, however, leaves unanswered a fundamental question: What happened to the old Roman taxes? The first part of the answer seems to be that the mildness of the tax regime of the early empire may have undermined the tax-raising efforts of later emperors. The new direct taxes inaugurated by Diocletian came as a shock to citizens accustomed to fiscal independence and semivoluntary contributions. Never was the ancient horror of direct taxation as the equivalence of servitude more clearly expressed than in the lament of a contemporary commentator:

> The census takers spread everywhere, overturning everything: it was an image of the tumult of war and of hideous captivity. The fields were measured clod by clod, the vines and trees were counted, animals of all kinds were registered, the heads of men were noted down; in each city the urban and rural commoners were assembled, all the public squares were full of families in flocks. . . . What the ancients had done by right of war to the vanquished, Galerius [Diocletian's successor] dared to do against Romans and Roman subjects.[75]

The new land taxes were charged at rates that led to the progressive abandonment of agricultural land. The government became so concerned that it took measures to force the peasants to remain on the land—the first intimation of the full-fledged serfdom that was to be the lot of their descendants. Many became unwilling to support either the military effort or the taxes necessary for it: "The true victory is that which will allow us to be equally unconcerned about the Scythians and about the tax collectors. . . . To a wretch it hardly matters whether his misery results from the act of a Scythian or from that of a Roman."[76] On one level this comment from a senator in Constantinople in the late fourth century is yet another example of the equation of taxation with conquest. But it also reveals a level of defeatism that makes one wonder how the Eastern Empire managed to survive any longer than the Western. It very nearly did not; only the skillful deflection of the barbarians into the West in the fifth century and a revival of the martial spirit in the sixth under Justinian saved it. In the Byzantine Empire, at least, the new tax system and the bureaucracy required for its collection established lasting roots. In the West, however, the principle of direct taxation scarcely seems to have acquired legitimacy. The senatorial class, which controlled so much prime agricultural land, managed to escape taxation almost entirely. In the words of one historian, "The local Roman aristocracies . . . sabotaged the whole system; by the time that the Germans established organized successor states, taxation was barely possible."[77] In 458 the emperor Majorian admitted fiscal defeat and remitted all arrears of taxes. By the seventh century a chronicler could write as established history that the Burgundians were invited into Gaul by Roman citizens "so that they might throw off the taxes of the empire."[78]

When the Germans first established their kingdoms, they experienced no financial shortfall. The treasuries of the early barbarian kings were bulging with the spoil of their conquests. The Ostrogoth treasury contained 2.9 million solidi (the equivalent of over 7,000 silver talents) at the time of its capture by Justinian. But while the new rulers initially maintained the old Roman taxes, they had less need for them. For one thing it was no longer necessary to pay the Roman armed forces. The Goths were not a paid army but had lived off booty and pillage like all tribal hordes. When such sources of income became less readily available, the warriors were assigned Roman lands for their support. But this strategy only accelerated the decay of the tax system. Because the Goths and Franks were not subject to tax any more than other successful tribal conquerors in past times, their settlement on the land led to an immediate fall in land tax revenues. Equally important was the inevitable temptation for other landowners to donate their lands to the invaders and receive them back in vassalage. In this way their lands, too, became tax-exempt. The dwindling number of taxpayers increasingly resisted their subservient position. Indeed, without a paid army, what purpose did taxation serve except the unwarranted enrichment of kings?

> In the seventh century, authors could take it for granted that the payment of tribute was incompatible with freedom and that its imposition constituted an act of oppression. Marculf's formulary officially defined the "truly free man" (*bene ingenuus*) as one whose name did not appear in a tax register.[79]

In this way the word *Frank* started to lose its connotation of nationality and took on a new meaning of "free"—and especially "free from tax."

It was perhaps not surprising, then, that the last glimmer of the old Roman taxes, and with them the old Roman coinage, faded during the seventh century, perhaps the very darkest point of the Dark Ages. The last record of land tax received by the Frankish kings is from 632, and in 674–679 the last gold coins were minted for Dagobert II.[80]

For the peasant farmer, however, the tax burden had not entirely disappeared. He simply paid his "taxes" to his Germanic overlord rather than to the state. The allocation of lands to the invaders and the consequent demonetization of society was the start of a process that ended up in the fully elaborated system known as *feudalism*. In its purest state—in which political and landholding relationships are based on oaths of allegiance rather then money exchange—feudalism may indeed have existed only in western Europe, as Marx maintained (allowing only the possible exception of Japan). But it is clear that somewhat similar processes took place in other societies confronted with the difficulty of maintaining a large, salaried army. Reduced to its fiscal core, feudalism may be defined as the simplification of state finances by turning soldiers into tax collectors and allowing them to keep the proceeds in lieu of wages. In this way an enormous bureaucratic effort could be avoided, but only at the cost of a considerable weakening of the central powers of the state. Unlike the twin practices of division of spoils and "gifts," fiscal feudalization did not represent the intrusion of tribal customs, although it was often provoked by tribal pressure on mature civilizations. In fact it generally depended on the preexistence of the land taxes typical of centralized civilizations. The degree of breakdown of central tax authority involved in feudalization varied greatly and depended on such factors as whether the land grants represented all or only part of the pay; whether they were hereditary; how easily they could be reclaimed or reassigned; and whether the king made grants directly to the common soldiers or allowed them to become subgrantees of a relatively few powerful grant holders. In western Europe the state's tax authority disappeared almost entirely. There was no residue of central pay, the fiefdoms became hereditary, and the common soldiers became subvassals of the great feudal lords, whose power was very often greater than that of the monarch, whatever his abstract claims to overlordship. This was not the case elsewhere.

By the end of the first millennium, the kings of western Europe had almost entirely lost the right to tax their subjects. The limited authority of the Carolingians is paradoxically revealed in the first glimmerings of a return to taxation in the ninth century, when Charles the Bald, successor to the French portion of Charlemagne's empire, had to raise special levies to pay off the Vikings. His inability to put his hands on periodic sums of between 3,000 and 6,000 pounds of silver out of his regular income during the 860s is almost astonishing when it is considered that "such sums cumulatively would not have presented any difficulty . . . even to a reasonably wealthy [Roman] landowner."[81]

In no other part of the civilized world was the process of breakdown so prolonged or extreme. The eastern half of the Roman Empire successfully transformed itself after a mere century of setbacks. Under Justinian and his successors the Byzantine Empire was still the foremost power of its day, rivaled only by the Sassanian Empire of Persia on its eastern border. The seventh century, however, witnessed massive losses of territory to the Muslims, and in the wake of this disaster Byzantium underwent a process of fiscal decentralization that some have compared to feudalism. A system of military "themes" allocated state lands to soldiers. These lands were hereditary, but dependent on continued military service. Most important—and here Byzantium differed sharply from western Europe—the "themes" represented only part of the soldiers' pay, the rest being made up in cash payments that may have averaged 9 solidi a year over his total period of active duty. Even the reduced Byzantine Empire of the ninth century, no larger or more populous that Charlemagne's at its height, had revenues in excess of 3 million solidi, nearly one hundred times the amounts that Charles the Bald struggled to raise in order to pay off the Vikings. The Byzantine budget was compatible with maintaining a standing army of 120,000 and the accumulation of a treasury of 13.7 million solidi in 856, equivalent to nearly five years' expenses.[82] Clearly "feudalization" did relatively little to weaken the Byzantine state at the initial stage of its introduction. Only after the setbacks of the eleventh century, when much of modern Turkey was lost to the Seljuk Empire, did it take on a more aristocratic form and the state start to lose direct contact with its farmer-soldiers.

The Arab conquest of the Sassanian Empire and of the Byzantine possessions in Egypt and the Middle East was so fast that no real breakdown of central authority occurred. The Arabs simply took over the land and poll taxes of the Romans and the Sassanids, reformed them along proper Islamic lines, and probably increased them. According to a contemporary eyewitness, Bishop John of Nakiu, "The Moslems took possession of all the land of Egypt, southern and northern, and trebled their taxes."[83] Certainly the early caliphs did not want for income. At its zenith under Harun al Rashid in the late eighth century, the Abbasid caliphate is recorded as having revenues that may have exceeded 35 million dinars.[84]* Even allowing for a population two and one half times as large as that of Byzantium, this sum is truly impressive and would exceed the largest known figure for the

---

*The dinar was the Byzantine solidus (or "gold denarius") inherited and adapted from the conquered provinces of Egypt and Syria.

revenues of the Roman Empire at its height, in spite of a population probably no more than half as large.

In later centuries, however, Islam, too, went through a process that has sometimes been compared to feudalism. Initially it was easy to reward the soldiers of Allah with the spoils of war. Under the caliphate the stream of booty was replaced by salaries that may have been the highest in relative terms in recorded history. Each foot soldier was paid around 65 dinars per year (a figure which has to be compared to 9 dinars per year for contemporary Byzantine soldiers, the equivalent of about 18 dinars for the legionaries of the early Roman Empire).[85] Such pay scales made the army effectively a ruling elite. As the fortunes of the caliphate waned and its income fell—to around 20 million dinars in the ninth century, and to under 15 million in the early tenth century—this financial burden became untenable. The state now resorted to the *iqta* system, which allocated specific land tax revenues to its soldiers in lieu of pay. This system was taken up in varying degrees and forms by all the later Islamic empires, including the Seljuk, the Ilkhan, the Ottoman, the Safavid, and the Moghul. The state never lost total control of the underlying land, however. The grants were rarely hereditary and could generally be revoked and reassigned at will:

> With the solid intellectual and administrative traditions of the East, the distinction between private and public rights was never obscured as it was in the West. . . . Economically the *muqta* [holder of an *iqta*] differed from the western lord in that he lived in the town and did not have to organise his rural lands. . . . He drew an income from the soil, and that is all.[86]

The Indian subcontinent, too, felt the impact of the Huns. Here, however, the nomadic invaders were less successful. The Gupta empire successfully repelled their assaults, and though the the empire did not long survive the effort, the result was political fragmentation rather than social and economic regression. In less than one century, northern India was largely reunited under Harsha, the last of the great Hindu empire builders.

Only in northern China did central tax authority decline to levels similar to those of western Europe. In the early fourth century a wave of invasions by mounted tribes from the steppes broke the defenses of the Great Wall. A period of unstable barbarian regimes was accompanied by a collapse of the cash economy and a return to payments in kind to support a warrior aristocracy. The south avoided barbarian rule but experienced a succession of short-lived dynasties that, although politically weak, preserved Han culture. However, the Chinese breakdown was not so prolonged as that of western Europe. By the late fifth century the wave of invasions had passed and the surviving barbarian regimes started, like so many others in Chinese history, to "sinicize." In the late sixth and early seventh centuries, just as Europe was entering its darkest phase, China was reunited under strong, centralized, tax-gathering regimes—the Sui and their successors, the T'ang. These dynasties came from the "barbarian" north but were nonetheless the restorers of political, cultural, and economic progress. How was it that they were able to reestablish central authority so completely? Perhaps the answer lies in the southern part of the country, which had never quite lost the Han traditions of culture and government. The Sui and the T'ang were able to use these traditions when they reunited the empire. The imperial bureaucracy was revitalized and warrior aristocracy was struck a permanent blow by the creation of the examination system, which was to last until the twentieth century. Equally important was the restoration of central tax powers. The T'ang reimposed the old land and poll taxes, and at its zenith the dynasty enjoyed the largest revenues of their time. By the ninth century imperial revenues had reached the impressive total of 57 million "strings,"* an income almost double that of the caliphate at its height, although from a population probably twice as large.

Just how far the tax base of western Europe declined compared to that of the civilized world (in which it could no longer reasonably expect to be included) is shown in the table below, which relates some of the figures mentioned above to estimates of population.

POPULATIONS AND TAX REVENUES, 350 B.C.–A.D. 1200[87]

	Population *Millions*	Revenue *Tons of silver*	Revenue per Head *Grams of silver*
Persia, c. 350 B.C.	17	697	41
Egypt, c. 200 B.C.	7	384	55
Rome, c. A.D. 1	50	825	17
Rome, c. A.D. 150	50	1,050	21
Byzantium, c. A.D. 850	10	150	15
Abbasids, c. A.D. 800	26	1,260	48
T'ang, c. A.D. 850	50	2,145	43
France, A.D. 1221	8.5	20.3	2.4
England, A.D. 1203	2.5	11.5	4.6

*A string consisted of 1,000 copper coins and was officially valued at 39 grams of silver. Only a very small proportion of the government's revenues were paid in coin. The majority was paid either in lengths of silk that also served as a general means of exchange, or in grain.

Of course, these figures are only the broadest approximation and make no allowance for variations in the purchasing power of silver at different times and places.[88] But the overall picture remains clear—especially when it is considered that the figures for France and England are from a later period, when monarchs were starting to recover some of their lost powers of taxation. If it were possible to come up with a valid figure for the empire of Charlemagne in 800, the comparison would probably look even more extreme.

TWO

CITIZEN CREDITORS

> The Monte [public debt fund] is the heart of this body which we call city. . . . Every limb, large and small, must contribute to preserving this heart as the guardian fortress, immovable rock and enduring certainty of the salvation of the whole body and government of your state.[1]
>
> —Budget of the Florentine Republic, 1470

THE RETURN OF THE CITY-STATE

Rather neatly, the corner was turned in time for the millennium. The Magyars were defeated. The Norsemen were converted to the civilizing truths of Christianity and turned from pillagers into state builders. The empire of Charlemagne was refounded in Germany under Otto I. Trade started to flourish and coin output grew rapidly. Yet Europe did not follow the example of T'ang China and reconstitute the Roman Empire in spite of an almost universally held belief that it ought to do so. To pull off the Chinese trick and reverse centuries of disintegration, it would have needed first to reconquer the Byzantine east with its well-preserved bureaucratic and fiscal traditions, and then to use these traditions to reestablish a powerful and centralized state in the west. This was most certainly not possible: Byzantium was enjoying a long period of revival and expansion under the Macedonian dynasty, and its armed forces, with disciplined formations of heavy cavalry on land and the terrifying "Greek fire" at sea, were probably the most effective in the Mediterranean world. Even greater obstacles lay inside western Christendom itself. The Holy Roman Emperor, the great white hope of western reunification, was bound by two fatal legacies from the intermingling of the Roman and Germanic worlds: the papacy and the Electoral College. The papacy in Rome was the most significant relic of the old empire, and, by careful manipulation of the facts, not to say falsification, the popes were able to pass themselves off as the official legatees of Constantine the Great in the west. Leo III skillfully inserted himself into the recreation of the Western Empire by unexpectedly placing the imperial crown on Charlemagne's head on Christmas Day, 800, and thereafter no emperor could ever achieve full legitimacy without the reenactment of this ceremony. Yet, while the popes were dedicated to the revival of the empire in theory, in practice they were reluctant to accept the loss of power to a centralized state. The battle for supremacy between the emperors and the popes lasted from the birth of the Holy Roman Empire until the fall of the Hohenstaufen, the last of the great medieval imperial dynasties, in 1250, and ended with the resounding defeat of the empire. Thereafter a weakened empire had to contend with the other side of its parentage—a revival of the Germanic tradition of elected kings. Before he could achieve the imperial crown, the would-be emperor now had to run a double gauntlet: first the German Electoral College, and then the pope. The upshot was a series of feeble monarchs who were unlikely to reignite the Western Empire, let alone take over the east.

As a result the original imperial territory—essentially Germany, the Netherlands, western France, Switzerland, and northern Italy—far from becoming the core of a new centralized superstate, became the most fragmented and decentralized area of Europe. The last emperor to exert any meaningful control over the original imperial territory was Frederick Barbarossa in the twelfth century, and even he was unable to sustain the effort in the end. Only the fortunate inheritance of the Kingdom of Sicily from the Normans in 1190 saved the Hohenstaufen for a few generations more. Sicily had never lost the Roman traditions of government. It was reconquered by Justinian in 535 and remained under the control of Byzantium until it was occupied by the Arabs in the ninth century. The Normans, with an eye for a good tax base, seized it more or less simultaneously with their takeover of England. It was this new private possession that allowed Frederick II to make a final bid to assert imperial power in Italy. The original imperial territories had disintegrated into a smorgasbord of petty states that in both Germany and Italy had to wait seven hundred years for reunification.

The importance of this history does not lie solely in showing how far Europe was from emulating the Chinese experience of reconstituting itself as a centralized tax-gathering empire. The revival of trade throughout Europe, and especially in the Mediterranean, created new cities and revitalized the old ones. The breakdown of nominal central authority in the imperial territories allowed the cities in those areas to develop into a new generation of independent city-states. By the twelfth century northern and central Italy resembled ancient Greece, with almost every town of over ten thousand inhabitants, and several of less, exercising de facto self-government. As the chronicler Otto of Freising wrote in 1150, before Frederick Barbarossa's brutal assault on their independence:

> The entire land is divided among the cities. . . . Scarcely any noble or great man can be found in all the surrounding territory who does not acknowledge the authority of his city. . . . They are aided . . . by the absence of their princes, who are accustomed to remain on the far side of the Alps.[2]

This unintended re-creation of the classical world had far-reaching consequences. The city-states of the ancient world had attempted in various ways to adapt tribal financial customs to the requirements of statecraft. The twin principles that they sought to preserve were the avoidance of the insult of direct taxation and the distribution of surplus assets. The citizens of the Italian cities showed an instinctive attachment to these ideas that would have done their forebears proud, but there was a profound difference in their social makeup that radically affected their public life. The Greek cities were largely based on farming; only a relatively small part of the population were merchants, and a large part of those were foreigners. This was not surprising in societies composed primarily of the descendants of settlers. The same was true of republican Rome. Senators were forbidden to take part in trade, and the legend of Cincinnatus, the farmer soldier, was handed down to future generations and reawakened in the breast of American republicans two thousand years later under not entirely dissimilar circumstances. In contrast, the medieval European cities were largely mercantile concerns. Although the Italian cities incorporated feudal nobility, often very uncomfortably, into their populations and many citizens owned land outside the walls, the attitude toward the surrounding countryside was largely restricted to its military control and fiscal exploitation.

There therefore arose, for the first time since the fall of Carthage, a group of states run by merchants. For the long-term significance of this development it is only necessary to recall the assertion of President Coolidge that "the business of America is business." He may subsequently have been held up to some ridicule for this statement but should properly be seen as a clairvoyant who expressed what has emerged as the essence of modern government. The medieval city-states were the first to see the business of states as the furtherance of business. They effected a revolution in statecraft, and especially in public finance. To the basic dislike of direct taxation shown by the free citizens of the classical cities, the merchants of medieval Europe added the principles of sound—and sometimes not so sound—business finance.

The epicenter of this development was northern Italy. This area was by far the most urbanized in Europe. By 1300, it had three or four cities of 100,000 or more inhabitants—Milan, Venice, Florence, and possibly Genoa. Outside Italy, only Paris was equal in size.[3] These cities were the first to establish true fiscal autonomy. The seminal moment appears to have been the appointment of consuls in a reawakening of the Roman spirit. Pisa made this leap in 1085, Milan in 1097, Arezzo in 1098, Genoa in 1099, Bologna in 1123, and Siena in 1125.[4] By the middle of the twelfth century, the area was a patchwork quilt of city-states which had not only achieved de facto self-government but had also established their control over the feudal barons of the surrounding countryside. In 1158, Frederick Barbarossa descended onto the Lombard plain in an attempt to reassert imperial authority. His fury at the resistance of Milan, the leading city of Lombardy, led him not only to sack it in the accustomed manner but to raze it to the ground, stone by stone, in 1162. In the long term it did him no good. The northern cities formed the Lombard League and cooperated to rebuild Milan five years later. Frederick threw in the towel and signed the Treaty of Constance in 1183, recognizing all the cities' previous rights and a few others for good measure.

The appointment of consuls was paralleled by two other developments: the definition of citizenship and the assertion of financial independence. The first involved the creation of a body whose membership conferred electoral rights and military duties. Often, as in ancient Athens and Rome, citizens with wealth above a fixed threshold were obliged to serve as cavalry.[5]

Financial independence could be achieved by simply stopping payment of imperial dues and tolls (by now generally to feudal nobles since the emperors had long since lost control of them). Alternatively, the right to collect the dues could simply be purchased.[6] Scarcely had the cities gained fiscal autonomy than the first signs of public loans started to appear. Genoa appears to have incurred debts in Rome in 1121. The first record of Venetian borrowing is dated 1164; Florentine records start in 1166.

Little can be inferred from these scattered fragments of the beginnings of public debt, and the full flowering of the idiosyncrasies of communal public finance did not take place until the late thirteenth century and beyond. Only a handful of republics survived into that era. The rest fell victim to the collapse of their republican institutions, or to conquest by one of the largest cities. The weakness of democratic forms of government was soon exposed as rival factions sought to monopolize office. The cooperative spirit so evident in the rebuilding of Milan lasted no longer then one generation. By as early as 1190, the *Genoese Chronicles of Caffaro* had to record:

> Civil discords and hateful conspiracies and divisions had arisen in the city on account of the mutual envy of the many men who greatly wished to hold office as consuls of the commune. So the *sapientes* [wise men] and councilors of the city met and decided that from the following year the consulate of the commune should come to an end and they almost all agreed that they should have a podestà.[7]

The institution of the podesta is one of the most interesting, and yet most sad, to emerge from medieval Italy. Unable to resolve their antagonisms through the ballot box, the citizens appointed a magistrate from another city whose impartiality could be relied upon.[8] He was paid a salary for a fixed term, usually no more than one year, after which his accounts were rigorously audited before he was allowed to leave. In Modena, the podesta was not allowed even to dine with local citizens during his tenure for fear of impairing his impartiality. The podesta became the common form of government in Lombardy after 1200. Some men took it up as a profession, and John of Viterbo wrote a manual of advice to aspiring applicants.[9] Even this institution, however, was not sufficient to save the republics. Perhaps the resulting form of government was too bland to inspire the loyalty necessary to keep out the old signorial families, who were always waiting in the wings to reclaim their lost power. Gradually the republics were taken over by the *signorie*—generally maintaining the fiction of republican institutions just as Augustus had maintained the fiction of the Roman Republic. By end of the century, most of the cities of the northern plain and in the Papal States were ruled by *signori*, and Dante would lament that "all the towns of Italy are full of tyrants."[10]

The public finances of the *signorie* diverged very clearly from those of the surviving republics. Although the new rulers of the cities often borrowed, they did so as personal rulers, and their financial habits resembled those of the kings of Europe rather than those of the cities. It was great surviving republics that were to organize public borrowing into a system.

What were the surviving republics? The greatest number remained in

Tuscany, at least until they were taken over by Florence, one of Italy's four urban giants by 1300. The largest, Milan, was no longer republican. The remaining two were in almost identical positions in the two opposite corners of the Italian peninsula as it joins the European landmass: Venice to the east and Genoa to the west. Both remained republics until Napoleon did away with their institutions in the interests of his "new world order."

LA SERENISSIMA

Venice deserves pride of place. It did not need to win independence from the emperor. The city had enjoyed self-government since the election of the first doge in 727. This early independence was a reflection of its origins as a refuge for mainland Italians from the barbarian invasions. The barren islands of the lagoon provided safety and de facto autonomy. By an exercise of the kind of political savvy for which they were to become famous, the Venetians carefully remained attached to the waning power of Byzantium. This attachment provided unimpeachable legal protection from the Carolingian takeover of the rest of northern Italy, and the Venetian lagoon provided the necessary physical backup. In the twelfth century the Venetians could sit quietly by as Barbarossa cut a swathe across the Lombard plain. Later they could blithely offer their city as a neutral forum for the signing of the treaty of reconciliation between the emperor and the pope and his allied cities. No other Italian city had anything like such unchallenged independence for so long. The long tradition of republican institutions and physical isolation from the mainland gave Venice a social and political stability never approached by any mainland city. It never needed a podesta and never fell under the sway of a *signore*. As a result its finances could share in some of the cohesion and discipline of the rest of its public life.

Like the Athenians of ancient Greece, the merchants of Venice disliked taxing themselves. Indirect taxes were easier to collect and fell on every resident and visitor; and certain tolls could be used to manipulate trade for the benefit of the citizen merchants. The regular revenues of Venice, as of all other cities, consisted of a combination of taxes on trade, such as gate and market dues, and excise taxes on essential commodities, most notably salt. In a vibrant commercial economy these could provide ample support for normal expenses and might go some way toward providing for defense. But they could never be enough to cover the expenses of warfare, which was as constant in medieval Italy as it had been in classical Greece. Since the largest concentrations of wealth were in the hands of the citizens, some means of tapping them in time of need had to be found. The alternatives to direct taxation were gifts or loans. The ancient tradition of public donation had vanished by A.D. 300, never to reappear. The merchant citizens of the Middle Ages preferred to lend their money.

The earliest known Venetian loan of 1164 was raised on a voluntary basis from twelve wealthy families.[11] In 1167, there was the first instance of the practice that was to be the hallmark of Venetian and Italian borrowing throughout the Middle Ages—the forced loan. The loan was subscribed by a large number of names (ninety in all) in very uneven amounts, which suggest that it was allocated on some proportional basis. More telling is the pledge not to raise another loan for two years, which suggests that the subscribers were not looking forward to the next installment with any great pleasure. A loan of 1171 was clearly compulsory and carried an interest rate of 5%, which later became the standard for all Venetian state debt. That rate seems low even by modern standards, and it would certainly have been lower than the prevailing market rates of the time. In 1152, Genoa paid 40% interest for a far smaller sum. The rate of 5% probably represented an ideal rather than a reality, but it is an indication of the astonishing speed at which the western European credit market was recovering. Less than a century earlier, mortgage rates of 100% had been recorded in France.

More important was the compulsory nature of the loans. How these earliest examples were levied is not known, but a system emerged from the surviving records of the following decades. An increasing number of loans were raised on a compulsory basis, and voluntary loans largely disappeared. In Venice the loans were assessed as if they were direct taxes. The original basis of the assessment may have been the *advevaticum*, a tax paid by those who wished to exempt themselves from the military service owed by citizens. In 1228 citizens had to swear to accept to pay the *advevaticum* and the forced loans as a condition of citizenship. The loans (or *prestiti*, as they were called in Venice) are in reality best seen as repayable taxes. In Florence similar levies (*prestanze*) were divided into those *a riavere* (to be returned), always the majority, and a lesser number *a perdere* (to be lost), which thus make the concept quite clear. These repayable levies were a medieval response to the perennial question of how to tax free citizens. They neatly expressed the duality of the position of citizenship in a small state: the obligation to undertake extra burdens and responsibilities to ensure the survival and prosperity of their state; and the exemption from the insult of direct taxes. In the city-states of medieval Italy to be a citizen was, by definition, to be a creditor of the state.

The records of the early Venetian *prestiti* are sparse, but it seems that each loan had slightly different interest and repayment terms, and that the loans were not repaid with any great speed. The city appointed two permanent officers—*iudices prestitorum*—to supervise its debts in 1252, and in 1262 it regularized the entire system. All future loans were to be made on the same basis. Interest was to be at 5% and to have priority over other city expenses. Repayments were limited to whatever surplus the city had on hand. In other words, in exchange for security of interest the citizens gave up any fixed commitment to repayment of principal. The consolidated permanent national debt had been born.

Not surprisingly, the Venetian debt fund (the Monte, as it was called) followed the city's fortunes in war. In 1279, there were already 154,000 ducats outstanding.* Wars with its arch rival, Genoa, and with Ferrara brought the total to 1,077,000 ducats in 1314. Thereafter a prolonged period of peace with regular repayments in principal reduced the debt to a low point of 423,000 ducats in 1343.[12] Throughout this period interest of 5% had been regularly paid and softened the blow of the very high levies needed in time of war. But even more important for the future history of finance, both public and private, was the development of a trading market. In this crucial development, the native ingenuity of the Italian merchants was aided by a serendipitous by-product of the usury laws.

The Middle Ages inherited a total ban on lending at interest. The ancient Jewish laws forbidding usury between fellow Jews had won out over the more realistic Roman tradition of interest rate limits. It was all right for the earliest Church Fathers to adapt the Jewish tradition into a ban on interest taking between fellow Christians when the Christians were neither very numerous nor very rich. Unfortunately, the moment when Christianity became the official religion of the empire, coincided with the breakdown of

*In the late thirteenth century gold coins started to reappear in Europe after a gap of six hundred years. Florence and Genoa started producing gold coins in 1252. The Venetian gold ducat was first minted in 1284. The model for all of these coins was the late Roman-Byzantine solidus (usually called the *nomisma* in the east). By the thirteenth century this had lost some 22% of its original gold content and contained no more than 3.55 grams of pure gold. The coins produced by the Italian city-states all followed this example in shape, weight, and, in the case of Venice, design. They became the standard coins of European trade, remaining largely unaltered for centuries, and were later imitated by most other states. For the rest of the Middle Ages and the early Renaissance they provide the best basis for international financial comparisons; and although each city had a different name for its coin (the most famous of which was the Florentine *florin*) the term *ducat* is used throughout the text to prevent an unnecessary proliferation of names.

the credit market due to inflation in the third and fourth centuries. In the west, the return of the loan shark made the universalization of the ban seem reasonable. The entire history of the Middle Ages and the Renaissance was spent in a struggle to return to the Roman tradition. Only in the sixteenth century was the battle largely won. During the Middle Ages merchants and even theologians might understand that reasonable interest between consenting adults was not the same as rates of 50% or higher inflicted on those in need; but the biblical prohibition was so total that they could not find a way to express their conclusions. The only solution was to find loopholes in the concept, and the ingenuity of certain theologians has led one historian to describe their efforts as "the first attempt at a science of economics known to the West."[13]

Some loopholes were quite easy to come by, such as the acceptability of taking interest from the enemy. Obviously this included Muslims, and since Islam had a similar loophole in its equally stringent ban, the important and profitable eastern trade of the Italian cities could continue unimpeded. Interest might be concealed as a gift. The word *interest* itself was the result of a loophole allowing payment of "damages."[14] Venice and most other Italian cities availed themselves of the concept of damages—easily justifiable if the loan was a forced one at below market rates of interest. Florence made its payments to creditors as "gift and interest," so as to insure itself with a double line of moral defense.

Another way to circumvent accusations of usury was simply to bypass one of the basic characteristics of a loan—the obligation to repay. If repayment of principal was entirely at the option of the borrower, then it was hard to claim that he had fallen into the snare of debt slavery that the usury laws were designed to prevent.[15] From the point of view of financial history, this was a crucial advantage. Loans without fixed maturities are particularly well suited to trading markets for two reasons. The first is that their yields are easy to calculate and compare, since the only possible basis is the current yield.* This is a simple calculation, quite within the means of medieval mathematics. By contrast, loans with fixed maturities can be compared only by reference to their yield to maturity†—the mathematics of

*This is the yield received by an investor without any consideration of capital appreciation or depreciation. (One calculates it by dividing the nominal interest rate by the purchase price and multiplying by 100.)

†If a bond is selling below (or above) its face value the yield is affected by the increase (or decrease) of capital when the bond is repaid. The yield to maturity of a bond represents the total return to an investor, including not only the annual interest payments but also the eventual increase (or decrease) in the investor's capital.

which is so complex that it was not mastered until the nineteenth century and is now safely left to computers. The second advantage is that, precisely because they have the same maturity (i.e., no fixed date), undated loans are identical from a trading point of view regardless of when they are issued. As long as the interest rate is kept the same, each successive loan is like a further issue of shares in a company. One market and one price cover the whole amount outstanding.

From the point of view of the citizen creditor, the ability to sell his loans compensated for the very long—potentially indefinite—postponement of repayment by creating a new source of liquidity. As debts mounted, it was this liquidity that made the whole system bearable. The first evidence of a market price comes from 1285, when the city converted some short-term debts into permanent *prestiti* at what were intended to be market rates. At the conversion rate of 75% of par,* the effective current yield would have been 6.67%, already an impressively low figure. Only a few prices have survived from the period before 1315, but they show clearly how demand would fall in time of war and rise with the return of peace. In 1299 and again in 1311, prices were as low as 60 (a current yield of 8.33%). After 1315 prices advanced steadily with the regular repayments of capital made by the city. By 1323 they had reached 90, and from 1333 to 1350 they ranged from 92.5 to as high as 102.[16] An unblemished record of interest payments and increasing scarcity due to repayments of principal had led to Venetian government debt's losing its role as a privileged way of paying direct taxes and gaining the novel one of an investment vehicle attractive to citizens and noncitizens alike. This trend was already evident in 1325, when a bequest to the monastery of San Daniele was made in the form of *prestiti*. The terms of the bequest specified that any funds received from repayments should be reinvested in further *prestiti* in order to maintain the yield.[17]

The *prestiti* had started as an adaptation of the underlying principles of tribal finance—the contribution of assets during time of war and the distribution of spoils afterward. Like the repayable taxes of the Roman Republic, the Venetian *prestiti* modified this ancient idea by specifically tying distributions to the amounts contributed. By paying a fixed and regular interest,

*Par value is the official ("parity") value of a bond or other financial instrument. The par value of bonds is the principal that the bond represents. Prices for bonds are expressed as a percentage of this value, so that when dealing in bond prices par means 100%. Prices are generally expressed simply as numbers rather than percentages; that is, a price of 80 means 80% of par value. (Shares also have par values, but their prices are not generally expressed in this way.)

however, and by consolidating the levies into a simple unified form that could be bought and sold, the Venetians had transformed the original idea and given it an entirely new meaning. They had invented the bond market.

LA SUPERBA

The Genoese are rich but the Republic is poor. —Genoese saying

Not all the credit should go to Venice. Its rival, Genoa, followed a parallel course. The city gained independence in 1099. Its early war finances were a mixture of taxes and loans that reflected a period of experimentation, but the citizens' preference for loans soon asserted itself. Genoa's earliest compulsory loans appear to have been without interest, but to have had fixed repayment terms. In 1200, the first loan was levied using tax registers as the basis of assessment. From then on the loans were with interest but without repayment terms; in other words, they were moving in the same direction as the Venetian *prestiti*. In 1257–1259, just a few years ahead of Venice, Guglielmo Boccanegra consolidated the city's debts at a nominal 8% yield. In 1262, the city's preemptive right of repurchase was ended and a free market started. In 1263 prices of up to 110.5% of par were recorded, which suggests a current yield of 7.24%.[18]

In spite of these similarities of development, Genoa was a profoundly different city from Venice. It had no lagoon to protect it from surrounding feudal aristocrats, who participated in its commerce but who never quite accepted the rules of republican life. Like the Lombard cities Genoa soon needed the services of a podesta, and the city's political history was one of constant turmoil and infighting. Genoa may have been *superba* (an adjective combining the English meanings of *splendid, proud,* and *arrogant*), but it would never have qualified as *serenissima*. Although the city never quite lost its republican institutions, its government was bandied back and forth between opposing aristocratic and popular factions. Often a losing faction would offer the city to some outside ruler as a means of regaining political power. That the city avoided the fate of Milan in falling under a *signoria* seems almost surprising: one of the great families of Genoese history—the Grimaldi—managed to impose permanent signorial rule on nearby Monaco.

Not surprisingly, the early coherence of Venetian public finance was absent in Genoa. The weakness of the state was reflected in the almost total "privatization" of public life. Whereas the Venetian fleet was built in the state arsenal—probably the largest manufacturing organization of medieval Europe—Genoa was dependent on private merchant vessels for its protection. The most stark example is the idiosyncratic Genoese institution of the *maona*. This represented the simultaneous privatization of both warfare and public finance. The Saracens of Ceuta made the mistake of plundering Genoese goods in the city in 1234. Genoa organized a *maona* of more than one hundred private ships to attack Ceuta in retaliation, and to make the sultan pay the compensation demanded. The participants were inscribed in a special ledger in the same manner as public creditors, but instead of money they were contributing ships, and they were to be repaid not out of tax revenues but out of booty.[19] The operation was successful. The venture looked both backward to the fitting out of the final Roman fleet of the First Punic War and forward to the gunboat diplomacy of the nineteenth century.

Genoese public debt was similarly privatized. When Genoa wished to raise money it "sold" some part of its tax revenues to a syndicate (*compera*) of its citizens. The "selling" of revenues was another loophole in the usury laws dreamed up by the wealthy monasteries of the eleventh and twelfth centuries, when they became one of the earliest lenders of the European revival. They were mainly interested in lending against lands, and they decided that if an income stream from the land—a "rent"—was sold to the lender in exchange for a certain sum, then the transaction was one of purchase and sale, not of borrowing.[20] This ingenious, not to say casuistic, theory neatly sidestepped the whole problem. That the transaction was, in reality, a loan rather than a sale is made clear by the fact that the "buyer" never enjoyed full and perpetual rights of ownership. His entitlement to the income would either expire at his death; on if it was agreed that he could bequeath the "rent" to his heirs, the "seller" would retain the right to repurchase it at cost at any time (effectively turning the "rent" into an undated loan on Venetian lines). On the other hand, it was essential that the "buyer" have no countervailing right to demand the return of his capital. Otherwise, what was the annual rent payment but his interest? This fine example of delicate legal drafting so as to exploit a loophole is surely worthy of a modern Wall Street law firm. The application of these principles to other streams of income—such as tax revenues—provided another theological umbrella under which public debt was able to flourish.

The *compera* was another idiosyncratic Genoese invention. If the loan was voluntary, rival syndicates would bid against each other in a public auction, and the syndicate offering the highest price would win. More often the loans were compulsory and were distributed among the citizens on the basis of the direct tax registers. The city would then allocate tax revenues sufficient to produce the agreed-on yield to a *compera* consisting of the whole citizen body. Yet Genoa went further in the rigorousness of its pursuit of the "sale" analogy than any other borrower or lender. In northern Europe, borrowers sold "rents" that were fixed. Lenders did not take the risk that the yield from the land or tax might fall below the specified level. Genoa, however, made a more extreme compact with its creditors. They truly bought the taxes and took the risk that the yield would fall below that theoretically offered. The risk was minimized because Genoa, like most cities, farmed out the collection of its taxes, thus converting them into fixed revenue streams The creditors' returns were therefore reasonably predictable, but they could not be quite sure how much they would receive or when.

Syndicate interests were divided into shares—*luoghi*—which could be traded publicly. (If the loan was compulsory, fractional shares would have to be issued.) The differences in their underlying revenues gave the shares in the various syndicates quite different market values. Because of the relative uncertainty of their returns and their subdivision into shares, the Genoese *compere* have been often seen as the true precursors of modern joint stock companies. In some ways, the Genoese became citizen shareholders as opposed to citizen creditors.

The system was highly fragmented, and consolidation occurred only as a result of periodic restructurings in periods of financial and political crisis. The first consolidation under Guglielmo Boccanegra was followed by others after almost every major period of warfare. The successful war against Venice in 1294–1299 led to a forced levy at 6% in 1303 to consolidate war debt incurred at higher rates. A further consolidation took place in 1332, after decades of intermittent civil war, to regularize the debts incurred by rival aristocratic governments. Boccanegra's grandson, Simone, the hero of Verdi's opera, made the most important and traumatic reorganization in 1340 after a popular uprising. By this time, the nominal debt was nearly 2.4 million ducats. As a result of the way that the various syndicates were valued in the consolidation, however, the effective debt was only 832,000 ducats, and the taxes pledged to the creditors were 75,000 ducats.[21]

The dire straits of Genoa contrasted with the financial strength of Venice at the same date—with most of its public debt repaid, and the remainder trading over par. Even when the Venetian debt rose toward 1.5 million ducats in the 1350s, the interest burden still represented less than

30% of the public revenues. By contrast, after 1340, Genoa had reached the stage where its revenues were so far pledged to cover its debt that it was living on a virtual stipend from its creditors.

A situation such as this is explainable only in terms of Genoa's social fragmentation. To the divisions between the noble families—broadly grouped around the signorial Grimaldi and Fieschi, on the one hand, and the more urban Spinola and Doria, on the other—there was the third element of the common citizens: the *popolo*. These not only wished to enjoy public office themselves but also had their distinct views about public finance. Undoubtedly the concept of repayable taxes would have appealed to all citizens at the outset. But as assessments increased, the poorer among them (the *popolo minuto*) found it increasingly necessary to sell their shares to the wealthier at below par. This resulted from the unavoidable facts that (1) the interest rate on forced loans was almost always lower than the free market rate, and (2) the market always fell at times of high wartime levies. The inclusion of interest exacerbated the distress since the wealthy were able to collect increasingly large shares of the city's regular revenues, forcing an inexorable increase in regressive taxes on essential goods such as salt. Little of this social tension was visible in Venice, although in 1350 the Senate took the precaution of passing an act fining anybody who rashly proposed reducing interest payments the very large sum of 2,000 ducats.[22] In Genoa, as in several other cities, these effects of long-term interest-bearing debt led to repeated popular demands for its replacement by nonrepayable direct taxes. This was the background of the uprisings of 1256, 1321, and 1339. In each case the populace was doomed to disappointment. The main weakness of their cause was that their leaders were always wealthy—as in the case of the Boccanegra family. Guglielmo was a successful international banker, scarcely the ideal champion of the opponents of debt, one might think. The wealthy commoners were more interested in ousting the nobles from power so as to enjoy it themselves than in altering the structure of public finance in the interests of the *popolo minuto*.

The result of the political uncertainty created by this three-way struggle for power was that the public creditors of Genoa sought to increase their control over the taxes that secured their income. In 1323 they ensured that the government officials responsible for debt service would be appointed by the creditors—in fact, had to be creditors themselves. In 1326 the tax farmers had to put up shares in loan syndicates in order to secure their farms—they, too, became creditors. In 1352 the full implications of the creditors' "purchase" of the all-important salt monopoly were laid bare: the city could not even increase the tax without the consent of the Compera Salis.[23] In 1339 the enraged *popolo minuto,* who had installed Simone Boccanegra as doge, burned the records of the city's debts and taxes. The following year Boccanegra disappointed his followers by reinstating the debt by negotiation with the creditors' syndicates. Mindful of what they had just witnessed, the creditors agreed to a significant reduction of debt and interest so that the city could lower the tax burdens that were afflicting the populace. It was in exchange for this debt reduction that the city accepted that all its remaining revenues should be pledged to the syndicates, and that it would receive in exchange the meager sum of 16,000 ducats for its day-to-day running costs. Genoa was to remain a virtual pensioner of its citizen creditors for the rest of the history of the republic. Moreover, the city had learnt that however attractive public lending might be as a way of expressing the political freedom of the citizens, it could also become intertwined with internal class warfare.

THE MONTE COMUNE

Florence took longer to join the ranks of the great city borrowers. Though its first recorded borrowing was in 1166, and in 1224 the city was stated to have a "large debt" by one of its chroniclers, Florence in the early fourteenth century had less than 50,000 florins* in debt. This low level of borrowing was largely due to the enormous success of the city in dominating the cloth trade of Europe. This trade generated revenues that were recorded at over 300,000 ducats in the balmy days of the 1330s and allowed the city a healthy peacetime surplus. In the thirteenth century the city, like its peers, had developed an assessment system—the *estimo*—on which it could levy direct taxes or forced loans in time of need, but in 1315 the citizens had abolished the *estimo*, relying on the ease of access to credit from its wealthy merchant-banking elite, led by the Bardi and the Peruzzi. The interest that the city paid was relatively high, generally between 10% and 15%, but the citizens did not mind as long as the debt was low, credit was readily forthcoming, and the economy was generally flourishing. By the 1340s none of these conditions were true: the debt had risen to 800,000 ducats, the Bardi and Peruzzi were bankrupt, and the economy was in a

*The Florentine florin was identical in gold weight and value to the Venetian ducat. In order to prevent unnecessary multiplication of names, however, the word *ducat* is used throughout this section.

deep deflationary crisis as a result of their insolvency.[24] The economic misfortunes of the city were compounded in 1347 by the Black Death, which swept across Italy and reduced urban populations by as much as one half. In 1342 the short-lived despotic regime of Walter of Brienne reinstated direct taxes and suspended payments of interest on the debt. After his overthrow in 1343 the new government set about consolidating the debt on the Venetian model. After various disallowances the principal of the new fund was established at 500,000 ducats. Interest was reduced to 5% secured by the salt and wine taxes, and the shares in the new Monte Comune (Communal Fund) were fully tradable.

It was not a promising start. The Venetian consolidated debt had benefited from eighty years of punctual payments and was now selling at over par. In Florence, the savage cut in interest, the lesser cut in principal, and the general economic crisis did not encourage investment, and the Monte Comune started life at prices as low as one-third of par or less. Had the city been able to return to the easygoing fiscal practices of the early decades of the century, it would undoubtedly have done so, but the days of approximate fiscal balance based only on indirect taxes were over. Thus the Florentines, like the Venetians, came to depend on a system of repayable direct taxes, and the Monte Comune became the centerpiece of Florentine public financial life. By the early fourteenth century, two-thirds of households in the city owned shares in the public debt.[25] Florence, like Venice and Genoa, had become a republic of citizen creditors.

But if Florence's finances were similar to those of Venice, its political life was a great deal less tranquil than that of La Serenissima. The public creditors may have constituted the dominant part of the citizenry, but they did not form an overall majority of the population even within the city. Florence witnessed struggles over public finance quite as fierce as those of Genoa. The first battle was about interest rates. The instinctive desire of the wealthier citizens in the following decades was to restore the yield to free market rates. Yet since 5% retained an almost unassailable prestige as a coupon rate, it was necessary to circumvent it by using a legal fiction to offer creditors interest on more than the amount they actually lent. In 1355 the Monte Uno Due (the Two-for-One Fund) was born, which inscribed citizens for twice the true amount of their loans. In 1358 the Monte Uno Tre inscribed them for three times, raising the yield to 15%. The wars of the 1360s and 1370s led to a rapid increase of debt and a wave of speculation. There were a number of different issues available at different prices. A surviving letter of 1375 from a highly placed official to an expatriate friend seeking to invest in the Monte shows the flavor of the times. The writer will invest his friend's money in shares of the Monte Uno Due

> since they are low at this price of 32, and it is certain that a year will not pass before they rise to 42, and then I will sell them and place [your funds] in another *monte* that yields more than 16 percent. . . . And if you say: "Oh why do you not place me in the one that provides the higher yield?" I will tell you the answer. The latter is a *Monte Uno Tre,* in which an investor of 100 is inscribed for 300, and pays 5 percent per year on the amount inscribed, and costs 28 per 100. . . . But these will never be worth more than the current price even with peace or any other improvement in the city's fortunes, and the reason is this: because there is a rule that anyone who owns them is obliged to sell them to the city, whenever it wishes, at 28 percent of par. And since the city has money it is repurchasing this issue, because it pays more than any other, and to reduce the debt of the commune.[26]

The letter is very revealing on a number of levels. The vast expansion of the number of public creditors since the events of the 1340s had led to a true financial marketplace. Intelligent citizens had learned to play the market to improve their returns. The city was also using the market as a means of reducing debt by repurchasing it at a discount. Equally striking are the very high yields, reaching 17.86% on the Monte Uno Tre, which attracted a number of foreign investors, including the Genoese, whose local debt rarely yielded more than 10%, and even the pope.

(Finally it is hard to avoid comment on the obvious conflict of interest of the writer. Not only does he act for a private investor while a member of the highest body of public finance, but he also offers to make the investment in his own name so as to avoid its being known that the true holder is a member of the discredited Bardi family. By comparison, Venice had passed a law in 1322 banning public officials from trading in its debt.)

As a result of this fiscal policy, the city's interest bill, which had been reduced from probably over 70,000 ducats in 1342 to 25,000 ducats in 1345, had risen to new highs.[27] To cover the extra cost, indirect tax rates were raised. The lot of the poor was made harder by the monetary policy of the governing elite. While international trade and the public debt were denominated in gold, the everyday currency of wages and retail trade was silver. From 1350 to 1378 the silver currency was debased 20% against gold, an action that increased both the profits of the merchants and the indirect taxes needed to secure the interest on the debt. The result, certainly not surprising in hindsight, was the popular uprising of 1378 known as the revolt of the Ciompi. One of the first acts of the new government was the removal of Ser Piero Grifi, the inventor of the Monte Uno Tre, from office and the confiscation of most of his fortune. The Ciompi demanded the reinstatement of direct taxes, the repayment of all public debt over twelve years, and the progressive meltdown of silver coinage until it had appreciated by 10%.[28] But as was always the case in such uprisings, the popular cause was rapidly weakened by the defection of its wealthier supporters, and its radical program was never carried out. All the Ciompi achieved was a new consolidation of debt at the standard interest rate of 5%. In this way the city's interest burden was reduced to the tolerable level of 50,000 ducats, but direct taxation remained abhorrent to the majority of citizens, and debt continued to increase.

THE TWILIGHT OF REPAYABLE TAXES

By the end of the fourteenth century, the bloom may be said to have been off the rose. The idea that borrowing was a painless way of levying money from citizens was severely dented. Florence had experienced two forced consolidations with drastic reductions in interest and concomitant falls in prices. Genoa had gone through similar convulsions, and the market value of the shares of several of the loan syndicates, especially those created for compulsory levies, had fallen to under 30% of the original contributions. The War of Chioggia (1378–1382), the final showdown between Venice and Genoa for dominance of the eastern Mediterranean trade, had left Venice eventually victorious but with its finances in tatters. Public debt had risen to 4.73 million ducats, and prices had plunged from over 90 to as low as 18. Interest payments were suspended in 1378, and when they were reinstated in 1382, it was only after deduction of a new 20% withholding tax, that reduced the interest rate to 4%.[29] In none of the three cities could the public credit record be said to be unblemished. The original concept of "repayable" taxes had become largely a myth. After 1363 repayments at par were never made by any of the cities. In 1389 Venice started a sinking fund* by setting aside a 38,000-ducat increase of customs duties. Florence started its own fund, financed by a 25% withholding tax on interest in 1392.

*A sinking fund is set up by a borrower to reduce debt by repurchasing it in the market. Generally such funds operate only if the debt is selling below par. Sinking funds appeal to borrowers and lenders for somewhat different reasons. Borrowers are able to reduce their debt more cheaply than by redeeming it at face value. The bondholders have the advantage of a reliable source of liquidity in the market.

The compact with citizens had changed subtly. The twin aspects of the levies—as loans and as taxes—were in theory easily distinguishable by the market price. To the extent that a citizen could recoup his levy by selling it on the market, it was effectively a voluntary loan; the rest was effectively a tax. This had always been so, but until 1378–1382 market values had been sufficiently close to the amounts subscribed that it was possible to ignore the "tax" element in the hopes that it would be eliminated by a rise in the market. After 1380, prices were too low, and the decision to limit any redemption of debt to its market value implies an unconscious acceptance of the loss of the remainder as tax.

This altered compact remained unstated, however, and an enormous amount of emotional energy was expended on supporting the myth of the ultimately repayable nature of all levies. In his *Istoria di Firenze,* written around 1400, long after debt levels had ceased to do anything but rise, Gregorio Dati was still giving the traditional answer to a rhetorical question of why Florentine citizens paid such large sums so willingly:

> The citizens do not lose [the sums paid], but rather lend them for the needs of the commune, and when the commune is at peace and in surplus, they have them returned; and while they wait to have them back, they do not waste time, but instead they have a return of 5 percent each year, as if they had spent them on land.[30]

Even in the second half of the fifteenth century, when their respective *monti* had passed the point of possible repair, the Venetians rather pompously continued to refer to theirs as "the principal foundation and continual and perpetual stability of our state, wherein lies the glorious reputation of our dominion."[31] The Florentines, perhaps as much in desperation as in pride, referred to theirs as *il cuore di nostro corpo, che si chiama città* ("the heart of our body, which we call city"). Perhaps the most striking statement of all was made in 1432 by the Florentine banker Giovanni di Piero Baroncelli: "The Monte and freedom are the same thing: therefore supporting the Monte will make the citizens willing to pay."[32] This stark association of freedom and public debt was made in support of a direct tax paid *a perdere* to fund continued market repurchases. In other words, the illusion that levies were not direct taxes was so important to the citizens' willingness to contribute that it was worth suffering the indignity of a small direct tax in order to support the market and therefore to make the remaining levies more palatable.

It was not all downhill after 1380. Debt levels in Venice slightly declined until 1403, and market prices rose to into the 60s. From 1404 to 1415, renewed wars on the Italian mainland increased debt to a new record of over 8 million ducats, and prices fell again to the low 40s. But this was the period in which Venice finally established itself as a mainland power, and its conquest of Verona, Padua, and Friuli brought it extensive new revenues. Under the careful tutelage of Doge Tomaso Mocenigo, these revenues were added to the resources of the sinking fund so that, by his death in 1423, debt had been reduced to 6 million ducats and prices had risen to 67.[33] Through laws enacted in 1386 and 1411, interest to secondary holders had been reduced from 4% to 3%, so as to compensate primary holders for the involuntary nature of their holdings.* This meant that the free market yield of *prestiti* had reached a new low of 4.48%. The revenues of the city had increased to over 1 million ducats. Total debt service, including the sinking fund, was around 300,000 ducats, with interest probably little more than 200,000 ducats. Clearly Venice was more than capable of servicing its debt.

Florence had followed a similar path. By the late fourteenth century, the fragmented political map of northern Italy was starting to simplify itself as the larger cities absorbed the smaller. Giangaleazzo Visconti, Signore of Milan, made a bid to extend his control of Lombardy to the whole region in the 1390s. Florence fought a series of desperate wars against this despotic threat and was given breathing space only by his sudden death in 1402. By 1394, interest on the debt had again risen above 100,000 ducats and was never to fall below that level again. The levies were so heavy that it was sometimes necessary to offer rates above 5% again, but this time no higher than 8–10%, and never high enough to prevent the citizens from incurring losses if they needed to sell. By 1414, the public debt had risen to over 3 million ducats.[34] Florence's early experiment with a sinking fund was not successful, but by 1415 the 25% withholding tax had become firmly established in any case, reducing interest on the basic 5% Monte Comune to 3.75%. From 1415 to 1423, the city, like Venice, enjoyed a relative respite, and prices rose to as high as 61, reducing the market yield to 6.15%.[35]

This was probably the lowest yield of Monte Comune shares on the free market at any time, but it is striking that it was still considerably higher than the 4.5% yield of the Venetian Monte at the same time. The explanation is not hard to find. In spite of becoming a large territorial state in the

*Primary holders are those who lend their money directly to the state. Secondary holders are investors who purchase their bonds in the market.

process of the wars, occupying almost all of modern Tuscany with the exception of the still independent republics of Siena and Lucca, Florence had not managed to increase its revenues. While Venice had seen its revenue base increase fourfold to over 1 million ducats, Florence still had the same income of around 300,000 ducats that it had enjoyed in the 1330s. Venice, therefore, required only 20% of its revenues to pay its debt interest, as against 60% for Florence.

Round two of the wars against the Visconti opened in 1424 and lasted with intermissions until the overthrow of Filippo Maria Visconti by the condottiere Francesco Sforza in 1450.* The wars destroyed the Venetian and Florentine debt funds. The last Venetian levy was made in 1454, the year of the Peace of Lodi; and the fund entered a state of suspended animation. Total levies from 1425 to 1454 amounted to a further 6–7 million ducats, 60–70% more than the entire assessed wealth of the citizens. The state took to making only one semiannual interest payment, and even that was often made after a long delay. In 1439 direct taxes were assessed, but the measure was so unpopular that it was repealed the next year. In the same year, the 3% interest paid to secondary holders was reduced to 2%.[36] The 4% rate paid to primary holders was protected for longer, but from the 1440s even this was paid only once a year, and with increasing delays. Not surprisingly, prices collapsed, reaching as low as 20 in 1440, and would have fallen further if the market had not been supported by the operation of the sinking fund. In fact, the Venetian ruling elite became more concerned to reduce the debt by repurchasing it at a discount than to continue to pay interest to its creditors. When the Monte Vecchio (the Old Fund, as it was now called) was finally abandoned as a means of raising money in 1482, it had been reduced by the sinking fund to just over 8 million ducats, but interest was twenty-one years in arrears, and prices had fallen to little over 10.[37] Thereafter the state made intermittent interest payments of 1% for an-

---

*The condottieri (mercenary captains) need a brief explanation. At first, the communes had been defended by citizen militias, but as they grew wealthy, their citizens found their time too profitably employed in business to be wasted on fighting. Adventurers, both Italian and foreign, were happy to take over this burdensome occupation from them at a profit. The result was a rapid escalation of military costs. In 1260 a *lancia*, consisting of a knight, a squire, and a shield bearer, could be hired for 6 ducats per month. By the 1430s, however, some of the top condottieri charged up to 65 ducats per *lancia*, and the business was turning into a racket. In 1432 Sforza was paid 50,000 ducats by his employer, Florence, just to remove his troops from its territory. Machiavelli had no doubt in blaming the misfortunes of Italy after 1494 on the use of mercenaries, with their lack of loyalty and their reluctance to expend the lives of their valuable soldiers. In the meantime, their use exacerbated the strains on the budgets of the cities.

other 100 years, but as a vehicle of public finance the Monte Vecchio had outlived its usefulness.

THE RISE AND FALL OF THE MONTE VECCHIO[38]

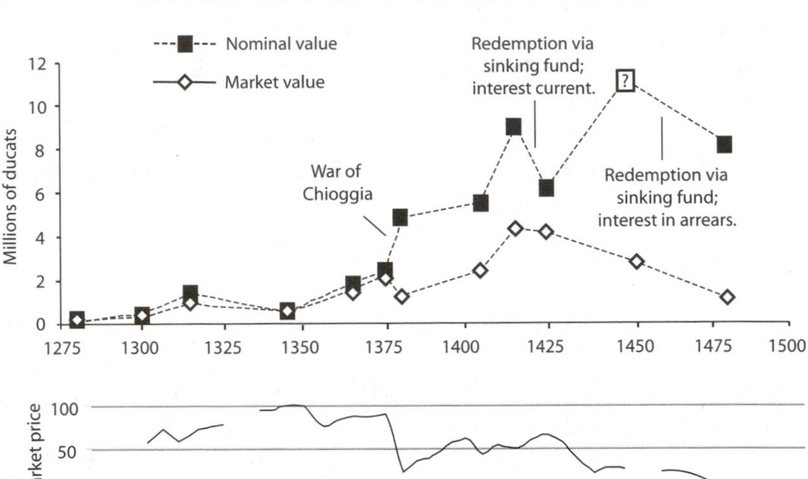

The situation in Florence was no better. By midcentury total debt had risen to 8 million ducats, and by 1470 it was over 10 million. Interest in that year, had it been paid in full, would have been 355,600 ducats—a figure not only higher than the taxes pledged to the Monte but higher than the entire public revenue.[39] Clearly a point of no return had been reached some time earlier, and the life of the Monte was being preserved only by the desperation of the citizens.

In order to maintain market values the citizens had accepted levies *a perdere* to finance the sinking fund, paid on average in two out of every three years. Without them, the debt would have been several millions higher. But this was not sufficient as a remedy. The Florentines, with the same ingenuity that went into the building of the dome of their cathedral without scaffolding, had turned their public debt into the world's first pension fund in an attempt to reduce its cost.

The Monte delle Doti (Dowry Fund) was originally set up in 1425. It allowed citizens to deposit fixed sums with the city which would mature after periods of between five and fifteen years. The deposits could be made either in cash or in Monte Comune holdings at their market value. Cash deposits were used to repurchase Monte Comune shares in the market, so the result either way was a reduction of the public debt held by citizens. No interest would be paid during the life of the deposit, but the amount paid at maturity would represent a compound rate of return more or less comparable to current yield of Monte shares. The rates of return offered were extravagant—often 11–15%—and reflected the depths to which the public debt market had sunk. In order to accumulate sufficient assets to pay the promised amounts at maturity, the interest on the Monte Comune shares held by the Dowry Fund would be used to accumulate yet more public debt in the market. Matured dowries would be paid by selling the necessary Monte shares in the market.

This scheme gave the city two advantages—one illusory and the other real. The Dowry Fund would retire large amounts of debt from circulation and would thus appear to reduce the interest payable to public creditors—at least until the dowries came due. The city's true profit, smaller but real, would derive from the significant number of girls who failed to marry as a result of the plague or other fatal illness, or because they elected "to join the celestial spouse in marriage"[40] by becoming nuns. In this case, the original deposit would be returned to the family or the nunnery, but not any accumulated increase. Since between 20% and 25% of girls generally failed to make it down the aisle, the scheme represented a significant profit opportunity for the commune.

Unfortunately, the expected panacea failed to materialize. In the 1430s, the purchases of the Dowry Fund stabilized the public debt market at around 25, but when the fund became a seller as the first dowries matured, the market sank to the mid-teens making forced loans even harder to raise. As a result it was decided in 1458 to stop selling assets to pay matured dowries, and to rely on the interest on the accumulated Monte Comune shares, now with a face value of 4 million ducats, or no less than half the total public debt, to pay dowries as they came due. Not surprisingly Monte Comune prices now rose, reaching 30 in 1463, although they had fallen back to 24 by 1470. New dowry deposits were still being used to accumulate Monte Comune shares, and by the 1470s when the crisis hit, the Dowry Fund held about 60% of the total debt. The ingenuity of the Florentines had not reduced the city's debt by any significant amount. True, the majority of the debt was no longer in private hands and was owned by the city itself. However, the money raised to repurchase it was owed to the citizens' children on their wedding days.

The city now faced a grim situation. Revenues were quite insufficient to service all the debt; choices had to be made. Tellingly, the Florentines chose to support the Dowry Fund at the expense of the Monte Comune. Already the reform of that year stated that Monte officials would pay only interest on the privately held debt "from time to time, as conveniently as they can from the revenues of the Monte."[41] Interest was reduced to 3.25%, then to 3% in 1478, and then to 2.25%. After 1480 payments were subject to the new direct tax, the *decima scalata,* so that they rarely exceeded a net payment of 1–1.5%. Finally, in 1491 investors in new dowries had to sell an equivalent amount of their Monte Comune holdings to the city at a price of 10. These would form the basis of a new sinking fund, which would accumulate Monte Comune shares "so that this *monte* [the sinking fund] shall increase . . . while the Monte Comune of private persons shall diminish, so that in time the interest shall serve the public and not private persons."[42]

Even with this reallocation of priorities, the state finances were inadequate to pay all dowries at maturity, and married couples were waiting for their endowments for up to sixteen months after their wedding. In 1478, it was decided to pay only 20% of dowries in cash, and to credit the remainder to a new 7% fund. Unlike that of the Monte Comune, interest on this fund was not taxable, and the 7% fund became the only public debt vehicle to retain public confidence. Its shares were officially valued at seven times those of the old Monte Comune in 1492. By 1542, the ratio had risen to fourteen times.[43]

Why did the Florentines give precedence to the Monte delle Doti? Obviously the social significance of dowries in the lives of Florentines made tampering with the fund hard to contemplate. But then the receipt of Monte Comune interest was of equal importance to just as many citizens. The true explanation is that the city had made a different compact with its creditors when it started the Dowry Fund. The Florentines understood instinctively that their old Monte Comune shares were really only a contingent liability of the city, and that the city would repay the levies only insofar as it was able. If it was not in a position to do so, the levies would become taxes pure and simple. By contrast, subscriptions to the Monte delle Doti were made on a purely voluntary basis, and the city's obligations to depositors were absolute, not contingent. Of course, Dowry Fund depositors were not repaid on the terms that they had anticipated, but they fared far better than the holders of Monte Comune shares. This explains why Florentine citizens were willing to take the significant risk that their daughters might not marry and happily contributed their public debt holdings to the Dowry Fund. Any risk that they took was more than compensated by the improvement of the "quality" of their assets.

The fate of the Monte Comune exposed a fundamental flaw in the system of repayable taxation. The commercial genius of the Italian merchants had transformed the primitive, and essentially political, principle of surplus distribution into an economically viable system of finance. But for all its elegance, the Italian formula ultimately failed the test of market efficiency.

For the system to work well, there had to be a flourishing secondary market.* Indeed, the creation of trading markets for long-term financial assets was one of the most important and lasting achievements of the Italian republics. The secondary market was needed for two reasons. First of all, large-scale debts could be sustained only if they were long-term, and long-term obligations were far more palatable if they could be sold in case of need. Second, the market was also needed because repayable levies, however skillfully devised, were only moderately efficient in tapping available liquid wealth. The levies failed to take into account the relative liquidity of the citizens, some of whom needed to sell their loans while others, whose ships had come in, had surplus funds to invest. Furthermore, there were many sources of funds that lay entirely outside the system of assessment, such as foreign residents (and foreigners in general) and religious and charitable foundations. These groups were important potential investors in the public debt. In 1375, a Venetian official estimated that as many as two-thirds of the shares in the Monte were owned by nontaxpayers.[44]

But there were fundamental incompatibilities between forced loans and free markets which became apparent at times of crisis. The levies collected from the citizens were in reality only contingent liabilities of the cities. Like the Roman contributions during the Punic Wars, they would be repaid if success in war (and international trade) permitted. It was therefore acceptable, if painful, to allow that the levies might be repaid only in part, after a very great time, or even not at all. What seemed unacceptable was that secondary-market purchasers, who bought their bonds at deep discounts, should receive yields so much higher than the citizens themselves. Venice, in particular, could never stop itself from feeling justified in discriminating against the rights of secondary holders for just this reason. Interest paid to secondary holders had been reduced to half that paid to primary holders by 1440. Clearly this was no way to encourage the development of a thriving marketplace. Investors either left the market entirely or demanded higher yields in order to compensate for such risks.

*When governments sell their bonds to investors, they create a primary market (i.e., one in which the "producer" receives money from the "consumer"). When investors subsequently buy and sell these bonds between themselves, they create a secondary market.

A further problem became apparent as debt levels rose. The idea that it was offensive to impose direct taxes on citizens meant that their contributions should be repayable. If such debt was viewed as a contingent claim only, then there was no limit to how much could be raised in this way. By contrast, the operations of free markets require that debts should not rise beyond the tax resources available to service them if credit standing is to be preserved. These two opposing principles did not collide as long as debt levels were reasonable. But by the middle of the fifteenth century, it was clear that the Florentine debt, at least, had long passed the threshold of creditworthiness.

Information on medieval economies is still too scanty to make GNP estimates more than informed guesses. However, a calculation based on Florence's tax returns for 1427 gives a figure for Florentine GNP of 3–3.5 million ducats.[45] It is not hard to see that public debt levels of 10 million ducats, or 300% of GNP, by 1470 were way beyond the capacity of even a modern state to service, let alone a medieval one, however advanced for its time.* With debt at these levels, it was scarcely surprising that the market collapsed.

The essential point was this. The market was sustainable only by the confidence of secondary holders—who were, by definition, *voluntary* lenders. But potential investors were unlikely to attribute a triple-A credit rating to a borrower whose obligations were only contingent, and a large portion of whose potential tax base could be tapped only by further borrowing. What was needed, then, was the explicit separation of loans and taxes, as well as a move to wholly voluntary loans, where the commitment to repay was absolute rather than contingent, and where there was no latent conflict between the claims of primary and secondary holders. It was this hard truth, understood perhaps only subliminally by the Florentines, that accounts for the demise of the compulsory Monte Comune and the survival of the voluntary Monte delle Doti.

Yet the ideal of repayable taxes died hard. The Venetians, in particular, showed considerable reluctance to move to a system of voluntary debt. In 1463, when the Monte Vecchio had ceased to be a viable method of raising money, the state enacted a direct tax, the *decima*. But gradually some of the new taxes started to have repayment terms attached, albeit without interest.

*It is interesting that the market value of Florence's debt appears never to have risen above 3 million ducats. As the face value soared, the market price sank. Perhaps this market valuation, equivalent to around 80–90% of GNP, represented the highest debt level it was possible to sustain at the time.

Then, in 1482, Venice attempted to revive the old idea on a clean slate, and the Monte Nuovo—the "New Fund"—was born. Interest was again set at the magic rate of 5% and was secured by the *decima*. The fund's active life lasted until 1509, and its capital rose to 3 million ducats.[46] During its last years it traded at par or better, having recovered from as low as 52 in the crisis year of 1500. Yet, with the experience of the Monte Vecchio still fresh in memory, Venice made little attempt to persist with the new fund once it ran into serious trouble. At the start of the War of the League of Cambrai, the city suspended interest, and prices fell to 40. Instead, the government started yet another fund—the Monte Novissimo. In the 1520s, this was in turn abandoned and replaced by the Monte di Sussidio. But these last two *monti* raised little over 2 million ducats between them.

By 1529, when the years of crisis were over, the Monte Nuovo had traded as low as 10, the Monte Novissimo as low as 25, and the Monte Vecchio as low as 3. The republic now had the chance to put its fiscal house in order. Its methods of doing so provide a further example of the incompatibility of the concepts of repayable taxes and voluntary loans, and of the republic's reluctance to accept the transition from one system to the other.

It would have required around half the public revenues to service the debt at the uniform rate of 5% in 1530. This was not beyond the capacity of the state, but it did not accord with the Venetian view of debt as a contingent obligation. Moreover, the Venetians could never accept that full interest be paid to those who had bought at low market prices. Many bonds of the Monte Nuovo had changed hands at around 20, and payment of 5% on face value would have yielded these speculators (who included several of the most prominent Venetian patricians) a return of 25%. One solution would have been to pay secondary holders a lower rate. This solution had been applied to the Monte Vecchio, but the bitter experiences with that fund had made the government forswear tampering with the coupon rate in its subsequent *monti*. Another solution would have been to compel secondary holders to sell their bonds to the state at the purchase price. This possibility had been provided for by law in 1491 and had already been applied to the Monte Nuovo when it fell temporarily to 50 in 1500. But of course, this solution, too, was incompatible with the principles of a free market, and in 1509 Venice had been forced to forswear the application of this law to the Monte Nuovo in an attempt to support the market.[47]

In the circumstances the Senate decided that it had best treat all Monte Nuovo holders equally, but at least, the secondary holders should be prevented from profiting from their speculations. The money that should have gone to pay interest was applied instead to redeem the principal, and 100,000 ducats* was allocated for this purpose—sufficient to redeem the whole issue over thirty years. The Monte Novissimo and the Monte di Sussidio were refunded by an issue of new bonds at 83.33 (a yield of 6%—the current market rate), and then application of the law of 1491 to repurchase bonds from secondary holders at 40–60. This operation neatly encapsulates the two conflicting principles of debt management. The compulsory repurchase of bonds at below-market prices was part of the psychology of repayable taxes, while refinancing at market yields effectively converted the two *monti* into voluntary loans. Arrears of interest were made up (which would have been unusual for forced loans), and current interest was thereafter paid regularly. Not surprisingly, prices rose to around par. The Monte Vecchio continued to be treated on the old principles. Interest was paid at a rate of 1%, but with no attempt at punctuality. In 1518, for example, the payment for September 1477 was finally made. At the end of the sixteenth century the old fund was finally redeemed. Once again, the prices paid were a reflection of the traditional order of priorities. Original holders received 5% of the face value of their claims, while secondary holders received no more than 2.5%.[48] With the disappearance of the Monte Vecchio at the beginning of the seventeenth century the era of repayable taxes finally came to and end.

SAN GIORGIO

Genoa has not figured in this tale because it took another course. The city did not enter into the internal power struggles of Italy. It controlled only parts of the thin Ligurian coastline and often surrendered its nominal independence in exchange for protection by either Milan or France. In the eastern Mediterranean it was hemmed in by Venice, and later by the Ottomans. In the western Mediterranean it faced the rising power of the Aragonese, who had transformed the area into a Spanish lake by the middle of the fifteenth century. Its opportunities for ruinous military expense were therefore somewhat limited as compared to those of Venice or Florence. Nonetheless,

---

*The Venetian ducat was by now no longer a gold coin, but a silver-based unit of account designed to represent an amount of silver equivalent to the value of a gold ducat. Unlike the medieval gold ducat, however, the silver ducat was not stable. By 1600 it had lost 22% of its original silver value.

the public debt continued to grow—as was not surprising for a city with its revenues almost entirely consumed by its interest bill. By 1509, the total nominal debt had reached the equivalent of 6.5 million ducats. The important aspect of this extra debt was that it was almost entirely voluntary.

Genoa had always had a larger component of voluntary lending in its public finance than the other Italian cities. As long as the fiscal and military situation was not critical, the citizens had always preferred not to be subject even to the compulsion of forced levies. The relative isolation of the city from the enormous costs of mercenary armies on the mainland allowed it to avoid some of the financial crises that plagued the mainland powers and that made the process of raising money so coercive. But the main reason that Genoa was able to make the transition to a purely voluntary debt was the extreme disunity of its political life, which had caused its creditors to take the reins of public finance almost entirely into their own hands. This process was completed in the fifteenth century with the establishment of that most idiosyncratic of all Genoese creations: the Casa di San Giorgio. The Casa was born in 1407 as another consolidation of part of the debt—in this case almost all of the debt created since 1340. Its initial capital of 2.9 million lire* (2.34 million ducats) was already the largest of any of the loan syndicates. By 1454, it had absorbed virtually all the remaining syndicates and represented almost the entire public debt of the city. By this stage the organization had become a state-within-a-state, arguably more powerful than the republic itself. It collected almost all the taxes, ran the salt monopoly, operated the mint, and governed the largest part of the city's overseas territories in Corsica, Cyprus, and the Black Sea. Its eleven thousand shareholders represented almost the entire citizen body.[49] Its powers included the right to torture suspected tax evaders, and to adjudicate claims against tax farmers. Apart from its quasi-governmental operations, it maintained the ability to act as a trader in its own right. In 1418 the state renounced the right even to inspect its books. The Casa di San Giorgio was not only the largest collective commercial enterprise of the Middle Ages, but also by far the best-run. Its meetings and elections for offices were held regularly and fairly; its accounts were perfectly maintained. The disorder and ferocity of Genoese public life were entirely missing from its opera-

*Gold ducats were not the official currencies of the Italian cities. These were based on the lira, a unit of account introduced by Charlemagne that originally contained one pound of silver. When the cities won financial independence they managed their own currencies, and over time the lira started to have quite different values in different places. The history of the £.s.d. monetary system is described in greater detail in the appendix on currencies.

tions. Machiavelli regarded San Giorgio as "the preserver of the country and the republic." In fact he could only wish that its influence might grow:

> It is a truly rare phenomenon, never yet seen in any of the real or imagined republics of the philosophers, to see within the same circle, within the same citizen body, both liberty and tyranny, life both civilized and corrupt, justice side by side with license: because such a combination is maintained only by that city so full of ancient and venerable customs. . . . If it should ever occur, as in time it probably will occur, that San Giorgio takes over the whole city, the Genoese Republic would be more memorable even than the Venetian.[50]

Machiavelli was right. It was indeed a strange phenomenon. The Genoese, unable to form a cohesive polity on the basis of one-man-one-vote, had effectively formed a parallel polity based on formalized power-sharing that largely excluded the two most disruptive elements in city life: the ex-feudal aristocracy and the urban poor. The Fieschi and Grimaldi familes, so dangerous politically, were almost unrepresented in its administration, whereas the urban mercantile nobility, such as the Spinola family, featured prominently. The organization of San Giorgio was certainly not democratic by any normal definition of the term. The eight "Protectors of San Giorgio" were appointed, not elected. They held almost total power for their year of appointment, and at the end they appointed their successors. Their posts were rigorously divided not only on social lines but also by the outdated political divisions of the imperial-papal struggle: two Protectors for the pro-imperial nobility, two for the propapal nobility; the two for the merchants and two for the artisans were again divided between the propapal and proimperial parties. The same proportional division was applied to the wider bodies of the Casa, the Council of Twenty-four, and the Council of One Hundred, and to the administrative officials of the colonies. In this way the antagonisms of factional politics were diluted by means of an ancient form of *partitocrazia**—crude, but without the hypocrisy and resulting corruption of the modern equivalent. Perhaps more than any other institution of the Middle Ages, San Giorgio represented the rule of merchants freed from aristocratic and popular pressure.

So how did the merchants of Genoa run their city's finances when they had them under their control? The idea of public finances run by a credi-

---

**Partitocrazia* was the term used to describe the political system of Italy from 1947 until 1994. Under the appearance of democracy, the parties tacitly agreed to divide the offices of government and nationalized industry between them in a manner that rendered the outcome of elections largely irrelevant.

tors' committee is anathema to the modern mind, as one too narrowly selfish to contemplate. Yet the results were not at all that might be supposed.

First of all, there was the self-confident generosity with which the Protectors progressively reduced the real* returns paid to the San Giorgio shareholders. They did this by allowing increases in debt without concomitant increases in underlying tax revenues. Even more important, the Genoese continued to denominate their debt in silver lire of constantly declining value, rather than copying the Florentines and Venetians, who ensured that their claims were denominated in gold ducats. Throughout the fifteenth century, cities and kingdoms devalued their currencies in the hope of alleviating a severe silver shortage that lasted until the opening of new mines in Austria, Saxony, and Bohemia after 1460. While the gold ducat/florin standard remained unaltered, as it needed to in the interests of international trade, the Venetian lira was devalued by 30% during the course of the century, the Florentine lira by 40%, and the Genoese lira by a full 60%. In 1407 the ducat was worth 1.25 Genoese lire; by 1509 the ducat had risen to 3 lire. The results are best seen in the table below:

THE COST OF GENOESE PUBLIC DEBT, 1407–1509[51]

	1407	1509
Debt (in lire)	5,900,000	19,300,000
Interest (in lire)	280,000	540,000
Debt (in ducats)	4,720,000	6,440,000
Interest (in ducats)	220,000	180,000

While the debt denominated in lire had risen sharply, the interest cost in ducats had, if anything, declined. The Protectors of the public creditors had effectively allowed the city to borrow free of charge. What is more, they had reduced the real interest paid by the city until it represented 2.8% of the face amount of the debt—and probably less than 2.5% of the amount actually borrowed. This has to be compared to the rates of 7–10% originally agreed on. The Genoese creditors, in spite of controlling the whole financial apparatus of the state, had voluntarily given away almost as much as the Venetian and Florentine creditors had lost in the collapse of their *monti*.

*Throughout the book, when the word *real* occurs in the context of finance, it means "adjusted for inflation" or, more precisely, "adjusted for changes in the value of the currency."

Not content with displaying such largesse in the matter of interest, the Genoese citizens were equally profligate with their principal. Their role model was Francesco Vivaldi, who in 1371 bequeathed 90 shares (9,000 lire face value) in the Compera Pacis to a sinking fund (known as a *coda*, or tail) to accumulate at compound interest for the public benefit.[52] The sting in the tail was that any attempt to divert the fund to cover current public expenses would cause it to revert to the family. By the miraculous workings of compound interest, the Vivaldi fund had managed to buy up 99.8% of the shares of the Compera Pacis by 1454, almost 1 million lire in face value. This represented around 12% of the entire public debt at the time. In 1467, the city showed its appreciation by erecting a statue of its benefactor (just as Greek cities had often done to honor creditors who remitted their claims). The Vivaldi example was taken up by many others in Genoa—but significantly, not in Venice or Florence. So many funds were started, not only for debt reduction but also for charitable purposes such as churches, hospitals and universities, that the matter of commemorative statuary had to be formalized. Up to 25,000 lire, donors were rewarded by a simple plaque; up to 50,000, by a bust; up to 100,000, by a small statue; and over 100,000, by a full-size statue overlooking the council hall of the loan syndicates.[53]

Clearly the Genoese public debt was no longer serving merely as a source of income for the citizens. Its yields were too low to attract the merchant classes, which preferred to aim for the returns of 12–15% or better available in trade or through regular commercial lending rather than the 5–8% market yield of San Giorgio shares. Beyond its use as an investment vehicle for charitable foundations, San Giorgio developed a more important role as a secondary source of money for the Genoese economy. Of course, one of the virtues of all public debts was that they avoided the economic wastefulness of public treasuries, which reduced the money supply. Debts such as those of the Italian cities that had active trading markets were also able to act as outlets for spare liquidity and as alternative means of payment for large transactions. They were of little assistance, however, to small-scale commerce. The critical development occurred in the 1440s, when San Giorgio started to pay its dividends not in cash but by means of paper notes—*paghe*—payable four years after the close of the year of account. These notes were very actively traded and were used to settle all kinds of commercial transactions and tax liabilities. Taxes were paid to the tax farmers in *paghe*, and the tax farmers then paid them to San Giorgio (to which all the taxes were now pledged). As a result, the *paghe* were slowly retired from circulation. By the end of four years only a relatively small number would remain to be presented for payment in hard money. The notes traded at a discount that reflected both their remaining life and the conditions of the money market at the time. The discount rates were usually far lower than commercial rates, reflecting the notes' primary use as a means of settlement of accounts rather than as income-producing assets. Apart from relieving the city from the deflationary consequences of the silver shortage of the fifteenth century, this highly original use of its public debt made Genoa the first European state to approach an effective paper economy.[54]

The city's reward went beyond the ability to increase its money supply. It was now able to raise debt more cheaply than its rivals. Nowhere is this more obvious than in a comparison of the interest rates paid by Venice and its erstwhile rival during the sixteenth century. In 1508, the Monte Nuovo reached its brief peak. Its shares traded at par and therefore yielded 5%. Venice had a debt of 3 million ducats, with an interest charge that represented only 13% of the public revenues. At exactly the same time, the Genoese debt of 6.5 million ducats, whose interest consumed the entire revenues of the city, traded at a yield of 4.5%.

Even when Venice raised debt by voluntary means, its disadvantage did not entirely disappear. During the War of Cypress in 1570–1573, the republic raised 6 million Venetian ducats by allowing interest-bearing long-term deposits at the mint. Yet these funds came at a heavy cost. The first deposits, offered at 6% and 7%, were largely ignored. Most of the money was raised at 8%, and some cost as much as 14%. The Ottoman Turks were as frightening to investors as to soldiers, but it is hard to avoid the conclusion that Venice's past track record did not engender the same confidence as Genoa's. Between 1509 and 1531, the far smaller Ligurian republic had borrowed a similar sum through San Giorgio at between 4% and 5%. The great French political theorist Jean Bodin, who wrote his *Six Livres de la République* in the 1570s, showed himself to be aware of this interest differential, and of the reasons behind it:

> Private men had rather take five in the hundred of the colledge [of San Giorgio], to bee assured of their principall, than much more of private men, who oftentimes become Bankerupts: the Venetians have alwaies lost, and shall loose, so long as they shall take eight in the hundred or more: or else they must abate their interest, as they have little and little abated the Mount Vecchio, cutting the creditors so short, as they dare not so easily put in their money as they were woont.[55]

The most remarkable interest rates recorded by Genoa came at the end of the sixteenth century. The city had little reason to borrow after 1530, but the sinking funds that had been set up to reduce the debt continued their preprogrammed repurchases of San Giorgio shares. By 1597, they held nearly 28% of the shares and threatened to swallow its whole capital in little more than a generation.[56] The situation was made more severe because another 40% of the shares was owned by religious foundations, which had no interest in selling. Since, like everything else in Genoa but unlike those of Venice, the sinking funds were private concerns, they had no power to force the religious foundations to sell, even at par. The inevitable result was an inexorable reduction in the float and an equally inexorable rise in the price of the shares. By 1582, they had reached par, reducing the effective yield to under 3%. In 1603 they soared above 200, and in 1621 they reached their all time high of 278. From 1603 to 1625 the average yield was no more than 1.5%.[57]

After 1625, the shares were pushed back under 200 by the combined effects of the Thirty Years' War, the general economic crisis, and the Spanish bankruptcy of 1627. But during the first decades of the seventeenth century, Genoa set benchmarks for public finance that are unlikely to be challenged. In 1624 the yield reached a low of 1.03%.* At a price of 278, San Giorgio had a market capitalization of 30 million ducats. In a state with a population of only 350,000, this was a huge figure. Even with a generous estimate of Genoese GNP per capita, it would still mean that San Giorgio had a market capitalization of well over 200% of GNP.[58] One hundred and fifty years earlier Florence had incurred a nominal public debt somewhere in the region of 300% of GNP, but the market valued it at under 100% of GNP. Genoa's situation was the inverse: a nominal debt less than total GNP was now valued by the market at more than double the national income.

SELFISH CITIZENS

The citizens of the Italian republics have not had a very good press from economic historians. They are generally accused of running selfish and narrow oligarchies at the expense of the disenfranchised majority. Of course, it is impossible not to admire their cultural achievements, which were to

*As of now the record still stands—just. The twenty-year Japanese bond (the longest available in the absense of perpetual debt) currently yields 1.375%.

transform the whole of European intellectual and artistic life. Nobody can remain unmoved in the Piazza San Marco or in front of the sculptures of Michelangelo. Perhaps the selfishness of the fiscal policies by which the citizens enriched themselves at the expense of the poor can be excused as a necessary evil required to fund these beautiful monuments.

Was anything else achieved by the enormous buildup of public debt beyond the enrichment of the wealthier citizens? From a Marxist perspective, the fiscal system of the republics was merely a new twist on the ancient game of "surplus extraction." The owners of the state—the merchant class—use its apparatus to pursue a fiscal policy that creates large-scale transfer payments—not, as in modern states, from the rich to the poor via social security payments, but from the poor to the rich via interest on the public debt.

In some ways it is hard to argue with this view. The pursuit of their narrow self-interest by the citizens was, in many ways, the downfall of the Italian republics. The cities wasted their resources in futile wars against each other, and against other Italian states. The financial exhaustion caused by this process made the invasions of Italy after 1494 by the far-less-advanced states of France and Spain harder to resist. Spain was the clear victor by 1530, and the whole of Italy had become a Spanish protectorate. Florence had ceased to be an autonomous republic and was now a puppet state under Medici grand dukes. Venice was the only state to retain true independence, but there was no question of her challenging Spanish hegemony. Even the popes, the great traditional defenders of Italian independence, had been cowed by the threat of the Reformation into exactly that subservience to the Holy Roman Emperor that they had fought so hard to avoid throughout the Middle Ages. It is striking that, during the final struggle for their republic in 1530, expatriate Florentines flocked back to the city. Michelangelo returned from Rome to design its defenses. But the city found no real support within its subject territories, which put up, at best, token resistance against the advancing Spanish army. This is a sad indictment of the restrictive citizenship of the Italian city-states. The citizen body became an ever smaller minority within a growing state and suffered the consequences.

In some ways, a better model existed north of the Alps. The cities there were insignificant compared to the Italian republics. In 1500, for instance, Hamburg had revenues amounting to a mere 12,500 ducats, compared to 250,000–300,000 ducats in Genoa and Florence and 1,150,000 in Venice. Not only were the cities smaller, but their financial independence was won later than in Italy and was in general less complete. Many continued to have a feudal or ecclesiastical overlord. Yet the northern cities were a vital link in the history of public debt and democracy for one main reason. It was they who set the pattern that was inherited and developed by the Dutch in the seventeenth century.

Like the Italian republics the northern cities financed themselves by borrowing. One advantage, however, of northern civic borrowing was that it was, like that of Genoa, largely voluntary. There was only intermittent recourse to the forced loans that formed the basis of public borrowing in Venice and Florence. As a result, the cities avoided the psychologically difficult transition from a system of repayable taxes. It was not that the northern burghers displayed any great desire to tax themselves. Like their contemporaries they viewed direct taxation as evidence of unfreedom. But it was easier to accept the need to do so if the issue was not complicated by the idea that all amounts collected from citizens should be viewed as contingent liabilities of the city.

The cities borrowed by selling "rents" on their revenues. At first, these expired with the life of the buyer (in other words, they were life annuities of the type first used in Miletus in 205 B.C.). Later the cities tended to sell rents that were inheritable, since they fetched a far higher price.* These inheritable rents were the ancestors of the perpetual annuities (*losrenten* in Holland, *rentes perpétuelles* in France, consols in Great Britain) that were to become the core of all European public borrowing until the wars of the twentieth century.

Historically, perhaps the most important feature of northern borrowing was that significant parts of the debt of each city were held externally. This was never the case in Italy. Some privileged foreigners were entitled to invest in the *monti* of Venice or Florence, or to buy shares in the Genoese *compere*, but their holdings never represented more than a small fraction of the total. In northern Europe it was not uncommon to find 50% of the debt held by foreign investors.

The main reason for this distinctly un-Italian feature was the lower intensity of intercity rivalries. The Italian cities had histories extending back into the classical world. The peninsula never lost its urban traditions even during the Dark Ages. Its cities commanded a fierce patriotic loyalty from their citizens. (To this day anybody who experiences the Palio of Siena can

*In the fourteenth century life annuities were generally sold at a yield of 10–12%. By contrast, perpetual annuities were sold for yields as low as 3% by Cologne in the fifteenth century.

feel the pulse of these ancient passions.) Once settled in a city, its inhabitants almost never left, except for business purposes or if exiled. In addition, after the defeat of Frederick Barbarossa, the cities' independence was complete and unchallenged. By contrast, the northern cities were often relative newcomers. Many were medieval foundations; and even those of Roman origin had become almost entirely depopulated in the following centuries. Their inhabitants were more recent and less deeply rooted than their Italian counterparts.

External investment in the public debts was usually provided by the burghers of friendly or allied cities. It was here that the looser ties of citizen and state proved to be a boon. The absence of the intense mutual jealousies of the Italian republics allowed the northern cities to form themselves into leagues—most famously the Hanseatic League founded in 1282.[59] Such leagues of republics had a long history going back to classical Greece, and to the leagues of Indian republics reported by the writers accompanying Alexander the Great. By banding together, city-states were better able defend themselves against far larger and more powerful empires. The Panhellenic confederation repulsed the assault of the Persian Empire, and in India, the Vrijjian league held the rising power of the Magadhan Empire at bay for a century. In medieval Italy, the Lombard League was highly effective during its brief periods of existence; but after the death of Frederick II its members returned to the mutually destructive warfare that was the normal pattern of communal life.

The northern tradition of intercity cooperation was handed down to the Netherlands in the sixteenth and seventeenth centuries. The Dutch Republic was essentially a league of cities. Its successes in fighting for independence against apparently overwhelming odds can only make one wonder what the history of Italy might have been if the intensity of local rivalries had not been so great.

Yet while future generations of republics would certainly learn to extend citizenship more widely than did Florence, Genoa, or Venice, one cannot say that their citizens did not shoulder the burdens of supporting their states. Certainly the Italian republics designed fiscal policies with their citizens as the main beneficiaries. They clung as closely as they could to the principle that free citizens should not suffer the indignity of direct taxation and should be repaid any contributions that they might have to make to the costs of government. Yet this was not how matters turned out. In each of the cities the public debt was supposedly sacrosanct, yet during the fifteenth century the citizens came to accept the loss of most of its value. In Venice and Florence the loss was 90% or more by the end of the century. The creditors fared somewhat better in Genoa, but they still ended the century with a public debt whose market value was almost certainly less than 50% of the amounts originally loaned.

The repayable taxes of the Italian cities were Janus-faced. Insofar as they were repaid, they were loans; if not repaid, they became taxes. The financial legacy of the Italian city-states to the modern world was not only their public debt markets but equally the principles of direct taxation that they developed and perfected. In order to distribute loans equitably, the cities based them on the individual wealth of the citizens. At first, these assessments were rather arbitrarily imposed by a less-than-impartial panel of assessors. The potential unfairness of this system led Venice to develop the first system based on citizens' own declarations. Assets were capitalized at ten times income, and various exemptions were allowed, as in modern tax systems. For instance, those with assets below 50 lire were exempt, and in 1383 charitable institutions could capitalize assets at only seven times income. In 1427, Florence adopted the Venetian system for the first time. All sources of income were taken into account, including both commercial assets and Monte Comune shares (at the prevailing market value). There were deductions for the primary residence of the taxpayer, and for the family members he supported. For the first time, the city was ruled "by laws rather than by men," as Machiavelli put it. A modified tax, the *diecina graziosa,* introduced the concept of progressive tax rates in 1442, and five years later the *diecina nuova nuova* extended the principle.[60] With rates from 8% to as high as 50%, it is perhaps not surprising that this new form of assessment was supported by the middle-income and less wealthy citizens, but opposed by the Medici and their wealthy friends. They could not stop its enactment but ensured that its life was brief. The *decima scalata,* a further reform, continued the principle of progressive rates after 1480, but the wealthy merchants succeeded in excluding commercial assets from its compass.[61] Of course these strikingly modern methods of assessment were designed originally to distribute forced loans more equitably. The collapse of the Monte Vecchio and the Monte Comune turned them into the most sophisticated direct taxes yet seen in the history of the world. This may not have been what the citizens originally intended, but it was nonetheless the logical corollary of citizenship.

THREE

SOVEREIGN DEBT

The king has no credit . . . no-one does business with him except in the belief that he must declare bankruptcy.[1] —Jean-Baptiste Colbert in 1660

KINGS AND MERCHANTS

In spite of any impression given so far, cities were not the only public borrowers in medieval Europe. In the later Middle Ages, the kings of Europe were rarely out of debt; but there was no market in their bonds. In general, the royal debts consisted of short-term loans from merchants and bankers, each with a different interest cost (often unstated), maturity (often vague or meaningless), and collateral.* These were clearly not the building blocks of a system. In fact the kings had no desire to turn their debts into a system. They wished only to be out of debt, and like all monarchs before them, they dreamed of the joys of a well-filled treasury. It is not fair to say that they were necessarily bad borrowers, looking only to defraud their creditors; but they were certainly reluctant borrowers, and in this they stood in stark contrast to the city-states. In the cities, both north and south of the Alps, the borrowers and lenders (who were virtually identical) conspired to make borrowing the core of their public finances. Kings borrowed only because they had to.

---

*Although royal debts were not "public" in the sense of representing the clear legal obligation of their subjects, it is not accurate to view them as purely "private," as is sometimes stated. Thanks to the revival of interest in Roman law in the thirtenth century, a distinction came to be made between the king's private and public finances, based on the Roman distinction between the private treasury of the emperors (the *fiscus*) and the public treasury of the empire (the *aerarium*).

One does not have to look far for the reason. The kings of medieval Europe emerged from the Dark Ages with almost nonexistent tax bases, as the table at the end of Chapter 1 showed only too clearly. Even in the relatively centralized kingdom of England, the monarch disposed of revenues equivalent to no more than 4.5 grams of silver per head around the year 1200. In theory kings could mobilize enormous unpaid armies via the feudal system. The system witnessed its moment of greatest glory in the First Crusade in 1099. Thereafter it slowly decayed, and wars started to require increasing amounts of hard cash. During the later Middle Ages most soldiers were paid. Mercenaries were employed as early as the twelfth century by such powerful rulers as the emperor Frederick I and Henry II of England.

There were several possible responses to this situation: to reconvert the feudal rights of the king into cash revenues; to establish new powers of taxation; or to look for alternative means of finance. The kings tried all three, since none was individually sufficient to cover the growing costs of government. The commutation of feudal dues into cash took place throughout western Europe but never seemed to produce revenues that would equate historically to those lost in the process of feudalization during the Dark Ages. It was generally difficult to commute more than the minor ancillary rights and dues. The only time that the core of feudal landholding arrangements could be converted into cash was when the king, on some excuse or other, was able to confiscate the entire fiefdom of his vassal. Only the strongest kings were able to do this, and even then only occasionally, since widespread confiscations led to instant revolt. The master of these arts was undoubtedly Henry VII of England at the very end of the Middle Ages. He not only was an exceptionally shrewd and parsimonious ruler but had the advantage of inheriting a country desperate for strong rule after years of civil war, and with almost all his potential rivals already dead, he was able to keep the goods he confiscated without having to redistribute them among potential supporters. He died with the largest treasure of his day, and possibly of the Middle Ages, estimated by the Venetian ambassador at almost 6 million ducats.[2] Not only was Henry VII quite exceptional in his success, but his main achievement was in accumulating assets rather than increasing revenues. He restored royal income to its pre–civil war level, but little more. The underlying tax base was still insufficient—around 6 grams of silver per head—for the needs of a Renaissance state, as his profligate son was to prove only too quickly.

Greater success was generally achieved through the second strategy: seeking altogether new powers of taxation. It was one which at least had the long-term flow of history on its side. But in the meantime, it appeared to encounter as many obstacles as the first. At the height (or depths, depending on how you view it) of feudalism, the king's only substantial residual source of income was his own estate—the royal domain. This was supposed to be adequate for the day-to-day costs of government, which were extremely limited, while he could meet emergencies by calling on his vassals for aid. As feudalism waned, the first part of this theory was left dangling without its corollary; nevertheless, it continued to be much quoted in the later Middle Ages. When Edward IV told Parliament in 1467, "I purpose to lyve uppon myn owne," he was not discussing his marital arrangements, but only repeating a commonplace of the time, which reflected a belief that kings should be satisfied with their inherited revenues and not go bothering their subjects for extra funds.

This attitude was itself an obstacle to creating new tax revenues. An even greater one is revealed by the fact that it was Parliament to whom Edward was speaking. In medieval Europe it was almost impossible for kings to raise new taxes without the consent of representative assemblies. The principle of consent had never completely disappeared from European political life, even during the centuries when it had been subsumed into councils of the great feudal landholders. The gradual growth of urban life meant that a full consultation of national interests required the presence of representatives of the towns (and, indeed, the kings viewed the towns as useful allies against the pretensions of the barons). The English Parliament likes to consider itself "the mother of parliaments"; but in fact, not only were such bodies common throughout Europe, but precedence lies elsewhere. Henry I of France held an assembly at Paris in 1059 which included not only lords and bishops but "lesser people."[3] The kingdoms of Christian Spain were particularly rich in parliaments, and in 1188 the assembly at León included representatives of the towns and other commoners for the first time. Although gradually sidelined during the centuries of "absolute monarchy" after the Middle Ages, the Spanish parliamentary tradition was never entirely lost, and when Napoleon attempted to impose his version of "democratic" rule on Spain the Cortes was summoned to Cádiz to set up a rival representative government: "things that we Spaniards know how to do . . . without any need for the French to come and teach us."[4] The role of the medieval assemblies varied, but there was little doubt that the most common reason for summoning them was a need for extraordinary taxes.

The problem for kings was not that their parliaments refused to grant them extra revenues ("aids," as they were carefully described). It was rather that, with the idea that the king should "live upon his own" in their heads, they almost always offered less than the amount needed. They also took care to make the taxes as provisional as possible and tended to write themselves ever more deeply into the fiscal process with every authorization. Generally rulers had more success with indirect taxes. The English kings were eventually granted customs duties for the duration of their reigns; but to fund full-scale warfare, direct taxes were unavoidable. In the first years of the Hundred Years' War, Edward III managed to increase his regular income of £30,000 (about 200,000 ducats), mostly derived from customs, to over £100,000 by means of parliamentary grants of extraordinary direct levies. During the later part of Edward's reign, government revenues rose as high as 15 grams of silver per head, from no more than 6 grams at the beginning of the century.[5] It seemed for a moment that the fiscal limits of the medieval monarchy were about to be broached. But such levels of per capita taxation were merely an unsustainable by-product of the drastic fall in population after the Black Death. By the end of the reign, the peasant population was ready to break out in revolt, and the dynastic wars of the following century rapidly reduced the monarchy's income to early medieval levels. In any case, Edward's income was largely due to the cooperation of a Parliament that looked favorably on his imperial ventures. As a French writer of the 1690s remarked—at the beginning of another century of Anglo-French hostilities—

> The English, who are always the people most jealous of their liberty, and whose history horrifies by the terrible measures that they have often taken to conserve it, offer freely of themselves all that is necessary to support those enterprises on which they feel that they should embark for the good of the State; and amongst these, throughout the centuries, war in France has always held the first place, according to Philip de Commynes [the fifteenth-century chronicler]; in that this celebrated author remarks that this people, so proud of themselves, never pay any subsidy under ordinary circumstances to their prince, who is forced to survive from his estates in peacetime, but never refuse him anything when it is a question of crossing the sea to come and trouble the peace of our kingdom.[6]

The only kings to finally break the barrier of parliamentary consent were the French monarchs of the fifteenth century. After 1436 Charles VII stopped obtaining permission to levy indirect taxes (the *aides*), and after 1439 he collected the taille (the all-important direct tax) with a similar disdain for legal niceties.[7] Under the pressure of constant war to free the country from English occupation and the equal threat of peasant uprisings, it was easy to find excuses for not recalling the assembly, and the will of the

Estates General to resist was rapidly broken after a century in which it had wielded as much power as any other parliament in Europe. Charles VII was the true founder of "absolute" monarchy in Europe, and the fiscal implications were plain by the end of the century: by escape from the need for authorization, both the inadequacy and the impermanence of parliamentary taxes were resolved. By 1483 Charles and his successor, Louis XI, had unilaterally increased the yield of the taille from the 100,000 livres* originally granted in 1439 to no less than 4 million livres per year (around 2.25 million ducats), giving France a budget almost twice the size of Venice's and more than four times the size of England's.[8]

Yet even this enormously increased income only represented about 8 grams of silver per head, and after the death of Louis XI popular discontent forced a sharp reduction in the taille to about 2.5 million livres, leaving revenues per head at about 5 grams of silver. This was certainly an improvement on the 2.4 grams of 1221, but it was still relatively unimpressive. The incomes of English and Castilian kings actually declined in the fifteenth century after reaching a peak in the fourteenth. The Holy Roman Emperors ended the Middle Ages as the poorest monarchs of Europe, scarcely able to cover even the day-to-day expenses of government and dependent on the charity of their wealthy subjects.

Since neither the commutation of feudal dues nor the search for new tax powers proved sufficient, there was no alternative but to seek other financial resources. The new credit markets beckoned, and kings found it hard to survive without them whether they liked them or not. The earliest forms of royal borrowing were ad hoc loans from Jewish moneylenders, or (incongruously, given that usury laws made the Jews the only legal lenders in Christendom) from monasteries. The rise of the Italian merchant bankers in the thirteenth century put a new complexion on matters. Under Edwards I, II, and III, the use of public credit by the English monarchy started to take on the appearance of a system. The wool production of the island was immensely attractive to the merchants of Tuscany, and they were happy to take the risks of sovereign lending in exchange for preferred access to this all-important raw material market. They had two potential sources of repayment: the proceeds of extraordinary taxes granted by Parliament and the

*The livre was introduced into France by Charlemagne, and was the French equivalent of the lira and the English pound. The history of the £.s.d. monetary system is outlined in the appendix on currencies. The value of the livre was not stable. In 1300 it was worth around 2 ducats. By 1500 it had fallen to little over 0.5 ducat.

yield of the customs duties. The first was able to produce far larger sums, but the second had the advantage of being under the merchants' control, since they insisted on its administration as a condition of their overall relationship with the government.

The first merchant bankers to try their hand were the Riccardi of Lucca, who financed Edward I's campaigns.[9] In 1294, however, they suffered the fate that was to characterize most royal financiers. The King of France seized their assets in his kingdom to punish them for supporting his adversary. As a result, they suffered a withdrawal of deposits by their Italian backers and were no longer able to satisfy Edward's needs. Their uselessness rendered them vulnerable, and it comes as no surprise to learn that their English assets soon suffered the same fate as their French ones.

Undaunted by the experience of the Riccardi, the Frescobaldi of Florence stepped in to take their place. They lasted until 1311, when baronial jealousy of their influence and wealth forced Edward II to expel them. The Frescobaldi were rapidly replaced by the Bardi and the Peruzzi. They, too, enjoyed considerable success for over twenty years and must have made enormous gains from the combination of profits from the wool trade, surpluses from the customs farm, and high interest rates on the royal debt. Like the Riccardi's, their downfall was caused by war with France. In 1337 Edward III launched the campaign that was to start the Hundred Years' War, and although he was later to enjoy dramatic victories, his initial attempt at invasion was a dismal failure. He was forced to retreat to England in 1340, having scarcely set foot in France. In the meantime he had run up debts totalling £300,000 (over 2 million ducats), of which nearly half came from the Bardi and the Peruzzi.[10] Edward's debts were now nearly ten times his normal revenues and were larger than any other public debt of the time except that of Genoa. Inevitably he defaulted, and his bankruptcy heralded the end of the Bardi and the Peruzzi. News of Edward's bankruptcy traveled rapidly to Florence and started a run on their banks. These troubles were combined with setbacks in the kingdom of Naples and by the continuing fall of gold against silver. The Peruzzi went bankrupt in 1343. The Bardi were supported for a time by the city government, which feared the consequences for the Florentine economy if its preeminent firm was to fail. But it was of no use, and the Bardi, too, declared bankruptcy in 1346. The event has been described by Carlo Cipolla as the first international debt crisis:

> In an over-simplified version, the paradigm may run as follows: the large companies of the dominant economy (Florence), which operate in the underdeveloped country (England), have a vital interest in securing the local raw

> material (wool) for the home market. By logic of events they are led to grant increasingly larger credits to the local rulers, on whose benevolence the licenses for the export of raw material ultimately depend. The rulers of the underdeveloped country, however, instead of using the credit to finance productive investment, squander the funds in war expense and are soon forced to declare bankruptcy. . . . [The paradigm] could be applied to the events of the 1970s simply by altering the names of the chief actors and changing the kind of raw material used.[11]

The English use of public borrowing never recovered during the Middle Ages. Edward was left with his crown in hock to Flemish merchants for £2,250. The crown passed from hand to hand and was finally redeemed seven years later at a total cost of £14,000.[12] This represented a compound rate of 30% per annum, probably not untypical of interest rates paid by royal borrowers. Generally these rates were invisible, since lower ones were quoted and lenders made up the difference by extracting higher profits in their parallel business dealings with the royal government. (In order to circumvent usury laws, the Bardi and Peruzzi loans were nominally interest-free and relied on prearranged "gifts" from the king. This made defaulting on interest all the easier.) The later Middle Ages contain regular references to royal debts, but there was no semblance of a system. Henry VI was stated by one account to have accumulated £372,000 (around 2.9 million ducats) of unpaid obligations by 1450 as a result of his fruitless campaigns in France and his extravagant building projects.[13] The inevitability of his default only encouraged merchants to support his rival, Edward of York. Edward restored some semblance of order to royal finances and was able to borrow money from the Medici bank in London, the first time that Italians had accepted an English sovereign risk since the events of 1340. The experience of the Medici was scarcely better than that of their predecessors. In 1478, the London branch of the Medici bank was closed down as a result of its losses on royal loans. The English crown ended the Middle Ages virtually without credit.

The Kings of France disliked borrowing even more than their English counterparts. Interest, even expressed as a gift, was an offense to their sense of propriety. Their financiers, therefore, charged no interest but were more than able to compensate themselves in other ways, since they were simultaneously tax farmers and suppliers of the royal armies. In this they were little different from the Bardi or the Frescobaldi, but the lack of even a nominal interest or "gift" rate made French finances even more opaque than the English. The financiers accumulated ever greater profits until their inevitable day of reckoning arrived; they then usually lost not only their wealth, as in England, but their lives. The first significant provider of financial services was the Order of Templars. Other than certain Italian firms, the mysterious and powerful Templars were the most important single source of credit in Europe in the thirteenth century. After 1294, the Italians joined them in the guise of the Fransezi brothers, Musciatto and Albizo, from Florence, who lent 200,000 livres to Philip IV (about 400,000 ducats) to fund the war against Edward I of England (who, of course, was similarly financed by Italians). Mouche and Biche, as they were familiarly known in France, met their doom in 1307, and their execution coincided with a coup against the Templars, who were summarily slaughtered, while the order was disbanded and its assets annexed to the state.[14] The regular seizure of the goods of Italian merchants on the excuse of usury made them largely withdraw from the French market by 1350. Native financiers fared little better. Gérard Gayte, who operated under Philip V from 1316 to 1322, ended his days in prison. The most famous French financier of the Middle Ages was Jacques Coeur. From 1438 to 1451 he was Charles VII's most indispensable minister, financing Charles's reconquest of Normandy, supplying the royal household, and acting as roving ambassador. In 1451, he was accused of usurious profiteering on his advances to the king by charging undisclosed interest at 15–20%. In vain did he plead that he was merely covering his own interest payments to his backers in Florence and Barcelona, and that money was expensive throughout Europe at the height of the silver famine. He, too, was publicly executed and his goods were confiscated.

When willing lenders could not be found, the kings looked for unwilling ones. The practice of forced loans was the result—not the carefully distributed levies of the Italian cities, but interest-free sums exacted from merchants or towns that were suspected of harboring surplus wealth. Small amounts were sometimes repaid so as to keep the illusion of lending alive, but for the most part these loans were simply a form of disguised taxation.

Royal borrowing was mired in a vicious circle. Short-term borrowing from merchants at high interest rates (whether stated or not) was bound to be unsustainable in the long term and led almost inevitably to default. The threat of default pushed the merchants to increase their short-term profits in turn. This cycle raises the question of why kings did not raise money in the more intelligent fashion of the cities by selling rents. The practice was well-understood by the fourteenth century, and there is some evidence of the existence of "rentes" on the French revenues as early as 1316.[15] Alternatively kings could tap the superior borrowing power of the cities themselves. In the late fourteenth and fifteenth centuries, the Dukes of Burgundy were sometimes able to raise money by pledging revenues to one of the wealthy semi-independent cities within their extensive possessions. The city (Bruges, perhaps) would then sell a perpetual or life annuity against these revenues on the duke's behalf, but with the city's name attached.

It was by developing such techniques that the monarchs of Europe were able to turn their debts into a viable (if still flawed) system of finance in later centuries. In the meantime, however, there were too many obstacles. First, kings sufficiently disliked borrowing so that they preferred to see their debts as merely temporary. Their dislike of interest was just as great, and they instinctively preferred it to be hidden from their view even if that meant paying higher rates in reality. Selling long-term annuities in imitation of the cities did not satisfy either of these deeply felt prejudices. Second, kings viewed borrowing as merely one of a repertory of financial expedients, which included forced loans, sales of royal estates and offices, fines and confiscations, and currency manipulation. They cared little that some of these might be at odds with others. The most important conflict was between currency manipulation and borrowing. For kings viewed the mint not merely as an institution whose purpose was to ensure a functional money supply but also as a source of profit. The process needs a brief explanation.

In order to make substantial sums from currency manipulation, the level of debasement had to be extreme. Debasement for profit, therefore, had nothing to do with the normal devaluation of medieval currencies, for which economic justifications could generally be found.* The process was, as far as possible, shrouded in secrecy. The king would attract coins to the mint by making a tempting offer (say, 11 livres of new coins in exchange for 10 livres tendered). The old coins would then be melted down and alloyed with a significant quantity of base metal so as to produce a new and larger series of coins with less intrinsic value but the same nominal value. Part of

*A certain amount of devaluation was necessitated by the normal wear and tear of coins, which was made worse by their deliberate "clipping" by profiteers. Periodic remintings at slightly lower weights or fineness were required simply to keep a functional currency in circulation. A loss of value of up to 0.3% per year can easily be explained by this process. (This applied only to silver and copper coins. Gold coins were not subject to wear and tear since they were used only for large-scale transactions and were generally traded by weight.) Additional devaluations might occur from time to time to compensate for a general shortage of coin in the economy. The typical 50% loss of value over 100 years evinced by medieval currencies represented no more than a 0.7% annual rate of devaluation—considerably less than the levels of inflation considered acceptable nowadays.

the new currency would suffice to pay the suppliers of old coins; the remainder was the king's profit. Normally the suppliers were merchants who were well able to palm off the new coins before their loss of value was generally realized and discounted through inflation. Since surprise was to some extent of the essence, debasements for profit were almost always conducted by mixing in base metal rather than merely reducing the size of the coins, since this would have been too readily noticed. The old coins not reminted would invariably disappear into hoards, since their holders were unwilling to part with them at parity with the new debased ones. This was the basis of Gresham's Law: that "bad money will always drive out good."* Generally the devaluations were not permanent and were followed by revaluations, partly as a result of aristocratic and parliamentary pressure, and partly so as to prepare the currency for the next round of debauchery. There were no profits to be made in this case, but the government forced the acceptance of the revalued coinage by demonetizing the old, debased coins, thus placing the cost firmly on the shoulders of the holders of existing currency.

It was the kings of France and Castile who were the masters of this art. As long as the rulers were sufficiently ruthless, the amounts that they could collect were impressive. In 1288–1289, for example, French mint profits were 1.2 million livres against 800,000 livres from all other sources. (Interestingly Mouche and Biche advised strongly against this financial strategy and advocated the use of loans backed by taxes, displaying the typical preferences of Italian merchants in public financial policy.) In 1342, the French currency was devalued by 75% in a single year, and in 1349, the mint produced two-thirds of all royal revenues.[16] Economically the revaluations were almost as devastating as the devaluations. In 1357, the hardship caused by restoration of the currency led to riots in Paris. After six violent cycles of currency manipulation in the period from 1285 to 1429, perhaps it is not surprising that the French population was willing to accept the lesser evil of direct taxation as a method of government finance.

Nor is it surprising that potential lenders had little interest in long-term annuities at moderate rates of interest. Until such time as rulers stopped viewing the currency as their personal property and started viewing it as a means of promoting the well-being of their subjects, there could be no

*The law is attributed to Sir Thomas Gresham, the financial agent of successive Tudor governments. In fact, the principle was well understood in the Middle Ages and is even to be found in the writings of Aristotle.

question of affordable long-term borrowing.* With so many financial (not to mention physical) risks attached to sovereign debt the main concern of lenders could only be to make as much money as they could as quickly as possible.

THE TREASURE OF THE INDIES

> Do not forget that the introduction of credit has done more change among the powers of Europe than the discovery of the Indies.
>
> —John Law to the Regent of France after his exile in 1720

To the dispassionate observer it might have appeared that the heyday of public debt was over by the end of the Middle Ages. The cities that had been its pioneers were floundering, in part, at least, because they had pushed their credit beyond the point of solvency. The great consolidated debt funds of Venice and Florence were in default, and the Genoese debt was trading at a discount of 40–50%. The situation was little better north of the Alps. Cologne, the greatest city of Germany, was heading toward bankruptcy by the end of the century because of a reluctance to impose direct taxes that rivaled that of the Italian cities. The cities of the Netherlands were so heavily indebted by the 1490s that Mary of Burgundy and her husband, Maximilian, had to grant several suspensions of payments.

The problems of the cities went beyond their financial straits. The period of their greatest flowering appeared to be over. The Mediterranean had for centuries been an Italian lake, but by the end of the century its western end was largely under the control of a newly united Spain, whose flag also flew over Sardinia, Sicily, and the Kingdom of Naples. The situation in the eastern Mediterranean was even more alarming, with the Ottomans controlling the old Byzantine territories right up to the shores of the Adriatic. The gloomy outlook of 1500 was to be confirmed in the coming decades. Under Suleiman the Magnificent the situation was to deteriorate further, the Ot-

*It is noticeable that the two countries with the best record of currency stability in the later Middle Ages—England and Aragon—had kings who had already given promises to their parliaments not to tamper with the coinage without consent. In 1247 James I of Aragon swore not to alter the currency without the consent of the Cortes. In 1307 James II made a similar committment when the Cortes authorized him to make a small debasement to alleviate the shortage of coin. In 1351 Edward III of England debased the pound by 10%, and the next year he was forced to sign the Statute of Purveyors, which declared that any further alterations should be made only with the consent of Parliament. The next English devaluation, in 1411 (16.5%), was made with proper authorization.

toman Empire fully encircling the eastern end of the Mediterranean, and with active plans to become a naval power as invincible as it was a land power. On land, the Italian position looked equally dispiriting. More than two centuries without major foreign incursions had ended in 1494 with the invasion by Charles VII of France, the precursor of others to come. The newly united kingdoms of France and of Spain battled for supremacy in Italy until the outcome was decided in favor of Spain at the Battle of Pavia in 1525. By 1530, only Venice may be said to have been truly independent. Charles V had become Duke of Milan, Genoa and Florence were largely satellites of the Habsburg power, and the popes were too cowed by the sack of Rome in 1527 and by the threat of the Reformation to renew their old fight against imperial pretensions.

Economically, the prosperity of the Italian cities was threatened by the voyages of discovery of the 1490s, which had opened a direct route to the Asian spice markets and led indirectly to the discovery of hitherto unknown continents. The Genoese and Florentines, sensing the importance of these developments, may well have lent their services as navigators and financiers, but they were in no doubt that the major beneficiaries would be the Iberian kingdoms, not their native cities.

If the future appeared to belong to kings, then it was not at all clear that they would be borrowers. The major kingdoms of Europe were largely out of debt by the last decades of the century. Louis XI of France had capitalized on the success of his predecessor in asserting the right of permanent direct taxation to build up the largest income of any monarch of the period. Henry VII of England was using (not to say abusing) the legal niceties of the feudal system to build up the most impressive treasury of the era. If anything, he was a lender, not a borrower. Ferdinand and Isabella of Spain, who had joined the two kingdoms of Aragon and Castile, had recovered most of the revenues alienated in the previous century, and Isabella left strict instructions for her successors never to indebt themselves again. Frederick of Habsburg, the Holy Roman Emperor, although disposing of modest means, was almost as parsimonious as Henry of England and managed to bequeath his crown without debts and with a replenished treasury to his son Maximilian in 1493.

Furthermore, in what appeared to be a replay of the cycle played out in classical antiquity, just as the city-states were waning, the monarchies were gaining new sources of revenues and looked to be heading for that absolute power that they had dreamed of but never achieved during the Middle Ages. During the sixteenth century the revenues of Spain and France were to undergo a dramatic expansion that removed them permanently from the medieval parameters within which they had fluctuated. European kings were finally in possession of incomes that could match those of the Grand Seignor, the Ottoman emperor—public revenues that had not been seen in western Europe since the days of Rome.

THE GROWTH OF GOVERNMENT REVENUES, 1500–1600[17]

		Population *Millions*	Revenues *Tons of silver*	Revenues per Head *Grams of silver*
France	1500	12.0	65	5.4
	1600	16.0	372	23.3
Castile	1500	4.5	51	11.4
	1600	6.0	423	69.3

Thanks to the breakthrough achieved by their fifteenth-century predecessors, the French kings were able to increase their revenues almost without reference to the Estates General, although they had to negotiate on some fiscal matters with various regional assemblies. When Francis I, who ruled France from 1515 to 1547, was asked by the Venetian ambassador to describe his financial resources, he replied tartly that they were "everything that I need, according to my will."[18] Without the control of the power of the purse, the future of representative assemblies was dim. The French Estates General met for the last time in 1614. Its demise set the pattern for most of the remainder of continental Europe, where, one by one, the parliamentary institutions of the Middle Ages were set aside during the course of the century.

The Spanish monarchs of the sixteenth century did not enjoy quite the freedom of action of their French rivals. They still needed approval of the representative assemblies of their constituent kingdoms for tax increases; but they were fortunate that the most important of these, the Cortes of Castile, was cooperative to the point of subservience. This was one of the reasons why the center of power in Spain shifted almost entirely to Castile, ignoring the supposedly equal partner in the marriage—Aragon. Aragon's deputies were made of sterner stuff than those of Castile, and Isabella of Castile had once protested to her husband, Ferdinand of Aragon, "It would be better to reduce the Aragonese by force than to suffer the arrogance of their *Cortes*."[19] In any case, notwithstanding the need to seek parliamentary assent, by 1600 the Spanish crown was able to increase its revenues to levels undreamed of in earlier centuries. The reason was America.

There has rarely been any doubt that the discovery of America in 1492 was one of the two or three most significant events in the known history of humankind. The sudden appearance on the map of continents unknown to any civilization of the Eurasian landmass opened up vast new economic horizons to the nations of Europe—especially those lucky enough to border the Atlantic. The process of discovery, and its consequences, created a whole new area of technological and economic advance—long-distance navigation and transport—an area in which Europe now held an undisputed global superiority. But of more immediate significance for this book was the discovery and exploitation of the silver mines of Mexico and Peru. According to Earl Hamilton, the main historian of the phenomenon, "No other period in history has witnessed so great a proportional increase in the production of the precious metals as occurred in the wake of the Mexican and Peruvian conquests."[20]

In an era in which money was still virtually identical with precious metals, the fluctuation of supply of these metals was of an importance that has no parallel in the present day. Even in the late nineteenth century, when gold formed merely the foundation of a large and flexible superstructure of paper money, the opening of the mines of South Africa was sufficient to turn the world economic cycle from deflation to inflation. In the sixteenth century the impact was even more extreme. The first shipments started early in the century, mostly of gold looted in the initial conquests. Truly significant amounts started arriving in the 1540s with the opening of the major silver mines. The pace accelerated until the end of the century and declined thereafter, but it never dried up. Between 1540 and 1660, a total of 16,900 tons of silver and 181 tons of gold was imported, of which over one-quarter went directly to the Spanish crown.[21]

By the last decades of the century, the Spanish monarchy enjoyed revenues of well over 2 million ducats* per year just from its silver imports. This revenue alone helped to free them from parliamentary restraints. But the American mines had other, more subtle effects. Just how much the money stock of Europe was increased by the vast influx of silver is a subject of some debate, but conservative estimates suggest a figure of around

*The Spanish ducat started life as a gold coin weighing 3.55 grams—copied, in other words, from the Venetian original. After 1529 it was no longer coined but was retained as a unit of account containing a more or less equivalent amount of silver—35.5 grams. Until the end of the sixteenth century its silver content remained unaltered. During this period, in which Spain was the dominant power in Europe, the Spanish ducat is used as the basis for international comparisons, although it has to be borne in mind that its purchasing power declined sharply in the period.

50% by 1660.[22] One of the results was that silver suffered a permanent devaluation against gold, falling from a relatively stable ratio of about 10:1 in 1500 to around 15:1 in 1660. Another result, not surprisingly, was inflation. From 1520 to 1600 prices rose about three times in most of Europe in terms of silver, and rather closer to four times in both Spain and France.

The effects of inflation do much to explain the increased revenues enjoyed by the powerful new monarchies. But inflation was also capable of undoing many of their superficial gains. The French revenues of 372 tons of silver in 1600 were probably equivalent to around 100 tons in terms of late medieval prices, an improvement on the 60 tons collected by Louis XII in 1500, but no more than Louis XI's income in 1483 and rather less in per capita terms. Spain, or at least Castile, appeared to do far better, but even here appearances are deceptive. Thanks to Isabella's very shrewd backing of Christopher Columbus (perhaps the world's single wisest investment decision), it was Castile—not Aragon or any other part of the Habsburg imperium—that enjoyed the fruits of conquest and exploitation. The Castilian income of 423 tons of silver in 1600 looks highly impressive, and the per capita figure of 70 grams of silver looks even more so. But if the revenues from American silver are removed and inflation is discounted, the Castilian population was paying in the region of 15 grams of silver per head, certainly more than in the late Middle Ages, but not quite the royal bonanza that it might have seemed. Even more significant was that the Castilian revenues, based on a population of around six million, had to act as the financial backbone of an empire of at least twenty million, in the remainder of which revenues discounted for inflation had not increased at all.

This rapid overview is enough to demonstrate that even the monarchies most successful at increasing revenues were not thereby liberated from financial constraints. Warfare was becoming even more expensive as standing armies and navies became the norm, and as technology pushed equipment costs (especially for artillery and ships) ever higher. The nirvana of a well-stocked treasury remained as elusive as before, and temptation to have recourse to the financiers remained no less strong than in the late Middle Ages.

An ongoing lack of revenues commensurate with their ambitions could explain a continuation of the sporadic and untidy pattern of royal borrowing that had evolved in the Middle Ages. But this was not how matters turned out; instead, the sixteenth century witnessed a veritable explosion of debt unimaginable in 1500. It is again to the discovery of America that one must look for an explanation. The influx of American silver played into the second of Europe's relative global strengths, possibly the only other field in which it outshone the civilizations of the East: finance.

From 800 to 1600, China was the most advanced society in the world. Yet its record in matters of finance was mixed at best. It was true that between the eleventh and the fifteenth centuries successive Chinese dynasties had issued paper money, many centuries ahead of Europe. But these experiments with paper were required, in part, because of the backwardness of Chinese metallic currency, which was based exclusively on copper, while gold and silver served only for hoarding. And, in matters of credit, China was far behind Europe. Even under the Sung dynasty (960–1279), the very zenith of the Chinese "economic miracle," credit remained primitive and interest rates remained high. The government occasionally made loans at 20% per annum from its silver reserves, but generally charged more. Private loans ranged from 36% to 60% per annum.[23] There was no long-term debt. Moreover, the Chinese were the first to discover that paper-money experiments always seemed to end in hyperinflation and the need for total monetary reform. As a result the Ming dynasty abandoned paper money in the fifteenth century, and Chinese government finances now operated largely in kind.[24]

The Islamic civilizations suffered from a ban on usury perhaps more severe than that of medieval Christendom. This did not keep them from developing quite sophisticated forms of trade finance, using credit sales at prices higher than those for immediate payment as the main vehicle.[25] It is impossible to know what level of interest was charged, but it was probably comparable to the rates charged in medieval Europe before merchants felt increasingly able to "come clean" about their financial practices. In any case, by the late Middle Ages, Europe was finally moving away from any pretense of a total ban on interest-taking and was starting to think in terms of interest rate maxima instead. During the sixteenth century, this new idea (actually a return to Roman practice) swept the old definition of usury away even in the most Catholic of countries.

Like China, the Islamic civilizations had no long-term debt. It was precisely in long-term finance that Europe was truly in a league of its own. The use of "rents" as a vehicle of long-term lending for both agriculture and governments had resulted in a gradual reduction in long-term interest rates to levels that are still impressive. By the late fourteenth century, 5% had become the benchmark rate for secure long-term loans, whether against land or government revenues. One or two northern cities had borrowed for as little as 3%. Additionally, the Italian republics had led the way in the creation of trading markets for long-term financial assets.

It was into this already relatively sophisticated financial sector that the bullion of the Americas was poured. The result was a considerable further stimulus to its development. The credit markets of the sixteenth century operated on a scale quite different from those of the fifteenth, both in terms of the quantity of the financial instruments created and in terms of the speed at which they circulated. The macroeconomic figures themselves bear witness to these developments. The increase in precious-metal money was around 50%, while prices rose by 200% or more. The only possible explanation of the difference—assuming that these figures are approximately right—was that nonmetallic forms of money rose even faster than metallic, or (and) that the velocity at which money circulated also rose. Both these possibilities appear to be true. The velocity of circulation was significantly increased, for example, by the advent of bearer paper, and by the gradual acceptance of the practice of endorsement to third parties.*

The very presence of such flourishing credit markets made it less likely that the European monarchies would be able to operate without recourse to them. Although the kings of Europe may have found borrowing distasteful, an empire as far-flung as that of Spain necessitated the services of financial specialists in order to operate at all. The troops required monthly pay, while the treasure fleets arrived only once or twice a year. This in itself virtually ensured that Spain would depend on short-term finance. It would always be a temptingly small step from using short-term debts to smooth the operation of a basically balanced budget to forgetting about balancing the budget altogether. One might think that, after the bitter experiences of the Middle Ages, the financial community would be reluctant to get involved with kings. But in the sixteenth century the anticipation of continuous increases in their revenues was enough to turn monarchs into at least tolerable credit risks. Here, again, the influence of America made itself felt. In the Middle Ages the sight of so much as 100,000 ducats in any one place would have been a great rarity. Yet, after 1550, the Spanish treasure fleets were starting to bring back silver amounting to several million ducats at a time. The sheer sight of such riches would have been enough to turn the head of the

*Financial instruments come in three forms in terms of their ease of transfer: Registered securities are made out to a specific owner, and if they are sold, new certificates have to be made out. Endorsable securities may be transferred to a new owner by the signature of the previous owner on the back of the document confirming its transfer. Bearer paper requires no endorsement at all. It is simply payable to whoever possesses it.

most hardnosed banker. It was in the sixteenth century that an era began—not yet entirely ended, it would seem—in which the financial markets of Europe were periodically fanned to the point of overheating by dreams of American wealth.

More important still was a new political paradigm. The discovery of America coincided with a return of the flood tide of autocracy. Yet for some reason history did not repeat itself. In this third cycle of civilization the pressures that had always pushed toward autocratic government did not prevail. This time, it seemed, the forces of democracy had a secret weapon. That weapon was public debt.

ANTWERP AND LYONS

However much the kings of France and Spain may have wished to avoid the credit markets, their good intentions did not survive long into the sixteenth century. The turning point came in 1519 with the death of the Emperor Maximilian. The heir to Maximilian's domains was his grandson Charles. In previous times no one would have cared very greatly about the prospect of another Habsburg emperor, for the family was not powerful enough to threaten the balance of power in Germany, let alone in Europe. By a remarkable series of marital coincidences, however, Charles had already inherited vast domains throughout Europe and beyond. Through his maternal grandmother Charles had received the Kingdom of Castile with it new American possessions. From his maternal grandfather he had inherited the Kingdoms of Aragon, Naples, and Sicily; and from his paternal grandmother he had received the Duchy of Burgundy with its wealthy cities in the Netherlands (the present-day Benelux countries). And now, from his paternal grandfather, Maximilian, he was to inherit the Habsburg possessions in Austria and a shot at the title of Holy Roman Emperor.

Even before Maximilian's death, Charles was the most powerful monarch in Europe. The new vacancy on the imperial throne opened a stark choice to the Electors. For two centuries after the fall of the Hohenstaufen the empire had been considerably less powerful than the other major monarchies of Europe. Now, suddenly, there arose the possibility of an emperor even more powerful than either Frederick Barbarossa or Frederick II. Francis I of France felt especially threatened, since his kingdom was almost surrounded by Habsburg possessions. The result was a bidding war to secure the votes of the German Electors.

The war started even before Maximilian lay on his deathbed. Charles offered 94,000 German florins (around 73,000 ducats), backed by Jacob Fugger.* Francis upped the stakes by a factor of about thirty with a dramatic offer of one and one half years' revenues. Since this offer was not backed by any reputable bankers, it failed to impress the Electors. The two kings now made a series of overtures to the main sources of large-scale finance in Europe at the time—Florence, Genoa, and Augsburg. Of the two, Charles was more successful—especially with the German financiers—and the final offer ("bribe" is more appropriate) was 850,000 florins, of which Jacob Fugger raised 543,000.[26] The main point of the story lies not in the amount of the debt, in itself quite containable, but in the psychological forces behind it. The very presence of a well-developed financial sector would always make it impossible for the kings of Europe to avoid debt if one of their rivals was willing to tap the market for short-term advantage. The election of Charles (now Charles V) to the imperial throne marked the beginning of a new era of dynastic rivalry. The financing of its inauguration showed that it was unlikely that the great powers would be able to stay in the black. The question was, however, whether the kings of Renaissance Europe would be able to improve on the desultory credit record of their medieval predecessors.

At first blush the outlook appeared favorable. In the late Middle Ages the Kings of France and Spain had had the worst record of currency manipulation of any rulers of Europe. In the sixteenth century, however, the Spanish ducat was entirely stable, and the livre was devalued by little more than could be justified by regular wear and tear. As a result, the French and Spanish kings were able to begin raising money by selling annuities. The Castilian kings had a slight head start here, for in the Middle Ages their predecessors had regularly issued life rents on specified revenues as pensions to favored supporters. Charles V transformed the process into a form of public debt by selling rents (*juros*, as they were called in Castile) rather than granting them. The *juros* representing indebtedness were always inheritable (i.e., perpetual) rather than for life. They were sold at yields that started out at around 10% and then declined in tandem with interest rates in general in the first half of the century. After 1530, rates of 5% were quite

*Jacob Fugger was one of the leading merchant bankers of Augsburg, a town that had been propelled to the forefront of European finance as a result of the opening up of silver mines in the Habsburg possessions in Austria and the Tyrol in the fifteenth century. The Fuggers' role in financing the rise to power of the Habsburgs was to make them the preeminent banking house of their time.

common, and some earlier issues were even redeemed (as was always the borrower's right with perpetual annuities) to be refunded with cheaper issues. Some 7 million ducats of long-term debt was outstanding at an average interest of approximately 6.1% by the early 1550s. This was not expensive by any standards, except possibly Genoa's.

A similar process was taking place in France. In 1522, a date which is traditionally viewed as the birth of the French public debt, Francis I issued 200,000 livres of inheritable rentes. Unlike the kings of Castile, he did not do so directly but followed the alternative strategy of using the credit of a major city. Francis's rentes were issued through the Hôtel de Ville of Paris and were the first of a major series of such issues that lasted until the French Revolution. By 1562, annual rente payments were 630,000 livres, implying a capital of some 7.5 million livres (about 3 million ducats) at a standard interest rate of 8.33%.[27]

Equally encouraging were signs that expensive and opaque loans from merchants and financiers could be replaced by cheaper and more transparent borrowing in the money markets. These markets were a spin-off of the medieval trade fairs and were yet another example of the precocious development of finance in Europe. The fairs of Champagne, which flourished in the thirteenth and fourteenth centuries, were gradually replaced by those of Bruges and Geneva in the fifteenth. By the sixteenth, it was to be Lyons and especially Antwerp that set the pace. The critical innovation of these markets, originally designed to trade goods (in particular wool and cloth) around Europe, was the concept of settlement days. The fairs were generally quarterly, and it came to be accepted that transactions concluded at one fair, or even between fairs, could be settled at the next. This practice gradually gave rise to a new form of short-term finance. The church looked on suspiciously at these developments, but as usual it was clerics who were at the forefront of finding subtle justifications of the practice. By the late thirteenth century, the fairs of Champagne had developed into the earliest form of money market in Europe, and the Riccardi—then bankers to Edward I of England—were able to borrow up to 200,000 livres (about 400,000 ducats) at a time between fairs so as to refinance themselves. Some local rulers, whether feudal, ecclesiastical, or municipal, were able to tap the resources of these markets directly.

Business at Antwerp was so flourishing by 1484 that the markets were open almost continuously—much to the irritation of competitors. Yet the practice of quarterly settlement days was maintained. These were the tenth of February, May, August, and November.[28] The near identity of these dates with those of present-day futures markets makes not only the historical parentage clear, but also what vast possibilities of speculation, and equally of securitization, were opened up by this invention. Indeed, by the early sixteenth century Antwerp had assumed many of the familiar characteristics of modern financial centers. Trading occurred in buildings constructed for that purpose, and a new exchange specialized in financial instruments such as bills of exchange and deposits. The throng of merchants from every country required the services of a variety of local specialists, such as brokers, translators, and—perhaps most strikingly of all—market forecasters. The digestion of large quantities of American silver created sharper periodic expansions and contractions of money supply than experienced before. This gave one Christofer Kurz the opening to sell his services:

> You may have often noticed in my writings to you how great a daily variation there is in bills drawn on Germany, Venice or Lyons, so that in the space of eight, ten, fourteen, or twenty days a man can make a profit of 1, 2, 3, 4, 5, or more per cent with other men's money. . . . For this I have developed a system so that I can foretell the tightness or easiness [of the market], not only from week to week, but also for each day and whether it will be before or after midday.[29]

This rapidly developing marketplace was handily placed in the center of Charles's Netherlands possessions. It was natural for him to tap its resources for his short-term financial needs. Generally this borrowing was performed by the Netherlands government under a female relation acting as regent, or by the city of Antwerp acting as intermediary. In the decades before the crisis years of the mid 1550s, the rates paid by the Habsburgs fell continuously, especially once imports of American silver started in earnest after 1530. At the beginning of Charles V's reign, interest rates averaged between 18% and 20%. By the 1530s they had fallen to around 15% and, in the 1540s, to as low as 10%.[30] During this whole period the credit of the Habsburgs remained solid, and they were able to borrow at rates not far above those of the merchants themselves. It was cheaper to borrow in this way than from merchant bankers, since they expected to be able to refinance themselves on the Bourse at a profit.

Antwerp was effectively closed to the French kings; Charles was not about to allow his chief rival access to his principal source of credit. Francis, however, had alternative means at his disposition. The fairs of Lyons had been growing in importance throughout the fifteenth century and Lyons now became the French equivalent of Antwerp. The south Germans were natural allies of the Habsburgs; the Genoese had seen the writing on the wall in 1528 and had thrown in their lot with the new hegemon. The Florentines, though, refused to do likewise and fled to Lyons in scores after the fall of the republic in 1530. At first, however, Francis used their services sparingly. The early part of his reign he relied on Jacques de Semblançay, an indigenous financier in the tradition of Jacques Coeur. His reputation started to totter after the Battle of Bicocca in 1522, where a shortage of promised funds led to the desertion of the Swiss mercenaries. His fate was sealed by the Battle of Pavia, and his public execution and the confiscation of his property followed the traditional French pattern. Thereafter Francis vowed to eschew debt and instead to build up an old-fashioned war chest. To avoid the temptations aroused by the sight of this treasure, the chests in which it was stored were endowed with "piggy bank" slots and no fewer than four locks, whose keys were in the hands of four different officials. By 1535, this reserve amounted to 1.7 million livres—quite inadequate for the requirements of war, but sufficient to keep Francis out of debt.[31] After 1540 new rounds of war against the Habsburgs put an end to such good intentions, and the war chest was kept full only by means of short-term loans raised from the Florentines in Lyons—clearly a travesty of the original intention. By the time Francis died in 1547, his short-term debts amounted to 6.8 million livres (around 3 million ducats).[32]

The accession of Francis I's son Henry II was a watershed. The war chest was finally abandoned, and the crown borrowed increasing amounts on the Lyons money market, generally at a rate of 3–4% per quarter (12–16% per annum). Perhaps as a result of Henry's marriage to a Medici, the crown's relationship with the Florentine bankers entered a new phase of cooperation and experimentation. In 1548 the Florentines proposed the establishment of four banks in Lyons, Paris, Toulouse, and Rouen that would collect deposits on which interest would be paid at 8%. The king would have priority of access to these funds, but in the absence of royal needs, they would also be reloaned at 11% to other borrowers. This proposal did not come to fruition but led at least to the establishment of the Paris Bourse.[33]

The most significant Florentine innovation, however, was the Grand Parti of 1555. The money market was certainly an improvement on the old system of relying on opaque loans from financiers. It supplied only short-term finance, however, and an excessive reliance on short-term borrowing was bound to be dangerous. The Grand Parti was a bold attempt to place the royal finances on a sustainable basis by consolidating short-term debts into a tradable long-term security. Holders of all existing royal debts on the

Lyons market, currently paying interest at 4% per quarter, could exchange them for a new fund paying 5%. The extra 1% per quarter was to be used for a sinking fund, which would in theory be able to retire the debt over a period of ten years. There was a general pledge of revenues as security (but, significantly, no mechanism for getting access to the funds). Shares in the Grand Parti were to be traded on the exchange so as to provide liquidity—not to mention speculative appeal. The idea was an instant success, collecting subscriptions from sources as far afield as the Ottoman Empire. (At this period the Turks and the French were often happy to make impious alliances with each other against their common enemy, the Habsburgs.) The total consolidation of French debt was never achieved, but by the end of 1557, a total of 9.66 million livres (about 4.4 million ducats) had been issued.[34]

The promising experiments with financial markets were not destined to last. The wars of the 1540s and 1550s led to an unsustainable explosion of royal borrowing, most of it short-term, not only in France and Spain but throughout Europe. Charles V decided to abdicate in favor of his son, Philip II, in 1554. He wished, so he said, to retire into monastic seclusion to set his spiritual house in order during his waning years. In his will he gave spurious advice to his heir to avoid debt. Perhaps there was a touch of *après moi le déluge* in his action. Philip took over the government of the Netherlands in 1555 and of Castile in 1556. He can scarcely have been pleased with what he found. The Castilian revenues were around 3 million ducats, while debts were no less than 20 million. The situation in the Netherlands was no better. Short-term debt was 7 million guilders (approximately 3.5 million ducats) and rising.* Borrowing costs in Antwerp had risen from 10% in 1550 to 14% or higher, so that interest now consumed almost the entire royal revenue. By early 1557 the market had virtually dried up. In April, when Philip was in England in a second unsuccessful attempt to impregnate his wife, Mary Tudor, he made the decision to suspend payments on all his short-term debts. On June 10, after his return to Spain, he announced his decision. The market duly collapsed.

Unlike Antwerp, the Lyons market had been strong during the early months of 1557, with the shares of the Grand Parti trading at 98–99. When

*Like a number of currencies known as *ducats*, *florins*, or *gulden* (*gulden* is German for "golden"), the Flemish guilder started out in the Middle Ages as a gold coin based on the ducat-florin standard, and subsequently became a depreciating silver currency. In the 1550s the Flemish (later Dutch) guilder contained around 18 grams of silver, and was worth half a ducat. It finally stabilized at approximately 10 grams of silver around the end of the century.

the Spanish move was announced, Henry hastened to reassure the market that his credit was unaffected. By this stage the Florentines were feeling a little queasy and had no wish "to bear the risk alone," but they were able to encourage some German bankers to lend another 525,000 ducats. "I am myself amazed at their openhandedness in such a situation," declared Henry, shortly before his own suspension of payments at the beginning of 1558.[35]

The crash of 1557–1559—the first general financial market collapse in European history—did not mark the end of Franco-Spanish rivalry. It was therefore unlikely to mark the end of their use of debt. It did, however, represent a major setback to their use of public markets to raise money. In both France and Spain, the next hundred years of the struggle were to be financed by other means. The Antwerp market still continued its operations, but it was no longer central to Habsburg operations. The German merchant bankers were dealt a blow from which they never truly recovered. In the 1540s and 1550s, a great deal of money had been invested in obligations of the Receivers General—Habsburg government officials responsible for collecting tax revenues. They were invariably businessmen of good credit standing, but they did not represent the true credit of the government, and their obligations were accepted with a certain reserve by all well-informed investors. Yet, in the early 1550s, even the most experienced investors were persuaded to accept them. The Fuggers ended up with 600,000 ducats' worth. After the crash of 1557, none of these loans were repaid.

SERIAL BANKRUPTCY

> I have never been able to get this business of loans and interests into my head. I have never been able to understand it.
>
> —Philip II of Spain to his Minister of Finance in 1580[36]

Philip's suspension of payments in 1557 is generally referred to as a bankruptcy. But the phrase gives a somewhat misleading picture of what actually occurred. What Philip wished to achieve was the restructuring of his short-term debts on a sustainable long-term basis. Apart from the obligations of the Receivers General, for which the crown was not legally liable, all short-term debts were recognized as valid state liabilities. Their holders were simply forced to accept payment in perpetual annuities bearing interest secured on revenues specially set aside for the purpose. Existing annuity holders were unaffected by this process. The operation clearly constituted an act of default, but compared to the fate of many lenders to medieval kings, the Habsburg creditors can be said to have escaped quite lightly. The credit of the crown recovered considerably faster than might have been expected given the vast sums involved. The operation was sufficiently successful in restoring the state finances so that over the following century it was repeated at regular intervals and became almost a system of public finance in itself—a system of "debt management by bankruptcy." It is necessary, however, to distinguish two phases in the Spanish system. The first, under Philip II (and to a lesser extent under Philip III), can be regarded as a marginally successful attempt to apply the techniques of the city-states to royal finances. The second, under Philip IV, witnessed Spain's descent into the worst features of ancien régime public finance.

The cyclical recurrence of bankruptcy was inevitable because the the market for perpetual annuities was never adequate to cover the Habsburgs' borrowing requirements. They always needed to have recourse to financiers. Indeed, after the failed experiment with the money markets, the services of the *hombres di negocios* ("businessmen") became more important than ever. But this posed two problems. In the first place, the interest rates and other fees charged by the financiers were always higher than the cost of long-term debt. In the 1550s the perpetual annuities of the Spanish crown had an average cost of just over 6%. By contrast, short-term borrowing costs were far higher. The direct borrowing of the Habsburg government on the Antwerp Bourse was generally at rates of around 12–14% and reached its lowest level of 10% in 1550–1551, before rising again to 14–16% before the crisis.

The borrowing costs of the Habsburgs in Castile were considerably higher, and on one calculation rose from 17.6% in the 1520s to 28% in the 1540s, peaking at almost 50% just before the crisis of 1557.[37] These figures do not exactly represent per annum interest rates. Although the loans were generally for one year, there were undoubtedly periods of late payment which would distort the figures. The figures also include fees for foreign exchange and other costs of remitting the funds from Spain to the various theaters of war. One thing is clear, however: between 1520 and 1550, while interest costs on the Antwerp Bourse were falling, the merchant bankers were increasing their profits. The average interest of 48.7% paid in 1552–1556 can only have represented desperation on the part of the crown. The total interest paid on these loans—*asientos*, as they were called in Spain—was 9 million ducats, of which 4.7 million was paid in the five years leading up to the crisis. If the money had been borrowed at the same interest rate as the long-term debt (say, 6%), the savings would have been 7 million ducats—a figure almost as great as the short-term debts that brought on the crisis in the first place.

The problem of reliance on expensive short-term debt was interwoven with a second feature of Habsburg borrowing. The crown's ability to sell perpetual annuities at moderate rates of interest was based on the fact that their payment was secured by the pledge of specific revenues and therefore had priority over other government expenses. In many ways, of course, this was a positive feature; but it also limited the revenues available to service short-term debt. Since short-term loans were generally for one year, it was unlikely that they could rise very much above one year's free revenues without the risk of a crisis. It was this that had brought on the bankruptcy of 1557.

Because the market for annuities was never large enough to finance the government, the process was to repeat itself. Short-term debt would gradually build up to crisis levels (a process accelerated by compounding at high interest rates), which would then require another "bankruptcy" or forced conversion. A rhythm of twenty years emerged as the typical cycle. Under Philip II there were further bankruptcies in 1560 (essentially a secondary tremor of the major quake of 1557), 1575, and 1595. Philips III and IV continued the series in 1607, 1627, 1647, 1652, and 1662. The trigger for default was the buildup of short-term debt to levels substantially above the revenues available to repay them.

Spanish Bankruptcies, 1557–1607[38]

	1557	1575	1595	1607
Total revenues (millions of ducats)	3.0	8.5	9.8	11.5
Long-term debt service (" ")	0.9	2.6	3.8	5.2
Net revenues (" ")	2.1	5.9	6.0	6.3
Short-term debts (" ")	7.4	15.2	14.0	12.0
—as a multiple of net revenues	3.5	2.6	2.4	1.9

Under Philip II, at least, the Spanish system was not without its virtues. In the first place, Charles and Philip had managed to break forever the medieval pattern of royal borrowing, both in scale and in sophistication of management. Furthermore, at each stage, the large majority of Philip's debt was in the form of cheap perpetual annuities. The very regularity of his bankruptcies meant that the adverse effect of compounding on the expensive short-term debt was kept somewhat in check. During his reign, interest on the large majority of *juros* was paid regularly, without deductions, and in good coin. By the time of Philip's death in 1598, the long-term debt had risen to no less than 68 million ducats, with an annual interest cost of 4.6 million ducats (6.75%).[39] The large majority of this debt had been created in the course of the three major bankruptcies. Yet, at the end of his reign, it was still possible to sell *juros* on unencumbered revenues for yields of 5%. Since total revenues had just risen to over 12 million ducats with the introduction of a new series of indirect taxes, the *millones*, free revenues were a very substantial 6 million ducats. The last of Philip's bankruptcies, in 1595–1596, had converted 14 million of short-term debt into *juros*, so that short-term debt in 1598 was well within the amount of free revenues. The situation looked reasonably healthy.

Healthy, perhaps, by modern standards of public accounting; but certainly not by traditional ones. Nothing is more striking than the contrast between the financial position of the Spanish empire and those of its major non-European contemporaries. The Ottoman Empire was somewhat past its prime since the death of Suleiman the Magnificent in 1566, but it still disposed of a public treasure of some 16 million ducats in 1596. The Moghul emperors of India were undoubtedly the wealthiest rulers of their day. At Akbar's death in 1605, the treasury at Agra contained 198 million rupees in coin and bullion (equivalent to over 60 million ducats) and another 30 million ducats of worked gold and silver and jewels. In addition there were reserves in other major fortresses. The Ming dynasty of China was in terminal decline by the late sixteenth century, and its bullion reserves were very low. Nonetheless, when Chang Chü-cheng died in 1582, he left almost 12.5 million taels of silver in the central treasury, equivalent to nearly 14 million ducats, and the contents of the provincial treasuries must have increased the overall amount by another 1–2 million. More significantly, in a society that still operated largely in kind, the imperial grain reserves amounted to no less than nine years' consumption. The Tokugawa shoguns of Japan also favored ample bullion reserves. Ieyasu left a treasury of 2 million *ryo* in 1616, equivalent to over 10 million ducats. The table below sets the comparison in clear relief.

NET RESERVES OF THE GREAT EMPIRES, c. 1600[40]

	Millions of ducats
Moghul India	62.0
Ottoman Turkey	16.0
Ming China	15.0
Tokugawa Japan	10.3
Habsburg Spain	–68.0

What an accountant from some intergalactic IMF would have made of this situation, had he visited Earth around 1600, is anybody's guess. Perhaps, coming from some highly evolved civilization, he might have seen that the future belonged to the most indebted.

The success of the Spanish financial system depended on the continuance of some critical preconditions. Each time there was a forced conversion, the financiers would find themselves holding large quantities of unwanted *juros*. If they could not off-load these onto more suitable long-term investors, the financiers became entirely illiquid and were unable to continue to offer short-term finance. In this case, the only possibility of securing finance would be if there was another unaffected group of financiers ready to take their place; but even then the situation would be inherently unstable. It was perhaps for this reason that the period of the Spanish system's greatest success is associated with the financial dominance of the Genoese. They were largely immune from the problems of 1557 and were therefore able to offer their services at an opportune moment, when the Germans were reeling from the problems in Antwerp. In the seventy years between 1557 and 1627 the Genoese financiers were to be found all over the empire. Many established themselves in Spain, where their names were hispanicized (Stefano Spinola becoming Esteban Espinola, just as Cristoforo Colombo had become Cristóbal Colón). Others operated in Naples, Sicily, and the Netherlands. Their preeminence was not the result of the low cost of their services. In fact, they invariably seemed to charge more than their rivals. They were able to get away with this because they were uniquely able to juggle the complex requirements of Habsburg finance. Their skills were twofold. First, their experience with a paper money economy was more profound than that of their rivals, thanks to the pioneering operations of the Casa di San Giorgio in the fifteenth century. "To deal with the Genoese is to deal not in cash, as we do, but in paper," observed the Fuggers.[41] As both the size of the Habsburg military forces and the shipments of American silver required to finance them continued to expand, the need for flexible short-term finance rose commensurately. Remittance by paper was always faster and more flexible than by other means. The Genoese would subsequently be repaid out of the cargo holds of the treasure fleets. To some Spaniards it seemed that most of the silver so laboriously mined in Mexico and Peru was ending up in Genoese vaults. Francisco Gómez de Quevedo, the seventeenth-century writer (and sometime secretary to Philip IV), wrote a little verse to describe the life cycle of the precious metal:

Nace en las Indias honrado,
donde el mundo le acompaña,
viene a morir en España,
y es en Genova enterrado.[42]

It is born with honor in the Indies,
where the world pays it court,
it comes to die in Spain,
and is buried in Genoa.

The second advantage enjoyed by the Genoese was perhaps even more significant than the first. Since it was hard to avoid being obliged periodically to accept large quantities of *juros* in lieu of payment, the secret of survival was to be able to place them as fast as possible with more appropriate investors. Centuries of accumulated experience and capital gave Italy and her bankers a decisive edge over other Europeans. The Fuggers were never able to unload their unwanted *juros* with the agility of a Centurione or a Spinola.* Thus the Genoese were able to maintain their liquidity through several bankruptcies, and to be the first to offer new finance after a forced conversion. It was symptomatic of the impending collapse of the Spanish system that the Genoese were no longer able to bounce back from the bankruptcy of 1627 and found themselves replaced as financiers by the Portuguese Jews.

Even when functioning at its smoothest, a system of periodic bankruptcy had its drawbacks. The forced conversions were not instantaneous operations but required months of negotiations. The bankers could not avoid receiving long-term debt in payment of their *asientos*, but they could refuse any further extension of credit unless they were given bonds with adequate yields to make them saleable. These delays could have disastrous military consequences. In 1576, the Spanish armies were enjoying such success against the Dutch rebels that their bid for independence appeared doomed. Then came the decree of bankruptcy, and the campaign ground to a halt. As the news of the bankcruptcy spread, the rebels lit fires of celebration, but the governor, Don Luis de Requesens, was in despair:

*Given their experience of their native city, it remains something of a mystery that the Genoese did not propose a consolidation of the Spanish long-term debt. One of the problems with the *juros* was that they were secured on revenues with different degrees of reliability. As a result the *juros* were sold for varying yields. A surviving list of market prices in 1594 implies yields all the way from 3.57% to 8.21%, confirming a wide divergence of quality. One solution would have been to consolidate the *juros* in a fund in which investors would own shares, on the lines of the Casa di San Giorgio (or, for that matter, a modern bond fund). In this way the liquidity of the market could have been significantly improved.

> The Decree of Bankruptcy has been such a blow to the [Antwerp] Exchange here that no one in it has any credit. . . . I cannot find a single penny. Nor can I see how the King could send money here, even if he had it in abundance. Short of a miracle, all this military machine will fall into ruins . . . and all this at a time when, if the King could have delayed for three months, I hold it certain that in that time we could have recaptured all the rest of Zealand and even the other provinces.[43]

The stalling of the campaign was not the only disaster. In November, Spanish troops mutinied for lack of pay and sacked first Aalst and then Antwerp itself. As a result Antwerp sided with the rebels, depriving Spain of its invaluable services. When it was recaptured in 1585, it was so thoroughly ransacked that it was of no further use to anybody.

Apart from the military risks, a near certainty of future crises could only increase the interest rates (whether open or hidden) charged by the *hombres de negocios,* as they instinctively added a risk premium to their expected overall return on investment. In the short term this only accelerated the buildup of short-term debt to unsustainable levels. In the long run, it was bound to perpetuate the unproductive atmosphere of mutual distrust that had characterised royal borrowing in the Middle Ages, and that was to mar Spanish finance for centuries.

Given these inherent shortcomings there can be little doubt that the Spanish system would have collapsed earlier if it had not been for the temporary illusion of wealth created by American silver. The most important precondition for the system to work was that there should be constant additions to the royal revenues so as to secure the periodic increases of perpetual annuities. In Philip II's reign, royal revenues grew spectacularly from 3 million to 12 million ducats. The main source of this growth was increased domestic tax revenues that now totaled 9.5 million ducats; but even this latter was to some extent the indirect product of the American silver mines. Less than one-third of the silver imports had gone directly to the crown. The remainder went to the private sector to pay for exports of Spanish manufactured goods to the new colonies. The result was an inflationary economic boom in the mother country, which helps explain the willingness of Castilians to pay continually rising taxes without complaint.

That said, the per capita tax burden in Castile was around 55 grams of silver by 1600. This was high by any standard, especially for a primarily agrarian society. Taxes in France were little more than 20 grams of silver per head. Even the Venetian Republic, with a far more urban and productive population than Castile's, collected only around 34 grams per head. In the absence of a further rise in silver imports, the Castilian level of taxation was likely to prove unsustainable.

Perhaps the silver mines could be persuaded to produce more, but instead, silver production started to decline after 1620. This decline produced a triple blow to the Spanish finances. It not only reduced the direct income of the crown but led indirectly to the stalling of price rises, and then to a gradual price fall toward the middle of the seventeenth century. The Castilian economic boom was over, and the high tax burden started to take its toll. The population, which had peaked at around 6.5 million in the late sixteenth century, fell to no more than 5 million by the middle of the seventeenth, as agricultural depopulation and new outbreaks of the plague started to take their toll. As a result the real per capita burden of taxes rose even further, accelerating the process of economic and demographic decay. The fiscal results can be seen clearly in the chart below.

Castilian Public Revenues, 1500–1675[44]

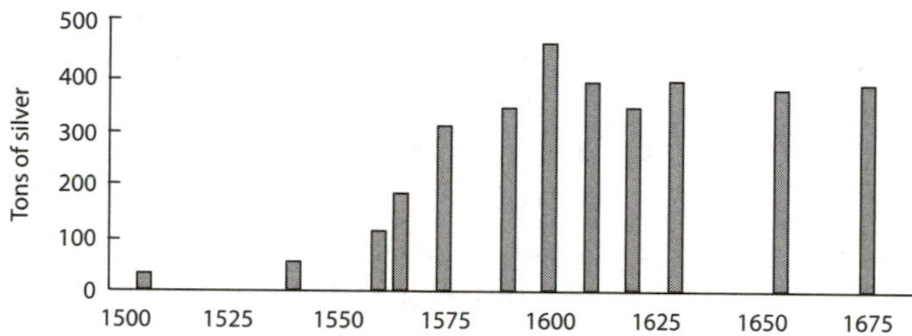

Stagnant or declining revenues were no basis on which to approach the devastating period of European warfare that started in 1618 and did not finish until 1659. The result was the collapse to the two pillars of Philip II's financial system: a sound currency and the regular payment of the long-term debt. The first to go was the currency.

Part of the problem was the perennial migration of silver to the Netherlands, which throughout the period was the epicenter of Spanish military operations. It was from here that campaigns were launched against the Protestants in Germany, the rebels in Holland, or the great rival dynasty in France. But the drain of silver to the Netherlands was not the sole reason for the collapse of the Spanish currency. As early as 1600, the monetary rectitude of the old reign was abandoned by Philip III. The Castilian kings reverted to the ways of their medieval predecessors and started using monetary manipulation as a means of taxation. The everyday currency of Spain was not the silver *peso de ocho*,* which served for international remittances, but coins made from a silver-copper alloy known as *vellon*. When the crown needed money, it simply minted large quantities of these coins at face values far higher than were merited by their metal content. From 1599 to 1626, for example, 41 million ducats of *vellon* coins were minted at a profit that can be estimated at 25–30 million ducats.[45] The value of the currency fell by 70% before an equally disruptive revaluation in 1628. This pattern of debasement followed by periodic revaluation continued throughout the war. In 1650–1651 the government resorted to a practice first employed by the Roman emperors of the fourth century. Coins were not even reminted but merely called in and restamped with a higher nominal value. Thanks to the profits from debasement and other counterproductive expedients, the crown's income appeared to rise. But devaluation rendered these nominal increases in government revenue meaningless. In 1630, revenues were 14.5 million ducats; in 1654, they were 18 million; and by 1674, they had reached 23 million. Yet, as the chart shows, they were stable or declining in silver terms.

If the kings were no longer willing to keep their hands off the currency, then their ability to sell long-term debt was likely to erode. This was made an absolute certainty by the lack of new revenues on which to secure new *juros*. After the bankruptcy of 1627, the Genoese bankers were no longer able to find takers for their unwanted securities, for the market had dried up. From then on any additions to the long-term debt debt consisted entirely of *juros* forced on short-term lenders and other government creditors in settlement of their claims. Inevitably, then, long-term debt service rose without pause. It had reached 11.2 million ducats by 1667, and by 1714 it was 19.6 million.

Yet, apart from the fact that the ducat was worth a great deal less than its nominal value after 1620, even these amounts were increasingly illusory. As more and more annuities were issued, they were increasingly secured on revenues that were already fully pledged. As a result, the *juros* on certain revenues were only partly paid. By the middle of the century it was

*After the opening of silver mines in Austria and Bohemia in the late fifteenth century, a new generation of unprecedentedly large coins weighing between 24 and 28 grams of silver was created to assist large-scale transactions. The first was minted in 1486, but the most famous of them was first coined in 1519 at the mines of Joachimsthal. As a result it was called the *thaler*. This was copied in most countries, including England, where it became the crown, and in Spain, where it became the *peso de ocho* (8 reals, an older-generation silver coin weighing just over 3 grams). Most famously of all, the peso was later to provide the basis of the American silver dollar—derived, of course, from *thaler*.

almost impossible to find any *juro* that was fully secured. Moreover, as the government's finances worsened, it became desperate to get its hands on some of the underlying taxes that it had pledged to its creditors. By 1637, the practice of withholding part of the interest had started.[46] In that year 54% of the interest due was taken by the government. After 1676, at least 50% of interest was withheld on a regular basis. In a futile attempt to maintain the appearance of good faith, the interest withheld was compensated by further *juros*; but this was meaningless in the absence of revenues to service them and only necessitated even greater withholding in later years. Thus, by 1714, nominal debt service had escalated to 19.6 million ducats, but the bondholders received only 14% of that amount, or 2.74 million. In silver terms this amount was worth only 1.22 million ducats—less than a quarter of the amount paid one hundred years earlier.[47]

The Spanish system of public borrowing had now turned from one that was at least marginally successful into one that was totally unsuccessful. Bankruptcy was no longer a periodic tactical move, undertaken with some regret; it became a pattern of behavior so ingrained as to constitute almost a pathology. By the nineteenth century Spain had probably the worst credit ranking of any European state.

As the real value of normal taxation and borrowing declined, the king looked to alternative sources of funds by exploiting his "regalian" rights, however counterproductive this practice might prove in the long term. One of these rights was currency manipulation. Another was the ability to sell offices, titles, and jurisdictions. By the 1660s some eight thousand offices and jurisdictions had been sold as freeholds (in other words, without the right of repurchase), mostly to the sort of purchaser who in better days might have bought annuities. The process has led historians to write of the "refeudalization" of Castile in this period.

In the sixteenth century, the ability of the Spanish Habsburgs to borrow had appeared to be a source of strength. Instead it turned out to be a poisoned chalice. The problem for the Habsburgs, as for all princes of the Renaissance, was that however much they managed to increase their revenues, it was still not enough to render them as "absolute" as they would wish. Even as the ties of the parliamentary institutions of the Middle Ages were loosening, they were being replaced by the less visible, but no less effective, financial restraints of public debt. Compared to the wholly deleterious effects of the outright sale of offices, jurisdictions, or taxes, the policy of selling "rents" at high prices while retaining the right of repurchase was an altogether lesser evil. In fact, in some hands public borrowing could turn out to be a positive source of strength; but these hands were not royal ones. It might be that by 1674 the state had so far privatized its finances that it "proceeds more in the manner of a republic than a monarchy" (in the judgment of the ambassador of the Republic of Lucca, who should have known).[48] But what the ambassador failed to point out was that, whereas the financial system of the republics had grown up by design, its Spanish counterpart had occurred, all too literally, by default. While the republics were simultaneously governed and financed by citizen creditors, monarchs and their lenders were separated by a wall of suspicion. The result was not the low interest rates enjoyed by the republics (by the late seventeenth century the public debt of Lucca had a market yield of around 3%) but a credit standing so low that *juros* could scarcely be sold at any price.

FOLIE DES OFFICES

During its heyday, the Spanish system of finances was undoubtedly the most successful attempt by a monarchy of its time to reap the benefits of public borrowing. It was France, however, that most clearly displayed the characteristics that, for good or ill, typified ancien régime finance. Since the French Revolution, the finances of the Bourbon monarchy have been held up to almost universal criticism and even ridicule. The failings of the French system are beyond dispute. Spanish bankruptcies were no more than forced conversions of short-term borrowing into long-term annuities. French bankruptcies, by contrast, generally involved the wholesale repudiation of debt, both long-term and short-term. However, the failings of the French system should not be allowed to obscure the hidden strengths that not only allowed it to survive repeated crises at least as severe as those of Spain, but that also underpinned a period in which France became the preeminent nation of Europe.

The public debts of the medieval city-states were a profound reflection of their sociopolitical structure. To be a citizen of such a state was, almost by definition, to be its creditor. By contrast, medieval monarchs borrowed only out of necessity and had little or no rapport with their creditors except for feelings of suspicion and mistrust. The achievement of the French financial system was to combine these apparently incompatible features into one.

The most characteristic feature of the French system was the sale of offices. Like the sale of rentes this started under Francis I. It was not that Francis was the first ruler to sell an office, but he was the first to embed the practice in France on a systematic basis. Indeed, he set a whole government department, the Bureau des Parties Casuelles, to handle this exciting new branch of revenue. In exchange for the purchase price, the officeholder was paid a fixed salary, or *gage*, usually 10% of the sum paid, which represented his return on investment. In theory, the office could be redeemed by the crown for the original sales price (although this was rarely done). Thus far the officeholder was no different from any other long-term creditor, and the idea had been created by Pope Sixtus IV in the late fifteenth century as yet another wheeze to avoid the appearance of usury. The papal offices were purely honorary. In France, however, the officeholder was generally expected to perform some administrative function as well. This dangerous idea made for a far more complex set of relationships between crown and officeholders than between crown and rentiers. (In practice, of course, the two were very often the same men.)

An idea of the significance of officeholding is given by the fact that officers' *gages* were already 2 million livres in 1549. This implied a capital of 20 million livres, whereas all other debts at that time scarcely amounted to 10 million. The idea of venal offices came into its own after 1557. By the end of the sixteenth century, almost every post connected with the royal finances and the administration of justice was for sale.

An officeholder was de facto a long-term creditor of the crown. His financial relationship did not end there, however. He was generally required to finance the government on a short-term basis as well. If his post involved the collection of revenue, he would have to anticipate its collection. If, on the other hand, it involved the expenditure of funds, he would have to anticipate the disbursement and wait for reimbursement as and when the revenue filtered through the system. To support this part of his operations, he would often have to borrow money on the Paris money market. Conversely, he might find himself with a float of funds that he had received but was not yet committed to disburse. These funds might be reloaned on the money market.

The officeholders were at the center of a wider network of men known variously as *financiers, partisans, traiteurs,* and *gens d'affaires.* They were subcontractors for the collection and disbursement of funds but did not necessarily hold venal offices. On the other hand they might at any stage be bidders for an office that was up for sale, and the term *financiers* was popularly used to describe the group as a whole.

What the French kings achieved by this system was the very close integration of their financing arrangements into the fabric of French society. A whole class came into existence that depended for its livelihood on lending to the state. The same men provided long-term debt through their investments in offices (and often in rentes) and short-term credit through their anticipations of revenues or disbursements. Moreover, their operations on the Parisian money market made them central to the whole credit structure of the kingdom, in which there were as yet no banks.

By the seventeenth century, the more important offices carried with them an added prize: entry into the aristocracy. A new class of nobility was created for this purpose—*la noblesse de la robe.* Unlike the old feudal nobility—*la noblesse de l'épée*—this was not a warrior aristocracy; but it shared one notable and telltale feature: exemption from direct taxation. The exemption of the feudal nobility from the payment of the taille derived ultimately from the freedom from taxes enjoyed by the old Frankish conquerors of Roman Gaul. As such, it embodied the ancient notion that direct taxation was a symbol of subjugation, and therefore that "conquerors do not pay." In the Middle Ages, this idea had transmuted into a parallel notion that unpaid military service, undertaken as an obligation of class, was a form of payment-in-kind of communal obligations. (This concept can be seen operating in reverse in medieval Venice, where the *advevaticum* was a tax paid by those exempting themselves from the military duty owed by all citizens.) By the seventeenth century the *noblesse de la robe* was providing another form of public service—the financing of the Renaissance state—more important than that of the *noblesse de l'épée* in a period when most soldiers were mercenaries, and when the most common platitude of statecraft was "Money is the sinews of war."

By granting nobility to the new class of officeholders the French kings were doing more than merely increasing the value of the offices that they wished to sell, whether by appealing to the snobbery of the bidders or by improving their potential return on investment. They were offering their creditors access to a higher form of citizenship, of which freedom from taxation was as emblematic as the high-sounding titles themselves. By doing so, they were embedding their credit arrangements ever more deeply in the social structure of the ancien régime. Of course, the *noblesse de l'épée* was no more performing its feudal duty of unpaid military service by the seventeenth century than the *noblesse de la robe* was performing unremunerated service in the administration of the country. Yet medieval notions died hard in Europe even when superseded by reality.

No single aspect of the financial system described above was unique to France. Short-term lenders and long-term annuity holders were categories that often overlapped. The selling of public offices and of titles was common practice both in Spain and throughout the rest of Europe. But venal officeholders were nowhere quite so prevalent as they were in France, nor so integrally tied into the public finances of the kingdom both as short-term and as long-term creditors. For most of the sixteenth and seventeenth centuries, the capital value of venal offices constituted the largest part of the long-term public debt of France.

Thus France had created a system of credit almost as "organic" as that of the Italian republics. Indeed the fates of the monarchy and of its financial system were intimately connected: the Revolution of 1789 was to sweep away both with the same broom. In spite of periodic French bankruptcies—more sweeping though less frequent than the Spanish—the creditor class remained loyal to the regime and continued to finance it to the best of its ability. There was no question of the rather suspect loyalties of the Genoese or the Portuguese.

The ties between the crown and the officeholders worked both ways, however. In exchange for tying its creditors so closely to the state, the crown lost control of much of its finance. The officeholders held the reins of tax collection in their hands—in fact, they were its legal owners. Not only did they own their offices, but their *gages* were also paid before any funds were remitted to the central treasury. These were not the only payments made before the crown got its hands on its revenues. In legal theory, rentiers were the owners of parts of specific taxes, and their annuities, too, were always paid first. Related to the rentes, but even more debilitating for the monarchy, were the *droits aliénées*. These, too, were taxes that had been sold, but unlike the rentes, which represented a fixed annual entitlement, the *droits* were for a percentage of the amount received. As taxes rose, so did the sums taken by the holders of the *droits*. By the 1630s, if the central treasury sought an extra 1 million livres in tax, it had to raise taxes by 1.8 million. The *droits aliénées* were also paid before any money was remitted to the central treasury.

Thus the situation in France was in many ways not dissimilar from that of Genoa. The state had so far "privatized" its finances that it no longer had control of the apparatus. Its creditors were also the tax collectors and paid themselves first before remitting any surplus to the central coffers. The following description of ancien régime France would also be a perfect depiction of late medieval Genoa:

> When the system reached its fullest stage of development only two partners remained—the tax-payers on the one hand, and the State creditors on the other, with the revenues raised from taxation no longer even passing through the hands of the public authorities.[49]

The creditor/tax-collector class could neither be removed from their offices, since they had purchased them, nor be taxed. Their power was such a severe brake on the supposedly absolute power of the state that one is forced to conclude that much of the bombast surrounding the idea of royal absolutism was only so much wishful thinking.

Yet France was not a republic of merchants—far from it. The creditor class was not synonymous with the population as a whole, or even with its more wealthy elements. In fifteenth-century Genoa, the eleven thousand shareholders of San Giorgio represented the large majority of households in the city. In seventeenth-century France, by contrast, the forty thousand to fifty thousand officeholders and rentiers represented at most 1.5% of the households in the country. The French kings saw the new class as a necessary evil. The feudal aristocracy may have been content to profit indirectly from the operations of the officeholders by surreptitiously financing their operations, but they also disliked them as parvenus. To the wider population they were merely a group of bloodsuckers.

This meant that, for all its intimacy, the relationship between the *financiers* and the state was little improved from the medieval pattern of mutual mistrust. As has already been seen in the case of Spain, this mistrust created a vicious circle. The financiers instinctively sought to increase their short-term returns to compensate for the perceived risk of default. This in turn made such a default more inevitable and laid the *financiers* open to the charge of usurious profiteering. But the situation in France was even worse. That a system based on venal offices was likely to lead to corruption scarcely needs to be stated. The *financiers* had means of increasing their short-term returns that would have made the *hombres de negocios* jealous.

The crown had several weapons to combat corruption. The Chambre des Comptes was a central auditing office that scrutinized the accounts of the officeholders. This was a perfectly sensible institution, in no way incompatible with modern theories of good government. But if the government accounts that it scrutinized were as impenetrable as the ones that have survived for the inspection of historians, then it is not surprising that it was scarcely able to fulfill its function. Failing the Chambre des Comptes the crown had a more potent weapon at its disposal: the Chambre de Justice. As its name suggests, this was a court set up to probe into the finances of suspect officials and to exact retribution. From the fall of Semblançay in 1523 until that of Nicolas Fouquet in 1661, Chambres de Justice were set up no fewer than thirteen times. Most of their victims got off with fines, others with imprisonment. Semblançay was the last finance minister to lose his head. Some of the accused were undoubtedly guilty of extravagant peculation; others were mere scapegoats for an endemic and pervasive corruption. The Chambres de Justice acted like miniature defaults, more frequent and more specifically directed than the major bankruptcies, but nonetheless a further destabilizing factor in the financial system. Their operations could only push interest rates higher. Yet there can be no finer illustration of the pervasiveness of the system than the decision of the Chambre de Justice of 1607 to farm out the collection of its fines to three *traiteurs* who offered 400,000 livres up front in exchange for 50% of the total proceeds.[50] Indeed, *justice* may be an entirely inappropriate descriptor for the role of the 1607 Chambre. Sully, the minister of finance, took the skeptical view that, while it raised some money for the crown, it was largely "the occasion for a shameful traffic between those who needed protection and those who were in a position to sell it."[51]

Although the Chambre de Justice was a technique of financial control in its own right, it operated most effectively when it coincided with the ultimate weapon in the armory of the French kings: bankruptcy. There were five major bankruptcies in the century from 1557 to 1661, the last four of which, in particular, were accompanied by massive repudiations of debt that were given legal sanction by the Chambres de Justice that accompanied them. The first occurred in the wake of the general market collapse of 1557. When Catherine de Médicis took stock of her position as regent at the death of Henry II in 1559, she had inherited accumulated debts of 42 million livres (about 17.5 million ducats). Of these some 16 million livres represented the Grand Parti and other debts in Lyons. These were eventually renegotiated for rentes at heavily reduced rates of interest, but the creditors had to double their original investments in order to qualify. Although there were no further bankruptcies during the remaining decades of the Valois dynasty, debts continued to mount at an alarming rate under the pressures of civil war and Spanish invasion. By the time the ex-Protestant Henry IV was able to establish his authority in 1594 with the immortal phrase "Paris is worth a mass," total debts had reached the enormous figure of 296 million livres. This was equivalent to 97 million ducats, 30 million ducats more than the debt of Spain. The long-term debt was around 150 million livres, with an annual interest cost of 14 million livres, leaving only some 16 million livres of revenues to meet short-term obligations of 146 million.[52] This implied a ratio of floating debt to free revenues of 9:1, far higher than the ratios leading to Spanish bankruptcies.

It was quite clear that a debt overhang of this magnitude could not be resolved simply by the forced conversion of short-term into long-term obligations. Over the following decade, Henry—described by the English ambassador as having an "oeconomical faculty of looking into matters of profit"[53]—"renegotiated" these debts in what amounted to an unofficial bankruptcy of major proportions. In this he was aided by his finance minister, Sully, whose "oeconomical faculty" was at least equal to his master's. The long-term debt was reduced by the expedient of repudiating any portion not paid for in cash. Since many rentes had been issued either at a discount or in exchange for unsatisfied government obligations, a very considerable reduction of debt was effected by this means. Subsequently the interest paid was cut in half, to 4.167%. Henry's other creditors suffered a variety of fates, depending on their political clout, the most fortunate being the leading aristocrats, the least fortunate the Swiss mercenaries. By 1608 the total debt had been cut by almost one half, and interest by at least two-thirds. Debt service was now around 9.5 million livres on revenues of 30.3 million. The French monarchy was back on an equal footing with Habsburg Spain.

Free Revenues of the French and Spanish Crowns in 1608[54]

Millions of ducats

	Gross Revenues	Free Revenues	% Free
Spain	11.5	6.3	55%
France	9.6	6.6	69%

The bankruptcies of 1634, 1648, and 1661 are harder to quantify, not because of a lack of French budgets to analyze. Thanks to the diligence of Jean-Roland Malet in the early eighteenth century, a more or less complete set of annual budgets survive for France after 1600, a record unique for any state in Europe in the seventeenth century. Unfortunately, they are almost useless for this purpose, and in their uselessness lies a tale. The French monarchy had a method of accounting that makes it impossible to tell whether it was running a deficit or not. Beyond that, it is impossible to tell how much was being borrowed or repaid, or the size of its interest bill. Perhaps advisedly: these were figures that the monarchy certainly did not wish to make public and possibly did not wish to know itself. Deficits were obscured by the refusal of France to accept the principle of double-entry accounting developed in Italy in the late Middle Ages. More significant was the classification of borrowing as revenue, and of repayments as expenses, in accounting categories that commingle them impenetrably with genuine income and expenditure. Overdue loans were often recorded as paid at the end of the year and then reinstated as income in the next. Malet fumed at such practices:

> These are not remotely actual receipts; on the contrary, all these sums are little more that false finances, created by remittances of imaginary funds that the Treasurers of the *Épargne* made reciprocally from one year of account to another.[55]

Interest was not recorded as a separate category but was included with principal—unless, that is, it was the kind of extravagant interest that the crown paid in moments of desperation, and that they preferred to hide even from the Chambre des Comptes. Then it was included in the *comptants*, a series of secret accounts that included bribes and other dubious expenses of the monarchy. Given the impossibility of knowing the true credit position of the government, perhaps the most indicative illustration of its financial plight is the growth of this hidden spending. During the war with Spain (1635–1648), the secret expenses had grown so far that they exceeded even the military budget.[56] In such circumstances it is scarcely surprising that the crown was obliged to default.

The bankruptcy of 1634 was a relatively humdrum affair by Bourbon standards, largely caused by the growth of *droits aliénées* to unsustainable levels. Any attempt to quantify the *droits* as if they were normal debts is meaningless; but the best estimate is that total long-term debt service, including the *droits*, was some 30 million out of a gross revenue of 60 million livres. The *droits* were forcibly converted to rentes in a manner that reduced debt service by around 50%.[57] As usual, a Chambre de Justice accompanied the default to demonstrate that justice was being done.

The 1648 bankruptcy was more serious. The crown decided unilaterally to end the *paulette*, a decision that struck at the very core of officeholding. The *paulette* was an arrangement made by Henry IV whereby officeholders could ensure the heritability of their offices in exchange for an annual payment of 1.67% of their original cost. The significance of the decision was vividly captured by Charles Loyseau, an officeholder himself, who witnessed the excitement of his colleagues as they signed up for the new arrangement:

> I noted that the moment they were finished they went straight to the place of a nearby notary to hand over their certificates of reversion; and they seemed to be walking on ice, mortally afraid of making a false step and dying on the way. . . . Contemplating this state of affairs, I had to say to myself, Merciful God, would we were as anxious to save our souls as our offices.[58]

At the time, the government calculated, correctly, that it would gain more than it would lose, since not only would it reduce its annual payments of *gages*, but the value of the offices that might sell in the future would also increase in value. This was a correct calculation since the sales price of offices doubled by the 1630s, reducing the market yield from 10% to 5%. The annual cost of *gages* was 26 million by 1640, and the crown had sold all the offices that it could dream up, down to the most superfluous. The abolition of the *paulette* and the general suspension of debt payments led to a revolutionary situation, the ominous precursor to 1789, the only moment when the *financier* class deviated from its allegiance to the crown. The royal bankruptcy was one of the main causes of the civil war known as the Fronde, which lasted until 1653 and nearly cost the young Louis XIV his throne. The extent of the resulting debt reduction is impossible to calculate with precision, but some indication is given by the debts annulled by the Chambre de Justice of that year, which totalled 100 million livres according to Cardinal Mazarin, Louis's chief minister at the time.[59] Interest payments on the remaining debt were subject to unilateral reductions of up to 40%.

By 1661, debts had risen to 451 million livres according Jean-Baptiste Colbert, Mazarin's successor. This figure would obviously have been far larger if it had not been for the preceding bankruptcies. (It would have been larger still if the capital value of offices sold by the crown—estimated at no less than 420 million livres by Colbert—had been included.) Again the Chambre de Justice was wheeled into action and improved the financial situation by more than 135 million livres.[60] This was only the start of a general restructuring of the crown's finances by Colbert, who, for the first time since Sully, achieved a balanced budget and drastically lowered interest costs. The only thing that can be certain about the justice meted out by the Chambre was that the biggest fish escaped its net. This was surely Mazarin himself, who died in that year, leaving net assets of 37 million livres. This was the greatest recorded fortune of the ancien régime.* Since Colbert rose to power as Mazarin's financial agent, he was to be believed when he stated that Mazarin had had no more than 8 million livres in 1658. This statement implies that the old man embezzled no less than 29 million in the last three years of his life.[61] Even Cardinal Richelieu could not compete with his pro-

*If Mazarin's fortune is regarded as if it had been held entirely in gold and then valued at $400 per ounce, it would now be worth around $300 million—already a substantial sum. However, this method of calculation fails to give a true impression of its value. Taken as a multiple of GNP per capita, perhaps 100 livres in Mazarin's day, it would translate into around $10 billion in today's money.

tégé, leaving a mere 20 million livres, of which 4 million was in cash.[62] One thing the two chief ministers had in common: a notable diffidence in regard to investments in royal obligations. The large bulk of their assets comprised cash, land, and diamonds. It was left to the naive Nicolas Fouquet, the minister of finance, to lend most of his rather smaller fortune to the king; and yet it was he who ended up as the chief scapegoat of Colbert's Chambre de Justice.

How was Mazarin able to accumulate his vast wealth? The answer may lie in the defaulted debts left over from the 1648 bankruptcy. Some 25 million livres of unpaid treasury bills (*billets d'épargne*) were in existence, trading at no more than 10% of their face value. Many rentes were selling at discounts that were almost as great. A minister could easily buy these debts up at bargain prices and then have them discreetly redeemed at face value. The possibilities were endless in a world of secret accounts.

FOUR

RESISTANCE TO THE HEGEMON

THE LEAGUE OF CITIES

The financial systems of the monarchies may have been flawed. Nonetheless, it was France and Spain, rather than any city-state, that set the pace in the sixteenth century. In 1500, Venice, the greatest of the mercantile republics, had enjoyed revenues that rivaled those of any state in Europe. By 1600, this was no longer the case.

Government Revenues, 1500–1600[1]

Tons of silver

	1500	1600
Castile	51	423
France	60	372
Venice	41	68

By the end of the sixteenth century it was clear that single cities, even if controlling a substantial territory, were no longer able to compete with the power of the great monarchies. The question was: Would they still be able to preserve their autonomy? This was especially true of those cities that, unlike Venice, acknowledged the nominal sovereignty of a king—particularly if the king was one whose ambition was to reverse the process of political fragmentation that had characterized Europe since the fall of Rome and had thereby allowed the cities to flourish.

The fate of Catalonia, for instance, suggested that the future of such autonomous areas was dim. In the late Middle Ages, Catalonia and its dominant city, Barcelona, had been a virtual city-state within the Kingdom of Aragon. In its commercial prosperity Barcelona had rivaled the merchant republics of Italy. In the sixteenth century, however, the area became mired in a vicious circle with its new Habsburg sovereigns. Perhaps out of jealousy of the rising power of Castile—in many ways a lesser power than Aragon in the fifteenth century—the Aragonese, and the Catalonians in particular, refused to contribute to the costs of empire and were increasingly excluded from its counsels. During the sixteenth century the continuous growth of their revenues from Castile and the Americas had allowed Charles and Philip to ignore the recalcitrant Catalonians. But as the Thirty Years' War took its toll, and the Castilian economy began to stagger under the Atlas-like task of supporting the empire, the monarchy could no longer tolerate the situation. A war of words about taxation and ancient rights gradually escalated into a full-blown rebellion in 1640. However, it is notable that, confronted with the military might of Castile, the Catalonians did not feel sufficiently self-confident to bid for full independence; they took the more prudent route of transfering their allegiance to France "as in the time of Charlemagne." This was no solution at all, however, for France was now governed by Cardinal Richelieu, a man even more determined than the Count of Olivares, the first minister of Spain, to stamp out regional autonomy. By 1652, the Catalonians were almost relieved when the French withdrew their troops to confront domestic rebellion and the Castilians reentered the province. In theory the Spanish crown agreed to respect the rights of the area. But it was not without significance that the Catalonian parliament met for the last time in 1653; and it was only because of the terminal debility of Habsburg rule in the second half of the seventeenth century that the province's nominal independence survived. When the Bourbons inherited the Spanish crown in the early eighteenth century, it was not long before Catalonia was forcibly united with Castile.

A city-state on the traditional model, then, was no longer a match for the new nation-states of Europe. Only a league of cities might still succeed in holding back the advancing tide of absolute monarchy. Where might such a league arise? Within the Habsburg empire the most likely region was undoubtedly the Netherlands. Not only did the area contain a greater concentration of self-governing towns than any other since the heyday of medieval Italy, but it had the added advantage of being part of the northern tradition of interurban cooperation, rather than the southern tradition of internecine urban rivalry. It is not surprising, therefore, that in the sixteenth century it fell to the Dutch to hold up the banner of civic freedom against the centralizing ambitions of their rulers.

The best way to limit the pretensions of kings was, as ever, to restrict their access to money. There were two ways of doing this. The first, inherited directly from the Middle Ages, was parliamentary stonewalling. The second, a more sophisticated technique, available above all to areas with strong traditions of urban self-government, was to agree only to lend the money, while retaining control of the fiscal apparatus necessary for servicing the debt. The Netherlanders availed themselves of both of these techniques.

Like the Catalonians, the inhabitants of the Netherlands were reluctant to tax themselves in the interests of what they saw as a Castilian empire. They had a strong hand in negotiations with the central government, for the royal domains in the region were very limited, and the Habsburgs depended on parliamentary grants for 80% of their local revenues. These grants were agreed to only after seemingly interminable negotiations and with special reductions conceded to the larger towns. From the Habsburg perspective the gravity of the situation was aggravated because the Netherlands was the military epicenter of the empire, the launching pad for invasions of France, Germany, and eventually England. Like the equally urbane and businesslike northern Italians, the Netherlanders were too profitably occupied to perform military duties, and the Habsburg forces there were almost entirely foreign. The behavior of the foreign troops only increased the reluctance of the States General, the regional parliament, to fund their presence:

> It was, then, a vicious circle. Because the States would not consent without wrangling, the regent could not pay her troops, who then behaved in such a way as to make the States absolutely unwilling to consent. As Margaret of Austria [the local regent] once complained to her imperial nephew, "In the long run, I do not see how it is feasible to conduct a war in these countries."[2]

In the 1520s, the situation was still tolerable, with the crown receiving an annual parliamentary grant of around 1 million guilders (about 500,000 ducats), giving it total revenues of nearly 1.4 million guilders. This grant would have represented about 7.5 grams of silver per head, scarcely a large sum for such a wealthy area even then.[3] But even this amount is deceptive, for the Netherlanders were also adept at the second financial strategy available to opponents of royal pretensions. The towns of the Netherlands had a tradition of funding their contributions by selling annuities (*renten* in Dutch) instead of raising taxes. The major towns of Holland, for instance, were all heavily indebted, with around 60% of their revenues pledged for debt service. Charles V only encouraged this trend by asking the provincial parliaments—hitherto not borrowers—to sell *renten* secured by their own subsidies. Failing that, the crown would use the subsidies as security for its own borrowing on the Antwerp exchange.

The combination of rising military costs and static basic revenues squeezed ever more tightly by debt service could lead only to a crisis. In 1539, the government faced a deficit of 1.4 million guilders. By 1543 the deficit had risen to 2.4 million. In 1540 Charles V had occupied Ghent to force it to rethink its refusal to pay its annual levy, in a foretaste of the tactics of his son Philip, but in the long run it did little good. The towns would consent to extra funds only in amounts less than required, and generally in the form of debt secured by new excise taxes that they themselves would administer. As a result their grip on the fiscal system closed ever tighter. By 1558, in the wake of Philip's general bankruptcy of the previous year, the Netherlands government had short-term debts of 9 million guilders. What was the proposal of the States General to remedy this situation? New issues of *renten* of 2.4 million, a similar sum raised by the States General on the Antwerp exchange, and the whole to be serviced out of a new grant of 800,000 guilders per year in taxes administered by the states themselves.[4] Not only was this grant less than the average amount received in the 1520s in nominal terms, but it was also paid in a currency of reduced value and probably represented no more than 5 grams of silver per head. Worse still, the revenue offered was to be almost entirely consumed in the servicing of debts—owned, of course, by the same merchants who dominated the States General. No wonder Philip found the situation intolerable.

Eventually the cold war, involving only money and words, was bound to turn into a hot war conducted with gunpowder and steel. In 1568, after another decade of deficits, supported only by remittances from Castile, Philip sent a new governor, the Duke of Alba, to impose fiscal (and religious) discipline. His radical proposal of a 10% sales and export tax was enough to start a revolt headed by the Prince of Orange. Even though the "tenth-penny" tax was temporarily withdrawn in exchange for an increase in the basic grant by the States General, the damage was done. The eighty-year war for independence had started. By the time the guns fell silent in 1648, the northern provinces of the Netherlands had transformed themselves into an independent and extraordinarily wealthy republic. Spain, however, was in precipitous decline, and many Spaniards agreed that "the war in the Netherlands has been the total ruin of this Monarchy."[5]

How were the Dutch able to take on an empire of twenty million and win? The Dutch were fighting on their home territory in the cause of their own freedom, but this is not a sufficient explanation. The Dutch had also to raise sums that could match those of Spain, sums that seemed almost unimaginable for a nation that numbered less that one and one half million.[6] The only way to approach the problem was to draw in full on the inherent financial advantages of a republic of merchants and borrow to the hilt. By the end of the war, the province of Holland alone had borrowed 133 guilders, the equivalent of around 38 million silver ducats.* The debt of the republic as a whole is not known but was probably equivalent to at least 50 million ducats.[7] The Dutch came to view the war as a battle not only of soldiers and guns, but also of credit ratings. In the words of one observer:

> Even if the country has no money, it still has its credit, and the enemy has neither funds nor credit, that I could not deny that we might wear out the enemy through this war, because this land has sufficient funds.[8]

There was no doubt who won the war of finances. The credit of the republic was looking a little ragged in places by 1648, and the admiralty boards were up to three years in arrears on the sailors' pay, but after the peace, credit was soon restored. By the mid-1650s the 5% perpetual annuities (*losrenten*) that constituted the bulk of Holland's debt were selling above par, and the government of Johann de Witt was able to reduce the interest to 4% by proposing immediate redemption for those who refused to accept the new rate. The debtholders may not have liked this, but by the middle of the century nobody wished to have his bonds redeemed since no one could imagine a safer storehouse for so much capital. The *losrenten* started to trade above par again, and by 1664 the deputies at the States General were pressing for a further reduction to 3%. In the meantime Spain was tottering from bankruptcy to bankruptcy, and its long-term debt was paid in a debased copper currency after deductions amounting to around 50% of the amounts due. The secondary market had virtually disappeared.

The Dutch achievement was truly impressive. The republic was able to sustain a per capita debt that was a multiple of the levels that bankrupted the Bourbon and Habsburg regimes, as the table below makes clear:

PUBLIC DEBT IN HOLLAND, CASTILE, AND FRANCE, c. 1650[9]

	Population *Millions*	Public Debt in Local Currency *Millions*	Public Debt per Capita *Grams of silver*
Holland, c. 1650	0.8	133 (guilders)	1,663
Castile, c. 1650	5.0	150 (ducats)	607
France, 1661	18.0	870 (livres)	376

*By 1648 the Spanish ducat had been devalued by about 40% from its sixteenth-century silver parity. In order to keep a sense of continuity, however, the Dutch debt is given here in nondevalued ducats.

The ideal would be to express the figures not in terms of silver, but in relation to the GNP. Unfortunately, national income figures in this period are still in the realm of informed guesses, but the per capita income of France around 1660 has been estimated at no less than 100 livres, or around 800 grams of silver.[10] Therefore a debt of level of less than 50% of GNP was still sufficient to cause bankruptcy. The GNP of the Dutch Republic at midcentury has been put at 1,100 grams of silver per capita,[11] while that of Holland itself would undoubtedly have been higher—perhaps 1,300 grams. This means that the Dutch were able to sustain a public debt higher than their national production and still prosper—a feat of some note even in today's world.

The Dutch Republic seemed to have squared the circle. It was the only country to emerge from the Thirty Years' War with its credit intact. It seemed to bear its enormous debts effortlessly and could boast of its ready access to more capital in case of further hostilities. It had endured a struggle that was arguably more severe than those of the Italian republics in the late Middle Ages. Yet it had survived without its public debt market collapsing as in Venice and Florence. What was the secret of its success?

A partial answer lies in the remarkable economic expansion that the republic experienced in the first half of the seventeenth century. It was during this period that Holland inherited the mantle of the Italian mercantile republics, which were no longer able to compete in a world where oceanic trade routes had displaced the commercial primacy of the Mediterranean. The Dutch venture into international trade had started in the 1590s with the fitting out of the first fleets to the Far East. The East India Company was founded in 1602, and its commercial success was so rapid that its share price doubled by the end of the decade. The Bank of Amsterdam was founded in 1609, and the exchange started year-round trading in 1611. By the time the Thirty Years' War started in 1618, the Dutch were already the wealthiest trading nation of Europe and had attracted capital from all over Europe—from the refugee merchants and bankers of Antwerp, to the Iberian Jews who had fled rather than face forced conversion, and the Venetians and Florentines who were prominent shareholders in the East India Company. The result was not only an influx of liquid capital but also the doubling of GNP at the same time as the struggle for independence was being waged. Both these developments made it far easier to raise the loans required to take on, and eventually wear down, the Habsburg armies.

The Dutch economic expansion was only part of the picture. The success of Dutch finance depended on two interrelated improvements that they made in the old Italian system. In the first place the Dutch managed to avoid the contradictions inherent in a system of repayable taxes, even though at times they were obliged resort to compulsion. In theory, Holland abandoned the practice of forced loans in 1553, but such loans were occasionally levied at times of crisis, as in 1586–1687 and 1600–1602. The financial pressures during the early part of the struggle were so intense that the Dutch were sometimes obliged to suspend debt service.[12] By 1575, interest had not been paid for three years, and a general suspension of all payments was decreed. In 1577, arrears of interest were capitalized, but by 1581 interest was suspended again and arrears were not finally settled until close to the end of the century.[13]

Like forced loans, the suspension of debt service was part of the philosophy of repayable taxation—in which the public debt was seen as a contingent liability of the state, to be paid only insofar as circumstances permitted. But the Dutch avoided taking this principle to its logical, and ultimately self-defeating, consequence. Crucially, the concepts of direct taxes and debt were always kept separate. The Dutch understood that it was necessary not only to ensure that loans would always be backed by taxes, but also to levy direct taxes on the citizens to complement to the usual welter of indirect taxes that were the backbone of republican finance. Excises on items of common consumption were supplemented by the *verponding*, a tax on land and houses. In 1584, the *verponding* was applied to annuity income as well. At the beginning of the seventeenth century direct taxes provided 30% of the total revenues of Holland. The important point here is that the temptation to make all direct taxes repayable was avoided and, with it, the inevitable skyrocketing of debt to unsustainable levels, as would surely have occurred by the beginning of the seventeenth century.[14] In fact, by 1603, debt service consumed a lower proportion of revenues than in 1567—little more than the income from direct taxes.[15]

The growth of tax revenues in tandem with the debt was crucial to the success of the system. One of the paradoxical aspects of the revolt of the Netherlands was that, while opposition to taxation played a large part in its outbreak, the outcome was massively increased taxes regardless of its success or failure. The revolt of the northern provinces (the future Dutch Republic) gradually spread throughout the whole region, especially after the Spanish bankruptcy of 1576 and the resulting sack of Antwerp. In the long run the southern provinces (present-day Belgium) were not able to resist Spanish reconquest, and the fiscal results of their subjugation were plain and clear. By the end of the century, the Habsburgs were collecting 4 million guilders from an impoverished and depopulated region, where they had

had difficulty collecting 500,000 before the revolt.[16] Even allowing for a further devaluation of the currency, this still amounted to some 27 grams of silver per head. But the result in the northern provinces was even more extreme. The Dutch, who had protested so vigorously about their very low tax payments to the Habsburgs, ended up paying unimaginably greater sums to their new autonomous government. By 1600, the province of Holland, whose normal subsidy to the Habsburgs had been 100,000 guilders, was collecting taxes of 3.6 million.[17] This sum would have represented around 60 grams of silver per head. In 1595, an English observer commented on this political paradox:

> The Tributes, Taxes and Customes, of all kinds imposed by mutuall consent—so great is the love of liberty or freedome—are very burthensome, and they willingly beare them, though for much lesse exactions imposed by the King of *Spaine*. . . . They had the boldness to make warre against a Prince of such great power.[18]

When the war with Spain resumed in 1621 after an eleven-year truce the relentless rise in taxes continued. Taxes in Holland had grown to 10.8 million guilders by 1640, or close to 130 grams of silver per head.[19] Even though the Dutch Republic was almost certainly the wealthiest society yet to flourish in the history of the world, this level of taxation was quite remarkable and was to give political philosophers of the following century much pause for thought.

In the Italian cities, the system of repayable taxes went hand in hand with restrictive citizenship. This, too, was a pitfall that the Dutch were able to avoid. The republic was able to create, and tap, a larger pool of capital than that available to any previous republican borrower, largely because it had a more widely dispersed power base. By midcentury the population was probably around 1.8 million—similar to that of the Venetian Republic. But whereas Venice was a single metropolis dominating a disenfranchised empire, the Dutch Republic was a league of cities. The Dutch Republic's extreme decentralization caused many to wonder whether it could operate at all, let alone flourish, but its decentralization created many more committed citizens and made every town into a potential source of long-term finance. This indigenous pool of capital was further increased by the republic's openness to foreign merchants displaced by the operations of the Inquisition—whether Iberian Jews or German Protestants. Many of Antwerp's merchants and bankers also migrated north in the wake of the sack of their city.

In the final analysis, however, the foundation of the strength of the

Dutch system remained the same as that of the medieval republics. The state and the citizens were more or less symbiotic. It may not have been compulsory to lend to the state in the Netherlands, but the results were little different than if it had been. The well-informed English observer William Temple estimated that there were sixty-five thousand public creditors in Holland in the mid-seventeenth century. The level of diffusion implied by this figure can be appreciated when it is remarked that the number of urban households at the time was probably in the region of 100,000. Equally important was the heavy investment in government debt by the leading merchant families. The Dutch Republic was certainly not a democracy in the modern sense. Political power was concentrated in hands of an urban elite. But this did not affect the public finances. Because the officers of the state themselves held large portions of their fortunes in government debt, every public creditor could be sure that his investment was safe. The whole system was based on the kind of trust that was so conspicuously lacking in the credit arrangements of the monarchies. The Dutch published no financial figures by which investors could tell if their government was solvent or whether their *renten* were properly backed. As debt continued to grow into the eighteenth century, the solvency of the republic appears, in hindsight, to have been questionable. After 1715 it is unlikely that the Dutch debt was ever much less than 200% of GNP.[20] Yet the citizens, protected not only by their blissful ignorance of this state of affairs but also by their unshakable trust in the good faith of their government, continued to lend at ever lower rates. The best borrowers, such as the province of Holland, were able to borrow long-term funds for as little as 2.5% per annum.

At the Treaty of Westphalia in 1648, the Habsburgs finally recognized the independence of the rebel provinces. But the Dutch were not able to rest easy for long. The republic's domination of maritime trade had become a provocation—and its "embarrassment of riches" a temptation—to its larger rivals on the Atlantic seaboard. Commercial rivalry with England led to two wars in the 1650s and 1660s. But although England might represent a long-term challenge to the undisputed commercial supremacy enjoyed by the Dutch in the seventeenth century, it did not threaten the very independence of the nation. The same could not be said of France, however. The Battle of Rocroi in 1643 may have ended Spanish military ascendancy in Europe, but by the same token it ushered in a period of French predominance no less worrying to neighboring states. In 1672, the new European hegemon had invaded, and the republic was saved from annihilation only by the extreme measures of flooding the dikes and recalling the Orange family to office in spite of lingering suspicions about their monarchical aspirations. The population and resources of France were so much greater than those of the Dutch that the superiority of Dutch public credit was barely able to compensate. Certainly there seemed little reason for France to address the chaos of its financial arrangements just to counter a threat from the Netherlands. For public borrowing to become a force that would challenge autocratic rule at its very core, a further revolution was needed.

REGICIDE

A year after the Treaty of Westphalia there occurred an event even more remarkable than the formal recognition of Dutch independence from Spain. In 1649 the ranks of republican Europe were suddenly swelled by the arrival in their midst of England.

That a region such as the Netherlands, with its tradition of urban self-government, should have become a republic was perhaps no surprise. Even the Dutch did not create a totally pure republic, however. In the early years of the revolt there was much discussion about the possibility of replacing Philip II with a new king, invited to take over the throne on terms that would strictly limit his powers. This, after all, was what happened in England in 1688, when William of Orange was offered the English crown by Parliament. By a nice piece of historical symmetry the putative Dutch crown was nearly handed to an Englishman, the Earl of Leicester; but he proved to have unacceptable views about the sweep of his prerogatives, even daring to attempt the centralization of tax powers. The Dutch finally ended up with a subtle compromise by maintaining the office of Stadtholder—the old provincial representative of royal power. This position was not theoretically hereditary but was almost always vested in the Orange family, which had led the initial revolt of 1569. The Stadtholder's powers were a mix of military and ceremonial rather than governmental; but they provided that crucial sense of continuity, and even of mystique, which prevented intercity rivalries from getting out of hand. Yet the relationship between republican urban governments and the Stadtholder were never comfortable, and the tensions had come to a head between 1654 and 1672, when no Stadtholder was elected and the republic was run by the Councillor Pensionary (the legal secretary of the provincial parliament) of Holland, Johann de Witt.

In these circumstances, it seemed deeply implausible that England should become a republic. In many ways the country was a more likely candidate for participation in the general trend toward absolute monarchy than for republicanism. It had a predominantly rural economy. It had no tradition of urban self-government. Not only was its monarchy well-established, but it was one of the most centralized in Europe. The nobility, who in England and elsewhere had always formed a bulwark against royal absolutism, were cowed by the end of the civil wars of the fifteenth century. There remained the English Parliament. But who was to say that that this body would not share the fate of most other European representative assemblies in the seventeenth century?

The sixteenth century, moreover, commenced with good prospects for royal power in England. Henry VII managed to accumulate probably the greatest royal fortune in Europe since the fall of Rome. His treasure was reputed to be at least £1.3 million (6 million ducats) by the time of his death—enough for around ten years' normal expenses. Henry's regular income remained relatively modest, but it was nonetheless a golden inheritance that he handed down to his son Henry VIII. Unlike his father, however, the new king had no interest in husbanding his resources. Nor did he have any fear of European entanglements; and his treasure chest tempted him to try his hand at international power politics in that giddy period when the whole of Italy and the imperial crown appeared to be up for grabs. By 1514, £892,000 had already been spent on military campaigns in France to no visible effect.[21] By the 1520s, Henry's inherited fortune was dissipated.*

Even then, Henry managed to lay his hands on another treasure even greater than his father's. The decisive moment came with the pope's surprising reluctance to annul his marriage to Catherine of Aragon. In the old days such a vital matter of state would almost certainly have been nodded through, especially for a prince who had showed himself such a strong defender of the papacy, whether from the sword of the French kings or from the pen of Luther. Unfortunately, since the capture of Rome in 1527, the pope had become a virtual prisoner of Catherine's nephew, Emperor

*In one of the nicer ironies of history, a minor part in the relentless fall in Henry's assets was due to the bankruptcy of the Frescobaldi banking firm in London in 1518. This was the same Florentine family that had financed Edward I and whose assets had been brusquely expropriated by his son, Edward II, some two hundred years earlier. It was a reflection both of the sheer size of Henry VII's treasure and of his commercial mind-set that he lent a portion of his assets to merchants in the hope of improving his customs receipts. The Frescobaldi owed his son £60,000 (around 270,000 ducats) at the time of their failure.

Charles V. In one of the most decisive moments in English history, the way simultaneously to resolve both the marital and the financial impasse suggested itself to Henry's new eminence grise, Thomas Cromwell. By repudiating the authority of the pope in 1532 and installing himself as head of a purely national church, Henry opened the way not only to the royal divorce, but also to the confiscation of vast church assets. The suppression of the monasteries and chapter houses brought lands with an estimated income of £135,000 to the crown—enough to double its normal revenues.[22] This scarcely enabled Henry to take on the two great powers of Europe on equal terms, but it was more than sufficient to make him independent of Parliament under any normal circumstances.

But the break from Rome was a poisoned chalice for the Tudor, both financially and politically. Perhaps the very ease with which the monastic lands had been acquired encouraged a cavalier attitude toward their management. They might have provided a stable base for a borrowing policy based on the selling of rents. Yet lands would always be a more tempting target for outright sales than the less tangible tax revenues of the crown. In any case, Henry proceeded to dispose of his new fortune almost as soon as he had acquired it. By the end of his reign in 1547 two-thirds of the church lands were gone. Having squandered its assets, the crown now resorted to debasement of the currency. From 1542 to 1551, the pound lost 83% of its silver content, and under Edward VI, currency manipulation became, for the first and only time in English history, the principal source of government income.[23]

Politically the Reformation produced equally unintended consequences. The only way to give the appearance of legality to the break with Rome and the suppression of the monasteries was to dignify them with the formal approval of Parliament: a process which was unlikely to give that body a diminished sense of its importance. When the dust settled, the crown was once again dependent on parliamentary subsidies for any expenses beyond its day-to-day needs. And Parliament showed no sign of granting taxes for more than one or two years at a time. Nor were the Commons, the allies of the crown, made any more subservient by the purchase on the cheap by its members of the lands that it had cooperated in confiscating. The long-term effect of Henry's financial policies was merely a transfer of economic resources from the upper house to the lower.

Just as significant were the long-term results of adjuring the authority of the pope. Henry may have intended no more than a national "Catholic" church, but he unleashed a process which led inexorably to the spread of

Protestant beliefs. Perhaps these beliefs would have spread anyway, as they did in France; but perhaps without the break with Rome, the outcome would have followed the French pattern and witnessed the final victory of Catholicism. In any case, by the 1570s, in the wake of the Duke of Alba's repression of Protestantism in the Netherlands, and of the St. Bartholomew's Eve Massacre in France, Catholicism became inextricably linked (in the minds of Protestants at least) with authoritarian state power, and Protestantism with civil liberty. The addition of this emotive brew to the long-standing tradition of fiscal foot-dragging by Parliament was as dangerous to the Tudors and Stuarts in England as it was to the Habsburgs in the Netherlands.

It was, as elsewhere in Europe, the power of the purse that provided the most potent weapon of the opponents of absolutism; and the English Parliament proved itself to be quite as obdurate as the States General of the Netherlands. Probably no monarchy in Europe was so effectively starved of funds in the later sixteenth and early seventeenth century as that of England. Whereas the revenues of the French monarchy had risen to the equivalent of 300 tons of silver by 1600, and those of Spain had soared to over 400, the English crown was still operating with an almost medieval income of around £400,000 (approximately 44 tons of silver)—and more than one-quarter of this modest sum required the assent of Parliament.[24] Even states with half the population of England had larger incomes.

Government Revenues in England and on the Continent, c. 1600[25]

	Population *Millions*	Revenues *Tons of silver*	Revenues per Head *Grams of silver*
England	4.5	44	10
Castile	6.0	420	54
France	16.0	370	23
Dutch Republic	1.5	70	47
Venice	2.0	68	34
Naples	2.6	90	34

The long run-up to the English Civil War has many elements of similarity to those leading to the Dutch war of independence: parliamentary stonewalling on taxation, an emphasis on "ancient liberties," opposition to standing armies, and the defense of religious freedom. One element missing in England was the means by which the Dutch burghers siphoned off the crown's revenues by funding their tax payments with *renten*. Perhaps the greater centralization of political power in medieval England was the cause, for there was relatively little tradition of urban self-government which might have encouraged such a form of finance. In fact, the continental practice of borrowing by selling "rents" scarcely existed in England. Loans against land were traditionally made by means of mortgages—a far more severe bargain, where the lender took immediate ownership and possession of the whole property, while the borrower retained merely the right of redemption by repaying the loan before a stipulated date. This form of lending did little to encourage long-term finance, since lenders looked mostly to the possibility of acquiring land cheaply, and borrowers resorted to it only in case of direst need.

The English crown, therefore, had almost no long-term debt. It could raise only short-term finance, which, by its nature, limited indebtedness to little more than one year's normal revenue (which, as we have seen, was meager indeed). Henry VIII managed to borrow £150,000 in Antwerp from the Fuggers. This was a tiny sum compared to the debts of the Habsburgs, but it still threatened to bankrupt the English crown, especially since it was denominated in foreign currency at a time when sterling was being rapidly devalued. It was the role of Thomas Gresham, agent of three successive English monarchs in Antwerp, to extricate the crown from its debts. After a period of mass expropriation and relentless debasement, the appointment of Gresham as agent and of William Cecil as chancellor in 1552 inaugurated a long period of teamwork between men committed to sound finances. The temptation to default was resisted, and when Elizabeth came to the throne, sterling was revalued and stabilized.*

With the outbreak of the Netherlands revolt in 1569, Gresham foresaw the inevitable decline of the Antwerp exchange. In 1571, he funded the building of the Royal Exchange in London—copied almost directly from the Flemish model—so as to encourage an indigenous capital market which the crown could tap in time of need:

> I would wisshe that the Queene's Majestie in this time shud not use anny strangers [as lenders] but her owne subiectes whereby . . . all other princes may se what a prince of powr she ys.[26]

---

*Elizabeth's recoinage of 1560 fixed the value of the pound at 111.4 grams of silver, about 30% less than in 1540, before the start of the "Great Debasement." The pound was now worth approximately 3 Spanish ducats. From the Elizabethan recoinage until the First World War, with the exception of the Napoleonic Wars, the pound remained an essentially stable currency. During this period it forms the obvious standard for international comparisons, even if it remained a relatively insignificant currency in international terms until the eighteenth century.

This was a prescient idea; but it was a forlorn hope at the time. The crown was indeed forced to rely on local lenders, but this scarcely transformed Elizabeth and her successors into "princes of power." The lack of a serviceable form of long-term debt meant that even low debt levels were enough to threaten bankruptcy. From the time of the Armada to the outbreak of the Civil War, the crown lived in an almost continual financial crisis. It was squeezed on one side by Parliament's stranglehold on any additional revenues and its anachronistic insistence that the king should "live of his own." It was squeezed on a second side by the opposition to any meaningful attempt to make "living of his own" viable by increasing existing fiscal rights. It was squeezed finally by its inability to borrow except on terms so short that punctual repayment was almost impossible. The emphasis by Charles I on his "divine rights" and his attempts to impose a high-church Anglicanism that smacked of Catholicism could only exacerbate his already intractable problems by increasing parliamentary determination to prevent his financial independence.

The £420,000 of debts bequeathed by Elizabeth were finally reduced by a series of grudging subsidies from Parliament. They reached a low point of £160,000 in 1610 and then started an inexorable rise.[27] By 1629, Charles had become so exasperated by the recalcitrance of a body whose role, in his opinion, was to support him in the running of the country that he decided to follow the example of the French kings and simply dispense with it.

It seemed for a time that he might succeed. The budget was in modest surplus by 1636, thanks to the tenacious exploitation of long-forgotten royal rights. Regular revenues were now over £600,000; and the most successful of all Charles's reinterpretations of ancient rights—ship money—brought in another £200,000.[28] In the past ship money had been a periodic levy in seaports to assist the king in his naval ventures. As applied by Charles and his ministers, it became an annual, nationwide direct tax, the first ever to be levied without the consent of Parliament. And yet, underneath these apparent successes of the regime, the fiscal situation was little less precarious than before. Ship money was possible to collect only as long as it was genuinely applied to building up a navy that would further the cause of English maritime commerce. There was no question of diverting the money to a standing army without creating massive internal opposition. Even with ship money, Charles's revenue base represented little more than 90 tons of silver. By contrast, taxes in France represented between 450 and 500 tons of silver at this time, those of Castile between 350 and 400 tons. The Dutch Republic was operating on a budget of nearly 230 tons of silver.

Nor could the royal income be much increased by borrowing. It was not just that there was no system of cheap long-term debt. Even the short-term facilities of the monarchy had decayed. James I and Charles I had destroyed whatever credibility Elizabeth had enjoyed with her creditors. An unfailing inability to meet stipulated repayment dates and an increasing resort to forced loans had turned relations with the merchants of London frosty. The final insult was to come in 1640, when Charles absconded with the contents of the mint, including the bullion deposits made by merchants. The only source of credit available to Charles in the 1630s was the advances of the Farmers of the Customs. These were a small syndicate of three to four entrepreneurs and their backers, who operated in a manner similar to the French *traiteurs*. Of course, such men had extra incentives to lend and were in control of their own sources of repayment. But at his time of need in 1640 Charles was unable to borrow more than £250,000 from the Farmers of the Customs.[29]

In the absence of a workable credit system, the fundamental weakness of the Stuart finances was bound to be exposed if there was any attempt to wage war. The outbreak of rebellion in Scotland in 1637 heralded the end of Charles's attempt to rule without Parliament. By 1639 the war was costing over £900,000 per year, an amount clearly beyond the financial capacity of the crown.[30] Yet this level of spending, even though sufficient to bring down the Stuart regime, was modest in international terms. The Dutch were spending £2 million per year in their military operations. The Spanish and French were spending closer to £3 million. There was no alternative other than to summon Parliament.

One thing was certain: after its suppression for eleven years the recall of Parliament was bound to be explosive. It was finally time for the English to follow the Dutch example of eighty years earlier. However firmly the English believed that they were fighting to restore their ancient, monarchical constitution, the inexorable logic of events would force them to remove their king from office and replace him with a commonwealth. But here the parallel ends.

The Dutch rebels inhabited a region with a long tradition of municipal self-government. By the time the Dutch revolt broke out, the merchant class had extended its reach to include most of the public finances. The merchants voted and administered the taxes and paid themselves the greater part of the amounts collected as interest. It is, therefore, not surprising that they displayed considerable maturity in their running of the public finances of their new republic. They were also helped by the fact that their king was a foreigner, who never set foot in the rebel provinces in an attempt to maintain his rule. He had many other kingdoms, and the loss of one, although embarrassing and certainly costly, was not a life-and-death matter. There was no need for the rebels to find themselves cornered into that ultimate act of political impropriety: regicide. For the same reason, their war was only marginally a civil war, and they were saved from the inevitable confiscations of opponents' property that sully the legality of most revolutionary regimes. Finally, the overpowering position of their king in international politics assured him of many adversaries who were delighted to fund any promising challenge to his power, thus saving the Dutch revolutionaries from some of the more extreme fiscal and monetary measures that they might otherwise have had to take.

For all these reasons the Dutch revolt displayed few of the normal attributes of revolutionary finance. The English parliamentarians were confronted with a very different situation. The powers that they had historically exercised had been entirely negative in character: they could maintain a long-term financial stranglehold on the king, but they had absolutely no experience of running public finances. While Charles's part-Scottish ancestry did not endear him to all his English subjects, he most certainly was not, like Philip II, a distant hispanophone foreigner. Charles fought long and hard to retain his throne in a conflict that split the country in two. He could not safely be exiled, but his execution in 1649 alienated even those, such as the Dutch, who might otherwise have supported the parliamentary cause.

It was England, therefore, that was to provide the first true example of a pattern of revolutionary finance that was to become familiar in the following centuries. The dialectic of revolution meant that, far from creating a more responsible form of government, capable of tapping the country's growing economic potential, the English Civil War ushered in a period of government arguably less responsible, at least financially, than the monarchy it had overthrown. The Long Parliament lived off a diet of forced loans, unpaid bills, fines, and confiscations. Creditors were issued with "public faith" bonds with interest at 8%, which traded at discounts of 50–70% in the absence of any likelihood of their redemption. Deficits might have been excused during the war itself, but after 1649 they continued at a rate of £400,000–500,000 a year under the cost of the revolutionary army, in spite of a considerably increased tax burden. Fines imposed on royalists to avoid confiscation of their lands raised £1.3 million. Lands actually confiscated were worth over £5 million, but only some £400,000 was raised by direct sales, since most purchasers were dubious about the long-term validity of the titles. Most of the confiscated land was used for "doubling." This was a technique that allowed creditors who paid in cash a sum identical to their claims to swap their debts for confiscated lands. Alternatively they could continue to hold the debt but have it secured against the same lands. Some £1.7 million was raised by this means, but since the land was overvalued by the government, even "doubled" debts traded at a 25–30% discount.[31] Even the soldiers of the New Model Army were paid in "public faith" bonds and, since they rarely had the wherewithal to double up, were generally forced to sell at desperation prices. In 1654, a member of the first Protectorate Parliament complained that "The Public Faith of the Nation is now become a public despair."[32]

In 1654 Oliver Cromwell disbanded the Long Parliament and took over the reins of government himself. The way that his precursor had treated its backers made it unlikely that he would have any greater success in raising loans on a voluntary basis. The merchant community of London, perhaps the single most important constituency of the 1688 revolution, would lend no support. Confiscations were by now an exhausted, as well as a counterproductive, source of funds. The Protector inherited debts of some £700,000 from the Long Parliament. He died in 1658, leaving £2 million in unpaid liabilities to his son Richard, who could scarcely find the money for his funeral.[33] The Commonwealth was by this stage truly bankrupt. The financial practices of the parliamentarians had contributed in no small part to the eventual failure of their cause. The policy of confiscations and fines prevented any reconciliation with the royalist community. The failure to service its debts gradually alienated its most crucial supporters.

The Interregnum left one significant financial legacy, however. Under the Long Parliament, taxes were radically reformed and placed on a footing that would serve as one of the bases for the success of the country in the eighteenth century. In 1641, Parliament introduced an excise tax. This form of revenue, by far the most stable foundation of a long-term edifice of public debt throughout Europe—from the Italian republics to the Dutch Republic, and to France—had hitherto been lacking in England. In the next year a new system of direct tax, the "assessment," was introduced. This updated the outmoded medieval "subsidy" along the lines of Charles I's much maligned ship money. Simultaneously the old feudal dues of the crown were abolished. In conjunction with the customs duties that had long formed the backbone of royal finance, the government now had a full complement of taxes that compared favorably with any in Europe in their modernity, efficacy, and sweep. Equally important was the sharp rise in total regular revenues, from around £600,000 in the last years of Charles's personal government to an average of £1.5 million under Cromwell.[34] This sum represented 165 tons of silver, or around 30 grams per head, finally bringing England more or less in line with other European countries. The revolt had led, as so often, to taxes far higher that those that had provoked it. In this case, at least, the English experience of revolution was no different from that of the Dutch.

GLORIOUS REVOLUTION

> Where is the Man that having lent his Money on the Credit of Parliamentary Security, will upon a whim, Discharge that Fund and take a precarious Company of Private Men for the Money?[35]

The creditors of the Long Parliament, confronted with this rhetorical question, would surely have shaken their heads in disbelief. Any one of them would most certainly have swapped his claim on the government for any halfway decent private credit that was offered in exchange. Yet by 1720, when the question was posed in an anonymous pamphlet published in London, the writer could assume as beyond dispute that the credit of Parliament was sounder than that of any private borrower. Clearly, substantial changes, amounting perhaps to a revolution, must have taken place in the interim.

In 1660, Charles II was restored to the throne of England on a tide of antirepublican sentiment. The Commonwealth had alienated the majority of the population by a combination of religious fanaticism, fiscal mismanagement, and the maintenance of a peacetime standing army. In its desire not to place the new king in the untenable position of his father, the titular head of an ungovernable country, Parliament made a settlement that set back the cause of representative government by several decades. The prerevolutionary financial straitjacket was deliberately relaxed so that the king should not be prevented from governing effectively. The reformed tax structure of the Commonwealth was maintained, and a permanent income of £1.2 million was granted to Charles for life. In theory this was enough to provide £200,000 for administration and £1 million for armed forces. (This sum was almost entirely devoted to the navy, because the New Model Army had been disbanded, the victim of the renewed aversion to standing armies.) As if this were not enough, in 1664, Charles even achieved the repeal of the Triennial Act of 1641, which had ensured the summoning of

Parliament every three years whether the king felt he needed its services or not.

Fortunately for the cause of representative government, in the early years of Charles's reign the theoretical revenues of the monarch were rarely collected in full. He was, therefore, periodically forced to fall back on parliamentary assistance, almost in spite of that body's initial reluctance to enter into oversight of the royal finances. During his reign the machinery of public finance continued to improve and became probably the most centralized and efficient in any European monarchy. Tax farming was ended, and collections and disbursements were centralized in the Treasury. As a result of these reforms and of the increase in English overseas trade, government income rose from no more than £1 million in the early years of Charles's reign to £2 million under his brother, James II. Strangely, in spite of whatever misgivings Parliament may have felt about the popish and antiparliamentary views of the new king, James was given a financial settlement if anything more generous than that given his predecessor. James called only one Parliament, in 1685, at the beginning of his reign, and thereafter ignored it. He scarcely needed its services when his income represented some 220 tons of silver, or around 40 grams per head. The day of absolute monarchy seemed finally to have arrived.

Yet so far had the costs of war escalated by the late seventeenth century that James could not be sure that he would never again need Parliament's services. It was his ruthless attempt to gerrymander parliamentary constituencies in 1688, turning against even his most natural supporters, that ensured that he would be almost universally opposed in the second English revolution. This time no mistake was made: James was exiled and replaced on the throne by his niece Mary and her husband, William of Orange. There was no regicide, no abolition of the monarchy, and no confiscation of property. The revolution was legally prudent and therefore secure. There was no mistake, either, about the new settlement made with the joint monarchs. The Triennial Act was reinstated, and Parliament was careful to make no generous grants of revenues for life. The mood was summed up by Sir William Williams, a former speaker of Commons: "If you give the Crown too little, you may add to it at any time; if once you give too much, you will never have it back again."[36] Parliament certainly did not give the crown "too much": only £1.2 million, and even that had to be regularly renewed. This was meager indeed on the eve of more than twenty years of almost continuous warfare that were to involve spending more than £6 million per year.

There is no doubt why William of Orange agreed to accept the invitation of Parliament to supplant James II on the English throne. After 1672, the Dutch never felt secure from the covetous gaze of Louis XIV and desperately needed to ensure that England would be at least neutral, and preferably allied. Given that the French king was only biding his time for another opportunity to overpower the republic, the offer of the English throne must have appeared a godsend to William and his compatriots.

Yet if 1688 was a year of some strategic significance in the history of Holland, it was to prove vastly more important to the history of England, and not only of England. Until 1688 only mercantile republics had succeeded in fully tapping the power of public credit. But in the late seventeenth century even the most successful of these republics was not able to stand unaided against the power of the greatest absolute monarchy of Europe. For all its financial defects the French political model appeared supreme in 1688. It could be challenged only if another monarchy managed to adapt itself to the requirements of "Dutch" finance. It was precisely this that was achieved by the Glorious Revolution of 1688.

In hindsight, it is temptingly easy to see the Revolution of 1688 as a clean break in English history: before, the struggle against would-be autocrats with limited means and no credit standing; after, the installation of a Dutch-style representative government (or perhaps, more accurately, a mercantile oligarchy) with the ability to leverage national power through cheap long-term debt. Yet the process was far more complex and hard-fought than this simple paradigm suggests. It would take until after 1720 for a stable form of parliamentary government to be securely established. It would take an equally long time to establish a stable form of abundant, affordable public debt.

It is scarcely surprising that this was so. The great achievement of the Dutch Republic was to deploy the political and financial institutions of the city-state within a confederation of cities large enough to compete with the monarchies of the Renaissance. Yet this achievement was easy compared to the task of England: to extend the same principles to a large, rural country in which the merchant class was a small, if growing, minority, and in which there was no tradition of self-governing towns.

It is not surprising, then, that the roles of Parliament and king in the government of England were not easily established. Even after the settlement of 1688 the role of Parliament was seen as merely legislative. There was no desire to repeat the unfortunate experiences of the Civil War and the Interregnum. It was the king's role to govern: William merely signed documents that made it impossible to do so without parliamentary consent. This was scarcely an improvement on the situation prior to the Glorious Revolution:

> The problem of the control of Parliament seemed to have been solved to the satisfaction of its backbenchers—that control was impossible. Parliament, it seemed, was free to harry monarchs, topple ministries, cut supplies, refuse taxation, concern itself with peace and war, formulate those constitutional changes that it felt necessary for its protection, and generally ride rough-shod over the administration. For the next twenty-five years the pattern of politics resembled this description: governments teetered on the edge of chaos, and party strife was as violent was as anything England had known since the Civil War.[37]

The tone of the debate is clearly shown in the 1701 Act of Settlement, passed by a Tory-dominated Commons, which established the succession after William's and then Anne's death. Its true title was *An Act for the further Limitation of the Crown, and the better securing of the Rights of the Subject.* Gradually a compromise was to evolve. The crown was to lose its right to appoint its ministers; and the executive, now liberated from royal control, was to gain a power to control unruly backbenchers that would have made the Stuarts weep with envy. The new system was to be completed after 1720 under the long regime of Sir Robert Walpole, England's first "prime" minister.

The immaturity of parliamentary government was not the only problem confronting England in its gradual adoption of the financial techniques of the mercantile republics. Whatever the size of London (and by 1700 it was already the largest city in Europe), England was still predominantly rural. The urban bourgeoisie, whose liquid wealth was the underpinning of public debt, was a growing but still small portion of the electorate. The landed classes, especially the Tory squires, were generally isolationist in their international outlook. They did not like the financial demands that war made; they did not like the inevitable increase in state power that so much money and so many soldiers represented; and most particularly they did not like the hocking of the future revenues of the country to Whig merchants and to foreigners so as to satisfy the insatiable demands of a Dutch monarch for instant cash. Indeed, their attitude toward the "monied men" and "stock jobbers" of the City of London was hardly less hostile than that of the French to the *financiers, traiteurs,* and *partisans* who financed the ancien régime, or of the Spanish to the *hombres de negocios.* Such hostility had always made royal defaults a popular act with large segments of the population, and therefore a temptation all the harder to resist. In England, the rhetoric of the pamphleteers, led by such pungent writers as Jonathan Swift and Daniel Defoe, would lead one to think that default was almost too good a fate for these drones and leeches. Yet in England the temptation was resisted, in spite of financial crises scarcely less dire than those that had led to bankruptcies in France and Spain. The gradual process whereby the Tories came to terms with a fiscal apparatus better suited to a merchant republic than to a monarchy parallels the achievement of a stable balance of power between executive and legislative. These twin processes were themselves exactly paralleled by the gradual improvement of the terms on which the country was able to borrow.

The country's borrowing terms certainly had a long way to improve. Under Charles II, it seemed, at first, that some progress might occur. In 1665, Sir Charles Downing, a senior official of the Exchequer and an admirer of the Dutch, arranged a special parliamentary grant of £1.25 million to back an issue of short-term receipts issued by the Exchequer at 6% interest. Downing conceived of the Treasury becoming a virtual state bank. The Earl of Clarendon, Charles's principal adviser, sniffily described this plan as "introductive to a commonwealth, and not fit for a monarchy."[38] The Exchequer receipts brought some discipline into Stuart finances by imposing a strict order of repayment on government obligations. But like all previous English methods of borrowing, they were short-term only and were therefore unsuited to raising large sums. In January 1672 Charles decided to stop payment on the receipts as a precautionary measure so as to free up income in anticipation of his impending declaration of war against the Dutch. Given that the Exchequer debt amounted to only £1.17 million at the time, and that the crown's total liabilities (including those semidormant ones inherited from the prior regime) were less than £3 million, the limitations of Stuart finance were again starkly revealed. After the "stop of the Exchequer," Charles continued to pay 6% interest from time to time on the principal. James reneged on even this commitment, but in 1705 the debt was reinstated at 50% of its old value. It thus became the first, albeit involuntary, component of the long-term national debt.[39]

Charles's credit was no better than his father's after 1672. In 1680, his adviser and future Treasurer, Sydney Godolphin, was rather pathetically passing the hat round to William of Orange:

> I have been informed (how truly I know not) that at this time no body gives more than 4 per cent for money in Holland; if that be so, your Highnesse may certainly dispose of [your money] here to much more advantage; for you may have 6 per cent with as good personal security as any is in England; you may have 8 per cent and be secured upon the Kings hereditary revenue,

> which gives you as good title in law as any man can have in England, though you had no trust at all in the Commissioners of the Treasury.[40]

Not only was the government's credit rating again worse than that of private citizens, but even the proposed 8% borrowing cost was optimistic. Charles was regularly forced by the city goldsmiths to pay 10–20% for his short-term needs.

After 1689, in the wake of war costs on a scale never before experienced in English history, there was an urgent need for more effective methods of raising money. Taxes were raised to unheard of levels of £4 million and over. This represented some 450 tons of silver and nearly 80 grams of silver per head. These were finally revenues fit for a contender in the European superpower struggle. Taxes never fell again to prewar levels, and that they could be paid year after year without strain showed only the extent of the country's growing wealth and how grossly undertaxed it had been before.

But even revenues of £4 million per year were not sufficient when spending was running at £6 million. Yet the ability of the government to raise cheap long-term debt was strictly limited by the insistence of Parliament in voting taxes for short periods only, so as to prevent William from gaining secure long-term revenues. The depth of the country members' concern to limit the tax-collecting power of the state is shown by the preference for taxes on land to excise duties. During the War of the League of Augsburg, which lasted from 1689 to 1697, the land tax represented 42% of all revenues.[41] The tax may have fallen directly on the assets of the Tory gentry, but at least its collection was in their hands. The tax was voted one year at a time, and the Commons had little doubt about its ability to abolish, or at least reduce, it after the war. By contrast, "excises are not likely to be got off again when the occasion ceases, they take root by their many officers . . . and tho necessity raised them at first, they are apt to find occasion for their continuance."[42]

This was clearly not the fiscal underpinning required for finance *à l'Hollandaise.* Out of the £18.2 million debt outstanding at the end of the war, only £4.9 million was long-term. The government fell back on sales of Exchequer tallies—those venerable notched sticks, sliced down the middle to provide debtor and creditor with a matching pair—now bearing interest until such time as they were paid. To be sure, most of the tallies were secured against specific taxes and were to be paid in order of priority as the specified revenues were received. Yet any theory that they might be paid within one year of issue receded rapidly as the war dragged on. Nominal interest was between 6% and 8%, but this rate was increasingly meaningless as the tallies were issued at ever-larger discounts. By 1696, tallies were typically sold at 70% of face or less, raising the current yield to 10% or more, and the yield to maturity far higher. Such rates were scarcely surprising when, by the end of the war in 1697, there was a £5 million shortfall in the revenues that were supposed to provide for their repayment. Total short-term debt was now £13.3 million, around three times revenues, a ratio which in Spain would most assuredly have led to default.[43]

Little succor seemed to be offered by the one promising innovation in this vicious spiral. The founding of the Bank of England in 1694 is generally, and rightly, seen as the herald of the country's eventual rise to worldwide financial predominance. It was certainly the first time England had made an innovation in public finance of long-term significance. The Bank of Amsterdam and the Casa di San Giorgio were not able to issue banknotes, but could merely deposit receipts against coin and bullion deposited. These receipts were far more convenient for trade than coin but did not add to the total money supply. The Bank of England was rather less conservative in its approach. Its "capital" of £1.2 million was represented by its advances to the government in the form of banknotes, against which it received perpetual annuities at 8%. The government was able to use the notes in payment of its liabilities, while the Bank was able to issue a further amount, up to the extent of its nominal "capital." Against these notes the Bank's effective reserves were the £720,000 paid in by the subscribers (who included the king and queen). The ability to manipulate the money supply implicit in this relative freedom of note issue was the foundation of modern central banking practice. In fact, the Bank of England was not quite the first public bank to experiment with paper money. It had been anticipated by the Bank of Sweden in 1661. The Swedish banknotes had rapidly fallen to a discount to specie, and the experiment came to an ignominious end in 1664.* In the straitened circumstances of the 1690s

*Like the paper money of Sung China, the Swedish experiment was the result of its dependence on a copper currency. Sweden was the largest producer of copper in Europe and in the seventeenth century sought to prop up the market for its main export by using copper for its currency. The result, as ever, was inconveniently heavy coins. The most massive coin yet minted in the history of the world was the Swedish 10-*daler* piece, which weighed an astonishing 19.7 kilograms. Even the 2-*daler* coin was as large as a letter-size sheet of paper. The number of these ponderous coins put into circulation merely reduced the exchange value of the Swedish currency and undermined its nominal objective. Until the country finally returned to the silver standard in 1772, it was to experience repeated bouts of currency instability as it sought to escape the consequences of its monetary policy.

the English paper looked to be destined for a similar fate. By September 1695, the Bank's notes were trading at up to a 25% discount in Amsterdam, and a £300,000 loan from the Estates of Holland was required to shore up reserves. By 1697, some notes were being protested for nonpayment in Amsterdam, and the Bank's shares had fallen by 40% on the London exchange.

The credit crunch in England was compounded by the decision of the government to remint the entire national currency in 1696. After Elizabeth's currency reform of 1560, sterling had remained unchanged in nominal silver value; but partly as a result of this admirable adherence to monetary stability, there had been no general reminting since 1601. Successive governments had thereby missed the opportunity to move to the new technology of milled rims, which prevented the age-old crime of "clipping" bits off the ill-defined edges of the old hammered money. Many coins were as much as 50% underweight by 1696, and the foreign suppliers to the English military looked suspiciously at these bedraggled specimens offered in payment. By 1695, sterling had declined by 25% against the Dutch guilder, and this decline made a general recoinage essential in spite of the unfortunate timing. Yet, to remint at the old silver parity was inevitably to reduce the money stock: £5.73 million of old coins taken into the Mint produced only £3.3 million of new currency. The £1.8 million taken to provincial mints suffered a similar reduction.[44]

Such drastic deflation was bound to increase the government's credit problems as cash rose to an ever greater premium over paper. Yet the government did not make the decision to remint unaware of the consequences, and this in itself is the single biggest clue to why England did not default on its debt. A considerable body of opinion, led by so eminently sound a thinker as William Lowndes, the First Secretary of the Treasury, preferred to remint at 20% lower weight so as to partially offset the deflation. In this he was supported, not surprisingly, by the landed classes—especially those with debts. Yet the debate was swayed by even greater heavyweights—John Locke and Isaac Newton, no less—who argued that, whatever the economic reasonableness of Lowndes's argument, to devalue the currency by 20% by parliamentary authority so soon after Parliament itself had authorized public debts of more than £10 million, would be to render that body's credit no better than that of the Stuarts (or, they might have added, that of the Commonwealth).

This argument was virtually unanswerable. Whatever Whigs and Tories might disagree about (and at times they seemed to disagree about almost everything), they were united in their belief in the sanctity of Parliament. It was this core of agreement, too, that ensured that, reluctant though they might be, the Tories would not derail the war effort against France. It is true that at least some of the isolationists could be persuaded of the need to prevent a Bourbon "universal monarchy" on the Continent, just as they had been persuaded by Elizabeth of the need to prevent the Habsburg variation on that theme a hundred years earlier. But the most persuasive argument for defending the Low Countries and taking on the greatest military power in Europe was the same in both centuries: to protect a now deeply rooted Protestant polity in England.

It is hard in this century to empathize with the post-Reformation equation of Roman Catholicism with absolutism, and of Protestantism with civil liberty. The exclusion of Catholics from office in England appears no better that the revocation of the Edict of Nantes by Louis XIV in 1685: relics of atavistic religious passions, properly discarded by a more enlightened age. Nowadays we are inclined to see religious divides as smoke screens for ethnic or social conflicts. Yet it would be foolish to disregard feelings so widely held in earlier times. In England, the politicoreligious equation had been indelibly etched in the national psyche by the plot to blow up Parliament hatched by the Catholic Guy Fawkes in 1605. Whatever their relative lack of political finesse, it is likely that Charles I and his two sons would have had no more trouble with Parliament than Elizabeth, had they not displayed an increasing desire to flirt with Rome. In James II's case, this flirtation went beyond dalliance to wedlock. It is possible that James and his brother and father were attracted by the aesthetics of the Catholic liturgy, or by the mysteries of transubstantiation. But it is more likely that, as kings, they appreciated the Catholic insistence on their divinely ordained role as "God's lieutenants on earth." Under this descending chain of authority, kings, like popes, received their power from God. Their subjects enjoyed their privileges, such as that of representation in parliament, at their king's good grace, in the same way that parish priests received their authority from their bishops. By contrast, Protestantism, especially in its more extreme forms, was unavoidably democratic in implication: people's relationship with God was direct and needed no intermediation by priests, who now became mere lay officials elected by their congregations. The political implications of Puritanism had become all too clear in the radicalism of Cromwell's army, and it is no surprise that Puritanism fell rapidly out of favor with the propertied classes as a result. The Anglicanism of the Restoration represented a political, as well as a theological, compromise. Both church and Parliament based their authority on ancient, established rights, not on papal or royal grace and favor, nor yet on sweeping philosophical claims about the "rights of man."

It is easy to argue that the incessant Anglo-French wars from 1689 to 1815 were the result of imperial rivalries. But this was not how it appeared in the late seventeenth century, when the Dutch still seemed far more of a threat to British commercial interests. The flight of James II to France and his welcome at Versailles turned English foreign policy anti-French almost overnight. It was not by chance that the first article of the Treaty of Ryswick in 1697, which ended the war with France, was the recognition by Louis XIV of William's title to the throne. While the Tories in the Commons heaved a sigh of relief after the end of the war and proceeded to dismantle William's war machine, Louis virtually guaranteed its renewal when James II died in 1701 by recognizing his son (the "Old Pretender" as he was later known) as King of England. Under such circumstances even the opponents of the "monied interest" could be relied upon not to destroy the fiscal machinery necessary for national self-defense.

It was indicative of the inherent strengths of the new system of government and of the English economy that financial order could be rapidly restored after the peace. In late 1697, most of the unsecured debt was converted into secured medium-term obligations. The capital of the Bank of England was almost doubled, and subscription was allowed in tallies, thus removing some £800,000 from the market. A further £2 million in perpetual annuities was contributed by the New East India Company. Additionally, from 1698 to 1700, the government ran a cumulative surplus of £2 million. By the end of 1697, Bank notes were trading at par. Exchequer tallies could be sold without a discount by 1700. At the beginning of the War of the Spanish Succession in 1702, the country's financial position was sound.

The new English state had weathered its first financial crisis. The second followed in 1710. It was in this year that two fundamental threats to its solvency, and perhaps, therefore, to its existence, came to a simultaneous head. From 1688 the persistent, if dying, ideal of separation of powers had allowed the government, however shifting and unstable its composition, to avoid falling into the hands of a strong "country" Tory majority in the Commons. Under William the government was dominated by the Whigs, an alliance of mercantile and aristocratic interests. After 1701, the government was nominally Tory, but ministers such as Marlborough and Godolphin were not committed party men and happily accepted the need to work with Whigs who could keep the City happy. There was no question of their threatening such vital appendages of the regime as the purely "Whig" Bank of England. Yet Marlborough, Godolphin, and their Whig colleagues were swept from power in 1710 by a new government under Robert Harley, backed by a newly elected Commons with 350 Tories and only 183 Whigs and independents. The main cause of this landslide was a financial crisis almost equal to that of 1697 in severity. The fiscal apparatus of the new mercantile state was now in the hands of its sworn enemies.

As ever, the problems derived from an excessive reliance on short-term debt. After the embarrassing position that the Treasury had found itself in during the 1690s, a concerted effort was made to control its issues of tallies. In 1710, they amounted to £5 million—too much, perhaps, for the market to sustain quite at par, but less than half the amount outstanding in 1697. Even more successful were the new Exchequer bills, whose circulation was underwritten for the government by the Bank of England. In 1697, these had required a yield of 7.6% to trade at par, in spite of their acceptance in payment of taxes. After 1710 there were £3–4 million outstanding at a rate of 3.04%, and they were coming to be seen as a form of alternative money for larger transactions. The total cost to the government was increased by the underwriting fees paid to the bank, but the Exchequer bills were probably the cheapest and most flexible form of short-term funding available to any government of the time. The skill of the Treasury in limiting its borrowing, however, only put more pressure on the government departments that supplied the armed forces to issue their own notes in compensation. By 1710, there was already another £6 million of unfunded departmental debt outstanding, and in the following year the new government was forced to declare a deficit of £10 million, including a full £7.5 million of hitherto unaccounted liabilities. Total short-term debts, had the true figures been made public at the time, were over £22 million, and income was little more than £5 million, a ratio worse than that of 1697.[45] No wonder the departmental notes had to be issued at discounts of up to 33% and traded even lower.

Yet this does not reveal the true extent of the government's woes. The picture does not yet take into account the considerable rise in long-term debt that had taken place since 1697. From 1704 to 1711 some £10.4 million was raised through the sale of long-term annuities.[46] Until 1708, these were on the apparently reasonable terms of 6.25–6.6% for ninety-nine years. In the growing crisis after 1708 the terms were adjusted to thirty-two years, and yields were raised to 9%. When these annuities were added to other long-term debt, such as the annuities held by the Bank of England

and the East India Company, the total long-term obligations of the government were nearly £20 million and generated an interest bill of around £1.2 million. The net revenues available to service the short-term debt, therefore, were less than £4 million. An Anglo-Spanish comparison based on Philip II's finances on the eve of his 1595 bankruptcy (at the very zenith of Habsburg power) puts the crisis of 1710 in stark light:

FISCAL CRISES IN ENGLAND AND SPAIN, 1595–1710[47]

	Spain	England	
	1595	*1697*	*1710*
Gross revenues (£ millions)	3.1	4.2	5.2
Long-term debt service (" ")	1.2	0.5	1.2
Net revenues (" ")	1.9	3.7	4.0
Short-term debts (" ")	4.6	13.3	22.0
—as a multiple of net revenues	2.4	3.6	5.5

This was the situation inherited by the Tories when they finally ousted the Whigs from power. The situation was made worse by their arrival. The market for government stocks collapsed, and in the words of Daniel Defoe, "the French laugh . . . they see your credit sinking and a Party prevailing that will Ruin the National Credit."[48] Given both the gravity of the situation and the accusations of mismanagement and misfeasance (often justified in the supply contracts for the armed forces), a Franco-Spanish pattern of show trials, partial repudiations, and compulsory conversions might reasonably have been expected. Under the withering phrases of Jonathan Swift, the whole French war was exposed as little more than a plot by Marlborough and the financiers to enrich themselves:

> What have we been fighting for all this while? . . . The answer is ready; we have been fighting for the ruin of the public interest, and the advancement of a private. We have been fighting to raise the wealth of a particular family; to enrich the usurers and stockjobbers; and to cultivate the pernicious designs of a faction, by destroying the landed interest.[49]

In his vitriolic but witty attacks on Marlborough, Swift compared the rewards obtained by Roman generals to the lavish perquisites that fell on the English commander. He valued the cost of a Roman triumphal procession in contemporary terms, giving "A Bull for Sacrifice" at £8, "A Triumphal Arch" at £500, and so forth. The total value of the Roman procession he placed, with exaggerated precision, at £994 11s 10d. By comparison, Marlborough's rewards—including the great and costly palace of Blenheim—he valued at £540,000.[50]

Yet, in spite of the gravity of the financial situation and the violence of their rhetoric, the Tories and the "country" interest singularly failed to act irresponsibly. True, the Duke of Marlborough was accused of embezzlement and retired into exile in disgust. True, also, that, in their overwhelming desire for peace, the Tories left England's European allies in the lurch and gave credence to the legend of "Perfidious Albion." But on the financial front Harley proved himself remarkably adept and managed to resolve the looming crisis without any resort to compulsion.

He resorted instead to temptation, in the guise of a debt equity swap. Holders of departmental notes were allowed to exchange them for shares in a new trading company, which was to enjoy a monopoly of trade in the South Atlantic—the land of El Dorado. The government would give the company 6% perpetual annuities equivalent to the short-term debts canceled by the exchange. No less than £9.2 million of short-term debts were voluntarily tendered for shares in the South Sea Company in a few months of 1711, in what was undoubtedly the largest operation of its kind to that date.[51] None of the later ill repute attached to the name of the company should be allowed to detract from the success of its initial flotation. Since the short-term trading prospects of the South Sea Company were limited, it traded strictly on the basis of its annuity income. At a price of around 70, the current yield was 8.6%—more or less in line with other government debt. Harley rounded off this achievement by raising a further £7.1 million via thirty-two-year loans with lottery prizes attached. These were rather more expensive for the government than the South Sea annuities (around 8% per annum overall), but cheaper than the thirty-two-year annuities issued by his Whig predecessors.[52] More important, they allowed the remainder of the war until 1713 to be financed while actually reducing short-term debt. By then a government supported by country squires could lay out a reasonable claim to having proved themselves no less competent than the Whig plutocrats they so despised. And the financial revolution that had been ushered in by the political revolution of 1688 was now secure.

FIVE

THE CHIMERA

> The credit of the French nation, concentrated in the person of its King, is infinitely superior to all other more feeble states governed by the multitude.
>
> —John Law, *General Idea of the New System of Finance,* 1719[1]

At the end of the second decade of the eighteenth century, France found itself caught up in an adventure that captured the imagination of the whole of Europe, and that continues to provoke astonishment to this day. Rarely has one man so swiftly and completely overturned the existing order as did the Scotsman John Law in 1719–1720. His plan was to effect a revolution that would transform France and make Paris the financial rival of Amsterdam and London. But his ideas, for all their virtues, were based on a number of false premises. Instead of creating a lasting transformation, Law merely stirred up a violent, but ephemeral, whirlwind. When the dust settled, the familiar landscape of French public finance reemerged, seemingly unchanged. And the fate of the ancien régime was sealed.

LE ROI SOLEIL

By the end of the seventeenth century, France found itself in a financial quandary quite different from any that had confronted it before. During the war against Spain from 1635 to 1659, it had been fighting a power whose financial arrangements were no less chaotic than its own. The war against the Dutch in 1672 had pitted France against a country that had mastered to the full the use of credit; but this scarcely mattered in light of the enormous disparity of populations. After 1689, however, France faced a grand alliance of countries whose resources matched those that the Sun King was able to put into the field. Furthermore two of those countries, Holland and, increasingly, England, were able to employ the techniques of "Dutch" finance. The result was that, by the time of the crisis of 1709–1710, whereas the credit of England was merely tottering on the brink of the abyss, that of France had already fallen over the edge.

That the crisis had taken so long to arrive was perhaps due to the legacy of Jean-Baptiste Colbert, chief minister of France from 1661 to 1683.[2] He inherited a country in a state of insolvency and left it in the strongest financial position of any time before the heyday of the Napoleonic empire. In 1683 total government revenues had risen to 113 million livres, while debt service, including officers' salaries, had been reduced to 23.4 million livres, leaving disposable income of nearly 90 million livres, equivalent to around £6.75 million sterling, or 750 tons of silver.[3] No other European country was in the same league. France's old rival, Spain, was at its financial nadir, its shrinking revenues wholly consumed by its debts. England was still a financial pygmy, the political stability of its regime as questionable as its credit.

Colbert's reforms operated on many fronts. Tax administration was improved, corruption was reduced, economic development encouraged, and the Sun King's love of war somewhat restrained. There were even, in the later years of his government, some improvements in the monarchy's credit arrangements.

For the first half of his tenure of office, Colbert operated with all the disregard for the fundamental rules of credit that his predecessors had displayed. The Chambre de Justice of 1661 resulted in the cancellation of 150 million livres of debt. But Colbert did not stop there. In 1663 he ordered the redemption of all rentes issued since 1656 on the basis of the actual amount received by the government less any payments of interest made to date. In the next year an edict called for the redemption of most other rentes on the basis of average market prices since 1639. This caused an outcry, and the Hôtel de Ville was thronged with rentiers. Finally, a deputation was sent to the palace to argue that such a procedure was an abuse of the legal right of reimbursement of debts. The rentes could be redeemed only at par, and not at the prices to which they fallen "as a result of public misfortunes, or the fault of an incompetent government." Colbert retorted that the king had to consider the interests of all his subjects, and that there were "no assets so useless to the king's subjects . . . as *rentes*." He darkly reminded the rentiers of their role in the Fronde, the revolt of 1648–1653 that had nearly toppled the regime. He also expressed his view that in many cases the market prices were little different from the amounts originally received by the government. In 1665, he put forward a "compromise" that ordered a general interest reduction of 20% (on top of the reductions already decreed in the wake of the Fronde) or redemption at prices around one half of face value, "after which, the *rentiers* should cease their complaints and content themselves with the glory of obedience to the will of a prince who is only making use of his legal rights."[4]

Colbert was not alone in his view of the legal position. The belief that repayment of principal greater than the amount invested by the creditor was inherently unjust has a long history. But such beliefs are incompatible with the principles of free credit markets, where discounts are considered merely an alternative way of increasing interest rates to their true market level. (And, of course, this was not the principle on which the English Tories chose to refund the floating debt in 1711.) Colbert's record was unlikely to help him raise debt in the future. At the outbreak of the Dutch war in 1672, he found no takers for rentes at the maximum legal interest rate of at 5.55%. Veteran rentiers were scarcely to be impressed by his puerile attempt to convince them that these would be serviced in full by the imposition of a fictitious reduction of 50% prior to issue. In the end, he was forced to twist the arms of the officers to buy them at a yield of 7.14%.

Perhaps this experience persuaded Colbert to change tack. After the war he decided, for the first time in French history, to attempt to reduce interest costs by voluntary means. Two million livres per year were set aside to start amortizing the old debt at face value, and market confidence was sufficiently restored by this act of good faith so that he was able to sell new issues at 5% so as to refund the rest. Colbert also took up the idea of a state deposit bank, first mooted by the Florentines of Lyons under Henry II, ignoring the "republican" associations of such institutions. The Caisse des Emprunts was opened in 1674, offering interest at 5% on demand deposits. The Caisse's life was brief, for it was abolished soon after Colbert's death, but it was nonetheless the forerunner of the state savings banks that, in France and elsewhere in Europe, were to prove so important a feature of nineteenth-century public finance.

But Colbert was unwilling, or unable, to grasp the root problem of Bourbon public finance. His rationalization of the fiscal system, by concentrating almost all excises in a single tax farm, the Farmers General, only strengthened the grip of the *financier* class on the tax-gathering apparatus of the state. Nor did Colbert manage to reduce the role of the venal officers in public finances. The most egregiously redundant offices were abolished, but the system as a whole was impervious to reform. To their holders, offices represented more than mere assets; they conferred status. While the value of rentes had fallen during the course of the century, the prices of offices had risen, and their yields were now considerably lower than those of rentes. To have attempted their wholesale suppression would most likely been to witness a return to the days of the Fronde. Only an outsider and a dreamer like John Law could contemplate such a move. Indeed, the system was to prove itself so deeply entrenched that only a maelstrom as violent as the Revolution of 1789 could sweep it away.

Nonetheless, Colbert left France in a position so strong that it survived the first phase of the wars against England and its continental allies after 1689 without major financial problems. It is true that Pontchartrain, the new minister of finance, had increasing difficulty in selling rentes in spite of raising the yield of rentes to 8.33%. As a result, he resorted to the merry ways of Louis XIII's reign by selling offices. The titles of his creations took on ever-increasing levels of absurdity—such as the Royal Sellers of Oysters. When asked by the king how it was possible to find buyers for such transparently superfluous functions, Pontchartrain cheerfully explained that "every time that Your Majesty creates an office, God creates an idiot to buy it."[5] But the financial system held together sufficiently well so that after the war Pontchartrain was able to refund the expensive wartime debt at 5.55% and then at 5% without resort to compulsion. The French credit record was, at this stage, arguably no worse than that of England, which was still in the early stages of its financial revolution.

Sometime during the War of the Spanish Succession, the relative credit standings of France and England crossed trajectories. Perhaps it was at the Battle of Blenheim, when suddenly France was on the defensive for the first time since the Thirty Years' War. When Desmarets became minister of finance in 1708, he reported that debts had risen to 2 billion livres, and that France was already insolvent.[6] By the end of the war the debt amounted to somewhere between 2.5 and 3 billion livres. This sum represented in the region 1,000 grams of silver per head. Whatever the success of Colbert in increasing the amount of per capita debt that France could maintain without default, it was inconceivable that it extended into these vertiginous regions, suitable only to mercantile republics. The chart below gives an approximate idea of how this indicator of solvency evolved over repeated cycles of borrowing and default:

French Public Debt per Capita, 1596–1725[7]

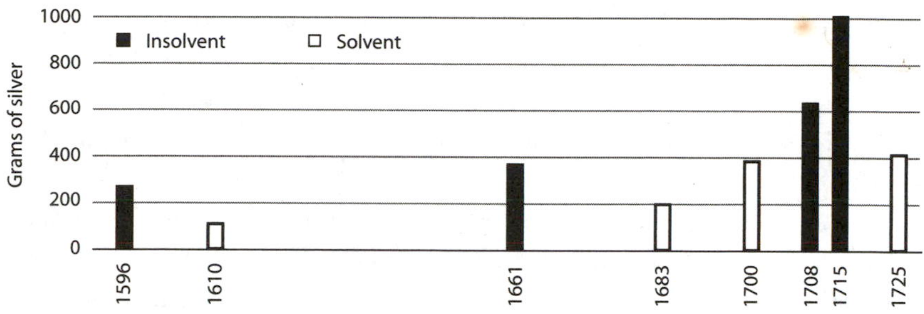

By 1710, England had also accumulated a public debt equivalent to over 600 grams of silver per capita, and although its solvency was certainly in doubt, it did not quite crumble. By the end of the war, debt had risen to around 750 grams, and the country was sounder than ever. These figures alone are enough to bear witness to the results of the country's political and financial revolution. But, of course, total debt does not in itself provide a complete explanation of the French credit crisis of 1709. The country's main problem, like that of England but to a far worse degree, was a growing imbalance between short-term debt and free revenues.

The Financial Crisis in France and England, 1708–1710[8]

	France	England
	1708	*1710*
Gross revenues (tons of silver)	756	572
Long-term debt service (" ")	460	133
Net revenues (" ")	296	439
Short-term debts (" ")	4,322	2,200
—as a multiple of net revenues	14.6	5.0

If England could barely survive when its short-term debts were five times available revenues, then France would surely be forced to default.

The financial woes of the French monarchy stemmed from its inability to adapt to the new world of Dutch (now Anglo-Dutch) finance. For instance, the willingness of investors to buy cheap long-term debt was unlikely to be improved by the return of the old French vice of monetary manipulation. Under Colbert the French currency had been reasonably stable. In the period from 1686 to 1709, however, more than forty changes were made in the value of the livre—the greatest number in any comparable period of its history. As before, the process involved revaluation as well as devaluation, but as always, the overall tendency was for devaluation, with the livre losing 27% of its silver content during the period. Continual currency manipulation not only deterred investment in rentes but also disrupted economic activity, thereby reducing the government's regular tax revenues. During the first decade of the eighteenth century, French revenues were nearly 20% lower than they had been in the 1690s.

The weakening market for rentes only made it more essential to find a cheap and effective way to raise short-term funds. In this period it was, above all, the ability of the Bank of England to circulate Exchequer bills at yields as low as 3.02% that constituted England's main financial advantage over its rivals. It was clear that the type of short-term finance which had sufficed for the wars of the Counter-Reformation was inadequate for the wars of the Enlightenment. The officeholders and *traiteurs* could not provide sufficient funds, and their charges were unaffordably high. France now turned to foreign bankers. The Protestants of Geneva, some of them the very Huguenots that had emigrated after the repeal of the Edict of Nantes in 1685, played a role comparable to that of the Portuguese Jews as financiers of Spain during the Thirty Years' War. They augmented the resources of the indigenous Catholic *financier* class, but their advances were not cheap, and by 1708 their means were exhausted. In 1709, the syndicate headed by Samuel Bernard, the leading Genevan financier of the French crown, collapsed, sending shock waves through the markets of Europe.

In order to compete with Holland and England, France needed to develop cheaper and more flexible methods of short-term finance. One attempt to do so was the Caisse des Emprunts, reestablished in 1702. More important, however, was the issue of money notes (*billets de monnaie*) by the Treasury. They were interest-free for the first year but were entitled to 4% (later 7.5%) if not paid when presented. But by comparison with the financial experiments in England, the French system was fatally flawed. Ultimately, the successful English pyramid of Exchequer tallies, Exchequer bills, and Bank of England notes rested on the credit of the private sector. The tallies were issued as anticipations of tax revenues, and if there was insufficient cash for their payment when due, they were repaid in Exchequer bills. These were effectively underwritten by the Bank of England, which, if it could not safely refinance them through issues of notes, had capital on call from its shareholders specifically for this purpose. Of course, the structure depended on (1) the care of the Exchequer not to overissue tallies and (2) the adequacy of the underwriting arrangements. But by 1710 £8 million of Exchequer debt was outstanding with minimal depreciation and with an average nominal interest of less than 5%.

The *billets de monnaie* had no underwriting support from the private sector, and of course, the government never had cash on hand for their redemption. The provision of interest in the case of nonpayment only encouraged holders to present them for payment as soon as they possibly could, after which they were in de facto default. For a few years they held their value simply because their amount was very limited. By 1708, however, there were 143 million livres of Treasury notes in circulation, trading at discounts of up to 75%.[9] Yet 143 million livres was equivalent to £8.75 million, scarcely more than the Exchequer debt of England, but in an economy close to three times the size.

When Desmarets took over as minister of finance in 1708, he inherited a bankrupt country with 687 million livres of short-term debts.[10] Fortunately Desmarets was a very different man from his incompetent predecessor, Chamillart. He was Colbert's nephew and had inherited something of his uncle's reputation for financial sagacity. Appointed to save the country's finances in their hour of peril, he approached the problems facing him with energy and determination. But it cannot be said the he was able to restore order—that would have been too hard even for his uncle. Desmarets was able to raise some money voluntarily, but his methods were largely a return to the arbitrary practices of earlier crises. In 1710, interest on the majority of rentes sold since 1702 was reduced to 5%. In 1713 this became 4%—and those paid for in depreciated notes were reduced by 40%. A considerable number of new rentes at the same below-market rates were forced on creditors to settle arrears of interest, to clear up the bankruptcy of Samuel Bernard's syndicate of 1709, and to retire some of the depreciated notes in circulation, in the hope that this would raise the value of those remaining. Of course, the creation of new notes in quantities considerably greater than those retired rendered such hopes illusory. Desmarets's great achievement was to finance the rest of the war and thus to enable France to salvage a reasonable peace settlement. For that alone, he deserved more credit than he was to receive after the death of Louis XIV. Nevertheless, in 1715 the country was no more solvent that it had been in 1708.

POST-BELLUM DEPRESSION

On September 1, 1715, Louis XIV finally gave up the ghost after a reign of seventy-two years, and, in the words of the Duc de Saint-Simon, "the people, ruined, overwhelmed, desperate, gave thanks to God." Le Roi Soleil had, as he admitted, "loved war too much." Now that he was dead it was possible for the ex-combatants to put their financial houses in order.

This was easier said than done. The total postwar debt of France has been variously estimated at between 2 and 3.5 billion livres. The most likely figure appears to be close to 3 billion—a sum approaching £200 million sterling.[11] In the meantime public debts in Great Britain had run up to £49 million, a small amount, perhaps, compared to that of France, but then the population of France in 1715 was three times larger than that of Britain. Moreover, £49 million was nearly twenty times the amount that had caused Charles II to default in 1672.[12]

A better sense of the scale of the challenge facing the two countries can be gained when it is understood that the GNP of Great Britain at this time was probably around £60 million.[13] The public debt, therefore, represented more than 80% of national production. French levels of GNP at this time are more conjectural, but two contemporary estimates put the figure at around 2.4 billion livres (or around £150 million at prevailing exchange rates)—a figure that matches reasonably well that of Britain.[14] Even if this were to be an underestimate, it is almost certain that French public debt was in excess of 100% of GNP. Even in the modern world, such figures would cause headaches in treasury departments.

The situation in Britain was not improved by the recentness of its conversion to the rules of mercantile public finance. Its debt was not only relatively expensive, it was also a ramshackle affair—cobbled together over a series of crises. In 1715 not one part of the debt had been raised in the form of unadorned perpetual annuities—the financial backbone of the merchant republics. True, the £16.4 million annuities held by the great chartered companies—the Bank of England, the East India Company, and the South Sea Company—were perpetual.[15] At rates between 5% (the East India Company) and 6% (the other two), they were also relatively cheap, although not by Dutch standards. But such rates had only been achieved by offering investors the added lure of profits from government-granted monopolies.

The remainder of the long-term debt had been issued on more quirky and less satisfactory terms. A total of £11.4 million had been raised in the form of lottery loans. These loans had tempted the investor with a minimum return of 6.84% over thirty-two years, but the lottery prizes increased the total cost to the government to 8%. It is true that the lottery loans were redeemable prior to their final maturity—but only by the expensive method of anticipating the return of capital.[16]

The ninety-nine-year and thirty-two-year annuities issued by Godolphin 1702 to 1710 were an even worse bargain. They had no right of early redemption at all. Like so many other aspects of European finance, this goes back to the medieval usury laws. The seller's right to redeem was specifically written into annuities that did not expire automatically; otherwise the borrower was "enslaving" himself to the lender in perpetuity. Because Godolphin's annuities expired automatically they did not need to be redeemable; yet ninety-nine years was so long as to constitute perpetuity in purely financial terms. By offering such privileged securities, Godolphin had been able to lower the initial annual cost to the taxpayer to a tolerable 6.67% or less, but only by sacrificing one of the main pillars of Dutch finance—the ability to lower interest costs in more prosperous times. In 1715 the "irredeemables," as they were called, amounted to £12.6 million, nearly one-quarter of the total debt. They were undoubtedly the Achilles' heel of British public finances, and were to be at the center of the financial whirlwind that swept over the country five years later.

Including a further £8.4 million of short-term obligations, English debt was high in relation to GNP, even by modern standards. But the Dutch experience had clearly shown that such levels were not beyond the means of a successful mercantile republic. Was England by now sufficiently close to emulating the Dutch—and before them the Italians—so that it could shrug off a similar burden? The answer is that it could. After the war, interest rates fell sharply, and in 1717 Robert Walpole, the new Chancellor of the Exchequer, could consider the possibility of refunding the entire public debt. The Bank of England and the South Sea Company were persuaded to lower the interest on their annuities to 5%, and the Bank agreed to circulate Exchequer bills at a rate as low as 1.5% per annum. But Walpole's greatest success was the conversion of the lottery loans into 5% perpetual redeemable annuities, the first true issue of this archetypal form of public debt in England without added incentives attached. The interest savings from the conversion were to be used for a sinking fund—another invention of the Italian republics of the fourteenth century that had been handed down via the Dutch. The strength of England's new financial system could scarcely have been made clearer than by the rapid rise of the new 5% annuities to 104 on the London exchange. The market was so strong that at the end of the year the excess short-term debt could be refunded with annuities paying only 4%. By this stage only the irredeemables remained to cloud the horizon.[17]

No such good fortune awaited the Duc d'Orléans when he became regent for the young Louis XV in 1715. The debt he inherited from the Sun

King was almost certainly in excess of GNP and, more significantly, even further in excess of the political capacity of the ancien régime. Of course, the usual solution for such a situation was a round of show trials, partial repudiations, interest reductions, and so forth. This policy had worked perfectly well before: the debt service was reduced to a tolerable level, the populace at large was satisfied, and the creditor class was so irrevocably tied to the government that it was incapable of uttering more than feeble protests. Indeed, a cynic might have observed that the whole cycle of borrowing and default was in reality a method of taxing the bourgeoisie—in fact, of undoing the very exemption from taxes that they had so carefully purchased along with their offices.

It was on this well-worn path that Desmarets had already been forced to embark in 1709. But the situation was no longer as straightforward as it had been for his predecessors. The sheer scale of the necessary write-offs constituted a problem in itself. When France had last experienced a major bankruptcy, in 1661, public debt was probably under 50% of GNP. Now it was close to 125% of GNP; but there was little to suggest that France was politically or financially equipped to handle a public debt even half that size. A debt reduction on this scale was a very large dose of taxation for the public creditors to swallow, one that might seriously jeopardize the stability of the regime.

It was not only that the debt was too big, however. Far too much of it was represented by depreciated short-term notes. After 1708, Desmarets had attempted to remove some of the overhang of paper money from circulation by obliging the holders to accept rentes in lieu of payment. But in the presence of continuing deficits, these measures were mere palliatives. By 1715, the volume of notes in circulation had more than doubled. Most were changing hands at less than half their face value. This was a far more serious problem than the depreciation of rentes. France was suffering from the effects of Gresham's law: the paper notes ("bad money") had driven coin ("good money") out of circulation. Far from booming under the stimulus of an increased money supply, the economy was grinding to a halt because of a death of a circulating medium that commanded popular confidence. The new government did nothing to improve the situation. Its first act, as so often in French history, was to sack the old administration, recall the Chambre de Justice, and start a new round of repudiation. Rentes were once again inspected for "usurious" origin, and those that survived scrutiny were reduced to 4%. In the meantime, the old notes were replaced by a new series, the *billets d'état,* restricted to 250 million livres, in a process that effectively wiped out two-thirds of their value. Yet any hope that this more modest circulation of paper money would restore confidence was soon disabused. The new notes fell almost instantly to a 40% discount, and coins remained as reluctant to emerge from their hiding places as ever. The economic slump continued.

Of course, in the climate of 1716, it was unwise to go on a spending spree—especially if one had had any connection with government finances in the previous decades. The Chambre de Justice had all such people firmly in its sights, and a display of wealth had always amounted in itself to evidence of guilt. In 1716, to the usual lineup of suspects, a new category had been added: the children of the new era of stock markets. The opening session of the Chambre was addressed by D'Aguesseau, the new Controller of Finance, in ringing tones:

> There is another class of men among whom there must be found some guilty ones. These are the usurers, to whom the trade in stocks has given birth in darkness and obscurity. They have raised sudden fortunes, the foundations of which they have robbed from the public. You will dive into those foundations, gentlemen, and you will destroy these detestable edifices of iniquity.[18]

As befitted the times, the 1716 Chambre operated on a scale unequaled in French history. Some 6,000 *financiers* were paraded before it, of which 4,410 were found guilty. No less than 400 million livres of their assets were declared illicit—a full third of all the assets investigated by the Chambre. Clearly there was something very rotten at the core of the fiscal system.

There was also something rotten at the core of the economy. With the parallel processes of show trials and debt repudiation in full swing, it is scarcely surprising that economic activity remained mired in a slough of fear and suspicion. A vicious circle was in play. The slump lowered tax revenues and ensured continuing deficits. The deficits could not be funded through issues of long-term debt whose market had been destroyed by the process of default. They therefore required constant additions to floating debt and eroded confidence in the ability of the government to maintain the value of the new paper money. The depreciated paper in circulation continued to "drive out" good money and ensured that the economy was starved by a shortage of cash.

The self-defeating nature of the cycle of default was mostly clearly revealed in the final results of the Chambre de Justice. Of the 400 million livres of assets declared illicit, only 219 million were imposed as fines. Of this amount, only 96 million livres was actually received by the state. But most of this was paid in depreciated paper money, and the real value of the amount collected was no more than 55 million livres. Some *financiers* went bankrupt. Others resorted, as in the past, to stalling, flight, and bribery to save their fortunes. Perhaps the process of default and recession would eventually have worked itself through. By 1717, the government was approaching a balanced budget by means of stringent economies and higher taxes. But the regent's patience was running out. Total debt was still around 2 billion livres and consumed half the state's revenues. The economy was as depressed as ever, and opposition to taxes was rising. The contrast with the economic strength of France's erstwhile enemies was galling. The old solutions did not seem to be working. Some fresh thinking was needed.

THE CHIMERA

> People with difficulty believe what they have seen; and posterity will consider as a fable what we ourselves look upon as a dream.
>
> —Memoirs of the Duc de Saint-Simon

The events that followed had an air of unreality that prompted more than one writer to compare them to fairy tale. One present-day historian has even provided a synopsis of the plot:

> A light-hearted and debonair prince, threatened by bankruptcy, sees the arrival one day of a handsome wandering sorcerer, who offers to change all his paper into gold; and without hesitating he delivers his kingdom to the stupefying experiences of the magician; the spell works, the orgy is unleashed, everybody is rich, but, alas! it was only a dream, and the next morning everybody awakes disenchanted with their *chiffons de papier.*[19]

The sorcerer in question was John Law, a Scotsman who thus enjoys an equivocal position in his country's history somewhere between the witches of Macbeth and the great Edinburgh school of economists. Underlying the surreal atmosphere of his brief career, however, was a very serious, if ultimately misplaced, attempt to effect a financial revolution in France. Although Law is most often (and quite rightly) associated with paper money inflation and stock market hysteria, this should not be allowed to obscure the rest of his ideas. At the peak of his power, his reforms were so sweeping in their scope that they affected almost every aspect of the financial structure of France and were referred to in awe as "the System."

The starting point of Law's ideas, beginning with his first published work, was undoubtedly the beneficent power of paper money. There was nothing very new in this. Contemporaries had long envied the Italian and Dutch republics their ability to alleviate the inconvenience, and often the shortage, of metallic money by the use of paper substitutes. The public banks of these republics were much admired, and their deposit receipts generally traded at a premium to cash. Interest rates in these states, it was observed, were uniformly lower than in other countries. Rulers of these other countries were constantly being urged to set up local equivalents, notwithstanding their "republican" associations.

The novelty of Law's thinking lay not in his advocacy of banks and paper money per se, but in the grand scale of his vision. His first, and still his best-known, work, *Money and Trade Consider'd; with a Proposal for supplying the Nation with Money,* was published in Scotland in 1705. It is notable for its analysis of the economic value of money, and for its proposal of a form of paper money secured by land. But more important than these features was Law's willingness to think in sweeping macroeconomic terms, even if his focus was still restricted to his poor and sparsely populated homeland:

> Suppose that the yearly Value [GNP] of Scotland is a Million and a half [pounds sterling], the yearly Value of England 40 Millions; the Value of Scotland is only about one 28th Part of the Value of England. Yet in Numbers of People considered, Scotland will be at least as one to 6; and if there was Money to employ the People we would be as one to 6, for we have Advantages peculiar to us, that do more than equal the Plantation and East-India Trades. . . . I don't doubt that the Paper Money propos'd being given out *equal to the Demand* [italics added], would bring the yearly Value of Scotland to 3 Millions.[20]

This was a grand vision indeed: GNP could be doubled by an increase of money supply! How much money would be needed for this miraculous economic transformation? Law suggested an answer with regard to England:

> England has been computed to have had 14 millions of Gold and Silver, and at the same time had paper money for a great sum, yet England never had enough money to employ the people: 50 millions would not improve England so far as it is capable of improvement.[21]

This passage is even more eye-opening than the last. Law's suggestion amounts to an increase in paper money greater than his estimate of English GNP at the time. A careful reader of this passage need not have been surprised by the events that were to unfold fifteen years later.

Some modern readers may also have picked up a salient feature of Law's thinking, which has prompted several historians to consider him the philosophical precursor of John Maynard Keynes. Law thought, for the first time, in terms of the "full-employment" economy and viewed monetary policy as a vehicle of demand management to raise output to its "full-employment" capacity. And like Keynes, Law rose to international fame as the man who could lead the West's largest economy out of a seemingly intractable economic depression.

Law was never able to put his theories into practice in his native land. For a decade after 1705, he traveled around Europe, exiled from Britain as a result of a duel. Significantly he spent much time in Venice and Genoa, witnessing at first hand the operations of the Bank of Venice and the Casa di San Giorgio, and the very low interest rates that prevailed in these republics. This confirmed his belief in the efficacy of banks and paper money and encouraged him to aim for a long-term rate of interest as low as 2%. Perhaps equally significantly, during his travels, he lived almost entirely by means of gambling, at which he was one of the most skilled operators of his day. His dual interests, macroeconomics and gambling, gave him no fear of the new era of stock markets. He was as comfortable with one form of speculation as he was with the other. Perhaps as a result, he never seems to have realized that there might be an inherent contradiction between the job of a central banker and that of a stock market operator. But then Law was a man of his time, and in the early eighteenth century, not even the Bank of England resembled its later image of the "Old Lady."

In 1715, Law arrived in France as an unemployed adventurer. Here was a new regime, an economy in crisis, and perhaps, therefore, a fertile field for economic experiments. His theories would have a special relevance to deeply indebted states. Without delay he sent his first proposal to the regent: a state bank with the power to issue paper money.

> An abundance of money which would lower the interest rate to 2% would relieve the King by reducing the financing costs of the debts, public offices, etc. It would relieve indebted noble landowners who would be enriched because agricultural goods would be sold at higher prices. It would enrich the merchants who would then be able to borrow at a low interest rate and give work to the people.[22]

Perhaps not surprisingly the regent's Council of State rejected Law's proposal. Their main concern was to resolve the ill effects of the last royal attempt to issue paper money. The Duc de Saint-Simon later wrote in his memoirs of his opposition to the scheme:

> An establishment of this sort may be good in itself; but it is only so in a republic or in a monarchy like England, whose finances are controlled by those alone who furnish them, and who only furnish as much as they please. But in a State which is weak, changeable, and absolute, like France, stability must necessarily be wanting to it; since the King, or in his name a mistress, a minister or favorites, or still more, such extreme necessities as we find in the years 1707–1710, may overthrow the Bank—the temptation to which would be too great, and at the same time too easy.[23]

Saint-Simon's assessment, although made with the advantage of hindsight, is quite remarkable. It is the juxtaposition of the adjectives "weak" and "absolute" that catches the eye. Far from repeating the old platitudes about *Dieu en terre* and so forth, Saint-Simon recognized, for perhaps the first time in European history, the inherent weakness of an absolute monarchy and the greater inherent strength of a republic of merchants (which he defined broadly—so as to include England—but with pinpoint accuracy, as a state "whose finances are controlled by those alone who furnish them"). It is not too much to say that the eventual fate of the ancien régime can be understood from these few simple sentences.

Notwithstanding his rejection of Law's ambitious scheme, in the next year the regent allowed Law to set up a private bank. He immediately set about proving what could be done on this more limited basis. The Banque Générale operated in a way that was entirely novel in France and derived from Law's admiration of Dutch and Genoese practice. It issued deposit notes that were repayable at a constant amount of specie—in other words, they were not tied to the notoriously unstable livre. This point was directly copied from the deposit receipts of the Bank of Amsterdam and the Casa di San Giorgio. The Banque lent money at 6%, and then at 4%. Such rates had been dreamed of only at a time when money could scarcely be found even at double-digit interest rates. Deposits poured in, and by the end of 1718, there were 149 million Banque Générale notes in circulation. This was pretty remarkable for a bank that had started out with only 375,000 livres of cash in its vaults (the remainder of its nominal 6 million capital was either on call or in depreciated state paper).[24] Still, the Scotsman ran his bank conservatively and always held adequate reserves against his notes.

However admirable Law's bank, it was not large enough to make a serious impact on the overall economic situation. Nor had it been able to raise the value of the *billets d'état,* which still circulated at no better than 35–40% of face value. In 1717, a new opportunity presented itself when the government concession for the colonization of France's North American possessions became available. However impressive the extent of these remote territories in the heartland of America, the licensee, Antoine Crozat, had become bored with a venture that offered so few prospects of short-term profit. Law seized his chance and offered to take over the concession.

It is unlikely that Law saw the Compagnie de l'Occident (the Mississippi Company, as it has become generally known) as anything more than a springboard for his wider schemes. In the words of an English observer:

> The Settling of a Colony . . . is a Work of time, and must take up not many Years only, but ages of Years; and the utmost he could have before him in such an Undertaking, was to die in the Faith of its Success, and to have the Satisfaction of having his Name very much talked about when he was Dead. . . .
>
> The first thing to be Enquir'd was to find out something to do, something to Trade in, for . . . it was plain that Mr. Laws never design'd a Hundred Millions of Livres should be Employ'd in peopling a Wilderness.[25]

A clue to Law's true intentions were given by the method of the company's flotation. The 100-million-livre capital (about £6 million) was entirely subscribable in *billets d'état.* The model here was obviously the South Sea Company, whose flotation in London six years earlier had been subscribable in the short-term debts of the English government. The *billets* received by the Mississippi Company were handed to the government in exchange for a 4% *rente perpétuelle,* just as the English debts had been exchanged for a 6% perpetual annuity. Like its English precursor, the Mississippi Company was short of immediate trading profits, and its shares therefore traded purely on the basis of its annuity income. As a result, its market price was little better than that of the notes it replaced. At around 200 livres per share, a 60% discount to the par value of 500 livres,* this gave a yield of 10%—probably indicative of the true market yield of rentes at the time. Clearly, Law had a long way to go if he was to reduce long-term borrowing costs to 2%.

While the Mississippi Company remained largely inactive after its flotation, the Banque Générale went from strength to strength, gradually improving Law's reputation. In early 1717 the government authorized the acceptance of its notes at face value for tax payments. By the end of 1718,

*Like bonds, shares also have par values. These are rarely referred to nowadays since they bear very little relation to market prices. However, this was not the case in the eighteenth century, and contempory accounts of the Mississippi Company generally give prices as a percentage of par value rather than as a price per share. In this account, however, the modern practice is followed, and prices are always given on a per share basis, rather than as a percentage of par.

the regent had become so impressed with the Scotsman that he reconsidered his earlier rejection of his first proposal of a state bank. On January 1, 1719, the Banque Générale became the Banque Royale, and the original shareholders reaped handsome profits when their capital was repaid in full—including the 83% that had never been paid in.

This was the turning point, the moment when Law could start to turn his dreams into reality. However successful the old bank, it was of relatively limited value in proving the miraculous powers of paper money. Not only were its notes restricted by the amount of specie deposited in its vaults, but they were not universally accepted as money. The notes of the Banque Royale were quite different. They no longer represented a fixed amount of precious metal; they were denominated purely in livres. The amount in circulation was no longer a function of the coin and bullion deposited in the bank's vaults but was authorized by simple royal decree. Equally important, they were made legal tender for all transactions throughout the kingdom. And, of course, whereas the notes of the Banque Générale, like those of the Bank of England, were only the private obligations of a private bank, the notes of the Banque Royale were a form of public debt.

The concept of "legal tender" needs some explanation. Historically, paper money has come in a number of forms, and with a number of different provisions to ensure its credibility as a means of payment. The most typical such provision, until this century at least, was its convertibility on demand into coin. The notes of the Banque Générale fell into this category, as did those of the Bank of England. To avoid the risks of a "run on the bank" implicit in convertibility on demand, notes were sometimes given specific maturity dates. In this case, they would generally bear interest. The *billets de monnaie,* the *billets d'état,* and the Exchequer bills of England were all of this type. Of course such notes were more cumbersome to use, and therefore less suitable as a means of payment, than non-interest-bearing notes.

As an alternative or an addition to convertibility, the government could encourage circulation by guaranteeing to accept the notes in payment of taxes. This was true of Exchequer bills and Bank of England notes, as it had always been of the deposit receipts of the state banks of the republics. The *billets de monnaie* had been only partially acceptable for taxes, and this had encouraged their decline in value. All these provisions, whether convertibility or acceptance for taxes, were what may be described as "self-imposed" obligations. The issuer or the state (sometimes the same, of course) gave specific undertakings to encourage the voluntary acceptance of the paper.

To make money "legal tender" is quite different. The state imposes the *involuntary* acceptance of the notes (or coins) as money, by stating that they may not be refused in settlement of any transaction. For the sake of good order, it has almost always been necessary to have "legal tender" money within an economy. In seventeenth-century Europe, the coins of every country were "legal tender" within that country. To make paper into "legal tender" was a risky business. Neither Exchequer bills nor Bank of England notes were legal tender in England. The closest approach to such a concept in Europe was the rules applying in both Genoa and Holland that transactions above a certain amount had to be made by means of transfer on the books of the state banks. But the coin and bullion in those banks remained the property of the individual depositors, not of the bank, let alone the state.

In France, the *billets de monnaie* had initially been made legal tender for 25% of any transaction above 4,000 livres. But, of course, unlike the vaults of the Bank of Amsterdam, the coffers of the state were very far from brimming with coin and bullion. As the *billets* proved to be effectively unconvertible, they rapidly lost value. The public was soon able to witness a fascinating example of role reversal: creditors fleeing from their debtors so as to avoid repayment in depreciated paper. Public opposition forced the government to restrict the notes' validity to Paris in 1706, and finally to drop it altogether. With a background such as this, it was a bold move to give the same royal fiat to the notes of the Banque Royale. But Law was nothing if not ambitious. His ultimate aim was the complete substitution of coin by paper; and as a first step, silver was banned from any transaction over 600 livres.

Law's new notes were still convertible on demand, however, and he was very concerned that they should appear the most stable form of currency in the land. They were therefore issued in limited quantities at first. In any case, his position was still very far from secure. The *financier* class viewed him with suspicion and dislike: another foreign banker (and a Protestant to boot) threatening their monopoly of royal finance. Their leaders were the Pâris brothers, who in late 1718 had formed a syndicate to take over the Farmers General (the consolidated tax farm established by Colbert) for 48.5 million livres per year. In the spirit of the times they had offered shares in the syndicate to the public—a far more attractive investment than those of the Mississippi Company with its distant swamps. Worse, the Pâris syndicate (the Anti-System, as it came to be called) would inevitably hold very large quantities of Banque Royale notes that it could present for conversion at any time, threatening the bank's solvency and Law's credibility.

Sometime in the first half of 1719, Law must have realized that he would never be able to put his theories to the test unless he had complete control of the public finances. His Mississippi Company was a lame duck, and the Banque Royale would always be vulnerable unless he commanded the two other "controlling heights" of the economy: coinage and tax collection.

It is not possible to know what negotiations took place behind the scenes. Law was a persuasive talker, but it is unlikely that abstract economic principles alone would win over the regent and his advisers. In the simultaneously skeptical and frivolous atmosphere of Versailles, it is almost certain that Law had to promise some extremely tangible gains to the crown and to influential courtiers in order to have his way. The shareholders of the Banque Générale, which included many influential courtiers, or their mistresses, had enjoyed impressive returns, albeit on a small scale. But the shares of the Mississippi Company, of which no less than 40% had been subscribed by the regent on behalf of the crown, had so far been a considerable disappointment. The events that were to follow can be explained only by Law's need to make the Mississippi Company an equally attractive investment for those in power.

In June and July, before the spectacular share issues of the autumn, the Mississippi Company made two share issues at rather low prices. These increased the capital from 200,000 to 300,000 shares. Of the 100,000 shares issued—all to existing shareholders—40,000 went to the crown. But by subtle manipulation, 20,000 of these went to influential courtiers. It is probably fair to say that, at this stage, over half the shares of the Mississippi Company were owned by "insiders."

At the same time, the company acquired some new sources of business. In May, it absorbed the other French chartered trading companies, with monopolies in the East Indies, China, and Africa. In July, it was granted the minting monopoly for nine years in exchange for a payment of 50 million livres. Law now had control of one of his two main objectives. More important, the prospect of some real operating profits was raising the share price fast. From around 200–250 livres at the beginning of the year, it now sailed past its original issue price of 500 livres to reach 1,000 and beyond. It was at 1,500 by July 29, making the second share issue at 1,000 only two days earlier look cheap. During August, public interest really started to take hold, and the shares traded as high as 3,000.

At the end of August, the "System" was unveiled in all its glory. The Compagnie des Indes, as the Mississippi Company was now called, offered to take over the Farmers General for 52 million livres per year—an increase of 3.5 million over the amount paid by the Pâris syndicate. In order to secure this privilege, the company made an offer that left all who read it aghast:

> That the better to show his Majesty the desire of the said India Company, to contribute by their credit to the ease of the State, they offer to lend to the King Twelve Hundred Millions of Livres at the yearly interest of three per cent, to be employed towards the reimbursing and redeeming the perpetual Rentes or Annuities, and other Debts secured by the Aides and the Gabelles, . . . the State-Bills, Bills on the Caisse and the sums advanced for the Offices already suppressed or to be suppressed.[26]

Given that the crown had hitherto been unable to borrow at less than 10% on the free market, this offer to refund almost the entire public debt at 3% seemed nearly fantastic. Law had created an institution the like of which had never before been seen—at least in France. It collected all the indirect taxes, not only those of the Farmers General, but ancillary ones like the tobacco tax. It controlled the mint and held a monopoly on the salt mines of Alsace; and the entire French trading empire was in its hands. It now planned to take over the national debt. A shareholder in Law's company would truly be a shareholder in the future of the country. The South Sea Company may have combined an association of public creditors with an international trading monopoly, but it was of limited scope by comparison. The true model for Law's creation, of course, was the Casa di San Giorgio, which had already combined all these functions in fifteenth-century Genoa, and which Law had been able to observe during his stay in the Ligurian republic. Was France now about to take on the character of Genoa, a state run almost as a private enterprise, with its citizens as shareholders? Was such a thing conceivable in a country whose last king's most famous dictum was "L'État, c'est moi"? No wonder people were amazed and exited. Law appeared to be contemplating a revolution in the raison d'être of French society. In March 1720 he wrote of his vision of France as a "body of merchants of which the *banque royale* is the treasury."[27] This, in the country whose ruler a century later was to sneer at England as "a nation of shopkeepers"!

It was one thing to make such a bold offer, quite another to put it into effect. Law had three parallel objectives: to ensure that all the debt was converted into company shares; to bring the long-term rate of interest down to 2%; and to ensure the profits promised to his patrons. These aims were not very easily reconcilable. To attract the public creditors, it was necessary to offer a 4% dividend rate—equal to the rate of their old annuities. To make such a promise affordable, it would be advisable to offer shares at a relatively low price—no more than the current market in any case. To translate a 4% dividend into his objective of a 2% long-term interest rate would require the share price to double after issue. This doubling would require speculative buying by the general public, which would have to be stimulated, but which would also be more easily achieved by a lower initial offering price. It was the third aim that mitigated against a low exchange price. The lower the price, the more the old shareholders would be diluted, and the lower their potential profits. The trade-off looked like this:

Distribution of Shares in the Mississippi Company
At different issue prices

Price (Livres)	2,500	5,000
Shares issued	600,000	300,000
Total shares	900,000	600,000
Percentage held by old shareholders	33%	50%
—of which the king held	11%	17%

But while the higher issue price increased the rewards of the existing shareholders, it also meant a substantially higher dividend payout of 120 million livres if Law's objective of a 4% yield was to be met. It is possible that at an issue price of 2,500 livres, Law might have succeeded. The necessary dividend would have been 90 million livres, which corresponds to two surviving estimates of potential profits made by Law, 88 and 91 million livres—the latter made at the shareholders' meeting at the end of the year. Yet Law chose to issue new shares not at 2,500 but at 5,000. The only possible explanation seems to be a desire to maximize the stake and the profits of the old shareholders.

Of course, a price of 5,000 livres could not be achieved by a simple offer of exchange at, or below, existing market levels. It required the unleashing of a speculative fever sufficient to unhinge the share price from reality. Here Law displayed the psychological acumen acquired during years at the gambling table, together with the understanding of credit gained by years of study. Unfortunately, these very skills were to destroy the edifice that he was trying to create. Law's twin tactics were rumor and credit: a well-nigh infallible combination in any age. To compensate for the inadequacy of identifiable near-term revenues, Law fed the rumors of longer-term profits from mining in the American territories. His personal concession of over 2,000 square miles in Arkansas was reported to contain a silver mine with the productive potential of Potosí. Yet again, the promise of El Dorado would unhinge the judgments of European investors.

Law's command of the more technical aspects of market manipulation was no less impressive. It was essential to attract the maximum number of investors, and to do so required that the rentiers should have no special priority in acquiring shares. They were given paper receipts by the Treasury, which they could tender for shares along with everybody else. Three issues were made from September 13 to October 2—a total of 300,000 shares at 5,000 livres. To make matters easy for outside buyers, subscriptions were payable in monthly installments: twenty months in the first issue, ten months in the other two. To make matters easier still, shares could be bought only with Banque Royale notes, and the note issue was obligingly expanded. By mid-October there were 620 million livres outstanding, up from 160 million in May. Naturally the bank also stood ready to lend money against the collateral of shares—even partially paid shares. Finally, to add speculative appeal, options* (known as *primes*, i.e., premiums) were created. With such a strong cocktail of stimulants it is no wonder that the market took off like a rocket.

Now the "orgy was unleashed." Of course, the boom and bust in Mississippi shares was not the first example of financial market excess in Western history. Exaggerated price rises and their correction are inevitable in all trading markets. But never before had so many people and so much money been involved. Men and women who had never before heard of shares joined in. The rue Quincampoix became the setting for the biggest stock exchange in Europe. Here there were no elegant, purpose-built arcades like those of the Antwerp Bourse or the Royal Exchange of London. Trading took place right there on a street that was little more than an alley. Dukes and duchesses, tradesmen, provincials, and foreigners jostled for space. Fortunes were made and lost—initially they were mostly made. A local waiter is reputed to have made 30 million livres, and to have retired in time to England. He next visited Paris—after a suitable interval—in the guise of an English "milord." It was estimated that over 300,000 visitors had rushed to Paris from the provinces and overseas, either to speculate or merely to watch. Almost no one seemed to be immune from the contagion.

*This was the right to buy a fixed number of shares at a specified price for a specified length of time. Once created, options could be traded in just the same way as the underlying shares themselves.

Rentiers, if they were not too busy speculating, protested that they were being defrauded by being denied priority for shares. Yet all state creditors who did not wish to purchase shares were repaid at par in Banque Royale notes, which in the general euphoria traded at a 10% premium to specie. Given the steep discounts that had so recently prevailed, creditors would have been wise to accept their good fortune like the incredulous noteholder

> to whom the Government ow'd Ten Thousand Crowns, which he would have been glad to have sold for Two Thousand Five Hundred . . . , that caused an Iron Chest to be brought, and put the Money into it, then drove Posts into the Ground in his Cellar, and chained it down to the Stakes, then chained it also to the Wall, and barricaded the Doors and Window of the Cellar with Iron, and all for fear, not of Thieves to steal the Money, but for the fear the Money, Chest and all should fly away into the Air.[28]

Ideally he should have taken his money overseas as well.

At the end of the year Law was at the height of his power. Mississippi stock had run up to 10,000, achieving his target of a 2% yield. At that stage he had started to sell shares into the market to stabilize the price at this semimystical round figure. At the beginning of 1720 he converted to Catholicism so that the regent could make him Superintendant of Finance. He now set about the wholesale restructuring of the French fiscal system. Venal offices were abolished, their capital cost to be repaid out of the seemingly inexhaustible coffers of the Mississippi Company. All direct taxes—the taille, the *capitation*, and the *dixième*—were repealed, to be replaced by a single, universal direct tax: the *denier royale*. Other tax rates were made uniform throughout the country. The most inequitable and unproductive taxes were abolished. The result of these reforms would have been the almost total extinction of the *financier* and officeholder class. In his memorandum on the new tax, Law answered the rhetorical question of what was to become of the these people with an unflattering analogy:

> What will become of the rats that live in my barn if I remove the grain so as to transport it to a safer location? I beg pardon of Your Royal Highness for the familiarity of the comparison.[29]

No wonder Law's system excited such profound opposition from within the old order. In the field of public finances even the Revolution of 1789 was scarcely more radical.

It must be admitted, however, that Law's wider reforms had little to do with the economic boom that was under way. The underlying cause was a massive dose of monetary stimulus. In May 1719 there were 160 million livres of Banque Royale notes in circulation. One year later the figure was 2.7 billion livres.[30] In *Money and Trade Consider'd* Law had suggested that England would benefit from the creation of paper money in an amount greater than its GNP. Law had now put into effect in France exactly what he had proposed for England fifteen years earlier.[31] Never had money been easier to come by in the history of Europe:

> Every thing at Paris then assumed a smiling Countenance; Money grew so common, that People did not know where to put it out at Three per Cent. The publick Debts, which before were at great Discount, now sold for Ten, nay, Fifteen above their intrinsic Value. The Tradesmen had a greater Vent for their Goods; the Workmen were better paid for their Work. The Value of Land about Paris rose to 50, and even 60 Years Purchase [i.e. fifty to sixty times annual rental value—a 1.67–2.0% yield]. Many Noblemen repair'd their broken Fortunes; and others grew very Rich by the great Advantages they made in dealing in the Actions of this New Company. . . .
>
> The King also has gained by it very considerably; since all the Branches of his Revenues must bring into his Coffers Sums infinitely beyond what was ever known before, because of the Circulation of the Species, which is certainly three times greater than it ever was, which is manifest from the Price of Provisions, Land, and Merchandizes.[32]

The king had indeed gained very considerably. His nominal profit on his shares was nearly 1 billion livres!

These quotes are from an anonymous pamphlet, but one that is understood to have had the blessing of the great man himself. Where the author is misleading is that it was not specie that was three times more plentiful than before, but money in general. The increase was entirely in the form of paper. The obvious inflationary consequences were already noted by the author. Perhaps strangely, to our minds, he thought that sharply rising prices were a positive sign; but then, so did those unfortunate enough to live through the Depression of the 1930s.

Of course, it could not last. The crux came, not surprisingly, as the monthly payments for share subscriptions came due. Investors started to take their profits, not least because they needed them to fulfill their obligations. The share price started to wobble in early 1720, when the Prince de Conti, the greediest of Law's aristocratic patrons, cashed in his shares and drove up to the doors of the Banque Royale with a convoy of wagons to convert his holdings into hard cash. In a desperate bid to maintain the price of the shares, and with it the profits of the royal court—not to mention his vision of a 2% interest rate—Law offered to buy all shares at 9,000 livres. To do so required merging the company and the Banque Royale. It also led directly to the final spectacular increases in the paper money issued by the bank, as notes were issued in exchange for shares.

With the share price fixed, speculation merely transferred itself to the notes. To prop them up, Law resorted first to the total demonetization of gold and silver, then to their confiscation. Informers could claim half of any hoard uncovered. Law had now assumed the role of economic dictator. In the words of the Duc de Saint-Simon, "Never before had sovereign power been so violently exercised; never had it attacked in such a manner the temporal interest of the community."[33] In a series of contradictory edicts decreeing the value of various types of money, Law managed to "carry monetary confusion to a point probably unequaled in history."[34] Gold and silver were progressively devalued against the livre in attempt to make banknotes seem more desirable, but the foreign exchange markets were not to be fooled. The French currency fell like a stone. By late May, it was obvious that the end had come. On May 21 Law himself dealt the coup de grâce by ordering the progressive devaluation of the banknotes and shares against the livre by up to 50% in order to bring them back into line with precious metals. This decree caused such an uproar that it had to be revoked a few days later. But the damage to confidence was fatal. In June, coin was allowed back into circulation again, and the unwinding of the System began. By the end of the year, Law was in exile, and the shares of the company were selling at less than 1000.

The spectacular collapse of the Mississippi Company appears in retrospect to have been the inevitable consequence of its equally spectacular rise. Was Law's grand scheme always doomed to failure?

In one view, Law's vision was wrecked by the greed and irresponsibility of those around him. The speculative boom in Mississippi Company shares made fortunes for many well-placed courtiers. In addition, there was the *trésor du roi*—the 100,000 shares owned by the king, which at their peak were worth no less than 1 billion livres. Contemplating the effects of Law's fatal decision to peg the share price at 9,000 livres, the historian Edgar Faure likened Law to the protagonist of Hemingway's *Old Man and the Sea*, threatening the stability of his fishing boat in the vain attempt to preserve his miraculous catch. Finally, of course, it would have to be cut loose anyway.[35] Law himself, while not immune to the attractions of wealth or the pleasures of gambling and speculation, viewed the antics of the rue Quincampoix with disdain. The feverish bull market in Mississippi shares was to him merely a necessary step in a greater game—and a sop to his aristocratic backers. Once his target price for Mississippi shares was achieved, Law planned to bring the orgy of speculation under control.

This view of events brushes too lightly over fundamental flaws in Law's thinking, however. For all his desire to emulate the mercantile republics, Law never seems to have understood that low and stable interest rates cannot be created through speculation. For the reduction of borrowing costs, like the colonization of a wilderness, "is a Work of time, and must take up not many Years only, but ages of Years." Public creditors will accept a long-term yield of 3% or less only when (inter alia) they have developed a profound confidence in the government's ability and willingness (1) to honor its debts under all circumstances, and (2) to maintain long-term monetary stability. There was nothing in the history of the ancien régime to make investors anything other than deeply skeptical on both these points.

With his profound (yet imperfect) understanding of the powers of credit creation and of the psychology of speculation, Law was able to create a boom that temporarily lowered interest rates to his desired target, but he was able to do so only by a vast increase in the total money supply that, in itself, negated any chance of fulfilling the second prerequisite of long-term stability. Under this shower of paper money, which fell on Parisians like ticker tape, prices rose by three times before the return of the old guard brought about a deflation more severe and prolonged than any in French history. In this sense the seeds of the destruction of the System were sown at its very beginning. Richard Cantillon, the expatriate Irish banker, speculator, and economist, saw the inevitability of the eventual collapse and sold out at around 2,250 in August 1719. Of course, he sold far too early and missed the great rise of the autumn. But his reasoning was impeccable. He observed how Law had expanded the note issue of the Banque Royale in June and July in order to accommodate the second and third share issues. From this expansion alone, Cantillon deduced the unsustainable nature of Law's project.[36]

But there was an even more profound defect in Law's political vision. He understood that France needed to copy the mercantile republics if it was to compete in the new era of public borrowing. His vision of the Mississippi Company was based on the Casa di San Giorgio of Genoa. He failed to grasp, however, that it was not sufficient to convert the French public creditors into passive shareholders in his grand design. San Giorgio (and effectively the Genoese state) was entirely controlled and run by its citizen shareholders. Under Law's scheme, political power was centered more firmly than ever on Versailles. The French court held a controlling interest in the Mississippi Company, and the French state owned all the shares of the Banque Royale. The extinction of the officeholder and the *financier* class removed one of the few remaining restrictions on royal absolutism. Law may have admired the financial strength of the mercantile republics, but just how far he was from grasping the political basis of this strength is shown by the following passage from one of his memoranda:

> In credit, just as in military or legislative power, it is necessary that the supreme power reside in a single person and that all subsidiary powers are united in it, because the secret, the obedience, the expediency, the order and the union so necessary in the administration of the State depend on the unity of a single will. The credit of all the members of this State, united in the single person of the prince is infinitely stronger and more sound than that which depends on a multitude of disparate individuals.[37]

Law thought that France could have a financial revolution and not a political one. He did not understand that, in the end, the two were inseparable.

THE BUBBLE

The Mississippi scheme was at least redeemed by a grandiose, if untenable, economic vision. The same cannot be said of the reaction that it provoked across the Channel.

After 1715 Englishmen had taken to congratulating themselves on the intrinsic superiority of their public finances. In late 1719, the anonymous author of *The Chimera: Or the French Way of Paying National Debts, Laid Open,* summed up the prevailing view:

> It was many years ago since the French Court regretted very much the height of the Publick Credit in England, they looked upon it as the Great, and perhaps the only Advantage that England had over them in the War. . . . No superiority in the Field, could be a Match for this superiority of Treasure; for Money being the Basis of the War, in the Modern way of carrying such things on in the World, it had long since been a receiv'd Maxim in the Case of War, that the longest Purse, not the longest Sword, would be sure to Conquer at last. . . .
>
> It was in vain that the late King of France, tho' he had an Absolute Command of the Greatest, and at first the Wealthiest Nation in the World, tryed all the Methods, all the Arts that human Wit could Invent to raise a Fund of Credit

in his Kingdom. . . . This coy Mistress, call'd Credit, could never be woo'd; the more he follow'd her, the faster she fled from him, and he had the continual Mortification to see his National Credit fall. . . .

Our Credit here grew daily, and at last encreased to such a height, that from paying Twelve and Fourteen per Cent for Money, and struggling to get it brought in, we came to reducing the Interest from Six per Cent to Five per Cent, and now have the publick Command of what Money they pleased at Four per Cent.

But now, to his horror, an expatriate Scotsman—a prophet without honor in his own home—had suddenly turned the entire situation upside down:

But Fate and the Fortune of France has now turned the tables on us. . . . And thus in a moment their Debts are all vanish'd, the substance is answer'd by the Shadow; and the People of France are made the Instruments of putting the cheat upon themselves . . . transposing the Debts from the King to themselves, and, being contented to Discharge the Publick, owe the Money to one another.

Yet, as far as our writer was concerned, there was no question of copying the French "chimera":

And thus for once in the World, Tyranny has the whip-hand of Liberty; for nothing can be done in England like this, even the Parliament itself is limited, and there are the redeemable and unredeemable Funds, the last of which are a Burthen, nothing but the Number *Ninety Nine* (Years) can put an end to. . . .

Let no Man mistake me here, as if I were bewailing the Incumbrances of National Privileges, and suggesting that it was a pity we should be a Nation of Liberty with such a Burthen of Debt; on the other hand, let us be, say I, a free Nation deep in Debt, rather than a Nation of Slaves Owing nothing. . . .

. . . The Goodness of the Publick Credit in England, is the reason why we shall never be out of Debt; for where is the Man that, having lent his Money on the Credit of Parliamentary Security, will upon a whim, Discharge that Fund and take a precarious Company of Private Men for the Money?[38]

Brave words; and in some ways an astute analysis. But unfortunately, there were only too many public creditors ready to exchange their parliamentary security for the "precarious Company of Private Men."

Like the Mississippi Company, the South Sea Company is most famous for the speculative stock exchange bubble associated with its name. But underlying this timeless example of crowd psychology lay a struggle for control of the financial affairs of the country that is often forgotten. Fortunately, the South Sea Company went under, and the Bank of England survived. What would have happened had events turned out otherwise is impossible to state with precision; but given the unscrupulousness and shallowness of vision displayed by the principals of the company, it is unlikely that the political and financial stability of the country would have been improved.

It is not at all surprising that the directors of the South Sea Company drew inspiration from the experiments of John Law. After all, it was the South Sea Company that had provided the model for the flotation of the Mississippi Company, a vehicle to permit the government to change short-term into long-term debt by adding the lure of trading profits to the basic interest income. After their initial flotations, the shares of both companies had languished, since the hoped-for profits singularly failed to materialize. In one respect there was, perhaps, a fundamental difference between the two companies. The French company did have some real, if long-term, prospects. The English company had almost none. It had been founded on the illusion that Spain could be induced, as part of the peace settlement at the end of the war, to open up its highly lucrative monopoly of trade with its American empire. Yet the final treaty disappointed on this score. Apart from one slave ship per year, no trade was conceded. Indeed, it is hard to see how any Spanish regime could have done otherwise than to protect its monopoly to the death. It was, after all, still the government's major financial asset—perhaps more important than ever, given the drastic decline of the domestic economy. Daniel Defoe put the matter succinctly:

> Unless the Spaniards are to be divested of common sense . . . throwing way the only valuable stake they have left in the world, and in short, bent on their own ruin, we cannot suggest that they will ever part with so valuable, indeed so estimable a jewel, as the exclusive power of trade to their own plantations.[39]

As it turned out, the South Sea Company was never to garner any significant income from its international trade. The opening of the South American market had to wait for the overthrow of the Spanish Empire (with British support) one hundred years later. By that stage, the era of the great chartered companies was over, and the era of "free trade" had begun. It is true that by 1719 the share price of the South Sea Company had risen from its early level of 70 to 100 or better. This was not the result of increased profits, but merely of declining interest rates in England. Even when the yield on its government annuities was reduced from 6% to 5%, the price continued to rise over par. By 1718–1719, it was stable in the region of 116, giving a yield of 4.3%—more or less in line with other government rates.

The directors of the company were ambitious men who were scarcely to be satisfied with such a situation. They came originally from the Sword Blade Bank, a Tory-controlled institution that had long sought to take the place of the Whig-controlled Bank of England. The South Sea Company had been founded by the Tories to overturn the Bank of England's increasing monopoly on government funding. Indeed, it is unlikely that its promoters ever considered the South Sea trade anything but a springboard for their wider financial ambitions. But much to their irritation, after the initial success of the South Sea flotation, the Bank had resumed its progress. Harley's later lottery loans had been managed by the Bank, and it was now responsible for the redeemable 5%s which had been issued to refund them. By 1719 the Bank was responsible for managing almost the entire short-term debt, as well as £16.5 million of redeemables and its own £3.4 million perpetual annuities. All this was in addition to its profitable private banking business. By contrast, the South Sea Company was little more than a passive holding company for £9.2 million of perpetual annuities. After 1718, England was at war with Spain, and such meager trade as had hitherto taken place halted entirely. The events of 1719 in France may have come as a very unwelcome surprise to most in England, but to the directors of the South Sea Company they were a source of inspiration. If they could employ some of John Law's tactics to alleviate the burden of the English public debt, they might finally oust the Bank of England from its stronghold.

The conundrum for any such undertaking was how to persuade the holders of the irredeemable debt to surrender their privileges. It was this problem that had defeated Walpole in 1717. What the directors of the South Sea Company now grasped was that, with the shares of the Mississippi Company doubled in price since the autumn, most French rentiers had made considerable capital gains. Whatever skepticism many in England professed about the underlying prospects of the Mississippi Company, the spirit of speculation was infectious. Never before had there been a better time to propose the South Sea Company as a vehicle for tempting the holders of the irredeemables to surrender their stock.

There was also a political opening. The events of 1715 had ruined the Tory Party, which until then had constituted the natural majority within Parliament. Its leader, Bolingbroke, had been in secret negotiations with the Old Pretender (James Edward Stuart) and had fled abroad at the arrival of George I. All Tories were suddenly tarred with the brush of treason; and for a party that prided itself on loyalty to the crown above all things, this was a death knell. Party members with an eye for self-preservation rapidly changed allegiance; and none had a keener sense of self-preservation than the directors of the South Sea Company. But, of course, none of this altered the old personal and institutional rivalries. In late 1717, the pure Whig government, in which Robert Walpole had been Chancellor of the Exchequer, fell out of favor. The new administration under the Earl of Sunderland installed John Aislabie as chancellor. Aislabie was a converted Tory from Harley's day whose views were far more favorable to the interests of his old party friends. In many ways the events of 1720 were the final opening for the erstwhile Tories to prove themselves capable of beating the Whigs at their own game.

The leaders of the scheme were a small group of directors and officers of the South Sea Company and the Sword Blade Bank, which was familiarly referred to as the Junto. At the very center of this cabal were Sir John Blunt, the founder of the company, and Robert Knight, its secretary. Blunt was now a member of Parliament and a well-known figure. Knight was less well-known, but no less important,

> a man of exceptional abilities, unlimited ambition and complete lack of scruple. . . . History has been slow to recognize him as a central figure. . . . But when the ruins of the scheme were examined, he was found to have made more out of it than anybody else. . . . Blunt provided cunning, bluster and technical draftsmanship, but Knight's was the power of innovation, charm and ingenuity that made the thing possible, and these he shared with Law, whom we now know to have been his close acquaintance, if not his friend.[40]

Knight may have been a close acquaintance of John Law, but to compare the two men is certainly to insult the Scotsman. Indeed, Law, with his capacious political and macroeconomic vision, understood that his plan was entirely inappropriate for England. France was in the depths of an economic depression and could easily handle (or so he thought) a strong dose of monetary stimulus. In addition, France required a radical change in its methods of public finance if it was to compete with the new Anglo-Dutch axis. By contrast, in 1719, England was enjoying an economic boom, which was already in danger of overheating. There could be no justification for the kind of credit boom that the Junto was to copy from Law's operations in France. Besides, England had already more or less completed its financial revolution. The irredeemable annuities were, from a long-term perspective, merely a minor inconvenience. The country had no need for wild debt-conversion schemes.

Throughout the second half of 1719, the Junto and the government ministers were in secret discussions. But although some rumors were in the air, when Aislabie announced in Parliament on January 21, 1720, that the South Sea Company was preparing a proposal to take over the entire national debt on favorable terms, his announcement was received in stunned silence. Some backbench enemies of the company proposed that the Bank of England should be invited to present a plan as well. This suggestion was little to the liking of the government, but they were forced to accede. As a result, on January 27, Parliament was presented with not one, but two proposals for refunding the entire £31.6 million of public debt not held by the chartered companies:

> The Corporation of the Gouvernour and Company of Marchants of Great Britain trading to the South-Seas and other Parts of America, and for Encouraging the Fishery, having under their Consideration how they may be most serviceable to His Majesty and His Government; and to shew their Zeal and Readiness to concur in the Great and Honourable Design of Reducing the National Debts.[41]

The South Sea Company's proposal was couched in roseate prose; the Bank's was rather more businesslike in presentation. But their substance was largely similar. Undoubtedly the Bank, which had been caught quite unawares, was merely concerned to outdo its rival at its own game. Both corporations proposed to exchange the debts in the hands of the public for their own shares. Both offered to cancel the debts thus exchanged for perpetual redeemable annuities paying 5%. Both sought authorization to issue shares with a nominal value equal to the debts exchanged. Most critically, neither specified the number of shares it would offer the debtholders. Because both their stocks were selling above par, they would be able to satisfy the debtholders with less than the total amount of shares authorized. The rest could therefore be sold in the market for cash.

This was the true excitement. The exchange of nonredeemable for redeemable debt was already a substantial benefit, which would lead to significant future interest savings. But both companies also offered a cash bonus to the state, which would derive from their ability to sell their excess shares in the market. The South Sea Company offered £3.5 million. The Bank offered up to £5.55 million, depending on the amount of debt exchanged. It was able to offer more than its rival for the simple reason that its shares were selling at around 150, whereas the South Sea shares were trading at no more than 130. It would therefore be able to satisfy the debtholders with fewer shares and have more left over to sell in the market. The Bank's offer had another advantage for the state. It proposed that each

£100 of ninety-nine-year annuities that it failed to bring in would automatically cancel double that amount in newly authorized stock. This would make it virtually impossible for the Bank to go ahead without exchanging the irredeemables, which was, after all, the original object of the exercise. The South Sea Company offered no such guarantee.

The Bank had delivered a very sharp setback to its enemy. But neither the Junto nor its allies in the government were about to surrender. Indeed, the inclusion of the cash offers to the state had made this a fight to the death. The money collected by the government could be used as a threat to force the redeemable annuity holders to convert or face redemption. If not needed for that purpose, the money could be used to redeem other debts—including the annuities held by the losing bidder. Both sides risked seeing the other end up with control of the very large majority of the national debt and themselves reduced to virtual insignificance. To make the stakes even plainer, the South Sea Company included an offer to underwrite £1 million of Exchequer bills free of charge—a direct challenge to the Bank's monopoly of this business.

A further round in this extraordinary auction of the national debt was ordered by the government. On February 1, the parties presented revised bids. The South Sea Company put its finger on the moving spirit of the times by focusing its improvements on the cash kickback. This was raised to £4 million fixed, plus a further amount of up to £3.57 million, depending on the number of the ninety-nine-year annuities exchanged. The state now stood to gain £7.57 million, or around 15% of the entire debt. In order to give some guarantee on the conversion of the irredeemables, the company offered to pay the equivalent of one year's interest for each amount not exchanged.

If the South Sea Company's second offer was far more daring than its first; the Bank's second offer was, if anything, more cautious. The cash offer to the state was slightly raised to £5.67 million, but unlike the South Sea offering, it remained entirely dependent on the number of annuities exchanged. More critically, the Bank now specified the number of shares it would offer to the various classes of creditors. For the £31.6 million of exchangeable debts, the Bank would give £26.9 million new shares (at nominal value). This would leave £4.7 million shares to be sold to the public. These were generous terms, which gave a reasonable assurance of success to the whole scheme. The break-even point was around 121—a price that would produce enough cash for the government's *douceur* and leave debtholders with shares worth no less than their old securities. Although the cash payment to the government would tend to dilute the share price, it is unlikely that it would have fallen this far. At a price of 130 the shares would still have yielded around 4%. Although this would have been a fall of 20 points from the price prevailing before the exchange, it would still have made sense to the Bank's directors. Their action was largely defensive, and it was far better to dilute the Bank's profitable banking monopoly by the addition of vast numbers of new shareholders than to risk the victory of its rival.

The South Sea Company's offer finished off with a plea for preference and an offer to match any other offer,

> flattering themselves that the Readiness and Cheerfulness that engaged them so much earlier than any other Society, to endeavour to reduce the great Debt under which this Nation is Oppressed, will Intitle them to the favour and preference of this House, since they are willing and do hereby declare they are ready to undertake this great work upon whatever Terms may be offered by another Company.[42]

They need not have bothered. Parliament paid scant attention to the details of the Bank's offer and focused entirely on the big figure of £7.5 million. Of course, there were many public creditors in Parliament, but the larger majority still consisted of the same country squires that had supported Harley in 1710. The country members had little understanding of the intricacies of finance, but they did understand that high public debt meant high taxes. Any offer that promised to reduce the land and excise taxes had their support, and the South Sea Company's offer seemed the most generous. They also had a deep and enduring suspicion of the Bank. There was not even a long debate on the issue: the South Sea Company's offer was carried by acclamation.

The next day South Sea stock rose to 160 and beyond, while Bank stock fell sharply. Everyone agreed that the Bank's era was over. This was not quite the end of the issue, however. An act of Parliament had to be drafted and given the formal approval of the Commons, the Lords, and the king. This was not ready until March 23, and the Bank and its allies fought a rearguard action. Their method of attack was to demand that the South Sea Company specify the terms of its offer to the debtholders—something that the company resolutely refused to do. The reason it refused goes to the heart of the debacle that was about to occur.

First, it is necessary to understand that there was no obvious reason why shares of the new megacompany should have a significantly different value, whichever of the two contenders won. The government would pay 5% on a capital of £31.6 million to either successful bidder. This income of £1.58 million would be added to the existing annuity income of the winner (also at 5%). The revenues of the successful bidder from its holdings of public debt were therefore quite predictable and would dwarf any other sources of income that it might have. True, the Bank had a slight advantage because of the profits from its banking business; but these profits would be totally insignificant compared to its interest income from the government.

The Bank, with considerable shrewdness, had pitched its bid at the highest possible level compatible with good sense. It had left itself just enough leeway to sell the residual shares at a price that reflected the likely long-term value of the enlarged company. By offering £2 million more, the directors of the South Sea Company had thrown caution to the winds. If they offered the public debtholders the same number of shares as the Bank, they would be left with the unenviable prospect of having to sell the residual shares at just over 161 in order to fund their obligations to the government. Yet who would buy them, when the underlying value of the company was unlikely to be more than 125?[43]

Of course, the directors of the South Sea Company were not about to allow themselves to be cornered into matching the Bank's offer—whatever the rhetoric of their second proposal. It would have been the end of their bid, and both they and the Bank's supporters knew it. The next weeks witnessed some of the most shameless acts of bribery in the history of Britain. Robert Knight opened a "green book" in which he recorded allocations of shares (shares that were not yet issued and did not have to be paid for until later) to those in high places. The Earl of Sunderland, the leader of the government, received £50,000 at a price of 175. Chancellor Aislabie received £20,000 at 170. Secretary of State Craggs was put down for £30,000 at 175. Twenty-seven members of Parliament "bought" £81,000. Six peers of the realm divided £38,000 between them. And to round matters off, the Duchess of Kendall—the king's mistress—and her two daughters were granted £12,000 each at a price of 154. Whether some also went directly to the king and the Prince of Wales is not known, but certainly not unlikely. The in-built profit on these shares was £400,000 at the time of issue.[44]

The debate in the Commons on March 23 lasted six hours. All the heavyweights were there. Sound financial minds such as Robert Walpole and Archibald Hutcheson led the opposition, but to no avail. The spirit of speculation had already taken hold. In vain, they warned that the current price of the South Sea stock—which fluctuated feverishly between 270 and 380 during the debate—bore no relation to underlying values:[45]

> If the truth be, as I verily believe it is, that there is no Foundation for the present, much less the further expected, high Price of South Sea Stock, and that the Frenzy which now reigns, can be of no long Continuance . . . is not the Duty of a British Senate to take all necessary Precautions, to prevent the Ruin of many Thousands of Families?[46]

An amendment was tabled to force the company to fix the terms of its exchange offer. Chancellor Aislabie endlessly repeated the party line that, if the offer were fixed, the price of the company's stock would fall and endanger the entire operation. Of course, this was true. In the absence of a valid financial justification for the South Sea exchange, the only incentive could be the possibility of speculative gains such as those enjoyed by the shareholders of the Mississippi Company. A falling price would soon erode the purely speculative appeal of the South Sea shares and expose the lack of fundamentals. But Parliament did not consider this implication of Aislabie's argument. The completion of the transaction seemed essential for the nation's future; therefore Walpole and his allies were ignored. The amendment was soundly rejected. To rub salt into the Bank's wound, the House voted two days later that all its annuities save the original £1.2 million would be redeemed in the next year.[47]

It is possible that the South Sea directors had originally planned a prudent exchange that might have succeeded. Certainly their original "sweetener" of £3.5 million was quite affordable. Perhaps the bidding competition with the Bank had forced up the ante to a point where the only way to complete the exchange was through a speculative boom. In other words, the company found itself in the same position as John Law when he set the issue price of the Mississippi Company at 5,000 instead of a more realistic 2,500.

Unfortunately, there is no evidence that this theory is correct. The inner ring of South Sea and Sword Blade directors had no grand economic vision such as that which inspired John Law. They were motivated by a desire for power and money. While they probably had little idea of how far the South Sea stock would rise in the heady atmosphere of 1720, they had always planned to have as much free stock as possible to sell at a "profit." Their idea was not to have just enough to satisfy the requirements of the sweetener, but enough to raise a very large amount of cash for the company.

It may seem odd to modern ears that the sale of shares should be viewed as a "profit" to the existing shareholders; but almost every pamphlet of the time expressed it in this way. Perhaps the world of joint stock companies was still too young for modern accounting principles to have taken root. Perhaps the fact that the cash offers by the company could be considered a "profit" for the public purse misled people into thinking of the entire proceeds of the share sales as a "profit" for the company. Whatever the reason, it was this misconception that was at the center of the general madness that was overtaking the country.

Taken to its illogical extreme, the failure to consider the dilution caused by the new shares issued in exchange for all this cash led to a belief in

> this extraordinary Paradox, *viz.* That the higher the Price is which is given for South-Sea Stock, the greater Benefit the Purchasers have thereby; and that 300 £ per Cent, it is intrinsically Worth 448 £, and at 600 £ is Worth 880 £.

In other words—if the new shares are not taken into account—the higher the share issue price, the greater the amount of cash raised, and the greater the assets per share. This was pure nonsense, and an anonymous MP (almost undoubtedly Archibald Hutcheson) railed against it in an answering pamphlet:

> [Under such reasoning] there is nothing left for the Purchasers of the said remaining Stock [sold to general public] but the Pleasure and Satisfaction of having made a generous Present to the Proprietors of the said United Capital . . . of the immense sum of 61,973,242 £ 13s. If this Computer intended to be understood thus, must he not think that the Purchasers of the remaining Stock . . . will be deprived of all Common Sense and Understanding? But if he intended to make them believe that their Stock would also be worth 448 £ 15s per cent, was there ever such a delusion from the beginning of the World to the 9th of April, 1720?[48]

Allowing for the shares that would be issued to the cash subscribers, the anonymous author recalculated the assets per share at £221 rather £448 and stated tartly that "this, surely is sufficient Gain to the Proprietors of the Old Stock, and sufficient Loss to the Purchasers of the New."

Well, even if this was the greatest "delusion from the beginning of the World to the 9th of April, 1720," it was to be handsomely surpassed by August. One's eye lights immediately on the fantastic sum of nearly £62 million that the company hoped to raise. To put this sum in perspective, it is only necessary to recall that the GNP of Britain at the time is now estimated to have been around £60 million. Yet, in spite of its inherent implausibility, the underlying calculation was simple enough. At a price of 300, £31 million pounds of public debts could be exchanged for only £10.3 million of South Sea shares. This would leave £20.7 million shares to be sold at 300 and hey presto! a value of around £62 million appears.

It is here that the South Sea Bubble most clearly differs from the Mississippi scheme. John Law never raised surplus cash from the public. All the 1.7 billion livres raised by the Mississippi Company went to the government to re-fund its debt (apart from a small portion to buy the right to operate the mint). The value of the Mississippi stock was based on its promise to pay a 4% dividend on the issue price of 5,000 livres—the same yield as the previous interest on the public debt. Even if 4% was hard to achieve in the short term, 3% was more than possible, and if dividends on the shares owned by the crown and the Banque Royale were deferred for at least the first year, the other shareholders could be paid in full. By contrast, the South Sea Company had revenues that would support a dividend of only 1.67% for debtholders who exchanged their annuities at 300. The only argument with even the superficial appearance of logic that could be made on behalf of the exchange was that the cash raised by the company through its issues of new shares would be reinvested in some highly profitable manner to increase this basic income or would perhaps be distributed to shareholders in an enormous dividend. Of course, most debtholders did not make any such calculation but merely acted in the hope of trading out at a profit.

Either way, it is hard not to suspect that the English investors were even more deluded than the French. It was not at 300 that the exchange was made and shares were sold, but at prices far—in some cases, almost unimaginably—higher. On April 14, a first share issue was made—to cash subscribers only—at 300. This served to raise some funds and to stoke up interest in the larger issues later. The bulk of the ninety-nine-year irredeemables were exchanged in the second issue on May 19 at a price of 375, while cash subscribers paid 400. After that, the market really took off, reaching 600 by the end of May and 950 by the end of June. The third subscription, again open only to cash subscribers, was made in June at a price of 1,000. In August, a final issue took place to mop up the redeemables and the remaining irredeemables as well as to raise still more cash. This issue, too, was sold at 1,000. The price of 300 mooted in late March appeared as the distant, and now outmoded, product of negative thinking.

In February, the Bank had offered £26.9 million of shares in exchange for £31.6 million of debts. By August, the South Sea Company had been able to exchange £26 million of debts for only £8.5 million of equity. It therefore had £17.5 million of shares left to dispose of, nearly four times the amount that the Bank had planned to sell. The company had been able to sell only half the shares by the time the bubble burst, but the amounts subscribed amounted to no less than £75 million.[49] The seemingly fantastic figures suggested in April had been considerably too low!

Subscribed, not paid. It was inconceivable, of course, that an amount considerably in excess of GNP could ever have been paid. The total money supply in the country was generally reckoned to be no more than £15 million. There was only one way of creating even the illusion of payment, and that was through credit. Here the Junto borrowed directly from John Law. Each issue was on progressively easier payment terms. The first was payable over sixteen months; the second over twenty-seven months. The third issue—by far the largest at £50 million—was payable over fifty-four months. The fourth witnessed a very slight shortening of terms to forty-five months. These were even more generous terms than those allowed by Law. In addition, the Junto used another of Law's tactics by employing the Sword Blade Bank to finance speculation. By June the bank was lending £400 per share, even against partially paid shares. In other words, a subscriber could put down £1,000 for £10,000 of shares (the rest payable over fifty-four months) and immediately borrow £4,000 against his investment.[50]

The scenes in London in 1720 rivaled anything that Paris had offered in 1719. Indeed, a great deal of smart money had now left Paris, dragging down the exchange value of the livre in its wake, and had headed for Exchange Alley. Like the informal chaos of the rue Quincampoix, dealings in South Sea stock avoided the Royal Exchange and took place in the narrow alleys and coffeehouses of the neighboring streets. As in France, the regular market participants were soon joined by a wave of foreign investors, and by every sort of local amateur, down to the least sophisticated. All sorts of rival promotions started up to take advantage of the seemingly endless supply of money and willingness to speculate. Some of these were valid and intelligent schemes, such as those for insurance or for ironworks. Some were far too futuristic for the time but have since come to fruition in other hands, such as gold mines in "Terra Australis." Others were mere hoaxes, none of which has become more famous than the "Company for carrying on an Undertaking of great Advantage, but Nobody to know what it is."*

More than one hundred of these lesser bubbles were started in May and

*Sadly, John Carswell, author of two definitive studies of the Bubble, states that he cannot find any clear evidence that this most notorious investment prospectus in financial history ever existed.

early June, and they threatened to siphon off money from the massive third issue planned by the Junto. Parliament obligingly passed the Bubble Act, banning joint stock companies except those already officially chartered.

Compared to the Banque Royale, the Sword Blade Bank was not a powerful tool of money creation. Nor was the Bank of England in a mood to help its rivals. This saved England from the rampant general inflation experienced in France. Indeed, the Junto had no desire to finance ventures other than its own; this was the reason for the Bubble Act, after all. But it was inconceivable that price rises could be confined to stocks and shares. Land prices rose to fifty times rental income, just as they had in France, as successful punters attempted to salt away their gains. Perhaps this was barely surprising when there were delirious pamphleteers proposing, in all seriousness, that the company "should purchase all the land in the kingdom."[51]

It was certainly very hard to keep one's head when all around were losing theirs. Isaac Newton sold out in April, stating that he could predict the motion of the heavens but not the madness of the people. Thomas Guy, an original shareholder from 1711, sold out in May and June, accepting prices significantly below the market in order to be paid in hard cash. His proceeds were £234,000, and it has sometimes been stated that the founding of Guy's Hospital was the only redeeming feature of the whole debacle.[52] Archibald Hutcheson continued to inveigh against the blindness of the speculators to the lack of underlying value. Some 20% of the irredeemable holders kept their heads on their shoulders and their assets in their safes. But many others had their judgment blurred by the contagion of the fever. Robert Walpole, who had sold out in March at below 200, could not prevent himself from being sucked back into the frenzy and avoided subscribing for the final issue only by pure good fortune. Even the Bank of England tendered £290,000 of its annuities in the last exchange offer.[53] This must have given the sweetest satisfaction to John Blunt and his coterie.

Of course, it could not last any more than the Mississippi Company boom could. The crunch occurred as the subscription payments started to take their toll in the autumn. It was accompanied by the rapid transfer of hard cash overseas by smart investors (many of them foreign) seeking to remove their profits to safe havens. The pound collapsed, just as the livre had collapsed in the spring. By late September, the South Sea Company was forced to seek the help of the Bank of England—little more than a month after the moment when the Junto had gloated over the Bank's apparent surrender. On September 24, the Sword Blade Bank closed its doors. The process of mopping up had started in England as it had in France. South Sea shares were selling for under 200 by the end of the year—although this price still reflected a certain residue of forlorn optimism. The shares were finally to settle back to the modest level of 100 at which they had started.

The subsequent histories of France and Britain have been enlivened by a considerable number of financial disasters and market crashes. The French Revolution was to create financial chaos every bit as devastating as that of the Mississippi scheme. But it is doubtful whether, in purely financial terms, even the Revolution surpassed the events of 1719–1720 for sheer exuberance and excess. In Britain it is impossible to find any other event that comes close to the South Sea Bubble. The scale of the figures involved speaks for itself. Several have been given already, but one more is worth including. At the time of the fourth share issue in August, the theoretical market value of the South Sea Company was in the region of £280 million. This was more than four times the GNP of the country at the time. To put this figure in perspective, it is only necessary to observe that the market value of all the British stocks and government bonds quoted on the London Stock Exchange at the height of the Internet bubble was no more than two and one-half times present-day GNP.

SIX

THE DILEMMA

Yes, Gentlemen, I have no fear of repeating it, . . . it is the public debt that is the germ of our liberty.

—Mirabeau, addressing the National Assembly, August 27, 1789

The storm subsided. Credulity gave way to incredulity as the speculators surveyed the debris of their shattered dreams. In Paris, the revulsion against the whole Mississippi episode was so deep-seated that all records of the great system were publicly burned. Gradually calm was restored, and as time passed, it became possible to see the events of the period as a timeless monument to human weakness and folly, and as a timely reminder to governments to confine themselves to financial orthodoxy. In the decades after 1720, at least until the memories of the scarred generation faded, both Britain and France pursued conservative financial policies in their different ways. War was avoided, budgets were balanced (or nearly balanced), currencies were stabilized, and debt reduction was left to the slow and automatic functioning of the sinking fund (in Britain), and to the equally slow and automatic death toll of rentiers (in France).

Did this mean that public debt would never again cause convulsions as great as those experienced in the years around 1720? Most certainly not. On August 16, 1788, the Bourbon monarchy announced the partial suspension of payments of its obligations. By the standards of some other Bourbon defaults, this was a mere hiccup. The financial situation was grave, but not as grave as in 1596, 1708, or 1715. After the initial panic, the markets stabilized. In the following months, investors appeared to see the suspension as a temporary and tactical move (the equivalent perhaps of the shutdown of the U.S. government during the budgetary standoff between President Bill Clinton and the Republican-dominated Congress in the winter of 1995) and remained relatively stable. Yet the ancien régime, which had proved so remarkably resilient in the face of the financial crises of the beginning of the century, could not survive an apparently lesser one at its end. The default of 1788 ushered in the revolution of 1789, and Mirabeau was not alone in blessing the debt that many saw as the Achilles' heel of the regime—the fatal weakness that finally led to its demise.

What had happened during the course of the century to alter so radically the political arithmetic of public finance? The impoverished France of 1710–1720, ruled first by an unpopular king, and then by a minor, was able to withstand probably the most serious financial crisis of the Bourbon dynasty without political upheaval. The considerably more prosperous France of the 1780s, ruled by a by no means unpopular king, then in his prime, was not able to surmount a lesser financial crisis without undergoing the greatest political convulsion in European history. The reason goes to the very heart of this book.

MOPPING UP

While it is true that both the English and the French governments returned to financial orthodoxy after 1720, their view of what constituted orthodoxy differed. In France, the fall of Law was accompanied by the return of the indigenous financiers, led by Pâris Duvernay, who now assumed the office of Controleur des Finances. At the height of his power, Law had suggested that the *gens d'affaires* and officeholders would be better employed in the private sector. Yet while history was clearly on his side in the long term, in the immediate aftermath of the debacle of 1720 the old order appeared to have had the greater foresight. The failure of the system could therefore only reinforce the grip of the *financiers* on the fiscal apparatus of the French state.

A return to the tried and true was accompanied by a suspicion of banks and stock exchanges that bordered on abhorrence. The informal market of the rue Quincampoix (which had moved on to several other temporary venues during the course of 1720) was closed. It was replaced in 1724 by a new, official exchange, a stodgy affair with licensed brokers and limited trading hours. The Banque Royale was closed down and had no successors. The very words *banque* and *banquier* became terms of abuse. The days when Paris appeared set to rival London and even Amsterdam as a financial center were over. The era of the archetypal Frenchman favoring a safe accumulation of gold under the mattress had begun.

A conservative mind-set was also evident in the methods used to unscramble the mass of paper and contracts bequeathed by the system. The objective, as far as was possible, was to return to the status quo ante. A start had been made, if reluctantly, by Law himself in his last six months in power from June to December 1720. Mississippi Company shares held by the Banque Royale were annulled, and banknotes were progressively exchanged for a new series of government rentes. In February 1721 a commission was established to inspect all contracts and claims. Land that had been sold for notes could be repurchased at the old prices. Officeholders returned to their offices, and the Mississippi Company was reduced to the level of a trading concern without further pretensions. Rentiers who had exchanged their old annuities for shares were given credit for an equal amount of the new rentes. Those deemed speculators (*Mississippiens*), however, were treated very differently. Their claims were subject to drastic reductions amounting to just over 1 billion livres; and in 1722 a special tax, levied on those new fortunes that had escaped the net, raised 188 million. (Needless to say, it was precisely the nouveaux riches who suffered most. Well-placed courtiers who had managed to augment their estates through speculation generally contrived to hold onto their gains.) After the commission had completed its work, its records were burned in great public bonfires so as to forestall any appeals and to close the whole distasteful chapter.

Equally traditional was the final resolution to the debt crisis inherited from Louis XIV's wars that had been the cause of so much chaos. The principle, as stated in a justificatory royal edict, was clear: "It was resolved to reduce the public debts to a proportion such as our State could support."[1] The financial turmoil of the years after 1718 had only served to increase total claims on the government. Some 3 billion livres of notes, company shares, and rentes were investigated by the commission. By 1724, this great mass of paper claims had been reduced to around 1.64 billion livres of rentes. But the interest on this debt was no more than 47 million—31 million on perpetual annuities paying 2.5% and 16 million on life annuities paying 4%. Including a small amount of life annuity debt that had escaped the Mississippi debacle, the government's total interest bill now came to 51.5 million livres—little more than half the (already reduced) amount payable at the death of Louis XIV.[2] Equally significant was the devaluation of the livre. The currency that Desmarets had struggled in 1714–1715 to restore to its prewar level of 8.3 grams of silver had sunk as low as 2 grams in mid-1720. The progressive cancellation of the Banque Royale notes allowed the silver parity to be raised to around 3.5 grams in 1721. The final stabilization was in 1726 at 4.45 grams—still an overall decline of nearly 50% from the days of Colbert.

It is impossible to calculate accurately the cumulative effect of all the debt reductions from Desmarets to Pâris Duvernay. But it is a fair assumption that for the typical rentier they would have resulted in a loss of at least three-quarters of the amount originally contracted in hard currency terms. This was almost certainly the most extreme financial setback suffered by the creditor class in the history of the ancien régime. Had the whole loss been imposed on them in 1715, there might truly have been a revolt of the rentiers reminiscent of the Fronde. But the main losses were incurred in the aftermath of the System, and in the wake of this failed experiment, the creditor class displayed an understandable aversion to radical action of any sort and was content to salvage what it could. In this unintended way alone, John Law may be said to have helped the regime to survive.

In some ways the results across the Channel appeared comparable to those in France. Many bondholders lost very considerable portions of their investments, and the government had to face the accusation that it had connived in, or at the very least failed to prevent, the defrauding of its creditors. The flight of John Law from France was mirrored by the flight of Robert Knight from England. The confiscation of Law's assets and the treatment of the *Mississippiens* were paralleled in England by the confiscation of the assets of the directors of the South Sea Company—parvenus and nouveaux riches to a man. As in France the highly equivocal position of the leading aristocratic members of the government and of the royal family itself was swept conveniently under the rug. It was Robert Walpole's subtle pirouette, appearing to seek the repatriation of Robert Knight while ensuring that he stayed safely abroad with his potentially embarrassing revelations, that ensured the enduring support in high places that was one of the principal props of his twenty-two-year regime. In the meantime, the £7.5 million public profit that had been the glittering prize at the end of the South Sea scheme was allowed to drop, just as the *trésor du roi* tacitly disappeared in the unwinding of Law's system. If the terms *banque* and *banquier* became anathema in France, so did the term *joint stock company* in England. It was not until 1802 that Napoleon founded the Banque de

France,* and it was not until 1824 that the Bubble Act, which required all corporations to be specifically authorized by act of Parliament, was rescinded.

Underneath these superficial similarities, the resolution of the crisis had fundamentally different implications in England. While the shareholders, creditors, and debts of the South Sea Company were not left to sort out their positions solely according to their original contracts, there was no attempt to return to the status quo ante. In October, Robert Walpole returned to office as the now-vindicated opponent of the scheme, and as the only influential Whig with the financial acumen to rescue the government from the hole which it had dug for itself and for the regime. Walpole soon realized that stability would never be restored if the web of claims and counterclaims were left to the workings of the legal system, and if the government did not take a lead in resolving the crisis. In the end, his solution followed the line of least resistance. Unpaid subscription installments were canceled entirely, as were 90% of all amounts borrowed against subscriptions. The company's newly authorized shares were then distributed as if the amounts actually received had been subscribed at a uniform £300 per share. This did much to alleviate the distress of cash subscribers, since they generally had paid in only their first installments. The remaining unissued shares were then distributed pro rata among the shareholders. In the meantime, the government dropped its claim to the £7.5 million that it was owed by the company, in spite of the howls from the Tory backbenches. The assets of the directors of the South Sea Company and the Sword Blade Bank were confiscated, apart from amounts deemed sufficient for survival, and assigned to the South Sea Company for the general benefit of the shareholders.

Walpole's actions did much to save the cash subscribers, and to a lesser extent the public creditors, from the consequences of their folly. But it did not save them entirely. There was no attempt to give the creditors back their old annuities, or the cash subscribers back their money. They were left with shares in a vastly expanded South Sea Company which now sank back to the price levels from which they had so recently risen. By late 1721 the shares were trading at no better than 100. Even allowing for the extra

*The Banque de France had been preceded by the Caisse d'Escomptes, founded in 1776. This performed a useful, if limited, service to the government during the last stages of the ancien régime. It is no coincidence, however, that the bank's founder—like Law, a foreign Protestant—did not use the dread word *banque* in its title. He preferred to refer back to Colbert's creation of the previous century, which was altogether less suspect.

shares that the new shareholders had received in exchange, they faced substantial losses on their investments. The ninety-nine-year annuitants had done best, since their annuities had been valued so highly in the exchange. But even they now held assets worth 25% less than before. The thirty-two-year annuity holders received only 43% of their old income, albeit now in perpetuity. The redeemable bondholders had suffered losses of nearly 50%—losses all the more painful since the government had never had any valid interest in refinancing this portion of its debt. The cash subscribers also found themselves the poorer to the tune of nearly half the amounts paid in.[3]

Who were the gainers? Since the government made no attempt to overturn private sales and purchases, there were many fortunes that had been made, to offset those that had been lost. These cannot be evaluated globally. The government itself must be counted among the winners, notwithstanding the loss of its £7.5 million windfall and the slight increase in its nominal debt. Its interest bill fell by £30,000 immediately, and more significantly by a further £370,000 when the interest rate was lowered to 4% in 1727. Moreover, it had achieved its original objective of making almost all its debt redeemable at will; here, at least it was unwilling to allow investors to recast their actions with the benefit of hindsight. Of course, the principal gainers were the old shareholders of the South Sea Company. Although the share price fell back to levels no better than those prevailing in 1719, the extra stock that they received in the distribution on 1721 allowed them to increase their income by better than 50%. The main financial result of the South Sea scandal was therefore a redistribution of income from one group of public creditors to another.

Thus the rules of the free market, and of the sanctity of private contracts, were not totally overturned. And it is also notable that there was, in England, a considerable reluctance to tamper with the due process of law at all. As the Commons noted in their resolutions:

> When we first entered into consideration of this extensive and perplexed affair, we thought it most advisable to leave every man's property to be determined by due course of law; and were of the opinion that no relief or abatement could properly be prescribed or given, but from the South Sea Company.[4]

This was in total contrast to France, where the guiding principle was to overturn as far as possible every transaction that had occurred in the past two years, and where the gains of speculators were deliberately annulled or taxed away. Any attempt to reduce the burden of debt through the operations of the free market was abandoned, and the government returned to the well-worn path of resolving its problems by partial repudiations of principal and by the unilateral imposition of below-market interest rates.

The South Sea Bubble therefore did less harm to Britain than the Mississippi scheme to France. True, the Bubble Act of 1720 acted as a drag on the Industrial Revolution in its early phase. True, also, that the government felt such residual embarrassment about the losses suffered by so many of its creditors that it delayed further reducing the interest on its debt even when the market permitted. But the main result of the debacle was, perversely, to reinforce the new political and financial order that had evolved since 1688. As in France, the government eschewed great financial experiments and returned to the tried and true. But in England this meant a return to the by now well-understood practices of "Dutch" finance, not to the considerably less flexible and more costly methods of the ancien régime.

Nowhere was the difference in outcomes more obvious than in the consolidation of the position of the Bank of England. Within the space of a few weeks, a threat to its very existence had been followed by the humiliation of its rival. By the second half of September, the South Sea Company had been forced to fall on its mercy. A tentative arrangement was made for the Bank to buy £3 million of the company's shares so as to provide it with liquidity. One of the conditions for this concession was that the company's cash should henceforth be kept at the Bank of England and not at the Sword Blade. "If the South Sea Company is to be wedded to the Bank, it cannot be allowed to keep a mistress," declared Sir Gilbert Heathcote, the Bank's chief negotiator, thus sealing the fate of the "mistress," which was forced to close its doors four days later. In the credit crisis that ensued, and that threatened even the Bank, this rescue package was never completed, but it marked the end to any further threat to the Bank's preeminence in government finance. A second proposal, to reallocate half the company's assets and shareholders between the Bank and the East India Company, also failed to materialize. In the end, the South Sea Company did indeed emerge as the single largest holder of the national debt, with £33 million out of a total of around £54 million,[5] but little good it did. By this stage the company was largely a shell. In 1723, half its capital was converted into perpetual annuities, since its new shareholders had little interest in anything more than the regular receipt of their reduced incomes. A decade later, most of the remaining capital was similarly converted, and in 1750, the company ceased trading and became a mere appendage of the Exchequer.

By contrast, the Bank of England emerged with an enlarged capital of

£9 million and a virtual monopoly of government borrowing. The Exchequer bills were found to be such a convenient and cheap method of short-term funding that others were sidelined. The issue and management of new long-term debt was also entrusted to this bulwark of the regime. By 1750, 83% of all public debts other than those of the South Sea Company were administered by the Bank.

THE RULING CLASS

The refunding of the public debt in the form of redeemable perpetual annuities, and its management by a bank controlled exclusively by mercantile interests, formed only one side of the political-financial equation that underlay "Dutch finance." The other side was political and is best expressed in Saint-Simon's description of England as a country, like the Dutch Republic, "where the finances are absolutely governed by those who furnish them." In other words, the government itself was also under the sway of the same mercantile class that controlled the Bank of England. This is obviously a more complicated proposition to sustain. The directors of the Bank of England did not feature as members of the cabinets of the eighteenth century. By and large, governments were formed from members of the landed classes, who continued to hold the vast majority of the national wealth. Certainly the government of Britain cannot be compared directly with that of the mercantile republics, where the rulers of the state were themselves merchants and bankers. In Genoa, the ten thousand shareholders of the Casa di San Giorgio were virtually identical to the citizen body. The same identity of citizens and creditors also prevailed in the Dutch Republic. It took a long time for anything similar to occur in Britain. In the middle of the eighteenth century, there were fifty thousand to sixty thousand public creditors. This was not an unimpressive figure, but it was modest in relation to an electorate of close to 300,000.[6] It took the massive borrowing of the Napoleonic Wars to expand the ownership of public debt to a point where the creditors constituted a majority of the electorate. In a primarily agricultural country such as eighteenth-century Britain, the modus vivendi that held together the very disparate elements of the ruling class was necessarily complex compared to the sociopolitical arrangements of the mercantile republics.

Robert Walpole was the architect of the compromise between the landed and mercantile interests which was the backbone of the country's new strength. That he was throughout his life a staunch Whig should not obscure this characteristic of his regime. He was helped, of course, by the near-total rout of the Tories. The ambivalence of some of their leaders toward the Hanoverian succession in 1714 had started their relegation to the status of a rump opposition. The bursting of the South Sea Bubble exposed as futile their hopes of a valid alternative to influence of the Bank of England. Even though it was a nominally Whig government that had proposed the scheme, it was commonly understood that neither the company's directors nor Chancellor Aislabie were true Whigs at heart. Any success that Robert Harley may have had in altering perceptions of the Tories as a party of financial naïfs was quite destroyed by the failure of his pet creation. Although there was still a considerable body of opinion that saw the national debt as a burden unnecessarily imposed by the alliance of William III with the Whigs, it was also acknowledged that, since they had got the country into its present mess, only they were capable of getting it out again. Walpole's masterful settlement of the financial chaos that he inherited and the rapid restoration of the credit markets only served to prove this point. His grip on power and the rout of the opposition were finally cemented by his exposure of the pro-Jacobite plot of Francis Atterbury, the Tory Bishop of Rochester, in 1723.

In these circumstances, the Tories were unlikely to obtain a majority in the Commons for the foreseeable future. To make such an outcome even less likely, the Whig government had already overturned the Triennial Act of 1694. This had been one of the main bulwarks of the power of Parliament, ensuring new elections every three years regardless of the financial situation of the government. The interval was now increased to seven years. Walpole also exploited the most glaring defects of the electoral system. The constituencies inherited from the Middle Ages bore little or no connection to existing population levels, so that many had vanishingly small electorates that could easily be bought by cash or favors. The government was always in a position to dispense greater favors than the opposition, and the Whigs, even if naturally representing the minority of the electorate, could therefore provide itself with a majority in Parliament. The "pocket" and "rotten" boroughs were not finally to be swept away until the Reform Act of 1832.

Yet it would be incorrect to see Walpole's system as depending merely on the exclusion of potential opponents of the regime from power. True, Catholics were specifically excluded from office by the Test Act. It is also true that the poor had no place in the system whatever; but then this was a characteristic of all known systems of government at the time, whether republican or monarchical, European or Asiatic. The real achievement of Walpole was to create the basis for some degree of compromise and consensus between the opposing elements within the Protestant ruling class. Nowhere is this more obvious than in his religious policy. Walpole perceived clearly that the Church of England was too important a vehicle of social cohesion, let alone political control, for the old Tory-Whig disputes about non-Anglican forms of Protestantism to be allowed to continue. (The Whig association with religious dissent derived not only from a tradition of indigenous Puritan radicalism, but also from the inevitable prevalence of non-Anglican Protestantism among the expanding continental element of the mercantile community.) In 1723, Walpole made an agreement with the Bishop of London that no further concessions would be made to dissenters if the church ensured that only clergy favorable to the government would be promoted. Walpole's foreign policy, too, coincided with the preferences of the country squires. Until 1739, he resolutely kept Britain out of all foreign entanglements, even when supposedly required to help its ally Austria in the mid-1730s. This was not merely a concession to his erstwhile opponents. Walpole himself had a visceral dislike of war, not only for its expense, but also for the political divisions that seemed to flow from it.

Walpole's resolutely pacific foreign policy allowed him to pursue a "Tory" financial policy by Whig means. The cost of the national debt fell by nearly £1 million per year from 1721 to 1739, a reduction of around one-third. This was partly the result of the agreed-on reduction of interest on the South Sea annuities in 1727, which was copied by the Bank of England and the East India Company. It was also because of a string of small but regular budget surpluses amounting to over £6 million, which were used to redeem expensive debt. A further £6.6 million was replaced by new perpetual annuities that paid as little as 3%. So strong was the government's credit that even the 3%s were selling over par by the mid-1730s. This prompted calls from the opposition to reduce the interest on the 4% annuities that still formed the majority of the debt. Here, however, Walpole gave priority to the feelings of his other constituents, the monied class, who were still licking their wounds from the South Sea debacle. But even his opposition to interest rate reductions in this case may be seen as a further example of his concern to soothe the passions of an earlier period.

Perhaps the clearest evidence of the reconciliation of interests achieved by Walpole was the support given by the landed classes to the reduction of the land tax and its replacement by excises. It will be remembered that after the Revolution of 1688 the Tory gentry on the backbenches had preferred to tax themselves via the land tax than to allow the creation of a permanent tax collected by a centralized body of excise officials. The Whigs, on the other hand, had always sought to rely on excise taxes, which provided the most reliable security for long-term debt in Holland and elsewhere. Since the economic, as opposed to political, interests of the gentry clearly did not lie with the land tax, all that was needed was a sufficient relaxation of the distrust between the two interests, the landed and the monied, for a mutually beneficial consensus to evolve. The land tax was halved in 1730, and in 1732 it was halved again. In the period from 1690 to 1715, 40% or more of total state revenues were provided by the land tax. After 1730 the percentage fell to around 20%.[7] Here, too, Britain was following—quite unconsciously—the example of Holland. In the early years of the struggle against Spain, the Dutch raised over 30% of their revenues from direct taxes. By the mid-seventeenth century, the zenith of Dutch prosperity, this had fallen to around 20%.

In other ways, too, the landed class came to appreciate the advantages of Dutch finance. The corollary of the fall in interest rates was an increase in the price of land and a reduction in mortgage costs. This trade-off had been suggested as early as the 1690s by the promoters of the Bank of England,

> for the falling Interest of Money to 3 per cent. per annum, to which Rates the Bank will reduce it, will unavoidably advance the Price of Land to above 30 years Purchase, which will raise the Value of Lands in England at least 100 Millions, and thereby abundantly reimburse the Nation all the Charges of the War, and will not only enable the Gentry to make better Provision for the Younger Children, but those who now owe Money on their Lands, to pay off their Debts, by the increase of the Value of their Estates.[8]

At the time, the gentry were deaf to such reasoning, partly because long-term interest rates took so long to fall. But as government borrowing costs finally reached the magic objective of 3% in the late 1720s, landowners could not fail to be impressed.

The essence of the eighteenth-century consensus was therefore as follows: the nation's finances would be run by the mercantile interests of London, while the reins of government remained in the hands of the landowners, who were able to ensure that their economic interests prevailed in other matters. This meant, for example, that they had a free rein to complete the modernization of agriculture by enclosing the old communal field systems. Earlier governments, under the Tudors and Stuarts, had often opposed this process because of the social disruption and unrest that it caused. In the later eighteenth and early nineteenth centuries, however, it was to be this development that underwrote the Industrial Revolution by providing the cities with cheap food and the industrialists with cheap labor.

The period of one-party rule ushered in by the Hanoverian succession and epitomized by Walpole lasted at least until 1760. It came to an end with the accession of George III and his counterproductive attempts to restore some of the power lost to the monarchy over the preceding seventy years. The instinctive royalism of the original Tory ideology was inevitably more congenial to his mind-set, and a new period of government started, initially overseen by such pallid Tory figures as the Earl of Bute and Lord North, and finally dominated by the genius of William Pitt. Under Rockingham, Burke, and Fox, the Whigs now reverted to the role of "liberal" opposition that they had performed before 1688. Yet so deeply was the post-1688 regime rooted in the country by this time that Lord North would blandly assert that the Bank of England was a "fundamental part of our constitution," as he renewed its charter without demur in 1781. Within Parliament, at least, there was no longer a serious challenge to the underlying premises of the financial system, however deep other political passions may have run, and however great the growing sense of alarm at the size of the national debt, which had now ballooned to over £130 million as a result of the Seven Years' War.

Perhaps it was the role of London that best demonstrates, and helps to explain, the success of the British formula. By midcentury London contained at least 650,000 people, not far off 10% of the nation's population. This was a far higher percentage than those prevailing in other large monarchies. Paris, for instance, contained less than 3% of the French population. In fact, the British capital had a position closer to that of Amsterdam within the Dutch Republic (250,000 in a population of two million), or of Venice within the Venetian Republic. Not only was it the seat of government and a great commercial center, but it also acted as a social fulcrum. Increasingly the landed gentry owned houses in London in addition to their ancestral manors. Taking up residence in London for the social season, they rubbed shoulders with the mercantile classes, whose objective, it seemed, was to buy country estates and build themselves grand Palladian mansions in imitation of their Venetian precursors. The two classes were slowly fusing.

The result was that Britain, although still predominantly an agricultural country, came to enjoy a system of public finance indistinguishable from that of a mercantile republic. It was not yet, statistically, a nation of citizen creditors, but it did exhibit the two other underlying principles of republican politics and finance. The first of these was the political logic of taxation and borrowing. In Britain, as in the merchant republics, it was the privilege of the ruling class to avoid (insofar as possible) the indignity of direct taxes, and to contribute to the common cause by means of lending. The second trait was the (equally political) logic of interest costs. Although the members of eighteenth-century British governments were primarily landowners, it became increasingly rare, as the century progressed, to find a government officeholder who was not also a debtholder. It was this identity of interest that, as in the merchant republics, underlay the implicit trust of creditors in the good faith of their government and therefore allowed the state to borrow so cheaply.

In some ways Britain was able to improve on the practices of its republican predecessors. For instance, it never toyed with the principle of repayable taxes, which the Venetians had never quite been able to shake off. Nor were its internal social and political divisions so great that they had to be resolved by handing over as much power to the Bank of England as that assumed by the Casa di San Giorgio within Genoa. The closest model for Britain was, not surprisingly, the Dutch Republic, which had already managed to avoid both these pitfalls. But even here the British financial system managed some improvements. The main one of these was the Bank of England, a far more flexible instrument of public finance than the Bank of Amsterdam, for instance, which, as a bank of transfer only, had no authority to finance the government directly or to increase the money supply by issuing banknotes in excess of deposits. This monetary flexibility was to stand the country in good stead in its hour of need at the end of the century.

The second advance was the presentation of detailed and reliable annual public accounts. All states prepared budgets of some sort by the eighteenth century, but they were universally treated as official secrets. It was therefore impossible for a public creditor to do more than hazard an informed guess about the financial soundness of his investments. In the closely knit communities of the mercantile republics, this may not have mattered very much since the government and the creditor class were virtually identical. The Dutch Republic operated in almost total secrecy, yet this did not stop its enjoying the lowest interest rates of the era in spite of its enormous debts. Indeed, some historians have suggested that being the sole nation to publish its budgets worked against Britain's interests, especially toward the end of the century, when its debt rose to levels as high as the Dutch. Be that as it may, the publication of budgets was to become a fundamental part of the development of open and responsible government. It therefore seems perverse not to count its introduction in Britain as an advance.

Armed with its now-stabilized political and financial system, Britain was well-equipped to handle the new wave of increasingly expensive wars that started in 1739. In each round of fighting, the annual cost of warfare ratcheted ever higher.

British War Spending, 1740–1784[9]

War	Total Cost £ *millions*	Annual Average £ *millions*
Austrian Succession (1740–1748)	40	4.5
Seven Years' War (1756–1763)	73	10.4
American Independence (1776–1784)	112	14.0

Inevitably taxes had to rise. From around £5.5 million per year in the mid-1730s, they rose to over £16 million in the mid-1780s. On the eve of the French Revolution, the government was collecting the equivalent of nearly 200 grams of silver per head. This made Britain the most highly taxed country in Europe, on a par with the province of Holland. That such amounts could be collected without significant unrest was proof not only of the increasing wealth of the country, but also of the extraordinary cohesion and strength of the political system.

Of course, as in the Dutch Republic, the increased taxes did not pay for wars directly. They served mainly to secure loans, which in turn paid for the wars.

British War Borrowing, 1740–1784[10]

War	Total Cost	Amount Borrowed	
	£ *millions*	£ *millions*	%
Austrian Succession (1740–1748)	40	29	71%
Seven Years' War (1756–1763)	73	57	78%
American Independence (1776–1784)	112	92	82%

Once the credit of the country was established, there seemed to be no limit to the amount of affordable long-term finance that was available. The price of the perpetual debt fell sharply during each of the wars, but the market never dried up. After the war, prices recovered rapidly, and the government was then able to fund the inevitable buildup of floating debt at rates more favorable than those available during the hostilities. In 1745, for example, with Bonnie Prince Charlie advancing into England, the 3% perpetual annuities fell to 74.[11] Yet by 1749 they had soared over par, and the government was able not only to refund its floating debt, but finally to convert all the 4% debt, now totaling £57.5 million, to 3%.* In 1754, most of the remaining annuities not owned by the great chartered companies were consolidated into a single issue, referred to, simply enough, as "Consols," which remains the oldest public debt issue still current and actively traded in the world. During the Seven Years' War, a similar pattern occurred. Prices fell below 70 in 1762, but with the return of peace in the following year, they rose to 90. The immense growth of the debt in these years started to take its toll, and prices never reached the highs of the early 1750s. The American War of Independence did even greater damage. Prices fell into the mid-50s after 1781, and even peace did not immediately improve the market. From 1785 to 1990, the 3%s traded generally in the mid-70s, a range that had reflected near panic in 1745. It was only in 1792 that prices finally recovered to over 90, reaching a peak of 97 just before the outbreak of the final and most cataclysmic round of Anglo-French warfare.

Such sums could have been produced only by a flourishing and substantially unfettered marketplace. This, in spite of the almost universal opprobrium heaped on stock jobbers and other such knaves, was what London enjoyed. With its attractive combination of liquidity and volatility, the exchange attracted funds from many sources—especially from Amsterdam. In the absence of an eloquent indigenous advocate of the virtues of speculation, it was left to an Anglophile Portuguese Jew living in Amsterdam to take up the cause of the stock market. In 1771 Isaac Pinto published his *Traité de la circulation et du crédit,* in which he claimed not only that the possibility of speculation had increased the funds available to Britain by as much as one half, but that those extra funds represented its very margin of success against a larger rival:

> If, without this *jeu d'actions,* the power that England obtains from loans would have been no more than two thirds, it would probably have lost those two thirds. . . .

---

*When interest rates fell, old annuity issues paying interest at above the current market rate traded above par. The government was now able to borrow more cheaply and use the proceeds to redeem the old debt at par. Rather than go through the time-consuming and expensive process of issuing new debt and then calling in the old, governments preferred to use the threat of redemption at below the current market price to persuade existing debtholders to accept a reduction of interest to a level more in line with market rates.

> The advantages, therefore, that come from speculators and foreign investors, are far greater that the drawbacks. Both [the speculators and the foreign investors] have been essential, and a great service to England, and have contributed in no small measure to the success of its military enterprises.[12]

When Pinto wrote his eulogy of the London market, Britain was riding high on its success in the Seven Years' War and it was easy to be optimistic. Ten years later the situation was rather different. It was easy to see why the market was becoming fatigued in the 1780s. Britain emerged from the American War of Independence with debts of £245 million, a level close to 200% of GNP. It had also managed to alienate the Dutch Republic, which had for so long been its ally, not only militarily but financially. The Dutch had long been significant investors in the Bank of England and in government debt, but they now started to redirect their funds toward France. The market was also left a little wary by the fact that Britain had, for once, emerged on the losing side, even if the damage was finally limited to the loss of the thirteen colonies. Under such circumstances the market for British debt was more remarkable for its resilience than for its relative weakness when compared to earlier wars. Even at a price of 75, Consols yielded no more than 4%. That they could have risen close to par in 1792 was quite remarkable and suggested that the country's credit was still not exhausted even at this vertiginous level.

British National Debt, 1690–1790[13]
As a percentage of GNP

The investor confidence required to support debts at these levels could come only from an absolute certainty that the taxes necessary to service it would always be raised. More particularly it depended on the demonstrable ability of the government to avoid deficits in peacetime, however high the cost of debt service rose. Even if the publishing of reliable annual accounts may not have been needed to satisfy a well-informed and largely London-based creditor class, it has certainly helped historians observe the punctiliousness of successive governments in this matter. Indeed, the peacetime budget was generally kept in surplus so as to support the operation of the sinking fund. It was undoubtedly the raising of the taxes by a further £1.5 million in 1791 and the achievement of a £1.7 million surplus in 1792 (the largest since 1769) that helped Consols to rally to 97 in that year in spite of the enormity of the debt.

British Peacetime Budget Surpluses, 1720–1792[14]

	Cumulative Surplus *£ millions*
1720–1739	6.3
1750–1755	2.9
1764–1775	8.4
1786–1792	2.9

The second pillar of investor confidence was monetary stability, although this has to be reckoned of less importance than fiscal probity. The avoidance of currency manipulation had not helped the Stuarts improve their dismal credit rating; nor was it to perform miracles for the Bourbon credit rating after 1726. It had not even prevented continual price rises in sixteenth-century Spain. Yet after 1600 there started an era, in England at least, that may be deemed to have lasted until the Second World War, in which prices were astonishingly stable over the long term. This did not mean that they were stable over the short term—very far from it. From 1650 to 1690 they fell quite sharply. From 1690 to 1711 they rose again under the influence of war, only to fall back again during the peace that followed. In the wars after 1739, they rose slowly to the levels of the mid-seventeenth century. Yet, reviewing the evidence from 1600, a public creditor would have been justified in concluding that, as long as the government eschewed a policy of debasement of the currency, prices could be expected to fall as far in periods of general peace as they had risen in wartime. Under such circumstances it is no wonder that the concept of "real" interest rates did not exist.* The market sometimes behaved as if it

*The real interest rate is the nominal interest rate less the rate of inflation. It is only with the onset of persistent inflation since the Second World War that this concept has come into focus. In earlier times the assumption that prices would fall as often as they would rise meant that investors were willing to accept low (or even negative) real returns on a temporary basis because they felt that had no reason to worry over the long term.

did, by demanding higher yields during wars, when prices were rising, and lower ones in peace, when they were falling. But this is not the most plausible explanation. Higher yields were needed in wartime partly because of the fear of the possible political and economic consequences of defeat, but mostly because of the sheer saturation of the market with government debt. In the eighteenth century it did not occur to the public creditors of Britain and the Dutch Republic that their governments might simply inflate away their problems. Such things did not happen in states "where the finances are absolutely governed by those who furnish them."

A rosy picture, it would seem. Even the critics of the system could not fail to be impressed, especially when confronted by the spectacular victories of the Seven Years' War. But this did not prevent a generalized anxiety as the debt rose ever higher. The anxiety was not confined to country gentlemen; the soundest thinkers of the day were equally disturbed. Walpole was on record as stating that Britain could never survive if debt went over £100 million. In 1752, David Hume confidently forecast the bankruptcy of the country by the end of the century if no action was taken: "EITHER THE NATION MUST DESTROY PUBLIC CREDIT, OR PUBLIC CREDIT WILL DESTROY THE NATION,"[15] he wrote, inadvertently echoing the words of the Florentine Francesco Guicciardini over two hundred years earlier: "*O il Monte disfarà Firenze o Firenze disfarà il Monte*" ("Either the Monte will undo Florence, or Florence will undo the Monte").[16]

By the end of the Seven Years' War, of course, the £100 million barrier had long been broken. In 1776, Adam Smith was little more sanguine about the situation than David Hume had been before him. But unlike his fellow Scot, he was not an advocate of returning to the principle of pay-as-you-go:

> The method of funding . . . hinders less the accumulation or acquisition of new capital, than that of defraying the public expense by a revenue raised within the year. Under the system of funding, the frugality and industry of private people can more easily repair the breaches which the waste and extravagance of government may occasionally make in the general capital of society.[17]

Smith put his finger on a quite different problem with reliance on debt: it made the society in which he lived excessively bellicose by disguising the true cost of war:

> In great empires, the people who live in the capital, and in the provinces remote from the scene of action, feel, many of them, scarce any inconveniency from the war, but enjoy, at their ease, the amusement of reading in the newspapers the exploits of their own fleets and armies. To them this amusement com-

> pensates the small difference between the taxes which they pay on account of the war, and those which they pay in time of peace.[18]

The difference between peacetime and wartime taxes was small precisely because of the new system of cheap public debt. In the absence of such a system,

> wars would, in general, be more speedily concluded, and less wantonly undertaken. The people feeling, during continuance of war, the complete burden of it, would soon grow weary of it.[19]

His conclusion, though reached by another route, was no different from Hume's:

> Great Britain seems to support with ease, a burden which, half a century ago, nobody believed her capable of supporting. Let us not, however, upon this account, rashly conclude that she is capable of supporting any burden. . . .
>
> The practice of funding has gradually enfeebled every state that has adopted it. . . . Is it likely that in Great Britain alone a practice which has brought either weakness or desolation into every other country, should prove altogether innocent . . . ?
>
> When national debts have once been accumulated to a certain degree, there is scarce, I believe, a single instance of their having been fairly and completely paid.[20]

When he warned of states "enfeebled" by reliance on public debt, Adam Smith was thinking most particularly of the Dutch Republic. By 1715, the republic had debts that amounted to more than 200% of GNP. The situation in that year was so grave that the central government had to stop payment on its obligations for nine months and then reduce the interest paid on its war debt to 3%. The province of Holland, which was responsible for the large majority of all Dutch borrowing, managed to survive with its credit standing intact, but only at the cost of continuing the emergency wartime taxes. For the rest of the century the debt was serviced punctually; in fact, it still commanded the most complete confidence on the part of the population. The bonds of the most trusted provincial issuers traded at yields as low as 2.5%—better than the lowest yield achieved by the British Consols. But payment of the debt came at a price. The Dutch could not but be aware that their country had reached the end of its fiscal tether. Entry into the War of the Austrian Succession ended in tax revolts. The Dutch were forced to pursue a passive and isolationist foreign policy, and thus to watch in resignation as Britain now took the lead in international commerce. At the same time, the domestic economy was stifled by excise taxes that were necessarily the highest in Europe. Under these twin constraints, it was no surprise that the economic growth of the previous century ground to a halt. The accumulated wealth of its citizens had not disappeared; but now Holland was to follow the path of Genoa before it, turning from an imperial trading power to a passive capital market for other, less-constrained states.

THE DILEMMA

Whatever anxieties were felt by the ruling class of Britain as the century proceeded were more than matched across the Channel. The success of the British system of government and finance—where representative institutions and seemingly unlimited borrowing capacity seemed to go hand in hand—posed an ultimately insoluble dilemma for the ancien régime. The moment of truth had arrived during the Seven Years' War. The disastrous outcome of that war had occurred, at least in part, because Britain was able to outspend its rival (£73 million versus £53 million[21]) in spite of the enormous disparity in populations. Its extra financial resources allowed Britain to support not only its own forces in the very expensive global struggle for empire, but also those of its allies in the more traditional European battleground (most especially the seemingly invincible Prussian army of Frederick the Great). That British finances recovered rapidly after 1763, while France lurched uneasily toward another bankruptcy at the end of the decade, only rubbed salt into the wound.

In the American War of Independence, France was again heavily outspent by Britain, this time by around £112 million to £40 million.[22] True, the war had ended badly for Britain, largely because it found itself fighting against erstwhile allies as well its longtime enemy, while France, for once, had no continental entanglements to distract it. But there was no guarantee that such a uniquely favorable strategic balance would offer itself in any future conflict.

In casting around for an explanation for England's extraordinary ability to pour money into global warfare, French statesmen did not look primarily to the economic strength of their rival. In 1782, for instance, Joly de Fleury, the minister of finance, was of the opinion that,

> from any standpoint, England's position is far from being as favourable as that of France, inasmuch as she has not a third of our money in circulation or our population; nor a soil so extensive or productive; nor as many manufactures of all varieties; nor a geography so favourable, which links us by land and sea to all parts of Europe and the globe.[23]

Recent research has tended to lend support to Fleury's contention. The old image of ancien régime France stagnating under the stifling weight of feudalism and absolutist bureaucracy, while England raced toward the Industrial Revolution, has been heavily rewritten. Eighteenth-century France is no longer seen as an economic underachiever. In many ways, and especially in manufacturing, its economy compared very well with that of England and certainly outperformed almost every other in Europe. This new image of France jibes with the cultural and intellectual dynamism of the era, the France of the philosophes and the great salons, of Lavoisier and Montgolfier.

There were good reasons why this should have been so. When the economic chaos of the regency had subsided and the costs of Louis XIV's wars had finally been written off, France found itself in a rather favorable economic situation. To its natural blessings, such as the privileged geographic position noted by Fleury, were added new stimulants to economic activity. One of these, paradoxically, was the drastic pruning of the public debt. By the mid-1720s the French budget was approaching balance. Revenue had increased to around 190 million livres, and long-term debt service was around 65 million, including the cost of venal offices. This left net revenues that were more or less adequate for peacetime purposes, and that could be expected to improve as the 20 million annual cost of the life annuities gradually declined. As a percentage of GNP, French debt service was now undoubtedly lower than that of Britain, let alone Holland.

Equally helpful to economic endeavor was the abandonment of monetary manipulation as a prop of government finance. After its stabilization in 1726, the livre remained unchanged for the remainder of the life of the ancien régime. The new parity of 4.45 grams of silver, or 25 livres to the pound sterling, became a new pillar of government policy. So powerful was the hold of the new orthodoxy that, after the destructive whirlwind of revolutionary finance had abated in the 1790s, the same parity was reestablished for the new franc. When France finally abandoned its old silver parity and followed Britain onto the gold standard, the old exchange rate with sterling was maintained. Only the ravages of the First World War finally forced France to abandon its commitment to *le franc fort.*

Even more significant, however, than the new stability of the livre was the 47% devaluation that had taken place since 1690. This would have been meaningless if prices had risen by the same amount, but the evidence suggests that this was not the case.[24] The devaluation of the livre had thus given France a distinct competitive edge for rest of the eighteenth century.

French manufacturers and merchants were not shy about taking advantage of this cost advantage, and the result was a long-term positive balance of trade, which had probably doubled the quantity of hard currency in the country by the 1780s.

The relative performance of the British and French economies has been a lively and even contentious issue among historians for some time.[25] This is not the place to enter into such debates, but the issue cannot be totally avoided because of the temptation to see parallels between the events of 1789 and those of 1989. Certainly never have two events provided a more striking visual parallel than the demolition of the Bastille and that of the Berlin Wall—the latter capping so elegantly the bicentenary of the former. It is inevitably tempting to see the fall of the ancien régime as the eighteenth-century equivalent of the collapse of the Soviet Union—as an admission of economic failure. Yet, in what might be described as the "high-tech" field, this was certainly not true. Eighteenth-century French technology and manufacturing were quite a match for the British. Only in agriculture (still, of course, the dominant sector of the economy) did France clearly lag behind its rival. Here, perhaps, there was something of a parallel to events two hundred years later. The series of poor harvests of the 1780s were a critical element in the buildup of revolutionary pressure. Undoubtedly much of the blame for the poor harvests was due to exceptional weather conditions. But at least some of the blame must go to the minimal growth of agricultural productivity in the preceding decades, followed by ill-timed attempts to liberalize prices.

In 1788, when the government announced the temporary suspension of repayments, it was easy to make a superficial case that the financial position of France was fundamentally sounder than that of Britain. The argument followed on the lines of Joly de Fleury a few years earlier: the economy was strong and debt levels were far lower than those across the Channel. The economic snapshot on the eve of the French Revolution looked something like this:

THE FINANCIAL POSITIONS OF FRANCE AND BRITAIN IN 1788[26]
£ millions

	France	Britain
GNP	280	135
Public debt	183	245
—as a percentage of GNP	65%	182%
Debt service	12.2	8.1[27]
—as a percentage of GNP	4.4%	6.0%

Certainly there was much that was comforting. GNP had probably more than doubled since the 1720s—an economic performance that compared favorably with that of Britain. In the meantime, public debt had also increased, the inevitable result of recurring Anglo-French warfare. But the increase was nothing compared to the spectacular growth of the British national debt over the same period—to levels that were surely verging on the unsustainable.

Yet even within this set of figures is one that reflected a different reality. The cost of servicing French debt was 50% higher in absolute terms than that of England. And this was in spite of the fact that not only was the total debt lower, but 30% of the debt still consisted of the very cheap perpetual rentes (paying only 1% or 2.5% interest) issued to the luckless public creditors in 1720. Obviously French borrowing since 1726 had occurred on terms far less advantageous than those available to Britain. In 1788, the government could console itself that, whereas successive British governments had borrowed in perpetuity, their French counterparts had made the wise decision to make much of the debt self-liquidating, so that a portion of the amount paid to its creditors represented capital repayment. But even so, it appears that, while Britain had managed to borrow since 1726 at an average cost of around 3.67%, France had had to pay closer to 7.3%.[28]

The high cost of French borrowing in the decades before 1789 has been the subject of debate ever since the Revolution, especially since it was well-known that it was an inability to service their debts that had brought down the Bourbons. The revolutionaries themselves set the pattern by arguing that the high cost was largely the result of a pervasive government incompetence that only served to illustrate the decadence of the old regime. More recently a number of historians have revised these ideas, asserting that French ministers were largely the victims of the political system in which they were forced to work.

What is certainly true is that French borrowing practices during the eighteenth century were very different from those of Great Britain. After 1750, Britain concentrated the majority of its new borrowing in the new 3% Consols. By the end of the American War of Independence, the Consols had become so dominant as to constitute the English equivalent of the Monte Vecchio of Venice or the Monte Comune of Florence: a single issue in which the entire credit standing of the nation was on public display, both to eighteenth-century investors and to twentieth-century historians. The price of Consols on the stock market was a proxy for government borrowing costs.

There was nothing like this in France. The events of 1720 had given *rentes perpétuelles* a bad repute that was to last until the nineteenth century. They were seen as the wastepaper of a century and a half of royal defaults. The cumulative deficits of monarchs from Francis I to Louis XIV, amounting to billions of livres, and financed at rates that ran from 5% to well into double digits, had ended up as a mere 1.4 billion of rentes paying 2.5% or even less. If *rentes perpétuelles* were unpopular after 1720, so, too, were financial markets. The monarchy did nothing to encourage the trading of its debt on the stock exchange and, at times, did its best to impede it. After 1764, for example, the transfer of rentes was taxed at the prohibitive rate of one year's interest. The combined effect of these twin aversions meant that France failed to take advantage of precisely the most important characteristic of perpetual debt—that it lent itself so readily to trading. Perpetual annuities had none of the risk of unpredictable loss of capital associated with life annuities. And because they had no fixed repayment dates, all perpetual annuities were effectively identical as long as two conditions were met: that any underlying security was held in common, and that the coupon rate was unchanged. To an investor on the London Stock Exchange, a 3% Consol issued in 1854 was no different from one created in 1754. Therefore each successive addition to the series only improved the size and liquidity of the market. The increased liquidity of their assets made investors ready to accept a lower interest return. By turning away from perpetual debt and financial markets, eighteenth-century France was already forcing its borrowing costs somewhat higher than they would otherwise have been.

A vicious circle was in operation. The royal government firmly believed that it should pay no more than 5% on its debt. This, after all, was the legal maximum; above this the rate was usury. Since investors were rarely willing to lend to the monarchy at this rate, the government attempted to disguise the true cost of its borrowing, and to prevent its true credit ratings from being exposed to view on a daily basis by the operations of the financial markets. Yet by these very policies, it managed to increase the interest rates that it had to pay.

It was not that there were no additions to the perpetual debt after the collapse of Law's system. A tabulation for 1789 included some 840 million livres that had come into existence since 1720.[29] Yet these new rentes were in no way comparable to the Consols. There were no fewer than thirty-eight different issues, with varying types of collateral and rates of interest. Many had not started life as perpetuals at all but had been issued to government creditors in settlement of their original claims. Almost all of them had been involved in the default of 1770. Their interest rates had been cut by a minimum of 10%, many by as much as 50%, and the rest had been reduced to a standard 4%. These rentes, like those of 1720, far from being the flagship of national credit, were no more than its flotsam and jetsam.

After 1720, French finance ministers operated on the conviction that no debts should incurred without their repayment being clearly programmed. There was, therefore, an increasing reliance on a loans with fixed repayment terms. Many of these had special features to improve the nominal yields (which were not allowed to exceed the usury threshold of 5%) such as initial discounts, early redemptions, or lotteries. Once or twice they may even have cost no more than the legal rate, but more often they ranged from 6% to 8%. Although these loans changed hands with a certain regularity, their market would never be very liquid, since each issue was different from every other, and since very few issues exceeded the equivalent of £1 million. By contrast, Consols came into existence at £9 million and were well over £100 million by the 1780s.

Somewhere in the region of 830 million livres was raised in the form of term loans from 1740 to 1788, yet they were not the main vehicle of French public finance.[30] That honor was undoubtedly held by life annuities (*rentes viagères*). Life-contingent debt had made its debut in France in the 1690s, paralleling the short-lived English experiments of that decade. The 34 million livres of such debt issued before the crisis of 1708–1709 had the good fortune to be almost the only government obligations to emerge unscathed from the subsequent debt reductions, partly because the amount was so small as to escape notice, and partly because of the conceptual difficulty of separating interest from principal so as to be able to justify a reduction. The difficulty of identifying the interest component of a life annuity was to prove as welcome to a borrower wishing to hide its true credit rating as it was to lenders hoping to avoid accusations of usury. Added to the self-liquidating nature of the debt, this advantage ensured that *rentes viagères* were to become the financial instrument of choice for the last seventy years of the ancien régime. After 1720 they assumed an ever greater importance with every decade, until after 1771 they dominated public borrowing. By 1789 1.4 billion livres had been raised in life-contingent debt, of which around 1.1 billion was still outstanding. But if small term loans with complex structures were poor candidates for building an active and liquid trading market, life annuities were even worse. Adam Smith put his finger on the reason in *The Wealth of Nations* when he observed, "No man will give for an annuity upon the life of another, whose age and state of health are nearly the same as his own, the same price that he would give for one upon his own. . . . It can never, therefore, make so convenient a transferable stock as a perpetual annuity, of which the real value may be supposed always the same, or very nearly the same."[31]

There are, then, some valid reasons to think that the high cost of French borrowing was partly the result of the mistaken policies of its finance ministers. This was not the argument of the revolutionaries, however. Their indignation was focused on a particular aspect of the life annuity debt and the innovative financial technique that it inspired. In 1771, an investment syndicate known as the Trente Desmoiselles de Genève ("Thirty Geneva Maidens") was launched. The syndicate and its successors have been described by their main historian as the epitome of "rococo finance," the fitting emblem of "that delicious *fin de siècle* before the deluge."[32] To the revolutionaries the Geneva Maidens were the most damning indictment of the financial incompetence of the ancien régime, the clearest evidence of the sheer "imbecillity of our old government."[33]

By the eighteenth century it was well understood that in order to make life annuities cost-effective it was necessary to offer annuity rates that varied according to the age of the subscriber. The statistical analysis of life expectancy, developed by the Dutch in the seventeenth century, had allowed Holland to issue life-annuity loans with rates that ranged from 4% for young children to 7.7% for senior citizens. In this way the dilemma that was first confronted by the Greek city of Miletus in 205 B.C. had been resolved.* In the first half of the eighteenth century, the French adhered to the principle of age-banding; and in 1746 the government sponsored Antoine Deparcieux to analyze the results of its oldest life-annuity issues from the turn of the century so as to further refine its future offerings. Not only was Deparcieux's work based on the lives of actual rentiers, but he also carefully calculated the different rates required for each single year so as to equalize returns over time. Yet in 1757, the government abandoned age-banding and started issuing flat-rate annuities in spite of the extra cost that they were bound to incur. It is here that posterity has heaped ridicule on the ancien régime. Surely only a government composed of imbeciles could ignore research that it had helped to fund.[34]

On closer analysis it is not at all clear that the criticism was entirely

*Miletus was the first state on record to borrow by selling life annuities. Because there was no differentiation in the return according to the age of the subscriber, it was not surprising that twenty-five of the thirty-nine subscriptions were made in the name of children—i.e., those with the longest possible life expectancies.

fair. In spite of their sale as single issues, life annuities appealed to two totally distinct markets. The first consisted of men and women generally between the ages of forty and sixty who wished to provide themselves with a pension. In eighteenth-century France they could usually obtain an income for life of between 9% and 10% by investing in a government annuity. Depending how long they lived, this might, or might not, be a good return on their capital; but they did not care overmuch. The income was higher than returns available on any other reasonably safe investment, and if they died prematurely, their immortal souls would, with luck, be too busy contemplating higher matters to worry about such earthly concerns as money. In fact, the cost to the government of these middle-class pensions was not excessive by French standards and generally compared favorably to other sources of new money. A recent study has shown that even during the American War of Independence the cost of annuities sold to fifty-year-olds was between 5.24% and 7.6%, compared to the yields of between 6.3% and 8% that were required to float term loans.[35]

The problem for the government was that the supply of pension money was not sufficient. Only one-third of the 1.4 billion livres raised on life annuities between 1730 and 1789 came from pension seekers. The remainder was raised by annuities issued against third-party lives. The rules for successful borrowing of this type were quite different. Unlike pensioners, the players in this market were extremely sensitive to the long-term rate of return on their capital. They were not especially interested in life annuities and would buy them only if their yields compared favorably with those of alternative investments. Indeed, in order to compensate for the risk that their third-party nominees would die prematurely, they inevitably demanded an above-market rate of return.*

Until the Seven Years' War, the government scarcely tapped this market. Investment in annuities on third-party lives was generally limited to parents attempting to set up their offspring. The rates offered on the younger age bands were simply too low to attract speculative investment. The cost of the Seven Years' War forced the government to rethink its policy. In 1757, it issued life annuities at the flat rate of 10%, regardless of

---

*The modern study of the psychology of risk evaluation has shown that as the size of a potential loss becomes greater, humans increasingly ignore the laws of statistical probability and overvalue the possible loss in relation to potential profits. The most obvious example is the attitude toward nuclear power stations. With third-party life annuities, the risk of losing up to 100% of the investment as a result of a unforeseeable accident could be offset only by potential profits above those required by actuarial probability.

age. The result, quite predictably, was that (1) the government was able to raise more than twice the amount garnered in any previous issue, and (2) most of the investments were made on the lives of children.[36] Yet the new policy of flat-rate annuities was not so foolish as it appeared on the surface. Rates of 9–10% were adequate to continue to tap the pensioner market as before. Actuarially accurate rates were simply not adequate to unearth other sources of investment. In the thirty years from 1757 to 1787, the government raised 1.1 billion livres on flat-rate annuities. Of this sum, some 25% came from pension seekers, who maintained a flow of investment similar to that of previous decades. The rest was from sources of capital which could not have been tapped at lower rates.

It was here that the Thirty Geneva Maidens came into the picture. The primary problem with third-party life annuities was the reluctance of investors to risk so much on the frail life of a single child. The solution, clearly, was to spread the risk. In the 1763 annuity issue, an ingenious Genevan banker called Jacob Bouthillier Beaumont set up a syndicate to invest on multiple lives. In 1771, his operations were put on a truly scientific basis. A doctor was employed to select young girls with the longest possible life expectancy. Generally they had to have reached the age of seven so as to be beyond the risk of smallpox. Later, the invention of inoculation allowed even younger girls to be selected. These maidens received the finest medical care, and Geneva's wealthy bourgeoisie followed their health in the newspapers—scarcely surprising, given the huge investments that rested on their shoulders. When Pernette Martin died in 1788 at the tender age of eight, no less than 212,000 livres of annual income disappeared overnight. The damsels were placed in groups of thirty to reduce risk and then syndicated to investors. One syndicate achieved an average life span of sixty-three years, far in excess of that predicted by the actuarial information available at the time.[37]

Beaumont had also helped solve the second problem associated with life annuities: the difficulty of selling them. Shares in his syndicates were quite easy to trade, and some rose to a premium in the aftermarket. Beaumont's invention was so successful that he spawned numerous imitators both in Geneva and outside. The Genevan share of investments made in the name of minors after 1771 was around one-third, a remarkable figure for such a small city. It is quite likely that syndicates of all kinds accounted for close to half of all the money raised by means of life annuities after 1771.

All this poses a new question: If the elegant Genevan system had resolved the problems associated with third-party life annuities, why did borrowing rates not fall? The revolutionaries were convinced that the foreign capitalists had simply taken the old regime for a ride and that a more competent government could have borrowed more cheaply. Yet this does not seem to be the case. Although sometimes the Genevan syndicates traded at a premium, it was almost never more than 5%. Generally they sold near par. By the 1780s, there were so many competing syndicates, and their overall share of the market was so large, that it is inherently unlikely that there was much arbitrage left in government incompetence. In fact, the evidence suggests that the Genevan syndicates did lower relative borrowing costs, despite the outrage of the revolutionaries. This can be seen by comparing life annuities with the longest-dated term loans.[38] In 1758, a thirty-year term loan was raised at 6.65% while annuities were offered at 10%. In May 1787, on the other hand, when life annuities were offered at 9%, the twenty-five-year loan of 1784 was selling at a yield of 8.2%. The gap between the two forms of borrowing had nearly disappeared. The effect had simply been masked by the rising cost of the French government's borrowing in a market that viewed its credit with increasing suspicion.

What is striking is that the rates paid by France in the decades leading up to the Revolution were higher not only than those paid by England or Holland, but also than those paid by such apparently less advanced powers as Austria. After the Seven Years' War, Austria, too, confronted a serious debt crisis. Its debts had more than doubled from 124 to 285 million florins (around 750 million livres). Yet Austria was able to resolve this crisis without default; and in the 1770s and 1780s Austria was able to borrow at rates as low as 3.5–4.0% both domestically and in Amsterdam. In the minds of Dutch investors, Austria was the prime foreign credit risk by the 1780s. It was followed by Denmark, Russia, Spain, and Sweden, all of which were able to borrow in Amsterdam at no more than 5%. The rates paid by the last two borrowers are particularly remarkable considering their less-than-impeccable credit records. Spain spent much of the eighteenth century repudiating the debts of the seventeenth. Only in the 1780s did it appear to be truly on the road to financial solvency and economic advance. Sweden spent the years between 1745 and 1766 experimenting for a second time with nonconvertible paper money. The currency fell by 55% on the exchange markets, and domestic prices rose correspondingly. An attempt to redeem the paper money in 1767–1768 proved too painfully deflationary to be sustained, and only after the royal coup d'état of 1772 was financial order restored by the ending of the copper-based currency that had plagued the country for more than a century.[39]

Comparing the rates paid on foreign loans floated in Amsterdam to those paid by France (or Britain) is not entirely straightforward. Neither country borrowed in foreign currency, and foreign investors had to factor in the risk of currency manipulation, which was absent in borrowings denominated in guilders. Certainly no one in their right mind would have wished to invest in loans denominated in Swedish dalers. Nonetheless, the discrepancy between the rates of 8% or more paid by France and those paid by other borrowers is too large to be explained by currency risk alone. If the extravagant rates paid by France were not merely the result of government ineptitude, perhaps they were the punishment for a reputation for fiscal irresponsibility that was unequaled in Europe.

Without wishing to whitewash the track record of generations of Bourbon defaulters, there is one major consideration which should be viewed in mitigation. The evidence can best be presented in the form of a bubble chart:*

DEBT PER CAPITA IN THE 1780S[40]

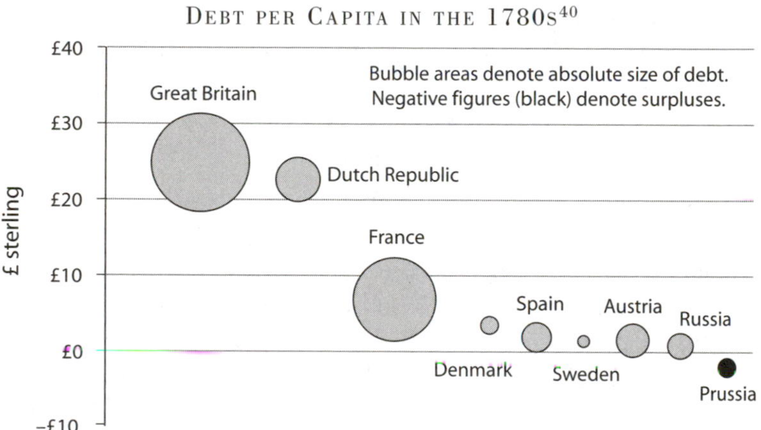

While the French per capita debt burden was far lower than the British or the Dutch, it was more than double that of any other continental monarchy. This alone put pressures on the French public finances that the political system was simply not equipped to handle. Moreover, the very size of the French debt—two and one half times the combined debts of the other major continental monarchies—strained the resources of the capital markets

*Bubble charts display an extra dimension of information beyond traditional bar charts. In this case, the vertical position of the each bubble shows the country's debt per capita, while its area shows the absolute size of the debt. Both these factors are important in understanding the dynamics of late-eighteenth-century public borrowing in Europe.

in a way that the Austrian debt, for instance, did not. Financially, France and Britain were the only true "great powers" of the century. The lesser states (and financially this category included Austria) were generally able to extract subsidies from one of these two in exchange for its support in the intricate game of rococo diplomacy. The financial burdens of the lesser states were thereby reduced, while those of the superpowers were correspondingly increased. In the hands of a ruler such as Frederick the Great of Prussia, who combined superlative diplomatic skills with a highly efficient tax system, the exploitation of foreign subsidies might help obviate public debt altogether.

For a combination of reasons, then, the cost of French public borrowing remained unsustainably high. Since long-term interest rates on private loans in France appear to have been no higher than in England, the rates required to fund the French government must have been the market's way of discounting the risk of bankruptcy. In the words of the historian James Riley, they represented a form of "prepaid repudiation."

That this was so is proved by a phenomenon peculiar to the ancien régime: the very different yields of superficially similar loans. While the old *rentes perpétuelles* inherited from 1720 might trade at yields of around 5%, more recent loans might offer returns of 8% or even higher. The only way to explain these apparent inefficiencies in the market is by the different likelihood of default on different categories of debt. The rentes of 1720 were understood by investors to be without serious further risk. They had already been purged of "usury" by the reductions of the early eighteenth century. It was later loans, which, precisely because of the regime's persistent record of default, could be placed only at yields of well over 5%, that were the most likely targets for any future reductions. And within this category it was always the longest-term loans that had the highest yields. It was for this reason that annuities taken out on the lives of children required such high yields. In the default of 1770, the government had unsettled investors by using Deparcieux's actuarial tables to arbitrarily reduce payments on some of its life annuity debt. From that time on, it must have been apparent that life annuities were no longer inherently safer than other loans. They, too, could now be declared usurious if necessary. The market was quite rational in its evaluation of risk. The nine-year term loan of 1780 sold for a yield of 6.3%. Since it was fully repaid by the time of the Revolution, investors had made a sound financial judgment in accepting a relatively modest yield. But an investor in a Genevan syndicate in 1781 was also quite right to demand a potential return of at least 9%. This money was still very much at risk by the time of the Revolution.

French finance ministers may have comforted themselves that they had wisely planned for the automatic reduction of debts over time, whereas their rivals had bound themselves and their country to its creditors in perpetuity. Superficially this was a sign of strength. But viewed from another perspective, it was merely a reflection of the reluctance of the market to make long-term commitments to the Bourbon monarchy. In some ways the annual burden of capital repayments was the straw that broke the camel's back. It inevitably served to increase the dependence of the government on the financial markets and made management of the debt all the harder. The 69 million livres due in 1788 added to an already growing imbalance between the short-term liabilities of the regime and the revenues available to meet them. It was these repayments that were the main target of the suspension of payments that led to the summoning of the Estates General in 1789.

So the market implicitly discounted another French default. Yet, curiously, with the accession of Louis XVI in 1774, default was explicitly ruled out of the repertoire of royal financial techniques. The first act of the new reign was to sack the successful ministerial team of Terray and Maupeou, who had dealt so ruthlessly with public creditors and political opposition alike over the previous four years. In 1776, the king went further and appointed a Genevan banker, Jacques Necker, as his minister of finance as evidence of his commitment to sound finance. What more could the public creditors ask for?

Nor can it be said that this public disavowal of default was skin-deep. The suspension of reimbursements of 1788 was not an act of debt reduction in the old style. Had the government wished to solve its problems by the tried-and-true methods of earlier generations, it could probably have done so—at least on paper. What would have been required was not a mere temporary suspension of repayments but the wholesale conversion of all debts whose cost represented "usury" (including the life annuities) into perpetual rentes paying no more than the legal maximum of 5%—or more possibly the level of 4% that had been enforced by both Desmarets and Terray.* Yet rather than start down this well-worn path, the king preferred to put the whole future of the ancien régime at stake by summoning the Estates General for the first time since 1614.

Whether the public creditors believed in the new royal rectitude cannot

*The amount that debt service could have been cut is hard to calculate accurately, but with the capital outstanding of all life annuities and term loans converted into 4% *rentes perpétuelles*, the reduction of total debt service (including capital repayments) would probably have amounted to 135–140 million livres. The residual deficit of 20–25 million livres could probably have been handled by some minor tax increases and spending reductions.

be proved one way or another. Perhaps they were willing to take Louis XVI's apparent conversion to their cause on trust. But even then a nagging doubt must have remained: Was this conversion sufficient in itself to ensure that their assets were safe? The king might wish to repay his debts, but did he have the money?

It was clear that he did not. The high cost of French debt was inextricably intertwined with another problem, equally serious in its implications for the ancien régime: the problem of taxation. In merchant republics, the citizens controlled taxation as well as lending and could therefore authorize whatever taxes were needed to secure the loans that they themselves provided. This was very far from the position in France. Taxes in the late 1720s had produced around 190 million livres annually. By 1788, this figure had risen to 475 million. This sum may have seemed impressive, but appearances were deceptive. Measured against GNP, taxes had remained virtually unchanged, at no more than 7%. Taken in combination with the rise in debt, this created a dangerous fiscal squeeze, which contrasted sharply with situation in the irritating pseudorepublic across the Channel. British taxes, which had already taken around 10% of GNP in the 1720s, had now risen to 13%, more than offsetting the rise in the cost of the national debt. In the 1720s, France had comparable spending power after debt service to that of Britain. By the late 1780s, this was no longer true.

FREE REVENUES IN FRANCE AND BRITAIN, 1725 AND 1788[41]

£ sterling millions

	France *1725*	Britain *1725*	France *1788*	Britain *1788*
Taxes	7.5	6.0	19.0	16.8
Debt service	3.5	2.5	12.2	8.1
Free revenues	4.0	3.5	6.8	8.7

Even before any consideration of the wide disparity in borrowing power, France was running at a £2 million–per–year disadvantage to its rival. Compared to the position bequeathed by Colbert, the relative decline of the ancien régime looks even more striking. Louis XIV was in a position to tap after-debt revenues of around 88 million livres in 1683, which at the higher currency value then prevailing was equivalent to £6.6 million. In those days, the Stuart kings of England had a net disposable income of no more than £1.2 million. All the growth of population and productivity that had occurred in France since the 1680s had barely sufficed to give Louis XVI the spending power available to his great-great-grandfather in his heyday.

The Bourbon monarchy may have been reluctant to make its affairs public—at least until Necker preempted the issue by publishing the budget for 1781, much to the horror of the old guard. But even before then, well-informed observers understood the conundrum of ancien régime finance. Adam Smith was among them:

> It might be expected that in France a revenue of thirty millions might be levied for the support of the state with as little inconveniency as a revenue of ten millions is in Great Britain. In 1765 and 1766, the whole revenue paid into the treasury of France . . . did not amount to fifteen millions sterling. . . . The people of France, however, it is generally acknowledged, are much more oppressed by taxes than the people of Great Britain.[42]

This was an astute observation. Taxes may have been lower in France, but, perversely, they aroused more opposition. The roles of France and England had been reversed. In the seventeenth century, it was the Stuarts who had struggled in vain to conjure a modest income out of their recalcitrant subjects, and whose regime had been brought down by financial starvation. In the following century, the Bourbons suffered the same fate. The amounts of money involved had grown beyond recognition in 150 years, but the graph shows just how neatly the index of taxpayer pliability had been turned upside down:

RELATIVE TAXATION IN FRANCE AND ENGLAND
Grams of silver per capita[43]

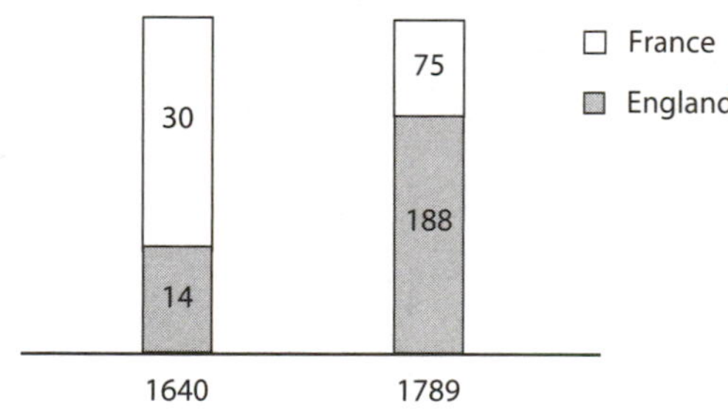

From figures such as these it would be only too easy to elaborate a counterfactual scenario in which it was France that resorted to regicide in the seventeenth century, and England in the eighteenth. Certainly the figures do little to support a simplistic view of revolution as the uprising of an oppressed people.

Yet, clearly, the French felt oppressed by their taxes. Two other possibilities have to be taken into account: that the figures understate the true burden of taxation, or that taxes were raised in a way that maximized popular resentment. Both of these appear to have been true. To the sums accounted for by the royal government, it is necessary to add others that were also felt as taxation. Local taxes, clerical tithes, feudal dues, and, above all, the profits of the tax farmers were all added to the taxpayer's mental accounting of the total drain on income. The total tax burden, including all such dues, may have come to as much as 700 million livres. This sum would have represented around 10% of GNP, far higher than the 6.8% accounted for by the Bourbon state, but still less than the 13% collected in Britain. Perhaps more important was the manner in which taxes were distributed and collected. Feudal dues, to give one example, had long been subsumed into rent in England and therefore no longer counted as tax. Indirect taxes were almost invisible in England, being largely levied at the point of production, whereas in France they were paid directly by consumers. Worse still, they were paid to private tax collectors operating for profit. The profits of the tax farmers, being secret, were subject to the wildest guesses. By some estimates, up to 80% of total revenues was skimmed, although modern research has tended to suggest collection costs of no more than 15%. So uniform was the loathing of tax farmers in France that direct taxes were more popular than indirect. Yet even direct taxes were resented because of the exemptions enjoyed by aristocrats and others. By contrast, the English land tax was paid by all without exception.

For all these reasons, the people of France, who lived under a tax regime that was not only lighter but probably less regressive, overall, than that across the Channel, could be "generally acknowledged" to be "much more oppressed by taxes than the people of Great Britain." Yet it is doubtful that the causes of the Revolution lie here. Tax burdens, whether real or perceived, were no higher in the late eighteenth century than they had been in the seventeenth. The glaring defects of the system had been even more glaring in the earlier period: the incidence of feudal dues had been higher, the profits of the tax farmers greater, and the direct taxes more unequally distributed. Compared to the extravagant corruption of Mazarin's period of office, the governments of the eighteenth century were squeaky clean.

The fall of the ancien régime, like the fall of so many others, is best explained not by revolt from below but by a vacuum above. The ruling classes no longer had confidence in the system by which they ruled. Indeed, it is not surprising that this was the case, for, in the final analysis, the only possible conclusion to be drawn from our graph of relative taxation is that absolutism was simply not working. After all, the rise of absolute monarchies in the Renaissance and the baroque period was explained by the greater ability of the new regimes to concentrate and project national power. They rose and fell by the taxes they could collect and the soldiers that they could thereby afford to pay. Yet now a monarchy even more limited than those of the Middle Ages was able to perform this feat more successfully than the most powerful kings in Europe.

THE LIMITS OF ABSOLUTISM

> General rule: one can raise higher taxes, in proportion to the liberty of the subjects; and one is forced to moderate them to the degree that servitude increases. This has always been, and will always remain so. It is a rule drawn from nature, which does not vary at all; one finds it in all countries, in England, in Holland, and in all States in which liberty becomes degraded, right down to Turkey.[44]

With these words Montesquieu threw a wrench into the works of absolutism. Of course, the empirical evidence on which he based his general law had been visible for some time. Writers had occasionally noted that, although Holland had the highest taxes in Europe, the Dutch seemed to pay them without protest. But no one had thought to turn such anecdotal observations into a fundamental rule so sweeping in its implications.

That Montesquieu was able to make such a generalization at all reflected an enormous change that had taken place on the international scene. Sixteenth-century Turkey, which by his rule should have had an extremely low tax burden, had revenues that were the envy of European monarchs. In the 1570s, Jean Bodin noted approvingly the order of Ottoman finances with their well-stocked treasuries and an income of 12 million ducats. This sum was not only considerably larger than those of France and Spain at the time, but it was unencumbered by debts. On the subject of the European monarchs' cash reserves, Bodin's sarcasm was biting:

> And as for the [French] treasure, it hath been so well husbanded, as in lesse than twelve years that king Henrie the second raigned, hee did owe more than his predecessors had levied fourtie years before.[45]

In the following century, it was the Moghuls who excited the awe of European observers with their even more lavish displays of wealth. In the 1650s and 1660s, François Bernier wrote about his travels in the empire of Shah Jahan:

> I have known many persons lost in amazement while contemplating the number of persons, amounting to millions, who depend for support solely on the King's pay. Is it possible, they have asked, that any revenue can suffice for such incredible expenditure? seeming to forget the riches of the Great Mogul, and the peculiar manner in which Hindustan is governed.[46]

The spectacular revenue of these despots was in no way attributed to the low taxes paid by their subjects. A slightly earlier traveler, the Dutchman Joannes de Laet, while detailing in awe the contents of Moghul treasuries, was horrified by the burdens of the peasants:

> When the crops ripen and are reaped, the royal officials are called, who take for the king's use about three quarters of all produce, leaving for the wretched peasant only one quarter, so that sometimes they get no advantage from their labour and expenditure.[47]

If Montesquieu had lived one hundred years earlier, it is unlikely that he would have formulated his general rule, but by the mid-eighteenth century everything had changed. It was not merely the rise of England that influenced Montesquieu's judgment, anglophile though he was. It was also that the salad days of the great Asiatic despotisms had passed. Their treasuries were largely empty. The Ottoman currency had lost 80% of its value, and the empire was well on the way to becoming the sick man of Europe. The remains of the Moghul dynasty were crumbling before the pressure of the European advance in India. Neither empire inspired awe and trepidation; nor did either appear to be worth emulating.

Even the earlier writers had seen the despotism of the Islamic empires as excessive. Bodin, although the great advocate of absolute and undivided royal sovereignty, was careful to distinguish the European "royal monarch" from the eastern "lordly monarch." The lordly monarch, in Bodin's view, was a despot who owed his power to conquest, whereas

> a Royal Monarch or king, is he which placed in souveraignty yeeldeth himself as obedient unto the laws of nature as he desireth his subjects to be towards himself, leaving unto every man his natural liberty, and proprietie of his own goods.[48]

Moreover, much as Bodin admired the sensible accumulation of reasonable reserves, he criticized the great hoarders of history, such as Darius and Tiberius (although one cannot but suspect that his praise of the French kings was tongue-in-cheek):

> The Law of God forbids to heape together much gold and silver; lest that thereby the prince should be allured to oppresse his subjects. . . . But our kings of France have not offended in this point against the lawes of God, by heaping up of too great treasures, and it is not to be feared that they will hereafter break it.[49]

De Laet and Bernier were particularly critical of the absence of private ownership of land in the East. The result was that no one cared about proper husbandry:

> For the rest, the government is purely tyrannical, for the king is sole master of the whole kingdom, and gives away estates at his will to his subjects, or takes them away again. . . . Hence it comes about that the whole country is carelessly cultivated.[50]

> The peasant cannot avoid asking himself the question: "Why should I toil for a tyrant who may come tomorrow and lay his rapacious hands on all I possess and value . . . ?" The Timariots, Governors and Revenue contractors, on their part reason in this manner . . . "Let us draw from the soil all the money we can, though the peasant should starve or abscond, and we should leave it, when commanded to quit, a dreary wilderness." . . .
>
> How happy and thankful we feel, My Lord, that in our quarter of the globe, Kings are not the sole proprietors of the soil! Were they so, we should seek in vain for countries well cultivated and populous, for well-built and opulent cities, for a polite, contented, and flourishing people.[51]

The "My Lord" whom Bernier was addressing in this letter was none other than the chief minister of France, Jean-Baptiste Colbert. Although Colbert's response, if any, is not known, the letter seems to sum up the most enlightened view of the virtues of the French absolute monarchy. Its government was strong and brooked no challenges to its power. It was quite capable of collecting a sufficient proportion of the national wealth to make its rulers the equals of any other on the face of the earth. But by recognizing private property rights and nurturing the economy through intelligent mercantilist policies, the kings of France ruled over a "well cultivated country" with "opulent cities" and a "flourishing people." Bernier noted that, in spite of the enormous abundance of gold and silver in Hindustan, there was very little coin in circulation. Whatever the other defects of mercantilism as an economic philosophy, it was always concerned to encourage the circulation of specie; and Bernier recognized at once that nothing discouraged circulation more than insecurity of property rights:

> When wealth is acquired, as must sometimes be the case, the possessor, so far from living with increased comfort and assuming an air of independence, studies the means by which he may appear indigent. . . . In the meantime his gold and silver remain buried at a great depth in the ground. . . .
>
> I have no doubt that this habit of secretly burying the precious metals, and thus withdrawing them from circulation, is the principal cause of their apparent scarcity in Hindoustan.[52]

By judiciously combining the virtues of absolute sovereignty, private property rights, and mercantilism, the rulers of the ancien régime in its heyday could reasonably feel that they had created the ultimate political model. Throughout Europe the majority of rulers agreed and set about that most sincere form of flattery: emulation.

Yet even the most apparently autocratic system of government depends on the support of a ruling class, whether landowning or bureaucratic, junker or mandarin, aristocratic or apparatchik. And the power of even the most self-important monarchs of Europe was considerably less absolute than they liked to suppose. The Estates General had been consigned to the history books and the feudal nobility had been confined within the gilded cage of Versailles, but the ancien régime was subject to other restraints, no less powerful because they were less visible. The "royal" finances turned out to be largely the property of others. Its owners were a disparate group composed of rentiers, venal officeholders, tax farmers, and *gens d'affaires*, whose backers, very often, turned out to be the great names of the *noblesse d'épée*. The two central institutions of the financial system were outside the control of the royal government. The Farmers General was the largest single employer in France outside the army and navy. Its thirty-five thousand employees included a paramilitary force of twenty thousand men. It collected and disbursed 150 million livres per year by the 1780s, yet the royal treasury saw only 18 million of this. Some 30 million was paid directly to officeholders and other salaried officials, and the remainder, over 100 million livres, was handed on to the other central body of ancien régime finance: the Hôtel de Ville de Paris. Here the funds received from the Farmers General and from other autonomous tax collectors, totaling around 160 million livres, were paid directly to the holders of government debt. Taken together, these two institutions constituted a virtual state within the French state: a closer approximation to the position of the Casa di San Giorgio within Genoa than even the Bank of England.

By these means, the privileged classes were able to siphon off a substantial proportion of the royal income before it reached the treasury; but the government was largely unable to tap their incomes in exchange. They were protected by the relative invisibility of financial assets, and by the ancient exemption from tax conferred by nobility (whether inherited or bought). In these circumstances it was not surprising that the government resorted to successive rounds of borrowing and default as a method of tapping a portion of this elusive wealth.

As the threat posed to the French political model by a monarchy acting as if it were a mercantile republic made itself clear, so, too, did the need for reform. Since the weakness of the ancien régime lay in the realm of finance, reform had to start here. Although reformers disagreed about the details, the essence of their proposals was remarkably unchanging. What was needed was a fundamental overhaul of the tax system, a drastic simplification that would raise more money with less opposition. Gone would be the whole paraphernalia of tax farming and the grotesque multiplication of excise taxes. Gone would be the impediments to internal trade caused by internal customs barriers and incompatible tax regimes. They would all be replaced by a single, uniform direct tax to be applied without exemptions across the whole country. Some reformers thought that this new tax need fall only on land. Others saw the need to include other sources of wealth. They all agreed on uniformity and simplicity, as well as the avoidance of the costly services of the tax farmers. The extra revenue that would flow into the treasury from this streamlined and equitable fiscal system would reduce the need for borrowing. All reformers agreed that, if debts were incurred, there should be no further recourse to the infamous practice of default.

It is easy to recognize the spirit of John Law in this manifesto. But the main ideas go back even earlier. In 1707, Marshall Vauban, the great French military engineer, published his *Dîme Royale*—an updated version of an unpublished document written as early as 1687. While Vauban allowed for the continuation of the salt tax at less than half its current rate, all other indirect taxes were to be replaced by the "royal tithe" on all income of whatever source—including rentes. Among his stated objectives was to liberate the crown from the clutches of the *financiers*. The tax exemption enjoyed by the nobility would also disappear. The pedigree of such ideas extends as far back as the works of Jean Bodin, who in the 1570s had already condemned the sale of offices as a practice than which "there is not any more pernicious nor base." According to Bodin, aristocratic tax exemptions for aristocrats were the peculiar vice of "our nation the French with whom, as Caesar saith rightly: *Nihil est plebe contemptius*. Nothing is more contemptible than the common people." To add to this catalog of national failings, the French were "easily gulled by the bankers of Italie [who control] the farms & all the best revenues of France, the taxes imposts, customs and doanne of Lion, by means of which farmes they ransome the subjects."[53] Bodin was in favor of taxation by means of an assessment of assets along Roman republican lines—although he did not go as far as to propose the abolition of all existing taxes.

It might be thought that proposals such as these would not go down very well with the holders of venal offices. Yet in 1763 Darigrand, a member of the Parlement of Paris, published *L'Anti-Financier*, calling for a virtually identical program to that of Vauban and Law:

> The expulsion of the Financiers and of all their Lackeys, leads inevitably to the suppression of that crowd of Taxes for whose collection one is obliged to employ an infinity of hands. This would be a double benefit of the King towards his People who long for a single and simple Tax which would cut the bonds that envelop them, give them back their freedom, & which would nevertheless adundantly furnish the needs of the State.[54]

For his suggestions, Darigrand was sent to the Bastille, a fate shared by several other reformers. He was perceived as an opponent of the government, even though similar ideas had been put forward by avid monarchists. His crime was largely that of rocking the boat. Given the persistence of this prescription for reform, it is not surprising to find that it formed the basis for the Revolution of 1789, and was formally sanctified by clause thirteen of the Declaration of the Rights of Man. Venal offices, tax farms, and all existing taxes and tax exemptions were to be swept away and replaced by new, equitable direct taxes (although with results that were not quite what proponents had anticipated).

If the changes needed were so obvious, why could they not be enacted?

The answer, of course, lies in the realm not of economics but of politics. The abolition of aristocratic tax exemptions, and of the whole apparatus of venal offices and tax farms, would remove the remaining limits on royal absolutism. In exchange for giving the state the freedom to increase its tax base, the privileged classes could reasonably expect to have their public debt holdings repaid without arbitrary reductions, but the fact that they were no longer liable to taxation by royal default would be offset by their new liability to other forms of tax. The financial trade-off was at best neutral. What of a political trade-off?

The problem was that there was no obvious political compromise. A solution *à l'anglaise,* which exchanged the informal limits on royal fiscal power for the more formal ones of representative government, was anathema to the crown. It represented such a clear overall loss of power that it could scarcely be considered a trade-off at all. For the privileged classes, too, the tactic of calling for the return of the Estates General involved a leap of faith. It required surrendering their very tangible financial privileges—tax exemptions, hereditary offices, tax farms, and so forth—in exchange for the far less tangible privilege of representation in a body of uncertain composition. And yet, of course, if France was to compete in an age of public borrowing, it was precisely this political revolution that was needed. It is a sign, perhaps, of the lack of cohesion of the privileged classes that they were not willing to make this leap of faith except as a last resort.

In the meantime, they fell back on assertions of their constitutional rights. Here, too, Montesquieu had much to say. His argument against reform imposed from above was that it would turn France from a monarchy subservient to the law into a Turkish despotism. Such a move would ultimately reduce tax revenues, not raise them. But his "general rule" was only Montesquieu's second line of defense. His first, like that of most of his contemporaries, was a historical claim: France had inherited its system of government from the Frankish invaders of the fifth century, and the Franks, like the other Germanic tribes, had brought with them a form of limited monarchy that separated Europe from the despotisms of Asia. The freedoms of Europe were born, in his phrase, "in the forests of Germany." France, in other words, had an ancient constitution that was being threatened by the overweening ambition of its kings.

This view of history was not new, and had formed a fundamental part of the case of the English parliamentarians against Charles I and of the Dutch against Philip II. The classic French statement of the theory was produced by the Comte de Boulainvilliers in 1721:

> Whatever little reflection we make on what passes in England, Germany, Poland, on what was practiced not long ago in Denmark and Sweden, and what has been done in France . . . we shall easily find, that all the governments of the kingdoms formed in Europe, on the dismembering of the Roman empire, had a particular attention not to abandon themselves so much to the power of their kings, as that their authority could not be tempered by that of the several tribunals, whose original business was expressly to share it. The same institution is found in every place, tho' under different names; as those of Diets in Germany and Poland; Parliaments in England; Estates in France, Sweden and Denmark; Cortes in Arragon, Portugal, and even in Castile, tho' a conquer'd country.[55]

This attractively simple theory was not without its problems, however. Alongside the concept of tribal political liberty lay another idea, if anything older and more widely accepted: freedom is enjoyed only by the unconquered. It might be true that the Franks were free, but how did this freedom relate to a country descended largely from Gauls and Gallo-Romans? To the aristocrat Boulainvilliers the answer was clear:

> No body is ignorant, that the French having conquered Gaul in the reign of Clovis, established a government in it altogether separate from that of the people subdued, who remaining in a middle state, between Roman servitude and liberty, were always viewed by the conquerors, as destined to labour and husbandry, and not to share the honours of government.[56]

The Gauls might well have been subsequently liberated ("enfranchized"*) from their semiservitude by their Frankish conquerors. But theirs was a lesser freedom than that enjoyed by the Frankish aristocracy, which had never been conquered. If a bulwark was sought against royal despotism, then it was only the old aristocratic families, the linear inheritors of the "freedom of the Franks," upon which all existing freedoms rested, who could provide it.

Clearly this was an unappealing view of history, unless you were a member of the *noblesse d'épée.* An alternative approach was preferred by the supporters of the Parlements. The Parlements were a group of regional supreme courts whose members constituted the highest echelon of the *noblesse de la robe.* In the hands of the *parlementaires,* the theory of the "Gothic constitution" underwent a subtle transformation. According to Mon-

---

*Literally, "given the rights of Franks." It seems tragic that the word *franchise* so appropriately and redolently used in the struggle to extend the right to vote in the nineteenth century, should now be confined to the right to open a fast-food restaurant.

tesquieu (who was a member of the Parlement of Bordeaux), Darigrand, and other writers, the Frankish tribal assemblies proved too cumbersome in such a large and sparsely populated country. They were gradually superseded by deputies, whose powers, since the demise of the Estates General, had devolved onto the Parlements. This might seem a tenuous chain of descent given that the *parlementaires* (or their ancestors) had purchased their positions, but it was more widely acceptable in eighteenth-century France than that proposed by Boulainvilliers. In any case, it allowed the Parlements to play the part of the representatives of the popular will with considerable aplomb in the decades before 1789.

Many reformers, however, despaired of the limitations of the opposition and sustained the *thèse royale* (the "royal thesis"), arguing that reform could come only from above. The advocates of this position could turn history to good account, too. The royalist version of the Dark Ages was most effectively expressed by Abbé Dubos in the 1734.[57] According to Dubos, whatever the political organization of the Franks in Germany, they had entered Gaul with the authorization of the Roman Empire, and their kings had therefore inherited the absolute power of the Roman emperors. The tribal assemblies were not embryonic parliaments; they had been no more than reviews of troops. It was feudalism which represented a usurpation of power, not royal absolutism. Taken to its logical conclusion the "Romanist" theory implied that all privileges, whether aristocratic titles or representative institutions, were no more than the blessings conditionally conferred on his subjects by a benevolent despot. Most monarchists, however, were uncomfortable with a view of history that portrayed kings as despots, and preferred to see them as paternalistic rulers conforming to Bodin's concept of "Royal Monarchy," where the ruler enjoyed absolute legislative sovereignty but where every man was left with "his natural liberty, and proprietie of his own goods." But this theory of sovereignty exposed the ancien régime to an insoluble philosophical dilemma—for the right to private property, in particular, could not be reconciled with the financial aspirations of the absolutists.

Since the rise of socialist and social-democratic thought, it has been fashionable to condemn John Locke and the philosophes for the unquestioning primacy they accorded to property rights. Private property is no longer considered to be at the core of democracy, and the early political thinkers are accused of somehow tacking it on unnecessarily in an unconscious justification of the rising tide of bourgeois capitalism. But this is to misunderstand the full implications of their thought.

Property rights were an essential part of a seamless and almost universally held view of the world, which started and ended with the contrasting poles of freedom and slavery. Slavery was the very antithesis of freedom. It was the ancient and inevitable result of conquest, of subjugation by force. According to John Locke, it was "the state of war continued, between a lawful conqueror and a captive." Yet what was the freedom that was forfeited by enslavement? It was none other than the loss of the ownership of one's person, the first and fundamental form of property that had existed since the Garden of Eden. "Though the earth, and all inferior creatures, be common to all men [in a state of nature], yet every man has property in his own person. . . ."[58]

If the unfree lost ownership of their persons, it was obvious that they could not own anything else.* By contrast, private property rights were the privilege of the unconquered—in other words, of the free (the connection is still enshrined in the word *freeholder* and the French *franc-tenancier*). Boulainvilliers, explaining the right of the descendents of the Gauls to be represented in the Third Estate, makes the matrix—slavery, property, political liberty—quite clear: "Thus, until the people arrived at liberty, to the right of possessing themselves, and having goods of their own, we must not be astonished at their not having any rank in the state."[59]

Equally clear were the fiscal implications of property rights. In the words of John Locke:

> If any one shall claim a power to lay and levy taxes on the people, by his own authority, and without [the] consent of the people, he thereby invades the fundamental law of property, and subverts the end of government: for what property have I in that, which another may by right take when he pleases, to himself?[60]

In an attempt to justify taxation without consent the Physiocrats—led by the finance minister Anne-Robert-Jacques Turgot—attempted to argue that

*Most writers did not seek to explain this connection. It seemed almost too obvious. Locke, however, took the matter head on and made everything derive from the ownership of one's person. Concomitant with this was the ownership of one's labor, and therefore of its product (in other words, exactly what was lost by a slave). Locke neatly resolved the apparent contradiction between an earth originally "common to all men" and its later subdivision into private property by emphasizing the value added by human labor and ingenuity. Natural value might be common to all men, but it represented a tiny fraction of the value added through human improvement: "An acre of land, that bears here twenty bushels of wheat, and another in America, which, with the same husbandry, would do the like, are without doubt of the same natural intrinsic value: but the benefit mankind receives from the one in a year, is worth 5£ and from the other possibly not worth a penny, if all the profit an Indian received from it were to be valued and sold here. . . ." [*Two Treatises on Government*, 1694, in *Collected Works*, Vol. IX, London, 1824, p. 363] landholders had surrendered a notional share of their property to the state in exchange for official protection of their property rights. (Exactly how large this notional share may have been was not defined.) When a landowner sold his land, he was in fact selling only his share in the property, while the state retained its separate stake. Taxation was therefore merely the income due to the crown on its own property.

Yet so convoluted a theory was bound to be a minority view. Most advocates of royal power admitted the absolute claim of private property rights. In France there was none more eminent than Bishop Bossuet, the silver-tongued tutor of Louis XIV's son and presumed heir, whose job it was to stroke the Sun King's ego from the pulpit of the royal chapel at Versailles. His studies of the Old Testament (and he sought the answer to all political problems in the Good Book with as much certainty as any Protestant fundamentalist) led him to distinguish, like Bodin, between European and Asiatic forms of rule:

> There is among men a kind of government which is called arbitrary, but which is not found among us in well-ordered states. Four attributes accompany these kinds of government. Firstly: subject peoples are born slaves, that is to say truly serfs; and among them there are no free persons. Secondly: no one possesses private property: all the sources [of wealth] belong the prince, and there is no right of inheritance from father to son.[61]

As a vivid proof of the need for legitimate/paternalistic rulers to respect property rights, Bossuet liked to recall the cautionary tale of King Ahab. In this memorable Old Testament story, Ahab was induced by his wife, Jezebel, to acquire Naboth's vineyard so as to round off the royal estates. As the story is careful to relate, Ahab offered Naboth at least the fair market value of the property, but Naboth still refused to sell and had the complete right to do so. In revenge Ahab resorted to false accusations of blasphemy and had Naboth stoned to death, so that he might get hold of the vineyard by confiscation. God's view of the matter was unequivocal:

> And the word of the Lord came to Elias the Thesbite (his prophet), saying: Arise, and go down to meet Ahab king of Israel . . . : behold he is going down to the vineyard of Naboth, to take possession of it. And thou shalt speak to him saying: Thus saith the Lord: Thou hast slain an innocent, moreover also thou hast taken possession. And after these words thou shalt add: In this place, wherein the dogs have licked the blood of Naboth, they shall lick thy blood also.[62]

If these were the arguments of the most eminent exponent of royal "absolutism" at its apogee, then it is reasonable to wonder whether the dispute about taxation without consent was not lost before it was joined.

ARISTOCRATIC REVOLUTION

The last true attempt of the Bourbons to assert their absolute power took place in 1770–1774. The attack came on two fronts. Joseph-Marie Terray, the Controller of Finance, took on the public creditors in a series of unilateral debt reductions that constituted the most serious default since 1720; and René-Nicolas de Maupeou, the chancellor, directed his aim at the Parlements. It was not just that these were the two principal restraints on the monarchy's freedom of action; they were also profoundly interconnected.

The Parlements are easily portayed as strange and antiquated institutions, which the Revolution was soon to consign to the dustbin of history. With their purchased offices, the *parlementaires* were poor representatives of even the ancient kind of liberty that they upheld. Moreover, by the late eighteenth century, the old ideas of differing degrees of freedom held by different ranks of society was starting to give way to more sweeping claims about the common rights of all. Beyond this philosophical limitation, the practical power of the Parlements under the ancien régime was almost entirely negative in character. They had the ability to obstruct, but not to enact. In this regard they were even more ineffective than the English Parliament of the early seventeenth century. Almost nobody saw them as the vehicles of positive reform, and it was in despair of this obstructionist role that several stalwart *parlementaires* deserted their colleagues to take up the royal cause—most notably Maupeou himself. But in the absence of any other body, the Parlements were a vital means of lending a cloak of legitimacy to a government that could never quite shake off the need to be seen as paternal rather than arbitrary. The registration of royal edicts by the Parlements—most critically those concerning new taxes and loans—was essential if they were to be regarded as legal by taxpayers and creditors. Of course, the king could always force registration by the notorious process of the *lit de justice*—in which he summoned the *parlementaires* to his presence and imposed his will from an ornamental bed. It was to avoid just this maneuver that the Parlement of Paris went on strike in 1771 and provoked Maupeou's coup. But acts so semiotically redolent of oriental despotism were best avoided if an image of paternal benevolence was to be maintained.

It is not clear whether the autocratic regime of Terray and Maupeou could ever have succeeded. Louis XV, who still liked to remember the early days of his reign, when he was popularly known as Louis le Bien Aimé, was a halfhearted despot and refused to extend Maupeou's reforms to most of the other regional Parlements. The coup was not complete. Nonetheless, most historians have tended to view this period as the last genuine opportunity for the ancien régime to avoid oblivion, and in evidence they point to the subsidence of opposition after 1771. There was certainly no obvious threat to the regime in 1774. But this is no different from pointing out the temporary success of Charles I of England in ruling without Parliament for eleven years of peace. The true test of the Maupeou-Terray regime would not have come until 1778, when France declared war on Britain in support of American independence. By that stage Louis XV was dead and had been succeeded by the young Louis XVI, who immediately renounced the old ways, dismissed Maupeou and Terray, and recalled the Parlements. Yet it is hard not to suspect that the autocratic experiment would not have lasted very long under the strains of war. The only major loan of Terray's regime was the life annuity issue of 1771, and at an expected cost to the government of around 10.5%, this was the single most expensive loan of the whole prerevolutionary period—issued, moreover, in a year of peace.[63] How much would Terray have had to pay ten years later?

The fundamental insolubility of the conundrum facing the ancien régime is nowhere better revealed than in a comment of one of the men mostly closely connected with the post-1774 government. J. M. Augeard was a long-standing member of the Farmers General, as well as a senior official in the royal household. He was offered the job of Controller of Finance by Maurepas, the chief minister of Louis XVI's new government. As a knowledgeable financier and a staunch royalist, he was well-placed to understand the vital role of legitimacy in public credit. In his memoirs he recorded an acute and revealing letter written to Maurepas in 1774 advocating the recall of the Parlements:

> It is necessary that the King should be absolute master in his kingdom, but what is even more necessary, not only for the happiness of his people, but for the support of credit operations, is that no one must worry that his power is above the law, since if the people believe him to be a despot, it will be impossible to open loans, or, if that route is taken, they will be so costly that England will always finish by having the last *écu* in any war. What is needed is that the King should be master of the Parlement but that no one should believe it.[64]

This was a tenuous fiction, but during the following decade, it worked moderately well. Partly mindful of their close encounter with extinction, and partly inspired by the wave of patriotic fervor that accompanied the anticipated humiliation of their rival in the American War of Independence, the restored Parlements registered the government's wartime edicts without significant protest. Under Necker's management, loans were raised and serviced without default. It is worth noting that, even under his successor, Joly de Fleury, whose relations with the credit markets was less intimate, and who faced a financial situation considerably more desperate, the cost of new loans never rose above 9%—significantly lower than Terray's annuity issue of 1771.

By 1786, however, the fiction was wearing thin. As memories of the 1770–1774 period started to wane, and as wartime enthusiasm receded, the Parlements started to revert to the same intransigence that they had shown after the Seven Years' War. The regularity with which ministers had to seek registration of new taxes and loans in an attempt to cover a deficit that was refusing to shrink only gave them a tool with which to hold the government to ransom. When Calonne, Louis's chief minister, sought a new permanent land tax without aristocratic exemptions in 1787, he was forced to see if he could overcome parliamentary resistance by first summoning a purely consultative Assembly of Notables. This entirely aristocratic body (which included the presidents of all the Parlements) showed a reforming zeal that the government could scarcely have anticipated. It was willing to accept the new land tax, and even the abolition of feudal dues, but only on the condition of the summoning of the Estates General to ratify the legislation. The significance of this aristocratic insistence on democratic reform was not lost on the economist Du Pont de Nemours, who was secretary of the assembly:

> On the 1st of May France was still a monarchy and the first in Europe. On the 9th of May . . . France became a Republic in which there remains a magistrate decorated with the title and honors of royalty but forever obliged to assemble his people to ask them to supply his wants, for which the public revenue without this new national consent would be forever inadequate. The King of France became the king of England.[65]

To consolidate the new accords, Louis replaced Calonne with leaders of the parliamentary opposition: Lomenie de Brienne, Lamoignon, and Malesherbes—veterans of the struggle against Maupeou. Strangely, when in power, they, too, were to despair of reform from below and to be transformed into Maupeou's spiritual successors. When the Parlement of Paris was invited to register the tax in July, it, too, was adamant that only the Estates General could authorize such a fundamental fiscal reform. The government refused to grant this demand for a period of five years, in which time it hoped to restore its finances and thereby avoid dependence on an elected body for its survival. When matters came to an impasse in September 1787, Louis converted a consultative séance into an impromptu *lit de justice* so as to force registration. That Parlement was sitting in expanded form with the representatives of the *noblesse d'épée* and the clergy in attendance made the coup all the more significant. In a memorable scene, Louis's action provoked an unprecedented rebuke from his cousin, the Duc d'Orléans: "Sire, I beg Your Majesty to allow me to place at your feet and in the heart of this court that I consider this registration illegal."[66]

Just whether the registration was, or was not, legal became the focus of the following six months. A mixed life-annuity/term-loan issue of 120 million livres, the last of the ancien régime, was part of the package of decrees—the essential measure required to cover the anticipated deficit of 160 million for the coming year. By November, it was already fully subscribed, but the Parlement had not yet voiced its opinion whether the registration of September was valid. Only in April 1788 did it finally opine that it was, unfortunately, invalid, and that the royal edict was therefore null and void. The judges had no doubt of the possible implications of their action for public credit:

> Your Parlement is not ignorant of the fact that capitalists in good faith, reassured by the external appearances of the annulled edict, have brought their funds to the 120 million loan opened for this year. Has their confidence been mistaken? That is not the intention of your Parlement. It is possible to insure their trust. In truth the means is no longer in the hands of your Parlement, but the lenders still have a resource in the Assembly of the Estates General. The Estates General will weigh up in their wisdom the public circumstances, they will hear everything that it required by the dignity of the nation, and their clear-sighted zeal will without doubt consolidate the loan already subscribed with the debts consecrated by the law.[67]

This remonstrance unleashed the fury of the new, supposedly reformist, government. The Parlements were again suppressed and their main leaders arrested. The intermittent downward trend in the credit markets that had been apparent since 1785 now accelerated. It was increasingly clear that the 120-million loan was the very last that the government would be able to issue this side of convening the Estates General. In June there was already a foretaste of the violence of the coming Revolution as the citizens of Grenoble sought to protect their regional Parlement from suppression. By August it was quite clear that Augeard had been right in 1774: no Parlements, no credit. On August 8, 1788, the government relented and brought forward the summoning of the Estates General to May 1789. But it was too late: the coffers were already empty. On August 16, payments in cash were suspended. In the ensuing panic Brienne was forced to resign and was replaced by Necker, the only minister in whom the markets had any confidence. Somehow he managed to engineer a partial resumption of cash payments, and to borrow enough here and there to keep the government afloat until the following May. But by now there was little reason to doubt that Du Pont de Nemours had been right in 1787. The King of France had become the King of England.

Perhaps there was no other solution. Perhaps the route advocated by the proponents of the *thèse royale* was a dead end. But before the idea of a successful royal absolutism is discarded, one should consider the case of Prussia. In the seventeenth century, the Electors of Brandenburg (after 1701 to be known as kings in Prussia[68]) had managed, like many of their contemporaries, to shrug off the parliamentary institutions inherited from the Middle Ages. The history of France has shown that it was of little use to remove the formal restraints on royal power if an informal, but no less restrictive, dependence on public credit remained. The Hohenzollern rulers of Prussia, however, achieved a freedom of political maneuver that the Bourbons could never match. They were therefore able to put into effect the sort of reforms from above that were repeatedly advocated, but never instituted, in France. Aristocratic tax exemption was abolished, and the nobles were encouraged to take up paid service in the Prussian army. The first professional and meritocratic bureaucracy in Europe was created, and the judicial system became a model of impartiality. It is no wonder that Voltaire, that most eloquent castigator of aristocratic privilege and advocate of its replacement by enlightened despotism, should hold up the regime of Frederick the Great as an example to the rest of Europe.

The Prussian example, on the other hand, was not one held up by Montesquieu. It was not just that Prussia seemed not to show that instinct for political liberty so fondly attributed to the Goths; it also singularly failed to provide support for Montesquieu's "general rule" of taxation and freedom. Under the Hohenzollern autocracy, Prussian tax revenues rose from 1.3 million thalers in 1714 to 7 million in 1740, and to 19 million in 1786. Whether the real burden of taxation of all types paid by the Prussians was higher than that paid by the French is hard to say. But what is certain is that taxes were more equitably distributed and therefore aroused less opposition, while a far larger portion of the amounts collected made their way into the central treasury. The fiscal policy of the Prussian state was so successful that it was, uniquely in Europe, able to maintain a large standing army without recourse to the moneylenders. Indeed, the congenital prudence of Frederick William I allowed him to bequeath a war chest of 8 million thalers at his death in 1740. His adventurer son played his diplomatic and military cards with such consummate skill that in spite of his wars he was able to increase his reserves to 51 million thalers (around £8 million sterling) by 1786.[69] On a continent on which no king since Henry VII of England had managed to accumulate any significant treasure, and on which all the others seemed only to accumulate debts, this performance was quite remarkable.

The translocation of the Prussian fiscal system to France would have produced striking results. The full "tax" burden on the French population was estimated to be as high as 700 million livres. Perhaps even a French state reformed from above would not have been able to lay its hands on that full amount; but even 600 million, collected centrally and unencumbered by debt, would have provided the Bourbons with resources equivalent to £24 million sterling—more than three times the net free revenues available to the crown in 1788. The financial advantage of Britain would have been reversed overnight. Yet it was not to be. In 1788, the forces of representative government were in the ascendant, and if the Bourbons were to increase their spending power, it would only be at the cost of their autonomy. France would follow the English rather than the Prussian model.

Or would it?

SEVEN

REVOLUTION

> Holland loaded itself with ten times the impositions which it revolted from Spain rather than submit to. Tyranny is a poor provider. It knows neither how to accumulate nor how to extract.
>
> —Edmund Burke, addressing the House of Commons, September 1774

> We will have done nothing for the peace and happiness of the nation, if it can believe that the reign of liberty is more onerous that that of servitude.
>
> —Mirabeau, addressing the National Assembly, April 1790

Edmund Burke, addressing the Commons in 1774, appeared to have no doubt that Montesquieu was correct. The experience of the Dutch showed that a free nation would always have a financial edge over a nation of "slaves." Not only would its citizens be willing to contribute more in way of taxes, but they would also happily lend extra funds at low rates of interest, confident in the good faith of their government. The political debate that led so inexorably to the Revolution of 1789 seemed to revolve around this fundamental proposition. The compromise fiction suggested by Augeard in 1774 was not, in the long term, viable. Taxpayers were perhaps slightly more willing to pay, and creditors somewhat more willing to lend, with the appearance of public approval lent by the Parlements. But neither taxpayers nor creditors were willing to contribute on the scale required to match the financial clout of England, where power rested definitively in an elected assembly (however imperfect the electoral system). And in any case, the Parlements were not prepared to play the role of a convenient rubber stamp indefinitely. By the 1780s the need for more fundamental reform was apparent to the large majority of the French ruling class; and the outcome that they anticipated was clear: not a slavish copy of the English constitution perhaps, but a Gallic version (perhaps more accurately a "Frankish" version) producing a similar financial outcome.

Yet was that outcome the only one possible from the transformation of France into a "free nation"? A glance at the words of Mirabeau in 1790 suggests that the question might not be so simple. A large number of Frenchmen, including Mirabeau, it seems, had not read Montesquieu or, if they had, were decidedly unconvinced by his equation of political freedom with happy and generous taxpayers. Political liberty in their view was supposed to lead to fewer tax burdens, not more. Were these people merely ignorant, or had Montesquieu missed something?

He had indeed missed something: an alternative interpretation of freedom whose roots lay deep in the past.

The ancients saw liberty first and foremost as freedom from conquest and as freedom from slavery—the second being the logical corollary of the first. Slaves, of course, did not pay tax as such. The totality of their surplus production was appropriated by other means. But very often the conquerors would be content merely to tax their victims in lieu of total enslavement. The ancients were not fooled: they saw taxation as a sure badge of subservience. The most coveted emblem of the free, therefore, was to pay no taxes. Of course, the preferred way to achieve this state of libertarian fiscal bliss was to conquer and subjugate others, who would pay taxes instead. When this course was not possible, or did not suffice, the free would be forced to dip into their own pockets. But they could still distinguish themselves from the unfree by a number of devices: by "giving" their money freely, *à la grèque*, or at least by consenting freely to a general levy; they might agree that any money contributed to the common cause would be returned by a distribution of the spoils of war, or they might their lend money on some more formal basis. The ancient world is full of examples of these and other adaptations of tribal finance to a monetary age. Public credit was not foremost among them, even if its origins are to be found in the great period of classical antiquity.

It was the city-states of medieval Europe, populated as they were by merchants, who first came up with a fiscal formula—an idiosyncratic brew of these ancient techniques—which approximated the modern system of marketable long-term government debt. Their ingenious creation enabled them to marry political liberty to commercial convenience. By doing so, they quite unconsciously set off a train of events with implications that they could scarcely have imagined. Their system of public finance based on cheap long-term credit was so effective that it could not be ignored by the monarchies of Europe. By the end of the sixteenth century, Spain and France had balance sheets so debt-ridden as to appear risible in comparison to those of their non-European rivals, let alone to those of past superpowers. Neither the Habsburgs nor the Bourbons were ultimately able to reconcile the political implications of the new financial system with the logic of absolutism. They ended up with a system of debt management by default and were unable to tap the full potential of the credit markets. Until 1688 it appeared that only a republic of merchants could manage this feat; but in that year England altered its political system to the degree that, although nominally still a monarchy, it could act in a manner that, financially at least, was as "republican" as any city of Italy or the Netherlands.

By the late eighteenth century the idiosyncratic invention of the Italians five hundred years earlier had evolved not only into a seemingly unstoppable force, but also into one that appeared to prove the validity of Montesquieu's "general rule." Resistance to tax might be all very well as a method of asserting one's freedom against an oppressive regime, but it was not the appropriate response to the defense and maintenance of liberty, once it was achieved. The reason was that, paradoxically, Montesquieu's rule was an essential precondition of republican finance, for the simple reason that there could be no successful reliance on credit without the reassurance of secure tax revenues.

Yet, in truth, public finance based on cheap long-term debt was not the only reinterpretation of primitive freedom from tax that was possible by the eighteenth century. It had merely acquired the apparent force of historical inevitability. There was another side to the politics of the mercantile-republican system which was not entirely lost on contemporaries. In its Italian origin the fiscal freedom that it represented was that of the citizen merchants. Only they had the privilege of paying their taxes as loans. Only they received the annual interest payments that made this privilege so attractive. The security for their interest was invariably indirect taxes—as always, felt to be less insulting than direct taxes to the dignity of those who were free. In theory this was not inequitable: the taxes were paid by citizens as well as noncitizens. But in practice they fell disproportionately on the poorer classes, who included not only noncitizen laborers but also the poorer citizens—the *popolo minuto*. The potentially regressive nature of the republican fiscal regime was accentuated as debts, and therefore, taxes rose. In the end, the system tended to conform to the ancient rule that freedom from taxation is hard to enjoy unless somebody less "free" pays instead. This political truth was perfectly well understood at the time and was behind both the uprising that propelled Simone Boccanegra to power in Genoa in 1340 and the revolt of the Ciompi in Florence in 1378. The popular parties in these revolts agreed in condemning reliance on loans and demanding increased direct taxes in their place.

The original Italian formula exhibited a conceptual purity unequaled by any subsequent variant. It neatly resolved the Montesquieu-Mirabeau paradox by making explicit the dual nature of freedom. If all went well, the levies on the citizens would function as loans. In this case, the fiscal burden would be minimal, as befitted the free in Mirabeau's opinion. Yet, in time of extreme financial stress, interest payments would be impossible to maintain, market prices would fall, and the levies would become de facto taxes. In this case, the fiscal burden on the citizens would rise very high, and the outcome would conform to Montesquieu's view of the matter. Perhaps better still, a three-stage paradigm for Italian debts can be outlined that exhibits the full range of possible financial outcomes compatible with political freedom. In the first, debts are low, as are the taxes required to service them, and market values remain close to par. In this case, the citizens enjoy fiscal freedom without excessively burdening any other group (except, of course, the inhabitants of rival cities, for whose defeat the loans would have been raised in the first place). In the second stage, debts have risen and are maintained at high prices only by onerous taxes that fall mainly on the poorer classes. Now the wealthy citizens maintain their fiscal freedom, but only by shifting the burden onto others less politically privileged. In the third stage, debts have risen to levels that are no longer sustainable by indirect taxes. Market values fall, and the fiscal burden on the richer citizens rises to levels that may match—or even exceed—those of the poor (since not only will their current contributions become de facto taxes, but the accumulated capital value of their past contributions will also fall toward zero).

The Italian system could not survive the fifteenth century. It had arrived at the third stage of our paradigm, and latent, but ultimately fatal, contradictions started to emerge. With ever-growing levels of debt, high market prices were sustainable only by the confidence of secondary holders—who were, by definition, *voluntary* lenders. But potential investors were unlikely to attribute a triple-A credit rating to a borrower whose obligations were only contingent, and a large portion of whose potential tax base could not be tapped except by more borrowing. What was needed was the explicit separation of loans and taxes and a move to wholly voluntary loans, where the commitment to repay was absolute rather than contingent, and where there was no implicit distinction between the claims of primary and secondary holders. This was the path taken by Genoa, and by the cities of the north (most notably by the ultimate league of cities, the Dutch Republic). In the interests of economic viability, the new variety of republican finance obscured some of the political principles that underlay its predecessor. Nonetheless, the essential political continuity of the system was visible in the relative roles of direct and indirect taxation. Direct taxes on the merchant creditor class were no longer entirely rejected but were simply kept to the minimum compatible with public solvency. Interest on the debt remained firmly secured on indirect taxes.

If the "republican" system of public finance was inherently associated with the rule of one class, then it was not certain that it would appear attractive to other societies seeking liberation from autocratic rule. The *popolo minuto* of those societies might well take the same dim view of the procedure as the Ciompi of Florence, or as the Genoese rebels of 1340. Of course, the *popolo minuto* had never (at least, not during the two previous millennia) managed to lay its hands on the reins of government for any extended period. But was the past a perfect predictor of the future?

This potential limitation on the applicability of the republican model was added to another. The system was the invention of merchants. Indeed, it was the perfect financial expression of government "of the merchants, by the merchants, and for the merchants." It had certainly never been, for instance, the ideal financial expression of aristocratic political power. It depended critically on high levels of liquid wealth, and on the diffusion of interest-taking as a norm of commercial interchange. It was this that had made the successful adoption of the system by England so significant. For the first time, a society still dominated by landed interests had managed to adapt itself to its requirements. But who was to say that England was not unique? First of all, by 1700, England had already become the most urbanized nation in Europe outside the mercantile republics. Second, the gradual reconciliation of the landed interests to "Dutch" finance had been possible partly because of the unusual structure of English landholding, with its dearth of smallholdings. Even with these advantages, the new financial system had not established itself without a struggle that had lasted a whole generation, and whose outcome had remained in doubt for many years.

These considerations were reasons to doubt whether the transition to finance *à l'Anglaise* would proceed smoothly across the Channel. France may have been no less oligarchic than England by the late eighteenth century, but it was certainly less urbanized, and its agrarian landowning structure was still largely medieval. On the other hand, it was probably no less urbanized than England had been in 1688, and it had accumulated a plentiful supply of liquid wealth, as well as considerable experience of financial assets—not least in the form of public debt.

But what if there were a society simultaneously less oligarchic *and* less urbanized than England or France? Would such a society be likely to take up the fiscal system of the merchant republics as the financial expression of its political freedom?

A NEW WORLD

> This Currency, as we manage it, is a wonderful machine. It performs its Office when we issue it; it pays and clothes Troops, and provides Victuals and Ammunition; and when we are obliged to issue a Quantity excessive, it pays itself off by Depreciation.
>
> —Benjamin Franklin, April 1779

> A bankrupt faithless republic would be a novelty in the political world, and appear among respectable nations like a common prostitute among chaste and respectable matrons.
>
> —Continental Congress, September 1779

The American colonists who gathered to declare their independence from Britain in 1776 needed no lessons in establishing a government based on representative institutions. Such institutions had long been soundly established along the Atlantic seaboard. Given that under the Articles of Confederation sovereignty was located almost exclusively in the individual colonies—now become independent states—the American Revolution was, politically, effortless. Not only did the necessary institutions already exist, as they did not in France, but they had also accumulated considerable experience of the practice of government. In this, they more closely resembled the provincial assemblies of the Netherlands in 1570 than they did the Parliament of England, whose experience of government in 1640 was largely confined to complaining about ministerial abuses and stonewalling on taxes.

In the century or so of their existence before 1776, the English colonies had established themselves as perhaps the "freest" places on earth to live. A happy fusion of historical and geographical factors had contributed to this state of libertarian bliss. There was the legacy of Protestant dissent.

Many of the colonists brought with them the practice of electing their pastors, a quintessential part of the Protestant revolt against the ordained power of Romish priests. The awareness that they were escaping intolerance and persecution in their native lands led many to support the toleration of all religious beliefs in their new homeland. One colony—Pennsylvania—was established for the avowed purpose of providing a safe haven for persecuted religious minorities. It was true that the Massachusetts Bay Company was initially closed to non-Puritans. It was also true that the founding spirit of some of the southern colonies was not religious at all, but rather the purely secular urge to make money. Nonetheless, few people would dismiss the long-term importance of the legacy of religious dissent in the establishment of a pluralistic and democratic society in America.

Whether the colonists sought spiritual or merely material welfare, they all brought with them a tradition of representative institutions from their native land. Almost instinctively they tended to re-create what they had left behind them. The Massachusetts Bay Company may not initially have wished to share power with outsiders, but its members were, significantly, known as "freemen" and participated in elections to a General Court. By the 1660s, the franchise had already been extended to other Protestant groups and after 1691 was based on property qualifications similar to those in England. The founder of Pennsylvania, William Penn, was a firm believer in the ancient freedom of the English, which, in line with the times, he traced back to the Angles and Saxons, and before them, to the Celts. His ideal commonwealth was to be not only a haven of religious toleration but also one founded securely on representative government. Political debate in the colony revolved around the role of the Penn family after the founder's death, the desirability of a semihereditary upper chamber, and the absorption of German and other non-English immigrants into the political system. But none of these issues brought into question the fundamentally democratic thrust of Penn's original creation. The other states followed varied paths to a similar goal, starting with some form of regular gathering of the original settlers to arrange their affairs, and finishing with an elected colonial assembly sharing the powers of government with a royal governor. Even Virginia, the most patrician of all the colonies, was no different in this regard. Its constitution centered on a two-chamber assembly elected on a property-based franchise. As Edmund Burke was to warn those in the House of Commons who insisted on a showdown with the colonists in 1775:

> In this character of the Americans a love of freedom is the predominating feature which marks and distinguishes the whole. . . . This fierce spirit of liberty is stronger in the English colonies, probably, that in any other people of the earth, and this from a great variety of causes. . . . First the peoples of the colonies are descendents of Englishmen. England, Sir, is a nation which still, I hope, respects, and formerly adored, her freedom. The colonists emigrated from you when this part of your character was most predominant; and they took this bias and direction the moment they parted from your hands.[1]

The legacy of history may have been primary, but it was amply supported by the contributions of geography. The tiny numbers and economic insignificance of the colonists ensured that they would for a long time be almost entirely ignored by the government at Westminster. Most interference in their affairs came only at the request of discontented groups within the colonies. Even in 1775 it was only slowly dawning on people in England that these tiny groups of emigrants had grown into flourishing societies with a combined population that was greater than that of the Dutch Republic, and that was doubling every twenty years. The great distance separating the colonies from Westminster not only contributed to their de facto independence but also made any attempt to assert greater control a venture of uncertain outcome as well as marginal utility.

Not only were the colonists used to relatively low levels of interference in their lives by the government in London, but their own local governments were also modest affairs. Their role was limited, in part, by the reduction of military costs afforded by the protection of the Atlantic Ocean, a vast moat patrolled by the British navy. Sporadic low-intensity warfare with the indigenous tribes was often adequately handled by militia forces. More serious exertions were required when the Indians were supported by the French, and a far greater financial strain was placed on colonial budgets; but as soon as there was any involvement of a rival European power, England could be relied upon to help, not only with military forces, but often with financial aid. In peacetime the colonial governments operated on minuscule budgets that in most colonies amounted to under £10,000 per annum.

Geography promoted the diffusion of political liberty in yet another way. The extreme sparseness of the population ensured that labor would be as scarce as land was plentiful. The result was a combination of high wages and low commodity prices that even before 1776 may have made Americans the possessors of the highest average per capita income in the world. This combination also reduced income disparities and therefore the possibility of a class of patricians living at the expense of the poor. In a world that had not yet conceived of true universal suffrage, voting rights were confined to the owners of property. But it was far easier to meet this basic requirement in America than it was in England, even if the hurdle was set at the same level. The result was a level of political participation that exceeded any other since the early history of some of the Italian communes, or of the city-states of ancient Greece. Of course, as so often in prior history, the freedom of one group came at the expense of another. Historians of the economics of slavery have often noted that it is precisely a shortage of free labor that has made people resort to its opposite. Like the political liberty of the Athenian demos, the freedom of Americans in at least five of the thirteen colonies was the logical corollary of their reliance on slave labor. But that was not yet an issue that clouded the political debate.

The undoubted political freedom of the American colonies was certain to find expression of some sort in their financial arrangements. But was this likely to be in the form created by republics of merchants? The background of the colonies gave them two further characteristics that suggested otherwise. The prevalent form of economic endeavor in a fertile and virgin land was inevitably agriculture. Some of the port towns along the Atlantic Coast had started to emerge as serious centers of commerce, but the day when America was to be dominated by urban interests was at least a century away. Not only was there a shortage of merchants, but there was also a shortage of that other essential ingredient of republican finance: liquid capital. The colonists had generally arrived with the bare essentials of life. A good portion of their liquid assets—and they were not often wealthy—had gone in the cost of the voyage. They started life in an immediate cash squeeze. Throughout the colonial period there was a constant trade deficit with the mother country, resulting from the import of manufactured goods. This deficit was only partially offset by a growing surplus with the Spanish Empire to the south.* Of course, the money stock was increased by other means, such as continuous streams of new immigrants and foreign capital investments. By the 1770s the total coin in the colonies has been estimated to have been between £2 million and £3 million. But this was less than half the amount circulating in England in relation either to population or to GNP.

*The result of these combined trade flows was that the majority of coins in the colonies were Spanish pesos of around 25 grams of silver. When the new republic chose, in the reforming spirit of an enlightened age, to avoid basing its currency on a unit of account unrelated to the coins actually in circulation, it inevitably chose the Spanish coins as its starting point.

What the colonies needed, therefore, was a form of emergency public finance that would satisfy an agrarian society with a fundamental dislike of big government and with a shortage of liquid assets. In earlier times this finance might have been found in a number of devices, but in the late seventeenth and eighteenth centuries the increasing prevalence of forms of paper money throughout Europe suggested a new solution. The first gleaming of what was to evolve into the characteristic colonial system of finance were to be seen in Massachusetts. In 1690, the New England colony planned an expedition against the French settlements in Quebec. The campaign was to be financed on lines that would have been easily recognizable in ancient Greece: the spoils of war would suffice to pay the troops and to make an overall profit. Unfortunately, the plans went awry; there were no spoils of war, and therefore there was no money to pay the soldiers. Rather than raise taxes immediately, the government decided to issue to the disappointed veterans £47,000 of notes, which would be gradually redeemed by future revenues. Most of the recipients of this paper, of course, could not wait for the promised redemption to materialize and were forced to sell at a loss. But the practice evidently found favor with the Massachusetts electorate, since it was followed by issues amounting to £430,000 during the Anglo-French wars of the following two decades.

There was nothing that was entirely novel in the action of the New England colony. The Long Parliament had paid its troops in paper, as had the Dutch Republic; and the French government had paid its suppliers with *billets d'épargne* during the Thirty Years' War. During the wars of 1689–1714, England and France had issued vast amounts of short-term paper of various kinds to pay for the escalating costs of war, with consequences that have been discussed in earlier chapters. The subsequent wars of the eighteenth century witnessed similar recourse to the printing press.

Yet there was a clear difference in the way that the American colonies applied the technique. In Europe, the combatants regarded short-term paper as only one of three tools of war finance. The other two—long-term debt and increased taxes—were generally considered the instruments of first preference. Short-term debt was ideally (although very rarely) kept to the minimum necessary to smooth the expenses of the war departments; and its issue in large quantities was a sure sign of the weakening of the long-term credit markets. In fact, the strength of the Anglo-Dutch formula lay precisely in its greater facility of raising long-term debt and its consequent ability to avoid the short-term cash squeezes that characterized Habsburg and Bourbon defaults. The American system, as it came to be practiced throughout almost all the colonies, relied almost exclusively on short-term paper, to the total exclusion of long-term debts and with precious little help from taxation.

This was not the only Atlantic schism. European short-term paper was generally interest-bearing and almost always convertible into coin—at least, in theory. Pure paper money in the modern sense—non-interest-bearing, nonconvertible, and supported solely by laws forcing its general acceptance—scarcely existed before 1789. Even John Law's Banque Royale notes were convertible into coin until quite late in the inexorable decline and fall of his system. This was not the transatlantic method of operation. The colonial notes were pure nonconvertible paper currencies, supported by laws making them legal tender for all transactions. Only in Sweden between 1745 and 1776 was there a similar reliance on nonconvertible paper.

There was a sound economic basis for this choice. If the colonies suffered from a shortage of hard currency, it made sense for them to issue paper money that did not tie up their reserves. Their economies were growing at rates far higher than any in Europe, and there was some reason to believe that the new currencies would help to nourish this growth without causing inflation. Encouraged by this belief, the colonial governments did not stop at the issue of paper to cover wartime expenses but kept the printing presses running in peacetime as well by setting up land banks.[2] Between 1712 and 1737 ten colonies set up public banks, whose purpose was to lend freshly minted paper money to landowners against mortgages on their land. The mortgages bore interest—generally at a favorable rate—and the notes (non-interest-bearing legal-tender money like other colonial issues) would circulate freely throughout the economy. Eventually they would return to the government in the form of interest and principal payments by the various mortgagees and would gradually be retired. Economically this was in no way a poor scheme. The money would be created as a result of economic demand and was relatively unlikely to cause inflation—although this unlikelihood depended on sound lending criteria, which were not always followed. The interest on the mortgages contributed to the government's budget, New York obtaining half its peacetime revenues in this way before the Revolution. Although the land-bank notes were a form of public debt in an abstract sense, they were not a tool of emergency government finance since they could not be issued in payment of goods and services. If anything, they complicated wartime fiscal management by further limiting the amount of wartime money that could be issued without inflation.

Mortgage demand was an imperfect guide for monetary policy, but at least it bore some relation to economic equilibrium. Wartime fiscal need was a rudder that regularly pointed the ship of state onto the rocks. There was absolutely no way to guarantee that the economically correct amount of money would be created by military expenditures, and the likelihood was always that too much would end up in circulation. Paper money of all sorts, including that of the land banks, would then start to depreciate in value, leaving the authorities with a familiar but unpleasant set of choices: They could reduce the amount of wartime currency outstanding by raising taxes payable in depreciated paper, or by refunding it with long-term debt. They could readjust its legal value to closer to its market level or merely leave things as they were. The one solution that the governments uniformly ignored was the second. They seemed to have a instinctive dislike of long-term debt and preferred some combination of the other methods available.

This system answered nicely to the predilections of the colonists. There was no need for increased taxation to cover the cost of interest payments. The growth of big government could therefore be averted. So, too, could the growth of a rentier class such as the one that appeared to hold the taxpayers of Europe in their thrall. It was a system that was markedly different from that of the mercantile republics; but it is nonetheless susceptible to analysis as a form of "tribal finance." Although the colonial system was without parallel in the recent centuries of European history, it had a distant ancestor in the iron drachmas of Clazomenae some two millennia earlier.[3] In 360 B.C. the Greek city of Clazomenae faced a debt of 20 talents to pay off its mercenaries. The solution was to assess the wealthier citizens for the necessary hard currency, and to give them some intrinsically worthless iron drachmas in lieu of their silver ones. These coins were declared to be legal tender in the city and were to be redeemed over five years by the saving of the interest (at the costly rate of 20% per annum) charged by the mercenary captains on their debt. The parallel with colonial currency lies, obviously, in the use of non-interest-bearing fiat currency as a form of emergency finance. The divergences lie in the method of distributing the currency, and in its method of redemption; and these reflected differences both of financial circumstances and political choices. The Clazomenians had incurred a hard currency debt, and there could be no question of satisfying it by handing some iron coins to the mercenaries—whose reaction can easily be imagined. The Clazomenians needed to collect a substantial sum of pure silver, and the only quick way to do this was by a special tax or a loan. Their solution was a forced loan (i.e., a loan that might turn out to be a tax) based on assessed wealth quite similar to the loans of the Italian republics of the Middle Ages. By contrast, the colonial paper currencies were used not to satisfy external debts but purely for domestic obligations. They could be put into circulation directly by being given out in payment for goods and services.

The same set of circumstances affected the redemption of the currencies. Assuming that the mercenaries took their money and left the city in peace—as was probably by this stage the dearest wish of the Clazomenians—the 20-talent payment to the mercenary captains would have reduced the local money stock. The issue of iron drachmas would therefore have restored the money supply to its original level and would have been unlikely to produce inflation. The colonial paper issues in America were inevitably a net addition to the domestic money supply and therefore almost always tended to depreciate. Thus their redemption was politically harder. No attempt was ever made to redeem them at par with hard currency. Redemption in any form immediately became a question of popular politics.

Yet although the colonial paper money was not allocated on the basis of assessed wealth, it was nonetheless a form of forced loan—a loan because it paid for services against a distant obligation of redemption; forced because the recipients had no choice in its acceptance. And like the repayable taxes of the Italian cities, the colonial paper money was Janus-faced. At low levels of emission, the paper's value would remain close to par, and it would appear as an interest-free loan. At higher levels, the paper money would inevitably depreciate, and it would assume its alternate role as a hidden tax—an inflation tax whose burden was assumed by the holders of the currency (by now widely distributed). If, finally, the government decided to reduce the depreciated currency by taxes payable in paper, the transformation of the loan into a tax would become quite clear, and the effective tax burden would be redistributed according to whatever criteria of taxation the government chose to apply.

Thus, underneath the marked superficial differences, the colonial system of finance shared a heritage with the *prestiti* of Venice and the *prestanze* of Florence. Indeed some could argue that it represented a superior evolution of the republican system, made possible by new developments in financial technique. For one thing the absence of interest made the colonial loan/tax package cheaper than the Italian original. Under ideal circumstances there was no tax cost at all to insult the liberty of the citizens. When circumstances were less than ideal—as, of course, they generally were—the citizens could be taxed via inflation; but even here there were advantages.

The workings of the inflation tax have never been better described than by Keynes in his *Tract on Monetary Reform*, written in 1923. In that year, of course, he was to have evidence at hand of the tax's devastating effectiveness, which had scarcely been dreamed of before. Keynes gave as an example a country whose money stock is worth $36 million in hard currency value and is composed of nine million notes worth $4 each. The government now decides to print three million more notes, bringing the total to twelve million. Logically, since the real value of the money stock is unchanged, the notes are now worth no more than $3 each, whatever their nominal value. In the meantime the government has been able to use the three million new notes in payment of goods worth somewhere between $9 million and $12 million in real terms—the exact figure depending on how far prices have risen before the government can disburse all the extra notes. This amount represents a tax exacted from the holders of the old notes:

> The burden of the tax is well spread, cannot be evaded, costs nothing to collect, and falls, in a rough sort of way, in proportion to the wealth of the victim. No wonder its superficial advantages have attracted Ministers of Finance.[4]

These same superficial advantages attracted the American colonists. The inflation tax was impossible to avoid and was distributed in a way that appeared to contain an element of rough justice; and perhaps most critically, its negligible cost of collection averted the insidious growth of governmental bureaucracy. Alongside the advantages listed by Keynes, there lay the near invisibility of the tax, which circumvented the need for overt taxation that would spoil the colonists' enjoyment of their freedom.

But recourse to the printing press is not a panacea for fiscal ailments. There are three profound problems with such a solution, regardless of its political appeal. The first is that the amount of currency that can circulate without depreciation is limited. The figure will vary according to the nature of the economy and the habits of the population but is unlikely to exceed 20% of GNP. By contrast, the mercantile republics had demonstrated that it was possible to borrow well over 100% of GNP by means of interest-bearing perpetual debt without notable depreciation.

An equally profound economic limitation on currency finance was described by Keynes. As depreciation sets in, the loan becomes a hidden tax. But gradually the population realizes that it is being taxed and reacts by holding ever smaller amounts of currency. The amount that the government can raise is therefore progressively reduced and eventually becomes negligible. The population can even overreact by avoiding the suspect currency so completely that its real value shrinks below that needed for economic activity. At this point total monetary reform is inevitable. The sums that can be raised by currency finance are very impressive for two or three years. But the ceiling imposed by popular avoidance tactics means that the total raised before the system implodes is again far lower than under the republican model.

A third problem arises as soon as depreciation starts. The free ride is over: it is time to pay the bills. But quite apart from the question of how to allocate the tax burden—as vivid in eighteenth-century America as it was in fourteenth-century Florence—the reliance on money as a form of debt creates other, more profound, problems. The depreciation of a currency that is also legal tender for private debts automatically calls into question every aspect of economic life. Monetary policy becomes a vehicle of social conflict.

The rules of this conflict were not new, even if they were colored by the advent of paper. In the late fourteenth century, the treasurer of the Kingdom of Navarre had analyzed them for his king in the following terms:

> Everywhere there are three sorts of men, each of which wishes the currency to be to their advantage, and there are four sorts of coinage. . . .
>
> The first sort of men are those who have rents. . . . This sort of men clearly wish one sort of money, that is, money of strong alloy. . . .
>
> The second sort of men are those who engage in commerce, who wish for . . . a middle sort of money. . . . Trade is always poor except when money is a middle state. To write all the reasons in this document would be too lengthy.
>
> The third sort of men are those who live from the work of their bodies. These would wish to have weak money. . . .
>
> The fourth sort of money is desired by lords when they are at war, and he [*sic*] can thus strike coin as feeble as he likes to have the means to pay his troops to defend him and his people and his land. But at the end of the war, he ought to take this money in again.[5]

This analysis has scarcely been bettered. Governments, both medieval and postmedieval, were regularly content to pay their bills in depreciated currency in time of war. Generally they attempted to restore the value of the currency after the war—if only so as to have a good base from which to restart the process in the next round of hostilities. They also had to reconcile the three-way social conflict described above. Landlords (and later creditors of all sorts) wanted their payments made in strong currency. Their tenants (or debtors) obviously had an interest in weak currency. Merchants and businessmen had a position somewhere in the middle—seeking a steadily growing money supply that would facilitate their commerce without causing price fluctuations. Generally, since kings were landowners as well as rulers, they tended, in time of peace, to side with the forces favoring a strong currency.

The balance of social forces in colonial America differed significantly from those in medieval Europe. The operations of the land banks gave a particular boost to the forces that sought to avoid any revaluation of the currency. As long as colonial currencies did not depreciate too far, there was generally sufficient common ground between the poorer, or indebted, colonists and those merchants who favored "a middle sort of money" to prevent strong deflationary measures after the return of peace. But this was not always the case. The trend setters in colonial finance were the New England colonies, lead by Massachusetts and followed closely by Rhode Island. By the 1740s, the paper money of those colonies had depreciated so far as to become both socially divisive and economically counterproductive. Massachusetts had £2.5 million outstanding worth less than 10% of face value in 1749. In 1739, William Douglass had already published a broadside in Boston, attacking the whole process of currency finance as a form of social warfare:

> To make a Bill of Note bearing no Interest and not payable till after a dozen of score of Years, a legal tender . . . in Payment of Debts, is the highest of *despotick* and arbitrary Government. . . . Our Paper Money Colonies have carried the Iniquity still further, the Popular or *Democratick* Part of the Constitution are generally in Debt, and their too great Weight of Influence in Elections, have made a depreciating Currency, a Tender for Contracts done many Years before; that is, *they impose on the Creditor side in private contracts*, which the most despotical Powers never assumed.[6]

It was the consequences for private contracts that outraged Douglas rather than the limitations of paper money as a means of government finance. His accusation of despotism on the part of the democratic elements is perhaps the earliest warning bell announcing the distant advance of the "dictatorship of the proletariat" (although ancient Greeks had been quite familiar with this idea, if not with the financial technique). But Douglass was also dimly aware of the phenomenon of the law of diminishing returns that Keynes was to analyze:

> [By] large and frequent Emissions of Paper Money, [the colonies] sink their own credit, and increase the Necessity of making more, by continued Increas-

> ing the Quantities to make good the Depreciating Qualities of the same: And this by a continued Progression, renders the Quantity vastly great, and the Quality of Value contemptibly small.[7]

Douglass was right about the "contemptibly small" value of the money. Massachusetts and Rhode Island issued so much paper that its value declined to a point where it became economically useless, constituting less than 5% of the total money supply, as opposed to nearly 50% in the more prudently run colonies of New York and Pennsylvania.[8] In 1751, the Westminster government stepped in and forbade further legal tender issues in the New England colonies. The intervention by London was timely, for Boston was by now one of the most commercially developed towns in America and the social structure of Massachusetts made it ripe for a move to more conventional "republican" financial techniques. The colony redeemed its old paper at 7.5:1 (which was considerably more than its market value), raised taxes, and, from that moment, became the American home of sound money, which it preached with the fervor of the convert. Subsequent colonial wars were financed by interest-bearing notes that were treated as investment vehicles, rather than as monetary instruments. These notes were supported by taxes that were higher than in any other colony—although they did not begin to approach those of England.

Massachusetts, however, was a lone voice. In 1764, Parliament banned all legal tender paper throughout the colonies. But most of them continued to emit non-legal-tender variants, which, in the absence of further military expenditure before the Revolution, were able to survive quite happily without this legal prop. The French and Indian War (the Seven Years' War, as experienced by the colonists) tested the system to its full. The notes of even the most successful colonies, such as New York and Pennsylvania, fell to discounts approaching 50%. But after the war a combination of financial aid from Britain and taxation of excess paper managed to restore market values to close to par. The strength of popular support for paper money was shown by the reaction to the 1764 ban on legal tender issues. Benjamin Franklin went so far as to propose a centralized land bank operated by Britain, whose interest could be collected by the Westminster government in lieu of the odious new stamp duty. The idea was turned down.

Even the relative success of the financing of the French and Indian War shows the limitations of the colonial technique. The total spent by the colonies was £2.8 million. Of this, £800,000 was raised by Massachusetts through its new Anglo-Dutch-style interest-bearing debt. Paper money accounted for £1.7 million. Only £300,000 came from taxation.[9] Yet given a colonial GNP of between £15 million and £20 million at the time, this financial effort was minuscule compared to that of Britain (or France). The total cost represented less than 20% of GNP, compared to around 90% of GNP in Britain. After the war Britain contributed £1.15 million of hard currency as reimbursement of the colonies' military efforts. These payments contributed handily to the colonies' return to fiscal solvency, and especially to Massachusetts's conversion to hard-currency finance. But the whole episode could not help but raise the question of whether paper money finance would withstand the strain of a more costly war.

THE FIRST AND SECOND AMERICAN REVOLUTIONS

The Seven Years' War brought the American colonies, hitherto an obscure blur on the periphery of their vision, to the center of focus of policymakers in London. They saw not only the growing wealth of the American possessions but also the heavy costs that had been incurred in saving them from French invasion. They may have been happy to reimburse the colonies for their wartime efforts at first; but with the rapid restoration of the colonies' economies and public finances, the next tendency was to seek a flow of funds in the opposite direction. This widespread feeling was not diminished by the accession of the young George III, the first monarch since 1715 to be born and brought up in England, and the first to plan to be considerably more than a rubber stamp for the inclinations of Whig politicians. He looked at those outlying parts of his empire that avoided contributing to the common cause by appealing to political rights with the same hostility that Philip II had viewed the Dutch towns that had used similar tactics two hundred years earlier. Some have attributed the Revolution solely to George's obstinate determination to reaffirm lost fiscal prerogatives in America (just as he was determined to reassert lost political prerogatives in England). While it is always possible that the dispute might have been resolved peacefully in his absence, there was certainly a mainstream of moderate opinion in Britain, which, while finding it hard to know how to tax the colonies either effectively or fairly, was also sure that the current situation was unsustainable. The explosion of public debt in England as a result of the Seven Years' War made the fiscal laxity of previous decades no longer acceptable.

One moderate was Adam Smith. In *The Wealth of Nations,* published in the year of the Declaration of Independence, he addressed the vexed issue of empire and public finance in depth:

> It is not contrary to the spirit of justice, that . . . America should contribute towards the discharge of the public debt of Great Britain. . . . The immense debt contracted in the late war in particular, and a great part of that contracted in the war before, were both properly contracted in defence of America. . . . It was because the colonies were supposed to be provinces of the British empire that this expense was laid out upon them. But countries that contribute neither revenue nor military force towards the support of the empire, cannot be considered as provinces. They may, perhaps, be considered as appendages, as a sort of splendid and showy equipage of the empire. . . . But if the empire can no longer support the expense of keeping up this equipage . . . it is surely time that Great Britain should free herself from the expense of defending those provinces in time of war . . . and endeavor to accommodate her future views and designs to the real mediocrity of her circumstances.[10]

Smith's solution was on a grand scale, but wholly impracticable: full representation at Westminster and the creation of an empirewide customs union with unified taxation that would increase tax receipts by over £6 million per year. Admittedly the extra revenues were not all to come from America, but given that the best offer from the colonies to date was £100,000 per year, there was clearly an unbridgeable gap. Other critics of government policy, like the radical Whig Richard Price, based their opposition on the desperate state of British public finances, still mortgaged in perpetuity for the cost of previous wars. In Price's view, "A KINGDOM ON AN EDGE SO PERILOUS SHOULD THINK OF NOTHING BUT RETREAT."[11]

Only Edmund Burke displayed a true appreciation of why it was best to leave the colonists alone. In his view, the colonists had inherited the same passionate resistance to taxation without consent that had characterized seventeenth-century England. A struggle to impose such taxation was therefore as ill-advised a venture as Charles I's experiments with ship money. More important than that, Burke saw, as even Adam Smith did not, that the benefits of trade with the world's most rapidly growing economies far outweighed the costs of their defense.

If the British government started to look more closely at the American colonies after 1755, so, too, did the colonies start to look more closely at Britain. They did not like what they saw. What they saw was a Parliament that, under the corrupting influence of Walpole, had lost its claim to represent the people and had become a vehicle of oligarchy. Worse still, under George III, the tricks that Walpole had used to control the Commons were now being used by a monarch to reassert the powers lost by James II. The oligarchy threatened to become an autocracy. They saw a state that had become astonishingly powerful, and whose taxes were the highest in Europe. They saw a highly stratified society, in which a wealthy rentier class was able to live off the misery of the unrepresented poor. In sum, they saw a society whose transplantation to the New World should be resisted at all costs.

The colonists did not have to dream up this critique for themselves. Since George III had ousted the Whigs from their long period of one-party rule, they had tended to revert to the role of opposition that they had held before 1688. The tradition of Walpole gave way to that of Burke and Fox within Parliament, and to that of more radical figures such as Wilkes and Price without. As interpreted by Americans, such as Benjamin Franklin, the radical Whig critique became one not only of the existing British regime but also of the whole essence of the republic of merchants. True political liberty was to be found only in agrarian societies, such as those of the classical world. The overpopulation of England, as of Holland and all other urbanized parts of Europe, must lead to the employment of surplus population in the dehumanizing work of manufacturing. Overpopulation led not only to social inequality but to constant warfare to annex limited resources. The payment for war by means of permanent, interest-bearing public debt only increased inequality by rendering one part of the population slaves to the other. The political freedom vaunted by the republics of Europe was only the freedom of an elite, and history proved that the greater the degree of their economic success, the more their political systems tended toward narrow oligarchy.

This was not a very optimistic view of the world. On the eve of the Industrial Revolution, Benjamin Franklin was of the opinion that "manufactures are founded in poverty. . . . It is the multitude of poor without land in a country, and who must work for others at low wages or starve, that enables undertakers to carry on a manufacture."[12] Manufacturing industry was likened to serfdom. Indeed, one writer declared that "the remains of that feudal system, which are to yet to be traced in the policy of European governments, enables the rich individuals to immerse in the deadly shades of their manufacturing houses, many thousands of miserable slaves."[13] And in one glimpse of an awkward truth, a writer in the *Gazette of the United States* in 1789 claimed that it was only black slavery that prevented a similar cancer from afflicting the new republic: "All Europe evinces, that where there are no *black slaves,* there must be *white slaves.*"[14]

Given such a dire prospect for human society, the best that could be hoped for America was that it would not develop too fast. Richard Price, for instance, prayed that America would remain in "that middle state of civilization, between its first rude state and its last refined and corrupt state."[15]

Americans, therefore, resisted the application of British taxes, however modest, to their country because they feared that it would eventually lead to the importation of the full political and social consequences of Anglo-Dutch finance: high taxes, a powerful state, a privileged rentier class, and a legislature corrupted by mammon. This was true of at least a good portion of the colonial population. But it is also worth pointing out that Massachusetts, which had by now caught the Anglo-Dutch disease—albeit at an early stage of infection—was at the very forefront of the rebellion. What the merchants of Boston wanted was not to avoid paying their own debts in hard currency, but to avoid paying those of Britain.

In any case, there was no question of applying anything other than the well-known rules of colonial finance to the alarming prospect of taking on the world's greatest financial power in 1775. If a considerable number of pages have been spent in describing the diminutive debts of the colonies, it is because the explosion of paper money during the Revolution should not be seen in a vacuum, as used sometimes to be the case—a youthful indiscretion, understandable in a small, impoverished country fighting for its life, but of no subsequent relevance. To take this view is to ignore the profound nature of the debates which rocked eighteenth-century America and, after America, Europe.

Jefferson put the total cost of American independence at $140 million. A more recent study has suggested a conservative figure of just over $100 million. However it is computed, the cost was very high in relation to a GNP of around $140 million. But it was no higher than British war spending in relation to British GNP. What was certain was that it would stretch the principles of colonial finance to the limit—and beyond. The audit of war looked something like this:

The Cost of American Independence[16]

$ millions

Continental dollars (legal tender notes)	37.8
States' spending (almost all in legal tender notes)	21.0
Certificates of indebtedness (short-term paper, not legal tender)	16.7
Domestic loans (interest-bearing)	11.6
Foreign loans (from France and Holland)	7.8
Taxes (remitted by states to the Congress)	5.8
Miscellaneous	2.9
Total	103.6

In 1774 Edmund Burke had warned Parliament that the Americans would follow the example of the Dutch—refusing to pay taxes imposed from outside while contributing freely to the defense of their own liberty. His views, however, seemed not to carry to the far side of the Atlantic. The Continental Congress had no power of taxation, and therefore depended exclusively on reimbursement by the states for its expenses. The states, however, made almost no attempt to raise extra taxes, with the result that both branches of government relied almost exclusively on the time-honored technique of paper currency. It is true that the revolutionary governments felt themselves to be in something of a quandary. Behind the official war against Britain there rumbled the civil war against loyalists—who represented up to 20% of the population. Almost everyone was forced to admit that British impositions, to date at least, had been negligible. Against a background of uncertain popular support, to raise taxes would have been risky. Commenting on the first emission of paper, Lieutenant Governor Colden of New York reported to the Earl of Dartmouth, "The Congress are well aware that an attempt to raise money by immediate assessment upon the people would give a disgust that might ruin all their measures."[17] Yet the same conundrum existed in Holland and England at an earlier date, when taxes imposed by revolutionary governments rose far higher than those that had caused the rebellions. The conclusion must be that the Americans were not followers of Montesquieu and took the same view as Mirabeau some years later. It was simply incompatible with the American view of freedom that "the reign of liberty" could turn out to be "more onerous than than of servitude."

The American War of Independence exposed both the effectiveness and the limitations of paper currency finance. Close to $60 million in real terms—by far the largest portion of the total cost of the war—was collected by this means. The nominal values of the Continental and state paper notes issued was, of course, far higher. The Continental currency totaled $240 million, while state currencies—which depreciated even faster—added another $209 million. The fate of these currencies demonstrated vividly Keynes's theory of the law of diminishing returns. The highest yield from Continental paper was in 1776, when $19 million of notes were issued for a real yield of $17 million. At around 12–13% of GNP, this was vastly higher than any previous tax on the colonies—even if it merely equaled the sort of peacetime taxes that the inhabitants of England and Holland had become accustomed to paying without complaint. It was particularly impressive because the notes were not yet legal tender. Since Britain had banned legal tender paper in 1764, the colonies had learned that it was possible to survive without this potentially divisive prop. Congress therefore resisted "forcing" the currency until 1777, when it had lost two-thirds of its value. That as much as $19 million could be circulated in one year without excessive depreciation aroused the reluctant admiration of even Robert Morris, the most important American opponent of currency finance:

> When the Continental money was issued, a greater confidence was shown by America than any other people ever exhibited. The general promise of a body not formed into, nor claiming to be a Government, was accepted as current coin, and it was not until long after an excess of quantity had forced on depreciation that the validity of these promises was questioned.[18]

It could almost be said that the patriotism that Burke had expected Americans to display in their tax returns was displaced onto their currency. The effect did not last much beyond 1776, however, and thereafter yields declined. In 1777, $13 million of paper yielded only $4.5 million of real value. The next year, revenues increased, but it already took $63.4 million of paper to produce $11.7 million in real terms. In 1779, the last year in which currency finance served any purpose, it took $125 million of paper to produce a mere $6 million of real income.[19]

By this stage, the final paradox described by Keynes had already taken over. The real value of the Continental paper money outstanding was $20 million at the end of 1776. By the end of 1779, this value had fallen to a mere $5 million. By the time it was removed from circulation in 1781, its value was a pitiful $1.4 million. The state currencies were probably worth no more. Given that prewar money supply was somewhere in the region of $20 million, the market value of Continental currency was way below the amount necessary for economic functioning. Ironically, the economy was by this stage largely surviving on the hard currency imported by Britain to pay for its military expenditures.

In April 1779 Benjamin Franklin was still describing the Continental currency as a "wonderful machine." A few months later, the machine was broken beyond repair, and was no longer a viable method of war finance. Not only had paper money proved inadequate as a method of war finance, but it had also led to social upheaval. This led inevitably to some profound soul-searching on the part of the leaders of the Revolution. A revisionist history was in the making that reckoned the costs of the struggle to have been unfairly distributed. "The dreams of the golden age were realized for the poor man and the debtor, but unfortunately what these gained was just so much taken from others," wrote David Ramsay in his *History of the American Revolution* in 1789.[20]

The most important revisionist was Alexander Hamilton. In 1775, he had optimistically opined that Britain was in no position to take on the colonists, since "it is notorious that she is oppressed with a heavy national debt."[21] He was no doubt impressed by the doom-laden forecasts of Richard Price and others. By 1780, however, Britain, though facing the concerted alliance of much of Europe, as well as of its colonies, was still solvent. Indeed, it was outspending all of its rivals. Now Hamilton was forced to admit that the British financial system "has done, and is doing wonders."[22] Hamilton's years in charge of the nation's finances were still a decade away, but the savior of the new nation's finances—and perhaps of the Revolution—was equally a convert to Anglo-Dutch finance. Robert Morris was a wealthy merchant who for a few years became the virtual incarnation of American public finance. He paid bills and raised credit on his own account; and although this was eventually to sink him amid the inevitable accusations of conflict of interest, even his direst enemies had to admit that he had kept the government afloat almost by levitation in the final years of the war.

While Morris temporarily managed the public finances with whatever impromptu measures he could lay his hands on, his ultimate aim was to convert the new republic entirely to the English system. "Admiring, we should endeavour to imitate," as he put it.[23] His vehicle of attack was the $20 million of interest-bearing debt that had already been incurred, $8 million of which had been raised in hard currency in Paris and Amsterdam. There could be no question of defaulting on this debt if European support was to continue. An additional $12 million had been raised domestically by interest-bearing loans. Now that paper money had been abandoned and demonetized, it was justifiable to pay the interest on this debt, too, in hard coin. The resulting annual interest was around $1.2 million. Morris hoped to use this interest bill to lever open the doors that blocked taxation by the Continental government. His proposal was a uniform 5% customs duty collectible by Congress that would provide the money necessary to pay interest on the national debt. Once this principal was accepted, he hoped to fund the floating debt—the certificates of indebtedness—on the same basis. Morris's plan would have raised the total long-term debt to over $35 million and would have secured the country's conversion to sound finance on Anglo-Dutch principles. Never again would the new republic have to appear as a "common prostitute among chaste and respectable matrons."

Morris very nearly got his way. By 1782, the general impost (as it was called) had been ratified by all states except Rhode Island—as always the great bastion of populist finance. The rhetoric of the *Providence Gazette* on the subject is ample demonstration of the philosophical chasm separating the two systems of public finance:

> What in the name of common sense have we to do with the financing of the trans-Atlantic world? What is it to us, by what methods the powers of Europe, Asia and Africa draw resources from their forlorn distressed and enslaved subjects? The science of modern financiering will suit a land of slaves, but Americans, I hope in God, will never consent to a scheme that opens the door for unperceptible draughts of money from their pockets.[24]

Britain had already given up the losing battle to retain the colonies by 1782, although peace negotiations dragged on until 1783. This was unfortunate for Morris, since the state of financial emergency had been his main lever against the stubbornness of his opponents. He even attempted to prolong the crisis by encouraging the army to refuse to disband until its paper notes representing back pay had been properly paid or securely funded. But it was to no avail, and the refusal of Rhode Island to ratify his taxes sounded the death knell for his grand scheme. Hamilton resigned from Congress in disgust in 1783, and Morris was left as an isolated figure increasingly vulnerable to accusations of misappropriation of public funds.

The nationalists—as the pro-Morris party was called—may have lost the battle, but the war was not over. After 1780, there were always to be forces on the side of "Anglo-Dutch" finance to counterbalance those on the side of "colonial" finance. It could be argued that this had been the case ever since 1751, when Massachusetts underwent its conversion. But the debate was not yet on a national level, and during the Revolution, Massachusetts had been forced to issue paper with almost as great abandon as any other state. It was from 1780 that a nationwide conflict over public finance began whose echoes could still be heard over a century later.

After 1782, the forces of "colonial" finance were clearly in the ascendant. The states resumed the well-worn path of issuing paper money and settling old debts at depreciated values. As usual there were several differences of technique and relative financial prudence. Pennsylvania and New York had non-legal-tender currencies that circulated at close to par. North Carolina and Georgia issued legal tender currencies that depreciated. The forces of populism were, as usual, most rampant in Rhode Island. Its new paper money had lost 90% of its value by 1788, and the state was causing widespread outrage by its attempts to enforce the currency's acceptance as legal tender outside its borders as well as within. Meanwhile, the Continental Congress received no more than $200,000–300,000 per year in annual revenues from the states—barely enough to pay its running costs, and certainly not enough to service its debts. Interest on the domestic debt was no longer paid in coin but merely in paper, which fetched no more than 20% of face value. Some foreign debts went into default, while others were merely provided for by means of new loans raised in Amsterdam.

Yet the forces of what, in the nineteenth century, was to be known as "sound money" had not disappeared. The Continental Congress, even though starved of revenues, nonetheless set about the process of refunding its floating obligations with long-term debt. By 1788, the interest-bearing debt had risen by $16 million, even if there was nothing to pay the interest with. In 1789, this debt was to provide Hamilton with his Trojan horse. Outside the peripatetic capital of the new nation, the battle raged even more fiercely. In Massachusetts, the sound-money men had managed to insist, uniquely, that the state's wartime currency should not be written down to its final miserable market value but should be refunded by interest-bearing debt at its market value at time of issue. Such principles, if applied nationally, would have given the Continental Congress an additional long-term debt of some $40 million, requiring hard currency revenues of $2.4 million just to pay its interest. Not surprisingly, taxes in Massachusetts rose to levels unheard of before the Revolution. But although the state was sociologically closer to a republic of merchants than any other, it still had its very own western frontier, where the spirit of agrarian independence held sway. In 1786, Daniel Shays led a rebellion in Northampton and Springfield against "the oppression under which the citizens groaned, from the imposition of taxes to satisfy the public creditors."[25] The uprising was suppressed, but the elections of 1788 swept the sound-money forces from power and installed a new government that drastically reduced taxation and left interest on the debt unpaid.

This alarming turn of events and the controversy surrounding Rhode Island's paper money convinced a majority of the propertied that, whatever their previous objections to the surrender of state power, their only hope of salvation lay in a strengthened national government. Such a government would need a monopoly of currency issue, and, most critically, the power to raise taxes. The new tax powers were needed to ensure that the future defense of the nation would be paid for in a manner that did not involve public bankruptcy and social upheaval. To achieve this assurance, the first step was to secure the debts of the last war, whether officially owed by the Congress or by the states. This was the hard political and economic reality underlying the new Constitution. Its carefully crafted articles were designed to ensure that the newly empowered federal government would restrict itself to this limited role and would otherwise leave its constituent states and their citizens in peace.

The Constitution represented a historic, if sometimes uneasy, compromise between opposing views of American public life that was to long outlast the temporary alliance that created it. The Federalist alliance centered around the figures of Alexander Hamilton and James Madison. By 1789, Hamilton had become an out-and-out advocate of the Anglo-Dutch system. His vision of the American state was not just of one with a sound currency and a securely funded debt. It was also to be a nation that would have a public bank frankly modeled on the Bank of England and financial markets as sophisticated as those of London and Amsterdam, which would finance the state and promote the development of commerce and manufacturing. Madison did not share this vision. He would support an invigorated central government as the only way to secure property rights and civil liberties, and to remove the threat of economic and social anarchy. But as the genteel product of a deeply agrarian state, he viewed the operations of the monied with the same distaste as did the Tory squires of England a century earlier. His ideal society was a republic not of merchants but of farmers. Madison was, in a sense, the pivotal figure in the 1789 compromise, as his subsequent career was to demonstrate.

During 1789, the Federalist alliance held together. Their debates centered on the creation of a new form of government, about which there was widespread agreement. In 1790 the new political machinery was in operation, and attention turned to the financial implications of the new Constitution. This was to lay bare the divide between the two visions of America, and eventually to split the coalition. Hamilton's objective was to refund the whole national debt on lines that would instantly, and irrevocably, restore the nation's credit standing. In exchange for this total restoration of credit, he expected to drive a very hard bargain on interest rates—bringing them down at a stroke to a level that would rival those of Britain. But Hamilton had no doubt that this bargain was possible only if creditors were treated according to the strictest rules of the market. This meant, first and foremost, that there could be no distinction between the rights of primary and secondary holders. Here was a rule that lay at the very foundation of public finances based on cheap long-term debt. And yet it was, as always, a bitter pill to swallow.

In 1789, the total domestic debt (including arrears of interest) was in the region of $67.4 million—$42.4 million owed by the Continental government and $25 million by the states. Very little of this debt was still in the hands of its original owners. Some of the $6 million originally raised in the form of loans had not changed hands, since the lenders had contributed from their surplus capital. But the vast majority of the remaining paper had been issued in payment for sums that the original recipients would have viewed as income and were therefore forced to sell for whatever they could get. The market prices of this debt varied considerably. A few Pennsylvania loan certificates, whose interest was being paid in paper that could be used for state taxes, traded as high as 40. The Continental loan certificates, whose interest remained unpaid, were worth between 20 and 25. The non-interest-bearing settlement certificates originally issued to suppliers and soldiers sold for as little as 10–12. If, therefore, Hamilton succeeded in raising the value of this debt to close to par by means of his refunding program, secondary holders and speculators would make profits of several times their investments. And these profits might amount to as much as $40 million.

This was more than Madison could stomach. In 1783, he had supported the assumption of state debts by the Continental Congress, and he had opposed discrimination between the primary and secondary holders. But the proposal had been rebuffed, and Madison had never had the chance to witness the wave of speculation that would inevitably have resulted. By early 1790, as it began to dawn on investors that the new federal government would be in possession of substantial new revenues, the prices of debts started to rise rapidly. Among the heaviest buyers were government officers led by William Duer, the Assistant Secretary of the Treasury. In disgust at the speculative orgy that was brewing, Madison decided to oppose Hamilton's policy of nondiscrimination between debtholders. His proposal was that secondary holders should receive no more than the highest current market price, the rest of the benefit being awarded to the original holders. This move would halt the activities of the speculators overnight. By this action, Madison created a split in the hitherto united ranks of the Federalists that would lead, ultimately, to their defeat at the hands of the Jeffersonian Republicans ten years later.*

The historical significance of Madison's proposal is made clear by its unconscious evocation of the Venetian law of 1491, which gave the state

*The Republican Party founded by Thomas Jefferson was quite different from the modern Republican Party, which was founded in the 1850s. The Jeffersonian Republican Party died out in the 1820s, and its spiritual heir was the Democratic Party founded by Andrew Jackson.

the right to repurchase its bonds from secondary holders at their cost. The reasoning of the Venetians was that, since their debt was a form of repayable taxation, it was wrong for the state to pay what were essentially tax rebates to speculators. This distant Italian ancestry is made clear by Madison's agreement that foreign (i.e., purely voluntary) debts should be rigorously treated according to their original terms. It was the domestic debt that Madison, and others, still could not help viewing as a form of contingent taxation. If it was now to be made good, it was the original "taxpayers" who should receive the benefit.

Against Madison's proposal, Hamilton made the fullest possible arguments for equal treatment of creditors—in other words, for debt as an absolute liability rather than a form of contingent taxation. His arguments rested squarely on the grounds of economic viability. He was easily able to point out a number of ways in which Madison's plan would not do justice to all creditors, even on its own terms; but this was not his main point:

> It will be perceived at first sight, that the transferable quality of stock, is essential to its operation as money; and that depends on the idea of complete security to the transferee, and a firm persuasion, that no distinction can, in any case, be made between him and the original proprietor. . . .
>
> And it will be readily perceived, that [discrimination against secondary holders] would operate a diminution of the value of stock in the hands of the first, as well as of every other holder. . . .
>
> For this diminution of the value of stock, every person, who should be about to lend to the government, would demand compensation, and would add to the actual difference between the nominal and the market value, an equivalent for the chance of greater decrease, which, in a precarious state of public credit, is always to be taken into the account.[26]

The fundamental reason why the original formula of the Italian city-states was not destined to survive has never found clearer expression. In the long run, it was just too expensive.

Hamilton had a fairly simple time defeating Madison's first objection to his plan. A harder battle was fought on the question of the assumption of state debts. For Hamilton, it was essential that the federal government have a monopoly of public borrowing, so as to stop the agrarian states from bringing the whole national credit into disrepute. Not surprisingly, the most vocal proponents of assumption were from Massachusetts, which had attempted to fund all its war debt, including paper money, on Hamiltonian lines but, as a result, now found itself in the hands of a populist legislature. Other states had already settled much of their debt at a discount. They showed little enthusiasm for taking over the debts of other states, even if the relative burdens of war finance were supposed to be equalized over time by a series of compensatory payments. Although many of the underlying divisions surrounding assumption were the same as over discrimination, the issue was clouded by horse trading between the states. Madison himself muddied the water by proposing that the state of Virginia, which had settled most of its debt, be allowed to tender the amounts redeemed to the federal government at face value. This proposal contradicted his earlier argument for discrimination against secondary holders, but Madison was at this stage mostly concerned to make assumption impossibly expensive, or at least to gain advantage for his own state. In the end, Hamilton got his way only after the famous secret bargain that was to site the new capital on the banks of the Potomac.

Hamilton struck a very hard bargain with creditors—one that stretched the terms *voluntary conversion* and *sanctity of contract* beyond their true limits. After an impossibly complex series of seven alternatives offered to creditors in January 1790, he settled on a single formula,[27] which maintained the nominal interest rate of 6% on the principal of the debt but reduced its effective cost by deferring interest on a portion for ten years. Certificates that had been issued in compensation for overdue interest were converted into capital but were entitled to interest at only 3%. Thus the total cost of the package was 4%, which was Hamilton's objective. In theory, acceptance was purely voluntary, but since only the converted debt was to be secured by the new tax revenues of the federal government, there were few who wished to retain their old paper. Curmudgeons complained that, if the conversion was to be considered truly voluntary, dissenters should have been offered redemption at par, as in the English conversion of 1749. But the vast majority of debtholders were more than happy with their profits.

And profits there were in abundance. By August 1790, the new nondeferred 6%s—representing debts that had sold for as little as 15 a year earlier—were trading at 75, and the speculation was only getting under way. Hamilton had offered one important carrot to investors: only a limited amount of the new bonds could be redeemed in any one year. Thus he could not convert the 6% debt to a lower rate even if it went over 100. The speculation centered on New York, where there were established contacts with the bankers of Amsterdam. Syndicates, such as that run by William Duer (now out of government so as to concentrate on making money) and Alexander Macomb, leveraged themselves to the hilt with foreign money in an attempt to corner the market. Throughout 1791, prices continued to rise, reaching a peak in early 1792. The 6%s were by now trading at 120, but given their immunity to redemption, Duer was convinced that they could only go higher. Even at 150 their yield would still be 4%, and his sights were set on the benchmark of 3% established by the British Consols. In the very long term, Duer's forecast was correct; but markets rarely behave linearly. In February, European investors started withdrawing their capital, scared both by the outbreak of war in Europe and by renewed Indian fighting in America. Prices started to fall, and by the middle of March, the Duer syndicate was in default on its debts. The news of his troubles led to the first-ever Wall Street crash in late March and April. Duer ended his days in debtors' jail.[28]

Hamilton hastened to stabilize the market by open-market purchases of government bonds. He was in no way personally implicated in the speculation (in fact, he was to leave government poorer than when he entered it); but the political damage was done. The boom in government stock was likened to the South Sea Bubble, and Hamilton was disparagingly referred to as the American Walpole. Many started to think that Madison had been right, and among those was Thomas Jefferson.

During George Washington's presidency, Hamilton, who held the post of Secretary of the Treasury, had de facto control of the direction of government. Under his administration, the government revenues increased rapidly. By 1796, they were over $8 million—thirty times higher than they had been ten years earlier—and supported a funded debt of over $80 million. This sum was tiny by British standards, but at least the principle had been established. Other Anglophile tendencies could be seen in the creation of a standing navy and the establishment of the Bank of the United States, Hamilton's American equivalent of the Bank of England. The stock market flourished, foreign capital poured in, and manufacturing advanced. Hamilton's long-term project included a standing army, a protective tariff to encourage infant industries, and a state that collected anything up to 25% of GNP in taxes.

As long as George Washington was president, opposition was relatively muted. But by 1794 John Taylor of Caroline, one of the leading voices of agrarian dissent, was already asking whether it was not "time to enquire whether the constitution was designed to beget a government, or only a British system of finance?"[29] The presidency of John Adams (which followed Hamiltonian policies even though Hamilton was no longer at the Treasury) brought the latent conflicts to the fore, and by 1798 there was a serious threat of civil war. Divergences of opinion that were already present were exacerbated by events in Europe. The Federalists' natural leanings toward Britain were even more unpopular after 1792, when France, America's ally in its struggle for independence, also became a republic. The citizens of the new sister republic were shaking off their shackles—not only the ancient chains of a despotic monarchy and a feudal aristocracy, but the new chains of the rentiers. Moreover, they were busy experimenting with their very own version of colonial finance in their fight against the united forces of European reaction, including the tyrant George III. It is in this light that the seemingly wild accusations of "monarchy" and "aristocracy" that were hurled against the Federalists have to be understood.

Jefferson called the election of 1800 the "second American revolution." The 1790s had taken the nation down a perilous path that had threatened to undermine all that had been fought for from 1776 to 1783. A new revolution was needed to return the republic to the path of virtue. The state must be taken out of the control of the merchant oligarchs and returned to the hands of yeoman farmers. The whole apparatus of the Hamiltonian state was suspect in the eyes of the Republicans. Rather than being to allowed to grow, it should shrink. Far from being a social bond and an economic boon, public debt was a "mortal cancer" that must be excised as soon as possible. Rather than encourage industry, with its inevitable social polarization, the republic should focus on agriculture. What was needed was not a tariff wall, but international free trade so that America's agricultural surplus could be exported to the overcrowded cities of Europe. This meant not a sycophantic admiration for Britain, but a direct challenge to its monopoly of sea trade, especially its wartime restrictions on neutral traffic with France.

More perceptive Republicans, such as Madison, saw that, in the long term, the process of urbanization could be delayed but not forestalled. The most effective method of conserving the republic's virtue was to ensure a plentiful supply of land for colonization. This made Jefferson's purchase of France's American possessions in 1803 not only the world's greatest real estate bargain but also the defining political act of his presidency. The 1807 embargo of British goods and the 1812 war were also the logical consequences of the Republican vision of an egalitarian agrarian republic exporting its surplus production to Europe.

But however bucolic their political vision, neither Jefferson or Madison was an extremist. In many ways it is not Hamilton who should have been called the American Walpole, but Jefferson. Just as the long period of Whig rule of Britain was made possible by Walpole's reconciliation of erstwhile

Tories, the long period of Republican rule in America was made possible by Jefferson's compromise with the Federalists. The compromise did not consist merely of the secret agreements that he may, or may not, have made with certain leading Federalists in order to break the tie in the Electoral College of 1800. These probably involved Jefferson's agreement not to disband the Bank of the United States or the navy, as well as to avoid the wholesale removal of Federalists from administrative office. Certainly these were the policies that he followed during his administration. A more subtle compromise, perhaps never openly discussed, evolved on the nation's public finances. Nothing would stop Jefferson from repaying the public debt as fast as Hamilton's restrictions permitted. In 1800, he inherited a debt of $83 million. By 1808, it was down to $57 million, and by the outbreak of the War of 1812 it had fallen as low as $45 million. By this stage, it was a mere 8% of GNP and scarcely constituted an aristocratic threat to republican virtue. But it was notable that the debt was repaid according to the strictest criteria of sanctity of contract. There was no question of undoing Hamilton's bargain, or of removing the federal monopoly of currency, or of a return to paper money, or any of the other characteristic features of colonial finance. The debt was repaid by means of tax increases paid in hard currency. Nor were there to be any impediments to the growth of the financial markets of New York, whatever the revulsion felt by the agrarian interests for the machinations of stock jobbers.

In essence, the compromise was not entirely dissimilar from that of eighteenth-century England. The nations' finances were to be run (at the federal level at least) as if the country were a republic of merchants. But the reins of government were to remain in the hands of the landed classes, who would otherwise follow policies suited to a republic of farmers. Neither in social composition nor in political interests did the American and British landed interests resemble each other. The flavor of the two governments was therefore quite different; and the American agrarian interests drove, perhaps, a somewhat harder bargain. But the compromise of 1800 was to prove resilient, even when put to the acid test of war. The outbreak of hostilities in 1812 put an end to the Republican dream of a debt-free nation. In three years all Jefferson's work was undone, and the public debt rose to $127 million. The republic's ability to raise long-term loans proved to be limited, and there was no alternative but to issue short-term paper. But this step was undertaken with reluctance, and there was no resort to legal tender currency.

If anything, the war further cemented the 1800 compromise. The Bank of the United States had not managed to outlast its charter, which expired in 1811. The tacit agreement that had left it untouched for the previous decade could not protect it from the forces of popular disapproval. It had been disbanded just when its services would have been most useful. The experiences of the War of 1812 made this quite apparent, and a successor bank was chartered in 1817. The trade war with Britain, so much part of Republican philosophy, had the paradoxical effect of stimulating American industry. It even brought into effect the protective tariff that Hamilton had always wanted. As Madison was wryly to admit in later years:

> It is true that under a great change of foreign circumstances, and with a doubled population and more than doubled resources, the Republican party has been reconciled to certain measures and arrangements which may be as popular now as they were premature when they were urged by the champions of Federalism.[30]

Perhaps the underlying truth was simply that the 1800 compromise was never truly tested. Hamilton's dream of a state with public debt as high as that of Britain or Holland was simply a nonstarter in a nation as geographically privileged as the United States. Its virgin territory encouraged continuous waves of immigration that gave it an in-built rate of economic growth beyond anything dreamed of in Europe. What was more, the majority of this virgin territory was in the hands of the federal government—a national treasure that exceeded the value of not only the existing but any foreseeable national debt.

Where was any future debt to come from? The same splendid geographical isolation that had sheltered the country from international conflicts while a colony continued to protect it as an independent nation. Even the War of 1812 was a minor affair financially. With a GNP that had already risen to $600 million, peak wartime spending of $35 million was little over 5% of national production. At its peak level of $127 million, the debt was no more than 16% of GNP. The taxes required to service and repay such levels of debt were never going to test the willingness of agrarian America to live up to its side of the unspoken Jeffersonian bargain. Even in 1816, when the government raised peak revenues of $48 million so as to pay off its floating debt, taxes were still less than 6% of GNP. Generally they were less than half that level.

Even before then, the logical impossibility of the country's following the path of Britain had become clear. Unlike Jefferson or Madison, Hamilton made no attempt to repay the debts of the United States. If anything, they rose during the Federalist era—from $75 million in 1790 to $83 million in 1800. But national production rose much faster, from $158 million in 1789 to $460 million. The rise was partly the result of the general inflation caused by the outbreak of the French revolutionary wars. But even in real terms GNP had more than doubled over the course of the decade to $325 million, as a result of continued rapid inflows of labor and capital. Paradoxically, the Federalists were more successful in reducing the debt burden than the Republicans. From 1790 to 1800 the ratio of debt to GNP fell from 40% to 18%. During the next decade Jefferson managed to reduce it only to 8%, in spite of his strenuous attempts to eliminate the "mortal cancer" entirely. Even more paradoxical is the only possible conclusion from this set of figures. Hamilton's unintended reduction of the debt ratio was the result of financial policies that stimulated economic growth. Jefferson's policy of tax increases to reduce the debt sharply slowed that rate of growth. The general inflation of the Napoleonic Wars still helped raise nominal income levels, but in real terms GNP rose only 16% from 1800 to 1810, against 106% in the preceding decade.

Public Debt of the United States, 1790–1810
As a percentage of GNP[31]

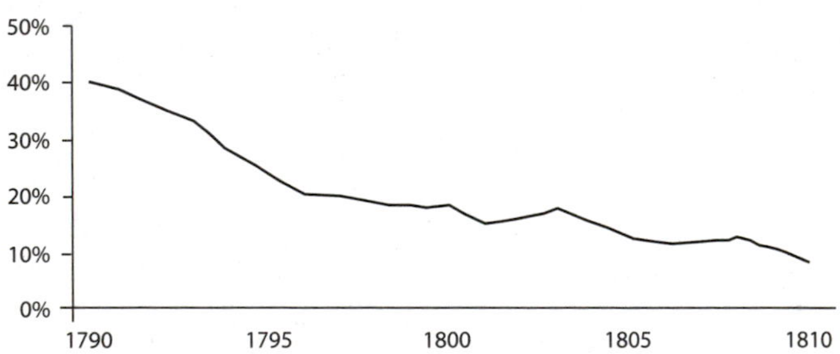

The paradoxical outcome of the Hamiltonian and Jeffersonian fiscal regimes is a reflection of a wider marvel of American history. By some fortunate operation of the laws of serendipity, the same geography that fostered agrarian hostility to mercantile finance also served to diminish the possibilities of conflict between the two models. In this way, too, America was surely a blessed land.

ENEMIES OF THE PEOPLE

> Sixty thousand capitalists and the ant-heap of the speculators decided the revolution. . . . They demanded that M. Necker should reign so that they might be paid; that a revolution be essayed so that they might be paid; that everything might be overturned as long as they were paid. They did not conceive that the National Assembly was anything other than a committee of finance.[32]
>
> —Antoine de Rivarol, royalist writer

The deputies who assembled in Paris in May 1789 were certainly not predisposed to be the initiators of another public bankruptcy. It was to avoid just such a bankruptcy that they had been summoned. Indeed, the deputies, whose ranks, as Rivarol noted sardonically, included large numbers of public creditors, were only too aware that they owed their newfound status to the inability of the old regime to avoid periodic default. They uniformly associated these acts of blatant disregard for legal obligations with the worst aspects of absolutism. Even if England was no longer considered a perfect model by reformers, the complete security enjoyed by public creditors there was still held up as an example. Accordingly, the first act of the National Assembly was to "place the creditors of the state under the protection of the honour and loyalty of the French Nation."[33]

This was a fine sentiment; but a closer reading of the resolution, passed unanimously by the deputies, might have given creditors pause for thought. Its longest passage was not about debt, but about taxes. The nation's first use of its reclaimed powers must be to "ensure the strength of the public administration." This assurance required tax revenues; but here the Assembly seemed to be in a quandary. Because public consent was the prerequisite for any tax to be legally enforceable, the Assembly was forced to declare that existing taxes, "never having been consented to by the Nation, are all illegal, and consequently null and void in their creation, extension or prorogation." Since, taken to its logical conclusion, this declaration would have led to instant bankruptcy, the Assembly also "consented provisionally, on behalf of the Nation, that the taxes and contributions, although illegally established and collected, should continue to be paid as before." But even here there was a sting in the tail. This provisional consent was valid only for the duration of the Assembly. If the king ever attempted to dissolve it, the deputies gave specific authorization for an immediate and total revolt by the taxpayers.

If creditors were not worried enough by a declaration that made no reference at all to the need for any new taxes, such as those proposed by the

Assembly of Notables two years earlier, they might have cared to consider the next paragraph. Action on the public debt was only to be taken once the Assembly, "in concert with his Majesty, has fixed the principles of the national regeneration." Unfortunately, the underlying principles of the national regeneration were already contentious, and were ultimately to prove impossible to fix "in concert with his Majesty."

The dispute over basic principles had started in late 1788. The Assembly of Notables had assumed that the Estates General, whose reconvening they had advocated, would be similar to those of the Middle Ages. Throughout Europe one principle had governed these assemblies: the idea of different orders in society—the different estates. The Estates General was so called when all three estates were summoned together. In some countries, such as England, the first two—the clergy and the nobility—had merged into one assembly (the Lords Spiritual and Temporal). More often they maintained their distinct meetings; and the third estate—the representatives of the towns—were almost always allocated to a separate chamber. The practice of voting by order ensured that the first two estates would maintain their privileged position. The proponents of a revived "Frankish" constitution assumed that this practice would be reactivated in France in 1789. In their view there was no need to fix any new principles. France already had a constitution. The Bourbons had ignored it for nearly two hundred years, to their peril. Now they had learned that absolutism was a blind alley that ended in bankruptcy. The example of England showed that constitutional government was more effective than unconstitutional.

The Enlightenment had given birth to another school of thought. The old idea of differing degrees of freedom held by different ranks of society was starting to give way to more sweeping claims about the common rights of all men. From the perspective of the Frankish aristocrats, their "freedom" was based on never having been conquered. From the perspective of the commoners of the Third Estate, on the other hand, the privileges of the nobles derived simply from having conquered others. If conquest was an unacceptable justification for the power of the monarch, then why should it be accepted for the privileges of the aristocrats. To men of enlightened views, the best that should be offered the first two orders was to sit in the same assembly with the representatives of the Third Estate. They would hold no more than one half of the seats—preferably one-third—and voting would be in common. A more radical view was put forward by the Abbé Sieyès (notwithstanding his ecclesiastical title) in his tub-thumping pamphlet *Qu'est-ce que le Tiers-État?* In his view, the Third Estate was not a mere order; it was the nation itself. Those who were not part of the Third Estate must therefore be parasites on it:

> It is impossible to say what place the nobility and clergy ought to occupy in the social order. This is equivalent to asking what place should be assigned to a malignant d[is]ease which preys upon and tortures the body of a sick man.[34]

When the situation is viewed with the benefit of historical hindsight, it is clear that the French elite was at the root of its own undoing. What was conceived of by the reformers of 1787–1788 was the control of the king by a broad-based ruling class that excluded those without property. This was true even of those who advocated the merging of the estates. In July 1788, Malesherbes had written to the king in the following terms:

> Let the King at the end of the eighteenth-century not convoke the three orders of the fourteenth century: let him instead call together the *proprietors* [italics added] of a great nation renewed by its civilization.[35]

Even Sieyès was an advocate of property qualifications for voting. The creation of just such a ruling class united by property was at the heart of Britain's success. In France it was not to be. The putative ruling class split almost at once.

In the autumn of 1788, the Parlements came out in favor of the 1614 formula for the forthcoming Estates General—with separate assemblies for each order (and with the *noblesse de la robe* safely ensconced with the *noblesse d'épée*)—and watched their previous popularity evaporate overnight. When the Estates convened in the following May, the dispute was still not resolved, but the deputies of the Third Estate refused to commence proceedings unless the other two sat with them. Finally, with the adherence of the more progressive members of the clergy and nobility, the Third Estate took matters into its own hands and declared itself to be the representative of the nation. By now the Revolution had already overstepped the limits decreed by the forces that had called it into being. And the recalcitrant members of the first two Estates had already implicitly declared themselves to be enemies of the nation, as now constituted.

Equally ominous for the character of the political debate was the underlying rumble of popular violence. The poor harvests of the late 1780s created a climate of tension, and increasingly of desperation, that did not help the prospects of bloodless political change. The need to import and subsidize expensive grain only exacerbated the strains on the budget, and bread riots merged imperceptibly into political riots. The Reveillon riots of April 1789, when the Parisian crowd fought the Gardes Françaises to sack the establishment of a noted advocate of grain price deregulation, had already threatened to undermine the policing of Paris. When, in late June, Louis XVI, advised by the hard-line members of his family and entourage, decided to put an end to the National Assembly, which had already threatened the conceptual underpinnings of the old order, the crowd took matters into its own hands. The eviction of royal troops from Paris on July 12–13 and the fall of the Bastille on July 14 marked the true beginning of the revolutionary dynamic that was about to take hold. It became clear not only that popular violence had saved the Revolution, but furthermore that it was a means of overcoming conservative opposition. The Parisian crowd was like a dangerous dog that could be used by revolutionary politicians to intimidate or attack their enemies; but whether the man or the dog at the other end of the leash was really in control was never certain. After July 1789, the political debate started to take on a tone of explicit ferocity and bloodletting that had already been implicit in Sieyès's diatribe against the nobility.

Was this likely to be a suitable ambience for the conversion of the ancien régime to Anglo-Dutch finance? The success of the English formula depended on a united ruling class and a quiescent population. But it was already apparent that the French ruling class was far from united, and that the populace was far from quiescent. Worse still, it was evident that one part of the ruling class was quite willing to incite popular unrest as a means of overcoming the other.

In these circumstances, it is perhaps not surprising that Necker and other proponents of Anglo-Dutch finance should have made little headway. The National Assembly may have been profoundly committed to avoiding another public bankruptcy, but that did not mean that the Assembly was happy to accept the prescriptions of the debt markets for the public finances of the newly liberated French nation. Its views on the sanctity of the debt were at variance with its feelings about the taxes necessary to pay it.

When the Assembly resumed its deliberations after the events of July, this ambivalence soon became apparent. The financial situation faced by Necker was already worse than it had been in May. The deficit was rising as a result of emergency grain purchases, and the 58 million livres of cash reserves that he had managed to accumulate between September 1788 and May 1789 had disappeared. He proposed a loan at 5% to cover the immediate shortfall, but the Assembly insisted on reducing the rate to 4.5% as a public demonstration that its credit was superior to that of the monarchy. Not surprisingly, given an interest rate so far below the current market, only a derisory 2.6 million livres was subscribed. The Assembly was already displaying an inauspicious dislike of the rules of the marketplace. Later in the month there was discussion of making interest payments subject to a new withholding tax. This proposal prompted Mirabeau to take a strong stance:

> Since you have not forgotten, gentlemen, that it is the good faith of the king towards the creditors of the State that has brought us to liberty; and if, listening to the murmurs of which I speak, he had wanted to be an unfaithful borrower, there was no need for him to have delivered us from our chains.
>
> Yes, gentlemen, I have no fear of repeating it, by a happy result of ministerial errors and depredations, *today the constitution is up for auction*; it is the deficit that is the treasure of the State, it is the public debt that is the germ of our liberty. Do you wish to receive the benefit, while refusing to pay the price?[36]

At this stage Mirabeau still appeared to be a disciple of Montesquieu. But the desire to pay the debt as contracted, which was still very much the majority view in the Assembly, was not matched by a coherent policy to collect the necessary taxes. The Parisian uprising of July was followed by the widespread rural violence of the Grand Peur. Taken in conjunction with the poor harvest and the inexorable rise in the price of bread, it was a brave soul who would have advocated increased taxes on the general public. Indeed, the French people were showing every sign of adhering to the classical pattern observed two centuries earlier by their perspicacious countryman Jean Bodin:

> It is an ordinarie thing in changes from a tyrannie to a popular estate, to abolish all imposts, taxes and subsidies for a signe of libertie, as they did in Rome, at the request of the Consul Valerius, after they had expelled their kings.[37]

The American reluctance to pay increased taxes in support of their revolution had been based on a profound aversion to strong government of any sort. The unwillingness of the French was based not on an aversion to government but on an equally profound belief that they were already overtaxed. From the summer of 1789, tax receipts, far from rising, were starting a drawn-out collapse that would reduce them by 84% in real terms by 1795. Even in 1789 less than 400 million livres were collected, against the 475 million budgeted by Necker. The only source of new tax revenues in the early period of the Revolution was the extra payments of direct taxes made by those liberal aristocrats and officeholders who had so generously joined the votes for the abolition of all venal offices and tax exemptions. But even here there was a sting in the tail. The actions of the Assembly, far from ameliorating the government's financial position, tended to make it worse.

In 1789, the Assembly inherited a public debt of approximately 5 billion livres, composed, more or less, of 3.1 billion livres of annuities, 1.3 billion livres of other medium- and long-term obligations (including term loans and the capital value of venal offices), and 600 million livres of miscellaneous short-term debts.[38]

The short-term debt was clearly not a stable number. It was already higher than in 1788 and was being constantly increased by the budget deficit. But it was not at a level that was beyond resolution and, had the deficit been resolved, it could have been reduced to a sustainable level of 200–300 million livres by issues of new long-term debt. Given the immediate difficulty of reducing the deficit, it might reasonably have been expected that the Assembly would decide to add the capital value of the abolished offices to the long-term debt. Yet no such plan was made, and the total cost of ending the old financial system—over 800 million livres—was declared immediately repayable. The equally enlightened abolition of feudal dues saddled the state with another 100 million livres, which was also to be paid as soon as possible. Virtually overnight, therefore, the floating debt grew to 1.5 billion. This was certainly not a piece of financial management that conformed to Anglo-Dutch principles.

By September, Necker had despaired of conventional taxes or loans. He had managed to increase the marketability of his August loan by convincing the Assembly to raise the nominal interest to 5%, and by allowing partial subscription in depreciated state paper; but the subscriptions were still very slow, and only 20 million in cash had been raised by the end of the year.

If modern prescriptions for public finance were unpopular, perhaps the people might respond to techniques borrowed from an earlier, more classical model. In September, Necker came up with proposals drawn from the ancient brew in which the citizens' commitment to their state was expressed as an ambiguous blend of gift, loan, and contingent taxation. His *contribution patriotique*, so called, was a semivoluntary, interest-free loan of 25% of net income (as voluntarily declared by the taxpayer), which would be redeemed by an issue of 4% rentes when the state's reformed tax base had been established. Since Necker reckoned the taxable income at around 800 million livres, this loan should have produced more than enough to tide the state over the first difficult years of its political transition. But out of the 200 million anticipated, only 9 million had been contributed after seven months. A parallel *don patriotique*, inspired by the Roman Republic, was to collect the free offerings of the citizens. It aroused the rapturous, but misplaced, enthusiasm of Louis Blanc, the socialist historian of the Revolution:

> Then took place one of those *élans* which are your strength and glory, oh my country! Patriotic offerings flooded into the office of the President of the Assembly from all points of the kingdom: gifts of the rich, sacrifices of the poor. Women offered their rings, children their toys. Workmen in manufacturing gave half their bread to the Revolution. And you, venal creatures, sullied by pleasure and crushed by scorn, unfortunate creatures of the night, you too were moved by this spectacle which left untouched the hearts of the bankers![39]

On inspection the flood turned out to consist of about 1 million livres in cash and a further 5 million in goods, jewels, and depreciated government paper. The finance committee of the Assembly was forced to admit in March 1790 that it was "struck by the size of the needs of the State, and the meager assistance offered by patriotic gifts."[40]

If the debt was not to be touched, but taxes were not to be raised, and neither loans nor gifts were forthcoming in sufficient amounts, a financial impasse loomed that could be resolved only if some hitherto undreamed-of expedient could be found. Already on August 8, the Marquis de Lacoste had broached the possibility of an alternative solution by declaring that "the goods of the church belong to the nation; it is time to take them back." By September his suggestion was taken up and successfully advocated by some of the strongest and most forward-looking voices in the Assembly, including that improbable cleric Charles-Maurice Talleyrand, Bishop of Autun. The confiscation of church property would provide the state with assets worth around 2 billion livres. By some curious piece of good fortune, this was almost exactly the amount of the debt that the Assembly had decided to repay: the 1.6 billion in floating debt plus the 500 million of term loans. This would leave only the *dette constituée*—the sacred funded debt historically administered by the Hôtel de Ville de Paris—safely under the "protection of the honour and loyalty of the French Nation."

It is hard not to be a little cynical about this neat coincidence of the assets of the church and the *dette exigible*—the repayable debt. It so happened that 45% of the deputies of the Third Estate were officeholders. They were joined by a not inconsiderable number of members of the two higher orders, who also held offices and who had investments in government affairs. These men were to be repaid very considerable sums out of the proceeds of sales of the confiscated lands. Even better, there might be an opportunity to buy these assets on the cheap. The first bidders for these properties, when they were placed on the market a year later, included a large number of officials of the old regime and even, it was rumored, the queen herself.

This was the background to the issue of the assignats, the paper money that was to become almost synonymous with the Revolution. Given the tenacious opposition to paper money that followed the collapse of Law's Banque Royale, it might seem odd that the Revolution should have had recourse of any sort to the printing press. The first issue of assignats was merely intended to replace the existing notes of the Caisse d'Escomptes (legal tender within Paris since 1788) and the private notes of the *financiers* by which they refinanced their advances to the crown. By November 1789, these totaled around 400 million livres. Necker's proposal was to increase the capital of the Caisse and makes its notes public obligations. The Assembly responded with suspicion to a suggestion that increased the power of an institution controlled by Genevan investors, and that would serve only to augment the number of legal tender notes in circulation. Their assignats were to be directly controlled by the French nation rather than foreign bankers. Furthermore, the assignats were to be issued only in denominations of 1,000 livres or more, were to bear interest at 5%, and were to be legal tender only in exchange for *domaines nationaux*—the public lands confiscated from the church. In other words, the assignats were not originally intended to serve as money, or as a means of paying current expenses. They were issued to refinance existing short-term obligations on a more secure (and politically correct) basis.

In 1790, the financial situation worsened dramatically. Tax receipts for the year fell a full 50% below the already meager revenues of 1789. It was thought necessary to make the assignats legal tender by April and to reduce their interest to 3%. In August, Montesquiou, the head of the finance committee, proposed increasing the issue to 1.2 billion livres. The new notes were to be without interest and were printed in denominations as low as 50 livres. The new notes were legal tender for all transactions but would be retired as they were tendered for sales of public lands that were to start in November. The value of the money was clearly understood to be secured by its convertibility into land, and each note had the legend *Domaines Nationaux* prominently displayed on it. The very word *assignat* implied the "assignment" of real assets to cover the sum promised on the note.

The events of the following six years were to display a parallel—at least financially—with the events of the American Revolution fifteen years earlier. The French Revolution, too, was to become synonymous with the issue of paper money. Looking back on events after 45 billion livres of paper assignats had been demonetized and burned, and the printing presses that created them destroyed, Ramel, the Minister of Finance, pronounced the following obituary:

> The assignats made the Revolution: they led to the destruction of ranks and privileges; they overthrew the throne, and founded the Republic; they armed and equipped those formidable columns which carried the tri-coloured banner beyond the Alps and the Pyrenees; they were worth our liberty.[41]

Yet despite superficial appearances, the French revolutionaries were not disciples of colonial finance. Their use of paper money had different connotations. Like the American colonists, the French ignored the anglophile wisdom of Montesquieu and looked back to earlier concepts of fiscal liberty. But as their historical and geographical situation differed from that of the Americans, so, too, did their interpretation of fiscal freedom. The American colonists had based their emergency finances on a system of interest-free contingent taxation. They understood perfectly well from extensive, and often painful, experience that paper money might become a tax on the population, either through depreciation or through its removal from circulation by overt taxation. They understood that the potential tax burden would fall on them because, unlike the tribal republics of antiquity, they had no other group to subjugate and thereby force to pay their taxes for them. The native tribes scarcely disposed of adequate resources to be worth taxing. The productive surplus of imported African slaves was already in the colonists' hands; it could be tapped only if the colonists themselves were tapped.

The French revolutionaries found themselves in a rather different position. By July 1789, it was already clear that a very substantial portion of the national assets was in the hands of groups that had implicitly declared themselves to be enemies of the new nation by refusing to sit and vote in common with the Third Estate. Confronted by this situation, the French took the classical position. The free should not have to dip into their own pockets until the resources of their enemies had been exhausted. Their paper money was intended to be no more than an advance on the assets expropriated from their enemies. This was how Joseph Cambon described the principles of revolutionary finance in late 1793:

> This revolution, considered solely from the point of view of finance, has given, and every day continues to give, the Nation immense properties which establish the credit of its assignats on a foundation which all the efforts of the coalition powers cannot shake, and which offer incalculable resources to ensure the conquest of its liberty.[42]

When Cambon spoke, the Reign of Terror was in full swing, and his claim about the daily additions to public assets was no exaggeration. The goods of those sent to the guillotine were automatically confiscated by the state. In Cambon's view, not only domestic revolution but even wars could be financed by the judicious use of Dr. Guillotin's invention. By 1793, the Revolution was in the hands of radicals who were themselves virtual hostages of the sansculottes to whom they owed their power. Many of the members of the Assembly of 1789 either had been executed or had saved themselves only by fleeing abroad. But the fundamental principle of revolutionary finance—a paper money supported by confiscated assets—had started not with the radical Jacobins of the National Convention (1792–1795), but with the moderate deputies of the first Assembly, half of whom had held office under the old regime. It was they who had preferred to ignore the tedious logic of balanced budgets and free-market interest rates propounded by Necker, and to resort instead to the convenience of expropriation.

The result was not immediate runaway inflation. Unlike the paper money of the American Revolution, the first assignats were not issued in time of war. They had only to cover an apparently short-term crisis. If the *dette exigible* could be repaid, the residual debt service would be around 160 million livres. The annual savings of 150 million livres would almost magically balance the budget. The assignats would be exchanged for the nationalized lands and then canceled, and the nation would be returned to sound finance. This was not what occurred. In 1790, the budget deficit started to mushroom as tax revenues fell to no more than 200 million livres. Assignats, originally planned as a stopgap measure to facilitate the repayment of debt, were issued simply to meet current expenses. Until the printing presses were finally destroyed in February 1796, the shortfall in tax revenues was offset almost entirely by means of paper. The amounts issued were the reflection—the mirror image—of the assertion by French taxpayers of their liberation from their burdens.

Revolutionary Budgets, 1788–1795[43]

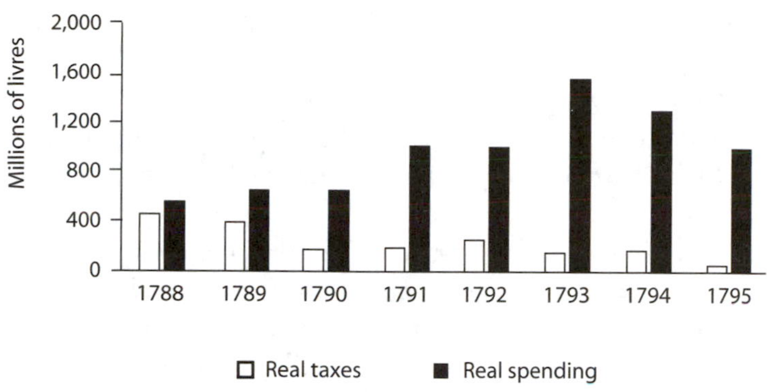

The final outcome, elegant in its inescapable symmetry, was that the amounts not contributed voluntarily through overt taxation were paid involuntarily through the covert operations of inflation. Yet the final collapse of the currency did not occur until 1795, when 16.5 billion livres were issued in one year and prices rose by 4,000%. Only then was the involuntary inflation tax paid. Until this final price explosion, the assignats more or less fulfilled their intended function of putting confiscated wealth into monetary circulation.

There were four distinct phases in the life cycle of the revolutionary currency. During the first—from August 1790 until April 1792—the king was still on the throne and the country was not yet at war. Total assignats issued were less than 2 billion livres, and of these many had been tendered for public lands and then burned, leaving just under 1.5 billion livres in circulation. Given that the prerevolutionary hard money stock was around 2 billion livres, a 75% increase in the money supply should have produced rapid inflation, but significant inflation had not occurred for the simple, if paradoxical, reason that the political and economic uncertainty that gripped the country had driven most hard money into hiding or overseas.

The Revolution entered its second phase in 1792. The military upheavals that were not to end until 1815 started in April, when war was ceremonially declared on the forces of counterrevolution led by the Austrian emperor. In the messianic oratory of the deputy, Anacharsis Cloots, the war effort was to be the symbol of French political and fiscal liberation:

> Kings make impious war on us with slave soldiers and extorted money; we will make a holy war on them with free soldiers and patriotic contributions.[44]

This was not at all how the war was to be financed, however. The declaration of war was accompanied by the confiscation of the possessions of all who had left the country since 1789. They had shown themselves to be enemies of the people and should suffer the consequences. The public treasure chest rose by another 2 billion livres or so and thus provided ample backing for the paper money issues that were the true vehicle of war finance. Cloots's "patriotic contributions" remained no more than an empty rhetorical flourish.

The third phase, the assignats, started in the summer of 1793. The revolutionary war, initially so successful, was suffering a series of terrible reverses. In January, the execution of the king had brought England into the counterrevolutionary alliance and had prompted the desertion of France's foremost general, Dumouriez, who followed his predecessor, Lafayette, into despairing exile. Within France, the revolutionary regime had to fight its opponents not only in rural backwaters such as the Vendée, but also in such major commercial centers as Lyons, Bordeaux, and Marseilles. In July and August, a series of major military setbacks in the northeast was followed by the capture of Toulon by the British fleet. Four billion livres of paper money were now in circulation, and confidence in the currency was collapsing. The looming defeat of the Revolution would inevitably mean the return of the confiscated lands that backed the paper, and its consequent demonetization. By August, the assignats were worth no more than 20% of their equivalent in coin. Some new method was needed to secure for the Revolution the means of its survival. Already in May, the Law of the Maximum had imposed price controls, but it was as yet largely without teeth. On May 31, the moderate Girondins in the Assembly were expelled under the threat of the cannon of the sansculottes, and power fell into the hands of the radical Jacobins, led by Robespierre. On September 5, a new political and economic totalitarianism was consecrated in a resolution of the National Convention: "Terror is the order of the day." "Rich egoists" and hoarders were now added to the enemies of the people, and the price controls of May were to be enforced by the guillotine.

The effectiveness of the new regime was beyond doubt. The forces of the counterrevolutionary coalition were repelled by conscripted armies larger than any hitherto witnessed in European history. Over one million Frenchmen were in arms during the following year. Spending reached levels unheard of under the old regime of the Bourbons—close to 1.5 billion livres per year in real terms. The value of the assignats stabilized and even rose. France was not alone in reinforcing the value of its paper currency with price controls and requisitioning laws when faced with financial meltdown.

The American Continental Congress had done the same in 1777 when its paper dollars fell to one-third of their face value. In the following year, the Continental currency stabilized, and the real income obtained from its issue more than doubled. But the Congress never commanded weapons of repression to rival those of the National Convention, and even in 1778, its income from note issue was only around 8% of GNP. During the Terror the Jacobins managed to extract sums equal to over 20% of prerevolutionary GNP and undoubtedly far higher in relation to the shrunken economic production of 1794.

Although the majority of the assets annexed to the state in 1794 were requisitioned from the general population at bayonet point, they were augmented by fiscal measures aimed at those with suspected royalist sympathies. The assignats issued under the monarchy, emblazoned with the royal portrait, were demonetized at the end of the year, in punishment of their owners for the insolent 5% premium at which they were valued in relation to their republican brethren. The rhetoric accompanying this act made the objective plain:

> In whose hands are these assignats? In the hands of aristocrats, of Austrians, and of all those who hope for the restoration of the monarchy. . . .
>
> The assignats with the head of the tyrant are accepted at 105 by the gentlemen of Lyon, Bordeaux, Marseilles and of Paris. I propose to punish them by the same means that they have sinned against the Republic.[45]

The demonetization was also timed to give impetus to another act of fiscal coercion directed at the wealthy with suspect loyalties: the forced loan. There was no trace here of the classical patriotic generosity invoked by Necker in his *contribution patriotique* of 1790. Cambon's proposal was an act of political hostage-taking:

> I would like the Convention to open a civic loan of one billion which would be subscribed by the rich and the indifferent. . . . You are rich, you have an opinion which is causing us expense [i.e., your royalist leanings are indirectly creating war costs]; I want to chain you to the Revolution in spite of yourself; I want you to lend your fortune to the Republic.[46]

The "loan"—interest-free and repayable only in public lands after two successive years of peace—was supposed to raise 1 billion livres. But it could be circumvented by subscription to a "voluntary" loan at 4%* interest,

*The nominal interest was 5%, but in 1793 all public debt interest was made subject to a 20% withholding tax.

which was immediately exchangeable for public lands. Those holding "royal" assignats also had the incentive to tender them in payment before the end of the year, when they would become worthless. In spite of these inducements, the results were less than satisfactory. The smart money was on subscribing to the voluntary loan and then using the bonds to buy public lands. But the policies of the Terror were at odds with any form of public credit—even the most coercive. Later Cambon was to bewail the malign effects of the Law of the Maximum:

> From the time it was decreed the voluntary loan was lessened. The forced loan which fell particularly on the commercial incomes of the year, had no more base. At the same time as we established revolutionary taxes, the revolutionary army carried terror everywhere. . . . Everything seemed to unite to paralyse the product of the voluntary and forced loans, which should have produced 1 billion, and which instead amounts to about 180 to 200 millions.[47]

In effect, the revolutionary regime had developed so many different methods of confiscation that they were in mutual conflict. This, anyway, was the explanation offered by the deputation of Fontaine de Grenelle for the shortfall of the sums due under the forced loan:

> The revolutionary tribunal has deranged our calculations by the punishment of a large number of traitors whose . . . goods have become the property of the nation, so that the Republic finds now that it has lent to itself.[48]

The paradoxical effect of the Terror was therefore to strengthen the assignats while weakening their link with sales of public lands. During a year in which the public display of wealth, whether inherited or recently acquired, invited the attention of the revolutionary tribunals, it was a brave soul who would be seen bidding for the confiscated goods of others. However tempting the prices for which they could be bought, the guillotine could always recycle them back into the public treasury.

The fourth, and final, phase of paper money was ushered in by the coup of Thermidor Year II (July 1794), which ended the Terror and sent its leaders to join their victims. The new regime quickly destroyed much of the apparatus of state repression. But as it had no obvious alternative scheme of finance, the economic terror did not end until December, when the Law of the Maximum was repealed. By this stage, it was becoming obvious even to the sansculottes that the result of the law was to reduce supply. Yet without price controls, the assignats were left with nothing to support them except the putative value of confiscated property. In December, Johannot optimistically declared this to be worth 15 billion livres—more than sufficient to cover the 7 billion livres of notes in circulation. But not only were the real values considerably lower than this, much of the property also came from more recent expropriations from families who had originally welcomed the Revolution. Almost any plan for a peace that would consolidate the gains of the Revolution involved the reconciliation of these important figures, and the return to France of those of them who had emigrated during the Terror. Not only would the national treasure chest be significantly reduced, but there were also unlikely to be any further expropriations to bolster it. Nothing so clearly illustrates the profound tie between the assignats and the confiscated lands than the fall of their value on rumors of a general peace in December 1794. Under any normal circumstances peace could have been expected to increase their value by limiting further issues. But holders looked only to the probable return of the émigrés and the repossession of their property.

Detached from their mooring on public land, the assignats were set adrift, and for the final fourteen months of their life, they became a tax pure and simple. As the population adjusted to this new and unwelcome function, it reacted (as predicted by Keynes) by refusing to hold more than the barest minimum of the money. The market value of the currency plunged to levels where it was no longer worth issuing, and where it was inadequate for economic functioning. At the end of 1794, the real value of the money supply was around 2.8 billion livres—a figure that still reflected the effect of price controls, and that was still far too high for the shrunken economy. By the end of 1795 the government had more than trebled the amount of money in circulation, but its market value had fallen to no more than 250,000 livres. By the time the printing presses were ceremonially destroyed in February 1796—in what one historian has called the last great festival of the Revolution—total monetary reform had become inevitable. The government attempted to postpone the inevitable by issuing a new currency also tied to public land—the *mandat territorial.* But the new paper was given an unrealistic exchange rate with assignat which doomed it to a depreciation so rapid that by June it was already worthless. In any case, it was too late for such measures. The population had already taken matters into their own hands and would deal only in coin.

The failure of successive revolutionary assemblies to collect taxes has continued to bewilder historians. By the end of 1791, the old, illegal, oppressive taxes had been replaced with new ones—enlightened, fair, and less burdensome. The deputies followed the prescriptions of earlier advocates of reform: no more tax farmers and the hideous morass of indirect dues that they collected. Instead, there were new direct taxes: the *contribution foncière* on land, the *contribution mobilière* on urban property, and the *contribution patriotique* on income. As Montesquiou presented his budget for 1792, he sounded positively optimistic:

> The collection will be easy from contributors who have already recovered the tithe for their own profit, who no longer have to pay the *gabelles,* the *droits* and *aides,* the tobacco tax, the tolls or customs, or a thousand other small dues. . . . [There is no comparison] between these clear, easy, direct and always certain receipts, and revenues which it was necessary to tear from the contributors and which were devoured in advance. . . . The united charges, which came to more than 700 million, and whose division was quite unequal, are now 100 million less, and are fairly distributed.[49]

Taken in conjunction with the planned repayment of 2 billion livres of floating debt out of the proceeds of the church lands, the result should have been a healthy budget surplus. Yet Montesquiou's optimism proved unfounded. In the words of one recent French historian, there was,

> surprisingly, a crisis of trust between the taxpayers and the institutions that they had just created: by now provided with legally established contributions and with a fiscal system entirely renewed according to their preferences, nevertheless the proprietors obstinately refused to pay their due, in spite of the pathetic exhortations of the office of the Public Revenues and by successive assemblies.[50]

In the absence of tax revenues, the Revolution was nourished on a diet of paper money that was intended to represent confiscated assets. There was, of course, nothing new about the conjunction of revolution and confiscation. In spite of the absolute and justified trust later placed in them by their creditors, the Dutch had not been above repudiating debts owed to Habsburg subjects at the time of the Dutch struggle for independence. The English Parliament had confiscated the lands of its royalist opponents without compunction in the 1640s. The American Congress had not been shy about applying a similar policy to loyalist assets in the War of Independence.

Yet the confiscations that were to fuel the French Revolution were of a quite different order from those that had preceded it. The Dutch repudiation of foreign debt is not possible to quantify exactly; but it would not have amounted to more than a few million guilders in a total cost of independence running into hundreds of millions. The English and American confiscations were higher and can be more exactly calculated. They amounted to around £5 million and $19 million, respectively—in each case, no more than 15% of GNP.[51] By contrast, the value of property confiscated in the first six years of the French Revolution has been estimated at between 4 billion and 5.5 billion livres in real terms.[52] The lower figure is probably closer to the truth but does not include the income from other forms of confiscation such as the demonetization of royal assignats and the proceeds of the forced loan on 1793. Even at 4 billion, the assets expropriated were equivalent to 57% of prerevolutionary GNP, and they may well have been as high as 70%. To put it another way, in the first six years of the Revolution total spending was around 6 billion livres in real terms. Of this, only one-quarter came from taxes, and a full three-quarters was covered by confiscations.

Of course, the confiscated lands did not pay directly for the Revolution. Only a portion were sold, and the buyers paid only a fraction of their real worth. At the first auctions, properties were sold for well above their estimated value; later, they were to be knocked down at bargain prices. In either case, the buyers got a bargain, since they could pay over a number of years in depreciating paper currency. The state received assignats worth around 1 billion livres in real terms, but even these were ultimately worthless. The importance of the public lands was as a psychological prop for the currency. Every time an issue was made, ministers were careful to make public a new and higher estimate of the value of the properties remaining in the national reserves, and to place some more of them on the market. The perception of underlying value helped maintain the value of the assignats and enabled the government to pay a greater number of expenses with each issue. The fiction was essential to the success of revolutionary finance, and when it crumbled in 1795, the currency crumbled with it.

Herein lay the root cause of the ineffectiveness of the tax-gathering efforts of the revolutionary assemblies. Until 1795, the Third Estate appeared truly to believe that it could pay the costs of its Revolution by confiscating the assets of the First and Second Estates. On some profound level it was simply incompatible with the French view of freedom that the newly liberated should have to pay taxes before the assets of their enemies were exhausted. The very name of the nation implied that political liberty was synonymous with freedom from tax. Now that they had cast off their chains, the Third Estate, too, wished to enjoy the "freedom of the Franks."

Nowhere was this fundamental truth more starkly stated than by François Guizot, who was to be prime minister under France's experiment with constitutional monarchy in the 1830s. Guizot was a true believer in the tribal origins of freedom, and his writing is steeped in the history of the "gothic constitution." Since he grew up during the Revolution, his beliefs were not far distant from those of the revolutionaries themselves:

> The Revolution was a war, a real war, such as the world recognises when it is waged between nations. For over thirteen centuries France contained two nations, a people of conquerors and a people of the conquered. . . . When in 1789 the representatives of all France met together in a single assembly, the two nations hastened to resume their ancient quarrel.[53]

In sum, the French view of fiscal *liberté* was not based on underlying assumptions of either *égalité* or *fraternité*; instead, it was based on old-fashioned *hostilité*. The Revolution was, exactly as Joseph Cambon claimed, an act of conquest—the conquest of liberty—to be paid for with the spoils of war.

The Thermidorian coup was, and has always been understood to be, a profound turning point in the Revolution. The Terror had stretched the definition of "enemies of the people" so wide that it had become, all too literally, a dead end. Not only aristocrats but successive leaders of the Revolution were now defined as its enemies. Whether they fled or were caught made no economic difference: their goods fell to the state either way. Producers were turned into potential criminals by the price-fixing and antihoarding laws. Their production was requisitioned at the point of a bayonet, and if they persisted in their hostility to the economic regime, they, too, might be deemed enemies of the people and suffer the same consequences as their erstwhile rulers. By July 1794, it seemed as if that there would soon be more enemies than people.

What was needed now was a process of reconciliation and the rehabilitation of those who had fled from the Terror. The implications for public finance have already been discussed. The *territoriaux nationaux*, the great public treasure chest that had appeared to pay for the Revolution, would no longer grow. It would shrink. In 1795, the assignats turned into a tax on the general public and suffered the fate of all hyperinflations. By 1796 there was no alternative to the return of more conventional financial arrangements. But were these arrangements to be, at last, on the Anglo-Dutch model that the 1789 Revolution had, superficially, looked set to inaugurate?

There were several practical obstacles in the way of a rapid conversion to credit-based public finance. The most obvious was the lack of a sound currency in which to conduct public affairs. So much money had fled abroad that the domestic stock of coin—even if enticed out of private hoards—was scarcely sufficient for normal economic functioning. Du Pont de Nemours estimated it at no more than 300 million livres. Then there was the total disintegration of the financial markets. Not only had the Paris Bourse been closed for well over a year during the Terror, but the French invasion of Holland in 1795 had dried up Europe's largest source of international finance. Even if the markets could be restored to life by a general peace, creditors were unlikely to forget the events of the past years overnight. Necker's warning to the Assembly in March 1790 was even more apposite six years later.

> Understand, gentlemen, that after having reestablished order in the finances, after having replaced the revenues which have disappeared, after having established a perfect balance between revenues and expenses, in sum after you are freed from the current embarrassment which so justifiably alarms us, it will still need some time before credit can recover its full vigour![54]

Quite apart from reviving the credit markets and awaiting their full recovery, it was a sine qua non that a "perfect balance between revenues and expenses" be established. This was an even more distant prospect. The average deficit in the public accounts since 1789 had been well over 700 million livres per year in real terms. Even with the return of peace, there was a prospective deficit of 300–400 million livres. Were French taxpayers suddenly to accept the trebling of their tax burdens so as to satisfy potential lenders? It seemed unlikely. Finally there was the problem of the old debt. Approximately 1 billion livres of the prerevolutionary debt had been repaid with assignats by 1795. But that still left an amount of more than 3 billion livres currently in default that would have to be settled to the satisfaction of the credit markets.

Perhaps, looking at this array of obstacles, it is not surprising that the Directory (the government that ruled France from 1795 to 1799) did not choose the Anglo-Dutch path. Yet the obstacles it faced were not so very much greater than those facing the Federalists in 1790 or, for that matter, the French Restoration government in 1815. Hamilton, too, had been confronted with a massive overhang of debt that had languished for years in default. The Restoration government of France faced not only a substantial existing debt—albeit smaller than in 1795—but the need to increase it to pay reparations to foreign countries and émigrés. In neither case was the population convinced of the need for a full settlement on terms acceptable to the credit markets; it was their leaders who took the initiative. After 1795, it was not that the Directory attempted to restore public credit and failed. It did not even try.

One if the most curious aspects of the French Revolution—regularly commented on by historians—is the juxtaposition of an apparently sincere belief in the sanctity of the public debt with policies that led inevitably to default. The National Assembly had taken the debt under the "guard of honor" of the French nation in 1789. In 1792, Antoine Lavoisier, the great chemist and erstwhile Farmer General, had produced a lengthy statistical analysis of the debt for the Assembly, which he had concluded with the observation that there was more to the debt than its mere enumeration. There was a moral element, too, and here Lavoisier was pleased to report that everywhere he found "that same severity of principles, that same loyalty which has so justly merited the trust of the nation."[55] Even the National Convention had not questioned this fundamental premise, and Cambon was proud to claim, "We will not act like the old regime, which looked only for ways to delay payments: we will overlook nothing in order to accelerate ours."[56] Interest payments and even some payments of principal were maintained under the Terror (albeit late, and only in depreciated paper money). In spite of the apparent ease with which Sieyès's imagery of parasitic disease preying on the body of the people could have been extended from aristocrats to public creditors, the leap was never made. Public creditors were never classified as automatic enemies of the people. It is true that the *financiers*, many of whom had welcomed the Revolution in 1789, were now to become its victims. In 1794, the Farmers General, or at least those of them who had remained in France like Lavoisier, were put on trial and condemned en bloc. But the rentiers were to remain a protected species—at least in theory—shielded by their image as victims of the Bourbon tyranny rather than as one of its props. True, like so many protected species in the twentieth century, the rentiers were to become virtually extinct anyway. But their extinction was not at the hands of the public executioner (although many of the guillotine's victims were incidentally rentiers) but rather, by a process of de facto expropriation of their incomes, undertaken always with a certain reluctance and with pithy words of exculpation.

At the risk of overburdening the analogy, the rentiers were simultaneously protected in theory and deprived of sustenance in practice because, like endangered species today, they performed no useful economic function within society to compensate for their consumption of resources. They were maintained only as evidence of the moral superiority of the new civilization to the old, and this was not enough to ensure their survival. It was not moral superiority that ensured the safety of the public creditors in England and Holland. It was the continued importance of public credit to the state. The reduction of the rentiers to totem status in revolutionary France was the inevitable corollary of the reluctance of successive regimes to embrace credit-based public finance.

It was the role of the Directory finally to reduce the sums paid to the rentiers to an amount commensurate with the diminished revenues of the state and with their merely totemic status. The process had started under the National Convention in 1793 with Cambon's consolidation of the debt in his *Grand Livre de la Dette Publique*. Cambon's consolidation trod the familiar path of ancien régime defaults. "Usurious" debts were relieved of their surplus interest. Life annuities had their returns reduced to a prospective yield of 5%, by use of the actuarial science that the old regime had sponsored and then so blithely ignored. The 125-million-livre lottery loan of 1784 had its bonuses removed. In addition, all debts were made subject to the new *contribution mobilière*, thus reducing their yields by a further 20% to a net 4%. So far, the revolutionary reductions were the equivalent, perhaps, of Terray's default of 1770.

The situation of the rentiers worsened after Thermidor. The assignats in which they were paid became entirely, as opposed to partially, worthless. When the assignats disappeared from circulation in 1796, two new forms of paper were created to cover interest payments, whose combined real value ranged between 15% and 25% of the amounts due. In 1797, the Directory put an official seal on a state of affairs that had existed in reality for some time by reducing the debt by two-thirds. It is not surprising to find that the speeches in support of this measure reflected the view of public debt as a contingent rather than an absolute liability:

> The repeated promises not to effect any diminution to the public debt are no more than a moral act, perhaps imprudent or indiscreet, which never engages the citizens beyond that portion of their revenue of which the State may legitimately dispose.[57]

The bankruptcy of 1797 was both the nadir and the turning point in the fortunes of the rentiers. The one-third of the debt that remained was to be paid in hard currency and without withholding taxes—although this commitment was to be fulfilled only after the fall of the Directory. In 1801, interest payments in cash were made for the first time since 1788. The repudiated two-thirds of the debt was converted into rentes at 5% of its old value, and the rentiers therefore received 36.67% of their old interest. The total debt service of France had been reduced from over 300 million livres to around 85 million. Taken globally, the revolutionary default was on a scale equivalent to that of 1708–1721.

It was the good fortune of Napoleon to inherit the results of the grubby work of the Directory, and thus to be able to parade himself as the savior of public credit. Under the Consulate and the Empire, the much reduced debt was serviced punctually and in good coin. The market value of the new rentes rose from under 10 in 1797–1798, to over 80 by 1807. But the rentiers were no more integral to the operations of Napoleonic finance than they had been to any previous revolutionary regime. Napoleon may have believed in honoring the debts of the state, but this did not imply that he believed in Anglo-Dutch finance. His view of public debt was quite as negative as Jefferson's:

> National debt is immoral and destructive; silently undermining the basis of the state, it delivers the present generation to the execration of posterity.[58]

Under Napoleon, therefore, as under the previous regimes, the rentiers remained a protected species with an essentially symbolic function. The imperial wildlife park was merely better protected from encroachment, and the animals were less mangy. Napoleon succeeded where his predecessors had failed in securing the "moral dignity" of France. It was precisely the loss of dignity that had been the chief lament of the opponents of the 1797 bankruptcy. As one deputy bewailed:

> That a people destined by its glory to become the model for others, should be reduced or that it should condemn itself, in the middle of its very triumphs and with resources superior to those of its enemies, to such an excess of opprobrium and degradation, is something that I fail to understand.[59]

Underlying this display of public morality lay a more subtle message. The protection of the public debt stood for the protection of property rights in general. In the words of Baron Louis, who oversaw the definitive restoration of French credit standing after 1815, rentes constituted "the vanguard of property rights. . . . When they are respected the others have nothing to fear."[60] By protecting the rentiers, therefore, Napoleon sent a message to the propertied classes that their interests were better protected with him than with either the Bourbons or the Jacobins, both of whom lay waiting in the wings for his regime to stumble.

But if Napoleon was not a convert to Anglo-Dutch finance, and if paper money was no longer an option, how was the state to finance its seemingly endless wars? No European state since the Renaissance, with the exception of Brandenburg-Prussia, had resolved this conundrum—and Prussia had had the advantage of foreign subsidies for which France was scarcely a contender. Perhaps Napoleon could create a valid alternative to the apparent supremacy of the republican model.

One possibility that must be considered is that Napoleon, in spite of his public disclaimers, was more dependent on borrowing than he let on. Public issues of long-term debt were certainly out of the question, but short-term finance was another matter. Like most features of Napoleonic finance, the underlying principles had been laid down in the apparent chaos of the Directory. *Financiers* may have been the single most despised group of the ancien régime, and Napoleon, like his predecessors, continued to castigate them as the "scourge of the nation"; but their services appeared to be indispensable. The Revolution succeeded in banishing them permanently from the realm of tax collection, but only temporarily from the area of spending. In 1793, the National Convention dismissed private army contractors in the interests of republican probity, only to find that the new system was more corrupt than the old. Reboul complained in 1796 that the "abuses and dilapidations are not partial; the rot is general, it is built into the system."[61] It had been easy enough to pay for military supplies with paper that could be printed on demand. The return to hard-currency finance posed more complex logistical demands, especially with France's armies operating at ever-increasing distances from its borders. So in 1796, a new generation of *financiers* took the stage, the most important of whom, Gabriel-Julien Ouvrard, became Munitionaire Générale in 1797 and continued to play a leading role until the fall of the Empire. As before, these private contractors offered a form of short-term finance, but one which was sufficiently disguised not to subvert too publicly Napoleon's official disapproval of indebtedness.

Yet the amounts contributed to the imperial finances by the *financiers* were relatively modest. They did not significantly leverage the amounts available to the state via taxation. The Empire did leave debts that were calculated at 1.3 billion francs* by Baron Louis, but these were accumulated only in the final years of decline and fall.

*The franc was the new French currency established in the wake of the collapse of assignats. It was more or less a re-creation of the post-1726 livre, altough with decimal subdivisions, and contained 4.5 grams of silver.

Nor was there to be any support from another Napoleonic institution taken from the repertory of Anglo-Dutch finance: the Banque de France, founded in 1803. Memories of John Law's Banque Royale, not to mention of the disasters of revolutionary finance, ensured that the bank would be privately owned—like the Bank of England and the Bank of the United States. But unlike either the English bank or the Caisse d'Escomptes, the Banque de France was specifically prohibited from financing the government directly. Indirect government finance was harder to control, since the army contractors could use the bank to refinance themselves. After a credit crisis in 1805, the bank was recapitalized, and the loophole was closed. In the final crisis of the Empire, the bank played no part. Napoleon preferred to have it pay off its notes and close its doors rather than risk another round of inflationary finance.

If there was to be any hope of surviving without borrowing, it was essential to reduce spending and increase revenues. The reduction of spending, in particular, was the legacy of the Directory, not only in the trimming of the public debt, but in the dismissal of redundant state employees, such as the 40,000 watchmen employed under the National Convention. The Directory also started the process of resurrecting the state's defunct tax base. The first requirement was to ensure that the basic land tax, the *contribution foncière,* would be collected. After 1797, this tax started to bring in around 240 million francs, rising to over 300 million by 1799. Napoleon did not materially increase its yield beyond this level. More significant was the gradual return of indirect taxes. These odious symbols of ancien régime injustice had been largely abolished in 1790, and the coup de grâce had been administered in early 1791, when the hated urban gate tolls also went. But by 1797, it was only too apparent that no modern state could survive on direct taxes alone, and this cornerstone of revolutionary ideology had to be abandoned. Navigation tolls were restored in 1796–1797, and gate tolls in 1798–1799. In 1803, wine returned to the list of taxed commodities, and finally, in 1807, the salt tax was reinstated. After 1810, over 200 million francs per year were raised by indirect taxation—sums, in other words, almost identical to those collected in the last years of the old regime. By that year, the negligible tax revenues that had been collected in 1795 and 1796, amounting to little more than 50 million francs in either year, had grown to 750 million francs. This sum was rather higher than had been typical at the height of the Empire, but revenues of over 600 million were regularly collected for many years.[62]

Even allowing for inflation, these sums were a significant improvement on the record of the Bourbons. Taking into account the reduction in debt service that had occurred as a result of the Revolution, the results were even more impressive. In 1788, the Bourbon dynasty had free revenues, after debt service, of around 170 million francs. By 1806, their Bonaparte successors had disposed of 500 million francs, and after 1810, this sum had increased to at least 600 million. What might Louis XV and Louis XVI have achieved if they had been able to spend such sums in their struggles against Britain? In 1788, France's free revenues were equivalent to £6.7 million, against the £8.7 million of Britain. Napoleon could throw the equivalent of £20–24 million into the fray, even at pre-1789 exchange rates. At the exchange rates that prevailed after 1810, this amount was equivalent to £30–35 million.

This was splendid enough, but it was not all. Even at these levels, France was not overtaxing itself. National production had recovered from the disasters of the 1790s and was in the region of 10 billion francs by 1810.[63] Taxation therefore represented around 7% of GNP. This rate was no higher than before the Revolution, and it was almost certainly less than the overall tax burden that had so incensed the prerevolutionary population, including tithes, feudal dues, and the profits of the tax farmers. These had probably consumed around 10% of GNP. The burden of taxation in France was far, far lower than that endured across the Channel.

Taxes at this level certainly did not represent that total "freedom of the Franks" that had been aspired to in the early Revolution, but there was some reason to believe that Mirabeau's assertion of 1790—that the reign of liberty should be less onerous than that of servitude—had not been contradicted—the more so since the principal means by which the French had managed to reduce their tax burdens in the 1790s had not been abandoned. By 1795 the idea of living off the assets of domestic enemies of the people had become a dead end and would not be resurrected. Napoleon even sought the return of émigré families by offering them their confiscated lands. But the principle of expropriation was simply transferred from internal to external enemies.

There was nothing new about the idea of living off the enemy: it was an accepted part of the realpolitik of the ancient world. In a limited, military sense, it was understood that since armies survived by requisitioning resources from the areas through which they passed, there was an in-built advantage in waging aggressive as opposed to defensive warfare. In a broader sense, it was also understood that extracting resources from other societies, whether by plunder, tribute, or taxation, was a sound method of reducing the taxes paid by one's own.

What was new in revolutionary France was not the elevation of pillage to the level of statecraft, but its justification by theories nominally dedicated to universal liberation. Even here the intellectual pirouette was not quite without parallel. First, by the reconquest of France from the enemies of the people and then, by extension, the conquest of their enemies abroad. Just as the Spanish conquistadors had been the logical outcome of the completion of the *reconquista* of the Iberian Peninsula, so the Napoleonic conquests were the outcome of the consummation of the revolutionary reconquest of France. And in both instances the external conquests were justified by the same doctrine that had sanctified the original reconquest.

As with other aspects of Napoleonic finance, the underlying principles had been laid down during the Revolution. In 1794 the lands of the Belgian church were expropriated by the National Convention. This was the simple extension of the confiscation of French ecclesiastical property following the annexation of the Austrian Netherlands to France. The same policy was later applied in Spain under Napoleon, and the illiquid assets thus obtained were put into circulation by means of paper very similar to the assignats of the early Revolution.

Expropriation of ecclesiastical assets might be an appropriate policy in Catholic countries, but it was less suited to Protestant ones. An alternative spin on revolutionary theory was required in such situations. In 1795, the Dutch Republic was overrun and then made to pay for the cost of its "liberation" from the House of Orange. A sum of 100 million guilders (200 million francs) was established as fair compensation incurred by the liberators, but this was the not the end of the affair. It is estimated that the Dutch had contributed 229 million guilders to the French budget by 1804. The same form of compulsory gratitude was imposed on the Italian territories conquered from the Austrians by the young General Bonaparte. The Orwellian newspeak implicit in these payments had already been elaborated in France two years earlier. Lyons, the second city of France, and for centuries proudly independent, was among the towns that rebelled against the increasingly Parisian thrust of revolutionary republicanism. When Lyons was overrun by the forces of the National Convention, its ancient liberties were annulled, together with its even more ancient name. It was now to be known as Ville-Affranchie—literally, Liberated Town.

The legacy of the Enlightenment was evident not only in the justificatory rhetoric, but in the more rational way that the French chose to live off their enemies. Ouvrard, for one, discouraged the old, haphazard practice of pillage, asserting, "There are only two ways to wage war: by pillaging or by paying. It is cheaper to wage it by paying."[64]

It was in the interests of efficiency, therefore, that France insisted on cash payments from its defeated opponents. Its overseas armies were almost universally supported at local expense, but the cost was thereby more equitably distributed than merely local pillaging would have allowed. Where the rhetoric of liberation faltered was with more distant enemies that were merely defeated as opposed to conquered and reformed. These, too, were forced to pay heavy indemnities, which could be justified, at best, as penalties for aggression against the advancing tide of universal freedom. Austria, for instance, was assessed 100 million francs after Pressburg and 250 million after Wagram. Prussia was compelled to pay 515 million francs after Jena "as punishment for its imprudent attacks."

The overall scale of these payments is contentious. As a rule of thumb they may be assumed to have paid for the cost of armies outside France and little more. Mollien was of the opinion that the payments did not even cover military costs. On the other hand, Gaudin, Napoleon's Minister of Finance, claimed that "victory powerfully assisted the extraordinary budget, and it permitted us even to consecrate more than 500 millions over four years to public works and domestic embellishments."[65] The sums involved were obviously liable to exaggeration—by Napoleon seeking to reassure his *financiers*, and by his enemies seeking reparations after his defeat. German historians claimed that French exactions amounted to 1 billion francs. Napoleon himself claimed to have gained more than 2 billion francs by his conquests. A more conservative estimate has put the figure for cash payments after 1799 at 785 million francs. The total of all expropriation would have been far higher, since it included goods of other kinds—such as those that made the Louvre Europe's foremost museum—and assets annexed to Napoleon's lieutenants rather than to the state.

Even if the amounts garnered from revolutionary conquests were limited to supporting overseas armies, they were impressive enough. Taken in conjunction with its solid domestic fiscal position, France was in command of resources that would have been the envy of any European monarch, past or present. Moreover, Napoleon's resources were obtained by means that other monarchs would have wholeheartedly endorsed (assuming that they were not among his defeated opponents). In a sense, the Napoleonic system may be seen as the apotheosis of ancien régime finance—more perfect even that its Prussian antecedent. The state was able to tax more or less without consent. The awkward conundrum posed by Augeard in 1774—that the king must be master of the Parlement for the sake of effective government, yet no one must believe it for the sake of affordable borrowing—no longer applied. The Parlements no longer existed, and the state no longer needed to borrow. Yet Napoleon was no Oriental despot. His rule was firmly based on the European tradition of absolutism limited by respect for private property rights. Such rulers were unlikely to amass the legendary treasure troves of past empires, but the reward for their moderation was a flourishing economy, not stifled by excessive taxes or depressed by deflationary hoarding of money. Nor was the foreign policy of the new regime out of character. The restless dynasticism of "old regime" Europe was manifested in a more or less ceaseless quest for territorial aggrandizement. In 1789, it was countered by revolutionary patriotism. The Napoleonic Empire can be seen as the Hegelian synthesis of these ideologies. Dynasticism meets Revolution and gives birth to revolutionary dynasticism. Charlemagne meets Cola di Rienzo* and gives birth to Napoleon. It was not without significance that, when war was declared on the Holy Roman Emperor in 1792, Francis II was not referred to by the title first enjoyed by Charlemagne, but only as the "King of Hungary and Bohemia." In these circumstances, it is not surprising that Francis thought fit to abolish his most august title in 1806 so as to prevent Napoleon's laying his hands on it.

But vital questions remained. However impressive Napoleon's financial resources, were they sufficient to take on the "nation of shopkeepers" across the Channel, that irritating pseudomonarchy that acted as if it were a republic of merchants? And beyond the issue of adequacy lay that of sustainability. Would a policy based on the expropriation of enemy assets suffer the fate of the Jacobin experiment—imploding under the weight of accumulated enemies?

THE ELEPHANT AND THE WHALE

Were the whole capital of the national debt, which at the time I write, is almost four hundred million pounds sterling, to be emitted in assignats or bills, and that whole quantity put into circulation, as was done in America and in France,

*Cola di Rienzo (1313–1354), the son of a Roman tavern keeper, aspired to restore the glory of ancient Rome. In a startling career, he led an uprising in 1347 in which he was acclaimed as Tribune of the People. His plans for a pan-Italian parliament to elect a new Roman emperor came to nothing, and he became a fugitive. After another trimphal return to Rome in 1354, he died at the hands of the mob. He became a hero of the Romantic movement, and Wagner wrote an opera, *Rienzi*, about him.

> those English assignats, or bills, would sink in value as those of America and France have done. . . . A nominal pound sterling in such bills would not be worth one penny.
>
> —Tom Paine, *The Decline and Fall of the English System of Finance,* 1796

Tom Paine, whatever his other virtues, was no expert on financial matters. His views on the subject were merely the expression of his political passions. Originally a devout believer in paper money, in the 1780s he had become a convert to the nationalist and Federalist belief in the importance of a strong central government with a funded debt. When he was writing from Paris in the 1790s, however, his only concern was to undermine, by whatever arguments came to hand, the main prop of his old enemy, the English establishment. Any writer who could still opine in early 1796 that "assignats have a solid property in reserve in the national domains" was clearly letting his prejudices blind him to the facts. Yet Paine did point out a fundamental truth: the English system depended critically on selling long-term debt rather than printing money. A national debt as large as England's would indeed be totally worthless if issued as banknotes along American or French revolutionary lines. In these circumstances, a polemic designed to discourage potential investors in Consols might do more damage to the country than the revolutionary armies. To unnerve the public creditors, Paine confidently forecast the impending collapse of England's debt market, and with it the fall of the country's despicable regime:

> I have now exposed the English system for the eyes of all nations, for this work will be published in all languages. In doing this I have done an act of justice to those numerous citizens of neutral nations who have been imposed upon by that fraudulent system, and who have property at stake upon the event.[66]

Paine's pamphlet was part of a "second front" in the Anglo-French struggle for supremacy—the war of public finances. By 1796, both sides sought victory as much in the financial as in the military downfall of its opponents. Viewing the chaos of French public finances, the English prime minister, William Pitt, claimed that he could confidently forecast the collapse of the French revolutionary war effort. "But who," his friend William Wilberforce is reputed to have retorted, "was Attila's Chancellor of the Exchequer?"

It is unlikely that Paine's pamphlet had much influence on the course of events; but his forecast was not so very wide of the mark. In the early years of the war, Pitt had done no more than apply the formula that had appeared to work in previous engagements: borrow heavily and raise taxes only sufficiently to pay the extra interest. But two factors made this a dangerous policy. Revolutionary France was able to outspend the Bourbon monarchy and thus further raised the cost of war. Additionally, Britain started the war of public finances with debts that already appeared to be at the very limit of sustainability. In 1795 and 1796, the government ran deficits of £20 million and £23 million, handily exceeding the average deficit of £10 million recorded in the American War of Independence. Not surprisingly, the upward trend in the price of the Consols that had prevailed from 1790 to 1792 went into rapid reverse. From a high of 97 in 1792, they fell to 70 in 1793, and to 60 in 1794. In 1796, they traded as low as 53¼—below even the worst prices recorded in the American War of Independence. The markets were so overstretched that Pitt was considering the possibility of a forced loan—albeit at a market rate of interest, and without the "soak-the-rich" rhetoric of its French equivalents.

If the long-term credit market was weak, the other pillar of the financial establishment was even weaker. The Bank of England had been among the beneficiaries of the flight of hard currency from France in the early years of the Revolution. When, after 1795, the Directory pursued policies designed to lure specie back into the country, the Bank's coffers were correspondingly drained. By the end of 1796, its reserves were no more than £2 million, compared to £8 million in 1791.[67] In early 1797, it looked as if the doomsayers were right, and the end was nigh. There was a small French landing at Fishguard in February, militarily insignificant, but sufficient to unnerve the credit market and start a dash for liquidity. The Bank's reserves fell to £1 million. They had been even lower in 1763 and 1783, but these were temporary credit crises brought about by postwar deflations. In 1797, there was no peace in sight and therefore no light at the end of the financial tunnel. On February 27, the Bank of England ended the convertibility of its notes into specie, and the decline and fall of the English system predicted by Tom Paine seemed set to unfold.

Even if 1797–1798 did not turn out to be the end of the road for Anglo-Dutch finance, it was most certainly a turning point. The deficit ballooned to £36 million in 1797, and the price of Consols fell below the psychological barrier of 50 for the first time in their history. Even with the extra liquidity provided to the system by the end of convertibility, it was apparent that the market would not sustain this level of borrowing. Tax increases were not even keeping up with interest costs: since 1792 revenues had risen by £3 million, while interest had increased by £4 million. The old policy of paying for war almost exclusively by borrowing was no longer possible. Britain had arrived at the end of the second stage of the paradigm of "republican" finance. The ruling class was no longer able to avoid a large part of the costs of war by a policy of borrowing supported by indirect taxes. If their political freedoms were to be defended against the new threat from the Continent, they would have to dig more deeply into their own pockets.

By 1798, it was already apparent that a new wind was blowing. Taxes falling on the rich were boosted by no less than £5 million in one year. Trebled taxes on such luxury items as carriages, horses, manservants, and hair powders provided £2 million, and a further £2 million was contributed voluntarily by those who felt themselves to be undertaxed. But Pitt had good reason to feel that, however morally admirable these results, they were an inadequate underpinning for the credit markets. In 1799, he introduced the general income tax that was to be the true savior of British war finance.

In its first year, the tax raised £6.5 million. By 1807, collection procedures were more efficient, and £12 million came into the Exchequer. This sum had risen to nearly £16 million by 1813—as much as the entire pre-1789 budget. The relative ease with which such large sums could be collected was all the more remarkable given the profound unpopularity of the tax with the propertied classes. This unpopularity was only partly due to the progressive nature of the levy, with incomes below £50 totally exempt and those below £150 partially exempt. Nor was the rate of 10% felt to be impossibly onerous, even to taxpayers not accustomed the exactions of modern governments. It was the invasion of privacy that aroused the maximum hostility.*

Direct taxation in the premodern world was always caught in the horns of a dilemma. It could be fairly distributed—especially in a commercially active society—only by a process of annual assessment. But such inquisitions were felt to be the greatest possible insult to personal freedom. A contributor to the letter column of *The Times* in 1816 expressed an almost universally held view:

*The tax covered all income, including interest on government securities. In spite of some claims that the tax constituted an act of default, the government was reasonably able to point out that, unlike blanket withholding taxes, such as the 20% deduction imposed by Cambon in 1793, not all holders of debt were liable for the tax. Foreign bondholders were exempt (even those under French dominion), as were those whose incomes were less than £150. The tax was not, therefore, merely a disguised method of debt service reduction.

> There is the despotic spirit of the inquisitorial impost, its horde of petty tyrants! A government exercising inquisitorial powers may easily extend them. . . . A single root will throw out shoots and suckers on all sides.[68]

The same horror had been shown in France at attempts to create a broad-based direct tax. Here, for instance, is the opinion of a government intendant charged with assessing the *dixième* on 1705.

> One should not believe that one has anything less than the most extreme repugnance to declare one's goods and to reveal the secrets of one's family. It is the very last of extremities, and so contrary to the genius of the nation, that nothing could occur to it that was more insupportable.[69]

So dreadful were the implications of assessment for political freedom that one writer claimed that he would be "a thousand times happier in Turkey." The profound opposition to assessment usually reduced direct taxes to fixed annual dues on certain easily identified forms of wealth, such as land. This, for instance, had been the fate of the Assessments of the English Commonwealth after the return of Charles II. But such reductions in scope undermined the taxes' raison d'être and encouraged accusations of unfairness, which were again assuaged only by limits on the amounts levied. Therefore the sums collected by the British income tax during the Napoleonic Wars are superficially as surprising as the repeal of the tax in 1816 is unsurprising.

It was not only the income tax that raised British revenues. Land taxes doubled, excises (including luxury taxes) went up two and a half times, and customs revenues almost trebled over the period. Total taxation, which had already been around 13% of GNP before the wars, rose to 20% or over. A tax burden that had already been twice that of France before 1789 was now three times as great.

But taxation was only part of the British response to Napoleon. Public borrowing was in no way abandoned. By the time peace returned, the national debt had soared to close to £800 million. The £36 million borrowed in 1798 was not even the record for the period. It was exceeded in 1807, 1813, and 1814, when deficits of over £40 million were recorded. As in the eighteenth century, increased taxes served first and foremost as security for further borrowing. Bolstered by the fact that revenues were now rising faster than debt service, Consols rose from their all-time low of 47¼ in early 1798 to as high as 69 in the following year and generally traded between 55 and 70 for the rest of the war. This meant that the £470 million borrowed during the entire war period was financed at an average cost of 5%, higher than the 4.35% interest cost of the American War of Independence, but still impressively low given the sums involved.

Such a favorable outcome was only possible at the price of a major modification of the old pattern of war finance. The days when 80–90% of the cost of wars could be financed had come to an end in 1797. Thereafter Britain returned to the more modest levels of borrowing of its earlier wars.

BRITISH WAR BORROWING, 1689–1815[70]

War	Cost *£ millions*	Borrowed %
League of Augsburg (1689–1697)	31	53%
Spanish Succession (1702–1713)	51	56%
Austrian Succession (1740–1748)	40	71%
Seven Years' War (1756–1763)	73	78%
American Independence (1776–1784)	112	82%
Revolutionary War (1793–1797)	100	89%
Napoleonic Wars (1798–1815)	772	49%

However, the most important change was neither the income tax nor the reduced role of borrowing. It lay in the deliberate pursuit of a policy of easy money. By 1798, the Bank of England's reserves had risen from their low of £1 million to over £6 million, and its directors offered to restore convertibility. It was Pitt who discouraged them from this step on the grounds of the uncertainty of the international position. If another crisis occurred, it would be more easily handled if there was no obligation to make payments in coin. For most of the period until 1809, the paper pound circulated at less than a 10% discount against bullion and foreign currencies. After that year, the combination of a frenetic boom in overseas trade, thanks to the opening of the Brazilian market by the Portuguese government, and the cost of financing the Duke of Wellington's army in Spain led to a fall of sterling to discounts of 20% on the exchanges.[71] In 1810, the Bullion Committee of the House of Commons criticized the Bank for excessive note issuing and demanded the resumption of convertibility within two years. The government, now Whig, but financially indistinguishable from its Tory predecessor, resolutely opposed the imposition of such a deflationary measure at least until after the return of peace. If anything, it was more determined to support the paper currency. From 1797, Bank of England notes had been accepted by the population as equivalent to coin without any legal obligation, but in the face of a level of depreciation that now approached 30%, some creditors started to demand payment in gold. In response, the Bank's notes were made legal tender in July 1811, in spite of voices raised against a measure that evoked memories of the assignats and the Continental dollars.

In spite of such fears, it was not government policy to finance the war through paper money. True, public borrowings from the Bank rose from £10 million in 1792 to a high of £35 million in 1814, but this was scarcely a significant contribution to wars costing nearly £700 million. Nor was the main purpose of easy money to devalue the public debt—since the majority of the debt was raised at higher price levels in any case. The underlying objective of successive governments was simply to avoid the risk of liquidity crises that might throttle the economy or the financial markets.

Thanks, at least in part, to this policy of easy money, the British economy enjoyed a boom during the war comparable to the spectacular commercial growth that had helped the Dutch finance their struggle against Spain two centuries earlier. In real terms, British GNP probably grew by two-thirds from 1790 to 1815—an annual rate of some 2.25%. This was certainly less than growth rates closer to 3.5% enjoyed across the Atlantic, where the productive capacity of the United States was continually boosted by immigration; but it handily exceeded any previous performance of the British economy. The growth of real GNP was augmented by the general rise in prices. Britain was not alone in experiencing inflation during this period, when commodity prices rose significantly even in gold terms. Even in Napoleonic France, where hard money was the order of the day, and where the effects of warfare were scarcely felt, prices rose by over 30%. In Britain, the easy-money policies of the government allowed them to double. This was not a shocking rate of inflation by modern standards—an average of 3.33% between 1792 and 1813—enough to stimulate the economy without deranging it. The result was that national income, which had been in the region of £130 million before the Revolution, had grown close to £400 million by 1814. It was this growth that allowed the government to raise £78 million in taxes and £60 million in long-term debt in 1814. The combined total of these sums was equivalent to the entire GNP of the country in the 1780s.

The "paper pound" might appear superficially to be a betrayal of the solid principles of Anglo-Dutch finance, but it is important to understand that the demonstrable success of the policy lay not only in the vigor of the economy, but also in the continued strength of the government's credit rating, without which the war effort could not have been financed. The willingness of creditors to ignore Tom Paine's warning of the imminent monetization of the public debt was the government's reward for decades of impeccable behavior. It was also based on the implicit assumption that the government would return to the straight and narrow after the war and would not abuse the trust vested in it.

Although regularly ridiculed and condemned by opposition politicians at the time, the financial policies of the British government during the Napoleonic Wars have received widespread praise from historians and economists. Was Britain, then, blessed with a singularly enlightened government? Before leaping to such a conclusion, one would do well to consider the case of the sinking fund. Notwithstanding William Pitt's role as the most resolute enemy of revolutionary France, he had early friends among radical thinkers. Not only William Wilberforce, the opponent of slavery, but Richard Price, the staunch supporter of both the American and the French Revolutions, was to be found in his circle. Price was a mathematical thinker of some note, and his *Treatise on Reversionary Payments,* published in 1771, had a lasting effect on the insurance industry. His *Appeal to the Public on the Subject of the National Debt,* published the following year, was to prove just as significant in the administration of public debt. A profound, almost mystical, believer in the power of compound interest for good or evil, Price had a dislike of the British public debt that was as mathematical as it was political. The only way to attack its exponential growth was at the roots. A sinking fund whose assets would not be merely canceled when bought but instead would be allowed to multiply by the mysteries of compounding would surely be able to attack the beast with its own weapons. So far, at least, Price's theories were foolish but not positively harmful. There was absolutely no mathematical advantage in holding on to repurchased debt. The interest received was exactly the same as the unnecessary extra interest paid by the state. But once separated from the moorings of common sense, Price floated off into more dangerous areas of speculation. Since the assets in the sinking fund would multiply faster at higher rates of interest, Price strenuously opposed the practice of converting debt to lower coupon rates. In fact, he proposed an upward conversion of the whole British debt from 3% to 4%, or even to 5%. That the extra interest paid on the total debt must vastly outweigh any increased interest collected by the sinking fund itself seemed not to occur to him.

In the nineteenth century, Price's theories were to be held up to almost universal ridicule. The most profound attack was on the very idea of a sinking fund at all. If the state was not running a budget surplus, the fund could be financed only by further borrowing, which would thus negate its raison d'être. But the idea of a fund at compound interest seemed even more ludicrous. The radical journalist William Cobbett was an early attacker:

> There is something so consummately ridiculous in the idea of a nation's getting money by paying interest to itself upon its own stock that the mind of every rational man naturally rejects it.[72]

If Cobbett was right, then William Pitt was clearly not a rational man. For it was he who had taken up Price's ideas in 1784 and started a new sinking fund. Walpole's old fund had fallen into disuse since the government had been unable to refrain from raiding it in time of war. Pitt's fund was protected from such acts by the provisions of the legislation. At Price's suggestion, it was to accumulate assets at compound interest. Fortunately, Pitt did not propose an upward conversion of debt, even though he expressed regrets at not doing so: "It was always my idea that a fund at a high rate of interest is better to the country than those at low rates."[73] Pitt's fund operated consistently throughout the war, and by 1813, it had accumulated no less than £238 million—almost the full amount of the debt in 1789.[74] The allure of Price's theories was starting to wear thin. A year earlier, the mathematician Robert Hamilton had argued that a sinking fund operating with borrowed money must be wasteful to the extent of the commission costs required to float the supplementary debt. On this basis, he calculated that the operations of Pitt's fund had cost the country £16.5 million during the course of the war. Impressed by his arguments, the government decided to cancel its stockpile of repurchased debt, although it refused to abolish the fund.

To further confuse the intellectual situation, Pitt disregarded his own advice when it came to funding the war. Far from selling debt at the highest possible coupon, as suggested by Price, he followed the line of least resistance and sold low-coupon debt at a discount. The markets liked low-coupon perpetuals because the government had no right to redeem (or convert) them until they reached par. Since the 3% Consols were generally sold for around 65, investors enjoyed potential long-term capital gains of 50% in addition to their current interest of 4.6%. After the war, the government was attacked by such intellectual heavyweights as the economist J. R. McCulloch for a policy that prevented it from lowering its interest costs, and that had added unnecessary millions to the face value of the debt. In its own defense, the government claimed that if it had tried to sell debt at par, investors would have demanded either an interest rate of over 6%, or 5% with a very long period of protection against redemption. Rightly or wrongly, the government chose the policy that provided the most money at the least current cost. After all, it reasoned, it was unlikely that so vast a debt would ever be redeemed at par.

Further intellectual confusion surrounded the government's monetary policy. The Bullion Committee, whose members included another of the founding fathers of modern economics, David Ricardo, attacked the Bank of England for overissue of notes, thereby causing sterling to decline against gold. The Bank responded that it had merely been seeking to accommodate legitimate demand for credit within the economy, and that the depreciation of sterling was the result of a Europe-wide demand for gold. But this justification was contradicted by failure of commodity prices to show similar depreciation. In the view of the Bullion Committee, there was no such thing as a body of experts who could intelligently manage the money supply. Perhaps its words should be engraved on the doors of modern-day central banks as a perpetual caveat:

> The most detailed knowledge of the actual trade of the Country, combined with the profound science in all the principles of Money and circulation, would not enable any man or set of men to adjust, and keep always adjusted, the right proportion of circulating medium in a country to the wants of trade.[75]

Far from operating with enlightened omniscience, the government was, as often as not, right for the wrong reasons. Price's theories on sinking funds were, to put it charitably, muddled. Yet the government was probably right to persevere with Pitt's fund, simply because of the psychological boost that it gave to the markets. It was also probably right to ignore both Price and McCulloch by selling low-coupon debt at a discount. A British government did eventually offer redemption of the 3% Consols at par, but that moment was so far off that it made virtually no difference to the overall cost of borrowing.* Ricardo and the Bullion Committee were undoubtedly correct, in the abstract, to claim that the depreciation of sterling against gold was a sign of overissue. But in time of war, it was undoubtedly wiser to follow a potentially overstimulative monetary policy at the risk of inflation than to risk deflation by adherence to strict logic.

*The offer was made in connection with Goschen's conversion of 1889. A simple calculation can be made that, if the government had been able to raise its war debt without discount by offering a 6% coupon, the annual interest payable would have been increased by £9 million by 1818, when a conversion to 5% would have been possible. Even after that, the interest would have been over £3.5 million higher than under existing government policy.

Was this financial strategy, whether the product of sublime reason, ordinary common sense, or mere fumbling, adequate to deal with the Napoleonic threat? Like many of his contemporaries, Napoleon was convinced that the war was not just between a nation of warriors and a nation of shopkeepers, nor between a nation of soldiers and a nation of sailors. He saw the struggle as one of opposing financial systems: the financial rectitude of his hard-money empire pitted against the fictitious wealth of the empire of debt. Militarily, the two nations were like different species—the elephant and the whale—who appeared invincible within their distinct habitats but could not reach each other. It was for this reason that Napoleon sought to add an economic dimension to the war by banning British goods from his empire. The drain of specie from England would surely force its financial system to bow, and ultimately to crack. Napoleon studied the foreign exchange markets for signs of the weakening of sterling with the same concern as the Bullion Committee. Its decline must be a sure sign that England was resorting to paper money, and that Tom Paine's forecast of 1796 was about to come true. In 1811–1812 his optimism must have seemed reasonable. Sterling had fallen from its historical parity of 25 francs to a mere 17–18 francs. Consols fell from a recent high of 70 to as low as 55. The outbreak of war with America in 1812 was damaging British foreign trade as well as its budget. In the meantime, Napoleon's armies were victorious throughout Europe and his budget was balanced.

By some analyses, it was only the disastrous invasion of Russia that brought down the Empire. Had Napoleon merely consolidated his gains, the financial strains on England would eventually have taken their toll. But the invasion of Russia was no casual mishap. It was the logical extension of everything that had occurred since 1789. A revolution that had financed itself by expropriation was succeeded by an empire that lived by its conquests. Such a state must always create new enemies, and eventually some combination of opposing forces will always prove too powerful. Nor is there any great reason to think that the financial resources of Britain were exhausted by 1812. In the following two years, the country increased its military spending from £57 million to £72 million per year. Even at the depreciated exchange value of sterling, this was equivalent to 1,260 million francs. Napoleon's highest military spending has been calculated at 817 million francs in 1814. The nation of shopkeepers could still outspend its old rival by better than 50%.

But surely, with its undertaxed population and debt-free balance sheet, France could have vastly increased its spending in time of need. It seems

MILITARY SPENDING, 1800–1814[76]

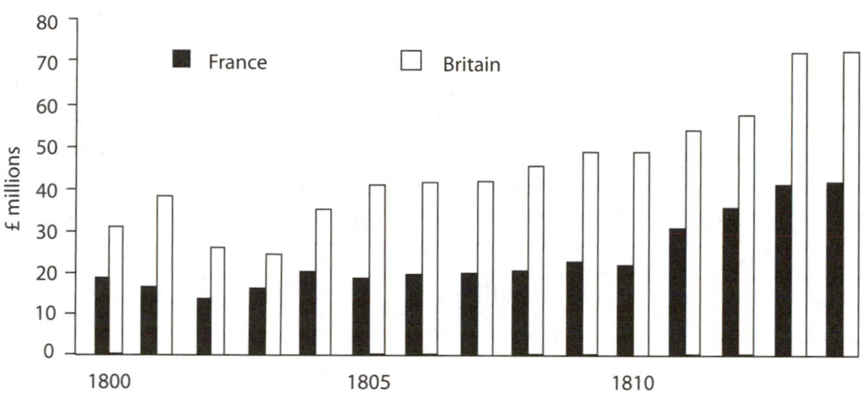

that this was not the case. Taxes were certainly raised in the final years of the Empire, but Napoleon found that the taxpayers' threshold of resistance was no higher than it had been under the Bourbons. By 1813 it had already been reached. As for the leveraging of available revenues by borrowing, it was quite out of the question. The long-term debt market was entirely atrophied, and this was certainly no time to revive it. The emperor refused to resort to paper money. The only alternative was to leave bills unpaid and run up the kind of floating debts that had characterized the bankruptcies of the ancien régime. By 1814, arrears amounted to more than 500 million francs and were rising fast. The total floating debt came to 1.3 billion francs, and was by now higher than the £60 million of Great Britain.[77] There was nothing in the history of France since the Revolution that had improved its ability to withstand such a buildup of short-term debt. Already the army contractors were going bankrupt. In the opinion of one French historian:

> One of the causes of the defeat of the Empire was without doubt the suspension of payments to suppliers, to workers, and to the army. . . . In spite of the sarcasms of the financiers of the Empire, the English finances, resolutely inflationary, were without any doubt better perfected than the French finances. In time of war, an excess of suppleness is evidently preferable to perfect rigidity.[78]

So, in the end, the financial system of the republic of merchants had shown itself yet again to be the superior model. It had proved to have the stamina to cope with a long fight and the flexibility to modify its own rules in times of crisis and to be more conducive to the economic growth that underpinned any system of public finance. And yet, there remained a profound question mark over British finances. Allowing for the inflation and economic growth of the war years, the national debt was equivalent to around 200% of GNP. This was not significantly higher than the peak reached in the 1780s after the American War of Independence. By accepting on trust that its inflationary policies were temporary, the markets had allowed the government to borrow fantastic sums without propelling the debt into territory that had throttled the Dutch economy in the previous century. But the hard part of this Mephistophelean bargain was now at hand. Would the country be willing, or able, to bear the pain of restoring sterling to its prewar level? What would happen if falling prices reduced the economy to a level where debts were no longer 200% of GNP, but 300%? Surely such a level of debt must prove unsustainable. Perhaps the postwar years would witness not the final victory of Anglo-Dutch finance, but its death throes.

EIGHT

BOURGEOIS CENTURY

It was the common practice of antiquity to make provision in times of peace for the necessities of war, and to hoard up treasures beforehand as the instruments either of conquest or defense; without trusting to imposts, much less to borrowing. . . . But [they] wholly overlooked the circumstance of its being necessary, in order to form such a treasure, to withdraw capital from productive employments. . . . For these and other reasons, this practice is now generally admitted to have been founded on erroneous principles.
—John Ramsay McCulloch, "The Funding System," *Edinburgh Review,* 1823

It is above all to representative and truly free governments that credit is useful: they are almost the only ones which have understood its true value, and which have harvested in abundance its fruits of wealth and prosperity. Credit and liberty are always united; they act to safeguard and support each other.
—Joseph-Dominique Louis, addressing the French Chamber of Deputies, 1815[1]

After 1815 there no longer seemed to be any doubt. The only solution to the immemorial problem of emergency finance was to borrow, not to save. The prudent principle of accumulation had been made to look foolish in the French revolutionary and Napoleonic wars. The vaunted treasury of Frederick the Great had been wholly consumed in the first round of hostilities, and thereafter the Kings of Prussia had endured the same fiscal straits as their neighbors. Napoleon was the last great ruler in Europe who appeared for a time to be able to finance his wars without recourse to the credit markets. Instead, the imperial military machine was fed on a diet of moderate taxation at home, and by the spoils of victory abroad. But at last, his empire succumbed to a vast alliance of accumulated enemies who cut off this last supply of vital energy. In the century that followed his defeat, the financial principles of France's great rival, England, reigned triumphant, and informed observers were inclined to the opinion that the advance of humankind must inevitably lead to the diffusion of parliamentary government and credit-based public finance. As Joseph-Dominique Louis, the French Minister of Finance, insisted to the deputies who assembled in the wake of Napoleon's exile, in a world of public borrowing only countries with political freedom secured by representative institutions would truly prosper.

The advance of parliamentary rule during the nineteenth century facilitated (and in its turn was facilitated by) the rise of the urban middle class. That the era between 1815 and 1914 belonged to the bourgeoisie is almost a commonplace of historical writing. It was agreed on not only by those paragons of industry themselves, but by their opponents to the right and to the left. The principle of public borrowing had been developed in the merchant republics of medieval and Renaissance Europe. The bourgeois ascendancy of the nineteenth century, however, was generally clothed in the guise of constitutional monarchy. But during that century, however regal their outward forms (and however great the reluctance of some of their crowned heads), the nations of the Europe came more and more to resemble republics of merchants.

Yet before that could be so, the originator of the very principle of republicanism disguised as monarchy, Great Britain, had to demonstrate that the practice of credit-based public finance was not, after all, a blind alley that must end eventually in default.

PAX BRITANNICA

> At every stage of the growth of the debt the nation has set up the same cry of anguish and despair. . . . [After the Napoleonic Wars] the funded debt of England amounted to £800 million. It was in truth a fabulous debt; and we can hardly wonder that the cry . . . should have been louder than ever. . . . Yet like Addison's valetudinarian, who contrived to whimper that he was dying of consumption till he became so fat that he was shamed into silence, she went on complaining that she was sunk in poverty till her wealth . . . made her complaints ridiculous.
>
> —Thomas Babington Macaulay, *History of England*, 1855[2]

It is possible, of course, that another war soon after 1815 would finally have vindicated the prophets of doom. Writing forty years later, Macaulay was able blithely to dismiss the concerns of an earlier generation. In 1855, the British debt was still over £800 million; but in the meantime, GNP had risen to £700 million.[3] Public borrowings were no longer more than 200% of GNP, but only slightly over 100%. No wonder he could be satisfied that there was no longer a threat to the solvency of his country.

That was not how it seemed in 1815. The national debt appeared almost unimaginably large. Yet the most immediate problem in the aftermath of the war was not the debt itself, vast as it was, but the currency in which it was expressed. In the last frantic years of the war, sterling had declined 25–30% against gold; but this decline did not tell the whole inflationary story. The prices of consumption goods had risen even faster than gold since 1789, and in Britain they had doubled. It was normal for commodity prices to rise against gold in time of war, and to fall back after the restoration of peace. Postwar deflations were painful but at least promised the end of wartime shortages. In Britain, however, the deflationary consequences of peace would be vastly increased if the country simultaneously decided to reduce its excess paper money supply so as to return sterling to its old gold parity in fulfillment of a Faustian (albeit unwritten) bargain with the credit markets.

Yet that was precisely what the government chose to do. The decision was not made without unawareness of the consequences, or without debate. In Parliament and outside it, there were many who advocated a policy that would have reestablished the convertibility of sterling at the level to which it had fallen. Among these were voices as eminent as that of David Ricardo, who had, surprisingly, been among the monetary hawks on the Bullion Committee of 1810, and the Reverend Thomas Malthus. But events preempted them. So great was the market confidence that sterling would be restored to its old level that by 1816 the currency was trading at a discount of less than 5%. At that point, Ricardo thought that it was better to complete the job.[4] A temporary setback to sterling occurred in 1817, but the old gold parity was reached in 1819, and full convertibility was restored two years later.

The economic cost was tremendous. The "revulsion"—as the business depression was called—lasted well into the 1820s. Prices nearly halved between 1814 and 1822, while the real economy stagnated. Soldiers returning from the war found no employment, while farmers and manufacturers who had borrowed heavily in the inflationary wartime boom went bankrupt, propelling laborers into vagrancy. Far from being a time of national euphoria, the postwar years were characterized by popular protest and official repression. The most enduring monument to the period is the Peterloo Massacre of August 1819, in which a troop of cavalry dispersed a radical meeting outside Manchester, leaving five hundred injured and eleven dead. No exact figures for economic output exist, but it is probably a fair estimate that, while GNP peaked at around £400 million in 1814, it was under £300 million by the early 1820s. The nominal national debt of £856 million was now verging on 300% of GNP.[5] This was surely a level at which default was inevitable.

The word *nominal* is critical. The actual amount borrowed was far lower than this figure. Because of the practice of selling bonds at a substantial discount, the redemption value of the debt was far higher than the amount received by the government. It was calculated that between 1794 and 1817 a total of £569 million of debt had been created in exchange for only £396 million in cash.[6] The government had sold bonds at a discount because, in exchange for the potential of a future capital gain, subscribers were willing to accept a lower current yield. But as so often in the history of public borrowing, the existence of bonds trading substantially below par was bound to encourage the insidious idea that the holders might be obliged to accept repayment at less than full face value. One has only to cast one's mind back to James Madison and the refunding of the American debt in 1790. Moreover, the scale of British wartime borrowing had been so vast that the difference between the sums borrowed and the face value of the debt represented in itself almost 50% of the country's GNP. The temptation to make use of this beguiling justification for debt reduction was, therefore, immense. It seems surprising, however, to find an economist and ex–bond trader such as David Ricardo taking up the cause. In 1816, he put forward the idea of a levy on all forms of capital (including government bonds), the proceeds of which would be used to redeem the bulk of the public debt at *market*—not *face*—value.* His proposal was voted down in Parliament.

As sterling rose and prices fell, another line of attack suggested itself.

---

*Unlike Madison's proposal of 1790, Ricardo's plan did not make any distinction between primary and secondary holders of the debt, but it was just as much a form of not-so-hidden default. This was not, however, the main reason for its rejection. Capital levies always fall on the horns of a dilemma. The public creditors can meet their obligations simply by surrendering a fixed percentage of their bonds. But it is not so simple for the holders of other assets. If these latter are forced to sell, the only purchasers with immediate liquidity will be the old public creditors, who will be able to buy their assets on the cheap. If they borrow rather than sell, their borrowing costs will be higher than that of the government, which has, in effect, hitherto been borrowing on their behalf. If, on the other hand, the government allows them to spread their payments so that they can be made out of income, the levy becomes no different from an income tax.

Yet again, its main proponent was an eminent economist: John Ramsay McCulloch. His idea was to index the debt to the price of wheat (which was falling rapidly):

> If the stockholder, therefore, is paid with half the sum he lent, when this half sum will purchase as much as the whole sum before, no injustice is done him; on the contrary, he is dealt with on the clearest principles of equity.[7]

Principles of "equity," perhaps; certainly not principles of law as hitherto understood. McCulloch's proposal was, like that of Ricardo, rejected. On the whole the British Parliament, however much it was awed by the enormity of the debt, was not willing to consider a retrospective and one-sided alteration of its contracts with its creditors.

The most obvious reason for the firmness of the British commitment to its public debt was the predominance of public creditors within the political system. By the end of the Napoleonic Wars, the debtholders numbered around 300,000, a sixfold increase since the mid-eighteenth century. At this level they represented a substantial majority of the electorate. Perhaps more important, it was hard to find a member of Parliament who was not also a debtholder. But if the ruling class was a class of citizen creditors, it was equally a class of landowners; and landowners were among those who suffered most from the postwar deflation.* Yet a Parliament still composed largely of landowners not only chose to adhere to the letter of its contract with the public creditors by rejecting semidisguised acts of default but also to adhere to the unwritten spirit of that contract by restoring the currency to its prewar level in spite of the increase of the real debt burden that such a policy entailed. One can only conclude that the public credit standing had come to be seen as a prop no less vital to the security and prosperity of the state than the British navy. A decade of economic hardship was not too high a price to pay for the assured ability to borrow in any future conflict.

But another question remains to be answered. Britain may have been *willing* to pay its debt, but how was it *able* to do so? In an era when public debts over 60% of GNP are considered imprudent, and those over 100% bordering

---

*An example of the scale of the losses incurred by landowners came my way when I chanced on a record of the changes in ownership of the Somerset house in which I spent part of my childhood. It so happened that Urchinwood Manor was sold in 1814—at the height of the wartime inflation—and again in 1834. The first sale took place at £18,826, the second at a mere £6,650. If William Codrington, the seller in 1814, put his proceeds into government stock, he was certainly a shrewd investor, for over the same twenty-year period Consols advanced from 54 to a high of 93.

on unsustainable, the thought that any country should be able to sustain a debt amounting to three times national income without default seems almost incredible. A unique combination of circumstances made it possible—and also made it a feat unlikely to be repeated. The first was the position of undisputed industrial and commercial supremacy that Britain had achieved, almost as remarkable as the economic predominance of the United States after the Second World War. The Royal Navy had swept all others from the seas. France was now deprived of most of its remaining overseas possessions. The Spanish Empire in Latin America was soon dismantled. While the wars had stimulated British manufacturing and commerce, Napoleonic rule had produced the opposite effect on the Continent. Britain's economic hegemony would not be seriously challenged for the next half century, by which time its debt burden had been reduced to manageable proportions.

Political considerations were equally important. The postwar British state was firmly in the hands of the propertied class, which was ready to use force to put down popular opposition to its economic policies. The Great Reform Act of 1832 gave more clout to the urban middle classes, but none to the urban or rural poor. It was not until after the electoral reforms of the 1860s and 1880s that these classes were represented in Parliament. By that time, the interest bill on the debt had fallen from 10% of GNP to less than 2% and was no longer a conspicuous target of popular discontent. It seems unlikely that the country's credit standing after 1815 would have fared so well if the government had been headed by, say, William Cobbett. Certainly, the next time Britain was to incur a debt that approached three times its national income, the financial outcome was to be very different.

Britain may not have defaulted on its debt, even by the hidden method of inflation, but for a long time, the government made almost no attempt to repay it. This was only partly because the idea of a sinking fund was now so entirely discredited. Other ideas were put forward, such as the exchange of perpetual annuities for terminable ones or even for term loans. All these ideas foundered on the objection that there was no true way to repay public debts except by budget surpluses. All other proposals were based on an dangerous illusion, dangerous because the alternative forms of debt proposed might be more costly to float than the tried-and-true 3% Consols that had served the country so well.

One accepted strategy for reducing the burden of debt remained: the voluntary conversion of interest to a lower rate. In the nineteenth century, the ability to negotiate large-scale debt conversion was the ultimate symbol of a good public credit rating. For voluntary conversion to be possible, however, the principal had to be trading above par, so that reluctant creditors could credibly be threatened with redemption (at a loss) if they refused to accept the government's proposal. Given that the bulk of Britain's debt had been sold at discounts of 30% or more, the idea that it would trade above par seemed a distant prospect. The market certainly recovered rapidly after the signing of the peace and the clear demonstration by the government that it remained committed to sound money policies. The relatively small amount of 5% debt could be converted to 4% as soon as 1822. By 1834, the 4% issues had been converted to 3.5%. But the bulk of the debt was in the venerable 3% Consols, and it seemed wishful thinking that a debt so vast as Britain's should trade at less than a 3% yield. Consols traded briefly over par in 1854, and Gladstone was thus enabled to convert the 3.5%s to 3%; but the outbreak of the Crimean War sent the market into retreat. It was only in the 1880s that the barrier was broken again. Finally, in 1888–1889, the market was so strong that £566 million 3%s could be exchanged for new Consols, yielding 2.75% at first, and then 2.5% after 1903.[8] By then, the interest on the debt had fallen from over £30 million in 1817 to under £16 million.

Interest conversions were fine, but they did not actually reduce the debt. If it was understood that debt reduction could be achieved only by budget surpluses, then why did Parliament not take steps to ensure that revenues would regularly exceed expenses? The answer is that, on the whole, Parliament preferred to lower taxes rather than redeem the debt. Money, according to the common wisdom, was "best left to fructify in the hands of the people." And fructify it certainly did. Thanks, in part, to a policy of almost continuous tax reduction, the national income continued to swell; and the national debt therefore shrunk on a relative, if not on an absolute, basis. By 1860 it was no more than 100% of GNP, but only because GNP had grown to £800 million. By 1880 the debt was just a little over 50% of GNP; but this more closely related to a further rise in national production to £1,400 million than to a modest reduction of debt to £770 million. By 1913 debt was still £710 million; but this represented only 25% of a GNP that had grown to more than £2,700 million.[9]

It is not fair to say, however, that no attempt was made to reduce the debt in absolute terms. The Parliaments of the first half of the century were content, on the whole, merely to pay the interest. A rather sterner attitude was, however, taken in the second half of the century. Gladstone set the tone in 1854 by declaring, with his customary thunderous sanctimony, his intention to finance the Crimean War by taxation rather than borrowing:

> The system of raising funds necessary for war by loans . . . practices wholesale systematic deception on the people. . . . The expenses of war are the moral check which it has pleased the Almighty to impose on the ambition and lust of conquest that are inherent in so many nations.[10]

The Crimean War was, however, financed in the traditional manner. So, too, was the far more expensive Boer War. Between them the government borrowed £190 million.[11] A further £15 million debt had been created in 1836 as compensation to colonial plantation owners whose assets had been effectively confiscated by the abolition of slavery. With this additional borrowing, the net redemption of debt achieved in peacetime during the century from Waterloo to Sarajevo came to around £360 million.[12] Of this, only a £70 million redemption was achieved before 1854.

In the 1860s Gladstone returned to office and to his attacks on the debt, which, he claimed, jeopardized the future of the country. Britain's national debt was twice the size of France's and 40% greater even than the awful burdens assumed by America during the Civil War. What Gladstone did not answer was why the country should suddenly take fright in 1866 when its debt represented little more than 75% of GNP—not so greatly different from levels of around 50% in both France and America. Surely the time for concern had been in the years after 1815, when British debt was nearly 300% of GNP, as opposed to 30% in France, and to no more than 15% in America. Perhaps, ironically, it was the diminished relative size of the debt in the 1860s that made it possible to imagine its repayment. Whatever the reason, Gladstone's words seemed to catch a new national mood that was willing to contemplate (marginally) higher taxation in exchange for long-term debt reduction. Sums were to be set aside within the budget for the repurchase of debt in the secondary market. Since the term *sinking fund* still invited ridicule, the new redemption technique was called a *fixed debt charge*—although in substance there was almost no difference between the two. A second tactic involved exchanging the low-coupon Consols held by the Post Office and savings banks for fixed-term annuities with higher annual payments.[13] Between these two techniques and regular small budget surpluses, a very considerable amount of debt was repaid: £200 million between the Crimean War and the Boer War, and £90 million between the Boer War and the First World War. By then Gladstone could have had no further cause for complaint. Britain was no longer the most but the least indebted of the major nations of Europe.

A couple of reflections on the remarkable history of the British national debt suggest themselves, before we move on. Between 1760 and 1860—one hundred years that may reasonably be termed the "British century"—

the national debt was never lower than 100% of GNP. For around two-thirds of that century—approximately 1780 to 1845—it was never lower than 150% of GNP. Simplistic notions that national power and national debt are mutually incompatible are disproved by this single historical fact. For states with an appropriate political structure and a dominant economic position, the constraints of national solvency are clearly far more flexible than is generally allowed.

BRITISH NATIONAL DEBT, 1690–1914[14]
As a percentage of GNP

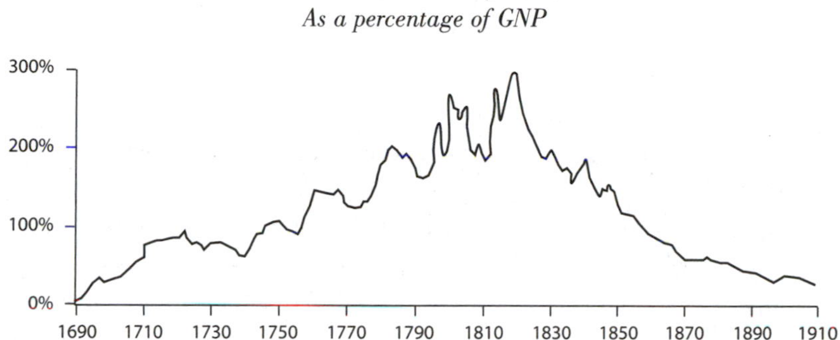

A second reflection: an investor who bought Consols during the Napoleonic Wars contracted to receive a yield of some 5% on the investment in perpetuity (or at least until the government chose to repay at par). In the following century, the real yield was far greater, since general prices fell almost continuously between 1814 and 1897. Even after the modest inflation of 1897–1914, they were still around half their Napoleonic peak. In the meantime, the market price of Consols rose from wartime levels of 55–70 to trade regularly over 110 in the last few years of the century. In a calculation made later by Keynes, the real purchasing power of government stocks almost quadrupled between 1815 and 1896.[15] No wonder they became known as "gilt-edged" investments.

THE HEYDAY OF BOURGEOIS FINANCE

> The fact is that since 1848, there had been an annual average deficit in the public accounts of the world of over $530,000,000. The constancy of this deficit shows a confirmed policy on the part of governments.
>
> —H. C. Adams, *Public Debts*, 1887

That Britain should have paid its debts after 1815 is not surprising, given its prior history, but the same can scarcely be said of its erstwhile rival.

Nowhere did the events of 1814–1815 have a more lasting effect than in France. In one way, at least, the fall of Napoleon constituted a revolution as profound as all the tumultuous changes of the preceding twenty-five years. The calling of the Estates General in 1789 had demonstrated the bankruptcy, both literal and metaphorical, of the old regime and had appeared to prescribe for France a diet of politics and finance *à l'anglaise.* "The King of France has become the king of England," as Du Pont de Nemours announced sententiously. He was wrong, of course; and for the next quarter century France resolutely refused to follow the path that history had seemed to lay out for the country.

All this changed after 1815. France appeared to retrace its steps to the turning that it had missed in 1789, and to set off down the route of constitutional monarchy and credit-based finance. While kings, however limited their powers, were ultimately to prove unacceptable to the majority of the French, the sanctity of the public debt was to become a fixed point on the French political horizon. And unlike the protection afforded to rente payments under Napoleon, this sanctity was not a cover for an underlying aversion to public borrowing of any sort. France was to make constant use of the credit markets.

The conversion of the nation to Anglo-Dutch finance is associated, above all, with the name of Joseph-Dominique Louis, first abbé and later baron. He had spent the years of the Terror in London and was determined that France, too, should, in the future, be in a position to avail itself of the miraculous powers of credit. He worked for Napoleon, but it is clear from his subsequent behavior that he was merely biding his time, waiting for a regime better suited to public borrowing to emerge. Above all, that emergence required the legitimacy afforded by free representative institutions. It also required, however, that the members of those institutions should recognize the need to pay *all* obligations with the most fastidious punctuality. In Restoration France, this was not a foregone conclusion. The early parliaments, elected on a highly restricted franchise of only ninety thousand voters, were dominated by royalists who would willingly have repudiated all Napoleonic debts. In late 1815, the ministry of Talleyrand, Louis, and Fouché, all of whom had served under Napoleon, was voted out of office and replaced by one less associated with the Corsican adventurer. But thanks to the support of Louis XVIII, the new government appointed a minister of finance equally committed to the public credit, Louis-Emanuel Corvetto, a Genoese ex-director of the Banco di San Giorgio (its four-hundred-year existence sadly brought to an end by Napoleon). Indeed, it was under the guidance of Corvetto that French credit standing was definitively restored. In 1817 an issue of 5% rentes was floated in London by Barings, the preeminent merchant bank of the time. The price was only 55, which to many in the ultraroyalist French assembly seemed an affront to national dignity; but this flotation was one of the seminal moments in French, and even European, financial history. In the eighteenth century, France had veered away from selling the perpetual annuities so heavily favored by the most creditworthy public borrowers in favor of life annuities that obscured the government's true borrowing costs. Necker had tried in vain in the summer of 1789 to persuade the National Assembly that it should accept the market rate of interest. Instead the Assembly had insisted on the wholly unrealistic rate of 4.5% in a futile attempt to demonstrate that its credit was superior to that of the old regime. The rente issue of 1817 therefore not only represented the final acceptance by France of the need to expose its credit standing to public scrutiny but also witnessed the triumphant return of perpetual debt to the center of French finances. The issue was a resounding success, and within a year the bonds were trading at prices better than 70. By 1824, in the wake of an even larger issue underwritten by the Rothschilds, rentes sold over par for the first time in the history of French public borrowing.

For the rest of the century, with one brief exception, the new French commitment to the preservation of public credit remained unshaken. This is remarkable not only because of the contrast with the events of the previous centuries, but also because the commitment was maintained through a political history that can only be described as turbulent. The Bourbon restoration lasted only until 1830, when a revolution overthrew the neoabsolutist Charles X. If Charles was the French equivalent of James II of England, then 1830 should have been France's Glorious Revolution, with Louis Philippe in the role of William of Orange. And it did seem for a time that under the "bourgeois monarchy" France had settled into a stable pattern of constitutional rule on English lines. Indeed, in many ways, the overthrow of Louis Philippe in 1848 seems hard to explain. His regime was certainly not financially insolvent; nor was it even especially unpopular, although it had never excited any feelings of passionate loyalty. France certainly enjoyed a form of government that was far more constitutional than that of any of the other states engulfed by revolution in that memorable year. Its Achilles' heel, other than a series of poor harvests and the general contagion of European revolt, which so easily rekindled the passions of the 1790s, was a franchise so restrictive (a mere 250,000 voters in an adult male population of around 9 million) that even the middle classes were largely excluded.*

For a few months in the first half of 1848, it seemed that France was on the verge of a financial meltdown similar to that of the 1790s. As before, taxes were repealed, and as before taxpayers seemed reluctant to pay those that were not. The price of the 5% rentes plunged from 116 on February 23 to 50 on April 7. An attempt to float a public loan raised only 500,000 francs. As Garnier-Pagès, the Minister of Finance associated with the collapse, recorded in his memoirs:

> Money flowed out of the Treasury as from an open flood-gate. Minute by minute, visibly, the level dropped, and one could calculate mathematically the moment when the drain would be complete. The director of the movement of funds and the central cashier never stopped warning the minister; they repeated sadly, morning and evening: We have only 15 days, 12 days, 10 days, 8 days. . . . Bankruptcy eight days away! Bankruptcy, that is to say universal ruin, the overthrow of everything, civil war.[16]

In reality, the bankruptcy so feared by Garnier-Pagès had already arrived. On March 16, the government defaulted on its short-term debt, and Bank of France notes were made legal tender, although in strictly limited amounts. The Caisses d'Épargne, established in 1818 to accept the deposits of small savers, were no longer able to meet their obligations. Only the rentes remained sacrosanct. On April 16, elections held by universal suffrage returned a conservative majority, but as in the 1790s, politicians remained overawed by the workers of Paris. Finally, in late June, General Cavaignac demolished the barricades in a few days of bloody repression, just as the young General Bonaparte had demolished them in October 1795. Under the more frugal and realistic administration that followed, the public finances were restored, and bond prices recovered into the 90s. In the following year, with Louis Napoleon now elected president, they approached par again.

The Second Republic was replaced by the Second Empire in December 1851, a transition barely noticeable in the credit markets. In 1870 the Empire was replaced by the Third Republic in far more devastating circum-

---

*By contrast, England's (still restrictive) franchise was probably more than five times larger on a relative basis. In France, voting rights were limited to those who paid over 200 francs per year in direct taxes. When François Guizot, the prime minister, was challenged on this point, he famously responded, "*Enrichissez-vous*" ("get rich"), a comment almost as politically foolish as Marie-Antoinette's purported "Let them eat cake."

stances, the country occupied by German troops and Paris in the throes of a socialist revolution. Yet the new regime managed to assert its credit standing almost immediately. The ease with which the supposedly prostrate nation managed to raise the 5-billion-franc indemnity demanded by Bismarck was one of the financial wonders of the late nineteenth century. France's national debt leapfrogged Britain's to become the largest in the world. Thereafter, although the Third Republic was to be notorious for the instability of its governments, its commitment to national solvency was never in doubt. Its reward was a continuous fall in interest costs. The 5% rentes issued to pay off Germany were sold at 82.5 and 84, producing a yield close to 6%. By the end of the decade, they were selling over par, and in 1883, they were converted to 4.5%. Four years later a second conversion reduced the cost to 4%. In 1894, this became 3.5%, and by 1902, virtually the whole French public debt was funded at 3%.[17] In the last decade before the outbreak of World War I, France's borrowing costs were no higher than Britain's. This was surely the ultimate monument to the financial revolution of 1815–1817; and it was made more remarkable by the opposing trajectories followed by their national debts in the intervening century. Whereas Britain's debt had fallen on an absolute basis—and even more sharply relative to GNP—France's debt had done nothing but rise. By 1914, it was around twice the size of Britain's on an absolute basis and three times larger on a relative basis.

France was not alone in finding itself paradoxically both more in debt and yet more solvent by 1914 than it had been one hundred years earlier. A Europe-wide pattern can be discerned after 1800. The French revolutionary and Napoleonic wars ushered in a period of financial chaos throughout the Continent. The result was that the Congress of Vienna was a gathering of nations that were, with the exception of Britain, in varying states of bankruptcy.

Austria, the darling of Dutch investors in the last decades of the eighteenth century, started off the chain of default by suspending payment on its debts in Amsterdam in 1796. After all, Amsterdam was now in the hands of the French. On its own, the Austrian internal debt market was not able to cope with the strains of war, and the only solution was to borrow from the Bank of Vienna, which then refinanced itself with demand notes. By 1797 note issues had risen from a prewar level of 18 million florins (about £1.9 million sterling) to 74 million florins, and the bank was forced to suspend convertibility. The suspension was a prelude to a downward spiral of paper money inflation. There were over 1 billion florins of banknotes in circulation by 1811, whose street value was no more than 12% of par. Formal bankruptcy was declared, interest payments were reduced by 50%, and the worthless paper money was refunded with almost equally worthless "redemption notes" that were later partly repudiated.[18]

The Austrian pattern (indirect default on internal debt via paper money and direct default on external debt, which could not be merely inflated away) was repeated with variations by the other continental countries that had participated in the war. None of them had domestic credit markets that were sufficient to support the costs of war in the age of revolution. Sweden resumed its experiments with nonconvertible paper money in 1789. In 1803 its notes were made convertible at a loss of 33%. In 1812 two-thirds of the kingdom's foreign debt was repudiated.[19] Its neighbor, Denmark, entered the downward spiral with a slight delay, but by late 1812 its paper money, too, was worth only 13% of face value. Bankruptcy followed in January of the following year. Foreign debts were spared, but domestic debt was reduced by 39%.[20] At the eastern end of the Baltic, Russia had been issuing its own very own assignats since Catherine the Great founded the Assignat Bank in 1768. Until the outbreak of the French Revolution, its notes circulated without a significant discount, and even in 1805 they were still worth 77% of face value. The strains of war took their toll, however, and by 1815 the assignats had fallen to under 26% of face. Foreign debt payments were suspended in 1812. Further south, Spain defaulted in 1809. By this stage its domestic state paper (the *vales reales*) had long ceased to have any significant value.[21]

Perhaps the most shocking default of all occurred in 1810. The Netherlands, bled dry by French exactions, could no longer bear the strain. The Dutch largely avoided paper money inflation, but the public debt doubled from its already astonishing pre-1789 level. In 1810, the enfeebled republic was absorbed into France, and its interest payments were simultaneously reduced by two-thirds. The state that, perhaps more than any other, had symbolized commitment to public credit was now a dissolved bankrupt.

In 1815, then, Britain stood almost alone in the world of public borrowing. Not only was it the only major European power still solvent, but its public debt also exceeded the combined total of all others. Gradually, during the course of the following one hundred years, a more even landscape emerged. By 1914, almost all the great powers of the old Continent had substantial public debts. In countries such as France and Russia, debt had increased tenfold over the course of the century. Britain's national debt, although still not insignificant in nominal terms, was now smaller than that of most of its rivals in relative ones.

PUBLIC DEBTS OF THE GREAT POWERS IN 1914[22]

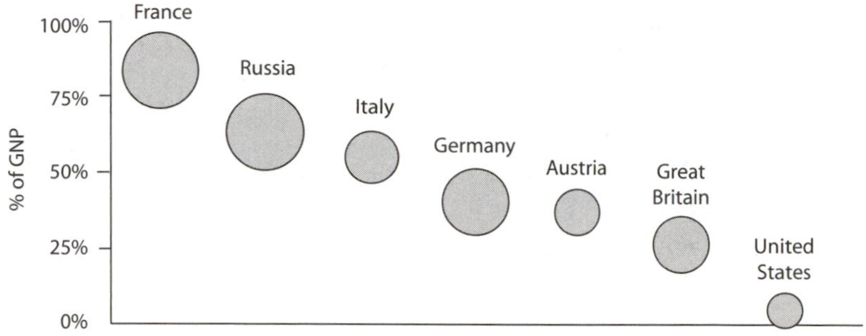

Bubble area denotes the absolute size of the debt.

According to this partial snapshot of the finances of the great powers of the Western world, there was no doubt that Henry C. Adams had been right in the 1880s. Borrowing had become the accepted norm of public finance. What was more remarkable was that states like Austria and Russia, which would have had a hard time sustaining debts significantly over 20% or so of GNP one hundred years earlier, were now solvent at levels of indebtedness that, while not coming close to the death-defying levels achieved by Holland and Britain in earlier times, reflected, without a doubt, a significant change in the way the world worked.

These changes concerned not only the proclivity to borrow rather than save, but also several other equally fundamental developments. There was, of course, the extraordinary extension of the capital markets during the course of the century; and there was the equally extraordinary explosion of industrialization, especially during the last fifty years before the First World War. The result was a worldwide increase of liquid assets that made it far easier for states to finance their deficits on reasonable terms. What was striking, however, was just *how* reasonable those terms were. In 1913 the range of borrowing costs of the great powers ranged from approximately 3.4% in Britain to 4.6% in Austria. These rates were all the more remarkable since there had been a modest but persistent inflation of around 1% per year in the major economies since 1897. The only exception to this very narrow range was the U.S. federal government, whose rapidly disappearing public debt was almost desperately sought after by banks since it formed the legal basis for their reserves. Federal debt therefore traded for yields as low as 2%, although the next rank of state, municipal, or corporate debt yielded around 4%—more or less in line with top-grade nongovernmental credits in Britain.

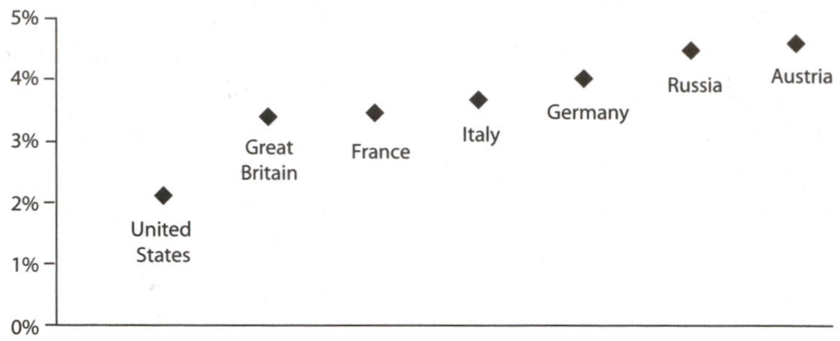

Interest rates at these levels undoubtedly reflected the growing sophistication and liquidity of the capital markets. They may also, in hindsight, have suggested an imprudent optimism on the part of investors, seemingly unconcerned about the gathering clouds of war. But more important, they also reflected the slow, but inexorable, advance of the English model of public finance.

Not all countries had adopted the model with the rapidity and success of France; but on the eve of the First World War it was easy to discern its characteristic traits in the public finances of all the great powers. First and foremost of these traits was parliamentary control of the national budget. In France, Holland, and parts of Germany, this was established in the aftermath of the defeat of the Napoleonic order. Farther east, however, the meticulous restoration of the pre-1789 status quo by Metternich with the support of Czar Alexander I ensured that it would take decades of revolution and war to achieve the same result. The Revolution of 1848, although largely suppressed by the combined armies of Austria, Prussia, and Russia, was instrumental in introducing parliamentary fiscal control in other parts of Germany, as well as in Scandinavia and in the Kingdom of Piedmont. Farther east, constitutional progress was altogether slower. It took the catastrophic military setbacks of 1859–1866 to force the Habsburgs to accept reform. Prussia, and thereafter the German Empire, although nominally subject to parliamentary fiscal control, managed to exempt the military budget from civilian oversight. Russia seemed almost immune to the advancing tide of constitutionalism. The wave of revolution that swept over Europe in 1848 left Russia unaffected. Defeat in the Crimean War suggested to Alexander II that the time was ripe to abolish serfdom (by autocratic decree), but not to write a constitution. It took the humiliation of defeat at the hands of Japan—a non-European country, for heaven's sake—

in 1905 to finally convince Nicholas II's advisers that reform was unavoidable. Even so, the new Fundamental Laws of 1906 that confirmed the constitutional position of the Duma reiterated that Russia was an "autocracy," removing only the word *unlimited*, which had hitherto preceeded it. Still, observers were largely of the opinion that it was only a question of time before a fully fledged constitutional monarchy must emerge in Russia, too, as it had elsewhere in Europe.

The second fundamental component of the English system was an independent central bank. Parliament was to be trusted with the budget, but not with the currency. Statutory independence being then an implausible defense against political control, the Bank of England was set up in 1694 as a private company with quoted shares. The Bank's unparalleled prestige by the end of the following century, and the financial meltdown of almost all its rivals during the period of revolution and war, forced other countries to follow the English model. When the Bank of France was founded in 1800, distant memories of chaos created by Law's Banque Royale as well as the more recent scars of the assignats ensured that its shares would be kept out of the hands of the state (although the government regained a limited level of control after the bank's near collapse in 1806). A decade later, in the aftermath of the Napoleonic Wars, the Netherlands and Austria set up privately owned banks to replace the informal central-banking roles of the city-owned Bank of Amsterdam and Vienna City Bank. A portion of the share capital of the new Bank of the Netherlands was initially retained by the state, but in 1847, this, too, was sold off. In the later nineteenth century, the resurgent states of Germany and Italy followed the same prescription. Bismarck founded the Reichsbank in 1871, and in 1893, the Bank of Italy was established to absorb the old regional banks of issue (although the Banco di Napoli and the Banco di Sicilia retained their independence in an attempt to placate the already chronically disaffected south). There was a gradual trend for the complete autonomy enjoyed by the Bank of England to be replaced by a more balanced approach, in which private ownership was offset by government appointment or approval of part of the governing bodies. The trend was reflected in the constitution of the Reichsbank, for instance. The only exception to private ownership was found, unsurprisingly, in autocratic Russia, where the State Bank was owned and controlled by the state. At the other end of the political spectrum, successive attempts to found an American central bank on English lines foundered on the shoals of populist opposition. The continuing agrarian suspicion of the apparatus of Hamiltonian finance left the country without any central bank for most of the nineteenth century. When the Federal Reserve was finally founded in 1913, it looked more to the German than to the British model.[24] But it was, nonetheless, privately owned.

The markets' reward for institutional responsibility was not only low interest costs but also the extremely long terms on which governments were able to borrow. Perpetual annuities were, as always, the vehicle of choice for the soundest borrowers, and no self-respecting European state would have chosen to issue any other form of long-term debt. The only exceptions to this rule were, yet again, on the periphery. Much of Russia's long-term public debt was contracted abroad and, although certainly long-term, was not always perpetual. In 1913 only 38% of Russia's total debt was in the form of rentes.[25] Across the Atlantic, the lingering suspicion of permanent public debt meant that the United States preferred its bonds to have fixed final maturities; but at the end of the nineteenth century this preference was put aside in the interest of monetary stability.[26]

The obverse of the prevalence of long-term borrowing was the minimal recourse to floating debt. In the parlance of the era, "floating" debt included almost anything that was not funded for the longest possible term and included issues that would nowadays be comfortably classified as medium-term loans. In Britain, on the eve of the First World War, floating debt constituted only £33 million out of a national debt of £706 million—less that 5% of the total. In France, the ratio was similar: 1.5 billion francs out of a total debt of 33.5 billion francs.

Investors were willing to lend large sums on such advantageous terms only if they were convinced that their interest and principal would be paid in sound currency. This is where the central banks came in. By the nineteenth century, it was no longer conceivable that economic growth could be financed by coined money alone. If that had been the case, there would have been little need for banks at all. Except for retail trade, economic exchange now depended largely on paper instruments, and in western Europe, payment by check was starting to make inroads even in this last area. The role of central banks, therefore, was to ensure that an ever-expanding superstructure of paper financial instruments would be made compatible with monetary stability. In the nineteenth century, it was taken for granted that there was no way to achieve this except by ensuring that all paper obligations would ultimately be convertible into precious metals. Contracts on paper were settled in money issued by the central bank; and the obligations of the central bank were payable, on demand, in coin. One thing was certain: any country that aspired to the temple of bourgeois finance had to ensure that all government obligations would be payable, if not in coin, at least in a currency convertible into coin.

At the beginning of the century, there was no particular reason to assume that coin meant gold coins alone. Britain had, almost by chance, adopted gold as its currency standard in 1696. Other currencies were pegged either to silver, or to both currencies equally. Gold became the centerpiece of nineteenth-century public finance only when the discovery of substantial new silver supplies after 1870—largely in the Rocky Mountains—disrupted the centuries-old ratio between the two metals.* By 1895, silver had lost over half its value—a fall accelerated as central banks successively abandoned convertibility of their notes into silver and then started to sell off their surplus stocks so as to shore up their gold reserves. By the end of the century, the adoption of the gold standard had become a sine qua non of great-power status.

For countries with bimetallic currency standards before the 1870s, the path to gold was relatively straightforward. Between 1871 and 1873 Denmark, Holland, Sweden, and Switzerland simply cut the tie to silver while retaining that to gold. In 1871 Germany easily adopted the new shibboleth of high finance by the simple expedient of draining a defeated France of a portion of its ample gold reserves. The path to gold was correspondingly more complicated for France, but it, too, had effectively abandoned silver by 1876.

Other countries had a harder route. Austria struggled for decades to remove from circulation the depreciated paper money issued during the Napoleonic Wars. A precarious convertibility was maintained until 1848, but the revolutions of that year soon put an end to this state of affairs. Thereafter the imperial finances never quite permitted a definitive restoration of the currency until the end of the century. Even when peace returned in 1867, the Austrian central bank had to face the problem of sitting on reserves composed almost exclusively of silver. Only in 1892 was it possible to contemplate full convertibility into gold, and even then not immediately. Russia's history more or less paralleled Austria's—a legacy of depreciated state paper from the Napoleonic Wars; a gradual return to convertibility until the midcentury; thereafter new issues of inconvertible paper money; and

*In the Middle Ages and for much of classical antiquity, gold had been worth ten to twelve times more than silver. The influx of Spanish-American silver after 1530 caused the value of silver to fall, but after 1650 the ratio between the two metals stabilized at 15–16:1 until the 1870s. The arrival of Rocky Mountain silver set off an even more radical decline in the relative value of silver. By the mid-1890s the ratio was 30:1. It is currently around 60:1.

finally, in 1894, the notes of the new State Bank made convertible into gold. The reborn Kingdom of Italy started life in 1860 with a convertible currency. By 1866, however, the accumulated costs of reunification (which were not, as in Germany's case, financed by hefty indemnities from defeated opponents) proved greater than the fragile political consensus could bear, and in the resulting financial crisis, the lira was allowed to float. Although the right to convert into gold was nominally reestablished in 1884, bureaucratic sleight of hand rendered it largely meaningless. As in Austria and Russia, genuine convertibility had to wait until the last years of the century, although even then the notes of the Bank of Italy retained their precautionary legal tender status. America's path was complicated by the fact the great new silver mines opened up after 1870 were largely located in the Rockies. The battle to secure the dollar's tie to gold was not finally resolved until the presidential election of 1896, with the defeat of the silver crusader Democrat, William Jennings Bryan, by the solid-gold Republican, William McKinley.

TIES OF IDENTITY

In 1913–1914, then, the impressively low interest costs enjoyed by the great powers could be said to be their reward for their adoption of an English formula of government and finance. Commentators inclined to this point of view could note with some satisfaction that in the chart of interest rates there was a distinct West-East trend line that corresponded, more or less, to the spread of constitutional government within Europe. The lowest interest rates were enjoyed by the countries with the most impeccable democratic credentials, the United States to the west, followed by Britain and France on the other side of the Atlantic. Only at the very eastern end of the slope was the geographical and political equation reversed. Russia, the most "Oriental" state both geographically and politically, and the most recent and partial convert to representative government, should, by rule of thumb, have had an interest rate higher than Austria's. This might have seemed a mere quibble, however; and the same graph drawn a few years earlier would have reversed their positions.

The attractive simplicity of this graphic picture of democracy and public credit hides a far more complex, and even contradictory, reality. America, for instance, may have been a democratic country, but for most of the nineteenth century its credit was viewed with considerable suspicion. In

1869, the Civil War was some years behind it, and its economic recovery was complete. Its GNP was already higher than Britain's on an absolute and a per capita basis. Public debt was 35% of GNP, as opposed to 75% in Britain. The bonds of both countries were serviced punctually in gold. Surely, in these circumstances, a U.S. bond should have yielded somewhat less than a British one. But no: in January 1869 British 3% Consols traded at 92, whereas American 6% bonds sold for no more than 82.

This was not the only paradox in the nineteenth-century credit landscape. Russia's low borrowing cost in 1913 was not simply its reward for enacting a constitution in 1905, nor for its adoption of the gold standard in 1894. Even as an "unlimited autocracy" czarist Russia had been able to borrow substantial sums at favorable rates. When General Hamilton arrived in Amsterdam in 1840 to negotiate a loan for the fledgling Republic of Texas, he found that the emissaries of the czar were raising funds at the same time. He was disconcerted, to say the least, to discover which of the borrowers was preferred by the Dutch investment public:

> The autocrat who wants this money to throw into the Black Sea or for the purpose of present violence or future destruction has had the Lists for his Loan filled in 3 Days when not one of the States of the American Confederacy could have effected a similar negotiation in 3 months or with 10 per cent of the rate at which the subscription was opened.[27]

The Russian bonds were sold at a yield of 4.45%. Not only was this rate lower than those that might have been available, if at all, for American states, but it was no higher than the interest paid by a reformed Russia in 1913. It is true that total Russian debt at that time amounted to no more than 460 million rubles, whereas by 1913 the figure had swollen to 13 billion rubles and represented around 60% of GNP. Also, Russia often had to pay considerably more in the intervening decades: after the Crimean War, after the surge of railway loans in the early 1870s, and in the wake of the Russo-Japanese War in 1905. Finally, not all investors were so generous toward autocrats as the Dutch. Russian loans were never very popular in London until the end of the century. However, it is hard to avoid the feeling that prima facie, in the light of the arbitrary and despotic nature of the czar's powers, the risk premium on Russian loans ought to have been higher.

Still, the Dutch were far from neophytes in their ability to judge credit risk. Of all the sovereign borrowers who had defaulted on their international debt in the Napoleonic Wars, Russia had been the first to resume payments in 1815 and had been the only borrower to make up arrears of interest. Such examples of good faith were not forgotten in Amsterdam. The Dutch were equally correct in their evaluation of General Hamilton's proposals. The remote and sparsely populated Republic of Texas had a credit record that was as poor as it was brief. By the time it became a state, its paper was selling for 10% of face value. Even when the U.S. government provided the means to settle its old debts, the state legislature was reluctant to do so. In the end the creditors could feel relieved to get back 77% of their claims in the face of popular hostility. Besides, in 1840, Texas was tarred with the same brush as the Southern and Western states of America, which were slipping into a downward spiral of default and repudiation that would make them a byword for bad faith among European investors, and that accounted, indirectly, for a good part of the exaggerated interest that would have to be paid by the federal government in the 1860s.

In the nineteenth century, therefore, a good public credit rating had to do with more than just democratic credentials. This is not surprising. In earlier centuries the few reputable public borrowers, almost invariably mercantile republics, were surrounded by would-be autocrats who borrowed only to default and, beyond, them by Asiatic despots who still depended on a bulging treasury. After 1815, both these models of public finance were permanently discredited. It was apparent even to rulers who opposed any form of parliamentary government that the only successful way to manage their public finances was to conform to the dictates of the credit markets. Moreover, public borrowing was no longer confined to Europe but was spreading rapidly across the entire globe. The British took it with them as part of the baggage that accompanied the flag. By 1900, almost every colony had significant debts. Where formal empire did not exist, the practice was spread informally—into the new states that emerged from the crumbling empires of Spain and Turkey, and then into the venerable despotisms of the Middle East and Asia, whose treasuries were now empty. In a world of almost universal public borrowing, it is not surprising that more subtle nuances started to emerge.

Surveying the world of public borrowing in 1870, Dudley Baxter (who may be credited with writing the first general history of the phenomenon) sought to explain the differences in national credit ratings according to the platitudes of racial stereotyping then current:

> From England we turn to the States most closely connected to her by race and institutions;—the United States her former colony; Germany, Belgium and Holland, the mother countries of the Anglo-Saxons; Denmark, Sweden and Norway,

> the sources of our Norse blood; and the free States of Switzerland. We shall find that all have common characteristics respecting their National Debts, differing considerably from those of the Celtic, Slavonic, and Turkish peoples; more thrifty and saving, and anxious for repayment. . . .
>
> Very different is the history of the Debts of the Latin nations inhabiting France and the two great southern peninsulas and the Spanish and Portuguese colonies of South America. Their people are careful and frugal, but their rulers are too often reckless and spendthrift, prone to overspend their income in time of peace and still more largely in time of war; trusting to sinking funds rather than to economy and surpluses; and sometimes unable to pay even the interest.[28]

Baxter also recognized the role of constitutional government in establishing sound credit. Of the Latin countries he suggested that "perhaps their tendency to arbitrary and therefore irresponsible government has much to do with the succession of deficits." But then, in the nineteenth-century worldview, democracy and race went hand in hand anyway. It was a logical heritage of the seventeenth- and eighteenth-century school of political thought that had looked for the roots of European parliamentary institutions "in the forests of Germany." Similar preconceptions showed up in the work of the eminent Austrian economist Eugen von Böhm-Bawerk, who argued in 1889 that a nation's interest rate was in inverse proportion to its collective intelligence.[29]*

While Baxter's racial asides are clearly an inadequate explanation of the credit records of different countries in the nineteenth century, there is no doubt that the idiosyncrasies of national histories may well have played a part. The financial stability of nineteenth-century France in the presence of so much political instability undoubtedly owes much to a collective wish to avoid the traumas and humiliations of the eighteenth and seventeenth centuries. Without doubt, the country's credit standing was saved from total collapse in 1848 only by the extreme rapidity of the move from revolution to counterrevolution. In the 1790s, the workers of Paris had held successive governments in their thrall more than six years. In 1848, they were left

*What Baxter apparently failed to notice was that in earlier centuries the city-states of "Latin" Italy had borrowed at the lowest interest rates of their time and had enjoyed credit ratings far superior to some of the states of "Anglo-Saxon" America in his own day. On the other hand, it is always possible that Baxter's sly inclusion of the Celts in his list of feckless races—at a time when there was no Celtic state in existence to prove or disprove his statement—was a subtle way of implying that the preponderance of Southern U.S. states in the list of defaulters in the 1840s could be explained by the presence of a disproportionate number of Irish and Scottish immigrants. It should also be said, in fairness, that Baxter's racial views were in no way central to his book, which contained a good deal of accurate information and intelligent comment.

in control of the streets for no more than four months. In most countries, on the other hand, the cumulative effects of history were more likely to embed a certain pattern of behavior rather than create a radical swing in the opposite direction. It is hard to avoid the feeling that in nineteenth-century Spain, for instance, the propensity to default had become an ingrained state of mind inherited from the pattern set up by the Habsburgs centuries earlier. The country defaulted in 1820, 1834, 1841, 1867, 1872, and 1882, under regimes both absolutist and constitutional. The obverse may well have been true in other countries: a good credit record, accumulated over decades, or even centuries, and rewarded by the markets by low borrowing costs, became part of a self-image that was hard to give up even when circumstances might have suggested otherwise. This must have played some part in Holland's willingness to live with a public debt in excess of 200% of GNP for a century and a half (roughly 1710–1860) in spite of an economy that was stagnating in relation to those of its neighbors. The same psychology needs to be invoked as a partial explanation of the Romanovs' virtually impeccable record of external debt service—as compared to, say, that of the Bourbons—in spite of periodic predictions of imminent default that circulated on the bourses of western Europe.

In order to get a better grip on this rather slippery matter, it is useful to return to the original connection between democracy and public credit that has been set out in this book. Democracy (even in its most partial and imperfect form) is a system in which the citizens control the state. As long as democratic states borrow from their own citizens, their good credit record is simply a reflection of the virtual identity of borrower and lenders.

Looking again at the credit records of nineteenth-century states with this in mind, it is fairly easy to see that the best borrowers were those countries that had accumulated substantial domestic capital over the centuries and were therefore able to finance themselves internally. These were the states where there was the greatest affinity between borrower and lenders and, moreover, where there was a natural constituency for the maintenance of a sound currency. For most of century the conspicuous members of this group were Britain, France, and the Netherlands. By 1914 America had finally joined their ranks, having depended for most of the preceding century on capital imports. This alone would account for the gradual fall in its interest costs over the period.

Where borrowers and lenders did not share a sense of identity, there was little inherent reason why a democratic form of government should be more creditworthy than a nondemocratic government. States that required foreign capital were invariably less creditworthy borrowers—not only because of their relative paucity of resources but also because of a latent hostility toward their foreign lenders that could bubble up from below in times of crisis. In many ways, this hostility was reminiscent of the antipathy felt by the kings of Europe for their creditors in earlier centuries and was equally counterproductive, being reflected in higher interest rates. The kings of Europe, however, now had some centuries of bitter experience behind them. Not only were they slowly being reduced to ceremonial roles as constitutional rule spread across the Continent, but they had learned that there was more advantage to be gained from the miraculous power of credit if one had a good reputation in the markets. Apart from the Iberian Peninsula there was no history of royal default in nineteenth-century Europe. The good credit record of the czar has to be understood in this light, too. Of two prospective borrowers, neither of whom had any ties of identity with their creditors, it was more likely that an enlightened, or even a semienlightened, eastern European despot would have learned the value of punctuality of payment than the volatile electorate of a poor and remote frontier state. Where inexperience, poverty, and despotism coincided, as they did in the majority of states outside western Europe and the United States, the credit record could be quite abysmal. Honduras, to take one extreme example, managed to be in default on its obligations for 91 out of 118 years of independent statehood prior to the Second World War.[30]

Even for states that could afford to borrow internally, the situation was not entirely straightforward. Where the legitimacy of the regime was questioned, no amount of domestic wealth could engender a good credit rating. It is only necessary to recall the financial weakness of the French monarchy in the eighteenth century to make this point clear. It was precisely the problem of legitimacy that the transition to constitutional government was supposed to resolve. But in the nineteenth century, the rise of representative institutions seemed to carry a sting in the tail. The new bodies gave voice to long-silent regional or ethnic groups that showed an increasing desire to break away from the states in which the tortuous turns of history had placed them. Insofar as separatism was not manifested in the form of actual violence, it tended to show up in the public finances of the affected states as a deficiency of taxes and, therefore, a weakening of public credit, for the simple reason that the separatists felt themselves to be "unfree" within their existing political body and responded in the traditional manner, by a reluctance to contribute to its upkeep. In most cases, the fiscal result conformed to Montesquieu's rule: Governments tended to go easy in their tax-raising efforts in the disaffected areas so as to avoid provoking more extreme manifestations of unrest—a policy that was not always successful. An analysis of the interest rates paid by countries throughout the century would tend to show that the states with the best credit ratings in relation to their constitutional credentials were those that suffered least from this dilemma. This is most obvious in a comparison of the two eastern powers Austria and Russia. The forces of separatism were so strong within the Habsburg empire as to threaten its very survival. It was a recurrence of separatist politics in the years before the First World War that lowered the price of Austrian bonds on the markets. Russia, on the other hand, seemed to gobble up whole ethnic groups without so much as a hiccup. Although there were periodic revolts by the chronically discontented Poles, few investors would have deemed them a threat to the survival of the czar's ever-expanding empire. By the same token, almost no one considered the "Irish question" a threat to the financial stability of Great Britain. Separatism was not always ethnic in origin. In the United States its causes were quite different, but the threat of a possible breakup of the union was no doubt one of the reasons why bonds of the federal government traded in the late 1850s at yields that did not seem to reflect the extraordinary soundness of its underlying financial position.

Even for that fortunate minority of states that were neither threatened by separatism nor dependent on foreign capital, the situation was no longer as simple as it had been before 1815. The formula for public finance that had been created by the mercantile republics and then adopted by Britain had been, and remained, the creature of the merchant classes—of those with surplus financial assets. The landed aristocracy disliked it in principle but had managed, more or less, to come to terms with it. It was a system, of course, well suited to a "bourgeois century," and its ideal political manifestation was parliamentary government based on a restricted franchise that excluded those without property. But although the nineteenth century undoubtedly represented the apogee of bourgeois principles of political economy—laissez-faire economics, underpinned by sound money, and overseen by a "night watchman" state—it was also the century in which the heyday of the property-based franchise came, and then rapidly went. In the second half of the century, the principle of universal male suffrage became an unstoppable force, and by the outbreak of the First World War, there was no great power whose electorate did not comprise the large majority of the adult male population. If the connection between public debt and representative government depended on the symbiosis of borrowers and lenders, then it was far from clear that this intimate relationship would continue to work once the state was no longer firmly in the hands of the propertied classes. Indeed, it took only a quick reminder of the type of public finance supported by the poorer classes in the American and French Revolutions (and the bourgeoisie of Europe did not need any such reminder) to understand why "democracy" was viewed for much of the century as a dirty word, virtually indistinguishable, conceptually, from demagoguery or mob rule.

Where the ideal of universal suffrage was associated with revolution, as it was in 1848–1849, it was scarcely surprising if its implications were wholly negative for public credit. But after the spectacular outburst of those two years, the nineteenth century settled into a more sedate pace. Visionaries like Karl Marx started to despair that the revolution would ever arrive and saw out their declining years as advocates of the trade union movement. In most countries, the passage to universal suffrage was achieved by a gradual and peaceful process of reform. Even so, few of the natural custodians of sound public finance welcomed its arrival. They anticipated, no doubt, a reactivation of the printing press—that tempting, apparently cost-free method of public borrowing that incidentally destroyed the fruits of decades of careful bourgeois accumulation. Yet, curiously, it was only in America that populist agitation expressed itself, for a time at least, in a cry for paper money. In Europe (and subsequently across the Atlantic), there was to be a new financial battlefield that took contemporaries almost by surprise.

It had long been a given of reformist opinion, whether moderate or radical, that it was spendthrift monarchs and cosseted courtiers who were the cause of excessive public spending. Constitutional government must, in the very nature of things, be cheaper than despotism, and republicanism must therefore be cheaper still. This was the view expressed, for example, in the pages of the radical *L'Ami du Peuple* in March 1848:

> The Republic will spend so little for the needs of its administration that its savings will grow in a manner that will soon see off all arrears. . . . the Republic will have to feed neither the luxury of horses nor the luxury of lackeys of all sorts of liveries, nor the luxury of mistresses: the sterile expenses of heads without thoughts, of idle and unproductive arms. . . . The taxes of a Republic in time of peace come to no more than one tenth of the taxes of a monarchy; be quite sure.[31]

The republican experiment of 1848 came to an end before this optimistic theory could be properly tested. It was replaced by the Second Empire, whose profligacy was easily explained, in the eyes of its opponents, by the absence of proper parliamentary controls. The inauguration of the Third Republic in 1871 was therefore accompanied by renewed hopes for frugal government. Such hopes were soon to be shattered. The political balance of the new assembly bore little relation to the parliaments that had taxed and spent so modestly before 1848. By 1882 the economist and statesman Léon Say was forced to take a stand against the new trend:

> We must . . . redress this strange deviation of the parliamentary regime which has made deputies, imagined and created as protectors of the assets of individuals against the excessive profligacy of governments, the agents of the excitation of spending.[32]

By the end of the decade the *Economiste Français* was sounding the same theme in even stronger language:

> The parody of a parliamentary regime which we enjoy is finally becoming grotesque. The deputies, thanks to the unfortunate right of parliamentary initiative which France grants them, but which England denies them, only seek to increase expenses. The whole management of the present assembly, and of its predecessor, and of the majority of the local assemblies as well, can be summed up in three words: *Vive la déficit*![33]

Notwithstanding the *Economiste*'s favorable reference to England, the French experience was in no way unique. The arrival of universal suffrage coincided with a reassessment of the role of the state in society. Before, it was more or less sufficient that it defended against invasion and assured the rule of law. Now, it was asked to provide a growing list of public services, including education, sanitation, and transport—the list was to be substantially increased in the century that followed. In some countries, such as Germany, the new order of things was accepted almost without debate. Bismarck is credited as the father of the welfare state, and it is in Germany that the new trend in public finance was first recognized and turned into a law. In 1877, Adolf Wagner published his ground-breaking *Finanzwissenschaft* (*The Science of Finance*) in which he argued not only that public spending was growing faster than GNP in western Europe and America, but also that this trend must continue since it corresponded to a fundamental law of social development.

The empirical data on which Wagner based his theory now seem beyond dispute. Much of the pressure for extra spending was felt on a local level, and it is only by including local budgets with national ones that the trend is made apparent. In Britain, spending by local authorities quadrupled between 1870 and 1910, while GNP merely doubled. At this stage, the expenses of local governments almost equalled those of Westminster. So, too, did their debts, which had risen to £640 million in 1913[34]—an astonishing tenfold increase since 1870 that rendered nugatory the stalwart efforts of Gladstone and his successors to reduce the legacy of Napoleonic borrowing. The same pattern was played out in other countries, with variations. The American experience more or less paralleled that of Britain. Successive Secretaries of the Treasury labored to pay off the debt incurred in the Civil War; and as a result, the federal budget in 1913 had shrunk to under 2% of GNP. But at the state, and especially at the municipal level, the old Yankee aversion to government activity of any sort seemed to be disappearing. Nonfederal spending had risen to 5.5% of GNP by 1913. And while federal debt had been reduced from $2.7 billion to $1.2 billion, the states and localities had more than compensated by increasing their own borrowing from $870 million to $4.4 billion.[35] On the continent of Europe the great powers displayed no attachment to old-fashioned thrift at any level of government. In decentralized Germany all levels of government seemed to compete to outspend each other. Total public spending sextupled from 1880 to 1913 in absolute terms, rising from 10% of GNP to around 17%. Total public debt had risen by more than seven times in absolute terms and had nearly trebled in relative ones, to around 55% of GNP.[36] In centralized France the increase of public spending and borrowing was attributable primarily to the national government, although the départements and communes did their best to contribute to the process. Total public spending at all levels of government rose from around 12–13% of GNP in the aftermath of the Franco-Prussian War to over 17% by 1913. Total public debt rose by around 15 billion francs, considerably outpacing the British record over the period, although scarcely competing with the German record.[37]

The growth of "social" spending may have been a natural result of rising GNP per capita, as Wagner argued, but a study of history showed that it could also be understood as an outcome of popular participation in politics. In the ancient world, the Athenian demos had shown itself adept at garnering the major portion of the revenues of the Periclean Age in the form of "jobs for the boys." According to Aristotle, twenty thousand Athenians were employed in some form or another by the state—over half the citizen body. A sharp swelling of the ranks of state employees had also occurred under the Jacobins in the 1790s, and again briefly under the Second Republic in the form of public workshops (*ateliers nationales*). Perhaps equally interesting were the implications of the methods by which these form of public largesse were financed. The Athenians were at first able to rely on the tribute of their "allies," but when these disappeared after the Peloponnesian Wars, there was an increasing tendency to finance public distributions by levies on the rich. In similar vein, the Second Republic, in its early radical phase, had abolished a number of indirect taxes and replaced them with a progressive income tax falling on the wealthy. The tax was soon abolished, and for the rest of the century, the propertied classes, led by the rentiers, fought a ferocious rearguard action against this political outrage, just as it was being grudgingly accepted elsewhere in Europe. The classical view of the politics of taxation was perfectly expressed by Jules Roche in the parliamentary debates of 1895:

> You dare to argue before the French Assembly that the tax that you are proposing will not address the whole nation, that you will seek out a small number of citizens, to make into a caste, in whose presence you will institute a "plebs" that you free [*affranchissez*] from the tax as unworthy to contribute towards the charges of the nation.[38]

It is his use of the verb *affranchir* that is so telling here. The plebs were to be given literally the "freedom of the Franks." The old political order was turned upside down. Now the erstwhile ruling class was to be taxed, while the poor were to enjoy the emblematic privilege of tax exemption. Who were the masters now?

The English ruling class, by contrast, had accepted just such a lopsided arrangement as the price of social and fiscal stability. In 1900, the electorate amounted to around eight million voters, of whom only just over one million were liable to income tax. But this did not mean that there was no potential for conflict between mass democracy and public solvency. Lloyd George's budget of 1909—the "people's budget"—marked a watershed. His proposal of a higher rate of tax on "unearned income" and a "supertax" on all incomes above £3,000 brought dire predictions from the senior English member of the house of Rothschild, the natural guardians of public bondholders everywhere: "The Chancellor of the Exchequer will . . . learn that the Socialistic taxation he talked of is not conducive to public credit. . . . Nothing is more likely to defeat socialistic legislation than the depreciation of Home Securities."[39] Lord Rothschild's forecasts were premature in 1909. The new patterns of "democratic" taxation and spending were starting from such a low base that Lloyd George's radical reforms now appear quite modest. Besides, his budget was balanced. The markets shuddered and then took his proposals in their stride. But the future battleground had been staked out.

A NATION OF RENTIERS

> By giving them for the first time a democratic character, and in calling on the whole nation to subscribe, the Emperor [Napoleon III] did for *rentes* what 1789 did for land; from now on the cultivator and the worker will not be less interested than the capitalist in the stability of credit. —*Moniteur*, June 9, 1857

In light of these considerations, it would seem foolish to argue that after 1815 public debt continued to be the main driving force behind the advance of democratic government. There were certainly times when the old rules applied. In 1818 the Prussian State Chancellor, Hardenberg, was in London, seeking to raise money by an issue of bonds. He was told firmly by Nathan Rothschild that, unlike the restored government of France in the previous year, Prussia would have to offer a mortgage on state-owned lands to secure any financing:

> The late investments by British subjects in the French Funds have proceeded upon the general belief that in consequence of the representative system now established in that Country, the sanction of the Chamber to the national debt incurred by the Government affords a guarantee to the Public Creditor which could not be found in a contract with any Sovereign uncontrolled in the exercise of the executive powers.[40]

Partly as a result of Rothschild's strictures, a decree was issued in the following year committing Prussia to convening the Estates to authorize any subsequent public borrowing, a decree that may be deemed the beginning of the retreat from enlightened despotism in eastern Europe. A later staging post on that retreat was the 1859 financial crisis in Austria, which marked the end of a decade of neoabsolutism following the suppression of the abortive democratic revolution of 1848 and started the empire down the path of constitutional experimentation that led to the reforms of 1867.

These were replays of old themes, however, helping to push reluctant autocracies over the threshold of reform. There is no visible connection between public credit and the subsequent advance toward true democratic government; that is, toward universal suffrage. In any case, after the advent of the Industrial Revolution, it is arguable that the rise of democracy did not need any further assistance from the credit markets. The spread of urbanization and rising educational and living standards were sufficient in themselves to fuel this historic process.

Yet if the advent of mass democracy was largely independent of public credit and potentially antithetical to it, this does not mean that the citizen creditor—the hero of our tale so far—had no further role to play in the history of the world. For one thing, there remains an obvious conundrum. If universal suffrage diluted the power of the natural supporters of sound public credit, how come the credit ratings of the Western nations seemed only to improve in the last decades before the First World War?

There are several possible answers to this question. The first is the force of inertia. The bourgeoisie had set their stamp so firmly on the century and had entrenched their values so deeply in the public consciousness that they were not to be easily displaced. Many of the new voters, especially those from rural areas, had centuries-old habits of deference that would take generations to fade. Against this theory it is possible to argue that, whatever the superficial trappings of the Belle Époque, the era of the frugal, bourgeois, "night watchman" state was over by end of the century. It was already being superseded by the spendthrift, plebeian, "nanny" state. There was no fallout from this transition in public credit rankings before the First World War only because social spending was growing from such a low base and was, by modern standards, quite negligible.

While this is true, it scarcely explains the *improvement* in credit ratings that occurred in the period. A more likely explanation lies in the general sense of well-being produced by a long period of peace and prosperity. The forty-five years that followed the Franco-Prussian War were a period of unparalleled general economic growth undisturbed by great-power military conflicts. It takes little knowledge of history to perceive that such conditions are not often associated with social conflict. Apart from the activities of a few cloak-and-dagger anarchists and the visions of scarcely more numerous avant-garde artists, there was little in the Gilded Age that suggested an appetite for radical change of the existing order. A few years of war and privation after 1914 would change all that.

Still, it is unlikely that the introduction of mass democracy into the cozy body of bourgeois constitutionalism would have taken place with so few financial repercussions if it had not been accompanied by a parallel development—one that neutralized a large part of its potential sting. The secret was the transformation of a large number of the new voters into public creditors.

The first significant step was taken in Britain in the immediate aftermath of the Napoleonic Wars. Though the borrowing of the Napoleonic Wars had made Britain a nation of citizen creditors, it did so only in the sense that the 300,000 public creditors represented the substantial majority of the electorate. In a country that contained nearly four million adult males, the enfranchised citizens were a small minority. Indeed the evidence suggests that the electorate had not even kept pace with population growth, so that it now represented only 10% of adult males as compared to 20% a century earlier. The rapid growth of the ranks of the destitute as a result of military demobilization and economic depression gave rise to a situation that was not only expensive (in increased "poor relief") but politically explosive. In 1817, Sir George Rose proposed legislation that would allow the establishment of savings banks throughout the country. The banks would entice the assets of the poor from under their mattresses and, more important, encourage habits of thrift that would eventually reduce the economic burdens on the state. In the visionary hopes of their promoters, the banks would rank among the great advances of modern society:

> As the practice of vaccination bids fair to eradicate the most loathsome diseases from the earth . . . so the establishment of Savings Banks may ultimately tend to banish poverty and wretchedness from society.[41]

The deposits collected from the public would be invested exclusively in government securities. This was based on a feeling that the government should take moral responsibility for the safety of the savings that it was trying to encourage, and should protect the unsophisticated from the hazards of risky or fraudulent investment schemes. Such altruistic hopes aside, the savings banks had another, less clearly stated objective. The deposits collected from the public were to be invested only in government bonds, and this last provision would ensure that an ever-larger portion of the population would have a stake in political stability and public solvency. This was well understood by the scheme's opponents, such as John Smith:

> For what real object? Why, that the hardy and industrious journeyman and citizens of the country may club their money together and have it placed in a thing called The Funds, that is to make it part of the great debt, by which means you would tie yourselves to the present system of mismanagement and would be silenced as to any reduction of those taxes required for paying the interest of those funds.[42]

Notwithstanding the objections of the radicals, the Trustee Savings Banks were an almost instant success—partly because of the relatively generous terms offered by the government. Within two years more than 250 savings banks had been founded, and by 1860 there were over 1.5 million depositors. In the following year the Post Office was allowed to offer its own savings accounts, which proved to be even more popular than those of the banks. By 1910, there were an astonishing 10,200,000 depositors (one-quarter of the total population, a figure larger than the total electorate, which by now comprised the large majority of adult males) within the national savings system. Their deposits totaled over £220 million and constituted by far the largest element in the national debt.[43]

The English savings banks were not the first in the history of Europe, but their very scale made them a model for other countries. France followed suit almost immediately with the establishment of the Caisses d'Épargne in 1818. The French savings system rivaled Britain's in scale, with over eight million depositors in 1910 and over 5 billion francs invested in rentes. The pattern was repeated throughout Europe. Italy, for example, was a latecomer, inaugurating its system only in 1875, but by 1910 there were already five million depositors with accounts totalling 1.5 billion lire.[44] By the end of the century, every major country had an extensive network of savings institutions whose assets were, with very few exceptions, funneled into the public debt. Only in America were savings banks given a significant level of freedom in choosing their investments, for the simple reason that for much of the century there was little federal debt for them to invest in.

The most obvious result of the remarkable growth of the assets of the savings banks was the increased latitude afforded to governments in the management of their borrowing. In Britain, Gladstone was able discreetly to increase the rate of national debt reduction by allocating term annuities to the savings institutions rather than Consols. This effectively forced Parliament to budget for a rather higher level of expenditure on debt service than it might otherwise have been willing to accept. Outside Britain there was little interest in debt reduction, but the savings banks gave other advantages. Governments were able progressively to reduce their dependence on the great banking houses, such as the Rothschilds, since they now had growing sources of investment assets under their own management. The presence of a large pliable mass of capital was especially useful in the mammoth debt conversions undertaken by Britain, France, and Italy between 1883 and 1906. For such operations to be successful, it was essential that bondholders face a plausible threat of redemption if they refused to accept a reduced rate of interest. The assets of the savings banks provided just such a credible threat.

The growth of captive savings was no doubt one of the reasons why interest rates on public debts were so low in the run-up to the First World War. It also had the effect of damping the enthusiasm of the new mass electorate for radical financial reform. This is certainly how its opponents viewed the system. In their view the encouragement of popular savings had purely political motives. In the eyes of Karl Marx, savings were "a golden chain on which the government holds a large part of the working class."[45] Lenin expressed the same idea more brutally:

> In Russia this capital serves primarily to strengthen the might of the militarist and bourgeois-police state. The Tsarist government . . . disposes of this capital just as arbitrarily as it does of all other public property it lays its hands on.[46]

Without being as cynical as Marx and Lenin, one can say that it is certainly true that the savings banks performed an important political service in the transition to universal suffrage. But they had their limitations. On a political level, depositors were only public creditors at one remove, and it is not clear, therefore, how profoundly they identified their financial interests with those of the state. Many depositors were only dimly aware of how their money was invested.[47] Although savings-bank depositors were unlikely to become revolutionaries, they were undoubtedly less committed to the public solvency than were those with direct holdings of government bonds. To this must be added two potential financial limitations. The amount that could be raised by the savings banks was not very flexible. The large sums achieved by the end of the century were the result of slow, regular accumulation—a process that would not be of much use in the event of a major war. Worse, deposits that could be withdrawn on demand might even aggravate the financial situation at a time of crisis, as had occurred in France in 1848, when the government had been forced to suspend the right of withdrawal. Mindful of this history, perhaps, the Rollits Committee reported to Parliament in 1904 that the scale of savings deposits in Britain was "already so vast as not to be without some risk to the credit of the country in the event of a grave national disaster."[48]

For a number of reasons, therefore, the logical next step was to encourage mass direct ownership of long-term public debt. Here Britain was, for once, a laggard—perhaps because it was never confronted by a political or financial crisis of sufficient gravity during the century. It was France that established the pattern that all countries would be forced to imitate when the Belle Époque came to an abrupt end in 1914.

It was precisely because France experienced such great political upheavals during the century that it became a pioneer. During the Revolution of 1830 the neo-Jacobin aspirations of the radicals had been narrowly averted when the veteran Lafayette publicly draped the tricolor around Louis Philippe and offered him the throne. Thereafter the "citizen king" hastened to lower the minimum denomination of rente from 50 francs to 10 francs so as to encourage small investors. By 1847, there were nearly 300,000 rentiers—more rentiers, in fact, than there were voters. Their numbers were not enough, however, to prevent another political deluge. During the Revolution of 1848, the closing of the Caisses d'Épargne, while it proved the point of the skeptics who had argued against financing the government with demand deposits, was, in the long term, a blessing in disguise. The larger depositors were repaid in rentes, and by 1850 the number of rentiers had swollen to 824,000. Although some of these evidently sold their holdings, there were still 640,000 bondholders at the time of the outbreak of the Crimean War in 1854. It was then that Louis Napoleon made the crucial decision to bypass the great financial houses of Rothschild and Laffitte, and to raise money directly from the public. Three issues were sold to finance the war, the third of which attracted 317,000 subscribers who, among them, offered 3.65 billion francs—almost five times the amount requested. By 1857 the number of public creditors had risen to 900,000. It was the success of these issues that inspired the *Moniteur* to rhapsodize about the "democratization of credit" in its June 9 editorial:

> By giving them for the first time a democratic character, and in calling on the whole nation to subscribe, the Emperor did for rentes what 1789 did for the land; from now on the cultivator and the worker will not be less interested than the capitalist in the stability of credit; from now on all the classes will participate in all the advantages, as well as in all the expenses of the country. . . . One knows what the result has been for the conduct of war and for the prestige of France abroad; the enthusiasm with which the loans were subscribed right down to the smallest hamlets has produced no less effect that the heroism of our soldiers under the walls of Sebastopol, and Europe has seen, with an equal astonishment, the stretch of our financial resources and the strength of our arms.[49]

It seemed as if the messianic vision of Anacharsis Cloots in 1792—a nation of citizen soldiers funded by patriotic contributions—had finally been realized. The power of financial democracy was to be even more dramatically displayed fifteen years later. In 1871 the "strength of French arms" was unlikely to impress outside observers, but no one could fail to marvel at the ability of the nation to tap its citizens' resources in its hour of need. The indemnity demanded by Germany was financed by two public issues of rentes. The first, for 2 billion francs, was floated in June 1871 and was followed by a second, for 3 billion francs, in July 1872. The first issue was already three and one half times oversubscribed, but it was the second one that really caught the popular imagination. No fewer than 934,000 subscribers responded, of which 792,000 were from the French provinces. An astonishing total of 43.8 billion francs was subscribed.[50] To put this figure in perspective, it is only necessary to consider that it was equivalent to more than one and one half times the French GNP at the time, and more than double the total British national debt. Whether such a figure would have been forthcoming is of course unlikely, since many subscriptions were exaggerated in the knowledge that allocations would be limited. Even so, the final issue of 3.5 billion francs[51] was the largest public loan that the world had yet seen. For centuries the French had been storing gold under their mattresses as an insurance against public profligacy and bad faith. Now times had so far changed that they were willing to lift the bedcovers and entrust their hard-earned assets to the safekeeping of a fledgling republican government.

After 1872, there were far in excess of one million Frenchmen who owned a stake in the national debt. But this was by no means the high-water mark of popular participation in public finance. By 1909, there were 4,631,857 rentiers—a number equivalent to nearly half the households in the country. One can reasonably ask whether, after eighty years of revolution, the stabilization of French politics under the Third Republic did not owe a great deal to this phenomenon. The introduction of universal male suffrage in 1848 had created political tensions which were held in check only by a revival of Bonapartism—rather as the conflict between oligarchy and democracy in ancient Greece had so often led to government by tyrants. Under the Third Republic the electorate (again based on universal male suffrage) comprised some ten to eleven million voters, whose political views ranged from unreconstructed monarchism to radical socialism. Within this body the vast numbers of rentiers formed a solid ballast, committed to public solvency, which held in check the more violent lurches of the ship of state and kept it from capsizing.

The remarkable success of France in encouraging direct ownership of its debt caught the attention of outside observers. In 1909, C. A. Stanuell compared the prices of British Consols and French rentes and reported that the minimal (around 0.15%) difference in their yields was not justified on the basis of national fundamentals:

> The French are a smaller nation: 39,000,000 people as against 41,000,000; so that they have fewer people to pay taxes. The British are far more wealthy than the French. Their resources, not only in money but in mines, minerals, trade, commerce and manufactures, are far in advance. Thus they have better means of paying taxes. The French Debt is £1,000,000,000 as against the British £750,000,000, amounting to £25 per head of the population while the British is £18. . . . France has an exposed frontier, while Britain is protected by the sea, so that the French require a large and expensive army. Under all these circumstances, the British Consols, being so much better secured, ought to be worth about 20 per cent. in the market more than the French.[52]

In Stanuell's opinion, the conclusion was inescapable that if Britain were as heavily indebted as France, "the French funds would rank above the British in the money market of the world." This startling reversal of historical fortunes he attributed directly to the narrowness of the market for Consols, with scarcely more than 200,000 holders—fewer, even, than one hundred years earlier—and to the difficulty of trading them except in the City of London. His proposal was to emulate the French system and sell Consols in small denominations to the widest possible public. In 1911, his call was taken up by *The Economist*, which suggested selling Consols "like postage stamps across the counters of Post Offices."[53]

All too soon these proposals would have to be put into effect.

GREENBACKS AND 5-20S

> Held, as it is, for the most part by our own people, [the public debt] has become a substantial branch of national, though private, property. . . . Men readily perceive that they can not be much oppressed by a debt which they owe to themselves. —Abraham Lincoln, annual presidential address, December 1864

> We now pride ourselves upon having given freedom to 4,000,000 of the colored race; it will then be our shame that 40,000,000 of people . . . have suffered themselves to become enslaved, and merely exchanged slave owners for new taskmasters in the shape of bondholders and taxgatherers.
> —Andrew Johnson, annual presidential address, December 1868

Notwithstanding the excitement of the events of 1848 and 1870, the most divisive, and the most fascinating, nineteenth-century debates on national finance took place not in Europe, but across the Atlantic. Nowhere was it less certain whether the words *democracy* and *public debt* could be reconciled. The fault lines that divided the American nation could not be easily bridged, even by the Jeffersonian compromise of 1800. This tacit understanding, it will be remembered, ensured that the public finances of the union would be run on sound bourgeois principles—no paper money, and all debts serviced punctually in good coin—but only on condition that existing debts would be redeemed as fast as possible and *never* allowed to become perpetual. This compromise held during the War of 1812 against Britain, and thereafter the republic soon reverted to its path of debt reduction. In 1815, the national debt peaked at $127 million. By 1829, it had fallen to under $60 million—the same level as before the war. Eight years later, the debt had been entirely repaid. Even though there was some small-scale borrowing in the 1840s and 1850s, the republic approached its gravest crisis—spiritually, militarily, and financially—in 1860 with debts that amounted, yet again, to around $60 million, by now a derisory sum equivalent to only 1.5% of GNP.

It might be thought that the absence of borrowing in these decades would have rendered the old debates about public finance obsolete. But the agrarian disdain for the appurtenances of "English" public finance did not die out in 1800. It merely manifested itself in other ways. The first battle was about central banking. Jefferson had been content to leave the Bank of the United States alone in 1800. Many of its old opponents, such as James Madison and Albert Gallatin, had become supporters by 1810. When its charter was due for renewal, it was easily voted through the House of Representatives by a 75–35 majority. Matters were less easy in the Senate, where the electoral system favored the smaller frontier states. The Senate divided equally, and the decisive, opposing vote was cast by the vice-president, George Clinton.

The difficulties of funding the war with Britain that followed this act of financial retrogression convinced the majority of politicians that they had made a mistake. A second Bank of the United States was chartered in 1816—once again a private, joint-stock company on the model that was being adopted elsewhere in the Western world. This bank, too, was destined to survive only for the length of its initial charter. The granting of statehood to the first areas carved out of the Louisiana Purchase in the West and the simultaneous spread of universal suffrage in the East shifted the political balance once again toward agrarian populism. In the presidential election of 1828, the new political majority swept John Quincy Adams, the champion of the Eastern mercantile establishment, from power and replaced him with Andrew Jackson from the frontier state of Tennessee. Over the following four years relations between the government and the central bank degenerated into an increasingly ill-tempered shouting match; but still, when the renewal of its charter was debated in Congress in 1832, the bank won majorities in both houses. At that point President Jackson exercised his veto, and the future of the bank became the central issue of the election that followed. The Jacksonian Democrats won a decisive victory, which would establish them as the dominant force in American politics until the Civil War, and in 1836 the country found itself yet again without a central banking institution.

For the following thirty years, the monetary policy of the republic was both contradictory and chaotic. Jackson and many of his supporters were primitive souls who trusted only in hard coin and viewed all banks as inventions of the devil. Others within the Democratic alliance, however, disliked the central bank only because its insistence on sound money ran contrary to their preference for easy money. The federal government refused to deal in anything but gold and silver. At the same time, however, it left banking regulation to the states, which proceeded to act according to their preferences. On the Eastern seaboard, there were sound banks that redeemed their notes in gold on demand. In the West, there were unsound banks that issued notes that were either not convertible or convertible only in far-off places "where the wild cats howl." J. K. Galbraith neatly summed up the politics of frontier banking:

> The function of credit in a simple society is remarkably egalitarian. It allows the man with energy and no money to participate in the economy more or less on a par with the man who has capital of his own. And the more casual the conditions under which credit is granted . . . the more egalitarian credit is. . . . Thus the phenomenal urge in the United States, one that lasted through all of the last century and well into the present one, to create banks. And thus, also, the marked if unadmitted liking for bad banks. Bad banks, unlike good, loaned to the poor risk, which is another name for the poor man.[54]

Where Galbraith was on shaky ground was in arguing that the "bad" banks established in the West were better suited to its economic needs. By the early 1850s, suspicion of such banks was so great that there were no banks at all in Arkansas, California, Florida, Illinois, Iowa, Michigan, Wisconsin, Oregon, or Minnesota.[55] Thanks to the legacy of Jacksonian populism, the monetary system of the United States was quite inadequate to finance a major war in 1861. The country was fortunate enough to have a substantial stock of coin in circulation, thanks largely to the discovery of gold in California ten years earlier. But the rest of the money supply was composed of a motley assortment of no fewer than seven thousand types of local banknotes, very few of which commanded anything approaching nationwide acceptance, and a good number of which were the subject of extensive forgery.

The 1830s had left another legacy, too. The successful completion of the Erie Canal in 1826 convinced Americans and foreigners alike that all projects to tame the American wilderness must be profitable investments. The resulting wave of optimism led to the floating of large numbers of loans to American states on the bourses of Europe. Few of these loans had a significant real prospect of repayment in the time frame agreed on. On the other hand, the states themselves borrowed only on the assumption that their projects would be self-liquidating, like the Erie project. Their citizens would have been horrified at the prospect of actually taxing themselves to pay interest, had somebody suggested the possibility of such an outcome. Curiously, the crash that followed the boom was made inevitable by the contradictions inherent in agrarian politics. In 1836, President Jackson's insistence that all payments to the federal government be made in specie set off a deflationary spiral that brought a wave of default in its trail. The American states soon acquired a credit reputation little better than that of the countries of Latin America that had suspended payments en masse some ten years earlier. The refusal of the federal government to assume responsibility for the debts, as it had in the 1790s, while insisting that the states themselves, as sovereign entities, enjoyed immunity from suit in the U.S. courts, only tarred its own credit standing. Passions ran high on both sides of the debate. The proponents of assumption were the same as the supporters of the Bank of the United States. They were horrified by the damage inflicted on the national credit, which promised to turn the republic once more into a "common prostitute among chaste and respectable matrons." On the other side, the opponents of assumption, like Senator Allen of Ohio (whose state narrowly avoided default), saw the erstwhile Bank of the United States as no more that "a branch of the Bank of England." Assumption, if passed, would only complete the devilish work of Hamilton in the 1790s, whose desire to inflict a perpetual debt on the nation had been based on his aristocratic pretensions and his disdain for the common people. For investors in London it was the sense that at least some of the states were not even *trying* to service their debts that created the greatest sense of outrage. A much-quoted letter from a creditor of Pennsylvania, by far the wealthiest of the defaulters, to the House of Representatives ran:

> If the refusal to pay . . . had been the result of . . . the unjust aggression of powerful enemies . . . ; if it were the act of a poor state struggling against the barrenness of nature, every friend of America would have been contented to wait

> for better times; but the fraud is committed in profound peace, by Pennsylvania, the richest state in the Union, after the wise investment of the borrowed money in roads and canals of which the repudiators are every day reaping the advantage.[56]

With a few notable exceptions, such as Mississippi, whose debts remain a legal battleground to this day, the defaulting states had made settlements by the end of the 1840s. Foreign investors were once again willing to resume the westerly flow of funds across the Atlantic; but now they concentrated on private-sector investments. Nonetheless, the history of default left a bitter aftertaste that still lingered in the mouth in 1860.

When the Civil War started, it was not surprising that the South soon found itself in financial difficulties. Of the $250–300 million of coin in the country, only $25 million was to be found in the Confederacy. The breakaway states had no central government and scarcely wished to create one. Their constitution was a reenactment of the Articles of Confederation of 1776, and it took only a brief glance at the history of the Revolution to foresee the likely financial outcome. The North, on the other hand, not only had an enormous demographic and economic advantage but also held the reins of government. The U.S. Constitution was not exactly a model of Napoleonic centralization, but it had, after all, been specifically designed to make the defense of the nation possible without financial meltdown. Moreover, the federal government had an almost debt-free balance sheet, an advantage rarely enjoyed by any Western power since the Renaissance.

Nonetheless, within six months of the commencement of hostilities, the North, too, faced a financial crisis. The government did show an initial reluctance to raise taxes sufficiently to support a successful policy of cheap long-term borrowing, but that was not the basic issue. The government was prisoner of a Jacksonian policy of dealing only in specie. This was fine when the federal budget was scarcely more than 1% of GNP; but soon the government was forced to spend more than 10% of GNP on its war effort. It did not matter, in a sense, whether this expenditure was financed by taxes or loans. There was simply not enough coin in the economy to support such a level of government activity without the assistance of paper instruments. By the end of 1861, government demands had drained the East Coast banks of most of their gold, and they had been forced to suspend convertibility. This was the background to the return of legal tender paper money that many thought to have been banished by the Constitution. As Senator John Sherman, the most reasoned supporter of the "greenbacks" (as they came to be called), observed in the ensuing debate:

> Where will the purchasers of your bonds get the gold and silver coin . . . ? It is now driven out of circulation. There is no such thing as gold and silver coin circulating in the country to any large amount. It is stowed away. . . . [The only alternative to the proposed legal-tender government notes would be] to install as your national currency, as your standard of values, the inflated currency of all the local banks in the United States; banks over which you have no control, which you cannot regulate or govern in the slightest degree.[57]

Sherman was quite right. The war could not be fought without some sort of acceptable national currency. The idea of relying on the depreciated notes of local banks was nonsensical. The senator backed up his support for the greenbacks by reference to Britain's actions in the Napoleonic Wars:

> While we are in war specie payments are naturally suspended, as they always will be and always have been in every country involved in a great war. They were suspended in England during her wars with Napoleon.[58]

But here he was complacent. The Bank of England may have suspended convertibility during the Napoleonic Wars, but that was after four and a half years of warfare that had already cost around 50% of GNP. The United States was forced to move onto a paper money standard after only six months of relatively low-intensity fighting that had cost little more than 3% of GNP. Whether the country could have avoided a suspension of convertibility altogether, had it possessed a central bank whose notes commanded universal trust in 1860, is not clear. The Civil War was fought on an unprecedented scale of intensity in terms of both casualties and costs. The North's war costs over four years probably represented over 55% of GNP. On the other hand, the North had no burden of previous debt to service, so that its *total* spending over the four years was considerably lower than Britain's in the 1790s. Even after 1865, the national debt was still barely more than 50% of GNP.[59] Perhaps even with a central bank, convertibility would not have survived the last year of the war—by far the most costly. But a resort to irredeemable paper money at that late point would not have resulted in the massive inflation that ensued after 1862.

There were undoubtedly forces within the country that would have been happy to finance the war largely by means of paper. Perhaps there were even a few within Congress that harbored the idea in secret. But it was certainly not the majority position, and it was not the policy of the government. Paper money issues were kept, so the government liked to think, to the minimum necessary to carry on the war. In the final analysis, greenbacks covered only 13% of total expenditure. The remainder was financed by taxation (23%), bond issues (31%), and interest-bearing short-term debt (32%).[60] The problem for the government was that its rapid resort to the printing press, although to some extent necessary to create adequate liquidity in the economy and in the credit markets, only exacerbated its major financial problem: how to borrow large sums of money at less than ruinous rates.

In order to preserve something of its credit standing, the government promised to continue to service its debts in gold. Yet, as the greenbacks depreciated, this commitment, however necessary, became progressively more expensive. By the spring of 1864, paper dollars had fallen to less than 50 cents in gold, and for every dollar loaned to the national cause, the government was therefore promising to pay more than double the nominal capital at maturity, and more than double the nominal 6% interest rate until then. This was all the more curious since the main argument urged by the proponents of paper money in 1862 had been that it was an insult to the national dignity for the government to pay more than 6% for its money. "The experience of half a century has demonstrated that the use of money is not worth more than six per cent.; that sum the Government ought to pay," stated Senator Howe.[61] Representative Spaulding concurred: "When money can be obtained at par on six per cent. bonds, I would prefer to have done that to the issuing of a very large amount of legal-tender notes."[62] To drive the message home, Congress authorized $500 million of 6% bonds redeemable between five and twenty years from issue (the "5-20s," as they were called) that the government could sell at a price not below par—knowing full well, of course, that the public credit was not good enough to achieve this target. In order to "save its dignity," therefore, the North issued paper money instead of borrowing; and when that money had depreciated sufficiently, it was able to sell the 5-20s at par in paper dollars without having to admit that its true borrowing cost was far, far higher than 6%.

It only takes a brief glance at the chart to get a sense of just how much the North had to pay to finance the war. In the 1850s the U.S. government had been able to raise money at rates as low as 4.5%. The quantity of federal government bonds outstanding, however, was tiny. Their prices were not a good indication of the rates that would be required to raise large sums at a time of crisis. In 1861, it had already become clear that significant amounts of long-term money could not be had for less than 6.5–7.0%. This was before the suspension of specie payments. For the rest of the war the government's average cost of borrowing (excepting Treasury bills) was around 10.5%, and in the summer of 1864 it reached a peak of over 16%.

Only when victory was in sight did the cost start to fall, and even then the average for the last six months of the war was 13%.

YIELD OF U.S. 6% BONDS, 1861–1865[63]

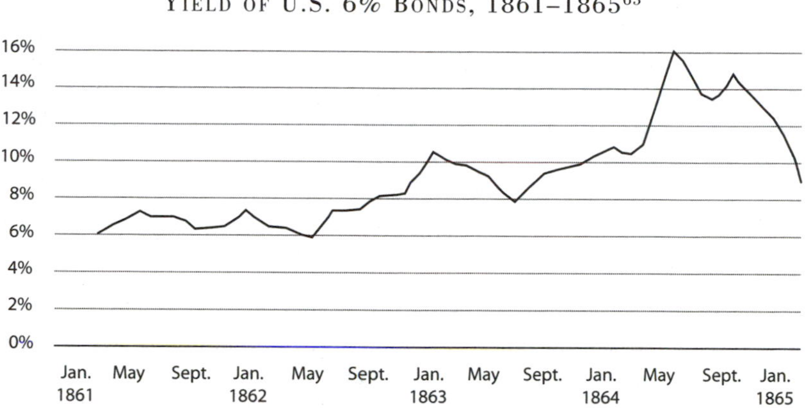

These were yields that implied an extremely high level of risk. To put them in perspective, it is necessary to recall only that the rates paid by the French monarchy in the late eighteenth century averaged 8% and peaked at 10.5%. Yet those were rates that historians have referred to as "prepaid repudiation," rates that led inexorably to the bankruptcy of 1788 and thus heralded the demise of the ancien régime. Is the message of the chart, then, that the United States was, when put to the test, likely to prove even less reliable a borrower than the Bourbon monarchy? Was this the penalty extracted by the credit markets for the legacy of Jacksonian politics?

It is possible to argue that it is not fair to compare eighteenth-century France and nineteenth-century America. Midcentury America was still dependent on foreign capital. It was simply not in a position to fund the unprecedented financial demands of the Civil War out of its own savings; and foreign markets were effectively closed for the duration of the war. This is not a complete explanation, however. The initial shortage of liquidity in the domestic credit markets was soon resolved, first by the issue of the greenbacks, and then by the National Bank Act of 1863, which allowed accredited banks to issue paper money against reserves held in government bonds. By the end of the war, the country was awash with liquidity. Indeed, it was precisely because of the fears aroused by American monetary policy that foreign investors were reluctant to lend.

It is also true that the threat faced by the North in 1861 was more serious than in the typical war of the eighteenth century. The secession of so many member states threatened the disintegration of the whole union. The North had a long, exposed frontier, and its capital was perilously close to the enemy armies. Many foreign observers were inclined to the idea that the war was unwinnable, and certainly not worth the cost. In October 1862 *The Economist* assured its readers that the independence of the South was "as certain as any future event could be."[64] Even as the military threat receded, the financial threat advanced. Every year brought higher spending and increased the risk that debt would reach unsustainable levels. High interest rates, according to this argument, may have reflected a high level of credit risk; but the risk concerned the country's *ability* to pay, not its *willingness*.

It is, of course, impossible to know the exact cost at which the North could have financed the war without the legacy of populist politics. But it *is* possible to eliminate the contributions of both wartime fears and capital shortage to high interest rates by shifting one's perspective forward. After Lee's surrender in April 1865, there was no further threat to the Union. Whatever interest rates were subsequently demanded by the market were no longer dependent on estimates of the likely duration or outcome of the war. Nor were they affected by fears that the government would be unable to rebalance the budget in its aftermath. By 1866, there was already a surplus in the accounts, and almost every informed observer was of the opinion that the extraordinary wealth and dynamism of the country would soon enable it to reduce a debt that, while very large in absolute terms, was quite modest in relation to the national income. Victory also brought with it the rapid return of foreign capital to the American market. International holdings of U.S. government securities were already over $300 million by the end of 1865, and three years later this sum had risen to $700 million—more than 30% of the amount outstanding.[65] It was certainly no longer possible to claim that the U.S. interest rates were affected by a shortage of capital—at least no more than those of any other borrower still partially dependent on foreign investment.

The cost of borrowing remained stubbornly high, however. From April 1865 to the end of 1868, the 5-20s traded at prices no higher than 80, giving a yield to maturity of around 8.5%. This was high compared to the borrowing costs not only of countries that were self-sufficient in capital resources and maintained convertible currencies, like Britain and Holland, but even of those that were not. Russian bonds, for instance, traded at yields of around 6% in the late 1860s. Yet Russia was a country whose debt was as high as America's in relation to its GNP, whose budget was in chronic deficit, and whose economic prospects generated nothing like the same enthusiasm. American credit standing in those years was on a level with that of Italy, whose bonds were then yielding as much as 9%. Like America, Italy had just secured its unity at the cost of heavy borrowing and of a suspension of convertibility. But unlike America, Italy's budget appeared out of control, and its debt was already over 70% of GNP and was growing fast. Furthermore, in 1866, Italy had already committed an act of default in the eyes of investors by imposing a unilateral withholding tax on interest payments, even those made to non-Italians.

In these circumstances, the high yields on American bonds can be explained only by lingering, and not unreasonable, fears of default. The secession of the Southern states in 1861 split apart the old Jacksonian Democratic Party. They were replaced as the dominant force in American politics by a new political coalition that, for the first time in decades, included the forces of sound money. But this did not mean that the old emotions of agrarian America had disappeared. Moreover, the payment of the public creditors in gold, while everyone else had to make do with depreciated paper currency, provided an all-too-obvious target for popular discontent. It was for this reason, in part, that the government initially sought to redeem the greenbacks as fast as possible after the war, so that the privileged position of the public creditors should disappear before their bonds came due. Needless to say, the deflationary consequences of this policy soon aroused widespread opposition. The monetary problem facing America was little different from that facing Britain after the Napoleonic Wars; but the political composition of the U.S. Congress in 1865 was far different from that of the British Parliament in 1815. It was scarcely to be imagined that the Peterloo Massacre would be reenacted across the Atlantic in the interests of public credit.

Moreover, the forces of agrarian America were far from voiceless between 1865 and 1868. Thanks to the assassination of Abraham Lincoln, the president of the country was one of their own. In Andrew Johnson's view, a war waged against slave masters had defeated its own purpose:

> An aristocracy based on nearly two and one half billion of national securities has risen in the northern states to assume that political control which was formerly given to the slave oligarchy.[66]

If Lincoln's term of office had seen a growth in the power of the executive to a level undreamed of by the Founding Fathers, Johnson's witnessed its nadir. Deprived of true power to control public financial policy, he could merely exercise a destabilizing influence from the wings. In his final presidential address of 1868, he publicly advocated a policy of default—the only time that an American president has ever done so. According to Johnson the public creditors had already been so well rewarded that they should now be well-satisfied if their interest payments were henceforth credited against principal. In this way, the whole debt could be paid off in little more than eleven years.* Both houses of Congress hastened to condemn this outrageous suggestion, but the markets continued, for the time being, to value American promises to pay at a precautionary discount.

In some ways Johnson was out of sync with his supporters. As a member of the old Jacksonian hard-currency school, he had little time for the greenbacks and argued strongly for their rapid redemption. The majority opinion favored a different approach. The deflation of land and crop prices that accompanied the redemption of the greenbacks was anathema to Western farmers. Most of the believers in the Jacksonian hard-money credo now found themselves converted to the paper that they had previously abhorred. In order to relieve the nation of the burdens of public debt, they proposed repaying government bonds in depreciated greenbacks. This view was facilitated by a loophole in the original Legal Tender Act that specifically committed only to paying interest on public debts in gold but made no mention of principal. Even though the bonds had been sold on the explicit basis (unchallenged in Congress) that principal would be repaid in gold, the presidential election of 1868 witnessed a wave of popular pressure, especially in the West, that unnerved even politicians who had hitherto taken a firm stance on matters of public credit. Senator Sherman, for instance, now suggested that

> equity and justice are amply satisfied if we redeem these bonds at the end of the five years in the same kind of money of the same intrinsic value it bore at the time they were issued.[67]

Repayment in greenbacks became a central plank of the Democratic platform.[68] Against the strong appeal of this battle cry stood the equally powerful pull of General Grant, the hero of the Civil War and a firm believer in the sanctity of the public credit. His electoral victory at the end of the year was followed by an inaugural address in early 1869 in which he clearly set out his position:

---

*There was, interestingly, a Venetian precedent for Johnson's proposal. The Monte Nuovo had been repaid in exactly this way between 1530 and 1560. Was Johnson a student of sixteenth-century Venice? It seems unlikely; but, then, who knows? His parting argument—that "the lessons of the past admonish the lender that it is not well to be over anxious in exacting from the borrower rigid compliance with letter of the bond"—seems to refer only too closely to a well-known, if fictitious, sixteenth-century Venetian moneylender.

> To protect the national honor, every dollar of Government indebtedness should be paid in gold, unless otherwise expressly stipulated in contract. Let it be understood that no repudiator of one farthing of our public debt will be trusted in public place, and it will go far toward strengthening a credit which ought to be the best in the world, and will ultimately enable us to replace the debt with bonds bearing less interest than we now pay.[69]

This speech was followed up in March by the Public Credit Act, which removed the loophole in the 1862 legislation by specifically pledging the redemption of public debts in coin. As Grant predicted, the price of American bonds rapidly rose, and their yields fell to 5.5%. The cost of borrowing would have fallen further if the country had been able to link its domestic currency to gold. But until that happened, America was classed with those middle-rank countries, like Russia, whose debt was sound, but whose monetary policies remained questionable. Such countries could never enjoy a triple-A credit rating in the eyes of nineteenth-century investors. The political pressure against deflation was too great even for Grant's administration. It was considered wiser to allow the value of greenbacks to rise of its own accord by the simple expedient of keeping their number constant while the economy grew. It was only in 1875 that it became possible to contemplate making them convertible into gold. An act was passed in that year specifying the general resumption of payment in coin by 1879. A further drop in borrowing costs was the not-so-surprising result. After 1877 long-term bonds traded for yields around 4%. By 1881 this rate had fallen to little more than 3% and now, for the first time in American history, equaled the yields on Consols. The startling transformation of American credit in those years is easily followed on the chart below:

U.S., RUSSIAN, AND BRITISH BOND YIELDS, 1865–1881[70]

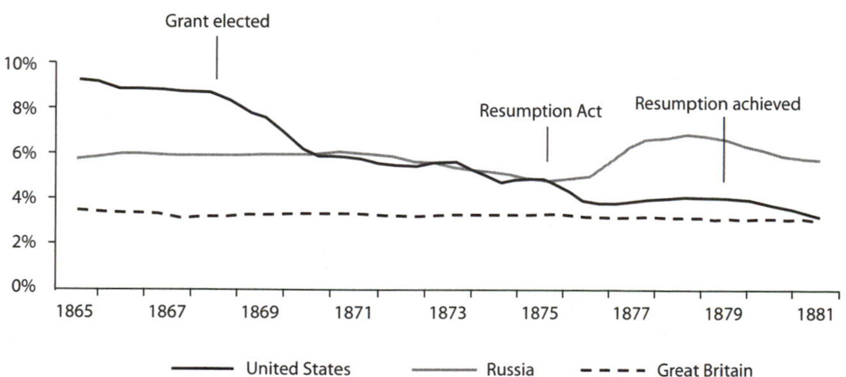

The easy-money/sound-money battle was not over even in 1878. Perhaps it was not finished even in 1896 with the electoral defeat of William Jennings Bryan, or even in 1913 with the establishment of the Federal Reserve system. But the events of the 1860s represented a major turning point in the epic struggle. In 1790, Hamilton had been able to persuade the Congress to shoulder a national debt that was, relatively, almost as large as that created by the Civil War. But in the days of the Founding Fathers, the electoral system was still based on a limited franchise, and the country still possessed something that saw itself as a "ruling class." Three-quarters of a century later the political landscape had changed. The opening of the West, together with the spread of universal suffrage and the virtual disappearance of old-fashioned social deference, made a Hamiltonian outcome far less likely. This was well understood by the more perceptive members of the government. Lectures on the virtues of sound credit were not likely to cut much ice with the forces of agrarian America if their old enemies, the Eastern bankers and capitalists, were seen to be establishing a permanent claim on the earnings of the nation. If a substantial public debt was to be made politically tenable, the only solution was to ensure that it would be as widely distributed as possible. This was certainly the view of Abraham Lincoln:

> For obvious reasons the more nearly [the public debt] can be distributed among all the people the better. . . . The great advantage to citizens being creditors as well as debtors with relation to the public debt is obvious. Men readily perceive that they can not be much oppressed by a debt which they owe to themselves.[71]

The man who deserves most credit for implementation of this policy, however, was not a politician, but a banker from Philadelphia, Jay Cooke. It was he who first understood the implications of the direct sales of public debt in France during the Crimean War. In 1861, he had already copied the French strategy in his home state of Pennsylvania—a state whose credit was still tarnished by memories of the default of 1840. A 6% loan that the bankers had refused to underwrite except at a discount of 25% was sold by Cooke to the public at par through a skillfully worded appeal to the "patriotism and state pride of Pennsylvanians in this hour of trial." Amounts as low as $50 had been sold to the wave of small investors who responded to the campaign. In early 1862, Cooke wrote to the Secretary of the Treasury, Salmon P. Chase, with a proposal to apply the same principle to the government's bonds. As supporting evidence, he enclosed a collection of cuttings about the French loan drives of 1854–1856 that told how the local government offices had been "besieged by crowds of peasant subscribers."[72]

From October 1862 to January 1864, and again from January to July 1865, Cooke was the government's loan agent. During the first period he sold the 5-20s. His success in placing no less than $500 million of these bonds at par over a period of fifteen months did not seem to entitle him to the gratitude of Congress, which was more concerned with the 3/8% commission earned by his sales organization. In January 1864 he was discharged from his role—an act of petulance that cost the country dear. The government's ability to sell long-term bonds virtually disappeared, and it was forced to resort to short-term issues, some of which were made legal tender. Lincoln's electoral victory at the end of the year allowed him to reinstate Cooke, but by then the public credit was so shaky that the best the government could hope for was the placement of three-year Treasury notes paying 7.3% that merely had the option of conversion into 5-20s. Again, the sums that Cooke raised were extremely impressive, totaling over $700 million in five months.

In each case, Cooke's marketing tactics were the same: the skillful use of the mass media of the day to disseminate messages that played on the apparently incompatible emotions of patriotism, calculated self-interest, and guilt. At one time his articles would call on national pride:

> What our Revolutionary Fathers are to us, WE will be to *coming generations,* if we fail not in our plain and simple duty [to buy government bonds]![73]

At other times he would harp on the high returns available on government securities; or he would promote them as "The Working Men's Savings Bank"—a safe haven where small investors could be sure that their savings were protected by the government. In the meantime, affecting stories of the contributions of the poor and wounded kept up the emotional pressure. As in a modern fund-raising drive, the public was kept constantly aware of how much had been contributed and how much remained to be raised. Cooke was in many ways the father of modern mass-marketing methods.

The mere filling of subscription lists was not all, however. Cooke was always mindful of the political dimension of his role. His twenty-five hundred subagents spread out into every part of the country. Strenuous efforts were made to sell bonds not only throughout the Western states but even, after April 1865, throughout the South. Small purchases were encouraged, and over two million subscriptions were taken in denominations of $50 and

$100. This crusade to spread the national debt as widely as possible reflected Cooke's profoundly held view of its importance for the stability and unity of the country. In a pamphlet of 1865 he went so far as to claim:

> Had we possessed a huge Union debt in 1860, and had as much of it been diffused among the mountaineers and planters of South Carolina as is now held in Rhode Island, as much in Alabama as now in Indiana, as much in Georgia as now in Minnesota, as much in Virginia as now in Connecticut, the war for slavery had never been waged.[74]

After 1865, Cooke's official role ceased. But he continued to take part in the debate over public finances that raged in the following years. As the controversy over the public debt peaked during the elections of 1868, he wrote a long, hard-hitting public letter on the question. He laid out just how large a percentage of the 7.3% Treasury notes had been issued in small denominations. Nearly 90% of total subscriptions were for amounts of $500 or less.

> The capitalists are in a very small minority, and any legislation repudiating in whole or in part the obligation of the bonds of the government would fall most severely upon widows, orphans and people of small capital. . . . It is common for public speakers who advocate the violation of the nation's faith by insisting on local taxation of bonds, their payment in greenbacks, etc. to designate the bondholders as "rich," as "privileged," . . . All this is demagoguery and willful perversion of the truth. . . . Out of the three million subscribers to our various public loans, over nine-tenths are of the class called *the people.* The West took $320,000,000 of the $830,000,000 7-30 loans, and I doubt not, holds a large portion of it now.[75]

Cooke then lashed out at the proponents of "repudiation," characterizing them as self-servers who had not cared to support the government in its time of need, preferring to invest in real estate rather than government bonds. They were now merely trying to protect the inflated value of their investments at the expense of loyal citizens. He finished by pointing out how counterproductive the agitation of the repudiators had been: "Yielding to [their clamor] has cost the nation . . . more treasure than can be estimated."

Whether Cooke's letter had any effect on the course of the election is uncertain; but his term as government loan agent may well have been vital. By Cooke's count there had been three million subscribers to government securities under his agency. Even allowing for some double counting, the number of American bondholders now exceeded the number of French rentiers by a substantial margin, at a time when the populations of the two countries were more or less the same. Some of the original subscribers may have sold by 1868, but who is to say that in an electorate of around 8 million (of which only 5.7 million actually voted), a nucleus of between 2 and 3 million public creditors would not have constituted the decisive element in the outcome of the election?

During the bond drive of 1865, one of Cooke's subagents in rural Illinois reported, "Farmers who live in little cabins, wear homespun clothes, and ride to church and town in two-horse wagons without springs, have in many instances several thousand dollars loaned to the Government."[76] This was a truly extraordinary transformation. Only a few years earlier, such yeomen farmers, the very core of the old Jeffersonian vision of America, would have been the natural opponents of public debt. But now, America, too, it seemed, had become a nation of citizen creditors.

NINE

NATIONS AT ARMS

TOTAL WAR (PART I)

> The failure of a single issue of Government bonds would be worse . . . than a disaster upon the field of battle.
>
> —U.S. Treasury, *Fourth Liberty Loan: A Handbook for Speakers*, 1918

The assassination of the Archduke Francis Ferdinand at Sarajevo on June 28, 1914, closed the door on the era of comfortable bourgeois optimism. Now the extraordinary advances of the past century were put through their paces in the harsh arena of war. The revolutions in transport and manufacturing allowed men to be carried to the front line and killed with unprecedented efficiency. But it was not only the mechanical arts that had progressed in the nineteenth century. Politics had also undergone profound changes: first, as the world of absolute monarchy had given way to parliamentary government; and then, as the limited, property-based franchise had given way to universal male suffrage. Public finance had changed in tandem with politics. The English system of borrowing, perfectly adapted to parliamentary government by limited franchise, had been successfully modified in France and America to suit the demands of mass democracy. The First World War would reflect these revolutions, too.

The war was not only the first "world" war, fought by nations that, between them, controlled the vast majority of the planet's landmass.* It was also the first "total" war, in which the full resources of the warring economies were deployed, and in which the full psychological commitment of their populations was brought into play. The participation of the popula-

*In fact, it was not definitively the first "world" war. The Napoleonic Wars and the Seven Years' War have both been nominated for that title at various times.

tion in the war effort was the logical corollary of their participation in politics. Warfare was now seen as the struggle between rival peoples. The vast conscript armies of the major combatants, now running into the millions, were indeed whole nations at arms. The war was thus the culmination of the work of the French Revolution, which had first unleashed the militarized power of "the people" onto the shocked gentility of the eighteenth century. Militarily, the Revolution had seemed unstoppable. Financially, it had been undone by its refusal to come to terms with the dictates of the credit markets. The Jacobins had relied on paper money and confiscation; Napoleon, on taxation and conquest. Both had been outspent by Great Britain with its seemingly inexhaustible supply of Consols. Napoleon's achievement had been to synthesize the force of revolutionary nationalism with traditional dynastic imperialism. The full potential of the power of the people, however, would be harnessed only through a synthesis with the bourgeois parliamentarianism of the nation of shopkeepers. It was precisely this reconciliation that the nineteenth century had brought about by means of mass participation in public debt. The First World War, then, was to be a showground not only for the products of the Industrial Revolution and for the forces of popular nationalism, but also for the power of democratic credit-based finance. The three were, in many ways, symbiotically related. The Industrial Revolution permitted a scale of conflict that was not sustainable without the psychological participation of the whole population, and that required the outlay of unprecedented sums of money. In turn, the psychological participation of the people encouraged the expenditure of human, material, and financial resources on an appalling scale. Finally, the powers of credit meant that there would be almost no financial limit to the struggle short of total exhaustion.

The sums borrowed by the major combatants from their citizens during the war were truly enormous. The United States, whose debt was barely over $1 billion in 1916, raised $24 billion in less than two years. Germany and Great Britain each raised around $27 billion. France, Russia, and Italy followed with $18 billion, $8 billion, and $6 billion, respectively.[1] Perhaps even more striking was the small contribution made by taxation. Tax revenues in France, Germany, and Russia actually declined in real terms over the course of the war. War expenditure in all three countries was financed almost exclusively through borrowing. But even in Great Britain and the United States, where taxes were increased sharply, the picture was not so very different. Borrowing accounted for 80% of war spending in Britain and 75% across the Atlantic. To put these figures into perspective, it is worth recalling that the record of Great Britain in the Napoleonic Wars. From 1792 to 1797 Britain financed almost 90% of its war effort out of loans. This policy ended with the near collapse of the credit markets, a run on the Bank of England, and the suspension of convertibility. Thereafter the country was forced to change tack. The remainder of the war was financed rather more prudently—only 50% provided by loans. In this light, it is not hard to see that the participants in the First World War were testing the now universally accepted practice of public borrowing to the limit.

The broad outlines of the financing of the war are shown in the chart, which reduces spending and borrowing patterns to prewar prices so as to avoid the distortions created by wartime inflation. France and Germany both borrowed amounts in excess of 150% of their prewar GNPs; Great Britain and Italy, only a little less. It is easy to see the extremes to which the major European powers pushed their credit, especially when war borrowing had to be added to high preexisting levels of debt, as in France and Russia. Only the United States, starting the war virtually unencumbered, could contemplate its cost with relative equanimity.

Spending, Taxation, and Borrowing, 1914–1918[2]

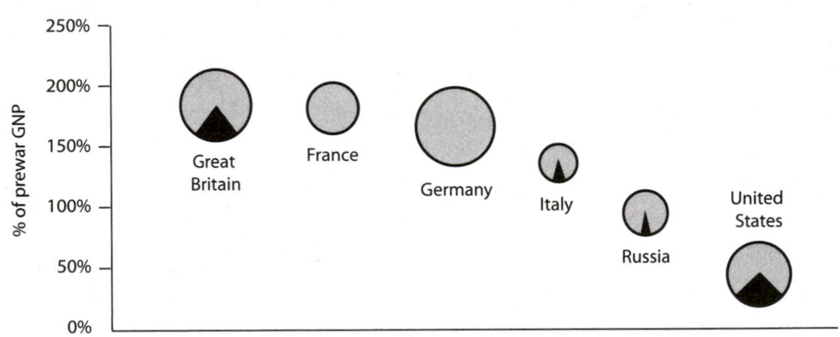

Bubble areas represent total war spending in prewar prices.
Black slices show the portion (if any) covered by taxes.
Grey areas show the amount of wartime borrowing.

The pervasiveness of public borrowing is reflected not only in the crude figures. In previous wars only one side had generally been willing, or able, to tap fully the resources offered by cheap long-term credit. Now everybody had got the message. The patriotic bond drive, first demonstrated in France in the last century, became the centerpiece of wartime financial planning.

Germany, still smarting, perhaps, from the ease with which the French indemnity had been paid in 1871–1872, understood the implications of popular bond drives straightaway. Other countries took a little longer. Until the middle of 1915, Britain appeared to think that it could rely exclusively on the wealthy investors who had financed its past wars, but thereafter the British small saver was courted as assiduously as those on the Continent.

But bond drives were more than just a means of collecting the greatest possible sums for the lowest possible cost. They were central to the psychology of the war effort. Never before had public lending been so unanimously proclaimed as the duty, the sine qua non, of citizenship. "ARE YOU 100% AMERICAN? PROVE IT! BUY U.S. GOVERNMENT BONDS," ordered a poster for the Third Liberty Loan. The Secretary of the Treasury, William McAdoo, went so far as to assert publicly, "A man who can't lend his government $1.25 at the rate of 4% is not entitled to be an American citizen."[3] Lending and fighting were seen as moral equivalents. "FIGHT OR BUY BONDS," "ENLIST OR INVEST," ran typical posters. Other messages were more ghoulish: "YOU WHO ARE NOT CALLED UPON TO DIE—SUBSCRIBE," and "There are only two alternatives. Either give your money or give your blood." Indeed lending was more than just the moral equivalent of fighting; it was part of the battlefront itself:

> The loans were presented as one of the forms of battle. The will to subscribe is for the civilian what the will to conquer is for the soldier. Not to subscribe or to subscribe too little is a desertion similar to flight before the enemy. The success of the loan is a victory to be won, which will depress the enemy not less than the retreat of his troops or the crushing of one of his allies.[4]

The "bond" war operated on two fronts. The oversubscription of a war loan showed that the nation had untapped reserves of money, and equally that it had untapped reserves of fighting spirit. Britain had always prided itself in winning wars because the solidity of its political and financial system ensured it the crucial "last million"—as Lloyd George put it in 1915. Under the new rules of democratic public finance, the "last million" would go to the country with the greatest ability to tap a deep groundswell of popular support through mass bond drives.

When America declared war on Germany in 1917, it was not only soldiers and artillery pieces that were sent into the fray—especially since it was many months before America had any to send. Instead, the two countries employed war loans to lob propaganda missiles at each other across the ocean. A poster for the Seventh German War Loan showed Woodrow

Wilson as a dragon being repulsed by a hail of German coins. The Americans responded in kind in the publicity for the First Liberty Loan:

> The Germans had the impertinence to call their last war loan an "Answer to Wilson." It was well subscribed. What is YOUR answer to Germany?[5]

Again in 1918:

> Ludendorff told the Germans recently that "the eighth war loan must prove our will to power, which is the source of everything." The Fourth Liberty Loan is up to the American people. It must prove our will to power. . . . The failure of a single issue of Government bonds would be worse for America than a disaster upon the field of battle.[6]

Public war loans had thus become an integral part of the struggle between nations. To some, the war appeared as a manifestation of the Darwinian battle for dominance between rival peoples in which, ultimately, the fittest would survive. To others, the level of carnage and the totality of the popular commitment brought to mind the wars of great tribal republics of the ancient world. Years before the postwar settlement became known as the "Carthaginian" peace the conflict produced allusions to the Punic Wars. Some of these specifically brought out the connection between democratic warfare and voluntary public lending. In the spring of 1917 Professor Lanciani of the University of Rome called attention to the voluntary donations of precious metals and jewels by the citizens of Rome during the Second Punic War (donations that were subsequently repaid out of the Carthaginian indemnity). He organized a march to the Forum on the anniversary of the city's foundation so that contemporary Romans could make public offerings to the state in emulation of their ancestors.[7] In America a prizewinning student speech, circulated to support the Fourth Liberty Loan, ran as follows:

> I am known all over the world and am hailed as the right hand of freedom's champions. Many scraps of paper has the Kaiser torn up but I am the scrap of paper that will tear up the Kaiser. I am, as probably you will have guessed, a Liberty Bond.
>
> Possibly you would like to know something about my family. My family tree is as old as time. Before Christ, my ancestors saved civilization when, thru their services, Rome was delivered from the clutches of Carthage.[8]

Perhaps, in their different ways, both the professor and the student were suffering from a surfeit of classical education. But the arrival of modern mass democracy did seem to suggest some striking full turns of the wheel of history. In ancient Athens and Rome it had been accepted that, because taxes were an insult to the dignity of free citizens, wars should be financed as far as possible by voluntary donations. Now it seemed that the same dependence on voluntary contribution by the whole citizen body had become an inherent characteristic of modern democracy. Other wars in modern European (and American) history had been financed almost entirely through borrowing, but none so publicly—it could almost be said, so deliberately—as the First World War.

There was, however, another side to the question. The war may have been, according to one interpretation, the first democratic war. But according to another it was merely the last of the stale battles for preeminence between the decaying dynasties of Europe. In the nineteenth century a rival ideology had grown up alongside democratic nationalism. According to Marxist theory, the nations of Europe were not unified "peoples" at all but were divided into irreconcilable classes. From this perspective, the ruling elites, of which the monarchs were the puppets, were waging an imperialist war merely to expand their spheres of dominion at each other's expense. Why should the working class have anything to do with a venture for which they would provide the cannon fodder? Their allegiance was to the toiling masses of all nations, not to their masters. In the years leading up to the war, the socialist parties of Europe had made their pacifist intentions clear, though when the moment of truth came in 1914 they were unable or unwilling to swim against the tide of patriotic war fever. For some, such as Mussolini, the outbreak of war came as a vision on the road to Damascus. But the majority, while going along with the new mood in public, held quietly to their old beliefs and waited for the moment when the fever would abate. A few maintained a staunch socialist internationalism throughout. As a result, the governments of Europe were always operating with one eye over their shoulders. They never quite knew when the newly enfranchised masses might start to see themselves as comrades rather than citizens. It was regularly rumored, especially in Germany, that socialist and pacifist elements were urging the boycott of war loans as a means of hastening the end of the conflict. It was this, in part, that made the failure of a war loan as alarming as a setback at the war front.

The common thread of war finance by public bond drive belied the claims of the Allied Powers to be waging a war against autocracy (a claim that was, in any case, pretty hollow until after the fall of the czar in February 1917). It may have been true that Wilhelm II enjoyed greater political autonomy than George V, and that after 1916 Germany was governed by generals. But this had little impact on the conduct of public finance where the powers of the Reich were heavily circumscribed. In a world in which wars could be financed only by taking a begging bowl to the general population on a six-monthly basis, it was impossible that an unpopular policy (or government) would long survive. The bond drives of the First World War were, in effect, financial plebiscites.

The battle for subscriptions had characteristic cross-border features. Because the war loans were a great test of the national will, voluntarism ruled the day. Teams of patriotic citizens were formed whose task was to ensure that no one would be left unaware of his or her financial duty. In the United States, regional bankers featured prominently in these organizations. They had the inestimable (if unspoken) advantage of knowing exactly what each local citizen was in a position to contribute. Propaganda films were made and distributed to cinemas. Rallies and other public events were organized, some of which achieved results that were impressive by any standards. A gala performance at Carnegie Hall featuring Enrico Caruso and other leading operatic stars in October 1918 raised no less than $4.8 million (this would translate into around $600 million in today's terms). Religion was brought into play. The Orthodox Church became, in effect, the financial agent of the czarist government. One hundred thousand clergymen delivered sermons in support of the American Victory Loan drive of 1919. In Germany, an old pagan ritual was invoked when subscribers were allowed to hammer iron nails into vast wooden statues of Field Marshal Hindenburg that toured the country in support of the Fourth War Loan. No one was exempt from the relentless demands of patriotic fervor. Even schoolchildren were called upon to contribute their pocket money, and their tiny contributions were used to step up the psychological pressure on their parents:

> Each one of you should ask your father tonight if he has bought a Bond, if he has done his part to feed the hungry little ones of Europe, or supply help so that the Allies can fight on, and to give our boys in the trenches all the guns and ammunition they need. Tell him that you will give him your spending money and everything else you can earn to him to help buy a Bond.[9]

Posters formed perhaps the most constant visual feature of the loan drives. They provide a fascinating study of the aesthetics and preoccupations of the time. Commissioned from a wide variety of artists, they run the gamut from neogothic fantasy to ultramodernism. Russian posters changed character sharply with the fall of the czar. Before 1917 they looked like murals on the walls of an Orthodox church. Under the Kerensky government, they took on the feel of the revolutionary art of the 1920s. Of course, this stream of visual propaganda concerned more than war loans. There were posters calling for volunteers (in those countries where there was no conscription), posters urging increased production or decreased consumption, and posters whose main purpose was to maintain the popular fighting spirit by revealing the enemy in his full beastliness.

The loan drives of the First World War were without doubt successful in terms of popular participation. In Germany, for instance, there were 1.15 million subscribers to the First War Loan, 2.7 million to the Second, 5.28 million to the Fourth, rising to nearly 7 million in the Eighth in April 1918. In early 1917, the Chancellor the Exchequer, Bonar Law, was at pains to compare Great Britain's record of popular participation with that of the enemy, arguing that the figures were "an indication of the spirit of the peoples where the loans are raised." He was pleased to announce that there had been over one million subscribers to his mammoth 5% war loan at the offices of the Bank of England and a further one million subscribers at the Post Office (*The Economist*'s 1911 suggestion of selling government bonds over the counters of the Post Office "like postage stamps" had come all too true). But this did not tell the full story of British public participation in the public debt. The Chancellor added estimates for the uncounted holders of War Savings Certificates and came up with a total number of public debt holders of at least eight million—thus (to his mind) satisfactorily trumping the Hun.[10] In France the highest number of subscriptions to a single war loan was seven million. By the end of the war, there can be no doubt that almost every family in the country had at least a few war bonds in the safe or under the mattress. The record for the largest total number of public creditors was, not surprisingly, held by the United States. The Fourth Liberty Loan of 1918 collected no less than 22.8 million subscriptions, of which 13.5 million were for the smallest $50 denomination.

The political success of war loans was measured in numbers of subscribers. Financially, however, the critical issue was to avoid a dangerous buildup of short-term debt. From the perspective of national solvency, long-term domestic debt ranked immediately after taxes. Thus the oversubscription of war loans meant that the national credit was still sound. This was a more important consideration, in substance, than borrowing at a lower interest rate than one's rivals—however useful the latter might be as a propaganda weapon. Even though rates rose during the war, as was scarcely surprising given the vast sums involved, they remained low by historical standards. The highest rate on long-term debt was paid by Austria at 6.04%; the lowest, by the United States at 4.25% (excepting the even lower rates offered on the earliest American and British war loans). Even allowing for different tax treatments, this was not a very high differential. Interest rates on short-term debts were invariably lower than those on war loans.

PEAK LONG-TERM BORROWING COSTS, 1914–1918[11]

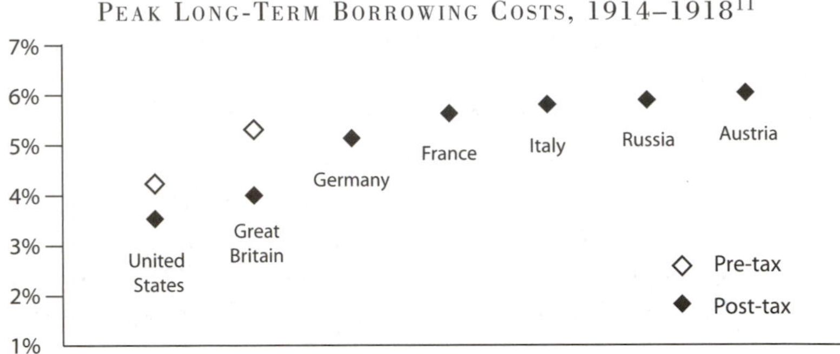

Note: Pretax yields are shown only in countries where government bonds were taxable.

If there was a threat to the wartime solvency of any of the combatants, then, it was not the result of runaway interest costs. A clearer indication of the relative success of the different countries in financing the war is revealed by the next chart:

SOURCES OF WAR SPENDING, 1914–1918[12]

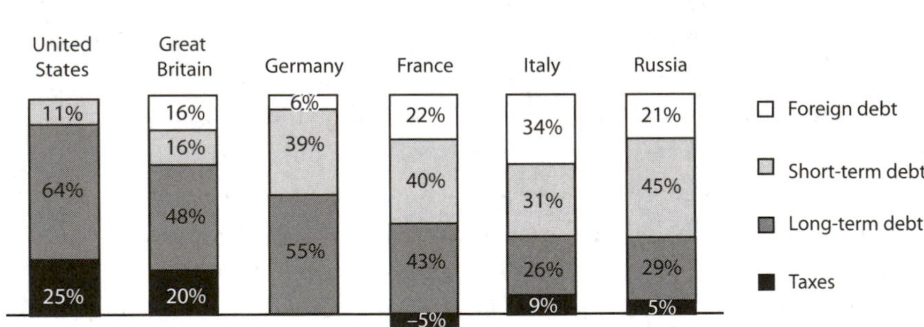

Given the position of financial and economic strength from which it started, not to mention its late entry into the war, it was scarcely surprising that the United States had the best record. Nearly 90% of American war spending was covered by taxes or long-term loans and barely over 10% by short-term debt. The American finances were considerably boosted by the introduction of the income tax in 1914, which supplied the bulk of the additional tax revenues available for war spending. But by far the most important and ubiquitous element in the war effort were the four Liberty Loans (so called because they "were to be used for the purpose of waging war against autocracy," according to Secretary of the Treasury William McAdoo).[13] The repayment terms of these loans varied but ranged from ten to thirty years from date of issue. In 1919 excess short-term debt was mopped up by a five-year Victory Loan sold with the same razzmatazz as its predecessors.

At the other extreme, Italy and Russia managed to cover little more than one-third of spending out of taxes and long-term debt. The relatively low yields at which their bonds had traded in the years before the war concealed the underlying shallowness of their financial markets. It proved impossible to sell adequate amounts of long-term debt to the general public, and both countries depended heavily on inflationary short-term borrowing. In Russia, 75% of the state's short-term debt was bought directly by the central bank. In Italy, the figure was only 36%, but the difference was more of form than of substance, since the Italian banks of issue were generally ready to lend against short-term government obligations held by the private sector. In addition, Italy managed to cover a greater portion of its war costs by interallied loans than any other combatant, significantly reducing the strains on its domestic finances.

The three major European powers—Great Britain, France, and Germany—fell somewhere between these extremes. On the surface, it appears that France performed little better than Italy or Russia. Only 38% of its total war spending was covered by taxes or long-term loans. Indeed, French tax revenues did not even cover its nonwar budget. Moreover, nearly 45% of the French short-term debt was held by the Bank of France. There were several offsetting factors, however, that cast the French performance in somewhat better light. First, a considerable portion of France's industrial heartland was under German control or destroyed by war, with a consequent reduction in national income and tax revenues. Second, France's borrowing requirements were increased by its loans to Belgium, Italy, and Russia. Most important of all, perhaps, France, unlike Italy or Russia, was able to sell a substantial portion of its short-term debt to the general public. At the end of 1914, France started issuing Bons de la Défense Nationale—a low-denomination Treasury bill that could easily be purchased at post offices across the country. The Bons found immediate favor with the public, and by the end of 1918 around 22 billion francs were outstanding, around 50% of all short-term debt. As a method of collecting public savings the Bons were as effective as the long-term war loans; but the failure of the French government to issue a long-term loan until one year after the sale of Bons was a considerable tactical error. Before 1914 French savers had never had the opportunity to invest in any government security except in the venerable form of rentes. By late 1915 they had already become accustomed to the attractions of a government obligation that offered the privilege of early redemption. This made it harder for the government to sell its four wartime rente issues, the Emprunts de la Défense Nationale, than would otherwise have been the case. As it was, France did well to raise 56 billion francs in perpetual debt by the end of 1918.

If the French borrowing program was somewhat haphazard, the German program was a model of Teutonic efficiency. War Loans were floated at regular six-month intervals. Each issue consisted of 5% perpetuals, protected against redemption until 1924 and offered at a small discount. Some of the issues also offered term loans with maturities from five years to as long as fifty years. These loans generally had a 4.5% coupon, but issue discounts and maturity premiums ensured that yields would be comparable to those of the perpetuals. A total of 97.6 billion Reichsmarks was raised during the war, although sinking funds and the use of bonds for tax payments reduced the overall growth of long-term debt to 87.5 billion. In September 1917, Dr. Rudolf Havenstein, the head of the Reichsbank, was gleeful over the (to his mind) superior financial performance of Germany over that of its archrival. Just as Napoleon and Pitt had viewed the war as a test of the financial prowess of the contestants, so Havenstein analyzed the outlook for the Great War:

> It is in the economic sphere that the ultimate decision lies. . . . Our U-boats draw an iron ring around the neck of our most hated and most formidable foe . . . stone by stone they remove the foundation of his world-trading power by destroying his mercantile marine. His last hope rests on our economic and financial vulnerability. That hope also, often and severely shaken already, must be shattered should this Seventh War Loan enjoy the overwhelming success for which I hope, and Great Britain will be forced to recognize the flaming fact that . . . the "last million" with which Lloyd George once boasted he would inevitably win the war, lies in the hand of Germany. . . .
>
> The financial and economic situation of our enemies is far worse than our own. Russia is in complete dissolution; France and Italy are nearing the end of their resources; and Great Britain is more heavily burdened than we are. Only

> one third of the total cost of the war . . . falls on Germany, and two-thirds on our enemies. . . . Reckoned per head of population, Great Britain's expenditure is incomparably higher than Germany's, amounting to 2,500 marks as compared with our own expenditure of 1,400 marks. Moreover the rate of interest in Great Britain has had to be increased from 2.5% and 3 per cent to 5 per cent and more, whereas in Germany the rise has only been from 4 to 5 per cent. . . . Finally, Great Britain has financed the war to the extent of only two-fifths by standing [medium- and long-term] loans; but Germany will, I hope, have obtained with the help of this Seventh Loan, seven-ninths or eight-ninths of her expenditure by means of standing loans.[14]

Havenstein's analysis was only partially convincing. The war was costing Germany far less than its opponents—a confirmation of the military proficiency that had so alarmed Entente statesmen before the war. In 1916–1918 Britain and France together were spending twice as much as Germany and yet only narrowly avoided defeat. It has been calculated that it cost the Allies $36,485 to kill an enemy soldier, as opposed to $11,345 for the Central Powers.[15] Germany had also performed remarkably well in raising long-term loans—far better, in fact, than the naysayers had believed possible before the war. But weaknesses were beginning to show. After the Fourth War Loan, subscriptions no longer kept pace with expenses and the floating debt started to expand. At the time that Havenstein spoke, some 70% of Germany's debt was long-term, not the 80–90% that he claimed. (In Britain, too, the ratio was around 70%, not 40% as he asserted). By the end of the war, 40% of Germany's debt was short-term, and half of this had been advanced directly by the Reichsbank.

But Havenstein was correct that the wartime financial performance of Great Britain was less impressive than its prewar reputation might have suggested. If any country might have been expected to been able to rely on cheap perpetual debt in support of its war effort, it was Great Britain. But in spite of the strength of the country's financial position in 1914, there was one significant impediment to her doing so. More than any other country, it was Britain that had suffered from the seventeen-year bear market in bonds that had started in 1897. In that year Consols had peaked at a price of 113⅞. By July 1914, they had fallen to 75. The prices of U.S. government bonds, although lower than in 1897, had been protected by their scarcity and their role as reserve assets, as well as by their fixed repayment terms. French and German rentes, too, had fallen less than Consols, largely because they had never risen so far in the first place.[16] The bonds of those countries, like those of Russia, Austria, and Italy, whose admission to the ranks of first-class borrowers dated only from the 1890s, had scarcely fallen at all. From 1898 to 1910, an investment in French 3% rentes would have produced a total return (including capital depreciation) of 2.5%, while Imperial German 3%s would have returned 2.05%—not much but at least positive. A similar investment in Consols would have yielded only 0.06%. This was scarcely an attractive record for what had for so long been the world's premier investment security.

As soon as the British government attempted to raise a war loan in 1915, the City made it clear that, after the experience of the past seventeen years, the market had lost its appetite for perpetuals. So sour had the market become, in fact, that not one jot of the British war debt was raised in this way. The first British war issue was made repayable no later than 1928. The government subsequently issued three major war loans. Since the first two of these allowed the conversion of preexisting debt, and since the terms offered improved with each issue, it was scarcely surprising that by the end of the war the long-term debt was concentrated in the two last issues: £2 billion in the 5% War Loan of 1917 and £1.4 billion in National War Bonds of 1917–1918. Both these yielded around 5.35%; but while the former did not have to be redeemed for thirty years, the latter were repayable between 1923 and 1928. By the end of 1918, the long-term debt had increased by £4 billion, of which nearly half was repayable in ten years or less. Although it posed no immediate liquidity problem, this was an uncomfortable situation for a country unaccustomed to the idea of fixed maturity schedules. Britain did compare favorably with the other major European powers in the relatively limited extent of its reliance on short-term borrowing. The £1.4 billion floating debt accumulated by the end of the war was considered a cause of great concern in Whitehall, but short-term borrowing covered a far lower percentage of total war spending than in Germany and France, and the depth of the London money market meant that only one-fifth of this debt was provided by the Bank of England.[17] On the other hand, it needs to be remembered that Britain, like France, had the advantage of the financial backing of the United States during the last eighteen months of the war, whereas Germany had to rely almost exclusively on its own resources. By the end of the war, Great Britain owed $4 billion to the American government.

The increasing reliance on short-term debt does not give a full picture of the inflationary impact of war finance. In order to encourage subscriptions to war loans, the governments took steps to provide their citizens with the necessary liquidity, largely by encouraging banks to finance the purchase of war bonds—the "borrow-to-buy" principle, as it was called in

America. Since borrowing from banks meant that bond purchases were not made out of savings, this process was bound to be inflationary, especially as the banks were allowed to refinance themselves at the central bank. Since the gold standard was one of the first victims of the war, collapsing even before the start of actual fighting, there were no constraints on the creation of money. By 1918, currency in circulation had risen by 91% in Britain, 386% in France, and 600% in Germany. The sharp increase in Germany was the direct consequence of the Reichsbank's purchases of government debt. By a broader definition, money supply had risen by 285% in Germany, 110% in Britain, and 78% in America. For the prospective settlement of war debts, these massive overhangs of purchasing power posed problems at least as great as those faced by Great Britain in 1815 and by the United States in 1865.

THE SETTLEMENT OF ACCOUNTS (PART I)

> "Either an indemnity or a national bankruptcy!" That's the slogan one hears again and again in all Pan-German propaganda. They're afraid of direct taxes, they're afraid of capital levies. That's why Dr. Roesicke and Dr. Stresemann insist that "whatever happens, we must have an indemnity."
>
> —Ewald Vogtherr, Independent Socialist deputy, addressing the Reichstag, 1 March 1918[18]

By the later stages of the war, the question of what was to happen to the enormous debts that were piling up around the continent of Europe was on everybody's mind. The war had been, among other things, an unparalleled experiment in popular participation in national finances. Every citizen of any means whatsoever had become a public creditor by 1918. With the partial exception of France, where rentes had been very widely distributed before the war, the vast majority of these debtholders were new to the experience, sucked in by the massive orchestrations of patriotic propaganda. What is more, in Europe, at any rate, they had significant portions of their patrimonies bound up with the public credit. The implications of this new phenomenon for public policy were vast and as yet unknown.

Of course, the matter would have been simple if the debts had been smaller. But the arrival of peace revealed that public debts had risen to heights of which only Britain had any meaningful prior experience. The only exception was the United States, where debt amounted to only 30% of GNP, scarcely a figure likely to challenge the capacity of what was by now clearly the world's dominant economy. The British debt had risen to over 130% of GNP. This was far less than after the Napoleonic Wars, but in those days Britain had occupied the position now held by America. Figures for postwar national income and production in Germany and France are elusive, but public debt may be tentatively estimated at around 150–160% of GNP in Germany and 170–180% of GNP in France.[19] For both countries this was uncharted territory.

Governments had most certainly not contracted these debts on the assumption that they would not be paid. Yet what was to happen to them now? How, it was asked, had such enormous obligations been allowed to accumulate? There were several well-understood economic justifications for a policy of borrowing. The ancient ideal of the war chest had, of course, been completely discarded (except for some vestigial homage paid to the notion in Germany, where the remains of the French indemnity, squirreled away for this purpose in the fortress of Spandau, sufficed to pay for barely two days of fighting). It was agreed that the resources required for war had to be found in the pockets of the citizens. It was also widely agreed that to attempt to obtain them entirely through taxation was unwise. Not only were taxes a disincentive to the extra work required, but they were also hard to implement and collect quickly.

However, a poll of international economists, had there been such a thing, would most certainly not have approved of the level of borrowing that occurred in the First World War. The borrowing was driven, as had always been true of public debt, by political motives. The issues that now confronted the belligerents can be easily understood by a review of the several millennia of public borrowing covered in this book.

In its most primitive origins, public borrowing was no more than the contribution of resources by a free people to the communal war effort and their subsequent repayment out of the spoils of victory. This process was an expression of the simple freedom of societies not yet converted, by conquest or revolution, into "pharaonic" autocracies, where the war chests of the rulers were fed by taxes on a subservient population. A considerable number of sophistications had subsequently accreted to this archaic tribal custom, but the original essence of the affair had not disappeared even in the early twentieth century. These sophistications had occurred largely as a result of the introduction of fixed interest payments, which in the Middle Ages had turned the primitive contribution-redistribution cycle into a financial system so powerful that it had cleared the way for the triumph of representative government in the eighteenth century. However, the payment of interest, although fundamental to the financial efficacy of the system, had brought with it (as interest always did) the risk of social conflict. Public borrowing may have originally been seen as merely an anticipation of receipts from defeated enemies abroad, but it now became intertwined with class warfare at home. From the moment of its medieval reinvention in Italy, public debt had always been the preferred fiscal policy of the propertied elite. Ideally the debts of the city would be repaid from victory in war; but if not, the interest burden was borne largely by the less politically privileged at home. Not surprisingly, then, the practice of public borrowing had been regularly opposed by those without property. The nineteenth century had witnessed a successful attempt to reconcile mass democracy to "bourgeois" finance by distributing the debt as widely as possible. But at high levels of borrowing, the issue was bound to reappear, the more so because the nineteenth century also saw the rise of an increasingly intense debate about the distribution of resources within society.

A quick consideration of these issues helps to clarify the actions of political leaders in the First World War. Because the war was initially opposed by socialists in most countries (except for Lenin, who saw it as the long-awaited orgy of self-destruction that heralded the end of the capitalist era), the desire of governments to lock the population into the war effort by participation in bond drives is easily understood. So, too, is their desire to forestall a potentially fratricidal internal debate about the distribution of war costs by recovering them as far as possible from external sources. It was not only in Germany that socialists were starting to press for a capital levy on the wealthy to pay down the war debt. Indeed, it seemed that, in their eagerness for internal redistribution of wealth, socialists were almost happy to forgo claims on the outside world.

As the costs of the war were added up, countries and social groups started a grim pirouette as they looked to see how best they could avoid paying them. The traditional way to avoid payment was to hand the bill to a defeated enemy. But as the halcyon days of the Belle Époque were disturbed by the gathering thunderclouds of war, an influential group of writers and thinkers sought to dispel the notion that this was possible. The emblematic work of this movement was Norman Angell's *The Great Illusion*, published in 1909. He argued that the indemnities imposed on France in 1871 had been of no benefit to Germany for the simple reason that national wealth could not be annexed. Somewhat more convincingly, he argued that national economies were now so intertwined that the economic disruption caused by a major war must outweigh any superficial advantage gained by the victor.

It has to be said that his arguments fell on deaf ears. Neither the Germans nor the French were convinced that the 1871 indemnity had been a meaningless piece of international accounting. And they were quite certain that the annexation of Alsace-Lorraine was a clear economic gain for the nascent German Empire, just as it had been a loss for France. In 1915 J. H. Jones debunked most of Angell's arguments in a short book entitled *The Economics of War and Conquest*, in which he concluded that, while an indemnity was unlikely to compensate for the entire cost of the war, it could most certainly help to offset it: "If Britain and her allies prove to be victorious in the present struggle, an indemnity to Belgium, if not also to France, will undoubtedly be provided for in the final settlement."[20] And this was quite apart from the clear gain that would accrue to France from the return of its lost provinces with their coal mines and manufacturing industries.

Neither the French nor the Germans had any doubts about demanding financial and other rewards if they were to prove victorious. The German government was quite explicit that the war debt would be paid by indemnities received from its defeated enemies. In 1915 the finance minister, Karl Helfferich, justified his refusal to raise taxes quite simply with the argument that "the enemy must foot the bill." Such views were held by businessmen as well. The Hamburg banker Max Warburg proposed a 50-billion-mark indemnity in 1914 on the assumption that the war would last no more than four months. Even in 1918 he was still asserting that a 100-billion-mark indemnity would be appropriate in the event of victory. This sum was only 25 billion marks short of the German public debt at the time. Given the old-fashioned annexationist peace treaty forced on Russia at Brest-Litovsk, there is little reason to question the type of terms that would have been imposed on Britain and France had they succumbed.

On the Allied side the position was more complex. The American president, Woodrow Wilson, had made his idealistic opposition to punitive indemnities plain. Still, his stand did not present enormous problems. France sought above all the return of its lost provinces. Moreover, there was no American inhibition against demanding reparation for war damages. Since the war in the West was fought largely on French soil, there was little reason to doubt that the figures involved would reach similar proportions to those attainable under the name of an indemnity. By contrast, Britain, true to the tradition of its earlier wars, had not thought of potential financial rewards, concentrating mostly on the less tangible, but equally fruitful, gains to be made by restricting or eliminating a dangerous commercial competitor and possibly annexing its overseas possessions. As victory loomed in the second half of 1918, however, the idea of covering some of the country's financial costs by claiming reparations started to take root. Only the United States disclaimed any interest in receiving financial or other compensation from its defeated enemies.

Enemies, however, were not the only potential source of funds to offset part of the war debt. There were also friends. Nearly 40 percent of the sums raised by the U.S. government had been reloaned to its allies. Indeed, the connection between the American war debt and advances to the Allies was specifically written into the congressional bills authorizing the Liberty Loans. Great Britain had also played the part of banker to the Allies, and its total advances of £1.74 billion ($8.5 billion) were only slightly lower than those of the United States ($9.5 billion). In practice, however, the British position was significantly diluted because around one-third of her advances were to Russia, and after October 1917, the likelihood of recovering these sums passed from low to infinitessimal. By contrast, the United States was fortunate enough to have almost no claims against Russia and instead to have over $4 billion outstanding from Great Britain, whose credit, although shaken, was still good. Still, there remained an amount of £1.2 billion that Britain could reclaim from countries such as France and Italy, whose credit should, at least in the long term, prove satisfactory. This sum was sufficient to cover the £850 million owed to the United States and still provide a 13% offset to the domestic debt. The calculations worked equally well the other way around. France's obligations to its allies represented 22% of its total debt; Italy's around 37%. If these amounts could be magically transformed into subsidies, their national balance sheets would be significantly improved.

It is with such calculations in mind that the parties approached the gilded halls of Versailles in 1919. The rules of the game were as follows: Germany sought to minimize the sums (now definitively to be labeled "reparations" rather than "indemnities") that were to be imposed on it. Those victorious countries that were nonetheless international debtors (e.g., France and Italy) sought to maximize their receipts from their erstwhile enemy while reducing their payments to their erstwhile allies. Great Britain, which was both international creditor and international debtor, sought to maximize its receipts from Germany, while taking an equivocal position in inter-Allied debt. The United States, which had renounced any interest in receiving reparations, merely insisted on the contractual sanctity of its claims against its allies. Perhaps it is not too cynical to see the two positions as interconnected. Had the United States staked out a claim to reparations, it would only have exposed how minuscule its sacrifices were when compared to those of France, while simultaneously opening up the issue (so dear to French hearts) of redistributing the costs of war equitably among the Allies. Safer, then, to emphasize the distinct, essentially idealistic, nature of the American participation in the war, while taking an equally "principled" stand on the debts of its allies—an issue, after all, where there was far more to be recouped for the American taxpayer.

In practice, the position was considerably more nuanced than this. Germany had almost no interests except the one outlined above. France, however, was not simply the vengeful harridan of conventional historiography (mostly Anglo-Saxon and German). Its main interest was to tame German militarism by whatever combination of methods, and while it expected to obtain compensation for war losses that were greater than those of any other (victorious) country, it was willing to moderate its monetary claims on Germany to the extent that its obligations to its allies were reduced and to the extent that German quiescence could be ensured by other means. Great Britain's calculations were equally complex. In order to receive any significant portion of the reparations pot, it had to expand the claim to include types of damage not originally considered appropriate—such as war pensions. This, after all, was almost the only kind of claim that could be lodged on behalf of its Canadian and Australian allies. The British Empire delegation, therefore, appeared even more intransigent than the French in the initial stages of negotiations. After achieving its objective of including pensions in the list of demands, it could afford to take a more emollient line thereafter. At the same time, while Britain would have liked to be released from its obligations to the United States, its overriding concern about reestablishing its position as the preeminent international financial and commercial center made it wary of upsetting a hard-earned reputation for punctilious settlement of debts. The position of the United States was, perhaps, second only to Germany's in its simplicity. Still, it could not afford to ignore the likelihood that receiving significant sums from such countries as France and Italy was contingent (in practice, if not in theory) on their obtaining adequate reparation payments from Germany. "Adequate" from the American point of view, however, was a sum far lower than those bandied about in the emotional atmosphere of Versailles.

The intricacies of the peace negotiations are beyond the scope of this book. As it turned out, the United States would not even allow the issue of inter-Allied debts to be discussed at Versailles, and the demands on Germany inevitably grew as a result. The initial claims of the victorious powers as presented to the Reparations Commission in 1920 were inflated not only by domestic electoral politics but by the desire to garner as high a portion of the eventual payments as possible. France claimed 218.5 billion francs—a figure higher than her entire public debt in December 1918. Italy was not far behind on a relative basis with a claim of 33 billion lire for damages plus a further 38 billion francs for pensions. British claims amounted to £2.5 billion of which £1.7 billion was for pensions.[21] It was tacitly understood that these claims were exaggerated and would be revised downward, but the eventual sum established by the commission in 1921 of 132 billion gold marks (equivalent to £6.6 billion, or $32.1 billion at pre-war exchange rates) was more than adequate to make significant inroads into the war debts of the victors—and, of course, to constitute a massive addition to the war debts of the losers. If reparations and inter-Allied debts are combined the putative outcome of international war debt settlements looked something like this:

THEORETICAL POST–WORLD WAR I CASH FLOWS[22]
$ billions

	Payments	Receipts	Net Addition to (Reduction of) Domestic War Debt	% of War Debt
Germany	32.0	——	32.0	+119%
Italy	4.1	3.2	0.9	+ 16%
France	6.3	16.6	(10.2)	– 53%
Great Britain	4.6	12.1	(7.5)	– 28%
United States	——	10.8	(10.8)	– 48%

The peace process, therefore, gave rise (in theory at least) to a general westward flow of funds, starting in Germany, passing through Rome, Paris, and London, and ending in Washington. In practice, transfers on the scale shown above were never made. The total of 132 billion marks was largely illusory. It was represented by three series of bonds, of which only the A and B series, totaling 50 billion marks, bore interest and were scheduled for payment in the foreseeable future. The remainder of the claim was documented by deferred C bonds, whose likelihood of eventual payment was such that George Theunis, the Belgian premier, joked that they could safely be left unlocked since no thief would be tempted to steal them. The realizable figure of 50 billion marks was not much greater than the amount proposed by the Germans themselves in 1921 or by Keynes in his legendary attack on the Versailles settlement, *The Economic Consequences of the Peace.* Not only were reparation payments to be stretched out over many decades but subsequent rounds of negotiations further diluted the near-term drain on Germany.

Payments of some sort started almost immediately after the war with the requisitioning of such assets as Germany had on hand—the merchant ships that Britain (and to some extent other countries) took in compensation for those sunk by U-boats, for instance. By the time the reparations bill proper was handed to Germany in 1921, some 4.5 billion gold marks' worth of assets had been taken, of which half were in as-yet-unsold German foreign investments. These sums did little more than cover the postwar costs of occupation and emergency credits for food purchases. Thereafter Germany was required in theory to pay amounts equivalent to 6% per annum on the 50 billion marks of A and B bonds (5% for interest and 1% for the reduction of principal). This target was reached in the first year, but thereafter, and especially with the policy of passive resistance to the Ruhr occupation, payments decreased sharply. In 1924, a new plan of payments was set up under the Dawes Commission, which for the first time took into account Germany's capacity to pay. For the next five years payments averaging 1.6 billion marks per year were made, but of course, this was less than the interest on the A and B bonds, so Germany's total debt on those bonds alone continued to grow. In 1929, a new "definitive" arrangement was drawn up by the Young Commission, which finally abandoned the pretense that the amounts originally claimed were ever going to be collected and established a stream of relatively modest annual payments averaging around 1.8 billion marks over the following fifty-nine years. Under the Young Plan, total payments by Germany over the 1919–1988 period would have been worth even less than the value of 30 billion marks that Keynes had put on the German counterproposal at Versailles.[23] Yet even the Young Plan was destined to last for less than two years before the economic crisis that now engulfed the Western world led to the Hoover moratorium on all war-related debts in 1931. In the final analysis, total payments by Germany over the 1919–1931 period came to 21 billion gold marks, but around 4 billion of those covered occupation and other postwar costs, leaving only 17 billion marks (just over $4 billion) for reparations. This was very far from realizing the expectations of the victors in 1919.

A similar deflation of expectations happened on the other side of the balance sheet: the inter-Allied war debts. Britain was an early convert to the idea of debt reduction, perhaps because it had relatively less to gain from the process than either France or America. In *The Economic Consequences* Keynes had proposed writing off all inter-Allied debts and reducing the reparations bill to 40 billion marks (an idea that provoked much outrage in every quarter except Germany—not least because it subtly managed to reduce French and American putative net receipts by more than Great Britain's). By 1922, opinion in London had moved even further. The government offered to drop all claims of any kind (including reparations) as long as the United States would do the same. When this idea met a glacial reception in Washington, it was modified to a "no net gain" position. In the Balfour Note of July 1922, Britain stated publicly that it would seek no more from its debtors than it was obliged to pay America.

American expectations shifted far more slowly. The Balfour Note, which effectively cast the United States as a Shylock standing in the way of world peace and prosperity, provoked an acid riposte in which the American government restated its position on war debts and pointed out that, unlike Great Britain, the United States had taken no part of the spoils of war—such as Germany's overseas colonies and her merchant marine. The United States clung to its position on the independent validity of its claims against its Allied debts with the same tenacity that France clung to the receipt of reparations. The reality of the situation, however, was that the Allies felt no *moral* obligation to repay their debts to the United States except insofar as they received reparations from Germany. After years of futile exchanges conducted in an atmosphere of barely disguised ill will and mutual incomprehension, the United States made settlements with Britain in 1923, and with its other major debtors in 1925–1926. In practice, these settlements ignored the strict instructions of Congress to respect the terms of the Liberty Loans and to grant no concessions. While lip service was paid to the nominal amount of the debts, the extension of payments over sixty-two years and the acceptance of interest rates much lower than 4.25% significantly reduced the real value of the debts. Britain managed to have its interest cost reduced to 3.3% on the argument that this had been its historically "normal" rate. France and Italy did even better, with 1.6% and 0.4%, respectively—implying debt reductions of as much as 60% and 80%.

These clearly concessionary terms were on based the borrowers' capacity to pay—the same principle, in other words, that was applied to German reparations under the Dawes Plan. The Young Plan of 1929, by establishing a schedule of reparations that terminated in exactly the same year as the American debts, made the de facto connection between the two types of payment even clearer. The Hoover moratorium of 1931 deferred both types of payments equally. In the end, the dogged American adherence to its war claims outlasted even the French adherence to reparations. Reparations were terminated by general consent in 1932, but the inter-Allied war debts ended only with unilateral default in 1933–1934. By that stage, the United States had collected little more than $2 billion on its war debts—an amount considerably less than the interest that would have accrued at 4.25% per annum. When postwar costs and the loss of interest are factored into the calculation, the United States recovered less than 15% of amounts it had loaned its allies, and had therefore managed to offset no more than 6% of its domestic war debt.

Moreover, it is arguable that payments made before the whole charade ground to a halt in the 1930s were based on pure illusion, since the real flow of funds was not westward, as required in theory, but eastward. One historian has gone so far as to write of "American reparations to Germany" to describe the process.[24] The way this worked was as follows.

When reparation payments officially started in 1921, the Weimar government nominally adhered to a policy of reluctant "fulfillment" of Allied demands but at the same time operated in a manner designed to show that fulfillment was practically impossible. The technique was quite simple. The government made only limited efforts to raise taxes and thus ran a massive deficit, which it covered by printing money. The mark therefore depreciated wildly on the exchanges, and the foreign exchange required to pay reparations was provided by foreign speculators banking on a return to monetary and fiscal policies more in line with Germany's prewar economic standing. The depreciation of the mark had the ancillary advantage of flooding Allied markets with cheap German goods, and thereby putting additional pressure on the Allied governments to reduce their demands.

This strategy was remarkably successful in the short term. In February 1922, Max Warburg could note with satisfaction the progress in softening international opinion. "If you consider that three years ago Cunliffe [the British banker and government adviser] demanded 28 billion gold marks a year; two years ago Klotz [the French Minister of Finance] demanded 18 billion marks; one year ago the Reparations Commission wanted around 8 billion gold marks; and the London Ultimatum demanded . . . around 4 billion, then the trend is clear. We are not so far removed from [achieving] what can ultimately be fulfilled, namely no cash payments."[25] It has been calculated that the losses of foreign speculators from 1919 to 1923 amounted to 15 billion gold marks, while reparations transferred abroad (including those in kind) amounted to 10 billion marks. In the words of the German historian Karl-Ludwig Holtfrerich, "Taking into account only the seven or eight billion gold marks . . . which Germany is estimated to have gained from foreign deposits in German banks between the end of the war and 1923, we have a sum which even in nominal terms exceeded the $1.5 billion received by West Germany after the Second World War under the Marshall Plan."[26] The role of currency depreciation in financing reparations on the cheap was not lost on contemporaries either. In August 1922, Keynes visited Hamburg and tacitly encouraged the inflationary spiral by his public appraisal of its positive side effects:

> One must not lose sight of the other side of the balance sheet. . . . The burden of internal debt is wiped off. The whole of Germany's payments to the Allies so far . . . have been entirely discharged by the losses of foreign speculators. I do not believe that Germany has paid a penny for these items out of her own resources. The foreign speculators have paid the whole of these liabilities and more too.[27]

The first, inflationary phase of reparations ended with French occupation of the Ruhr and the final disintegration of the mark in 1923. In the years of the Dawes and Young Plans, foreign exchange was provided by an influx of foreign loans and direct investment amounting to nearly 30 billion marks. Again, this sum handsomely exceeded the 11 billion marks paid in reparations. In the wake of the general German default in 1932–1933, these investments, too, had to be written off. The overall balance for the period from 1919 to 1932, therefore, was around 45 billion marks lost by foreign investors against 21 billion marks paid by Germany, of which little more than 10 billion marks filtered back to the U.S. Treasury. Whoever paid for such reparation as was made after World War I, then, it was not Germany.

It was clear, in the end, that whatever the initial hopes of the victors, the settlement of the huge debts of war would have to be decided by domestic, not foreign, politics. Class warfare could not, it seemed, be avoided after all. The question, then, was: Were the public creditors now so numerous as to ensure the payment of their war bonds even in an age of mass democracy? Not surprisingly the question had different answers in different countries.

At one extreme there was the United States, whose postwar public debt represented no more than 30% of GNP—less, proportionately, than after the Civil War. There was no reason to suppose that debt on this scale would overstrain the social consensus. In 1919 the economist Harvey Fisk wrote a short book for popular consumption entitled *Our Public Debt*, in which he confidently predicted a bright outlook for the new generation of citizen bondholders:

> Those who have bought bonds from patriotic motives will unquestionably be rewarded for doing so in hard dollars and cents profits, should they wish to realize upon their bonds prior to maturity. The present market return of nearly five percent from an investment in United States Liberty Bonds will fade away as did the big returns from similar investments after the Civil War. . . . The same relative enhancement in market value and of rapid debt reduction happened following the funding of the Revolutionary Debt, after the War of 1812 and after the Mexican War.
>
> It will not be many years before the United States will again be out of debt and in the interval the fortunate holders of the country's bonds will reap a bountiful harvest. This time, it is a pleasure to know that those to be benefitted will be the people at large, for there is scarcely a family today which does not own at least one Liberty Bond.[28]

The situation was not quite so simple as Fisk described. The country was faced with a monetary overhang as severe as in 1865. The armistice was followed by an unhealthy economic boom supported by this excess liquidity. By early 1920, prices were 30% above 1918 levels. The Federal Reserve was faced with an awkward choice: raise interest rates to stop the inflation at the cost of forcing down the market price of Liberty Bonds; or keep a policy of easy money so as to support the bonds' nominal price at the cost of further eroding their real value.* After much soul-searching, the first path was chosen. The result was a rapid collapse of prices and a severe but short-lived recession. The Fed found itself attacked on all sides: by those who felt that it had exacerbated the problem by waiting too long before taking action; by those who were unhappy with the (temporary) fall in bond prices; and by all the natural heirs to the Jacksonian tradition. The president of the American Cotton Association accused the Fed of acting like the Bank of the United States and forecast a return of Jackson's bank war. Benjamin Strong, the governor of the New York Reserve Bank, was forced to claim in front of a congressional committee that the deflation had occurred through natural causes quite independently of the actions of the bank. Still, the policy held, and Fisk's rosy forecast for the holders of Liberty Bonds came true. By comparison with the aftermath of the Civil War,

*One of the minor, but recurring, mysteries of investment psychology is the greater importance attached to nominal, as compared to real, value. The 1919–1920 inflation was aggravated by the concern of the government about avoiding depreciation of Liberty Bonds in nominal terms, even though this meant a far greater depreciation in real terms. The same problem ocurred after the Second World War.

the post–First World War restoration of monetary order was far more rapid and was achieved with far less public debate. No one dared to suggest, as they had in 1868, that the country's war debt should be repaid in anything but gold coin or its equivalent. This in itself was a tribute to the success of the Liberty Bond drives, "the most magnificent economic achievement of any people," as Robert Leffingwell, the wartime Assistant Secretary of the Treasury, proudly proclaimed in 1922.[29]

If America was at one end of the spectrum, it is not hard to see why Germany was to be found at the other. Domestic public debt was probably around 160% of GNP by the end of the war. Reparations (taken, for the sake of argument, as 50 billion gold marks) brought the country's total debt to over 300% of GNP. It is true that Great Britain had had a debt burden not so much smaller than this at the end of the Napoleonic Wars; but the Napoleonic debt was an entirely internal affair. Exactly what the outcome of the German domestic settlement would have been in the absence of reparations is impossible to say with certainty. But the combination of the massive wartime buildup of liquidity and the postwar threat of communism makes it implausible that the patriotic holders of the nine War Loans would have seen their bonds repaid except in depreciated money. The addition of reparations to the postwar matrix sealed their fate. The inflation of 1919–1921, followed by the hyperinflation of 1921–1923, reduced the value of all domestic financial claims to zero.

Germans excused the hyperinflation as the inevitable consequence of the need to avoid unemployment that could have handed the country to the communists, combined with the strain of attempting to fulfill impossible reparation demands. The French characterized the process as a *faillité frauduleuse*, a phony bankruptcy designed by the Germans to evade reparations by pretending that the taxes required to pay for them were beyond the country's means. One can safely report that both lines of argument are alive and well to this day. Either way, the German public creditors, however numerous, were simply not powerful enough to compete with the combination of forces that preferred deficits and inflation to the taxes that would have been required to satisfy the demands of debt service. After the monetary reform of 1924 confirmed the totality of the bondholders' loss, a battle was carried on in the Reichstag and the Supreme Court for at least a partial revaluation of the long-term debt. To little avail: bondholders received only valueless deferred-interest debentures nominally representing 2.5% of their original claims. Only those who had held on grimly to their war loans throughout the whole period were treated a little better, being offered a further 12.5% of their claims over thirty years with interest at 4.5%.[30] In this way, Germany's domestic debt, which had reached 179 billion marks at the end of the war, was reduced to 6.8 billion marks in 1925. At this level it represented no more than 10% of GNP.

The fate of the French war debt (to which there had to be added a bill for reconstruction higher than in any other country) was subject to psychological forces more complex and contradictory than those of any other major power. A well-informed American observer eloquently described the unraveling of the web of French hopes and fears:

> The Frenchman, in his capacity as a taxpayer, contributed nothing toward the costs of the war. . . . It was in his capacity as a bondholder that he made his financial contribution. . . . The collapse of Germany found his pockets full of *Bons de la Défense Nationale.* These, he felt, perhaps foolishly, were infinitely to be preferred to tax receipts. . . .
>
> The financial implications of victory had been impressed upon the French at the close of the Franco-Prussian War. Now the boot was on the other foot. Germany was defeated and Germany would have to pay. With victory, the financial problem had become Germany's problem. To France remained only the bother of making out the bill. . . .
>
> However, as time went on, it began to be whispered that Germany either could not or would not pay, at least in anything approaching the proportions called for by the bill. To the Frenchman with his pockets full of *Bons de la Défense Nationale,* such a whisper brought terror. This was because he realized that if Germany did not pay the bill, his *bons* would be transformed automatically into something closely resembling worthless tax receipts. . . . Thus to commit financial hara-kiri was certainly not his conception of the rôle of the conqueror.[31]

In this way, the fate of the public creditors of France became linked to the fate of those of Germany. At the end of the war the French Minister of Finance, Louis-Lucien Klotz, outlined a fiscal policy that was to remain an idée fixe of French politics for most of the following decade:

> Since the armistice the question of balancing the budget has assumed a new character. My essential duty as Finance Minister is simply to draw up the list of items which the enemy must be asked to restore and make good. That is my sacred duty. . . . If, after that, it appears that new taxes are unavoidable, if it still appears that the French people, who did not provoke the war, have still to tax themselves, either directly or indirectly, I will take the necessary steps.[32]

There was, then, no question of acting to balance the budget *before* the collection of reparations. Since the work of restoration could not wait, a special "recoverable budget" was created whose deficits would be covered once Germany started to fulfill its obligations. This device maintained the satisfying illusion that the underlying fiscal situation was sound. Once the idea was firmly in place, it became hard to dislodge when reparations failed to materialize in the amounts anticipated. To admit the need to balance the budget would be to admit that the country no longer expected to receive reparations. The whole period from 1919 to 1923 can thus be seen as one in which France and Germany indulged in a competition to see who could run the most convincing deficit.

For a few years the French participated in the fantasy of the "recoverable budget" and continued to buy the requisite quantities of Bons de la Défense Nationale. But the disappointing results of reparations collections from 1921 to 1924 led to a growing awareness that France would be lucky if it covered the costs of reconstruction and the Allied debts.* This would leave little or nothing to offset the debts contracted in the war. As elsewhere, the fate of the war debt would have to be resolved domestically. The resolution of the divisive internal debate that followed came only in 1926, after a massive credit and foreign exchange crisis led to the fall of the left-wing Cartel des Gauches and the return to power of the conservative warhorse Poincaré, who finally balanced the budget and "saved the franc." By this stage, however, the franc was worth no more than 20% of its prewar level, and it was inconceivable that, whatever the vain hopes of the rentiers, the domestic war loans would be repaid in anything except highly devalued currency.

Superficially it might seem that the French public creditors fared only marginally better than their German counterparts; but this would be inaccurate. The interest receipts of German bondholders were paid in currency that became entirely worthless in 1923, whereas French bondholders were able to reinvest their interest in further government obligations (indeed, the colossal postwar deficits made it essential that they do so) that retained a good portion of their value after the stabilization of 1926. In real terms the public creditors may be said to have been left with around 33% of their long-term war loans in 1926, compared to (at best) 10% in Germany.[33] The contrast is even more extreme for the holders of other government obliga-

*In the final analysis the German reparations did not even come close to covering the costs of reconstruction. These were calculated at 85.6 billion francs by 1926—equivalent to $6.6 billion. Total receipts from reparations were little more than $2 billion over the whole period to 1931. This calculation does not include the additional 44.5-billion-franc cost of war pensions, which the French also placed in the "recoverable" budget.

tions. The short-term war debt and all the postwar debts of the Weimar Republic were entirely wiped out in 1923. By contrast, the French postwar reconstruction debt had lost perhaps 30% of its real value in 1927.

In the first few years after the war, the inroads made by inflation into the French war debt had been more than offset by postwar borrowing. Domestic debt had grown from around 140–150% of GNP in 1918 to over 200% in 1921–1922.[34] Thereafter, renewed inflation reduced it to a more sustainable proportion of the national economy. In one of his more astute predictions, Keynes forecast that "the level of the franc exchange will continue to fall until the commodity value of the francs due to the *rentiers* has fallen to a proportion of the national income which accords with the habits and mentality of the country." He said this in 1923.[35] As it turned out, by 1927 the French domestic public debt was back to around 100% of GNP. This was the same level at which it had been stable in the late nineteenth century.

A rather different set of forces were in play across the Channel. The postwar financial situation, although scarcely comforting, was far better than in France. The British national debt had grown from a smaller prewar base, and taxes had played a greater part in war finance. The physical damage of war had been largely confined to shipping, and a portion of this was made up by confiscating the German merchant marine. It was felt by many that the greatest wartime injury to the country's prosperity had been the loss of international commercial and financial primacy to the United States.

The reparations illusion therefore lasted only briefly in Britain. The 1918 election was fought at an unparalleled level of demagoguery, as the forces of the conservative press barons sought to channel the passions of the newly enlarged electorate away from the socialist siren song of a capital levy into the safer slogan "Germany must pay." By 1920–1921, however, the appeal of the slogan had waned. Britain had less to gain from the postwar settlement than France or the United States and had done somewhat better than most in the immediate postwar asset grab. But more crucial than either of these calculations was the feeling that the country's interests were better served by a return to economic normality than by a vain chase after chimeras. Only in this way could the country seek to restore the bases of its prewar prosperity.

The first logical step in this process was to bring the budget deficit under control. In 1920–1921 a budget surplus amounting to a remarkable £238 million was run up—almost 5% of GNP. The second, equally logical, step was to seek a reduction of the tangle of postwar debts that was inhibiting world trade, even to the extent of a unilateral write-off of all Britain's war-related claims. Although this proposal had much support in the cabinet, it was abandoned in favor of the ill-fated compromise of the Balfour Note on the grounds that it was too much for a heavily taxed electorate to digest. The capstone of British policy, however, was the restoration of the historic link between sterling and gold that had been broken by the strain of war finance. Only in this way, it was felt, would it be possible for London to resume its place as the world's financial center. It was understood that a return to the old gold parity would inevitably involve the country in a painful deflation. The history of the Napoleonic Wars and their aftermath had not, after all, been forgotten. Unlike France and Germany, which believed that their postwar interests lay with a display of financial prostration, Britain acted on the conviction that its interests were best served by a demonstration of financial strength.

The British postwar political debate was deeply colored by this set of beliefs. Socialists in Britain, as elsewhere in Europe, favored a progressive capital levy as the most equitable method of distributing the costs of war.* But unlike many of their continental counterparts, they were not in favor of inflating the war debt away. This streak of financial conservatism has been attributed partly to the Methodist background of many of the movement's leaders, with its equation of financial laxity with moral degeneracy. But it was also true that in no other country were the canons of bourgeois public finance so closely bound up with national self-image. In terms of industrial unrest, the postwar political struggle was just as intense in Britain as elsewhere in Europe; but the common acceptance of the dictates of financial probity meant that there was never a serious threat to the interests of the public creditors. Precisely because wartime inflation had been more severe than in the United States, the deflation that took place in Britain after 1920 had to be deeper and more prolonged if the old exchange rate was to be restored. Popular discontent with unemployment that refused to sink below two million handed the election to the Labour Party in 1923. But the new Chancellor, Phillip Snowden, turned out to be as avid a deflationist as his

*In theory there was nothing inherently socialist about a capital levy. The levy would reduce people's apparent wealth, but it would also reduce the tax burden. If the taxes reduced were those that fell on the wealthy (i.e., the progressive income tax, the surtax on "unearned" income, and the estate duty), then there was little implicit redistribution in the process. This, however, was not what socialists had in mind, and everybody knew it. A frequent objection to the idea of a levy was the disruption of market values caused by the simultaneous sale of vast amounts of private property. This opened up a second line of attack, since the state might agree to accept assets in lieu of cash and thus effect a backdoor nationalization of wealth.

predecessor; and his tenure in office was instrumental in paving the way for the definitive return to the gold standard in 1925.

Surely Karl Marx would have choked with disbelief at the paltry results of handing the reins of power to the British working class. In Russia, however, the advent of the "dictatorship of the proletariat" produced financial results more in line with socialist principles. One of Lenin's first acts in 1917 was immediate and total repudiation of all public debt, both domestic and foreign. Only holdings under 10,000 rubles were exempt, and soon even this small concession to the petty bourgeoisie was rendered meaningless by the deliberate depreciation of the currency. These policies were not merely expedients of financial desperation; they were revolutionary acts designed to destroy the capitalist system. Since, by the time of the Revolution, the public debt was around 33 billion rubles, equivalent at prewar prices to around $17 billion, this was an event without historical precedent both in scale and in deliberation. The Bolsheviks went far further than the Jacobins in their clear-sighted understanding of the workings of paper money inflation. Indeed, they were the first (and only) regime to list the proceeds as a tax pure and simple, without any of the self-exculpatory rhetoric that was to be heard in Paris in the 1790s. In 1920, a leading communist thinker waxed positively lyrical on the subject in the introduction to a work on revolutionary finance:

> I would like to dedicate this imperfect work of mine to the one who, by the perfection of his own work and by its unbounded abundance, gave me the impulse to write these pages. I refer to the printing press of the People's Commissariat of Finance. . . . To be sure, its days are numbered now, but it has accomplished three-quarters of its task. In the archives of the great proletarian revolution, alongside the modern guns, rifles, and machine guns which mowed down the enemies of the proletariat, an honorary place will be occupied by that machine gun of the People's Commissariat of Finance which attacked the bourgeois regime in its rear—its monetary system—by converting the bourgeois economic law of monetary circulation into a means of destruction of that same regime, and into a source of financing the revolution.[36]

The Soviet inflation was one of the main sources for Keynes's *A Tract on Monetary Reform*, published in 1923. He noted that the Bolsheviks had recorded the proceeds of the inflation tax as falling steadily from 525 million gold rubles in 1918 to 58 million in 1922. In Keynes's analysis this fall reflected the ability of the population to learn how to avoid the tax by minimizing its use of money. In Russia, however, the progressive return to barter did not upset the more radical elements in the Communist Party. Instead, it was celebrated as the "naturalization of economic relations." In the communist paradise that was waiting to be built, there should, after all, be no need for money.

In spite of the high drama of events in Russia, the impunity with which the Bolsheviks were able to repudiate the czarist debt was not the most significant blow to the old certainties in the postwar years. Nowhere, except possibly in the United States, could it be said that the wartime reliance on borrowing from the general population had proved a success. It had not been possible to hand the bill for the war to defeated enemies, or even to one's friends. Instead, the bill had had to be presented to the electorate; and however widely the war loans had been distributed among the population, it became clear that class conflict would not be avoided in the final settlement. On the continent of Europe, the outcome had involved all the belligerents in a loss of hard-won credit standing. Their war debts, if not repudiated, had been largely inflated away. Only in England had there been a determined effort to conform to the old rules. And yet, paradoxically, it turned out that the British attempt to restore its prosperity by a display of financial strength had been counterproductive. When the accounts were added up, it appeared that the French refusal to put its house in order, so disdained by all believers in financial probity, had been the more successful strategy. In 1928 the French real GNP was some 25% higher than in 1914, in spite of falling during the war. By contrast, the British real GNP, which had actually risen during the war, was barely at prewar levels in 1928, after falling 20% in the recession of 1920–1922.

If the events of the 1920s were bad enough, the 1930s were worse. In September 1931, after a decade of relentlessly high unemployment, Britain finally gave up the unequal struggle to stay on the gold standard and let sterling float again. This time, however, the act was far more significant than in 1919. It represented a watershed in the history of the country. For the past one thousand years (with the sole exception of the decade 1543–1553), sterling had been a strong and stable currency—the strongest in Europe. The people generally approved of this state of affairs and could therefore be relied upon to support the sometimes difficult measures necessary to maintain it. Now, it seemed, all had changed. The idea of a strong currency was discredited. In the following decades, the political consensus would always seem to favor the easy path of devaluation. In August 1931, the Labour government had resigned en masse rather than face the national humiliation of abandoning the old gold parity. Now, it seemed, they need not have bothered.

The British desertion of gold was followed the next year by the termination of all war-debt payments, by agreement or otherwise. That Britain and

France could, in the end, default on their written obligations with impunity did little to support the old concepts of public credit. The end of reparations came too late to save the Weimar Republic. If the cost of financial rectitude in Great Britain had been a decade of economic hardship, in Germany it was something far worse. The rise of Adolf Hitler was the product of many postwar traumas, not least the destruction of middle-class savings in the early 1920s. But the straw that broke the camel's back was the refusal by the Brüning government to undertake any reflationary measures to counteract the global depression that started in 1930.

Only in the United States had it so far been possible to repay the war debt in real terms without provoking social discontent. The wounds of the postwar deflation were soon forgotten in the economic wonderland of the 1920s. By early 1929, a succession of budget surpluses had reduced the debt to $17 billion, a figure that represented no more than 16% of a rapidly growing GNP. In the wake of that fateful year, however, American views on the subject of public debt changed. Over the following three years, a 30% reduction of economic activity in real terms was accentuated by falling prices. The public debt had suddenly become 50% of a shrunken GNP—higher than at the end of the war. In the following year, the total public debt, including state and local borrowing, rose above 100% of GNP for the first time in American history.

When President Franklin Roosevelt took office in 1933, one of his declared aims was to raise prices to their old levels. He decided that the best way was to devalue the dollar against gold (in spite of advice from the Federal Reserve that this policy would have little effect on domestic prices). However, a policy of devaluation ran up against the stone wall of the "gold clause" that required the payment of all public debts (and many private debts) in gold coin of a fixed weight. This clause had become standard practice as a result of the monetary "civil war" of the 1860s, but its strict application in the 1930s, it seemed to the Democrats, would hand unjustified windfall profits to bondholders.* In such circumstances it was not surprising that the old rhetoric started to reappear. No longer were the public

*The hole in the argument of the Democrats was that, if prices had risen as predicted, the debt burden would have remained unchanged in real terms, even with the retention of the gold clause. It was precisely because of the failure (as predicted by Marriner Eccles of the Federal Reserve) of the devaluation to make any significant impact on prices that the abolition of the gold clause could be said to be fair. In the opinion of many economists, the devaluation actually prolonged the Great Depression by so far undervaluing the dollar in international terms that the growing tendency to protectionism was increased, and world trade further eroded.

creditors seen as the people as a whole, whose patriotic contributions had financed victory; rather, they once again appeared as a class of "aristocratic" parasites whose pretensions must be kept in check. Undaunted by legal niceties, Congress passed an act in June nullifying the gold clause. Defending the legality of the act, the U.S. Attorney General warned that, if it was overturned by the Supreme Court, the decision "would create a privileged class, which in character, in immunity in power, has hitherto been unparalleled in the history of the human race."[37] Such language had not been heard from a high U.S. official since the days of Andrew Johnson. The Supreme Court waved aside the Attorney General's rhetoric but supported the government on the grounds that its constitutional right to regulate the value of money took precedence over its constitutional obligation to respect private property rights. But this did not mean that there had been no default, merely that the Constitution, as now interpreted, allowed the government to default under certain circumstances. The advocates of the bondholders desolately predicted financial mayhem.

As it turned out, however, their doom-laden jeremiads were stillborn. The near-complete failure of the 41% devaluation of the dollar to reflate the economy meant that the bull market in government bonds continued unabated. Yields on long-term government securities fell from 3.6% in 1929 to just under 2% in 1941. The same pattern occurred across the Atlantic. After a decade in which the yield on British war loans had stubbornly refused to fall below 5%, the government was finally able to return to its customary technique of debt conversion in the 1930s. In 1932 the bulk of the outstanding war debt was consolidated into a 3.5% perpetual annuity. By 1935 the venerable 2.5% Consols were moving to within sight of par. So persistent was the fall in interest rates throughout the decade that some commentators (especially those on the left) started to talk of the "euthanasia of the rentier."

These blows to the traditional status of public credit were lent academic respectability by a new generation of economists, led by John Maynard Keynes. It was he, after all, who had listed the elimination of the German public debt as a *positive* side effect of hyperinflation in 1922, and who waxed lyrical about the euthanasia of the rentier in 1936. In Keynes's view, "the fact that in time of war it is easier for the State to borrow rather than tax, [cannot] be allowed permanently to enslave the taxpayer to the bondholder."[38] Although Keynes's preferred solution to excessive public debt was a capital levy, inflation was an acceptable second best. This would have been one thing if Keynes had set himself against public borrowing in the first place. But when questioned in 1925 about the advisability of paying down the British war debt, he rejected the idea:

> I think the argument for extinguishing the National Debt is partly an aesthetic argument, that it looks nice to have a clean balance-sheet, and I think it is partly from a false analogy from private account keeping: an individual likes to be out of debt. But for the nation as a whole it is merely a book-keeping transaction.[39]

The thrust of the Keynesian argument was to undermine the moral aspect of the budgetary debate, which had for so long equated deficits with profligacy. Now public borrowing was referred to, euphemistically, as "the Treasury's net contribution to purchasing power." In Keynes's view, public borrowing had become a necessary part of government macroeconomic control, required to replace the discredited workings of the "invisible hand":

> I bring in the State; I abandon *laissez-faire*—not enthusiastically, not from contempt of that good old doctrine, but because, whether we like it or not, the conditions for its success have disappeared.[40]

In 1936, the new creed received definitive intellectual underpinning in *The General Theory of Employment, Interest and Money.* Here Keynes redefined the purpose of the state budget. In the nineteenth century, when it was deemed sufficient for the state to protect the realm and maintain law and order, the budget was not considered of particular economic significance. Now, since the free market had proved itself unable to balance the macroeconomic equation of production, consumption, savings, and investment in a manner that would ensure full employment, it was left to the state to do so by adjustments to its pattern of taxing and spending, as well as by direct control of the rate of interest. Keynes was not an advocate of the idea of complete state planning. His libertarian (and elitist) instincts put limits on how far he was prepared to go down the road toward socialism. But his economic theories merged seamlessly with more extreme theories of state control.

Keynes's recurring theme throughout the 1930s was that full employment could be maintained only by unabashed deficit spending. At the time, it has to be said, his advice fell on deaf ears. Britain ran a budget surplus for every year between 1921 and 1939, with the exception of 1934, when balance was missed by a small margin. Across the Atlantic it appeared that the new gospel was more warmly received. The U.S. budget was in deficit by significant amounts in every year from 1931 to 1941, and the public debt rose by $27 billion. But this result does not appear to have come from any revolution in theory, since the administration continued to advocate the goal of budgetary balance, being forced to fall short of its ideal by sheer weight of circumstances. Curiously, it was only in Nazi Germany that Keynesian economics were fully applied in the 1930s (although not by that name). And it was in the monumental struggle to defeat Nazi Germany that they were to be proved elsewhere.

TOTAL WAR (PART II)

> The financial conduct of the war in all belligerent countries has given us new insight into the operation of modern economies. Much more clearly than during the last war do we realize today that nowhere is the war effort limited by financial resources. The proverbial saying that money is the sinews of war has lost much of its significance. —Otto Nathan, *Nazi War Finance*, 1944[41]

The "war to end all wars" turned out to be only the first round in a great thirty-year struggle to decide if Germany was to achieve hegemony in Europe. The second round started in 1939. Once again, the nations took up their arms. This time the rhetoric of popular mobilization was amplified by the rise of a new ideology that declared war to be the supreme test of national character. "War alone brings up to its highest tension all human energy and puts the stamp of nobility upon the peoples who have the courage to meet it,"[42] as Mussolini proclaimed enthusiastically. By now the participants were well prepared for the economic and psychological rules of "total war." The military battlefront was mirrored by the "home front," where the civilian population participated in the great national struggle. Public bond drives were one of the main features of this second front. They constituted not only the principal method of war finance, but also a parade ground for popular commitment to the war effort. It could fairly be assumed, then, that the subscription lists of a new wave of patriotic war loans would soon be opened.

Yet matters were not quite so straightforward. Much had changed since 1914. For one thing, Russia was now under a regime whose response to the debts of the First World War had been to repudiate them totally in the name of the people. The communist economic system was so foreign to anything known in the West that it was safe to assume that Russia would follow a different path in war finance, too. In Germany, a rival ideology reigned, which had so far successfully managed to flout most of the conventions of bourgeois finance. It, too, refused to play the game of war finance by the old rules. Only in the United States and Great Britain (and in the Commonwealth countries) was there some sense of déjà vu about the experience of total war. These countries had emerged victorious from the first war. Their form of government was unchanged; and they had managed to survive the interwar years with their credit (more or less) intact. It was here that popular war loans came into their own again.

The bond drives of the Second World War used all the same tools of persuasion as the first. The posters proclaimed the need to liberate the world from the forces of barbarism. "BONDS vs. BONDAGE—BUY FOR VICTORY," read a Canadian poster featuring an SS officer driving slave laborers with a whip. As before, vast corps of volunteers distributed leaflets, knocked on doors, and made speeches at local rallies. The number of volunteers reached five million in America (compared to the twenty-five hundred who had sold bonds for Jay Cooke in the Civil War—a sales force that had provoked astonishment at the time). The roll call of volunteers seemed to embrace the whole panoply of popular culture: Humphrey Bogart, Cary Grant, Judy Garland, Bing Crosby, Frank Sinatra, and Duke Ellington—not to mention Bugs Bunny and Donald Duck.[43] A new medium of delivery was introduced with the radio, but the message was the same. More than ever before, the selling of bonds played on feelings of patriotic self-sacrifice rather than those of rational self-interest. In a postwar study of bond drive psychology, Robert Merton coined the apt phrase "guilt-edged" bonds:

> The act of buying a bond is redefined. It is imbued with pathos. It celebrates self-sacrifice. Removed from the plain and unadorned context of transactions in the market-place, the bond purchase is sanctified as a sacrificial rite.[44]

It was sometimes thought that men, especially businessmen, were less susceptible to sentiment than their wives. The CBS bond drive presenter Kate Smith had words for her male listeners:

> It's been said that listeners who pride themselves on being rational don't phone in pledges for bonds because they feel such a purchase is the result of emotional pressure. . . . Bond-buying is a careful investment decision, not to be undertaken at the sound of a voice, at the stories of atrocities committed on American boys who are prisoners of the Japanese, Americans boys lying in hospitals, wounded and maimed. That's emotionalism. . . .
>
> That's what they say, and gentlemen, I tell you now, I . . . DON'T . . . BELIEVE . . . IT! I say THEY LIE, these people who think our American

> businessmen don't like emotionalism, don't harbor sentiment in their hearts. . . .
>
> How about you, Mr. America? Are you going to count the cost, and add up careful investments, and do planned bookkeeping when our kids overseas have some accounts of their own to balance—to balance in blood? How about you? Will you listen to your heart—now?[45]

With forces such as these in play, it is scarcely surprising that the dollars flowed in. There are fewer statistics on the exact distribution of public debt in the Second World War, partly because the types of instruments did not lend themselves so readily to tabulation, and partly because it was taken for granted that almost every household owned some government securities. In Britain, for example, there were no fewer than twenty-three million depositors with government savings accounts by 1944. In America, the Fourth War Loan issued sixty million individual bonds (although the number of actual subscribers was undoubtedly smaller than this). The Canadian War Loans regularly collected three million subscriptions from a total population of only twelve million.

And yet, underneath the familiar features of Allied wartime finance, there lurked subtle but profound shifts in emphasis. The scale of the economic mobilization demanded by the First World War had caught countries by surprise. It took some time before they adjusted themselves to fighting a "total war." There could be no excuse for such unpreparedness in 1939. It was clear from the start that levels of spending would be at least as great as they had been twenty-five years earlier, and in all probability greater. Much had been learned during the First World War, and the events of the postwar era had given rise to further rethinking.

There was now a far greater reliance on taxation. American tax revenues rose from under $6 billion in 1940 to nearly $48 billion in 1945—an increase proportionately as great as in the First World War, but this time from a far higher base. In Britain the rise was from under £1 billion to £3.4 billion. In both countries the growth of revenues was aided by the rapid expansion of economies (which still had much slack after a decade of depression) under a level of "Keynesian" fiscal stimulus greater then anything its originator had dreamed of. But tax rates were also raised sharply, and it was in the Second World War that government taxes rose to levels of GNP (around 20% in the United States and 35% in the United Kingdom at which, more or less, they still remain. This did not mean that taxes were more important than loans in financing the war. Around 60% of war spending was financed by borrowing in both countries. But this was a far "better" performance than in the First World War.

AMERICAN AND BRITISH FINANCING OF WORLD WARS I AND II[46]
$ billions

	World War I		World War II	
	United States	Great Britain	United States	Great Britain
War spending	32	42	328	106
Borrowing	24	33	200	64
— as % of spending	75%	80%	61%	60%

The increased emphasis on taxation was not just a reflection of a new fiscal prudence, let alone a reassertion of Victorian morality. Under the influence of the new macroeconomic thinking, there had been a change in the whole theory of war finance. It was now seen that it was not enough merely to raise the sums necessary by the most politically convenient method. In order to prevent a recurrence of the inflationary spiral of the First World War, it was essential that the amounts raised be provided by a surplus of production over consumption rather than by a diversion of existing capital. A study by the National Bureau of Economic Research in 1942 stated the new doctrine clearly:

> The immediate task of war financing consists largely in reducing civilian use of resources needed for the military program and in preventing the inflation that might develop because civilians have more money to spend on fewer goods.[47]

The ubiquitous posters of the two world wars were intended to influence public behavior in three fundamental directions: to enlist, to lend, and to save. The first objective remained a constant,* but the second and third were promoted in inverse proportions in the two wars. In the First World War, the main thrust was to encourage people to lend; in the Second, to save. Once the money was saved, it was not hard for the government to lay hands on it. As Henry Murphy, a U.S. Treasury economist, wrote after the war:

> It should be emphasized that it is the stimulation of savings and not the procurement of the investment of these savings in government securities which is essential. If the money is saved it is only a matter of the niceties of finance that

*Enlistment remained a prime objective even after the introduction of conscription. Women were exhorted to join their parallel military organizations and others were encouraged to join ancillary programs such as war loan promotion. In the Second World War an additional focus of posters was the prevention of "loose talk" that might be overheard by enemy agents. The advent of long-range wireless communications made espionage a far greater threat than in the First World War; and especially in a polyglot society like the United States, the allegiance of all citizens was not taken for granted.

it should be invested directly in government securities by the saver. If he does not so invest it, this will be done for him by the banks or other institutional investors whose liabilities he is holding.[48]

If the resources for war were to be procured from incomes rather than capital, it followed that a greater portion of resources would have to come out of the pockets of the poorer classes than in the First World War, for the reason that incomes were less unequally distributed than capital. Keynes made this point clear in late 1939, when he wrote *How to Pay for the War,* the pamphlet that encapsulated the new macroeconomic thinking about war finance. He rejected the idea, put forward by some socialist leaders, that the working class should not be asked to shoulder the financial burdens of war:

It is not sane to suppose that the war can be financed without putting some burden on the increased war incomes of the class with £5 a week or less. For this income group accounts . . . for more than 60 per cent of the total personal incomes of the country . . . and for two thirds of current consumption. . . . The only question is, therefore, how large the contribution of this class must be, and how it can be obtained with least sacrifice and most justice.[49]

Keynes understood that there was a psychological limit to the amount that could be raised in taxes, just as there was to the amount that could be raised by voluntary savings. He therefore came up with the novel idea of "compulsory savings." Since the working class was less inclined to voluntary saving than the middle class, he proposed tapping a portion of their incomes via taxes that would be repaid with interest after the war. An ancillary benefit of his proposal was that the repayments could be timed to help counteract the postwar recession that many feared to be inevitable. The idea became highly controversial, many attacking it as "repugnant to the intellect" and even "antidemocratic." This was incorrect. As this book has shown, repayable taxation has played a long and honorable role in the history of democratic public finance. The most intriguing feature of Keynes's proposal, from this perspective, was its complete inversion of the old rules of the Italian republics. In medieval Italy it was the privileged citizens who were entitled to have their taxes repaid with interest, while the less privileged were forced to pay *à forfait.* In the topsy-turvy world of mass democracy, the formula was reversed.[50]

The idea of compulsory savings appealed to economists but was so foreign to politicians that it made only a marginal impact on war finance. Small-scale schemes (far smaller than those advocated by Keynes) were introduced in Britain, Canada, and South Africa. A push was also made to introduce the idea in America. But though there was already a model for the concept in the Social Security system, it aroused the determined opposition of Franklin Roosevelt and his Treasury Secretary, Henry Morgenthau. They felt strongly, and probably rightly, that compulsory schemes would conflict with the all-important voluntary bond drives that were under way. The war loan program was not just an important method of raising money; it was essential for public morale. Morgenthau put it this way:

> There are millions of people who say "What can we do to help?" . . . Sixty percent of the reason I want to do this thing is . . . to give the people an opportunity to do something . . . the hard way . . . the democratic way.[51]

Henry Murphy, a strong supporter of Keynes's ideas, dismissed this equation of voluntarism with democracy. Were not taxation and conscription perfectly in accordance with democratic principles? Furthermore, he pointed out:

> Voluntary borrowing as viewed by the theorists is not identical with the voluntary way in practice. Indeed, the more voluntary borrowing is stressed as a *way*, the more it tends to lose its truly voluntary character and to become semicoercive. This occurs, of course, because the stress on the voluntary-borrowing program *as such* leads to its being required to carry a greater load than is compatible with its strictly voluntary character. . . .
>
> The coercion of social pressure and of employer pressure (particularly in the payroll savings plan) runs, of course, through the entire spectrum of persuasion from mild pleas to buy to threats of discharge or of social obloquy. . . . Such coercion is fundamentally more distasteful to democratic ideals than the coercion of forced saving.[52]

Murphy was, of course, right that voluntarism was, in practice, only semivoluntarism. This had been quite as true in the First World War as in the Second. But he was wrong to see social obloquy as undemocratic. Repayable taxation and semivoluntary donation both had classical antecedents. The liturgies of ancient Athens were only semivoluntary, but the force of social obligation, backed up where necessary by ostracism, was the glue of Athenian democracy. Beyond that, Roosevelt and the supporters of voluntarism understood a fundamental, if unelaborated, truth. Compulsory schemes are democratic only insofar as they are agreed to by elected assemblies. But elections take place only rarely. They may not take place at all during a war. Bond drives give the population the chance to demonstrate its support for the war effort on a regular basis. They were, in effect, financial plebiscites, just as they had been in the First World War.

The debate between the advocates of voluntarism and compulsion goes to the heart of a fundamental divide between the two wars. The First World War was the last in which the old maxim "Money is the sinews of war" held sway. It was the truth of this maxim that underlay the crisis of legitimacy that brought down the Bourbon monarchy: "If the people believe [Louis XVI] to be a despot, it will be impossible to open loans, or, if that route is taken, they will be so costly that England will always finish by having the last *écu* in any war." The same point resonated through the First World War, when Lloyd George claimed that Britain would win because the country would always be able to raise the "last million," and when the failure of a war loan was viewed as "worse . . . than a disaster on the field of battle." War was a test not only of military proficiency, but also of the soundness of the political and financial system. And it had been proved to everyone's satisfaction that a only a system of cheap long-term debt backed by an elected government could extract that magical last dollar, pound, or mark that would win the war.

Between the wars, a different view took hold. Events in communist Russia and Nazi Germany had proved that resources could be extracted by means other than conventional finance. The new economic theories of Keynes and others emphasized the role of the state as economic engineer. As a result, public finance, in the conventional sense, was now seen as only a part of a wider process by which the state could acquire control of the resources it needed for war. The rationing of goods and services could force people to save rather than spend their incomes. The closure of the credit markets to private borrowers could force these savings directly into the coffers of the state without the need for time-consuming patriotic bond drives. The introduction of payroll schemes that deducted income taxes (or compulsory savings) at source allowed levels of direct taxation that were unheard of before. With a judicious exploitation of these new techniques, there seemed to be no limit to the portion of the national product that the state might commandeer. No wonder that there arose a new maxim of war finance: "The limits of an all-out war are physical and psychological, not financial."[53] In other words, it was no longer the last dollar that tipped the scales but the last bullet and the last drop of blood. As Henry Murphy put it, "The war, of course, would have been financed in any event whether there had been a savings bond program or not. Modern nations do not turn themselves over to the enemy for financial reasons."[54] In a wartime publication entitled *Where's the Money Coming From?* Stuart Chase expressed the idea even more pungently: "Money is the slave, not the master now."[55]

If the old method of raising money was still used, then, it was largely as a means of giving voice to the patriotic spirit of the population and demonstrating the democratic nature of the war. It might have been true, as Franklin Roosevelt declared in a radio address to launch the Third War Loan in September 1943, that "Every dollar that you invest in the Third War Loan is your personal message of defiance to our common enemies."[56] But the message transmitted to Berlin signaled untapped reserves of fighting spirit rather than unused reserves of dollars.

Patriotic war loans were all very well; but the experiences of the past decade had made clear that they were easier to raise than to redeem. One thing was certain: no one seriously assumed they would be reimbursed by defeated enemies. There were proposals for postwar reparations of some sort, mostly put forward by the Russians, who saw themselves as the prime beneficiaries. But these proposals largely involved the removal of German industrial plant with the objective of permanently disabling its war machine. The idea of cash transfers was almost entirely discredited and had no effect on American or British financial calculations. Nor was there any assumption on the American side that the war matériel it was shipping to Britain and others would be repaid in cash with interest. Roosevelt's Lend-Lease Act of 1941 tacitly accepted the failure of past American policy on this issue. Yet if there was to be no external source of repayment, it was clear that the whole burden of the war debt would have to be resolved by domestic politics. It may have been true, as the economist Alvin Hansen optimistically noted, that "under modern conditions [the ideal identity of taxpayers and creditors] is more closely approximated than was formerly the case."[57] But the First World War had shown that, however widely the war debt was distributed, taxpayers and creditors were *not* wholly identical, and it was therefore impossible to avoid class conflict altogether when the cost of debt service rose above a certain point. And whereas in 1914 Britain and America had enjoyed very low levels of borrowing, this was most certainly not the case in 1940. It was perfectly clear that this time even America would finish the war with a debt considerably in excess of its GNP.

If, then, there was to be debt, its social divisiveness must be kept to a minimum. The most straightforward way to achieve this objective was to reduce the interest cost. In the First World War, interest rates had been allowed to rise to a level where the appeal to patriotism could be enhanced by an appeal to the pocketbook. In the Second World War, such a strategy was ruled out by the determination of governments to finance the war on the cheap. In Britain it was decided that this would be a "three percent war" even though prewar rates were slightly above this benchmark. In America, where interest rates had fallen even lower in the 1930s, the maximum yield was fixed at 2.5%. In neither country were there any tax exemptions (apart from modest amounts of tax-free savings bonds aimed at the small investor). Nothing like this had even been attempted before. But of course, such very low interest rates could be achieved only by pressing to the full the "guilt-edged" obligations of patriotism and thus increasing the tendency toward semicoercion that Henry Murphy rightly noted.

A higher than usual current yield had not been the only traditional attraction of wartime lending. Long-term debt had also offered the possibility of capital gains—especially if the bonds were issued below par. Furthermore, the historical pattern was for general prices to rise in wartime and then fall back with the return of peace. This pattern increased the real returns of bondholders—particularly on investments made in the later stages of the war. Under the new dispensation, none of these ancillary gains were considered politically acceptable since their ultimate source was the taxpayer.

The reduction of potential capital gains was facilitated by the aversion of small savers to market risk. In the aftermath of the First World War, they had been unnerved by the swings in the market value of their investments. They were more than happy to accept a lower yield in exchange for security of principal. To satisfy this need, they were now offered unmarketable savings bonds that could be redeemed before maturity with an interest penalty. Investments of this sort had existed in the First World War in both countries, but the emphasis on single all-embracing war loans had limited their use to a small percentage of total debt. In the Second World War, by contrast, the American Series E Savings Bonds and the British War Savings Certificates were the most ubiquitous financial instruments of the era. In line with the new philosophy, they offered the highest rates of any government security; but they were available only in quantities that inhibited their purchase by the wealthy investors. Their relatively generous yields (2.9% in the United States and 3.17% in Great Britain) were partly explained by the fact that the funds that they siphoned off from workers' pay packets were the ones most critical to the fight against inflation. But the reallocation of rewards in accordance with the priorities of mass democracy also represented an attempt to offset a possible postwar backlash against rentiers.

For wealthier investors, more traditional long-term loans were offered, but their very low coupons and the absence of issue discounts made significant speculative capital gains inherently unlikely. Even so, there was concern in political circles about the practice of "free riding," whereby some members of the public bought bonds only to sell them for a marginal profit in the aftermarket rather than to hold them to maturity. In the old days, such activity might have been seen as a useful lubricant to market liquidity, but in the "antimarket," almost socialistic, atmosphere of the war it was seen as politically unacceptable. The change in war borrowing patterns is easily seen in the chart below:

Allied Borrowing Patterns in World Wars I and II[58]

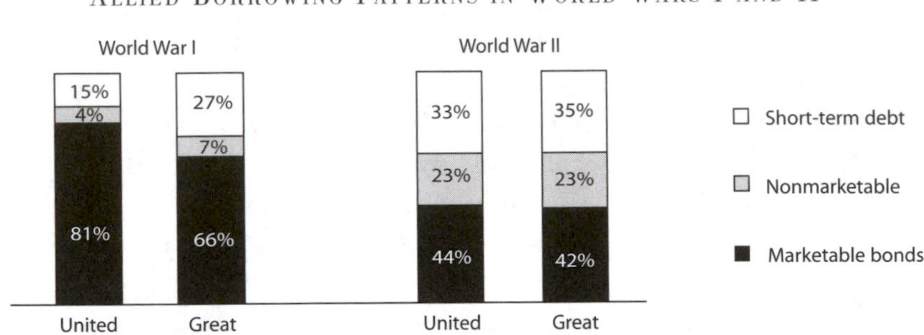

The ultimate barometer of the success of war finance was the price level. The central theme of Keynes's *How to Pay for the War* was the need to steer clear of the twin perils of inflation and deflation. This was partly to minimize economic disruption; but there were other reasons. Inflation would hand windfall profits to businesses, while breaking the bond of trust between the state and the citizens who were placing their savings in its hands. Deflation would exacerbate the postwar conflict between public creditors and taxpayers, just as it had after previous wars. The Holy Grail, therefore, was price stability. There were two threats to this much-desired objective. The analytical tools of Keynesian economics exposed the danger of the "inflationary gap." If consumers did not save a sufficient portion of their incomes to cover the government deficit, the "surplus" would be subtly but inexorably removed from them by inflation.* But even voluntary savings were "safe" only as long as they were locked up in government bonds (or other long-term investments). If they were kept in bank accounts, they cre-

*The process was described by Keynes in *How to Pay for the War.* The surplus income would inevitably accrue to businesses whose "excess" war profits would be partly taxed away and partly saved—thus completing the macroeconomic circle.

ated a further inflationary hazard by setting up a monetary overhang that might spark a postwar boom. A second crucial test of sound public finance, therefore, was how far governments could avoid borrowing from commercial banks. On this score, it seemed, the British (and Canadian) governments performed rather better than the American. Banks (including the central bank) accounted for 40% of American wartime borrowing, as opposed to around 20% of British. This admirable demonstration of economic self-control by Britain, however, conferred fewer advantages than supposed. The greater overall level of borrowing meant that, as a percentage of GNP, the amount of bank lending was only a little less than in America.

On the surface, it appeared that wartime inflation had been tamed by these miraculous advances in economic understanding and financial technique. After an initial surge from 1939 to 1941, retail prices remained quite stable during the years of maximum war spending. In America they rose by 10% between 1942 and 1945. In Britain prices rose only 3% in the last four years of the war. Yet the truth was that these comforting figures were due mainly to price controls that masked the underlying inflationary potential. The only reason that Britain recorded lower wartime inflation than the United States was that its economic controls were stricter. The balance sheets of the banks revealed that a monetary overhang was building up that was almost as large as at the end of the First World War. From 1941 to 1945 British GNP rose by 10% while bank deposits grew by nearly 60%. The story across the Atlantic, where inflation was less efficiently repressed, was only a little less worrying. In the last three years of the war, GNP grew by one-third while bank deposits increased by nearly two-thirds. In both countries, currency in circulation increased by 50% more than economic production. Over the horizon the problem of the postwar settlement loomed ominous as ever.

TOTALITARIAN WAR

There is no deficit in the State Budget, there is a permanent surplus of revenue over expenditure.

—Statement of basic socialist principles, *The Soviet Financial System*, Moscow Financial Institute, 1966

If the democracies borrowed from their citizens as a matter of course, the same could not be said for their communist allies. Karl Marx had not considered the question of public debt very deeply, but there had been no doubt in his mind that it formed one of the cornerstones of the early capitalist system, playing, in his words, "a great part . . . in the capitalisation of wealth and the expropriation of the masses":

> England at the end of the 17th century [creates] a systematical combination, embracing the colonies, the national debt, the modern mode of taxation, and the protectionist system. These methods . . . all employ the power of the state. . . . Public credit becomes the *credo* of capital. . . . The public debt becomes one of the most powerful levers of primitive accumulation. . . . The modern system of taxation was the necessary complement of the system of national loans. . . . Over-taxation is not an incident, but rather a principle. In Holland therefore, where this system was first inaugurated, the great patriot, DeWitt, has in his "Maxims" extolled it as the best system for making the wage-labourer submissive, frugal, industrious, and overburdened with labour.[59]

With views such as these voiced by the Master, it was no surprise that one of Lenin's first acts was to repudiate the prerevolutionary debt. But what to do thereafter? Marx and Engels had bequeathed tomes on the historical origins, current iniquities, and inevitable downfall of the capitalist system, but little in the way of a blueprint for the socialist era that was to follow. One thing was certain, however: the first priority of the dictatorship of the proletariat would be to expropriate the assets of the capitalists. There was, then, little reason to suppose that public borrowing would feature prominently, or even at all, in communist public finance. After all, if wealth was nationalized, where was the need to borrow it? Communist dogma always refused to accept the notion of deficit financing as practiced in the West. Since the state budget was "the budget of the whole economy" the idea of a deficit was a logical contradiction. It was with pride that communist writers asserted that the only years in which the USSR had failed to run a surplus were from 1941 to 1943. Even in 1943, goes the official story, "the State Budget met 97.3 per cent of budget expenditure out of revenue. From 1944 the budget was again in surplus, as in pre-war years."[60]

Yet matters were not so simple as they appeared on the surface. In the late 1970s, the defector Igor Birman exposed Soviet budget surpluses as a long-term "statistical trick," created by the concealment of money emission within the annual accounts.[61] But beyond such subterfuges, there is also the unconcealed fact that each year from 1922 to 1956 the Soviet government issued bonds for sale to the population. The amounts involved were modest by Western standards, amounting to only 20% of GNP in 1957, when Khrushchev stopped the practice and deferred debt payments for twenty years.[62] But even though the state budget insisted, in line with communist dogma, on classifying the proceeds of bond sales as income rather than borrowing, the very presence of public debt in the midst of the Stalinist dictatorship is a curiosity that requires explanation. On inspection, the history of the Soviet state bonds reveals the limitations of even the most extreme form of totalitarianism.

The story starts with the unraveling of the first period of revolutionary hopes and aspirations. The hyperinflation of the civil war period may have encouraged radicals to dream of a moneyless society; but Lenin was more realistic. He was aware that support of the peasants, crucial to the survival of the regime, was waning after years of requisitions at gunpoint. He also understood that barter was generally seen as an act of desperation, and that the population preferred more traditional forms of exchange. In October 1921 he admitted defeat:

> Nothing has become of commodity-exchange; the private market has shown itself stronger than us, and instead of commodity-exchange we have ordinary purchase and sale, or trade.[63]

The truth was that the conditions for a successful socialist economy did not exist. Not only was the bulk of the national wealth now in the hands of uneducated peasant proprietors of dubious loyalty, but production had also fallen below prewar levels. The quickest way to revive it was to allow the despised profit motive to work its evil magic. This was a strategy of *reculer pour mieux sauter*—a necessary retrogression to gain strength for future battles. Lenin's plan was that

> a certain amount of freedom in the exchange of goods and services would economically motivate the farmers to increase their productivity and lead to a rapid revival of agriculture; that nationalized industry could be rebuilt on this basis and private capital forced out; that after the gathering of forces and means a mighty industry could be built up as the economic foundation of the socialistic State, after which the final offensive against the last remnants of capitalism remaining in the country could be launched and these latter be destroyed.[64]

This reluctant decision to allow, and even encourage, a capitalist sector of the economy, entailed the revival of all the old accessories of bourgeois finance: money, banks, taxes—and even public loans and bond markets. The first state loan was issued in 1922 and had to be forced on a reluctant population. This reluctance was scarcely surprising when free-market interest rates were running as high as 16% per month. In the words of the People's

Commissar of Finance (breathtaking as evidence of the volte-face that had occurred): "Accumulation of money capital was only in its inception. . . . Stock and bond exchanges, which enable the supply and demand of securities to establish their current prices, did not yet function properly."[65] After 1924, however, the (temporary) combination of monetary stability and economic liberalism allowed the raising of modest sums by wholly voluntary means. Under the NEP (New Economic Policy), then, public borrowing was a reflection of the inability of the communist state to do without the private sector.

Reliance on the free market was never intended to last, however; and after 1928 Stalin decided to force the pace of change rather than wait on events. An industrial society would simply be imposed from above, and there would be no more kowtowing to the interests of peasant landowners. The result was the Five-Year Plans and the forced collectivization of agriculture. By the mid-1930s, the private sector had withered into relative insignificance, just as Lenin had hoped. Logically, public borrowing should have withered with it; yet this was not the case. In the early years of industrialization, the state needed access to all the funds that it could lay its hands on; and by the deduction of bond subscriptions from wage packets, substantial amounts could be collected. But this is not an adequate explanation in later years. The state had far more powerful means of extracting savings from the population than by borrowing them. The Five-Year Plans focused national production on capital goods, leaving only modest amounts of goods to be sold to consumers. The prices of these goods were then raised to a level where the excess incomes of the population were effectively taxed away. In this manner, the Soviet state enforced a policy of forced savings that approached 50% of GNP. Sales of government bonds were peripheral to this process.

Yet perhaps it was the very extremity of the measures needed to create the communist paradise that ensured the survival of public loans. In order to conceal the level of sacrifice involved, it was considered prudent to pay the population more than it could, in practice, spend. The excess income was then borrowed back by the state at interest, thus nurturing hopes of higher spending power in future years and the illusion of a level of economic freedom. Public borrowing in the 1930s, then, constituted a disguise for the true nature of Soviet economic control.

It is unlikely that the population was greatly deceived by the disguise. "Investors" did not appear to place enormous faith in the steady accumulation of purchasing power that their bonds were supposed to offer. It was soon found that their preferences ran to lottery prizes rather than interest. This was an entirely rational response in an era when inflation averaged 22% per annum while bond payouts were progressively reduced from over 10% to 4% or less. Moreover, bonds which qualified for lottery prizes were immediately redeemed, while the rest, which could not be sold, were subjected to periodic mandatory deferrals of their nominal maturity dates. Nor did the population appear to view its participation in public lending as convincing evidence of economic freedom. Although enrollment in payroll deduction schemes was ostensibly voluntary, it was a brave soul who dared to opt out when the trains for Siberia departed regularly. Where payroll schemes did not exist, as in the countryside, it proved hard to sell bonds. The peasants, their traditional diffidence in matters of finance now compounded by the traumas of collectivization, preferred to keep their rubles hidden under the mattress rather than entrust them to the state that had so recently dispossessed them.

The illusory nature of Soviet public borrowing was noted by an American observer in 1936:

> Since the total volume of . . . consumption goods is fixed by the [Five-Year] Plan, no expansion of total consumption would follow if direct taxation and loans were abolished. The only result would be a general rise in prices. . . . Compared to the sums taken from the people by price manipulation, the amount taken directly by taxation and loans is comparatively small. There appears to be no particular reason for resorting to direct taxation and issuing loans when popular consumption can be equally well restrained by raising prices, but no doubt there are psychological considerations which make the Government unwilling to let these methods of raising revenue fall into abeyance.[66]

Whatever psychological considerations may have affected the calculations of Soviet planners in the 1930s, the decision to leave a residue of the private economy came into its own in the Second World War. Whereas the outcome in the West was an unprecedented increase in the role of the state, the obverse was true in the USSR. It was the private sector that was allowed a temporary renaissance. The catastrophic territorial losses on the summer of 1941 placed almost one-third of industrial capacity in German hands. In order to stimulate alternative production—and especially agricultural production—greater economic freedom was given to private enterprise and to collective farms. The resulting rise in private incomes was then tapped by special war taxes and war loans. Whereas revenues from the state sector actually fell in the war years, revenues from direct taxes and loans rose sharply.

Soviet Sources of Funds During World War II[67]

Billions of rubles

	1940	1944
State sector revenues	128	116
Direct taxes	9	47
Public loans	9	30

In all, public loans raised around 100 billion rubles during the war. The bulk was still collected by deductions from payrolls, but it is likely that these were more willingly tolerated in the atmosphere of the "Great Patriotic War." As in the 1930s, lottery loans predominated, their appeal now more speculative than ever since only 25% of bonds qualified for prizes. In comparison with its Western allies, however, Soviet reliance on borrowing was minimal. Public debt covered only 17% of war spending, whereas in the United States and Great Britain the figure was close to 60%.

Where taxation and borrowing proved insufficient, the burden of war finance was taken up by the printing press—hidden as usual in obscure parts of the budget. Official Soviet histories admit to a fourfold increase of currency circulation during the war. Much of this currency ended up in the hands of those sectors that had benefited from the wartime liberalization of prices. After the war a day of reckoning loomed. The 1947 monetary reform subjected privately held currency to a 90% reduction—justified on the grounds that substantial currency holdings must represent the illicit gains of war profiteering. Since it was the peasants who, as always, kept the vast majority of their cash holdings in currency rather than in state savings banks, it was they who suffered most from this step. From the point of view of the rural population, then, the war and its aftermath amounted to a small-scale reprise of the bitter cycle of the 1920s and 1930s. Not that the urban population with its accumulation of war bonds had much reason to feel happier. The 1947 reform mandated conversion of existing state debt into new 2% twenty-year bonds with a face value only one-third of the original amounts.

The truth of the matter was that, while the Stalinist bonds represented a nod in the direction of personal economic freedom, they were, in the final analysis, correctly categorized in the budget as a form of income. The state had no intention of repaying them, nor even of paying a meaningful rate of return. Stalin was happy to persevere with the system as long as two conditions applied: (1) inflation continuously reduced the real value of the debt, and (2) debt service remained substantially below the proceeds from new issues. Both these conditions held true from 1928 to 1947. Inflation averaged 20% over the period, while the progressive reduction of payouts and deferrals of maturity dates ensured that cash inflows would always handily exceed outflows even as nominal debt accumulated.

In the light of this history the 1947 reform was no surprise. The lowering of interest and deferral of maturity were entirely in line with previous Soviet practice. The only novel aspect of the reform was the reduction in the face amount of the bonds. Since postwar inflation had already reduced the real value of the public debt to little more than 25% of GNP by 1947, it was not clear why such a reduction was necessary.[68] The most likely explanation lies in a sharp reversal in Soviet economic policy in that year. Instead of continuous price rises, there was now a policy of price reductions intended to raise the standard of living of the urban population. In a deflationary environment, however, the economics of debt service would be altered to the disadvantage of the state. Better, then, to reduce the value of bonds first, while the measure could still be justified as a wartime sacrifice.*

Superficially it would seem that Nazi Germany lay at the opposite end of the financial spectrum from the Soviet Union. No country relied more on borrowing to support its war effort. Almost three-quarters of German war spending was covered in this way. But appearances are deceptive. In spite of an ideology that would seem to lend itself perfectly to demonstrations of nationalistic fervor via public bond drives, Nazi war borrowing was shrouded in secrecy. There were no giant wooden statues of Hitler paraded through the towns of the Reich. There were no posters and no subscription lists. No oversubscribed war loan was trumpeted as a "message to Roosevelt" in the way that the Sixth German War Loan of 1917 had sent "a message to Wilson."

There were, it has to be said, good reasons for the German government to avoid stirring up unpleasant memories of the First World War. The loyal

*The subsequent history of Soviet borrowing is worth outlining briefly: Stalin restarted the bond issues—perhaps because of force of habit. But their days were numbered. Initially, high net cash inflows outweighed the disadvantages of the increasing real value of the debt. But in 1956 outflows already came to 87% of inflows. Khrushchev decided to grasp the nettle, just as some foreign observers had predicted. However, the government was still unable, or unwilling, to avoid paying the population more than was available to consume. Without the outlet of bonds, the government now funneled surplus popular income into state savings accounts. These had the advantages of appearing less forced, and of having no fixed repayments; but they only stored up problems for the future. The vast overhang of unspendable purchasing power in the hands of Soviet citizens was one of the many elements that led to the demise of the communist system at the end of the 1980s. Needless to say, the wealth nominally represented by the savings accounts was wiped out by the hyperinflation of the 1990s.

citizens who had subscribed so readily to the war loans of 1914–1918 had witnessed the near-total loss of their investments. It was not clear what the popular response would be to an appeal for new subscriptions, even if presented by the world's greatest masters of propaganda. On the other hand, a similarly inauspicious history existed in the Soviet Union, but it did not inhibit Stalin from using public borrowing as one of his financial tools (albeit a relatively minor one) during the war. In some ways, the Nazis' position was easier than that of the Bolsheviks, since the elimination of the previous war debt was in no way their doing. Indeed, the Nazis regularly compared their own sound finances with the criminal abuse of the printing press by the Weimar Republic.

The real problems for the Nazi regime lay elsewhere. While there was strong domestic support for a reversal of the humiliations of 1919, it was not clear how far this support extended to the grandiose gamble into which Hitler swept the German nation in 1939. The recurring nightmare of the Nazi leadership was the "stab in the back"—the belief that it was a socialist-inspired collapse of morale on the home front that had led to defeat in 1918. As masters of public relations they understood that bond drives worked both ways. While they might offer a Nuremberg-style rallying ground for the national cause, they also allowed the population to vote with their wallets, and thereby offered an indirect public forum for dissident elements. Furthermore, there could be no claim, this time, that Germany was fighting an essentially defensive war. A war of aggression could be justified only by the rewards of victory. If the German people were to be persuaded of the virtues of being the Master Race, they had to see the beneficial results in their pocketbooks.

Hitler had a strategy for this. The notable success of the German economy in recovering from the slump of 1929–1932 had been based on the adoption of the new economic principles of state control and state spending. Large-scale rearmament and investment in infrastructure had helped bring about an 80% increase in national production between 1932 and 1939, at a time when most countries were still grappling with escaping the clutches of the Depression. The emphasis on armaments production meant that by 1939 the German economy was already on a semiwar footing. Hitler could therefore use a strategy of blitzkrieg—the application of overwhelming force to achieve a rapid victory without major dislocation of the economy. Once the intrinsic martial superiority of the Aryan race was rewarded with victory, any further resources required for the defense of the Reich could be supplied by defeated enemies.

It is not difficult to recognize the outlines of Napoleonic finances in this strategy. But the great strides of European "civilization" over the intervening century had brought about equal advances in economic technique and doctrinal ruthlessness. The sums that Napoleon levied from occupied territories were derisory compared with the resources extracted by Hitler. The total was substantially in excess of 120 billion marks.* To put this sum into perspective, it is only necessary to recall that the *total* bill for reparations demanded from Germany in 1921 was 132 billion marks, of which only 50 billion marks was expected to be paid within the foreseeable future, and of which only 21 billion marks was actually transferred.

In theory, it was in the east that Germany was to find the resources to support the Master Race. In practice the economic backwardness of the area, made worse by the effects of wartime destruction and by the ruthlessness of Nazi racial policies, hindered the systematic exploitation of local resources. Apart from the substantial quantities of raw materials looted from the area, the east was mainly of use as a source of slave labor. It was in the west that expropriation was raised to the level of science. In the 1920s, it had been loudly proclaimed that for Germany to pay more than 2 billion marks a year in reparations would cause economic ruin. Now France was subjected to "occupation costs" of 7.3 billion marks per year. In the 1920s reparations payments averaged around 3% of German national income. From 1941 to 1944 France paid Germany the annual equivalent of 26% of its prewar national income.[69] The amounts were extracted partly by taxes, partly by the use of overvalued paper money within France, and partly by the importation of French goods in exchange for clearing credits that were never settled. Similar principles were applied in Belgium, the Netherlands, Norway, and elsewhere.

But the tribute collected by the Reich was never sufficient. The military and economic odds never looked more favorable for Hitler than in late 1940 and early 1941. The prosperous northern Atlantic seaboard of Europe was under German control, as were Czechoslovakia and western Poland. The only opposition was the British Empire. Yet even then it proved impossible to finance the war effort from conquest alone. In the twelve months to April 1941, German war spending was 54 billion marks—a figure more or less comparable to the British expenditure of £3 billion if allowance is

*This figure covers only amounts for which there is statistical evidence. It does not include any estimate of such items as the goods looted from Poland and the USSR, the taxation of territories incorporated directly into Germany, or the value of forced labor.

made for the costs of occupation. But even when the system of exploitation was at its height in 1943, the occupied territories produced only 30 billion marks. The price of "total" war had escalated to a point where, even under the most favorable circumstances, it was impossible to off-load the costs onto others. After Russia and America joined the list of Germany's enemies, it was clear that the burden on the population could only grow. By the later stages of the war, Germany was spending more than 100 billion marks per year in an attempt to stave off looming defeat.

These vast amounts could be raised only by taxation or borrowing. If Hitler wished to hide the cost of the war from the German population, there were limits to how far he could make use of the former, especially since German tax rates were already high. A series of special war taxes was imposed at the outbreak of hostilities; but the Führer made his opposition to further substantial increases clear in 1940. Tax revenues rose by 70% in nominal terms during the war, but this was a small increase compared to that in Great Britain or in the United States and largely reflected the escalation of wage rates during the war. As a contributor to war costs, taxes were scarcely more significant than in the First World War.[70] The only alternative, therefore, was to borrow. Even in 1940–1941, at the height of its ascendancy, the Reich ran a deficit of 37 billion marks.

But it was not just tax increases that were excluded by the logic of military ascendancy. Public bond drives, too, implied a level of patriotic self-denial that did not entirely jibe with the enjoyment of the fruits of conquest. It was only later, after the setbacks in Russia, that Nazi propaganda started to demand ever-greater sacrifices from the population. But now it was not the prospect of victory but the specters of Bolshevik revenge, devastation by Asiatic barbarians, and exploitation by international Jewry that were raised to galvanize the population. Even if public loans were easier to justify in a war of defense, these were hardly images likely to encourage subscribers to risk their savings. It was easier, then, to pursue a policy of "noiseless borrowing." Already in the 1930s the government had stopped publishing budgets and had started to borrow from financial institutions rather than directly from the public. Now the principle was extended.

There was no special mystery to Nazi borrowing techniques. The regime had fully understood the new arts of economic control years before war had necessitated their adoption in America and Britain. The population was exhorted to increase savings, and a system of tax-advantaged savings accounts was set up, funded by semicompulsory payroll deductions. Since rationing limited consumer spending, it was not too hard to achieve the desired increase in the amounts deposited. The state then quietly borrowed the funds required for the war effort from the banks. "The saver became, indirectly, without realizing it, a creditor of the Reich," as the Finance Minister, Count Schwerin von Krosigk, put it in his memoirs.[71] Where the surreptitious appropriation of savings was not sufficient, the state borrowed directly from the Reichsbank, the result being a sevenfold increase in the currency circulation by the end of the war. The underlying inflationary time bomb, however, remained concealed by rigid price controls.

The unsurprising result was that public debt rose more dramatically in Germany than in any other country in involved in the war. From September 1939 to May 1945 it had increased more than twelve times, from 32 billion to nearly 400 billion marks—more than three times peak wartime GNP, and far higher in relation to the shrunken level of economic activity of the final months of collapse.

The Reich budget may have been secret, and public borrowing "noiseless," but a certain amount of financial information was bound to seep out. There were newspaper reports by 1943 that the public debt was reaching alarming proportions, and government ministers were forced to address the question. Schwerin von Krosigk was on record in April of the next year as stating that he understood the popular anxiety about the level of the debt, but he felt confident that a great portion could still be satisfied by allocation of lands in the remaining conquered territories. Even in early 1945, as defeat stared the regime in the face, a report by Ludwig Erhardt outlined the possibility of a postwar debt consolidation at an interest rate of 1%. By this time, however, the population had lost confidence in the whole monetary system, and Germany was fast becoming a "cigarette" economy even before the GIs arrived with their packets of Camels.

Otto Nathan wrote a study on Nazi war finance in early 1944 for the National Bureau of Economic Research. In his introduction, Ralph Young, the director of the bureau, felt compelled to note:

> Many of the methods [the Nazis] used are similar in outward respects to certain of those which have been put in operation in Great Britain, Canada and the United States. These similarities, however, are superficial and should not be permitted to obscure contrasts in values which are fundamental. Financial measures imposed under democratic processes of government are different in essence and in effect from those enforced by a tyrannical dictatorship.[72]

The similarities were, to say the least, striking. The Nazi economic and financial system was little different from the wartime controls imposed under the aegis of the new economics. Rationing, price controls, and the exclusion of private borrowers from the credit market made it easy for the state to borrow whatever it needed. Did it matter what system of government put these measures into practice? Young rested his case for the fundamental difference between democratic and totalitarian finance on "contrasts in values," without further elaboration. His assertion looks more than a little wooly and constituted precisely the sort of unthinking liberal embrace of state planning that Frederick Hayek was to attack in *The Road to Serfdom*, published in the same year.

There was, however, one area in which the war finances of the democracies differed visibly from those of the "tyrannical dictatorships." The distinguishing feature of democratic war finance was the much maligned "voluntary way"—cherished by Roosevelt and other old-fashioned politicians, but largely pooh-poohed by the economists. From the perspective of the new economics, it was "only a matter of the niceties of finance that [savings] should be invested directly in government securities by the saver. If he does not so invest [them], this will be done for him by the banks."[73] From the perspective of politics, however, the "niceties of finance" were crucial. It was precisely the ability—and willingness—of the democratic countries to finance the largest part of the war by persuading their citizens to entrust them directly with their money that separated the democracies from the totalitarian dictatorships.

THE SETTLEMENT OF ACCOUNTS (PART II)

> Whatever obscurity may cloud other post-war goals, one goal is clear. All over the world masses of people have determined that the future world must be a world of full employment and production. It is not too much to say, as did *The Economist* of London recently, that this aspiration overrides all other political and social ideas.
>
> —*New York Times*, 9 December 1942

The jubilation of the crowds on the streets at the end of the war in Europe in May 1945 was undoubtedly watched with more than a bit of reserve by the mandarins in the Allied treasury departments. The war in the Pacific was not yet over, and the costs of the military occupation of Germany were substantial. It would be at least another year before borrowing could be brought under control. But it was not only the victors and their vanquished opponents who were heavily indebted. The tribute exacted by the Nazis from the conquered nations of Europe was reflected in their balance sheets. France, Belgium, and the Netherlands all had debts that had risen to around four and one half times their prewar levels. Everywhere there was a sea of red ink.

When compared to national economies, the levels of public borrowing had reached unheard-of (in some cases almost absurd) heights, especially on the continent of Europe, where economic activity had shrunk during the years of fighting. It was calculated in Germany that the debt bequeathed by the Nazi regime was equivalent to 675% of national income. The ratio rose briefly over 400% in the Netherlands. Among the Allies the figures were scarcely less alarming. In Britain the national debt had risen to 270% of national income. In Canada and Australia the figures were 180% and 210%, respectively; and even in the United States the ratio was approaching 150%.[74] Debt ratios appeared less high in countries such as France, Italy, and Japan merely because inflation was already running out of control, thereby reducing the real value of the debt faster than it could be created.

Inevitably the question of reparations arose for a second time. Only the Russians expected to obtain anything material by this means. A figure of $20 billion was put forward by Stalin at Yalta; but there was no suggestion that it should be paid in cash. With memories of the Versailles debacle fresh in people's minds, it was agreed that payment could be made only in kind—either by the delivery of goods, by forced labor, or by the dismantling and transfer of industrial plant. This last idea found some favor in the west. Not only would Germany be permanently demilitarized, but the heavy industry that had supported the Wehrmacht would be destroyed. Although this would produce almost no material compensation for war damage, it had the advantage of eliminating Germany not only as a military threat, but as a commercial and industrial rival. Even in Whitehall and Washington the appeal of this strategy could be seen. At the Quebec Conference in September 1944 the Allies announced that they were "looking forward to converting Germany into a country primarily agricultural and pastoral in character." It was left up to Keynes and other skeptics to puncture this idyllic evocation of the land of Bach and Goethe. How was a country as densely populated as Germany to feed itself if its export industry was dismantled? The incongruity of the plan was brought into sharper relief once the Russians, firmly in charge of the whole of Eastern Europe, handed over one-quarter of Germany's best agricultural land to Poland, while expelling millions of Germans into the west to be fed. As Keynes put it:

> It seems monstrous that we should first de-industrialize and thus bankrupt the Ruhr to please Russia and then hand over the territory, or at least the industries, to an international body to please France, but that we alone should remain responsible for feeding the place. . . . Our present policy to Germany, by which we have become involved in paying her large reparations, might rank as the craziest ever—if one did not remember last time.[75]

In the end, the erstwhile Allies took entirely opposing lines of approach. In West Germany an amount estimated at $1 billion was collected in reparations, largely in the form of dismantled plant sent to the USSR in exchange for food supplies. As the implications of Soviet hegemony in Eastern Europe became apparent, the need to rebuild West Germany as a strong democratic (and industrial) nation became all too clear. The Marshall Plan and the ongoing Allied food aid funneled around $4 billion into the country in the process. Once again, Germany received "reparations" from America, this time with happier results. In East Germany, the Russians extracted whatever they could with a ruthlessness equal to Nazi occupation tactics. It has been estimated that the total amount collected by 1955 came to at least $7 billion in prewar values.[76] Dismantling was soon abandoned once the Russians realized that nobody at home knew how to work the equipment. Instead, large-scale deliveries from current German production were made, while the consumption of the local population was held substantially below prewar levels. Anyone familiar with the Five-Year Plans of the 1930s would have understood the processes at work.

Outside the USSR, then, reparations did nothing to alleviate the postwar fiscal plight. The process of financial stabilization varied from country to country. In the defeated Axis powers the public debt was simply wiped out, either by currency reform, as in Germany, or by hyperinflation, as in Japan. By the mid-1950s the public debt in both countries was no more than 10% of GNP. France and Italy had their own dynamic. Both countries had been extensively fought over. The discredit of their pro-Nazi or collaborationist regimes had given a huge boost to the credibility of the local Communist Parties, which had led the resistance. It was not immediately clear in which ideological camp their future lay. Until the political debate was resolved, there was no hope of returning the public finances to a semblance of order. By the time deficit spending was reduced to normal levels in the early 1950s, the fiscal landscape was unrecognizable. Public debt in France had risen to ten times 1939 levels, but prices had risen twenty-five times. As a result the domestic debt had fallen from 110% of GNP to a mere 30%. In Italy, debts had risen thirty-four times, but prices had risen fifty-five times. The public debt, which had started the war at around 80% of GNP, peaked at around 120% in 1943 before falling precipitously as inflation spiraled out of control. Prices rose by 340% in 1945. By 1947 the new Italian Republic inherited a debt that represented little more than 30% of GNP.

In other liberated countries in Western Europe, the position was not quite so dire. Less damage had been sustained either to the economic infrastructure or to the political consensus. A degree of fiscal and monetary order could therefore be reestablished with more modest doses of inflation. In Belgium a determined program of deflation undertaken (with the cooperation of the Communist Party) within weeks of the liberation of the country somewhat contained the looming inflationary spiral. Additionally the rapid pickup of economic activity after the end of the fighting soon reduced debt ratios to more normal levels. The Dutch economy had recovered so strongly by 1948 from its low point in 1944 that production was around one-third higher than before the war, even in real terms. National debt was now a more manageable (by Dutch historical standards at least) 160% of national income.

It was in the victorious Allied countries that peace posed the most interesting question. What order of priorities would regulate their postwar policies? The war had been, on some levels, an extraordinary financial achievement. Never had so much been borrowed from the public with so little economic and social disruption. In spite of the increased emphasis on taxation, the level of borrowing had exceeded that of the First World War, even in Britain.

ALLIED DOMESTIC BORROWING IN WORLD WARS I AND II[77]

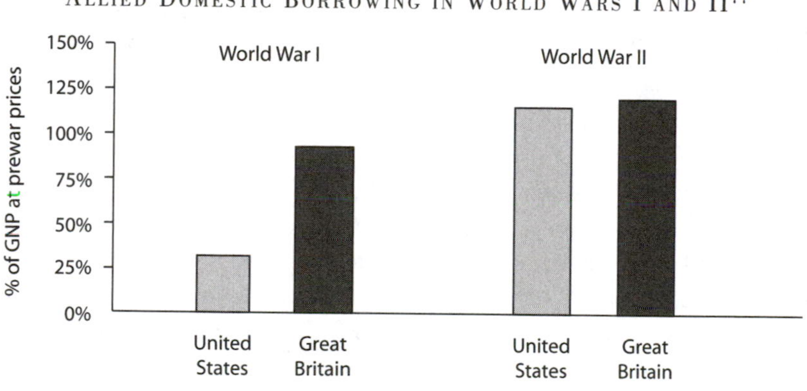

Equally remarkable had been the extremely low interest cost of the war debt. In the First World War, interest rates, although low by historical standards, had risen progressively throughout the war. In the Second World War, interest rates were not only considerably lower but were kept stable, or even falling, as the war progressed. In the First World War, the average cost of American and British borrowing was 4.2% and 5.1%, respectively. In the Second World War, both countries managed to borrow at just under 2%, not only by keeping a fixed ceiling on the cost of war loans, but also by ensuring that their short-term borrowing rates would be even lower (under 1% in the case of Treasury bills). The result was that even in Britain, where the national debt rose to levels not witnessed since the Napoleonic Wars, the interest burden was only 4.7% of GNP in 1946, as opposed to nearly 10% in 1816 and over 5% in 1919. Debt interest in America was only 1.7% of GNP in 1946, as opposed to 2.7% in 1866. On the surface, then, there seemed to be little reason to worry about the sustainability of Allied war debts.

There was, however, one area in which the financing of the war had not succeeded. The decisive economic test, according to the experts, was the avoidance of inflation. But it had proved impossible to finance the war entirely through taxes and long-term borrowing out of savings. Short-term debts had accumulated, and these were held to a worrying extent by the banking system (including substantial amounts held by the two central banks[78]). The result had been the buildup of hidden inflationary forces that threatened to erupt once wartime price controls were lifted. The financial situation was, in the end, little different from that confronted by governments after the First World War. Once again, the public had been called upon to contribute to the national cause by investing in war loans. Again, a substantial portion of their savings was now tied up with the national credit. If immediate steps were not taken to reduce the excess money supply that had built up during the war, it was inevitable that the citizens who had responded so staunchly to wartime appeals for loans would see the value of their savings rapidly eroded.

Even during the war it was clear that the postwar outlook for public creditors was somewhat murky. In contrast to the First World War, there was no appeal to the pocketbook by offering higher-than-normal interest rates. The best economic rationale that was now offered for wartime saving was that it helped provide for the future in a general sort of way. It was inconceivable that a Harvey Fisk of the 1940s would have proclaimed, "Those who have bought bonds from patriotic motives will unquestionably be rewarded for doing so in hard dollars and cents profits [when postwar interest rates fall] . . . as did the big returns from similar investments after the Civil War."[79] With interest rates already so low, the best hope was simply that they should not rise. Perhaps the repeated propaganda leitmotif of war bond purchase as patriotic duty was a subliminal signal to subscribers not to expect any return on their investment?

Then there was the redistributionist undercurrent of war finance. This had been quite explicit in Keynes's proposal for compulsory savings, in which the lower income brackets were to have their taxes repaid with interest. Even without his scheme, the highly progressive tax rates imposed during the war achieved the same result. As only one example, the number of British taxpayers reporting incomes over £6,000 had fallen from seven thousand in 1938 to just eighty in 1944. The share of income held by the wealthiest sections of the population fell sharply on both sides of the Atlantic, with a corresponding rise in the share received by wage earners.

The war had also given a boost to ideals of social cohesion and public welfare represented by the New Deal and by the Beveridge Report. In the United States, a 1942 report by the National Resources Planning Board proposed a "bill of rights" enshrining "freedom from fear of old age, want, dependency, sickness, unemployment and accident."[80] In Britain the new political agenda was firmly established by the summary ouster of the Conservatives in July 1945. By far the most important influence on the postwar debate, however, was the fear of unemployment. The dole lines of the 1930s left deep scars even when full employment had been restored by the stimulus of war spending. It is certainly not too much to state, as did the *New York Times* and *The Economist* in 1942, that the desire for full employment overrode all other political and social ideas. On both sides of the Atlantic, governments enshrined full employment as official public policy.[81] None of these political currents suggested that the traditional postwar retrenchment would occur.

And so postwar inflation was inevitable. Prices rose throughout 1946 and 1947, and then stabilized in 1948 at around 30% higher than 1945 levels. They might have settled there but for the Korean War. A further surge in price levels occurred in 1951, and again, there was no question of postwar deflation. By 1953 prices were around 50% higher than at the end of the Second World War. For the holders of government bonds the contrast between the two world wars was clear. In past wars it had been generally understood that the losers might fail to repay their debts. Now, it seemed, the victors would follow the same path.

Real Rates of Return on Allied War Loans[82]

Over a period of ten years from issue

	World War I *% per annum*	World War II *% per annum*
United States	+4.2	–1.7
Great Britain	+4.6	–2.0

The political and economic equation that led to this novel state of affairs was somewhat different on either side of the Atlantic. America left the war economically strengthened. Britain left it weakened. Internationally, Britain was temporarily bankrupt, and Keynes's last service to his country before his early death in 1946 was the negotiation of a large loan from the United States. In London, too, there was a government whose avowed intention was the redistribution of wealth. Hugh Dalton, the Chancellor of the Exchequer, justified his easy-money policies partly on the basis that they encouraged the "euthanasia of the rentier" and "fitted in well with our general policy of diminishing the inequalities of wealth."[83] Such language would not have been heard in Washington. It is important, however, not to overemphasize the differences between the two countries. The policy of easy money was carried on for the same *economic* motives and with the same inflationary results in America and elsewhere. Moreover, Britain's financial problems were temporary ones that resulted from the diversion of industry to war production, thereby reducing the possibility of exporting manufactured goods in payment for essential food and raw material supplies. The fundamental infrastructure of the country was sound, and GNP was higher than before the war. Domestically the country was not bankrupt.

The easy-money period of postwar finance lasted until 1951, but its climax was reached in 1946. The British government made a determined effort to force long-term rates to 2.5%, and this effort coincided with the short-lived peak of the bull market in long-term bonds. The investing public had become habituated both to low yields and to government "management" of the financial markets. Moreover, with memories of the 1930s still fresh, many were unconvinced that the private economy could replace the government as an outlet for their idle funds. The signs of an impending reduction in government borrowing requirements caused a brief scramble for long-term government bonds in early 1946 that caused yields to reach levels that rivaled those of the 1890s—around 2% in America and 2.5% in Britain—before falling back to wartime levels. The twenty-five-year bull market in bonds was over, and a thirty-five-year bear market was about to begin. Yet for some years, bond yields remained close to their historic lows.[84] It remains one of the mysteries of investment psychology that no one seemed to care in the late 1940s that inflation was running at well over 10% per year, whereas in the 1890s prices were falling.

The American government, falling into the same trap as in 1919–1920, persuaded itself that its policies were in the best interests of public credit. The Federal Reserve was required to support the market for long-term bonds at par regardless of the consequences for monetary growth and inflation. Matters came to a head in early 1951 in a seminal debate between the Secretary of the Treasury, John Snyder, and his opponents in the central bank and elsewhere. In John Synder's view the maintenance of the now hallowed rate of 2.5% on government savings bonds and long-term debt instruments had become a matter of national integrity:

> We have an obligation of the highest order not only to maintain the finances of the Government in the soundest possible condition but also to fulfill our responsibilities to the millions of Federal security holders throughout the Nation. A stable and confident situation in the market for Federal securities is our first line of defense on the financial front. . . .
>
> It is my view that a 2½ percent rate of interest on long-term Treasury bonds is a fair and equitable rate—to our Government which is borrowing the money, to the purchaser who is lending the money, and to the taxpayer who has to pay the interest on the money borrowed. . . . The 2½ percent rate of interest . . . is an integral part of the financial structure of our country. . . .
>
> The credit of the United States Government has become the keystone upon which rests the economic structure of the world. Stability in our government securities is essential. I do not think that we can exaggerate when we emphasize these matters. I think they are basic to our national survival.[85]

Fine sentiments, reminiscent in many ways of the official Venetian description of the Monte Vecchio as the "the principal foundation and continual and perpetual stability of our state."[86] Perhaps it is no coincidence that both assertions were made when the public debt was being progressively devalued. Against Snyder were ranged a number of voices that argued not only that it was impossible to contain inflation unless interest rates were raised, but that it was counterproductive to support the nominal value of government securities when their real value was declining. What was the point of pontificating about the global importance of American public credit if it was being undermined from within by inflation?

> Over the past decade, $1,000 invested in the highest-yield Government securities (United States Savings Bonds) would now buy only $750 worth of consumers' goods even after the large interest accumulation is added on to the principal. . . . In these circumstances excessive concern over nominal savings in interest cost is likely to go down as a classic example of fiscal shortsightedness.[87]

> The real threat to Government credit is that people will come to lose confidence in the future purchasing power of the dollars in which the debt is stated. . . . People have already seen the purchasing power of their dollars, bonds, and

> their fixed-price assets decline more than 40 percent during the past 10 years. We cannot be certain that they will continue to be willing to buy and hold Government bonds if they come to expect this trend to continue.[88]

In the end the government lost the debate, and interest rates were allowed to rise. A similar process took place in Britain, coinciding with the return to power of the Conservatives.[89] The rise in interest rates cemented the losses of the public bondholders but at least prevented further erosion of their position through inflation (for the time being).

The most striking aspect of the postwar inflation is the very modest amount of social discontent that it provoked. There were no mass protests by crowds of holders of savings bonds who felt defrauded by their government. The period was, on the whole, characterized by a fairly high level of social consensus. No one expressed support for inflation, but then no one ever voices support for inflation. The lower income groups were undoubtedly aware that the postwar world was more favorable to their interests than the prewar one. Whatever the difficulties of the era, at least there was full employment. The wealthy, with an eye on the looming menace of communism in Europe, were probably relieved that matters were not worse. For the millions of holders of government securities, the erosion of savings had been a gradual affair—less distressing than a partial default, or a capital levy. Their losses were relatively modest in the end, at least when compared to events in France, Germany, and Italy. Perhaps they understood subliminally that theirs was a final patriotic sacrifice for the war effort. The more reflective, or economically educated, may even have grasped that the underlying cause of the inflation was the failure of citizens to respond adequately to war loan campaigns.

EPILOGUE:
THE END OF THE AFFAIR

Was this, then, the ideal way to finance wars? Or was it a unique virtuoso performance that contained the seeds of its own destruction? The answer cannot be known, since, mercifully, there has been no Third World War to put the matter to the test. There is good reason to suspect, however, that the second hypothesis is the correct one. The successful financing of the Second World War would not have been possible without the persistence among investors of the traditional assumption (more than plausible in light of interwar history) that prices could go down as well as up. It was this assumption that made the holders of long-term fixed-interest securities willing to accept yields that fell, from time to time, below the level of inflation. The fly in the ointment in the 1940s, however, was that it was now official policy to ensure that prices would never fall again. While there was no consensus in favor of inflation, there was an absolute determination on the part of politicians of all stripes to avoid deflation. The only financial justification, therefore, for holding bonds that yielded 3% or less was the assumption that the politicians would fail in this objective, and that the Second World War would be followed, like its predecessors, by a period of falling prices.

As is now well-known, this did not occur. The immediate postwar inflation stalled in 1948; but the possibility of a sustained downturn in general price levels during 1949 was removed by the outbreak of the Korean War. This too was a conflict whose inflationary impact was not followed by a postwar deflation. In light of these events it seems almost perverse that long-term American government bonds should have rallied sufficiently by early 1954 to yield 2.5% again. A note of reality set in three years later, and new issues could not be raised for less than 4%. But even this rate was overoptimistic in a world where prices moved in one direction only. It was conceivable that inflation might average 1% in good times, thus making 4% a reasonable rate of return. But this was unlikely to be a prudent long-term assumption when any temporary economic shock would inevitably serve to raise the average. When low inflation (but not deflation) once again became a believable long-term hypothesis in the 1990s, the markets were willing to price long-term government bonds at yields of between 5% and 6%, not lower. These were rates that had American bondholders gasping for breath when they first established themselves in the late 1960s. In Britain, where inflation was consistently worse than in the United States, even during the years of the postwar "economic miracle," such levels were reached a decade earlier. By the end of the 1960s British bondholders were refusing to lend except at rates that approached double digits.

Between the restrained inflation of the years from 1953 to 1965 and the 1990s, moreover, there lie two decades in which inflation was anything but restrained. In one, largely liberal-Keynesian, view this unparalleled surge in prices was merely the unfortunate result of the irresponsible financing of the Vietnam War followed by the unrelated mishap of two successive oil crises. It is impossible, however, so entirely to absolve the revolution in economic and political thought that took place in the 1930s. It may be true, as J. K. Galbraith wittily put it, that "faced with a choice between unemployment and price increases the liberal politician unhesitatingly condemns both."[1] It is, however, undeniable that a climate of opinion took hold in the postwar years that led to a ratcheting up of inflationary expectations. The first element was a continual lowering of the acceptable level of unemployment and a raising of the acceptable level of inflation. Keynes's disciples in Cambridge started to argue that any level of unemployment over 2% was "cold-blooded."[2] If the maintenance of a long-term inflation rate of 1% required periodic bouts of unemployment of 5% or more, then perhaps the inflation target should be raised to 2% or 3%. In an article in the *New York Times* in 1959, the economist Sumner H. Slichter argued that "the problems of creeping inflation are a small price to pay for avoiding the much greater problems of unemployment and a rate of growth that falls far short of our potential."[3] It was clear to Slichter that such a policy implied long-term bond yields of 5% or more, but to others the modest rise in interest rates in the late 1950s and early 1960s was already excessive. The independence of the Federal Reserve was attacked, and in 1964 the *Washington Post* complained that "the United States is the only great power in which monetary policy is not subject to the firm control of the incumbent administration. . . . The time for thoroughgoing reform has arrived."[4]

To compound the effects of these shifts in popular economic thinking, there was the seemingly inexorable expansion of the role of the government. In the 1950s, the "social" budget (excluding military spending and debt interest) represented under 7% of GNP.[5] By the end of the 1970s, it had more than doubled to nearly 15%—the bulk of the growth coming in the decade from 1965 to 1975 as the "Great Society" programs kicked in. To some extent, the additional social spending could be financed by the "peace dividend" of falling military expenditure—especially at the end of the Vietnam War. But the peace dividend represented no more than 4% of GNP. Prudent finance, therefore, would have suggested an equivalent rise in taxes. The problem was that the limits of taxpayer tolerance had long since been reached. Federal tax revenues had risen from around 5–6% of GNP in the 1930s to around 20% of GNP during the Second World War. By some unspoken political consensus, they have refused to budge from this level ever since. In 1953 they were 18.8% of GNP. In 1963 the figure was 17.5%. In 1973 it was 18%, and ten years later it was 19%.

The inevitable result was a surge in public borrowing. As Robert Samuelson pointed out in an article in *Newsweek* in 1993, "We simply borrowed to pay for bigger government, because the tax burden has actually remained stable."[6] Borrowing was not the only means of bridging the gap in the 1970s, however. A significant part of the extra spending was financed by inflation, that is, by paying negative real interest on the public debt. From 1971 to 1980 the interest paid by the federal government represented a true cost of minus 1.3% per annum. The average budget deficit for the decade was 1.7% of GNP. Had a reasonable rate of return been paid on the debt, however, the figure would have been closer to 3% of GNP. This was a modest outcome when compared to that of America's wartime ally, Great Britain. Inflation rates that approached 10% seemed shocking enough in America; but in Britain, where prices rose by more than 25% in 1975, the average for the decade was 14%. The average budget deficit was 4.2% of GNP. If a positive rate of return had been paid on the debt, the figure would have been 11%.[7]

The inflation of the 1970s was so unprecedented that it took years for investor expectations to catch up with reality. Every time yields reached new highs, inflation rose still further. Finally, bondholders refused to buy except at rates that discounted the continuation of inflation in excess of 10% for the indefinite future. In America the bottom of the bear market occurred in the autumn of 1981, when the government was forced to sell twenty-year bonds at a yield of 15¾%. In Britain the trough came in the dark days of 1974, when Consols traded at a price of 13⅞ to yield a shade over 18%.

The importance of the great bear market from 1946 to 1981 lies in the progressive erosion of trust in government. High inflation could, perhaps, be excused in time of war, but not in a time of peace and unparalled prosperity. Moreover, while it was unreasonable to blame corporate borrowers for the negative returns experienced on investments in their bonds, the same indulgence could not be extended toward governments, in whose hands, ultimately, lay the power to determine the course of prices. Perhaps the most shocking thought was that governments were profiting at the expense of the unsophisticated, whose savings it had hitherto been their self-appointed role to nurture and protect.

As inflation rates continued to increase, there were some who began to question the sustainability of democratic government. Sydney Homer, the historian of interest rates and head of research at Salomon Brothers, expressed himself ironically on this trend in 1974:

> When I was a student in college, we were all taught that peacetime inflation was unthinkable in our great United States, or for that matter in any other first-class enlightened industrial state except perhaps France. Peacetime inflation was then to be found chiefly in banana republics with their pesos, escudos, and other queer-sounding currencies, and all they needed to save them from the disgrace of inflation was to obtain the monetary advice of any one of our distinguished economists and follow it. . . . Our [current] inflation is unprecedented in our economic history for times of peace. . . . What has happened to our stockpile of astute economists that used to lecture small South American countries on how to behave themselves fiscally? Indeed, a few of them are now telling us to emulate South American methods even though these often require a military dictatorship.[8]

At a Congressional hearing entitled "Crisis in the Bond Market" in March 1980, the treasurer of the State of South Carolina ominously quoted the eighteenth-century political theorist Alexander Tytler:

> A democracy cannot exist as a permanent form of government. It can only exist until the voters discover that they can vote themselves largess from the public treasury. From that moment on, the majority always votes for the candidates promising the most benefits from the public treasury with the result that a democracy always collapses over loose fiscal policy, always followed by a dictatorship.[9]

A British cartoon from 1974 neatly encapsulates the sense of betrayal experienced by those who had doggedly held onto their war loans in the postwar era.[10]

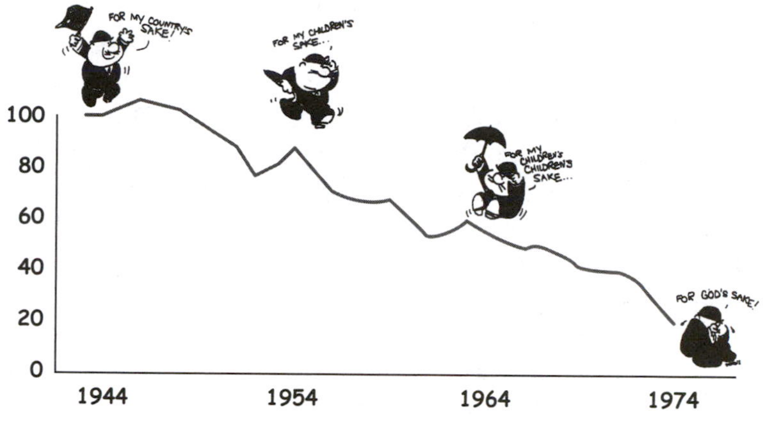

The Rewards of Victory
The Price of British 3.5% War Loan, 1944–1974

This brings us back to the question posed at the beginning of this epilogue. Was the financing of the Second World War a repeatable achievement? The unavoidable conclusion is that by the late 1970s a patriotic appeal to the public to buy bonds at negative real interest rates would merely have provided suitable material for Saturday-night television satire. This is not to say that another war on the scale of the Second World War could not have been financed. Governments can always raise money if they need to. Indeed, the bond markets did not dry up in the years of inflation, even though there were moments when observers predicted that they might. As early as May 1969, the respected magazine *Institutional Investor* featured a picture of a dinosaur on its cover in an issue that lamented the demise of the American bond market. There were periodic "buyers' strikes" on both sides of the Atlantic from the late 1960s to the early 1980s, but it was always found that, if yields were raised sufficiently, even long-term bonds could be sold. The question, however, is whether, in 1980, say, the U.S. government would have been willing to offer rates of 15% on war loans in the hope of finding voluntary subscribers. It seems highly improbable, and the strategy would soon have been found to be prohibitively expensive. It is far more likely that a familiar package of wartime controls would have obliged consumers to save substantial portions of their incomes, and these would then have been quietly funneled to the government through the banking system. The "totalitarian" system of war finance would finally have replaced the "democratic" one.

The obvious riposte to this argument is the one so often leveled at generals: that it attempts to fight the last war, not the present one. The Third World War would not have been a replay of the Second World War for the simple reason that nuclear weapons would have ensured that the encounter would be short and cheap (but not sweet). The undoubted validity of this argument gives rise to a nagging suspicion. Perhaps it was the subliminal knowledge that it was no longer necessary to nurse their credit ratings for the next great war that allowed governments to behave as they did in the decades after 1945.

This leads to another line of reasoning. In a world where any superpower conflict leads to mutual assured destruction, only small-scale conventional wars are possible. But such wars do not lead to sufficient levels of borrowing to qualify as heirs of the great wars of the past. Even a war on the scale of Vietnam is virtually invisible on a long-term chart of American public indebtedness. In the age of nuclear deterrence, the ancient connection between war and public debt has been broken.

This leaves peacetime borrowing—of which there has obviously been a great deal since 1945. But peacetime borrowing differs from its wartime equivalent in a number of crucial respects. Peacetime deficits, however much finger wagging they may incite, are relatively small. The highest of America's Reagan-era deficits represented only 5.5% of GNP, whereas in the Second World War the country was borrowing 25% of GNP annually for several years. A borrowing requirement of 5% of GNP is never going to require a great public bond drive for its fulfillment. The main concern of the credit markets in peacetime is the relatively mundane business of refinancing existing debt as it matures.

But there is a more profound difference between peace and war borrowing. Because great wars are moments of heightened national unity, the deficits to which they give rise enjoy a level of political legitimacy that peacetime ones can never attain. Some small level of legitimacy could conceivably be attributed to Keynesian deficit spending in time of economic recession or depression. But since these events are characterized by a popular desire to save and a flight to safety, the government has little difficulty in raising money without waving the patriotic banner. Indeed, since the whole purpose of government spending in these situations is to persuade people to save less and spend more, a public bond drive whose implicit message is to encourage saving would be inherently absurd.

One thing is certain. No legitimacy whatsoever can be ascribed to the most common cause of deficits in the postwar era, namely, the inability of society to resolve debates about the level (and distribution) of taxation and spending. Deficits in this case are merely the financial expression of a sociopolitical stalemate. The nation, far from having a common cause, is a house divided into warring economic interest groups. It is entirely inconceivable that there should be any connotation of patriotism or civic virtue in lending to the state in such circumstances.

The result is that public borrowing in time of peace is always more apolitical and impersonal than in time of war. The sense of depersonalization has been accentuated by dominant features of the postwar economic landscape. First among these is the continuing rise of institutional investment. In the late nineteenth century, the only important financial intermediaries were banks, and to some extent insurance companies. These familiar institutions have now been joined by pension funds and investment funds, whose role continues to grow with each year. The portion of public debts held by domestic financial intermediaries in recent years ranges from 37% in the United States to more than 77% in Japan.[11] Parallel to institutionalization is globalization. International ownership of public debts (again largely by institutions) is growing rapidly. In the United States, Germany, France, and Italy, the proportion is currently in the region of 30%.[12] As recently as 1970, by contrast, the figure was just over 5% in the United States, and less than 2% in Germany. In a striking turnaround from earlier times, a substantial foreign investment in the national debt is now seen as a proof of international credit standing rather than as a sign of economic immaturity or financial weakness.

The corollary of these trends has been the progressive disappearance of the hero of our tale, the citizen creditor, from the political scene. In the United States, the savings bonds that were once considered a vital part of national security now represent only 5% of public debt. Even when all other government securities are taken into consideration, the percentage owned by American citizens is under 10%.[13] In other countries the ratio is even lower. In France, the French citizen, whose name was once proudly inscribed in the *Grand Livre de la Dette Publique*, now owns only 1.6% of all public debt securities.[14] In Germany, where the era of the patriotic bondholder was snuffed out by the hyperinflation of the 1920s, the citizen has never regained a central role in the public finances. The Federal Republic has always preferred to borrow from banks.[15] In Japan only 2.3% of government bonds are owned by Japanese citizens.[16] Only in Britain, where the National Savings system still provides around 17% of the national debt, is there a modest residue of the old philosophy of public borrowing as an intimate compact between state and citizens. It is not that the citizens of modern states have no economic interest in their national debts; it is rather that, because of financial intermediation, they are scarcely aware of having one.

Perhaps a sudden shock or military threat can revive the old equations of democratic public finance—in other words, such an event as September 11. There was an immediate renaissance of public spirit in the wake of that terrible event, and the surge of patriotism led to calls in Congress for a new war loan to support the "War on Terrorism." In December 2001, the Treasury Department issued a "Patriot Bond" in response to the pressure. But while the Patriot Bond is a tribute to the bond drives of the Second World War and a reminder of the strength of the historic alliance of democracy and public borrowing, it is more in the nature of a snapshot from an old photo album than a realistic policy for the twenty-first century. It is unlikely that the War on Terrorism can ever be sufficiently costly for world's only superpower to require a new round of patriotic loans. The U.S. government's current borrowing requirements have more to do with recent tax reductions than with increased military costs. It is scarcely surprising, then, that the Treasury Department makes no claims that the funds raised from the Patriot Bond will do more than enter the general coffers of the state. Indeed, the new bond has received so little publicity from the government that its future seems as dim as that of the venerable Series EE Savings Bond that it was supposed to replace. After many years of atrophy, the U.S. Treasury appears to have lost track of the political dimension of public borrowing and to prefer to concentrate exclusively on administering the nation's finances with its undoubted technical proficiency.

The change in governments' view of public credit is mirrored by changes in the credit markets themselves. While the bond market in its infancy was simply the financial expression of the political freedom of medieval Italian republics, the mature bond market of the modern world has a life of its own. Indeed, the bond market is now feted as a supranational, almost godlike force that passes daily judgment on the behavior of governments without fear or favor—stampeding like a "galloping herd"* at the mere whiff of reckless policy. It was after enduring one such nerve-wracking stampede that James Carville, President Clinton's chief of staff, whimsically observed that, if there was such a thing as reincarnation, he would like to be reborn as the bond market. This aspect of the bond market

*This is the phrase used by Thomas L. Friedman in *The Lexus and the Olive Tree.*

is not entirely new, however. In the long years of peace during the nineteenth century, there were two contradictory tendencies at play. The first, described in Chapter 8, was the development of institutions that rooted the public debt as far as possible in the national polity by encouraging popular investment in government securities. The second, antithetical to the first, was the development of an international bond market with no special attachment to any single nation. In 1906 Nathan Rothschild, whose family were the high priests of this market, went so far as to comment in one of his letters to the Paris house that it was "a curious thing how investors & capitalists dread the stocks of their own countries particularly if they live in Europe."[17] His words reflected the globalization of finance and trade during the period before the First World War. As soon as war broke out, of course, Lord Rothschild's words were forgotten. For the duration of the fighting, the bond market ceased to be an impersonal supranational force and became the expression of democratic nationalism. With the return of peace and prosperity after 1945, it is not entirely surprising that some of the features of the late-nineteenth-century landscape should have been rediscovered. While it is too extreme to state that investors "dread" the bonds of their own countries, it is certainly true that an internationally balanced portfolio is becoming an axiom of modern investment philosophy.

Nowadays the relationship between treasury departments and bond markets is little different from that between any other participants in the financial marketplace. Governments seek to lower their interest and administration costs while managing their maturity schedules and widening the pool of potential investors. Bond buyers seek to increase their returns while maintaining liquidity and controlling their exposure to risk. There is nothing patriotic or intrinsically democratic about the process. It is not that democracy and bond markets are hostile to one another. The old ties, once so powerful, still linger somewhere in the recesses of memory. In the meantime, the two remain on cordial terms. Credit markets still generally rank democracies more favorably than other forms of government. For all practical purposes, however, the venerable marriage between public credit and democratic government, so vital a factor in the history of the world, has been dissolved.

A NOTE ON CURRENCIES

GLOSSARY

NOTES

BIBLIOGRAPHY

ACKNOWLEDGMENTS

INDEX

A NOTE ON CURRENCIES

I have attempted, insofar as it is possible, to limit the number of currencies used in the text. In so vast a historical time frame, however, there are inevitably a considerable number of them to deal with. Understanding historical currencies was considerably easier for readers in the days when money was still synonymous with precious metals. All that was necessary was to compare the weights of earlier coins and currency units to those of existing coins. For example, it was natural for nineteenth-century American writers to describe the ancient talent as equivalent to $1,000; for if you took 1,000 silver dollars you had more or less the weight of a talent of silver. Such simple relationships are hard for current readers to grasp, their monetary moorings cut adrift by decades of paper currency inflation. However, the simplest procedure, even nowadays, remains to reduce all coins and currency units to a standard unit of weight, and this is the procedure followed in this book. The most convenient unit is the metric gram, even if this is somewhat unfamiliar to American readers, for coins generally weigh far less than one ounce, and the traditional English subdivision of grains (7,000 per ounce) is even harder to follow. The book limits itself to two metric weights: grams for coins and currencies, and tons (1,000,000 grams) for large-scale amounts like state budgets. The American equivalents are as follows:

1 oz. = 28.35 grams
1 ton (U.S.) = 0.907 tons (metric)

The U.S. and metric tons are therefore close enough to be understood as equivalent by readers.

Apart from limiting the number of currencies mentioned, I have also attempted to find a currency in each period that can serve as a basis of international comparison. The currency had to be one that was stable for the period of its use, and one that would have been recognized by contemporaries as a true international standard. Additionally, throughout the first five chapters, I have periodically translated values into metric weights as a method of showing even longer-term relationships.

The Ancient World to A.D. 200

There are three important units used in the book: the talent, the drachma, and the denarius. The talent was a large unit of weight. The drachma and the denarius were small silver coins. The Roman denarius was copied from the drachma, and under the Roman Empire, *drachma* was merely the Greek word for denarius. The drachma-denarius standard depreciated so slowly as to be considered almost entirely stable from around 600 B.C. until A.D. 200, after which depreciation became so rapid that it destroyed the whole monetary system in the course of one century.

1 talent = 6,000 drachmas = 25,800 grams = 57 lb. (U.S.)
1 drachma = 4.3 grams of silver (around 400 B.C.)
1 denarius = 3.9 grams of silver (around A.D. 1)

A.D. 300–1600

There are two fundamental types of currency unit used in the book for this period: gold coins and the £.s.d. monetary system.

Gold Coins. These were based on the late Roman/Byzantine solidus, which weighed 4.55 grams of gold at the time of its introduction in the fourth century A.D. Because its weight was not far different from that of the old silver denarius, it was sometimes referred to as the *gold denarius.* When much of the Eastern Empire was conquered by the Muslims, this coin was retained by the new rulers and was the word *denarius* transmuted into *dinar*. In the West, there were no gold coins for many centuries after the Dark Ages, but when they reappeared in the thirteenth century, they all copied the Byzantine coin, which had now been reduced to 3.55 grams of gold. The Venetian ducat and the Florentine florin were the two most important. They were never debased and are by far the most convenient unit of international comparison during the period. In order to have an idea of their value in terms of Greco-Roman currency, it is necessary to understand that gold was generally worth between ten and twelve times silver. The reader will not go far wrong if he considers the Roman/Byzantine solidus to be worth between 12–15 drachmas/denarii and the medieval ducat/florin to be worth 10–12 drachmas/denarii.

In the sixteenth century international comparisons can still be made in ducats—this time the Spanish ducat, originally a gold coin on the Venetian model, but after 1537 a currency equal to 35.25 grams of silver (designed to be a silver equivalent of the gold ducat at the current gold/silver exchange rate of 10:1). In silver terms, the Spanish ducat was stable until 1600, but it is important to bear in mind that it had lost a great deal of value in real terms over the previous century. The importation of large quantities of silver from the Americas had resulted in a quadrupling of prices in silver terms and in the devaluation of silver against gold. The silver ducat of 1600 was probably worth no more than one-fifth of the gold ducat of a century earlier.

£.s.d. This designation stands for *libra, solidus, denarius.* The extraordinary persistence of names in monetary matters is shown by the fact that the word *denarius* lived on not only as the Islamic dinar, but as the Western European penny (*denaro* in Italian, *denier* in French). In the later Dark Ages, the only coins minted in western Europe were little silver pennies containing around 1.5 grams of silver. Two hundred and forty of those were struck from a pound (*libra* in Latin, *lira* in Italian, *livre* in French) of silver. The pound contained 12 (not 16) ounces and weighed anywhere between 330 and 410 grams depending on the region. Charlemagne standardized the system throughout his empire on the basis of a 1.7-gram penny and a 408-gram pound. The solidus in the £.s.d. system (*soldo* in Italian, *sous* in French) was inspired by the Roman/Byzantine coin, but in western Europe, it was not a coin, but merely an accounting unit of 12 pennies. The mark, which eventually formed the basis of many currencies east of the Rhine, was originally a subdivision of the £.s.d. system, equal to two-thirds of 1 pound.

From its promising start under Charlemagne, the monetary pound soon lost its connection with the pound weight and started to devalue. The rate of devaluation was faster in some places that in others. Whereas gold coins maintained their weights over centuries, the monetary value of the pound, the livre, the lira, and the mark varied sharply from time to time and from place to place. In Italy, with its proliferation of city-states, there was an equal proliferation of lira values. The process stabilized only in the late sixteenth century in England, and in the eighteenth and nineteenth centuries on the continent of Europe. Until such stabilizations occurred, the £.s.d. system is largely useless for comparing values over time or place and crops up in the text only in local contexts. The following data give an idea of some of the silver weights of the monetary pound.

Grams of Silver	c. 1300	c. 1500	c. 1600
English pound	319.0	174.6	111.4
French livre	81.0	21.7	12.4
Genoese lira	80.0	12.8	8.6
Venetian lira	14.0	6.2	4.3

1600–1914

During this period, with the exception of the Napoleonic Wars, the English pound sterling was a stable currency worth 111.4 grams of silver—later changed to 7.3 grams of gold. In specie terms, therefore, the pound was equivalent to approximately 2 gold ducats. (In purchasing-power terms, however, because gold had lost over half its value by the mid-seventeenth century, the pound was worth rather less than the medieval gold ducat.) From 1600 to 1914, the English pound forms the obvious basis for international comparisons, even if it remained a relatively insignificant currency in international terms until the eighteenth century.

The other currencies of the £.s.d. system started to stabilize after 1700. The French livre was fixed at 4.45 grams of silver in 1726. During the French Revolution, the livre was replaced by the franc, which contained 4.5 grams of silver. Both currencies had a long-term exchange rate with sterling of 25:1. The various Italian lire also stabilized in the eighteenth century at weights between 2.4 and 5.4 grams of silver. Napoleon introduced the franc with its decimal subdivisions into Italy; and the basic outlines of the new system were maintained after his fall. The new Italian lira was also set at 4.5 grams of silver in 1860. In Germany (and, most important, in Prussia) the mark stabilized at 5.55 grams of silver during the eighteenth century, which gave it a long-term exchange rate with sterling of 20:1.

Thaler/dollar/crown/peso. The opening up of new silver mines in the late fifteenth century enabled states to mint a new generation of large coins containing between 24 and 28 grams of silver. In Germany, these were called *thalers* after the largest of these mines in Joachimsthal, Austria. In various countries, most famously the United States, this name transmuted into *dollar*. Elsewhere the coins were known as *crowns* (in England), *kroner* (in Scandinavia), *écus* (in France), and *pesos* (in Spain). These coins were standards of international commerce in the seventeenth and eighteenth centuries, especially the peso minted from the Spanish mines in the Americas, and they were (almost) never debased. These coins had had exchange rates with the English pound sterling that ranged from 4.0 to 4.8:1, depending on their weights. By the end of the nineteenth century, the U.S. dollar had detached itself from silver and had became a gold-based currency with a sterling exchange rate of 4.87:1.

1914 TO THE PRESENT

The twentieth century was one of those periods, like the third century and the sixteenth century A.D., when there was no currency available to serve as a truly stable basis for international and intertemporal comparisons. The U.S. dollar was clearly the dominant international currency of the period and is used as the point of reference in this book; but its record as a store of value is worse than that of the Spanish silver ducat between 1520 and 1620. Indeed its record is not much better than that of the Roman denarius between A.D. 181 and 284. The dollar lost nearly 95% of its purchasing power in the course of one century, as opposed to around 75% for the Spanish ducat and 98.5% for the denarius. In mitigation, however, it has to be borne in mind that the whole concept of currency stability has changed now that the traditional ties with gold and silver have been broken. In the old days, a stable currency was one whose precious metal content remained unchanged. This did not mean that prices were stable. It was accepted that they might might rise or fall significantly over long periods. It was understood, however, that a currency with a fixed metal content would not depreciate significantly over the long term. Nowadays, a "stable" currency is one that is designed to depreciate consistently at a low and predictable rate. Central banks are given inflation targets of 2–2.5% and are expected to take action to prevent inflation from falling *below* this rate as well as rising *above* it. By this criterion, the ideal currency should lose between 87% and 92% of its purchasing power in the course of one century. The depreciation of the dollar is therefore largely the product of its place in historical time. Whereas the devaluation of the Roman denarius was a symptom of the near collapse of the empire, the devaluation of the dollar is, to some extent at least, merely the outward expression of a new theory of monetary rectitude.

The other point that needs to be made is that until 1945, at least, the purchasing power of the dollar was still within historically recognizable limits, even if it had fluctuated sharply over the previous fifty years.

Present-day Values in U.S. Dollars

Attributing present-day values to historical coins and currencies is a vexed issue. Quite apart from the difficulty of creating accurate indices, there is the added problem of the vast increase in wages relative to prices that has occurred since the Industrial Revolution. However, since the reader may reasonably wish to have some idea of what the currencies used in the book mean in modern terms, I have attempted to address the issue.

An approximate idea of present-day purchasing power of the principal currencies used in the text can be given by indexing them to the price of wheat until 1850, and thereafter to U.S. retail prices. This produces the following values:

1 Athenian drachma (c. 430 B.C.) = $7
1 Venetian ducat (c. A.D. 1400) = $100
1 pound sterling (c. A.D. 1850) = $90

These figures give a reasonable idea of what an Athenian or a Venetian would be able to buy in the modern world if he had one drachma or one ducat in his pocket. However, it has to be borne in mind that the city-states of ancient Greece and medieval Italy were very poor societies by modern standards. A living wage in fifteenth-century Venice would have been 12–15 ducats per year. In terms of relative social status, therefore, a ducat was worth far more than $100 dollars is worth in present-day Western society.

GLOSSARY

annuity A series of fixed equal payments, in theory annual (hence the name) but in practice often semiannual, quarterly, or monthly. Annuities are not necessarily connected to loans; for instance, they may represent a pension. A loan, however, may be repaid by means of an annuity. An example is a fixed-rate mortgage, which is repaid by regular equal payments that do not distinguish between principal and interest. It is in this context that annuities occur in this book. There are three fundamental types of annuity: (1) *Life annuity*: Payments stop when the recipient dies. (2) *Term annuity*: Payments stop after a specified number of years (as in a fixed-rate mortgage). (3) *Perpetual annuity*: Payments stop only if the borrower chooses to redeem the annuity for a preagreed sum. Unlike the other two kinds of annuity, in which interest and capital are not explicitly separated, the annual payment represents interest on the sum borrowed. The amount payable on redemption represents the principal.

bearer paper/bearer bonds Securities that are payable to the holder (bearer) of the paper rather than to a specifically named individual. Financial instruments of this type are obviously easier to trade than when changes in ownership have to be noted on an official register and new securities issued.

bills/*bons* Pieces of paper representing short-term obligations to pay. Treasury bills *(bons du trésor)* are short-term (under one-year) unsecured obligations of the Treasury.

bond Originally, the security for a loan that was redeemed when the loan was repaid. The term is now used to describe a share in a long-term fixed-interest-rate loan. The loan is divided into small-denomination "bonds" that can be sold to multiple investors and then traded on the "bond market."

Consols The name is an abbreviation of *consolidated* annuities, i.e., when a number of outstanding debts were aggregated into a single issue of perpetual annuities. Many countries had such consolidated annuities and sometimes used the word *consols* to describe them. In this book, the word refers only to the British Consols that first came into existence in 1754 and are still traded on the London Stock Exchange.

conversion The exchange ("conversion") of one type of security for another. In this book, the term almost always refers to the conversion of perpetual annuities into others paying a lower rate of interest. The process may be "voluntary" if the holders of the old annuities agree or "involuntary" or "forced" if they do not.

convertible Broadly, any financial instrument that is exchangeable for another at the choice of the holder. The most frequent use of the term in this book, however, is to describe paper money that is freely "convertible" into gold or silver coins.

coupon A detachable part of a bond representing a single interest payment. It is removed and canceled when the interest payment is made. In common terminology, the "coupon rate" is the nominal rate of interest on the bond—as opposed to the yield received by the investor, which varies depending on the price at which he bought the bond.

current yield The yield received by an investor without any consideration of capital appreciation or depreciation. (It is calculated by dividing the nominal interest rate by the purchase price and multiplying by 100.)

debasement The process whereby coins are reminted so as to produce a new series coins of equal face value but lesser real value in terms of their precious metal content. Debasement occurs either by the simple reduction of the size of the coins or, more commonly, by the addition of a quantity of inexpensive metal while the apparent size and weight are left unchanged.

funded debt/floating debt Long-term debt and short-term debt, but the distinction is rather more precise and stringent than that. Debt was considered "funded" if the money for its payment (both interest and principal) was clearly identified within the normal government budget. If not, the debt was considered "floating," since it would need to be refinanced when it came due. Annuities were invariably considered "funded" since there was no requirement to come up with additional sums for the repayment of principal. With the demise of annuities as a form of government debt, the terms have fallen into disuse, since most contemporary government debts are effectively "floating."

gage A fixed annual sum payable to the holder of a French government office under the ancien régime.

gilts British government bonds, originally given this name because of the gilded edges of the paper on which they were printed.

GNP/NNP Gross national product/net national product. The distinction between the two is that an allowance for depreciation is deducted from GNP in order to give NNP. NNP is therefore very close to **national income** (q.v.).

juro The Castilian term for **annuity** (q.v.)

legal tender Money that is declared by the government to be legally valid for payment of taxes, commercial transactions and debts within the country.

life annuity See **annuity**.

national income The sum of all wages, salaries, profits, interest, dividends, rent, etc., received by the population of a country. This figure is slightly lower than **GNP** (q.v.) because deductions are made for depreciation and certain government subsidies and indirect taxes.

option In financial terms, the right to buy (or, alternatively, the right to sell) a share or other financial instrument at an agreed-on price for a specified period of time.

par (value) The official (parity) value of a bond or other financial instrument. The par value of bonds is the principal that the bond represents. Prices for bonds are expressed as a percentage of this value, so that, in bond prices, *par* means 100%. A price of 80 means 80% of par. (Shares also have par values, but their prices are not generally expressed in this way.)

perpetual annuity See **annuity**.

perpetual debt The same as perpetual annuities.

rentes/renten The French and Dutch words for annuities. In nineteenth-century Europe (and throughout this book), the French word *rentes* was used widely to describe perpetual annuities—*rentes perpétuelles*. Life annuities were *rentes viagères* and term annuities were *rentes passagères*.

repudiation The most extreme act of default. The borrower not only fails to pay the debt but refuses to acknowledge its existence.

secondary market/secondary holder The market for bonds, or other financial instruments, after they have been first sold to investors. Investors who buy bonds on this market are secondary holders.

sinking fund A fund set up by the borrower to repurchase its bonds in the market. Generally such funds operate only if the bonds are selling below **par** (q.v.). Sinking funds appeal to borrowers and lenders for somewhat different reasons. The borrower is able to reduce the debt more cheaply than by redeeming it at face value. The bondholders have the advantage of a reliable source of liquidity in the market.

tax farming The government subcontracts the collection of a tax to a group of private investors. The tax farmers agree to pay the government a fixed sum and take the risk of how much they will eventually collect from the taxpayers.

term annuity See **annuity**.

yield to maturity/YTM If a bond is selling below (or above) **par** (q.v.), the yield is affected by the increase (or decrease) in capital when the bond is repaid. The "yield to maturity" of a bond represents the total return to an investor, including not only the annual interest payments but also the eventual increase (decrease) in capital.

NOTES

INTRODUCTION: THE FINANCIAL ROOTS OF DEMOCRACY

1. Anon., *The Chimera: Or, the French Way of Paying National Debts, Laid Open*, London, 1720, pp. 7–9. The quotation is given in more extended form in Chapter 5.
2. Joseph-Dominique Louis, addressing the French Chamber of Deputies in 1815, quoted in G. Ardant, *Histoire de l'Impôt*, Paris, 1972, p. 269. The quotation is given in more extended form in Chapter 8.
3. J. M. Augeard, *Mémoires sécrets*, ed. M. E. Bavoux, Paris, 1866, p. 81. The quotation is given in more extended form in Chapter 6.

1. TRIBES AND EMPIRES

1. H. B. Barclay, *People Without Government: An Anthropology of Anarchy*, London, 1990, p. 90.
2. L. Mair, *Primitive Government*, London, 1962, p. 58.
3. Mair, *op. cit.*, p. 60.
4. Judges 8:23.
5. T. Jacobsen, "Primitive Democracy in Ancient Mesopotamia," *Journal of Near Eastern Studies*, 1943, p. 142. After the unification of the region by Sargon of Akkad in the late third millenium B.C., Mesopotamia entered its imperial phase, and the role of the councils of elders was limited to local judicial matters.
6. According to the political anthropologist Robert Carneiro, "The possibility of producing a food surplus is inherent in virtually every agricultural village. Proof of this is afforded by the fact that villages in pre-industrial states were very commonly forced to pay a tax in kind which ranged between 10 and 25 percent of the food they produced. This indicates that among autonomous Neolithic villages there is always an unactualized margin of production, amounting to from 10 to 25 percent above subsistence, which can be squeezed out of them once they are conquered and taxed." R. Carneiro, *Political Ex-*

pansion as an Expression of the Principle of Political Exclusion, in: R. Cohen and E. R. Service, eds., *Origin of the State: The Anthropology of Political Evolution,* Philadelphia, 1978, note on p. 219.

7. M. Mauss, *The Gift: Forms and Functions of Exchange in Archaic Societies,* transl. I. Cunnision, London, 1954, p. 1.
8. Barclay, *op. cit.*, p. 81, citing the work of Pierre Clastres.
9. I Samuel 8:11–18.
10. I Samuel 30:20.
11. I Samuel 8:19–20.
12. Herodotus, *Histories*, transl. R. Waterfield, Oxford, UK, 1954, 1:96–98.
13. Mair, *op. cit.*, p. 93.
14. M. Wheeler, *The Indus Civilization,* Cambridge, UK, 1960, p. 25.
15. Information on early interest rates is taken from S. Homer and R. Sylla, *A History of Interest Rates,* 3rd edition, New Brunswick, NJ, 1991.
16. L.-S. Yang, *Money and Credit in China: A Short History,* Cambridge, MA, 1952 p. 96.
17. Herodotus, *op. cit.,* 1:88–89.
18. Herodotus, *op. cit.,* 1:6.
19. Herodotus, *op. cit.,* 1:126.
20. "They pay a land tribute to the king, because all India is the property of the Crown and no private person is permitted to hold land. Besides land tribute they pay into the royal treasury a fourth part of the produce of the soil." Megasthenes, the Greek ambassador, quoted in K. R. Sarkar, *Public Finance in Ancient India,* New Delhi, 1978, p. 56. Also pp. 90–91 on rates for irrigated land.
21. *The Cambridge History of China,* Vol. I, pp. 595–601.
22. Herodotus, *op. cit,* 3:91–2.
23. Herodotus, *op. cit,* 1:192. Herodotus states that the governor's total revenue was 55 liters of silver per day. Since this would equate to 22.4 talents per day the figure seems extraordinarily high, but Herodotus states that Babylonia was by far the wealthiest of the Persian possessions.
24. A. Andreades, *A History of Greek Public Finance,* Cambridge, MA, 1933, p. 96.
25. Quoted in M. H. Gopal, *Mauryan Public Finance,* London, 1935, p. 134.
26. Andreades, *op. cit.,* pp. 94–95.
27. Mauss, *op. cit.,* p. 40.
28. Leviticus 25:39–46.
29. F. Engels, *The Origin of the Family, Private Property, and the State,* London, 1891, pp. 173–174.
30. I Kings 9:20–22.
31. Diadorus, 3, 38 and 17, 104, quoted in B. Prasad, *The State in Ancient India,* Allahabad, India, 1928, pp. 169–170.
32. Polybius, 6, 51, quoted in S. Lancel, *Carthage: A History,* Oxford, UK, 1992, p. 118.
33. Aristotle, *Politics* IV, 13, in: *Complete Works*, ed. Barnes, Princeton, NJ, 1985.
34. Herodotus, *op. cit.,* 3:57.
35. Plutarch, quoted in J. J. Buchanan, *Theorika*, New York, 1962, p. 12.
36. Andreades, *op. cit.,* p. 266. The likely breakdown of the revenues was 200–300 talents

from liturgies, 50–100 from the silver mines, 50 from taxes on foreign residents, and the remainder from customs, fines, and other sources. See R. Goldsmith, *Premodern Financial Systems,* Cambridge, UK, 1987, pp. 32–33. The allied tribute was first fixed at 460 talents. By the beginning of Peloponnesian War it had risen to 600 talents. See Andreades, *op. cit.*, pp. 308–309.

37. Aristotle, *Constitution of Athens*, quoted in Buchanan, *op. cit,* p. 12.
38. Aristophanes, *The Knights*, quoted in R. Meiggs, *The Athenian Empire*, Oxford, UK, 1972, p. 392.
39. Isocrates, 15, 159–160, quoted in M. M. Austin, "The Finances of the Greek States," in *The Cambridge Ancient History,* Vol. VI, Cambridge, UK, 1994, p. 549.
40. L. Migeotte, *L'Emprunt public dans les cités grecques,* Quebec, 1984, gives details of 118 surviving records of public borrowing.
41. Aristotle, *Economics* II, 1348, 16.
42. Migeotte, *op. cit.*, p. 392.
43. J. W. Jones, *The Law and Legal Theory of the Greeks,* Oxford, UK, 1956, p. 156.
44. Thucydides, *Peloponnesian War* V, 89, quoted in C. H. McIlwain, *The Growth of Political Thought in the West,* London, 1932, pp. 17–18.
45. Plutarch, *Alexander the Great,* 1, 5, 329 A-D, quoted in J. W. Jones, *op. cit.*, p. 50.
46. Aristotle, *Politics* III, 9, 3.
47. Plato, *Republic*, 358e–359a, quoted in J. M. Kelly, *A Short History of Western Legal Theory,* Oxford, UK, 1992, p. 16.
48. Demosthenes, *Contra Leptinem,* quoted in Andreades, *op. cit.,* p. 171.
49. Aristotle, *Politics* II, 3, 5.
50. "When [the king], however, thinks that 'by taking a loan [*pratyadeya*] I shall cause my enemy's treasury, army, and other defensive resources to dwindle' . . . then he may take a loan." *Arthasastra*, quoted in M. H. Gopal, *op. cit.*, p. 136.
51. U. N. Ghoshal, *A History of Indian Political Ideas,* Oxford, UK, 1959, pp. 137–138.
52. Aristotle, *Economics* XII, 1349, 30.
53. Livy, *Ab Urbe Condita* V, 20, quoted in Y. Garlan, *War in the Ancient World,* London, 1975, pp. 75–76.
54. Polybius, 1, 59, 1–8, quoted in T. Frank, *An Economic Survey of Ancient Rome,* Vol. 1, Baltimore, 1933, pp. 63–64.
55. Livy, *op. cit.,* 26, 36 5–12.
56. Frank, *op. cit.*, p. 66, estimated the cost of quinquereme at 15,000 denarii.
57. G. de Sanctis, *Storia dei Romani,* Vol. III, 2, Turin, 1917, p. 629.
58. *The Wealth of Nations,* Book 5, Chapter 3.
59. Festus, quoted in M. Crawford, *Roman Republican Coinage,* Cambridge, UK, 1974, p. 612.
60. As early as 381 B.C., citizenship was offered to the people of Tusculum. See D. Heater, *A History of Citizenship,* Leicester, UK, 2000, p. 55.
61. Herodotus (3, 80–83) records a Persian debate on the relative virtues of monarchy, oligarchy, and democracy. However, the tale, even not entirely aprochryphal, never seems to leave in doubt their choice of monarchy.
62. Frank, *op. cit.*, p. 141.

63. See L.-S. Yang, *op. cit.*, p. 4. Wang Mang had 600,000 catties of gold, equivalent to 14,500 talents of gold. At the gold-silver exchange rate prevalent in Rome at the time, this would have been equivalent to around 175,000 talents of silver.
64. Goldsmith, *op. cit.*, p. 35.
65. W. Goffart, *Caput and Colonate,* Toronto, 1974, pp. 102, 30.
66. Aelius Aristides, speech delivered upon arrival in Rome in A.D. 143, sections 23, 36, 59, 64, in: J. H. Oliver, "The Ruling Power: A Study of the Roman Empire in the Second Century After Christ through the Roman Oration of Aelius Aristides," *American Philosophical Society,* 1953.
67. Tiberius left 675 million denarii (around 100,000 talents), Antoninus Pius left 725 million denarii, and of Septimius Severus it was said that he left more than any emperor before him. However, allowance must be made for the depreciation of the currency, which had reached 50% by the time of Septimius Severus. It is possible that in real terms Tiberius' treasury was the high-water mark of the empire. It also has to be borne in mind that the treasuries of Tiberius and Septimius Severus were largely the result of confiscation of opponents' fortunes—scarcely a sustainable policy over the long term. In each case, the following reign dissipated the accumulations of the three hoarders.
68. A.H.M. Jones, *The Roman Economy,* Oxford, UK, 1974, p. 79.
69. M. Hendy, *Studies in the Byzantine Monetary Economy, 350–1450*, Cambridge, UK, 1985, pp. 165, 171, and 224. The considerably reduced level of income compared to the early Roman Empire has to be understood in the light not only of a smaller population but also of a substantial fall in price levels. Wheat prices, for instance, had fallen by about 60% since the first century A.D.
70. A. Marongiu, *Medieval Parliaments: A Comparative Study,* English transl., London, 1968, p. 32.
71. *Annals of Lorsch,* quoted in T. Reuter, "Plunder and Tribute in the Carolingian Empire," *Royal Historical Society*, 1985, p. 84.
72. F. Lieberman, *The National Assembly in the Anglo-Saxon Period,* Halle, Germany, 1913.
73. Reuter, *op. cit.*, p. 75.
74. *Epitaphium Arsenii,* quoted in Reuter, *op. cit.*, p. 83.
75. Goffart, *op. cit.*, p. 45, quoting the Christian writer Lactantius.
76. Themistius, c. A.D. 368, quoted in W. Goffart, *Rome's Fall and After,* London, 1989, p. 16.
77. C. Wickham, *Land and Power: Studies in Italian and European Social History, 400–1200,* London, 1994, p. 74.
78. Fredegar, *Chronicon*, 2, 46, quoted in Goffart, *Rome's Fall and After,* p. 226.
79. Goffart, *Rome's Fall and After,* pp. 230–231.
80. The coins minted were *triens*—⅓ of a solidus, 1.5 grams gross weight, but by this stage heavily debased and no more than one-third gold. P. Spufford, *Money and Its Uses in Medieval Europe,* Cambridge, UK, 1988, p. 20.
81. M. Hendy, *The Economy, Fiscal Administration and Coinage of Byzantium,* Northampton, UK, 1985, 7, p. 38.
82. W. T. Treadgold, *Byzantine State Finances in the Eighth and Ninth Centuries,* Boulder,

CO, 1982, pp. 10–11 and 15–17. Theodora's treasury in 856 was not the highest in this period of Byzantine history. In 1025 Basil II left 14.4 million solidi.

83. J. B. Simonsen, *Studies in the Genesis and Early Development of Caliphal Taxation System,* Copenhagen, 1988, p. 138.
84. Goldsmith, *op. cit.,* p. 75. Estimates vary between 28 and 35 million dinars but do not include all taxes or amounts spent locally.
85. *Encyclopedia of Islam,* Leiden, 1960– , p. 1145. Foot soldiers were paid 1000 dihrem per year. The dinar was then worth 15 dihrem. The pay of Byzantine soldiers is from Treadgold, *op. cit.,* p. 97. The pay of Roman legionaries is from A.H.M. Jones, *The Roman Economy,* Oxford, UK, 1974, p. 192.
86. *Encyclopedia of Islam,* p. 1090.
87. Population figures from C. McEvedy and R. Jones, *Atlas of World Population History,* London, 1978. Revenues from various sources: Persia from Andreades, *op. cit.*; Egypt from F. M. Heichelheim, *An Ancient Economic History,* Leiden, 1958, p. 125; Rome from Goldsmith, *op. cit.*; Byzantium from Treadgold, *op. cit.*; Abbasids from Goldsmith, *op. cit.*; T'ang from D. C. Twitchett, *Financial Administration Under the T'ang Dynasty,* Cambridge, UK, 1953, p. 154; England and France from R. Bonney, ed., *Economic Systems and State Finance,* Oxford, UK, 1995, p. 67.
88. In general terms it may be stated that (1) prices were lower in Mesopotamia than they were in Mediterranean Europe, and that (2) prices rose in a discontinuous fashion until they reached a peak in the early Roman Empire. At the time of Hammurabi, barley sold for around 5–7 grams of silver per hectoliter. By the late Persian Empire, this had risen to 10–20 grams. In the fifth century B.C. in Athens, wheat (a more valuable grain than barley) cost around 38 grams of silver per hectoliter. By the time of Augustus, wheat prices had reached 55 grams of silver. The retreat of the classical world was accompanied by a retreat of prices. Under Justinian, wheat was around 22 grams of silver per hectoliter, and by the ninth century in Byzantium it was 15 grams. In western Europe prices fell even further than this during the Dark Ages. However, by the twelfth century they had started to rise again. In England around A.D. 1200, wheat was again selling for around 20 grams of silver per hectoliter.

2. CITIZEN CREDITORS

1. Quoted in L. F. Marks, *The Development of the Institutions of Public Finance in Florence During the Last Sixty Years of the Republic, 1470–1530,* unpublished D.Phil. thesis, Oxford University, 1954, p. 20.
2. Quoted in D. Waley, *The Italian City Republics,* London, 1978, p. 59.
3. M. Ginatempo and L. Sandri, *L'Italia delle città: Il popolamento urbano tra Medioevo e Rinascimento (secoli XIII–XVI),* Florence, 1990. Outside Italy there were few towns of over twenty thousand people, whereas Italy had twenty-three of them north of Rome.
4. Waley, *op. cit.,* p. 60.
5. Waley, *op. cit.,* p. 84.
6. In thirteenth-century Genoa, residual feudal dues were still privately traded, and even syndicated, for yields of about 5%.

7. *Annales Genovesi di Caffaro,* Vol. II, ed. L. T. Belgrano and C. Imperiale, p. 44.
8. This recourse to technocratic government as a result of the failure of the electoral system has a curious parallel in the nonpartisan technocratic ministry that governed Italy from 1992 to 1994 under the ex-head of the central bank, Carlo Ciampi.
9. *Liber de regimine civitatum,* written around 1260. See Waley, *op. cit.,* p. 71.
10. *Purgatorio* 6, 124–125.
11. The information on Venetian medieval public debt is taken from G. Luzzatto, *Il debito pubblico della Repubblica di Venezia,* Milan, 1963.
12. Luzzatto, *op. cit.,* p. 283.
13. John T. Noonan, *The Scholastic Analysis of Usury,* Cambridge, MA, 1957, p. 2.
14. The loophole derived from the Roman legal concept that allowed payment of damages as a result of breach of contract. *Quod interest* means "that which is the difference" between the lender's present position and his position had he not lent in the first place. The trick was to extend this principle not only to penalty interest when the borrower defaulted, but to all interest. The theory (highly contentious) was that the act of lending money was a loss in itself, or at least the loss of potential profit. The theological battle surrounding this issue was not resolved until the end of the Middle Ages. Noonan, *op. cit.,* pp. 105–132.
15. The practice of undated debts led to an intriguing defense of interest taking. Laurentius di Ridolfis, writing in 1403, argued that since public debts of Florence and other states had no fixed repayment date (and indeed were rarely redeemed), the city was, in effect, in default from day one, thus easily justifying the payment of interest. Noonan, *op. cit.,* p. 123.
16. Luzzatto, *op. cit.,* p. 271.
17. Luzzatto, *op. cit.,* p. 61.
18. H. Sieveking, *Studio sulle finanze Genovesi nel Medievo,* Vol. I, Genoa, 1906, p. 63.
19. Sieveking, *op. cit.,* p. 52.
20. Noonan, *op. cit.,* p. 155.
21. Sieveking, *op. cit.,* pp. 129–135, and J. Day, *Les douanes de Genes,* Paris, 1963.
22. Coincidentally, this was an almost identical sum to the 20,000-drachma fine that the city of Miletus threatened to impose on similar offenders in 205 B.C.
23. Sieveking, *op. cit.,* pp. 111, 133.
24. M. B. Becker, *Florence in Transition,* Vol. II, Baltimore, 1968, p. 151.
25. D. Herlihy and C. Klapisch-Zuber, *Tuscans and Their Families,* New Haven, CT. 1985, p. 102. Becker, *op. cit.,* p. 159, gives a figure of five thousand debtholders around 1380. There were around ten thousand households in Florence after the drastic reduction of population caused by the Black Death.
26. G. Brucker, "Un documento Fiorentino del 1375," *Archivio Storico Italiano,* 1955, p. 174.
27. Becker, *op. cit.,* p. 177, gives a figure 135,000 ducats' debt service in 1367, although this may have included an element of capital repayment.
28. Becker, *op. cit.,* p. 191.
29. Luzzatto, *op. cit.,* p. 181.
30. Gregorio Dati, *Istoria di Firenze,* quoted in E. Conti, *L'imposta diretta a Firenze nel Quattrocento, 1427–1494,* Rome, 1984, p. 36.

31. Luzzatto, *op. cit.*, p. 257.
32. Quoted in Conti, *op. cit.*, p. 158.
33. Luzzatto, *op. cit.*, p. 212.
34. A. Molho, *Florentine Public Finance, 1400–1433,* Cambridge, MA, 1975, pp. 70–72.
35. Conti, *op. cit.*, p. 32.
36. Luzzatto, *op. cit.*, p. 239.
37. Luzzatto, *op. cit.*, p. 258.
38. Luzzatto, *op. cit.*, pp. 271–272, 283. Luzzatto does not give a figure for the total debt around 1450. The figure of 11 million ducats in the graph is simply an estimate based on the total levies made after 1425, less an allowance for the reduction of debt effected by the sinking fund.
39. Income from Conti, *op. cit.*, p. 29. Monte Comune accounts from Sieveking, *op. cit.*, Vol. II, p. 149. Total public revenues were only 312,000 ducats, and taxes pledged to the Monte were only 256,000 ducats.
40. A. Mohlo, *Marriage Alliance in Late Medieval Florence,* Cambridge, MA, p. 35.
41. Marks, *op. cit.*, p. 47.
42. Marks, *op. cit.*, p. 124.
43. Mohlo, *Marriage Alliance,* p. 75. It was soon found that there was not enough money to support the 7% fund if 80% of all matured dowries was credited to it. In 1490, therefore, the city created 3% and 4% funds, to which dowries were credited while waiting for space in the 7% fund. These funds, too, were given priority over the Monte Comune, but they never sold for the prices of the 7% fund.
44. R. C. Mueller, *The Venetian Money Market: Banks, Panics, and the Public Debt, 1200–1500,* Baltimore, 1997, p. 547.
45. R. Goldsmith, *Premodern Financial Systems,* Cambridge, UK, 1987, pp. 148–149.
46. Information on Venetian finances in the sixteenth century is found in F. C. Lane, *Venice, a Maritime Republic,* Baltimore, 1973, and "Public Debt and Private Wealth: Particularly in Sixteenth Century Venice," in: *Mélanges in honneur de Fernand Braudel,* Toulouse, Fr., 1973. Also in L. Pezzolo, *L'oro dello Stato,* Venice, 1990.
47. Lane, *Public Debt,* pp. 320–321.
48. The redemption was based, more or less, on the average market price since 1520. The reason that the bonds traded at prices that appeared, on the surface, to offer a yield of 40% per year is that interest was many decades in arrears. In line with its general attitude toward secondary holders, the republic did not recognize the right of new holders to interest arrears. The new holders therefore had to wait many decades to receive a return on their investments.
49. J. Heers, *Gênes au XVe siècle,* Paris, 1961, p. 175. There were 11,315 shareholders in 1460 and 9,997 in 1500. There is considerable dispute about the Genoese population in the fifteenth century, with figures ranging between 50,000 and 100,000. The number of households would therefore range somewhere between 11,000 and 22,000. If a middle ground is taken, the shareholders of San Giorgio represented at least two-thirds of the total households (in which there were obviously a considerable number of noncitizen residents.)
50. N. Macchiavelli, *Istorie Florentine,* 8, 12.
51. Sieveking, *op. cit.*. The 1407 figure is the sum of the original capital of San Giorgio

(Vol. II, p. 18) and the nominal value of the debt in 1339. The 1509 figure is simply the capital of San Giorgio at that date (Vol. II, p. 164). The interest for 1407 is based on a rate of 7% for the debts consolidated in San Giorgio, and a rate of 6.7% for the remainder. See J. Day, *Les douanes de Gênes,* Paris, 1963, p. xxvi. The interest for 1509 is from C. M. Cipolla, "Note sulla storia del saggio d'interesse: Corso, dividendi e sconto dei dividendi del Banco di San Giorgio nel Secolo XVI," in: *Saggi di storia economica e sociale,* Bologna, 1988.

52. Sieveking, *op. cit.,* Vol. I, p. 199.
53. Sieveking, *op. cit.,* Vol. III, p. 233.
54. Heers, *op. cit.,* p. 162–173.
55. J. Bodin, *The Six Books of a Commonwealth,* 1576, transl. R. Knowles, London, 1606; Harvard University Press facsimile edition, Cambridge, MA, 1962, p. 673.
56. Sieveking, *op. cit.,* Vol. 3, p. 222–227.
57. Cipolla, *op. cit.*
58. There is no estimate of Genoese GNP per capita that I know of. But estimates have been made of the GNP of the Dutch Republic in the mid-seventeenth century that suggest a GNP per capita of around 1,100 grams of silver. (See R. Goldsmith, *Premodern Financial Systems,* Cambridge, UK, 1987.) The market capitalization of San Giorgio at its peak was equivalent to around 3,000 grams of silver per head of Genoese population.
59. In 1254 the towns of the Rhineland formed a defensive league. In 1376 the towns of Swabia made a defensive pact against the Counts of Württemberg.
60. Conti, *op. cit.,* pp. 196, 211.
61. Conti, *op. cit.,* p. 281. Conti gives details of an almost bewildering variety of experiments in direct taxation during the fifteenth century.

3. SOVEREIGN DEBT

1. *Lettres de Colbert,* Vol. VII, ed. P. Clement, Paris, 1861–1866, pp. 180–181. Quoted in R. Bonney, *The King's Debts,* Oxford, UK, 1981 p. 274.
2. F. C. Dietz, *English Government and Finance, 1485–1588,* Urbana, IL, 1921, p. 88.
3. A. Marongiu, *Medieval Parliaments: A Comparative Study,* London, 1968, p. 29.
4. Marongiu, *op. cit.,* p. 62.
5. R. Bonney, ed., *Economic Systems and State Finance,* Oxford, UK, 1995, pp. 140–147.
6. P. de Boisguilbert, *La Naissance de l'economie politique,* Paris, 1966. p. 666–667.
7. M. Wolfe, *The Fiscal System of Renaissance France,* New York, 1972, p. 34.
8. Wolfe, *op. cit.,* p. 58.
9. The total loans made to the English crown by the Riccardi amounted to £392,000 (equivalent to 3 million ducats). Because their loans were short-term, only a small portion of this amount was outstanding at any one time.
10. E. B. Fryde and M. M. Fryde, "Public Credit, with Special Reference to North-Western Europe," in: *Cambridge Economic History of Europe,* Vol. III, Cambridge, UK, 1963, p. 460.
11. C. M. Cipolla, *The Monetary Policy of Fourteenth-Century Florence,* Berkeley, CA, 1982, pp. 7–8.

12. E. B. Fryde, *Studies in Medieval Trade and Finance,* Ch. 7, London, 1983, p. 1165.
13. Fryde and Fryde, *op. cit.,* p. 470.
14. Fryde and Fryde, *op. cit.,* p. 478.
15. An edict of Philip V in 1316 specified that the proceeds of fines and confiscations should be used to redeem revenues from "personis habentis redditus perpetuos vel ad vitam super thesauro predicto" ("persons holding rents either perpetual or for life on the aforesaid treasury"). However, it is not clear from the text whether these rents had been sold to investors or merely granted as favors. See A. Vührer, *Histoire de la dette publique en France,* Paris, 1886, p. 4.
16. P. Spufford, *Money and Its Uses in Medieval Europe,* Cambridge, UK, 1988, pp. 302–305.
17. French revenues from Wolfe, *op. cit.,* and J. Collins, *The Fiscal Limits of Absolutism,* Berkeley, CA, 1988. Spanish revenues from P. Toboso Sanchez, *La deuda publica Castellana durante el antigua regimen,* Madrid, 1987, and I.A.A. Thompson, *War and Government in Habsburg Spain,* London, 1976.
18. A. Guéry, "Les finances de la monarchie française," *Annales*, 1978, p. 221.
19. J. H. Elliott, *The Revolt of the Catalans,* Cambridge, UK, 1963, p. 15.
20. E. J. Hamilton, *American Treasure and the Price Revolution in Spain, 1501–1650,* Cambridge, MA, 1963, p. vii.
21. Hamilton, *op. cit.,* pp. 34, 42, and 123.
22. F. Braudel and F. Spooner, "Prices in Europe from 1450 to 1750," in *Cambridge Economic History of Europe,* Vol. IV, p. 445.
23. L.-S. Yang, *Money and Credit in China: A Short History,* Cambridge, MA, 1952, pp. 97–98.
24. Yang, *op. cit.,* pp. 51–68.
25. A. Udovitch, "Bankers Without Banks: The Islamic World," in: R. E. Lopez, ed., *The Dawn of Modern Banking,* New Haven, CT, 1979, p. 262. Curiously, this loophole was explored but explicitly rejected as usurious by theologians of the West. European merchants used the alternative strategy of disguising interest as foreign-exchange costs in their "bills of exchange."
26. R. Ehrenberg, *Capital and Finance in the Age of the Renaissance,* London, 1928, pp. 75–77.
27. H. J. Shakespeare, *The Royal Loans,* Shrewesbury, UK, 1986, p. 4.
28. Ehrenberg, *op. cit.,* p. 237.
29. Christofer Kurz to firm of Tucher in Nuremberg in 1543. Quoted in Ehrenberg, *op. cit.,* p. 241.
30. H. van der Wee, "Monetary, Credit and Banking Systems," in: *Cambridge Economic History of Europe,* Vol. V, Cambridge, UK, p. 362.
31. Wolfe, *op. cit.,* pp. 87–89.
32. Collins, *op. cit.,* p. 58.
33. van der Wee, *op. cit.,* p. 365.
34. R. Doucet, "Le Grand Parti de Lyon au XVIe Siècle", *Revue Historique,* 1933, p. 500.
35. Ehrenberg, *op. cit.,* p. 306.
36. G. Parker, "Loan Hands," *Times Literary Supplement,* 23 May 1986, p. 571.

37. R. Carande, *Carlos V y sus Banqueros,* Vol. II, Madrid, 1943, p. 298.
38. Revenues are from Thompson, *op. cit.,* p. 288. Debt service is from Toboso Sanchez, *op. cit.* (1557, 1575, 1595) and Thompson, *op. cit.* (1607). Short-term debts are from Toboso Sanchez, *op. cit.* (1557 and 1575), G. Muto in: Bonney, ed. *Economic Systems and State Finance,* p. 257 (1595), and J. C. Boyajian, *Portuguese Bankers in Spain, 1626–1650,* New Brunswick, NJ, 1983, p. 3 (1607).
39. This is the total of *juros* listed in Toboso Sanchez, *op. cit.,* pp. 150–151. However, the figure does not include short-term debts and may be an understatement even of the long-term debt. Other accounts give long-term debt as 90 million ducats at this stage.
40. Moghul India from J. de Laet, *The Empire of the Great Mogol,* 1631, transl. J. S. Hoyland, Bombay, 1928, p. 107. Ottoman Turkey and Tokugawa Japan from Goldsmith, *op. cit.,* pp. 90 and 143. Ming China from R. Huang, *Taxation and Governmental Finance in Sixteenth Century Ming China,* Cambridge, UK, 1974, p. 295.
41. F. C. Spooner, *The International Economy and Monetary Movements in France, 1493–1720,* Cambridge, MA, 1972, p. 59.
42. Quoted in R. Carande, *El credito de Castilla,* Madrid, 1949, p. 27.
43. G. Parker, *The Army of Flanders and the Spanish Road, 1567–1659,* Cambridge, UK, 1972, p. 235.
44. Figures as already given except those for 1504 and 1674, which are taken from I.A.A. Thompson, "Castile: Polity, Fiscality, and Fiscal Crisis," in: P.T. Hoffman and K. Norburg, eds., *Fiscal Crises, Liberty, and Representative Government, 1450–1789,* Stanford, CA, 1994, p. 157.
45. Hamilton, *op. cit.,* p. 88. Profits on debased coins were typically around 75% of the nominal amount issued.
46. Toboso Sanchez, *op. cit.,* p. 178.
47. Toboso Sanchez, *op. cit.,* p. 191.
48. Thompson, "Castile: Absolutism, Constitutionalism, and Liberty," in Hoffman and Norburg, *op. cit.,* p. 217.
49. J.-C. Wacquet, "Who Profited from the Alienation of Public Revenues in Ancien Régime Societies?," *Journal of European Economic History,* 1982, p. 666.
50. J. F. Bosher, *French Finances 1770–1795,* Cambridge, UK, 1975, pp. 17–21.
51. *Memoires de Sully,* Vol. I, quoted in Vührer, *op. cit.,* p. 79.
52. Collins, *op. cit.,* pp. 58–72.
53. Sir George Carew, *A Relation of the State of France,* p. 480, quoted in Bonney, *The King's Debts,* p. 54.
54. Figures for Spain from Thompson, *War and Government,* p. 288. Figures for France from Collins, *op. cit.,* pp. 75, 234.
55. J.-R. Malet, *Comptes rendus de l'administration des finances du royaume de France,* London, 1789, pp. 249–50, quoted in R. Bonney, "Jean-Roland Malet: Historian of the Finances of the French Monarchy," *French History,* 1991, p. 202.
56. R. Bonney, *The King's Debts,* pp. 306–309.
57. Collins, *op. cit.,* p. 217.
58. Charles Loyseau, *Les Oeuvres de Maistre Charles Loyseau, avocat en Parlement,* Lyons, 1701, p. 143, quoted in Wolfe, *op. cit.,* p. 302.

59. Bonney, *The King's Debts,* p. 320.
60. Debts from J. Dent, *Crisis in Finance: Crown Financiers and Society in Seventeenth Century France,* Newton Abbott, UK, 1973, p. 43. Value of offices from K. W. Swart, *The Sale of Offices in the Seventeenth Century,* The Hague, 1949, p. 16. Debt reduction from Bonney, *The King's Debts,* p. 321.
61. Bonney, *The King's Debts,* p. 260.
62. J. Bergin, *Cardinal Richelieu, Power and Pursuit of Wealth,* New Haven, CT, 1985, p. 243.

4. RESISTANCE TO THE HEGEMON

1. Figures for France and Castile are as already given. Figures for Venice are from F. C. Lane, *Venice, A Maritime Republic,* Baltimore, 1973, p. 426.
2. J. Tracey, *A Financial Revolution in the Habsburg Netherlands, 1515–1565,* Berkeley, CA, 1985, p. 38, quoting Margaret to Charles V, April 1523.
3. Tracey, *op. cit.,* p. 30.
4. Tracey, *op. cit.,* pp. 100–101.
5. Don Fernando Girón at a meeting of the Council of State in 1632—while voting nonetheless for the continuation of the war. Quoted in G. Parker, *The Army of Flanders and the Spanish Road, 1567–1659*, Cambridge, UK, 1972, p. 266.
6. This is an estimate for the late sixteenth century. By the middle of the seventeenth century, the population was closer to two million.
7. The figure for Holland is from P. de la Court, *The True Interest and Political Maxims of the Republic of Holland and West Friesland,* London, 1702, pp. 208–209. By 1648 the union itself had a debt of around 8 million guilders—see M. t'Hart, *The Making of a Bourgeois State,* Manchester, UK, 1992, p. 169. Holland contributed around 57% of the budget of the union, but it is generally considered that it would have had a rather higher percentage of the overall public debt. The other states did not have the credit standing of Holland, but all issued debt to some extent. An estimate of around 180 million guilders is therefore not unreasonable for the total public debt of the republic.
8. Anon. pamphlet, 1632, quoted in t'Hart, *op. cit.,* p. 68.
9. Population figures derived from C. McEvedy and R. Jones, *Atlas of World Population History,* London, 1978. Holland is assumed to have half the total population of the republic. Dutch debt taken from de la Court, *op. cit.,* pp. 208–209. Castilian debt derived from debt service figures in P. Toboso Sanchez, *La deuda publica Castellana durante el antigua regimen,* Madrid, 1987, capitalized at 5%. The French debt is Colbert's estimate and includes 420 million livres for the capital value of offices sold.
10. F. Braudel and F. Spooner, "Prices in Europe from 1450 to 1750," in: *The Cambridge Economic History of Europe,* Vol. V, p. 446.
11. R. Goldsmith, *Premodern Financial Systems,* Cambridge, UK, 1987, p. 201.
12. t'Hart, *op. cit.,* pp. 161–162.
13. Tracey, *op. cit.,* pp. 205–206.
14. Given the paucity of information on fiscal matters in Holland, it is impossible to know

how much direct tax was paid during the war. A purely hypothetical illustration can be based on the fact that direct taxes were 1.1 million guilders in 1603. If, let us say, 800,000 guilders of direct taxes for twenty-five years were classified as debt at 6.25% interest, the total debt service would have been 3.9 million guilders in 1603, against only 2.5 million in revenues. (This calculation includes that 1.4 million existing debt service in 1603 recalculated at 6.25% instead of 8.33%.) The Dutch debt would certainly have gone the way of the Monte Vecchio and the Monte Comune under this scenario.

15. Tracey, *op. cit.*, p. 207.
16. Parker, *op. cit.*, p. 144.
17. t'Hart, *op. cit.*, p. 138.
18. Fynes Moryson, quoted in M. t'Hart, "The Merits of a Financial Revolution: Public Finance, 1550–1700," in: M. t'Hart, J. Jonker, and J. L. van Zanden, eds., *A Financial History of the Netherlands*, Cambridge, UK, 1997, p. 11.
19. t'Hart, *Bourgeois State*, p. 138.
20. Estimates for Dutch GNP from Goldsmith, *op. cit.* Public debt from J. Riley, *International Government Finance and the Amsterdam Capital Market 1740–1815,* Cambrudge, UK, 1980, p. 77, and t'Hart, Jonker, and van Zanden, *op. cit.*, p. 69. Most known figures are for the province of Holland, which probably represented around 75% of the total.
21. F. C. Dietz, *English Government Finance, 1485–1558,* Urbana, IL, 1921, p. 91.
22. Dietz, *op. cit.*, p. 117.
23. From 1544 to 1551 there was almost continual warfare. To finance it, Henry VIII raised £800,000 from sales of church lands, £650,000 from parliamentary taxes, and £363,000 from debasement. After his death in 1547, his successor, Edward VI, raised £258,000 from sales of church lands, £300,000 from parliamentary taxes, and £650,000 from debasement. See Dietz, *op. cit.*, pp. 147–183.
24. In 1600 the ordinary revenues of the crown amounted to £288,000, while parliamentary grants contributed a further £128,000. W. R. Scott, *The Constitution and Finance of English, Scottish and Irish Joint-Stock Companies to 1720,* Cambridge, UK, Vol. III, 1911, p. 520.
25. English revenues are from Scott, *op. cit.*, pp. 520–521. Naples from A. Calabria, *The Cost of Empire: The Finances of the Kingdom of Naples in the Time of Spanish Rule,* Cambridge, UK, 1994, p. 59. The figures for other countries have already been given elsewhere. The per capita figure for Spain excludes the revenues from the Indies.
26. Quoted in R. Ashton, *The Crown and the Money Market, 1603–1640,* Oxford, UK. 1960, p. 188.
27. F. C. Dietz, *English Public Finance, 1558–1641,* New York, 1932, pp. 113, 126. The figure for 1607 does not include provision for the last forced loans of Elizabeth's reign, which had been quietly forgotten in the interim and were never repaid. If they had been included, the total would have been £280,000. See Ashton, *op. cit.*, p. 37.
28. Dietz, *English Public Finance*, pp. 269, 279.
29. Ashton, *op. cit.*, p. 110. The figure of £250,000 claimed by the Farmers may have been an overstatement.
30. K. Sharpe, *The Personal Rule of Charles I,* New Haven, CT, 1992.

31. H. J. Habakkuk, "Public Finance and the Sale of Confiscated Property During the Interregnum," *Journal of Economic History*, 1963, pp. 77–87.
32. Sir William Strickland, in the Long Parliament, 1652. Quoted in M. Ashley, *Financial and Commercial Policy Under the Cromwellian Protectorate*, Oxford, UK, 1934, p. 104.
33. Ashley, *op. cit.*, pp. 105–106.
34. Ashley, *op. cit.*, p. 96.
35. Anon., *The Chimera: Or, the French Way of Paying National Debts, Laid Open*, London, 1720.
36. H. Roseveare, *The Financial Revolution, 1660–1760*, London, 1991, p. 32.
37. J. H. Plumb, *The Growth of Political Stability in England, 1675–1725*, London, 1967, p. 65.
38. Roseveare, *op. cit.*, pp. 14–15.
39. R. D. Richards, "The 'Stop of the Exchequer,' " *Economic History*, 1933.
40. Quoted in Roseveare, *op. cit.*, p. 85. This was in 1680.
41. J. Brewer, *The Sinews of Power: War, Money and the English State, 1688–1783*, London, 1989, p. 95.
42. Narcissus Luttrell, parliamentary diarist, quoted in Brewer, *op. cit.*, p. 147.
43. Short-term debt from B. R. Mitchell and P. Deane, *Abstract of British Historical Statistics*, Cambridge, UK, 1962. Long-term debt and revenue shortfall from P.G.M. Dickson, *The Financial Revolution in England: A Study in the Development of Public Credit 1688–1756*, London, 1967, p. 48, 354.
44. Dickson, *op. cit*, p. 349.
45. Figures for Exchequer and departmental debts from Dickson, *op. cit*, p. 526. Total short-term debt from Mitchell and Deane, *op. cit.*
46. Dickson, *op. cit.*, pp. 60–63.
47. Spanish figures are as in Chapter 3, note 58 (page 500), converted into sterling at 3.1 ducats per pound. English figures from Mitchell and Deane, *op. cit.*
48. M. Foot, *The Pen and the Sword*, London, 1957, p. 107.
49. J. Swift, *The Conduct of the Allies and of the Late Ministry in Beginning and Carrying on the Present War*, London, 1712. Quoted in Foot, *op. cit.*, p. 304.
50. Article in the *Examiner*, November 1710. Quoted in Foot, *op. cit.*, p. 152.
51. Dickson, *op. cit.*, p. 68.
52. Dickson, *op. cit.*, p. 72.

5. THE CHIMERA

1. In John Law, *Oeuvres complètes*, Vol. III, ed. P. Harsin, Paris, 1934, p. 80.
2. Colbert never held the title of Surintendant des Finances. Until 1665 he was merely the dominant member of the Council of Finance. After that he became the Controller General of Finance, a post which he held until his death.
3. French revenues from A. Guéry, "Les Finances de la monarchie française sous l'Ancien Régime," *Annales*, 1978. Debt service from R. Bonney, "Jean-Roland Malet: Historian of the Finances of the French Monarchy," *French History*, 1991, p. 190.

4. A. Vührer, *Histoire de la dette publique de France,* Paris, 1886, pp. 84–98.
5. Vührer, *op. cit.*, p. 117.
6. J. M. Fachan, *Historique de la rente française,* Paris, 1905, p. 39.
7. The figures for 1596–1661 are as given earlier. The figure for 1683 is a estimate based on capitalizing debt service at 5%. The figure for 1700 is an estimate of 450 million livres of rentes, 450 million livres of offices, and 100 million short-term debts. The figure for 1715 is explained in note 11 below. The figure for 1725 is explained in Chapter 6.
8. French revenues and debt service from Guéry, *op. cit.* Short-term debts from A. Seligmann, *La Première Tentative d'emission fiduciaire en France: Étude sur les billets de monnaie du Trésor Royal à la fin du règne de Louis XIV (1701–1718),* Paris, 1925, p. 99. The livre is converted at 6.31 grams of silver.
9. Seligmann, *op. cit.*, p. 99.
10. Of this sum, 143.3 million livres were Treasury notes, 60.4 million were certificates of deposit issued by the Caisse d'Emprunts, and 61.7 million were notes issued by the tax farmers and the Receivers General. In addition there was 87.1 million livres due to foreign bankers, and no less than 208.3 million in unpaid expenses. See Seligmann, *op. cit.*, p. 99.
11. Estimates as low as 2 billion livres do not take into account all types of debt. The figure used in this section is 2.85 billion livres, broken down as follows: rentes, 1,384 million; offices, 542 million; notes, 597 million; arrears and anticipations, 322 million. The figure for rentes is from Fachan, *op. cit.*, pp. 44–45. The others are from F. Marion, *Histoire financière de la France depuis 1715,* Vol. I, Paris, 1914, pp. 63–64. However, it is quite likely that the true figure was larger than this.
12. B. R. Mitchell and P. Deane, *Abstract of British Historical Statistics,* Cambridge, UK, 1962.
13. English national income in 1715 has been estimated at £53.8 million by P. O'Brien and P. Hunt, in "The Rise of the Fiscal State in England 1485–1815," *Historical Research,* 1993. This calculation excludes Scotland, and a reasonable estimate of the GNP of Great Britain would be around £60 million.
14. See F. C. Spooner, *The International Economy and Monetary Movements in France, 1493–1720,* Cambridge, MA, 1972, p. 313.
15. P.G.M. Dickson, *The Financial Revolution in England,* London, 1967, p. 80. The total of £16.4 million includes £664,263 given to the holders of debts that had been affected by Charles II's "Stop of the Exchequer" in 1672. The table also details the other long-term debts at the end of September 1714.
16. The lottery loans were a strange hybrid. All investors received interest for thirty-two years, and at the end of the period the principal was allocated among them by a lottery draw. Therefore the "losers" ended up with a self-liquidating 32-year annuity with an effective yield of 6.84%. Because the loans were issued at a 23% discount, the early repayment of capital substantially increased the cost to the government.
17. Dickson, *op. cit.*, pp. 84–87.
18. Quoted in P. A. Cochut, *The Financier, Law: His Scheme and Times,* London, 1856, p. 9.

19. H. Lüthy, *La Banque protestante en France: De la révocation de l'Édit de Nantes à la Révolution*, Paris, 1959, p. 288.
20. Law, *op. cit.*, Vol. I, p. 144.
21. Law, *op. cit.*, Vol. I, p. 158.
22. J. Law, *Memoire sur les banques*, 1715, in *Oeuvres complètes*, Vol. II, p. 307.
23. Quoted in Cochut, *op. cit.*, p. 42.
24. A. Murphy, *John Law*, Oxford, UK, 1997, pp. 158–159.
25. Anon., *The Chimera: Or, the French Way of Paying National Debts, Laid Open*, London, 1720, pp. 16, 21.
26. Edict of August 1719. Quoted in full in Anon., *op. cit.*, p. 51.
27. "Un corps de negociens dont la banque royale est la caisse," John Law, letter in the *Mercure*, March 1720, *Oeuvres Complètes*, Vol. III, p. 104.
28. Anon., *op. cit.*, p. 61.
29. Law, *Oeuvres complètes*, Vol. III, p. 53.
30. L. Neal, *The Rise of Financial Capitalism: International Capital Markets in the Age of Reason*, Cambridge, UK, 1990, p. 69, and Murphy, *op. cit.*, p. 289.
31. In 1705 Law estimated the GNP of England at £40 million sterling, and suggested that at least £50 million of paper money would be required for the economy to reach its full potential. Law did not appear to have a definitive estimate of French GNP. In his *Memoire sur le denier royale* of June 1719, he suggested a figure as low as 1 billion livres in one place. But this was largely for illustrative purposes. Elsewhere in the same memorandum he states that he has seen credible estimates of 2.4 billion livres. In either case, his paper money issues were higher than his estimate of GNP.
32. Anon., *A Full and Impartial Account of the Company of Mississippi: Otherwise Call'd the French East India Company, Projected and Settled by Mr. Law*, London, 1720, pp. 11, 25.
33. Duc de Saint-Simon, *Memoirs*, ed. W. H. Lewis, London, 1964, p. 202.
34. Lüthy, *op. cit.*, p. 309, n. 22.
35. E. Faure, *La Banqueroute de Law*, Paris, 1977, p. 241.
36. A. Murphy, *Richard Cantillon, Entrepreneur and Economist*, Oxford, UK, 1987, pp. 79–83.
37. Law, *Oeuvres complètes*, Vol. III, p. 80.
38. Anon., *The Chimera*, pp. 1–9.
39. Quoted in J. Carswell, *The South Sea Bubble*, London, 1993, p. 47.
40. Carswell, *op. cit.*, p. 52.
41. *The Schemes of the South-Sea Company and of the Bank of England, As Propos'd to the Parliament for the Reducing of the National Debts*, London, 1720, p. 3.
42. *The Schemes of the South-Sea Company*, p. 7.
43. This assumes that the shares traded at a 4% yield—more or less the market rate for government debt at the time.
44. Carswell, *op. cit.*, pp. 95–96, 101, 103.
45. Carswell, *op. cit.*, p. 101.
46. Archibald Hutcheson, 31 March 1720, quoted in Dickson, *op. cit.*, p. 102.
47. Carswell, *op. cit.*, p. 102.

48. Anonymous member of House of Commons, *Some Seasonable Considerations for Those who are Desirous, by Subscription or Purchase, to Become Proprietors of South Sea Stock: With Remarks on the Surprising Method of Valuing South-Sea Stock, Publish'd in the Flying-Post of Saturday, April the 9th, 1720,* London, 1720.
49. Dickson, *op. cit.*, p. 136.
50. Dickson, *op. cit.*, pp. 125, 143.
51. Anon., *A Letter to a Director of the South-Sea Company,* London, July 1720.
52. Carswell, *op. cit.*, pp. 108, 113.
53. Dickson, *op. cit.*, p. 277.

6. THE DILEMMA

1. Edict of June 1725, quoted in F. Marion, *Histoire financière de la France depuis 1715,* Vol. I, Paris, 1914, p. 110.
2. Marion, *op. cit.*, pp. 63, 111–112.
3. P.G.M. Dickson, *The Financial Revolution in England: A Study in the Development of Public Credit 1688–1756,* London, 1967, p. 185.
4. J. Carswell, *The South Sea Bubble,* London, 1993, p. 229.
5. In the immediate aftermath of the scandal, the Company's holdings of government debt totaled £37 million, but £4 million of this was sold to the Bank in the process of reorganization.
6. J. Cannon, *Parliamentary Reform 1640–1832,* Cambridge, UK, 1972, p. 30, estimates the 1754 electorate at 282,000.
7. J. Brewer, *The Sinews of Power: War Money and the English State, 1668–1783,* London, 1989, p. 98.
8. Michael Godfrey, *A Short Account of the Bank of England,* 1695, quoted in H. Roseveare, *The Financial Revolution, 1660–1760,* London, 1991, pp. 92–93.
9. Figures for British government finances are taken from B. R. Mitchell and P. Deane, *Abstract of British Historical Statistics,* Cambridge, UK, 1962. The cost of war is calculated by taking the total spending in the period less an allowance for the normal peacetime spending based on the average expenditure in the years preceding the war. By this method, the increase in debt interest resulting from the war is included in war spending, together with the direct military costs. From the British perspective, the American War of Independence merged into the fourth Anglo-Dutch War, which was not concluded until 1784, and some military costs were not accounted for until 1785. These figures are all included under the title "American Independence."
10. The amount borrowed is the total deficit recorded in the period rather than the nominal debt created, since the latter is liable to distortion. Figures from Mitchell and Deane, *op. cit.*
11. Prices of British government debt are taken from S. Homer and R. Sylla, *A History of Interest Rates,* 3rd edition, New Brunswick, NJ, 1991.
12. I. Pinto, *Traité de la circulation et du crédit,* Amsterdam, 1771, pp. 66–68.
13. The figures for GNP are extrapolated from a base figure of £43.5 million in 1689 (as per Gregory King), a figure of £110 million in 1780 (as per Arthur Young), and a figure of

£130 million around 1788. In 1707, £6 million is added to take into account the union with Scotland. A constant real growth rate of 0.7% per annum in applied until 1780, and 1.3% thereafter. The resulting figures are deflated by the consumer price index created by E. Schumpeter, "English Prices and Public Finance, 1660–1822," *Review of Economic Statistics,* 1938. The figures for debt are from Mitchell and Deane, *op. cit.* In the period 1702–1719 they are adjusted (1) to smooth out the sudden inclusion of accumulated but unaccounted short-term debts in: 1711 and (2) to include the capitalized value of the terminable annuities.

14. Figures from Mitchell and Deane, *op. cit.*
15. David Hume, "Of Public Credit," in: *Political Discourses,* Edinburgh, 1752.
16. F. Guicciardini, *Le cose fiorentine,* originally written in the 1520s, ed. R. Ridolfi, Florence, 1939, p. 109.
17. A. Smith, *The Wealth of Nations,* London, 1776, Book 5, 3, p. 11.
18. Smith, *op. cit.,* p. 8.
19. Smith, *op. cit.,* p. 11.
20. Smith, *op. cit.,* p. 13.
21. J. C. Riley, *The Seven Years' War and the Old Regime in France,* Princeton, NJ, 1986, p. 130.
22. R. D. Harris, "French Finances and the American War, 1777–1783," *Journal of Modern History,* 1976, p. 249.
23. Joly de Fleury, *Travail sur la situation générale de la dette du roi a l'époque de premier janvier 1782,* quoted in Harris, *op. cit.,* p. 249.
24. During the seventeenth century, the average price of wheat in Paris was around 86 grams of silver per hectoliter, compared to 73 grams of silver in England. In the period 1726–1730, average prices were 42 grams of silver in France and 70 grams in England. (M. Baulant, "Les Prix des grain à Paris de 1431 à 1788," *Annales,* 1968, and Mitchell and Deane, *op. cit.*). In the meantime, French wages remained stable in nominal terms from the 1680s to the 1720s, and therefore halved in real terms. (M. Baulant, "Les Salaires du batîment, 1400–1726," *Annales,* 1971).
25. A good discussion of the question of French economic performance in the eighteenth century is given in Riley, *op. cit.,* pp. 13–23.
26. Figures from D. R. Weir, "Tontines, Public Finance, and Revolution in France and England, 1688–1789," *Journal of Economic History,* 1989, p. 98. The figure for French public debt is the 4,580 million livres given by Weir, *op. cit.,* p. 98, note 17, before arbitrarily reducing the capital value of the *rentes perpétuelles* issued in 1720. His figure for debt service is increased by 13.5 million livres to allow for the annual cost of venal offices (see W. Doyle, *Officers, Nobles and Revolutionaries,* London, 1995, p. 108).
27. This does not include amounts of £1–1.5 million of sinking-fund payments that were made in the years after 1784. These are excluded on the grounds that they were not contractual obligations, but merely a voluntary program of debt reduction. Their abandonment would not have constituted an event of default, just as the failure to maintain the earlier sinking fund established by Walpole had not unduly upset the market.
28. The figure for Britain is based on the increase in interest from 1726 (factoring in the interest reduction that came into effect in that year) until 1788, set against the cumulative

government deficit for the period. Figures taken from Mitchell and Deane, *op. cit.* The figure for France is necessarily somewhat less precise. The interest figures for 1726 (from Marion, *op. cit.*) and 1788 (from Weir, *op. cit.*) are reduced by 15% of annual life-annuity payments so as to allow for the element of capital repayment. Officers' salaries are not included in the calculation.

29. Marion, *op. cit.*, Vol. I, Paris, p. 474.
30. F. R. Velde and D. R. Weir, "The Financial Market and Government Debt Policy in France, 1746–1793," *Journal of Economic History*, 1992, p. 20.
31. A. Smith. *op. cit.*, Book 5, 3, p. 7.
32. H. Lüthy, *La Banque protestante en France: De la revocation de l'Édit de Nantes à la Révolution*, Paris 1959 p. 469.
33. Lüthy, *op. cit.*, p. 469.
34. A. Deparcieux, *Essai sur les probabilités de la durée de la vie humaine*, Paris, 1746.
35. The cost of French government borrowing has been brilliantly analyzed by Velde and Weir, *op. cit.* Their figures are used throughout this section. The amount of life annuities still being paid in 1784 is from Marion, *op. cit.*, p. 473.
36. In 1784, the issue of 1754, the last under the old policy of age-banding, had only 19.6% of its original annuities outstanding—generally the ones that paid 7–8%. At the same date no less than 56% of the annuities issued in 1757 were still outstanding—all of them paying 10%.
37. In order to compete with the Genevans, the French government offered the possibility of taking out annuities on two, three or four lives; but the rates offered were generally 0.5% lower for each extra life named. Not surprisingly, sophisticated investors preferred the syndicate solution.
38. Because of the very long life expectancy of the Geneva maidens, only the longest-term loans offer a fair comparison. Shorter-term loans had a different risk profile (they were more likely to be repaid before the next default) and therefore traded at substantially lower yields.
39. The impossibility of financing warfare on an early-modern scale with a pure copper currency had led not only to the previous abortive experiment with paper money in 1661–1664, but also to a massive issue of copper token currency in 1718–1720. These coins had contained so little copper in relation to their nominal value that they were little different from paper.
40. Sources: Denmark, Sweden, and Russia from J. C. Riley, *International Government Finance and the Amsterdam Capital Market 1740–1815*, Cambridge, UK, 1980, pp. 138–139, 149, 157. Figures include government-issued paper money. Dutch Republic from Riley, *International Government Finance*, p. 77, plus an an estimated 140 million guilders for the debts of the other provinces and the union. Austria from P.G.M. Dickson, *Finance and Government Under Maria Theresia, 1740–1780*, Oxford, UK, 1987, p. 379. Great Britain and France as given earlier in note 26. Spain from J. F. Lazaro, "Deuda publica, evolución de la hacienda y crecimiento," Madrid, 1991. Prussia from S. B. Fay, *The Rise of Brandenburg-Prussia to 1786*, New York, 1937, p. 141.
41. Figures for France from Marion, *op. cit.*, Vol. I, pp. 120–121 (1725), and Weir, *op. cit.* (1788). Figures for Great Britain from Mitchell and Deane, *op. cit.*

42. Smith, *op. cit.*, Book 1, 2, p. 47.
43. The figures represent only the ordinary revenues of the government—that is, those that could be levied annually without question or dissent.
44. C. Montesquieu, *De l'esprit des lois,* Vol. III, Ch. 7.
45. J. Bodin, *The Six Books of a Commonwealth,* 1576, transl. R. Knowles, London; Harvard University Press facsimile edition, Cambridge, MA, 1962, p. 675.
46. F. Bernier, *Travels in the Mogul Empire 1656–1668,* London, 1891, p. 221.
47. J. De Laet, *The Empire of the Great Mogol,* 1631, transl. J. S. Hoyland, Bombay, 1928, p. 95. Originally published in Holland in 1631.
48. Bodin, *op. cit.*, p. 204.
49. Bodin, *op. cit.*, p. 683.
50. de Laet, *op. cit.*, p. 94.
51. Bernier, *op. cit.*, pp. 227, 232.
52. Bernier, *op. cit.*, p. 225–226.
53. Bodin, *op. cit.*, pp. 669, 675.
54. M. Darigrand, *L'Anti-financier,* Amsterdam, 1763, p. 24.
55. Comte de Boulainvilliers, *An Historical Account of the Antient Parliaments of France, or States General of the Kingdom,* transl. London, 1739, 1, p. 60. "The merit of whose works has caused them to be prohibited in France, and translated for the Use and Instruction of such British lovers of Liberty as cannot read the original." Original ms. around 1721.
56. Boulainvilliers, *op. cit.*, 1, p. 56.
57. J.-B. Dubos, *Histoire critique de l'établissement de la monarchie françoise dans les Gaules,* Paris, 1734.
58. J. Locke, *Two Treatises on Government,* 1694, in *Collected Works,* Vol. IX, London, 1824, pp. 352–353.
59. Boulainvilliers, *op. cit.*, 1, p. 57–8.
60. Locke, *op. cit.*, Vol. IX, p. 140.
61. J. B. Bossuet, *Politics Drawn from the Very Words of Holy Scripture,* transl. P. Riley, Cambridge, UK, 1990, p. 263.
62. Bossuet, *op. cit.*, pp. 256–265.
63. Velde and Weir, *op. cit.*, p. 20. The figure of 10.5% is based on an assumption that 25% of the loan was taken up by pensioners, and the rest invested in the lives of children.
64. J. M. Augeard, *Mémoires sécrets,* ed. M. E. Bavoux, Paris, 1866, p. 81.
65. Quoted in S. Schama, *Citizens*, New York, 1989, p. 253.
66. Schama, *op. cit.*, p. 267.
67. *Procés verbale du Parlement de Paris,* 11 April 1788, quoted in M. Bottin, "Le budget de 1788 face au Parlement de Paris (Novembre 1787–Avril 1788)," in: *État, finances et economie pendant la Révolution française,* Paris, 1991, p. 77.
68. This was a peculiar compromise title recognized by the emperor, who had little desire to cede nominal sovereignty over part of what was formally his empire. In 1772 the title was changed to King of Prussia.
69. Fay, *op. cit.*, p. 141.

7. REVOLUTION

1. Burke in the House of Commons on 22 March 1775, quoted in B. W. Hill, *Edmund Burke on Government, Politics and Society,* London, 1975, pp. 171–172.
2. The first recorded proposal for a land bank was published by William Potter of London in 1649. The idea was quite prevalent in England throughout the 1690s and led to the abortive founding of a land bank to rival the Bank of England in 1696.
3. Aristotle, *Economics* II, in: *Complete Works,* ed. J. Barnes, Princeton, NJ, 1985, p. 2138.
4. J. M. Keynes, *A Tract on Monetary Reform,* London, 1923, p. 43.
5. Guillaume de Soterel, quoted in P. Spufford, *Money and Its Use in Medieval Europe,* Cambridge, UK, 1988, p. 305.
6. William Douglass, *A Disourse Concerning the Currencies of the British Plantations in America,* Boston, 1739, quoted in R. W. Weiss, "The Issue of Paper Money in the American Colonies, 1720–1774," *Journal of Economic History,* 1970, p. 771.
7. William Douglass, *Essay Concerning Silver and Paper Currencies,* Boston, 1739, quoted in R. Vernier, *Political Economy and Political Ideology: The Public Debt in Eighteenth-Century England and America,* unpublished D.Phil. thesis, Oxford University, 1993, p. 184.
8. Weiss, *op. cit.,* p. 779.
9. Figures from E. J. Ferguson, *The Power of the Purse: A History of American Public Finance 1776–1790,* Chapel Hill, NC, 1961.
10. A. Smith, *The Wealth of Nations,* London, 1776, Book 5, 3, p. 22.
11. Richard Price, *Observations on the nature of Civil Liberty, the Principles of Government, and the Justice and Policy of the War with America,* London, 1776, quoted in Vernier, *op. cit.,* p. 134.
12. Benjamin Franklin, *The Interest of Britain Considered,* 1760, quoted in D. R. McCoy, *The Elusive Republic,* Chapel Hill, NC, 1981, p. 51.
13. *Independent Chronicle,* Boston, October 1785, quoted in McCoy, *op. cit.,* p. 111.
14. *Gazette of the United States,* New York, 2 May 1789. Quoted in McCoy, *op. cit.,* p. 119.
15. Price, *op. cit.,* p. 70, quoted in McCoy, *op. cit.,* p. 66.
16. B. Mitchell, *The Price of Independence: A Realistic View of the American Revolution,* Oxford, UK, 1974, p. 101.
17. Ferguson, *op. cit.,* p. 30.
18. Robert Morris, *Journals*, Vol. XXII, p. 434, quoted in Ferguson, *op. cit.,* p. 51.
19. Ferguson, *op. cit.,* pp. 30, 32, and 43.
20. D. Ramsay, *The History of the American Revolution,* Philadelphia, 1789.
21. A. Hamilton, *A Full Vindication of the Measures of Congress,* 1775, quoted in Vernier, *op. cit.,* p. 216.
22. Quoted in Vernier, *op. cit.,* p. 248.
23. Robert Morris, *Collected Papers,* Vol. III, p. 77, quoted in Vernier, *op. cit.,* p. 248.
24. "Thoughts on the Five Percent," *Providence Gazette,* 19, October 1782, quoted in E. J. Ferguson, "Economy, Liberty, and the Constitution," *William and Mary Quarterly,* 1983, p. 404.
25. Theodore Sedgwick in the House of Representatives, 1790, quoted in Ferguson, The *Power of the Purse,* p. 246.

26. Alexander Hamilton, *Report on the Public Credit,* January 1790, quoted in G. Taylor, *Hamilton and the National Debt,* Boston, 1967, pp. 14–15.
27. D. F. Swanson and A. P. Trout, "Alexander Hamilton, Conversion, and Debt Reduction," *Explorations in Economic History,* 1992. The options offered would not, perhaps, be deemed excessively complex in today's sophisticated capital markets. But in the late eighteenth century they were rejected as an invitation to further profiteering by stock jobbers.
28. R. Sylla, "William Duer and the Stock Market Crash of 1792," *Friends of Financial History,* 1992.
29. John Taylor of Caroline, *A Definition of Parties,* 1794, p. 7, quoted in Ferguson, "Economy, Liberty and the Constitution," p. 411.
30. Quoted in R. Hofstadter, *The Idea of a Party System,* Berkeley, CA, 1969, p. 185.
31. B. R. Mitchell, *International Historical Statistics,* Basingstoke, UK, 1992.
32. H. Lüthy, *La Banque protestante en France de la révocation De l'Édit de Nantes à la Révolution,* Paris, 1959, p. 559.
33. Assemblée Nationale, *Procès verbale,* Vol. I, 17 June 1797, pp. 11–13. The same source applies to the passages quoted in the two following paragraphs.
34. Quoted in S. Schama, *Citizens*, New York, 1989, p. 304.
35. Schama, *op. cit.,* p. 297.
36. H.-G. de R. Mirabeau, *Oeuvres: Les discours,* Vol. I, Paris, 1921, pp. 141, 153.
37. J. Bodin, *The Six Books of a Commonwealth,* 1576, transl. R. Knowles, London, 1606; Harvard University Press facsimile edition, Cambridge, MA, 1962, p. 668.
38. There is no definitive figure for French debts on the eve of the Revolution. F. Braesch (*Finances et monnaires revolutionaires,* Paris, 1936) came up with the same figure by the simplistic means of capitalizing all budgeted interest payments and officers' *gages* at 5%. Even though this is conceptually inadequate for annuities and for the value of venal offices, the truth does not seem to be far from his estimate. The figure for annuities is calculated from F. Marion, *Histoire financière de la France depuis 1715,* Paris, 1914, Vol. I, pp. 472–475. The figures for venal offices and farmers' bonds is from J. F. Bosher, *French Finances 1779–1795,* Cambridge, UK, 1975, p. 256. Braesch's estimates of other debts are accepted.
39. Louis Blanc, *Histoire de la Révolution française,* Paris, 1847, quoted in R. Stourm, *Les Finances de l'ancien régime et de la Révolution,* Vol. II, Paris, 1885, p. 261.
40. Stourm, *op. cit.,* p. 255.
41. Ramel, in the Council of Elders, 9 Pluviôse An 5, quoted in Stourm, *op. cit.,* Vol. II, p. 284.
42. Joseph Cambon, report on the finances since 1791 to the Convention, Germinal An 2, quoted in J.-F. Belhoste, "Le financement de la guerre de 1792 à l'an IV," in: *État, finances et économie pendant la Révolution française,* Paris, 1991, p. 342.
43. Figures from S. Harris, *The Assignats,* Cambridge, MA, 1930, p. 51. Harris's figures for real spending have been reduced by the real value of debt repayment in the period.
44. Quoted in Schama, *op. cit.,* p. 597.
45. Chabot, in the Convention on 30 July 1793, quoted in Stourm, *op. cit.,* Vol. II, p. 322.
46. Cambon, in the Convention on 27 April 1793, quoted in Stourm, *op. cit.,* Vol. II, p. 369.
47. Cambon, in the Convention on 3 Pluviôse An 2, quoted in Marion, *op. cit.,* Vol. II, p. 87.

48. Quoted in Marion, *op. cit.*, Vol. III, p. 88.
49. Montesquiou in the Legislative Assembly, quoted in Marion, *op. cit.*, Vol. II, p. 280.
50. M. Bruguière, *Pour une renaissance de l'histoire financière, XVIIIe–XXe siècles,* Paris, 1991, p. 375.
51. H. J. Habbakuk, "Public Finance and the Sale of Confiscated Property During the Interregnum," *Journal of Economic History,* 1963, p. 87, and Mitchell, *International Historical Statistics,* p. 34. The figure for the American Revolution was the amount subsequently established by the British government, which had agreed to compensate all those who were expropriated as a result of loyalty to the Crown.
52. Harris, *op. cit.*, pp. 80–84.
53. F. Guizot, *Du gouvernement de la France depuis la Restauration et du Ministère actuel,* Paris, 1820, pp. 1–2, quoted in L. Poliakov, *The Aryan Myth: A History of Racist and Nationalist Ideas in Europe,* London, 1971, p. 31.
54. Necker, to the Assembly, 6 March, 1790, quoted in Stourm, *op. cit.*, Vol. II, p. 270.
55. A. Lavoisier, "De l'état des finances en France au ler Janvier 1792," in: *Oeuvres de Lavoisier,* Vol. VI, Paris, 1864–1893, p. 492.
56. Quoted in Marion, *op. cit.*, Vol. III, p. 82.
57. Crétet, in Council of Elders, 20 September 1797, quoted in R. Stourm, *op. cit.*, Vol. II, p. 340.
58. Quoted in L. V. Birck, *The Scourge of Europe: The Public Debt Described, Explained, and Historically Depicted,* London, 1926, frontispiece.
59. Rousseau, quoted in Marion, *op. cit.*, Vol. IV, p. 58.
60. Quoted in Marion, *op. cit.*, Vol. IV, p. 384.
61. Quoted in H. G. Brown, "A Discredited Regime: The Directory and Army Contracting," *French History,* 1990, p. 51.
62. J. Delmas, *Histoire militaire de la France,* Vol. II, Paris, 1992, p. 314, and Marion, *op. cit.*, Vol. IV, p. 305.
63. T. J. Markovitch, *L'Industrie française de 1789 à 1964* in: *Cahiers de L'I.S.E.A.* (Series AF, No. 6), June 1966.
64. Brown, *op. cit.*, p. 52.
65. Quoted in J. Gabilard, "Le Financement des guerres napoléoniennes et la conjuncture du premier empire," *Revue Historique,* 1953, p. 558.
66. T. Paine, *The Decline and Fall of the English System of Finance,* Paris, 1796, p. 23.
67. J. H. Clapham, *The Bank of England,* Vol. I, Cambridge, UK, 1944, p. 275.
68. Letter to *The Times*, London, 16 February 1816, quoted in A. Hope-Jones, *Income Tax in the Napoleonic War,* Cambridge, UK, 1947, p. 114.
69. Lamoiginon de Basville, quoted in R. Bonney, " 'Le secret de leurs familles': The Fiscal and Social Limits of Louis XIV's Dixième," *French History,* 1991, p. 389.
70. The cost of the war is taken as the total spending during the war less an allowance for normal peacetime spending. For all wars until the Napoleonic Wars, this allowance is based on the spending in the years immediately preceding the wars. Since there were no such peaceful years immediately before 1798, an allowance of £10 million for peacetime defense is made for the period 1798–1815. This is simply an average of pre-1789 spending of £5 million per year and a post-1815 defense budget of £15 million per year.

For the purposes of this table, the Napoleonic period of the wars is defined as starting in 1798 rather than 1799, simply so as to coincide with the change in British fiscal policy. The amount borrowed is taken to be the cumulative budget deficit of the government, rather than the face amount of the debt created, since the latter is liable to distortion. Figures from B. R. Mitchell and P. Deane, *Abstract of British Historical Statistics,* Cambridge, UK, 1962.

71. A. E. Feaveryear, *The Pound Sterling,* Oxford, UK, 1931, pp. 228, 230.
72. W. Cobbett, *Paper Against Gold* (Letter VI), p. 95, quoted in E. L. Hargreaves, *The National Debt,* London, 1930, p. 137.
73. Hargreaves, *op. cit.,* p. 112.
74. Hargreaves, *op. cit.,* p. 127.
75. Report of the Bullion Committee, quoted in Feaveryear, *op. cit.,* p. 198.
76. British spending from Mitchell and Deane, *op. cit.* French spending (prospective military budgets rather than actual spending) from Delmas, *op. cit.,* Vol. II, p. 314. The French figures do not include amounts collected from foreign countries and spent locally. These may have been as much as £5–10 million per year between 1806 and 1812. However, they would not materially alter the underlying message of the graph.
77. Marion, *op. cit.,* Vol. IV, p. 375.
78. Gabilard, *op. cit.,* p. 563.

8. BOURGEOIS CENTURY

1. Quoted in G. Ardant, *Histoire de l'Impôt,* Vol. II, Paris, 1972, p. 269.
2. T. B. Macaulay, *The History of England from the Accession of James II,* Vol. V, London, 1914, pp. 2283–2285.
3. The debt was £807 million in 1855, and GNP has been estimated at £703 million. Throughout this section, the figures for debt are the gross liabilities of the state taken from B. R. Mitchell and P. Deane, *Astract of British Historical Statistics,* Cambridge, UK, 1962. GNP figures after 1855 are from C. H. Feinstein, *National Income, Expenditure, and Output of the United Kingdom 1855–1965,* Cambridge, UK, 1976.
4. "If in the year 1819 the value of the currency had stood at 14s for the pound note, which had been the case in 1813, he should have thought that, on a balance of all the advantages and disadvantages of the case, it would have been as well to fix the currency at the then value, according to which most of the existing contracts had been made; but when the currency was within 5 per cent of its par value, he thought they had made the best selection in recurring to the old standard." Ricardo, speaking in Parliament, June 1822.
5. Patrick O'Brien gives figures for national income of around £360 million for both 1809 and 1819 in his "The Rise of a Fiscal State in England 1485–1815," *Historical Research,* 1993. But retail prices were some 15–20% higher in 1814 than in those years, while in 1822 they were at least 30% lower. P. Deane and W. A. Cole (*in British Economic Growth,* Cambridge, UK, 1962) estimated gross national income at £291 million in 1821. The public debt was £838 million in 1821, but this figure does not include an allowance for the capital value of life annuities that cost £1.8 million during the year.

Capitalizing these somewhat conservatively at ten times annual payments gives a total peak debt of £856 million.

6. J. R. McCulloch, *Inquiries with Respect to the Influence and Operation of National Debts and Taxes,* London, 1827, p. 80, reprinted in: L. C. Kaounindes and G. E. Wood, *Debts and Deficits,* Aldsershot, UK, 1992. These were net figures, after the redemptions made by the sinking fund during the war.
7. J. R. McCulloch, *Essay on the Question of Reducing the Interest of the National Debt,* 1816, in: *Collected Works,* Vol. I, ed. D. P. O'Brien, London, 1995, p. 198.
8. The total amount available for exchange was £591 million; £25 million refused to convert and was redeemed.
9. GNP figures from Feinstein, *op. cit.*
10. Gladstone, budget speech of 1854, quoted in E. L. Hargreaves, *The National Debt,* London, 1930, p. 169.
11. The government borrowed £30 million in the Crimean War and £160 million in the Boer War.
12. This reduction is calculated from the peak debt of £844 million (£864 million including an allowance for the capital value of life annuities) recorded in 1819.
13. This was something of a political sleight of hand. It was clear that the savings institutions had no need for terminable securities. Each time they matured, they would have to be replaced by others. However, because the capital portion of the annuities was included in the budget, Parliament was forced to accept a higher level of debt service than if all the debt had been in the form of perpetuals. Between 1863 and 1883, £118 million of perpetual debt was converted into terminable annuities by this ruse.
14. Sources for the period until 1790 are as in Chapter 6, note 13. The information for the period after 1790 is from Mitchell and Deane, *op. cit.* The series for GNP is created by extrapolating from the decennial figures calculated by Deane and Cole, *op. cit.*, for the period until 1855, deflated by the retail price index, and then by using the annual GNP figures from Feinstein, *op. cit.*
15. J. M. Keynes, *A Tract on Monetary Reform,* London, 1923, p. 15.
16. L.-A. Garnier-Pagès, *Histoire de la révolution de 1848,* Vol. IV, p. 26, quoted in F. Marion, *Histoire financière de la France depuis 1715,* Vol. V, Paris, 1914, p. 242.
17. Marion, *op. cit.*, Vol. VI, pp. 51, 162, 261.
18. J. C. Riley, *International Government Finance and the Amsterdam Capital Market, 1740–1815,* Cambridge, UK, 1980, pp. 135, 203–207.
19. Riley, *op. cit.*, p. 207.
20. L. V. Birck, *The Scourge of Europe,* London, 1926, pp. 298–299.
21. Riley, *op. cit.*, pp. 209–211.
22. GNP/NNP figures: Great Britain, Feinstein, *op. cit.*; France, T. J. Markovitch, *L'Industrie française de 1789 à 1964*, Paris, 1966; Germany, B. R. Mitchell, *International Historical Statistics,* Basingstoke, UK, 1992; Russia, P. Gregory, *Russian National Income, 1885–1913,* Cambridge, UK, 1982; Austria, N. Ferguson, "Public Finance and National Security," *Past and Present,* 1994; Italy, B. R. Mitchell, *op. cit.*; United States, B. R. Mitchell, *International Historical Statistics,* Basingstoke, UK, 1983. Debt figures: Great Britain, Mitchell and Deane, *op. cit.*; France, *Annuaire Statistique de la France,* Paris, 1924; Germany, D. E. Schremmer, *Cambridge Economic History of Europe,*

Vol. VIII, Cambridge, UK, 1989; Russia, A. Michelsen, P. N. Apostol, and M. B. Bernatsky, *Russian Public Finances During the War,* New Haven, CT, 1928; Italy, A. Confaloniere and E. Gatti, *La politica del debito pubblico in Italia, 1919–43,* Bari, It., 1986; United States, *Historical Statistics of the United States: Colonial Times to 1957,* Washington, DC, 1952.

23. Yields of long-term debt. United States, Great Britain, and France are average yields for the year, from S. Homer and R. Sylla, *A History of Interest Rates,* New Brusnwick, NJ, 1991. Italy, Germany, Russia, and Austria are as of 11 October 1913, from *The Economist.*
24. This was partly due to the influence of Paul Warburg, the expatriate German banker who was, in many ways, the father of the Federal Reserve System.
25. Michelsen, Apostol, and Bernatsky, *op. cit.,* p. 240.
26. In order to resolve the monetary anarchy that followed the end of the Second Bank of the United States in 1836, the federal government passed the Nation Bank Act in 1863, which authorized qualifying banks to issue notes against amounts held in government bonds. The National Bank notes were legal tender for tax payments, and in the absence of a central bank, they became essential for the smooth running of the economy; but the supply of U.S. bonds was so low in the late nineteenth century as to threaten the ability of the national banks to issue sufficient money. There was therefore strong pressure to issue perpetual debt. A significant portion of the federal debt in 1914 comprised the Consol 2%s, which were protected against redemption until 1930.
27. D.C.M. Platt, *Foreign Finance in Continental Europe and the United States 1815–1870,* London, 1984, p. 69.
28. R. D. Baxter, *National Debts,* London, 1871, pp. 26, 48.
29. E. von Böhm-Bawerk, *Positive Theory of Capital,* Vienna, 1889. See J. A. Schumpeter, *Ten Great Economists,* Oxford, UK, 1951, p. 182.
30. C. Suter, *Debt Cycles in the World Economy,* Boulder, CO, 1992, p. 2.
31. *L'Ami du Peuple,* 19 March 1848, quoted in Marion, *op. cit.,* Vol. V, p. 237.
32. Léon Say, *Journal des Economistes,* November 1882, quoted in Marion, *op. cit.,* Vol. V, p. 49.
33. *Economiste Français,* December 1888, quoted in Marion, *op. cit.,* Vol. VI, p. 109.
34. E.J.P. Benn, *Debt (Private and Public, Good and Bad),* London, 1938, p. 46.
35. Figures for 1913 from U.S. Bureau of the Census, *Historical Statistics of the United States: Colonial Times to 1957,* Vol. II, pp. 1126–1127. Figure for 1870 state and local debts from H. C. Adams, *Public Debts,* New York, 1887, reprinted New York, 1975, p. 305.
36. Spending figures from S. Andic and J. Veverka, "The Growth of Government Expenditure in Germany," *Finanzarchiv,* 1964. Debt figures from R. Goldsmith, *Comparative National Balance Sheets,* Chicago, 1985 (for 1875), and Schremmer, *op. cit.*
37. Spending and debt figures from *Annuaire Statistique de la France,* Paris, 1926. GNP figures from Markovitch, *op. cit.*
38. Quoted in Marion, *op. cit.,* Vol. VI, p. 173.
39. Quoted in N. Ferguson, *The World's Banker: The History of the House of Rothschild,* London, 1998, p. 951.
40. Quoted in Ferguson, *op. cit.,* p. 132.

41. *Sheffield Mercury,* December 1818, quoted in H. O. Horne, *A History of Savings Banks,* Oxford, UK, 1947, p. 13.
42. John Smith addressing the Bolton weavers in 1816, quoted in Horne, *op. cit.,* p. 76.
43. Horne, *op. cit.,* pp. 389, 392.
44. U.S. National Monetary Commission, *Banking and Currency Systems in England, France, Germany, Switzerland, and Italy,* Washington, DC, 1910; and A. Valentino, *L'Emploi des fonds des Caisses d' & Épargne Ordinaire,* Paris, 1969.
45. Moscow Financial Institute, *The Soviet Financial System,* Moscow, 1966, p. 275.
46. Lenin, *Works,* Vol. VI, p. 92, quoted in Moscow Financial Institute, *op. cit.,* p. 275.
47. In 1859, for instance, Gladstone declared: "There cannot be a more gross delusion than to think that the funds in the hands of the Commissioners of the National Debt are the funds of the depositors in the savings banks. . . . They have no interest in the employment of the money; it does not signify to them if you fling it to the bottom of the sea." Quoted in J. Wormell, *The Management of the National Debt of the United Kingdom, 1900–1932,* London, 2000, p. 700.
48. Horne, *op. cit.,* p. 277.
49. Marion, *op. cit.,* Vol. V, p. 368.
50. Marion, *op. cit.,* Vol. V, p. 570.
51. The figures for the two rente issues are amounts raised rather than face amounts.
52. C. A. Stanuell, *British Consols and French Rentes,* London, 1909, p. 5.
53. *The Economist,* 16 December 1911. The article also emphasized the political aspect of wide debt distribution: the creation of a "more . . . instructed public opinion in matters of national finance."
54. J. K. Galbraith, *Money: Whence It Came, Where It Went,* New York, 1975, p. 71.
55. P. Studenski and H. E. Krooss, *Financial History of the United States,* New York, 1963, p. 121.
56. M. Winckler, *Foreign Bonds, An Autopsy,* Philadelphia, 1934, p. 9.
57. Quoted in R. E. Sharkey, *Money, Class, and Party,* Baltimore, 1959, p. 44.
58. This quote is from a speech in the Senate on 9 February 1863, in: *Speeches and Reports on Finance and Taxation by John Sherman,* New York, 1879, p. 51.
59. The federal debt was $2.68 billion in June 1865, against a GNP of $6.56 billion. However, the real value of the debt was higher since the interest-bearing portion was payable in gold, which traded at a 33% premium at the time. The full implications are discussed later in the text.
60. W. C. Mitchell, *The History of the Greenbacks,* Chicago, 1903, p. 129. Around $236 million (7% of total spending) of the interest-bearing Treasury bills were given legal-tender status, although they were not intended to circulate as currency.
61. Mitchell, *op. cit.,* p. 64.
62. Mitchell, *op. cit.,* p. 96. This statement was made in connection with the second issue of greenbacks in July 1862, but the debate was much the same.
63. The chart shows the yield to latest maturity (in 1882) of U.S. 6% bonds calculated in gold terms. Information for bond prices is from *The Bankers Magazine and Statistical Register,* New York, 1862–1865. Where prices for the 5-20s are not available, the series uses those of the 6%s issued in 1848 redeemable after 1868, since these were the

most similar to the 5-20s. The value of gold against paper currency is taken from W. C. Mitchell, *op. cit.*, p. 423.

64. H. M. Lawson, *Jay Cooke, Private Banker,* Cambridge, MA, 1936, p. 115.
65. M. Wilkins, *The History of Foreign Investment in the United States to 1914,* Cambridge, MA, 1989, p. 91. The figure represents 30% of the federal debt at the time (excluding the greenbacks, which obviously were not an object of foreign investment interest).
66. Studenski and Krooss, *op. cit.*, p. 161.
67. U.S. Senate, 27 February 1868. From *Speeches by John Sherman, op. cit.*, p. 165. Sherman's view was that bondholders who refused to convert into a new 5% 40-year gold bond would be left with the unresolved threat of repayment in greenbacks. Opponents argued that, since dissenters would not be redeemed in gold, the process was tantamount to a forced conversion.
68. Neither the Democrats nor the Republicans were entirely united on this issue, however. The leader of the movement to repay in greenbacks, George Pendleton, lost the Democratic primary to Horatio Seymour, a believer in hard money (who then had to live rather uncomfortably with the soft-money plank in his manifesto). On the other hand, several Republicans favored Sherman's plan of a forced conversion.
69. J. Richardson, ed., *Messages and Papers of the Presidents,* New York, 1897, p. 3961.
70. American and British long-term bond yields are from Homer and Sylla, *op. cit.* American yields are calculated to latest maturity in gold terms. Russian interest rates are derived from prices on the London Stock Exchange. These have kindly been provided by Niall Ferguson of Jesus College, Oxford, from his database of bond prices quoted in *The Economist.* The bulge in Russian yields in 1877–1879 was the result of the Russo-Turkish War of 1877–1878. Thereafter, Russian yields settled into their old pattern.
71. Richardson, *op. cit.*, p. 3348.
72. Lawson, *op. cit.*, pp. 106, 121.
73. Lawson, *op. cit.*, p. 130.
74. S. Wilkeson, *How Our National Debt May Be a National Blessing,* Philadelphia, 1865, p. 6. Wilkeson was a journalist who worked for Cooke. It is commonly understood that in this and other pamphlets he was merely Cooke's mouthpiece.
75. Cooke's letter is quoted in full in E. P. Oberholtzer, *Jay Cooke, Financier of the Civil War,* Vol. II, Philadelphia, 1907, pp. 44–53.
76. Lawson, *op. cit.*, p. 174.

9. NATIONS AT ARMS

1. These figures are calculated by conversion of the total amount borrowed in each war year at the average dollar exchange rate for the year. The figures are taken from the United Nations, *Report on Public Debt,* Lake Placid, NY, 1947, for Great Britain, Germany, and the United States; R. M. Haig, *The Public Finances of Post-War France,* New York, 1929, for France; D. Forsyth, *The Crisis of Liberal Italy,* Cambridge, UK, 1993, and F. A. Répaci, *La finanza pubblica Italiana nel secolo 1861–1960,* Bologna, 1962, for Italy; A. Michelsen, P. N. Apostol, and M. B. Bernatsky, *Russian Public Finances During the War,* New Haven, CT, 1928, for Russia.

2. The annual amounts borrowed are deflated by the average of the retail and wholesale price indices except for Russia, where only the wholesale price index is used. War spending is calculated to include the increased cost of debt service, but to exclude prewar levels of military spending. Source for prices: United Nations, *op. cit.*, except for Russia where the source is G. Y. Sokolnikov, *Soviet Policy in Public Finance*, Stanford, CA, 1931. Amounts borrowed are taken from the same sources as in the previous footnote, plus U.S. Bureau of the Census, *Historical Statistics of the United States: Colonial Times to 1957*, Washington, DC, 1960; B. R. Mitchell and P. Deane, *Abstract of British Historical Statistics*, Cambridge, UK, 1962; and W.J.E. Lotz, *Deutsche Staatsfinanzwirtschaft in Kreige*, Stuttgart, 1927.
3. Quoted in N. Ferguson, *The Pity of War*, London, 1988, p. 325.
4. Charles Rist of the Bank of France describing the German war loans, quoted in G. Jèze and H. Truchy, *The War Finance of France*, New Haven, CT, 1927, p. 283. Rist felt that France's bond drives had been haphazard compared to Germany's, but his description captures the spirit of wartime borrowing in every belligerent country.
5. Liberty Loan Committee, *The Liberty Loan of 1917*, New York, 1917, p. 12.
6. U.S. Treasury, *Fourth Liberty Loan: A Handbook for Speakers*, Washington, DC, 1918, p. 36.
7. T. Frank, *An Economic Survey of Ancient Rome*, Vol. I, Baltimore, 1933, p. 89.
8. U.S. Treasury, *op. cit.*, p. 63.
9. Speech to schoolchildren by William Mather Lewis, from *Fourth Liberty Loan: A Handbook for Speakers*, p. 87.
10. J. Wormell, *The Management of the National Debt of the United Kingdom, 1900–1932*, London, 2000, p. 340.
11. The chart gives the yield of the most expensive long-term loans floated in each country during the war. In the case of the United States and Great Britain, the figures are shown both before and after deduction of the base rate of income tax in order to give a fair comparison with continental countries where war loans were tax-exempt.
12. Sources of information for this chart are as in notes 1 and 2. The contribution from taxation is calculated by allocating the wartime increase of debt interest to war expenses, but excluding an allowance for prewar levels of military spending. The figure for France is shown as negative because French tax revenues did not even cover nonwar spending. The existence of inter-Allied loans complicates the calculation of war costs, not least because the question of how far they were repayable became the subject of considerable postwar debate To avoid a problematical sequence of second-guessing, they are shown as they were budgeted at the time. However, it has to be borne in mind that this creates as element of double counting, since the creditor countries—America, Britain, and, to a lesser extent, France—also classified the loans that they made to Allies as part of their own war spending. Germany's small amount of foreign war debt consisted of credits from foreign suppliers.
13. A. D. Noyes, *The War Period of American Finance, 1908–1925*, New York, 1926, p. 183.
14. Address of Dr. Havenstein at the Frankfurt Chamber of Commerce, 20 September 1917. From R. H. Lutz, ed., *The Fall of the German Empire*, Vol. II, New York, 1969, pp. 210–212.

15. Ferguson, *op. cit.*, p. 337.
16. It was extremely rare for perpetual annuities to rise very far above par because of the risk of redemption. In the 1890s, Consols were able to rise to very high prices because they were protected against redemption until 1923 as a result of the 1889 conversion. Consol prices were also affected by a change in the law in 1889 that allowed trustees, previously obliged to invest exclusively in government securities, greater liberty in their investment decisions. This gradually deprived Consols of what had been a large captive pool of savings.
17. E. V. Morgan, *Studies in British Financial Policy 1914–25*, London, 1952, pp. 160–162, 170. In Britain only 3% of war spending was accounted for by borrowing from the central bank, as opposed to 17% in France and 20% in Germany.
18. Quoted in B. Kent, *The Spoils of War*, Oxford, UK, p. 52.
19. France's prewar GNP was around 40 billion francs. This had probably fallen by 20% by the end of 1918, even allowing for the return of Alsace-Lorraine. Prices had risen by around 200% by that time, so that nominal GNP may have been in the region of 90–100 billion francs, compared to public debt of 173 billion francs. Germany's NNP fell from around 50 billion marks before the war to no more than 35 billion gold marks afterward. Prices were also around 200% higher by the end of 1918, so that nominal NNP would have been in the region of 100–110 billion marks. Postwar GNP may then be estimated at around 115 billion marks, compared to public debt of 180 billion marks.
20. J. H. Jones, *The Economics of War and Conquest*, London, 1915, p. 212.
21. Figures published by the Reparation Commission on 23 February 1921, as per J. M. Keynes, *A Revision of the Treaty*, London, 1922, pp. 195–6.
22. The figures for inter-Allied debts are taken from J. M. Keynes, *op. cit.*, pp. 219–220. Amounts due from Russia are excluded. Amounts due to Great Britain in sterling are converted into dollars at the prewar exchange rate of 4.86:1. The figures for inter-Allied debts are somewhat larger than those recorded in the immediate aftermath of war since they include postwar credits and accrued interest. The figures for domestic war debt are calculated from the annual increase of wartime debt at the average dollar exchange rate for the year in which it was contracted. Postwar domestic borrowing is not included.
23. The calculation is made by discounting German payments to 1919 values at a discount rate of 5% per annum. The resulting figure is 27 billion gold marks. The German counteroffer at Versailles had been 60 billion gold marks over thirty-three years without interest, which Keynes had valued at 30 billion marks in 1919 terms in *The Economic Consequences of the Peace*, London, 1919, pp. 206–207.
24. S. A. Schuker, *American Reparations to Germany, 1919–1933*, Princeton, NJ, 1988.
25. Quoted in N. Ferguson, *Paper and Iron: Hamburg Business and German Politics in the Era of Inflation, 1897–1927*, Cambridge, UK, 1995, p. 345.
26. K.-L. Holtfrerich, *The German Inflation 1914–1923*, Berlin, 1986, p. 295.
27. Quoted in Ferguson, *Paper and Iron*, p. 359.
28. H. Fisk, *Our Public Debt*, New York, 1919, p. 60.
29. Leffingwell testifying to a congressional committee in 1922. Quoted in C. R. Wittlesey, *The Banking System and War Finance*, New York, 1943, p. 31.
30. One-thirtieth of the debt was repaid annually by lottery draws. Interest was paid only at

redemption, and was not compounded. Payments continued until 1944. M. L. Hughes, *Paying for the German Inflation,* Chapel Hill, NC, 1988, pp. 189–193.

31. Haig, *op. cit.*, pp. 42–43.
32. Klotz addressing the Chamber of Deputies on 3 December 1918, quoted in Kent, *op. cit.*, p. 27.
33. This calculation is based on the assumption that the French investor received 5% interest compounded on an annual basis. The resulting values have been adjusted for relative prices, with 1927 used as representative of poststabilization price levels. Both the retail and wholesale indices have been used, since they produce somewhat different results. This process gives real present values that range from 21.6% for amounts invested in 1915 to 55% in 1918. The arithmetic average of all eight calculations is 33%. The same calculations have been made for Germany on the assumption that public creditors could reinvest their interest until 1918 but not thereafter, since all currency and short-term debt instruments issued after 1918 became valueless in 1923. The 4.5% lottery bonds that they received are reduced to present value at 5% per annum to compensate for the fact that interest was only paid upon redemption on a noncompounded basis. The base year used for stabilized values and price levels is 1925–1926. The range of resulting residual values is from 7.5% for amounts subscribed in 1915 to 16% for amounts subscribed in 1918, with an arithmetic average of 9.8%.
34. There are no accepted figures for French GNP during or after the war. Markovitch confines himself to an average figure of 188 billion francs for the period from 1920 to 1925. For the purposes of this calculation I have taken the figures for real NNP from B. R. Mitchell, *European Historical Statistics,* London, 1992. I have converted them somewhat arbitrarily into GNP figures by reflating them by the wholesale price index and comparing them to the generally accepted 1913 GNP figure of 40 billion francs. The resulting figure is very comparable to Markovitch's. The figure for 1918 is based on an approximate assumption that real NNP had fallen by 20% during the war even when the return of Alsace-Lorraine is allowed for.
35. J. M. Keynes, *A Tract on Monetary Reform,* London, 1923, p. 73.
36. F. Preobrazhensky, *Paper Money During the Proletarian Dictatorship,* Moscow, 1920, p. 4. Quoted in G. Y. Sokolnikov, *Soviet Policy in Public Finance,* Stanford, CA, 1931, p. 111.
37. Quoted in J. Grant, *Money of the Mind: Borrowing and Lending in America from the Civil War to Michael Milken,* New York, 1992, p. 231.
38. Keynes, *Monetary Reform,* p. 67.
39. Keynes, giving evidence to Colwyn Committee in 1925, quoted in S. Harris, *The National Debt and the New Economics,* New York, 1947, p. 68.
40. Keynes in 1924, quoted in J. M. Buchanan *et al.*, eds., *Deficits,* Oxford, UK, 1987, p. 130.
41. O. Nathan, *Nazi War Finance,* New York, 1944, p. 90.
42. A. S. Milward, *War, Economy and Society, 1939–1945,* London, 1977, p. 4.
43. L. R. Samuel, *Pledging Allegiance: American Identity and the Bond Drive of World War II,* Washington, DC, 1997.
44. R. Merton, *Mass Persuasion: The Social Psychology of a War Bond Drive,* Boston, 1945, p. 53.

45. Merton, *op. cit.*, pp. 180–182.
46. Figures for borrowing are from United Nations, *op. cit.* Figures for revenues are from U.S. Bureau of the Census, *op. cit.* (for the United States), and from Mitchell and Deane, *op. cit.* (for Great Britain). War spending is defined as total spending less an allowance for nonwar spending of $9 billion per year for the United States and £1 billion for Great Britain. These figures represent the governments' rate of spending in the final year before the war.
47. W. L. Crum *et al.*, *Fiscal Planning for Total War,* New York, 1942, p. 127.
48. H. C. Murphy, *The National Debt in War and Transition,* New York, 1950, p. 72.
49. J. M. Keynes, *How to Pay for the War,* London, 1940, pp. 25–26.
50. In Keynes's proposal everyone would have had a portion of his taxes classified as "deferred income." However, whereas for those at the lowest end of the income scale this would be the entire amount deducted, for those at the top end the portion would be very small. For example, incomes of £300 would incur a 30% tax rate entirely repayable, while incomes of £20,000 would incur an 80% tax rate, of which only 15% was repayable.
51. J. M. Blum, *From the Morgenthau Diaries: The Years of War,* Boston, 1967, pp. 19–20.
52. Murphy, *op. cit.*, p. 87.
53. J. L. Ilsley, Canadian Minister of Finance, in 1940, quoted in F. I. Ker and W. H. Goodman, *Press Promotion of War Finance,* Toronto, 1946, Introduction.
54. Murphy, *op. cit.*, p. 196.
55. S. Chase, *Where's the Money Coming From? Problems of Postwar Finance: Guidelines to America's Future as Reported to the Twentieth Century Fund,* New York, 1942, p. 26.
56. Radio broadcast, 8 September 1943, from the Franklin D. Roosevelt Library and Digital Archives website.
57. A. H. Hansen, *Fiscal Policy and Business Cycles,* London, 1941, p. 179, quoted in H. G. Moulton, *The New Philosophy of Public Debt,* Washington, DC, 1943, p. 58.
58. The figures are taken from the United Nations, *op. cit.*, and from the Federal Reserve, *Banking and Monetary Statistics.* Government agency holdings of U.S. debt have been excluded for the sake of comparability. The figures for Great Britain are taken from United Nations, *op. cit.*, and from H. O. Horne, *A History of the Savings Banks,* Oxford, UK, 1947. The total assets held in the postal savings system have been deducted from the increase in long-term debt reported by the UN.
59. Karl Marx, *Das Capital,* Vol. 1, Part 8, Ch. 31, "The Genesis of Industrial Capital."
60. Moscow Financial Institute, *Soviet Financial System,* Moscow, 1966, p. 112.
61. I. Birman, *Secret Incomes of the Soviet State Budget,* The Hague, 1981.
62. J. R. Millar, "History and Analysis of the Soviet Bond Program," *Soviet Studies,* 1975. Bonds outstanding in 1957 were 25.8 billion rubles versus a net material product (the Soviet term for national production) of 113 billion rubles.
63. Quoted in R. W. Davies, *The Development of the Soviet Budgetary System,* Cambridge, UK, 1958, p. 50.
64. Vladimir Lenin, *History of the Communist Party of the Soviet Union,* p. 223, quoted in O. Kushpeta, *The Banking and Credit System of the USSR,* Boston, 1978, p. 29.
65. Sokolnikov, *op. cit.*, p. 265.
66. L. E. Hubbard, *Soviet Money and Finance,* London, 1936, pp. 181, 191.

67. Figures from J. R. Millar, "Financing the Soviet War Effort in WWII," *Soviet Studies,* 1980.
68. In the immediate aftermath of the war, public debt had stood at around 45% of national production. However, a doubling of prices between 1945 and 1947 had reduced this ratio to 25% of national production by the time of the monetary reform of December 1947, in spite of additional postwar bond issues.
69. Reparations figures are from Ferguson, *Paper and Iron,* p. 477. French occupation costs are from Milward, *op. cit.,* p. 140. In the absence of figures for French national production during the war, the sums are translated into 1938 prices and compared to national income in 1938.
70. Domestic taxes raised 185 billion marks during the war. "Civil" spending was recorded at 200 billion marks. If the increased cost of interest on the public debt caused by war borrowing is excluded, civil spending would be around 176 billion marks—leaving only 9 billion marks net tax contribution to war costs in excess of 500 billion marks. The rest was financed by domestic borrowing (74%), occupied territories (23%), and credits from foreign suppliers in neutral countries (1%). However, it is possible that the "civil" budget includes certain indirect war costs. If the figures are recalculated with 1938–1939 spending as a fair estimate of nonwar spending during the war years, then the contributions are as follows: taxes, 11%; domestic borrowing, 67%; occupied territories, 21%; and foreign suppliers, 1%. The truth probably lies somewhere between these two figures. Either way, the contribution from domestic taxation was slight. The figures here are taken from W. A. Boelke, *Die Kosten von Hitlers Krieg,* Paderborn, Germany, 1985, pp. 98–114.
71. Graf Schwerin von Krosigk, *Staatsbankrott: Finanzpolitik des Deutschen Reiches 1920–1945,* Gottingen, 1974, p. 297.
72. Nathan, *op. cit.,* Introduction.
73. Murphy, *op. cit.,* p. 72.
74. Source: United Nations, *Statistical Yearbooks,* Lake Placid, NY, 1947–1950.
75. Keynes in February 1946, quoted in A. Cairncross, *The Price of War,* Oxford, UK, 1986, p. 100.
76. Figures from Cairncross, *op. cit.,* p. 219.
77. In order to show the ratio of borrowing to GNP, the annual additions to debt have been deflated to prewar prices. For the First World War, the resulting figure is then compared to prewar GNP. For the Second World War, the comparison is to peak wartime GNP deflated to prewar prices. A comparison to prewar GNP would give a somewhat false impression because there was so much economic slack in the American and British economies in 1939.
78. In 1919 the U.S. Federal Reserve held 9% of the relatively small amount of short-term government debt outstanding. In 1946 the Fed held 32% of a relatively far larger short-term debt. In 1919 the Bank of England held 20% of short-term government debt, as opposed to 23% in 1946.
79. See note 28.
80. National Resources Planning Board, *Post-war Agenda: Full Employment Security, Building America,* Washington, DC, 1942, quoted in A. S. Milward, *War, Economy and Society 1939–1945,* London, 1977, p. 340.

81. In the United States the seminal document was the Employment Act of 1946. In Britain it was the official policy document ("white paper") *Employment Policy* of May 1944.

82. These figures represent an average of rates of return for typical loans raised from the general public during the war years. There are a number of difficult choices to make when constructing tables such as these. For the Second World War, the figures are based on the U.S. savings bonds and the British savings certificates sold to small savers. These had the highest interest rates available on any government security during the war and were protected against depreciation. If long-term marketable bonds had been used, the rates of return would be substantially worse. For the First World War, the figures are based on the loans issued in each year of the war. Where conversion to higher-yielding loans in later years was possible (as it generally was), it is assumed to have occurred. Since interest on the American Liberty Loans was exempt from the base rate of income tax, their nominal yields have been grossed up by 4% in 1918 and 12% thereafter in order to make them comparable to British loans that were wholly taxable. Without this adjustment the average return would be 3.7% rather than 4.2%. In order to make a fair comparison with the Second World War, all American and British First World War loans are assumed to have been repaid at par after ten years. This is not unreasonable since their market prices were close to par in the mid-to-late 1920s. Since official consumer price indices diverge quite radically from wholesale prices in both periods (partly because of price controls), a composite price index based two-thirds on consumer prices and one-third on wholesale prices has been used. If only consumer prices or wholesale prices are used, the results change significantly, as shown below:

	World War I		*World War II*	
	CPI	WPI	CPI	WPI
United States	+2.4%	+7.8%	–1.5%	–2.4%
Great Britain	+3.8%	+6.4%	–0.3%	–3.8%

83. Article in the *New Statesman,* 21 February 1948. Among the more left-leaning economists of the Labour Party, such as Joan Robinson, the main worry about the policy of reducing interest rates was that it might hand unjustified capital gains to the holders of long-term bonds—the very people who were supposed to be candidates for euthanasia. See S. Howson, *British Monetary Policy 1945–51,* Oxford, 1993, p. 89.

84. The pattern of bond prices was somewhat different in the United States and Britain. In the United States, bond prices started to fall significantly from their wartime levels only in the second half of the 1950s, while in Britain the bear market started in earnest in 1949–1952 when Consols fell from the low 80s to the low 60s.

85. John Snyder in August 1950 and January 1951, quoted in U.S. Congress Joint Committee on the Economic Report, *General Credit Control, Debt Management, and Economic Mobilization,* Washington, DC, 1951, pp. 37–40.

86. Decree of Venetian Senate, in G. Luzzatto, *Il debito pubblico della Repubblica di Venezia,* Milan, 1963, p. 257.

87. G. L. Bach of the Carnegie Institute of Technology, testifying to Congress, quoted in U.S. Congress, *op. cit.,* pp. 61–65.

88. Lester V. Chandler of Princeton University, ibid.

89. In late 1951, the Bank of England lending rate was finally raised from the 2% level at which it had been held steady since 1940. By 1952 it had risen to 4%.

EPILOGUE: THE END OF THE AFFAIR

1. Quoted in S. Homer, *The Great American Bond Market*, New York, 1978, p. 280.
2. This was the phrase of Keynes's colleague, Joan Robinson, in 1966. See C. T. Rowley, "The Legacy of Keynes: From the General Theory to Generalized Budget Deficits," in: C. T. Rowley *et al.*, eds., *Deficits*, Oxford, UK, 1987, p. 159.
3. *New York Times Magazine*, 8 March 1959. From H. Wolozin, ed., *American Fiscal and Monetary Policy, from the Pages of the New York Times*, New York, 1970, p. 215.
4. Editorial in the *Washington Post*, 14 July 1964, quoted in *The Rising Toll of Interest Rates*, issed by the Conference on Economic Progress, Washington, DC, 1964, p. 83.
5. The interest on the debt owned by the Social Security agency is excluded from this calculation, since the operations of the fund are implicitly part of the "social" budget.
6. R. J. Samuelson, "Clinton's Nemesis," *Newsweek*, 1 February 1993.
7. For both the United States and United Kingdom, these calculations are based on the assumption that a fair rate of return would have been 3% above the rate of inflation.
8. "Myths and Facts About Inflation," a speech in Cleveland, Ohio, 10 June 1974, in: Homer, *op. cit.*, pp. 129–131.
9. "Crisis in the Bond Market," hearing before the Joint Economic Committee, Congress of the United States, 12 March 1980.
10. This cartoon is courtesy of the artist Frank Dickens. Unfortunately, although both the author and the artist remember the original cartoon, neither of them has been able to track it down. The present drawing is therefore a re-creation. The author provided the necessary graph to the artist, who then drew the figures from his memory. Both the author and the artist feel that the result, if not an exact facsimile, captures the spirit of the original.
11. The calculations exclude holdings by government agencies. The Japanese figures are for government bonds only. The rest of the Japanese debt consists of loans (21%) and Treasury bills (7%). Institutional holdings in other countries are as follows: Italy, 44%; Great Britain, 55%; and France, 68% (negotiable debt only—approximately 92% of the total). The figures are as of 1998 (United States and Great Britain), 1999 (Italy), and 2000 (France and Japan.)
12. The figures for 1999–2000 are as follows: United States, 33%; Germany, 34%; Italy, 33%; and France, 28%. The figures exclude holdings by government agencies. The exception to this trend is Great Britain. The proportion of foreign ownership has remained largely unchanged since the war, at around 15%. Foreign ownership of gilts was always important because of the role of sterling as a reserve currency. All that has happened is that foreign governments have been gradually replaced by private institutions.
13. No country has kept more complete figures for the distribution of holdings of the public debt than the United States, where there are continuous records back to the First World War. Unfortunately the amounts owned by individuals and corporations are separated only after 1940. However, it is reasonable to estimate that individuals owned around

45–50% of the debt in 1919, since a full 80% is recorded as owned by private nonbank investors. In the Second World War there was a far greater dependence on bank finance, and individuals furnished only around 27% of total borrowing. A ratio of around 25–30% lasted until the early 1970s, when a period of inexorable decline began. In 1999 the Treasury Department stopped publishing figures for individual ownership of marketable securities and started combining the figure with corporate holdings again. In June 1998 individuals held 9.3% of federal government debt. Source: *Treasury Bulletin,* March 1999.

14. This figure covers only marketable debt—some 92% of the total. If the deposits of French citizens at the post office and at the Treasury are included, the total increases to around 5%. Source: *Bulletin de la Banque de France.*
15. Domestic banks provided around 50% of German public debt in 1999, down from 65% in 1970. In the United States and United Kingdom, by contrast, the figures are 7% and 4%. German statistics do not break out the amount of debt held by individuals, but the total of all domestic nonbank holdings—including corporations, insurance companies, and investment institutions—is only 18% of the total. Source: *Bundesbank Monthly Report.*
16. Source: Japanese Ministry of Finance, *Japanese Government Bonds: Quarterly Newsletter of the Ministry of Finance of Japan,* No. 5, Tokyo, 2001.
17. N. Ferguson, *The World's Banker: The History of the House of Rothschild,* London, 1998, p. 806.

BIBLIOGRAPHY

Aalbers, J., "Holland's Financial Problems (1713–1733) and the Wars against Louis XIV," in: A. C. Duke and C. A. Tamse, eds., *Britain and the Netherlands,* Vol. VI, The Hague, 1977.

Acworth, A. W., *Financial Reconstruction in England 1815–22,* London, 1925.

Adams, Henry C., *Public Debts,* New York, 1887.

Aftalion, Florin, *The French Revolution, An Economic Interpretation,* Cambridge, UK, 1987.

Aldcroft, Derek H., *The European Economy, 1914–1970,* London, 1978.

Alesina, Alberto, and Mauro Maré, "Evasione e debito," in: Andrea Minorchio, ed., *La Finanza Pubblica Italiana dopo la Svolta del 1992,* Bologna, 1996.

Allen, Senator William, *Speech on the Report of the Select Committee in relation to the Assumption of State Debts by the Federal Government,* Washington, 1840.

Alsop, J. D., "The Politics of Whig Economics," *Durham University Journal,* 1985.

Anderson, B. L., and A. J. H. Latham, eds., *The Market in History,* London, 1986.

Anderson, J. L., "Aspects of the Effects on British Economy of the Wars against France, 1793–1815," *Austrialian Economic History Review,* 1972.

Anderson, Perry, *Lineages of the Absolutist State,* London, 1974.

Andic, Stephan, and Jindrich Veverka, "The Growth of Government Expenditure in Germany," *Finanzarchiv,* 1964.

Andreades, A., "The Finances of the Tyrant States in Ancient Greece," *Economic History,* 1930.

———, *A History of Greek Public Finance,* Cambridge, MA, 1933.

Angell, Norman, *The Great Illusion: A Study of the Relation of Military Power to National Advantage,* London, 1910.

Annuaire Statistique de la France, Paris, 1924.

Anon., *An Argument to Shew the Disadvantages that Accrue to the Publick, from obliging the South-Sea Company to fix what Capital Stock they will give for the Annuities,* London, 1720.

Anon., *The Chimera: Or, the French Way of Paying National Debts, Laid Open,* London, 1720.

Anon., *A Comparison of the Proposals of the Bank and the South Sea Company,* London, 1720.

Anon., *A Full and Impartial Account of the Company of Mississippi. Otherwise Call'd the French East India Company, Projected and Settled by Mr. Law,* London, 1720.

Anon., *A Letter to a Director of the South-Sea Company,* London, 1720.

Anon., *A Letter to Mr. Law, Upon his arrival in Great Britain,* London, 1721.

Archer, Leonie, *Slavery and Other Forms of Unfree Labour,* London, 1988.

Archi, Alfonso, ed., *Circulation of Goods in Non-Palatial Context in the Ancient Middle East,* Rome, 1984.

Ardant, Gabriel, *Histoire de l'Impôt,* Paris, 1972.

Aristotle, *Complete Works,* Princeton, NJ, 1985.

Artaud, Denise, "Le Gouvernement américain et la question des dettes de guerre au lendemain de l'armistice de Rethondes (1919–20)," *Revue d'histoire moderne,* 1973.

Ashley, Maurice, *Financial and Commercial Policy under the Cromwellian Protectorate,* Oxford, 1934.

Ashton, Robert, *The Crown and the Money Market, 1603–1640,* Oxford, UK, 1960.

Assemblé Nationale, *Procès Verbale,* Paris, 1789.

Augeard, J. M., *Mémoires sécrets,* ed. M. E. Bavoux, Paris, 1866.

Austin, M. M., "The Finances of the Greek States," in: *Cambridge Ancient History,* Vol. VI, Cambridge, UK, 1994.

Aziz, Abdul, *The Imperial Treasury of the Indian Mughuls,* Lahore, 1942.

Balbi de Caro, Silvana, *Roma e la Moneta,* Milan, 1993.

Balderston, T., "War Finance and Inflation in Britain and Germany, 1914–1918," *Economic History Review,* 1989.

Ball, Douglas B., *Financial Failure and Confederate Defeat,* Urbana, IL, 1991.

Bank of England, *Annual Statistical Abstract,* London, 2001.

Bank of Italy, *Annual Report,* Rome, 1963–2002.

Banque de France, *Bulletin de la Banque de France,* Pam's, 1994–2002.

Barbadoro, Bernadino, *Le finanze della Repubblica Fiorentina: Imposta diretta e debito pubblico fino al'istituzione del Monte,* Florence, 1929.

Barbour, Violet, *Capitalism in Amsterdam in the 17th Century,* Ann Arbor, MI, 1963.

Barclay, Harold B., *People Without Government: An Anthropology of Anarchism,* London, 1990.

Barducci, Roberto, "Politica e speculazione financia a Firenze dopo la crisi del primo trecento (1343–1358)," *Archivio Storico Italiano,* 1979.

Barrett, D. C., *The Greenbacks and the Resumption of Specie Payments, 1862–79,* Cambridge, MA, 1931.

Bauböck, R., and J. Rundell, eds., *Blurred Boundaries: Migration, Ethnicity, Citizenship,* Aldershot, UK, 1998.

Baulant, Micheline, "Les Prix des grains à Paris de 1431 à 1788," *Annales,* 1968.

———, "Les Salaires du batîment, 1400–1726," *Annales,* 1971.

Baxter, R. D., *National Debts,* London, 1871.

Becker, Marvin, "Problemi della finanza pubblica fiorentina della seconda metà del trecento e dei primi del quattrocento," *Archivio Storico Italiano,* 1965.

———, *Florence in Transition*, Baltimore, 1968.

Belhoste, J.-F., "Le Financement de la guerre de 1792 à l'an IV," in: *État, finances et economic pendant la Révolution française*, Paris, 1991.

Bellamy, C., *Administering Central-Local Relations 1871–1919*, Manchester, UK, 1988.

Benn, Ernest J. P., *Debt (Private and Public, Good and Bad)*, London, 1938.

Bergin, Joseph, *Cardinal Richelieu, Power and Pursuit of Wealth*, New Haven, CT, 1985.

Bernier, François, *Travels in the Mogul Empire, 1656–1668*, in: *Constable's Oriental Miscellany*, London, 1891.

Binney, J.E.D., *British Public Finance 1774–92*, Oxford, UK, 1958.

Birck, L. V., *The Scourge of Europe: The Public Debt Described, Explained, and Historically Depicted*, London, 1926.

Birman, Igor, *Secret Incomes of the Soviet State Budget*, The Hague, 1981.

Black, Anthony, *Political Thought in Europe, 1250–1450*, Cambridge, UK, 1992.

Blum, J. M., *From the Morgenthau Diaries: The Years of War*, Boston, 1967.

Bodin, Jean, *The Six Books of a Commonwealth*, 1576, transl. R. Knowles, London, 1606; Cambridge, MA, 1962.

Boelke, Willi A., *Die Kosten von Hitler's Krieg*, Paderborn, Germany, 1985.

Bogart, E. L., *War Costs and Their Financing*, New York, 1921.

Boisguilbert, Pierre de, *Pierre de Boisguilbert: La Naissance de l'economie politique*, Paris, 1966.

Bonney, Richard, *The King's Debts*, Oxford, UK, 1981.

———, "Jean-Roland Malet: Historian of the Finances of the French Monarchy," *French History*, 1991.

———, ed., *Economic Systems and State Finance*, Oxford, UK, 1995.

———, "The Failure of French Revenue Farms, 1600–60," *Economic History Review*, 1979.

———, *The Limits of Absolutism in Ancien Régime France*, Aldershot, UK, 1995.

Bordo, Michael, D., and Eugene N. White, "A Tale of Two Currencies: British and French Finances during the Napoleonic War," *Journal of Economic History*, 1991.

Bosher, J. F., *French Finances 1779–1795*, Cambridge, UK, 1975.

Bossuet, J. B., *Politics Drawn from the Very Words of Holy Scripture*, transl. Patrick Riley, Cambridge, UK, 1990.

Bottin, Michel, "Le budget de 1788 face au Parlement de Paris (Novembre 1787–Avril 1788)" in: *État, finances et economie pendant la Révolution française*, Paris, 1991.

Boulainvilliers, Comte de, *An Historical Account of the Antient Parliaments of France, or States General of the Kingdom*, London, 1739.

Boyajian, James, *Portuguese Bankers in Spain, 1626–1650*, New Brunswick, NJ, 1983.

Braesch, Frédéric, *Finances et monnaies revolutionaires*, Nancy, France, 1934.

———, *1789, L'An cruciale*, Paris, 1940.

Brandt, Hans-Heinrich, "Public Finances of Neo-Absolutism in Austria in the 1850s: Integration and Modernisation," in: Peter-Christian Witt, ed., *Wealth and Taxation in Central Europe: The History and Sociology of Public Finance*, Leamington Spa, UK, 1987.

Braudel, Fernand, and Frank Spooner, "Prices in Europe from 1450 to 1750," in: *The Cambridge Economic History of Europe*, Vol. IV, Cambridge, UK, 1967.

Brewer, John, *The Sinews of Power: War Money and the English State, 1668–1783,* London, 1989.

Brezis, E. S., and François H. Crouzet, "The Role of Assignats during the French Revolution: Evil or Rescuer?" *Journal of European Economic History,* 1995.

Brown, A. J., *The Great Inflation 1939–51,* Oxford, UK, 1955.

Brown, Howard G., "A Discredited Regime: The Directory and Army Contracting," *French History,* 1990.

Brucker, Gene, "Un documento fiorentino del 1375," *Archivio Storico Italiano,* 1955.

Bruguière, Michel, *Pour une renaissance de l'histoire financière, XVIIIe–XXe siècles,* Paris, 1991.

Brutus, Junius, *Vindiciae contra Tyrannos,* London, 1648.

Buchanan, James J., *Theorika: A Study of Monetary Distributions to the Athenian Citizenry during the Fifth and Fourth Centuries B.C.,* New York, 1962.

Buchanan, James M., *Public Principles of Public Debts: A Defense and Restatement,* Homewood, Il, 1958.

Buchanan, James M., Charles K. Rowley, and Robert D. Tollinson, eds., *Deficits,* Oxford, UK, 1987.

Bullock, C. H., *Politics, Finances, and Consequences,* Cambridge, MA, 1939.

Bunselmayer, Robert E., *The Cost of the War 1914–1919: British Economic War Aims and the Origin of Reparations,* Hamden, CT, 1975.

Burdekin, Richard C. K., and Farrokh K. Langdana, "War Finance in the Southern Confederacy, 1861–1865," *Explorations in Economic History,* 1993.

Burgess, Glen., *The Politics of the Ancient Constitution,* London, 1992.

Burke, Peter., *Venice and Amsterdam: A Study of Seventeenth-Century Elites,* London, 1974.

Burnett, Philip Mason, *Reparation at the Paris Peace Conference,* New York, 1940.

Cairncross, Alec, *The Price of War: British Policy of German Reparations,* Oxford, UK, 1986.

Calabria, Antonio, *The Cost of Empire: The Finances of the Kingdom of Naples in the Time of Spanish Rule,* Cambridge, UK, 1994.

Cambridge Economic History of China, Cambridge, UK, 1994.

Cannon, John, *Parliamentary Reform 1640–1832,* Cambridge, UK, 1973.

Canstrini, Giuseppe, *La Scienza e l'Arte di Stato,* Florence, 1862.

Canterbury, E. Ray, *Wall Street Capitalism,* River Edge, NJ, 2000.

Carande, Ramon, *Carlos V y sus Banqueros,* Madrid, 1943.

———, *El credito de Castilla,* Madrid, 1949.

Carswell, John, *The South Sea Bubble,* London, 1993.

Carter, Alice, "Dutch Foreign Investment, 1738–1800," *Economica,* 1953.

Castillo Pintado, Alvaro, "Dette flottante et consolidée en Espagne," *Annales,* 1963.

Chancellor, Edward, *Devil Take the Hindmost: A History of Financial Speculation,* New York, 1999.

Chandaman, C. D., *The English Public Revenue, 1660–88,* Oxford, UK, 1975.

Chandler, Lester V., *Inflation in the United States, 1940–1948,* New York, 1951.

Chase, Stuart, *Where's the Money Coming From? Problems of Postwar Finance: Guidelines to America's Future as Reported to the Twentieth Century Fund,* New York, 1942.

Cipolla, Carlo M., "The Decline of Italy," *Economic History Review,* 1952.

———, *Money, Prices, and Civilization in the Mediterranean World,* Cincinnati, OH, 1956.

———, *Le Avventure della Lira,* Milan, 1958.

———, "Currency Depreciation in Mediaval Europe," *Economic History Review,* 1963.

———, *The Monetary Policy of Fourteenth-Century Florence,* Berkeley, CA, 1982.

———, "Note sulla storia del saggio d'interesse: Corso, divindendi e sconto dei dividendi del Banco di San Giorgio nel secolo XVI," in: *Saggi di storia economica e sociale,* Bologna, 1988.

Claessen, Henri J. M., and Peter Skalink, eds., *The Early State,* The Hague, 1978.

Clapham, J. H., *The Bank of England,* London, 1944.

Clastres, Pierre, *Society Against the State,* New York, 1977.

Cochut, P. A., *The Financier, Law: His Scheme and Times,* London, 1856.

Cohen, Ronald, and Elman R. Service, eds., *Origins of the State: The Anthropology of Political Evolution,* Philadelphia, 1978.

Collins, James B., *Fiscal Limits of Absolutism: Direct Taxation in Early Seventeenth Century France,* Berkeley, CA, 1988.

Comité pour L'Histoire Économique et Financière de la France (CHEF), *État, finances et économie pendant la Révolution françoise,* Paris, 1991.

Confaloniere, A., and E. Gatti, *La politica del debito pubblico in Italia, 1919–43,* Bari, It., 1986.

Conference on Economic Progress, *The Rising Toll of Interest Rates. The One Great Waste in the Federal Budget,* Washington, DC, 1964.

Congress of the United States, *General Credit Control, Debt Management, and Economic Mobilization, Joint Committee on the Economy Report,* Washington, DC, 1951.

———, *Crisis in the Bond Market, Joint Economic Committee,* Washington, DC, 12 March 1980.

———, *Chaos in the Municipal Bond Market, Joint Economic Committee,* Washington, DC, 28 September 1981.

Conti, Elio, *L'imposta diretta a Firenze nel Quattrocento, 1427–1494,* Rome, 1984.

Cook, J. M., *The Persian Empire,* London, 1983.

Cooke, Michael, "Islam: A Comment," in: J. Baechler, J. A. Hall, and M. Mann, eds., *Europe and the Rise of Capitalism,* Oxford, UK, 1988.

Cooper, William J., *Liberty and Slavery,* New York, 1983.

Corley, T.A.B., *Democratic Despot: A Life of Napoleon III,* London, 1961.

Costantini, Claudio, *La Repubblica di Genova,* Turin, Italy, 1986.

Cozzi, Gaetano, and Michael Knapton, *Storia della Repubblica di Venezia dalla guerra di Chioggia alla rinconquista della Terraferma,* Turin, Italy, 1986.

Crafts, N.F.R., "British Economic Growth, 1700–1850: Some Difficulties of Interpretation," *Explorations in Economic History,* 1987.

Crawford, Michael, *Roman Republican Coinage,* Cambridge, UK, 1974.

———, *Coinage and Money Under the Roman Republic,* London, 1985.

Crum, William Leonard, John F. Fennelly, and Lawrence Howard Seltzer, *Fiscal Planning for Total War,* New York, 1942.

Dahlin, E., *French and German Public Opinion on War Aims,* Stanford, CA, 1933.

Dakin, Douglas, *Turgot and the Ancien Régime in France,* London, 1939.

Darigrand, M., *L'Anti-Financier*, Amsterdam, 1763.

Dashwood, Henry, *An Appeal by Dutch Creditors to the Finance Junta in Madrid, and to Their Fellow Sufferers*, London, 1850.

Davenant, Charles, *Discourses on the Public Revenues and the Trade of England*, London, 1698.

Davies, R. W., *The Development of the Soviet Budgetary System*, Cambridge, UK, 1958.

Davis, Lance E., and Robert A. Huttenback, *Mammon and the Pursuit of Empire: The Political Economy of British Imperialism, 1860–1912*, Cambridge, UK, 1986.

Davis, R. W., *The Development of the Soviet Budgetary System*, Cambridge, UK, 1958.

Day, John, *Les douanes de Gênes*, Paris, 1963.

Dean, P., and W. A. Cole, *British Economic Growth*, Cambridge, UK, 1962.

de Cecco, Marcello, *The International Gold Standard*, Oxford, UK, 1975.

de la Court, Pieter, *The True Interest and Political Maxims of the Republic of Holland and West Friesland*, London, 1702.

de Laet, Joannes, *The Empire of the Great Mogol*, 1631, tranl. J. S. Hoyland, Bombay, 1928.

de Pinedo, Emilio Fernandez, *Gasto publico y reformas fiscales*, Madrid, 1991.

de Roover, Raymond, *The Medici Bank*, London, 1948.

———, "Tratto di fra Santi Rucellai sul cambio, il monte comune e il monte delle doti," *Archivio Storico Italiano*, 1953.

de Sanctis, G., *Storia dei Romani*, Turin, Italy, 1917.

Delaporte, L., *Mesopotamia*, New York, 1925.

Delmas, Jean, ed., *Histoire militaire de la France*, Paris, 1992.

Dent, Julian, "An Aspect of the Crisis of the Seventeenth Century: The Collapse of Financial Administration of the French Monarchy (1653–61)," *Economic History Review*, 1967.

———, *Crisis in Finance: Crown Financiers and Society in Seventeenth Century France*, Newton Abbott, UK, 1973.

Deparcieux, A., *Essai sur les probabilités de la durée de la vie humaine*, Paris, 1746.

Deutsches Bundesbank, *Monthly Report*, 1985–2002.

Dickson, P.G.M., *The Financial Revolution in England: A Study in the Development of Public Credit 1688–1756*, London, 1967.

———, "War Finance," in: *Cambridge Modern History*, Vol. VI, Cambridge, UK, 1970.

———, *Finance and Government Under Maria Theresia, 1740–1780*, Oxford, UK, 1987.

Diderot, D., *Political Writings*, Cambridge, UK, 1992.

Dietz, F. C., *English Government and Finance, 1485–1558*, Urbana, IL, 1921.

———, *English Public Finance, 1558–1641*, New York, 1932.

Dominguez Ortiz, Antonio, *Politica y hacienda de Filipe IV*, Madrid, 1983.

Dombusch, Rudiger, and Mario Draghi, *Public Debt Management*, Cambridge, UK, 1990.

Doucet, Roger, "Le Grand Parti de Lyon au XVIe Siècle," *Revue Historique*, 1933.

Doursther, Horace, *Dictionnaire universelle des poids et mésures*, Brussels, 1840.

Doyle, William, *Officers, Nobles, and Revolutionaries*, London, 1995.

Drekmeier, Charles, *Kingship and Community in Early India*, Stanford, CA, 1962.

Dubos, Jean-Baptiste, *Histoire critique de l'établissement de la monarchie françoise dans les Gaules*, Paris, 1734.

Duchène, Albert, *Guerre and finances: Dépenses et liqidation d'une guerre—1914–1918–1939,* Paris, 1947.

Duggan, Anne J., ed., *Kings and Kingship in Medieval Europe,* London, 1993.

Dupriez, Léon H., *Monetary Reconstruction in Belgium,* New York, 1947.

Durliat, Jean, *Les Finances publiques de Diocletian aux Carolingians (284–889),* Sigmaringen, Germany, 1990.

Eagly, Robert V., "Monetary Policy and Politics in Mid-Eighteenth-Century Sweden," *Journal of Economic History,* 1969.

Economist, The, *The Consol Market,* London, 16 December, 1911.

Edie, Lionel, *Easy Money,* New Haven, CT, 1937.

Ehrenberg, Richard, *Capital and Finance in the Age of Renaissance,* London, 1928.

Eichengreen, Barry, *The International Debt Crisis in Prespective,* Boston, 1989.

———, *Golden Fetter: The Gold Standard and the Great Depression,* Oxford, UK, 1992.

Eichengreen, Barry, and Alessandra Casella, *Halting Inflation in Italy and France After World War II,* London, 1991.

Einzig, Paul, *Germany's Default: The Economics of Hitlerism,* London, 1934.

———, *Primitive Money,* London, 1949.

Elliott, J. H., *The Revolt of the Catalans,* Cambridge, UK, 1963.

———, *The Count Duke of Olivares,* New Haven, CT, 1986.

Encyclopedia of Islam, Leiden, 1960– .

Engels, Frederick, *The Origin of Family, Private Property, and the State, in the Light of Researches by Lewis H. Morgan,* London, 1891.

Fachan, J. M., *Historique de la rente Française*, Paris, 1905.

Faini, Riccardo, and Gianni Toniolo, "Reconsidering Japanese Deflation During the 1920s," *Explorations in Economic History,* 1991.

Faure, Edgar, *La Banqueroute de Law,* Paris, 1977.

Fay, S. B., *The Rise of Brandenburg-Prussia to 1786,* New York, 1937.

Feaveryear, A. E., *The Pound Sterling,* Oxford, UK, 1931.

Federal Reserve Bank, *Banking and Monetary Statistics,* 1916–1970.

Federal Reserve Bank of New York, *Annual Reports,* New York, 1975, 1982.

Feinstein, C. H., *National Income, Expenditure, and Output of the United Kingdom 1855–1965*, Cambridge, UK, 1976.

Feis, Herbert, *Europe: The World's Banker, 1870–1914,* New Haven, CT, 1930.

Felix, David, *Walter Rathenau and the Weimar Republic,* Baltimore, 1971.

Ferguson, E. J., *The Power of the Purse: A History of American Public Finance 1776–1790,* Chapel Hill, NC, 1961.

———, "Economy, Liberty, and the Constitution," *William and Mary Quarterly,* 1983.

Ferguson, Niall, "Public Finance and National Security," *Past and Present,* 1994.

———, *Paper and Iron: Hamburg Business and German Politics in the Era of Inflation, 1897–1927,* Cambridge, UK, 1995.

———, *The Pity of War,* London, 1998.

———, *The World's Banker: The History of the House of Rothschild*, London, 1998.

———, *The Cash Nexus: Money and Power in the Modern World, 1700–2000,* London, 2001.

Finlay, M. I., *Politics in the Ancient World,* Cambridge, UK, 1983.

———, *The Ancient Economy,* London, 1985.

Fisk, Harvey E., *Our Public Debt,* New York, 1919.

Foot Michael, *The Pen and the Sword,* London, 1957.

Ford, Franklin F., *Robe and Sword: The Regrouping of the Franch Aristocracy After Louis XIV,* Cambridge, MA, 1963.

Forsyth, Douglas, *The Crisis of Liberal Italy,* Cambridge, UK, 1993.

Frank, Tenney, *An Economic History of Rome,* London, 1927.

———, *An Economic Survey of Ancient Rome,* Baltimore, 1933.

Franke, Hans-Hermann, Eberhart Ketzel, and Hans-Helmut Kotz, *Handbook of Public Credit in Europe,* Berlin, 2000.

Friedman, Benjamin, *Day of Reckoning: The Consequences of American Economic Policy Under Reagan and After,* New York, 1988.

Friedman, Thomas L., *The Lexus and the Olive Tree,* New York, 1999.

Fryde, E. B., *Studies in Medieval Trade and Finance,* London, 1983.

Fryde, E. B., and M. M. Fryde, "Public Credit: with Special Reference to North-Western Europe," in: *Cambridge Economic History of Europe,* Vol. III, Cambridge, UK, 1963.

Fukayama, Francis, *Trust: The Social Virtues and the Creation of Prosperity,* New York, 1995.

Gabilard, Jean, "Le Financement des guerres napoléoniennes et la conjuncture du premier empire," *Revue Historique,* 1953.

Galbraith, J. K., *Money: Whence It Came, Where It Went,* New York, 1975.

Garlan, Yvon, *War in the Ancient World,* London, 1975.

Gatrell, Peter, *Government, Industry and Rearmament in Russia, 1900–1914,* Cambridge, UK, 1994.

Gay, Peter, *Voltaire's Politics,* New Haven, CT, 1988.

Goshal, U. N., *A History of Indian Political Ideas,* Oxford, UK, 1959.

Giavazzi, Francesco, and Luigi Spaventa, *High Public Debt: The Italian Experience,* Cambridge, UK, 1988.

Gibbons, J. S., *The Public Debt of the United States,* New York, 1867.

Gilbert, Charles, *American Financing of World War I,* Westport, CT, 1970.

Ginatempo, Maria, and Lucia Sandri, *L'Italia delle città: Il popolamento urbano tra Medioevo e Rinascimento (secoli XIII–XVI),* Florence, 1990.

Gioffrè, Domenico, *Il debito pubblico genovese,* Milan, 1967.

Girard, Albert, "La Guerre monétaire, XIVe–XVe siècles," *Annales,* 1940.

Glassman, Debra, and Angela Redish, "Currency Depreciation in Early Modern England and France," *Explorations in Economic History,* 1988.

Goffart, Walter, *Barbarians and Romans,* Princeton, NJ, 1980.

———, *Caput and Colonate: Towards a History of Late Roman Taxation,* Toronto, 1974.

———, *Rome's Fall and After,* London, 1989.

Goldsmith, Raymond, *Compartive National Balance Sheets,* Chicago, 1985.

———, *Premodern Financial Systems,* Cambridge, UK, 1987.

Goldthwaite, Richard A., *Private Wealth in Renaissance Florence,* Princeton, NJ, 1969.

Gopal, M. H., *Mauryan Public Finance,* London, 1935.

Grant, James, *Money of the Mind: Borrowing and Lending in America from the Civil War to Michael Milken,* New York, 1992.

Green, Peter, *Alexander of Macedon,* Berkeley, CA, 1991.

Gregory, Paul, R., *Russian National Income, 1885–1913,* Cambridge, UK, 1982.

Grellier, J. J., *The History of the National Debt, from the Revolution of 1688 to the Beginning of the Year 1800,* London, 1810.

Grossman, Herschel I., and John B. Van Huyk, "Sovereign Debt as a Contingent Claim: Excusable Default, Repudiation, and Reputation;" *American Economic Review,* 1988.

Guéry, Alain, "Les Finances de la monarchie française sous l'ancien régime," *Annales,* 1978.

Guicciardini, Francesco, *Le cose fiorentini,* ed. R. Ridolfi, Florence, 1945.

Guizot, François, *Histoire des origines du gouvernement représentatif,* Paris, 1851.

Habbakuk, H. J., "The Long Term Rate of Interest and the Price of Land in the Seventeenth Century," *Economic History Review,* 1952.

———, "Public Finance and the Sale of Confiscated Property During the Interregnum," *Journal of Economic History,* 1963.

Haig, Robert Murray, *The Public Finances of Post-War France,* New York, 1929.

Halpern, Louis, *British War Finance, 1939–44: A Comparison with United States, Germany and Canada,* Unpublished Ph.D. thesis, New York University, 1945.

Hamilton, Earl J., "Origin and Growth of the National Debt in Western Europe" *American Economic Review,* 1947.

———, *War and Prices in Spain, 1651–1800,* Cambridge, UK, 1947.

———, *American Treasure and the Price Revolution in Spain, 1501–1650,* Cambridge, MA, 1963.

Hammond, Bray, *Sovereignty and the Empty Purse: Banks and Politics in the Civil War,* Princeton, NJ, 1970.

Hanc, George, *The United States Savings Bond Program in Postwar Period,* New York, 1962.

Hansen, Alvin H., *Fiscal Policy and Business Cycles,* London, 1941.

Hardach, Gerd, *The Political Economy of Germany in Twentieth Century,* Berkeley, CA, 1976.

———, *The First World War,* London, 1977.

Hargreaves, E. L., *The National Debt,* London, 1930.

Harris, R. D., "French Finances and the American War, 1777–1783," *Journal of Modern History,* 1976.

Harris, Seymour, *The Assignats,* Cambridge, MA, 1930.

———, *Inflation and the American Economy,* New York, 1947.

———, *The National Debt and the New Economics,* New York, 1947.

Harrison, Mark, ed., *The Economics of World War II,* Cambridge, UK, 1998.

Harvey, William H., *Coin's Financial School,* Chicago, 1894.

Heater, Derek, *History of Citizenship,* Leicester, UK, 2000.

Hecksher, Elie F., *The Bank of Sweden,* The Hague, 1934.

———, *An Economic History of Sweden,* Cambridge, MA, 1954.

Heers, Jaques, *Gênes au XVe siècle,* Paris 1961.

Heichelheim, Fritz M., *An Ancient Economic History*, Leiden, 1958.

Hendy, Michael, *Studies in the Byzantine Monetary Economy, c. 300–1450*, Cambridge, UK, 1985.

———, *The Economy, Fiscal Administration and Coinage of Byzantium*, Northampton, UK, 1989.

Henwood, Doug, *Wall Street*, New York, 1997.

Herlihy, David, and Christiane Klapisch-Zuber, *Tuscans and Their Families: A Study of the Florentine Catasto of 1427*, New Haven, CT, 1985.

Herodotus, *Histories*, transl. Robin Waterfield, Oxford, UK, 1954.

Hill, B. W., "The Change of Government and the 'Loss of the City' 1710–1711," *Economic History Review*, 1971.

———, *Edmund Burke on Government, Politics and Society*, London, 1975.

Hobbes, Thomas, *Leviathan*, London, 1651.

Hocart, A. M., *Kings and Councillors: An Essay in the Comparative Anatomy of Human Society*, Chicago, 1970.

Hoffman, Philip T, and Kathryn Norburg, *Fiscal Crises, Liberty, and Representative Government, 1450–1789*, Stanford, CA, 1994.

Hofstadtler, R., *The Idea of a Party System*, Berkeley, CA, 1969.

Holtfrerich, K.-L., *The German Inflation, 1914–1923*, Berlin, 1986.

Holzman, Franklin D. "The Soviet Bond Hoax," *Problems of Communism*, 1957.

Homer, Sidney, *The Great American Bond Market*, New York, 1978.

Homer, Sidney, and Richard Sylla, *A History of Interest Rates*, 3rd edition, New Brunswick, NJ, 1991.

Hope-Jones, Arthur, *Income Tax in the Napoleonic War*, Cambridge, UK, 1947.

Horne, H. Oliver, *A History of Savings Banks*, Oxford, UK, 1947.

Hotman, François, *Francogallia*, 1573, transl. Julian H. Franklin, New York, 1969.

Howson, Susan, *British Monetary Policy 1945–51*, Oxford, UK, 1993.

Huang, Ray, *Taxation and Governmental Finance in Sixteenth Century Ming China*, Cambridge, UK, 1974.

Hubbard, L. E., *Soviet Money and Finance*, London, 1936.

Hughes, Michael L., *Paying for the German Inflation*, Chapel Hill, NC, 1988.

Hume, David, "Of Public Credit," *Political Discourse*, Edinburgh, 1752.

Humphreys, S. C., *Anthropology and the Greeks*, London, 1978.

Hutchings, Raymond, *The Soviet Budgetary System*, Albany, NY, 1978.

Ilseric, A. R., *Government Finance in Post-War Britain*, London, 1955.

International Monetary Fund, *International Financial Statistics*, 1953–2002.

Israel, Jonathan I., *Dutch Primacy in World Trade*, Oxford, UK, 1989.

Jacobsen, Thorgild, "Primitive Democracy in Ancient Mesopotamia," *Journal of Near Eastern Studies*, 1943.

James, Edward, *The Franks*, Oxford, UK, 1988.

Janeway, Elliott, *The Economics of Crisis*, New York, 1968.

Japanese Ministry of Finance, *Japanese Government Bonds: Quarterly Newsletter of the Ministry of Finance of Japan*, No. 5, 2001.

Jay, Douglas, *Who Is to Pay for the War?* London, 1941.

Jeffrey, L. H., *Archaic Greece*, London, 1972.

Jennings, Robert M, and Andrew P. Trout, *The Tontine: From the Reign of Louis XIV to the French Revolutionary Era*, Philadelphia, 1983.

Jèze, Gaston, and Henri Truchy, *The War Finance of France*, New Haven, CT, 1927.

Johnson, Brian, *The Politics of Money*, New York, 1970.

Jones, A.H.M., *The Decline of the Ancient World*, London, 1966.

———, *History of Rome Through the Fifth Century*, London, 1968.

———, *The Roman Economy*, Oxford, UK, 1974.

Jones, Aubrey, *The New Inflation*, London, 1973.

Jones, J. H., *The Economics of War and Conquest*, London, 1915.

Jones, J. W., *The Law and Legal Theory of the Greeks*, Oxford, UK, 1956.

Jones, S.R.H., "Devaluation and the Balance of Payments in Eleventh-Century England: An Exercise in Dark Age Economics," *Economic History Review*, 1973.

Kagin, Donald H, "Monetary Aspects of the Treasury Notes of the War of 1812," *Journal of Economic History*, 1984.

Kaletsky, Anatole, "Professionals Who Forgot That Bonds Can Also Fall," *The Times*, London, 24 February 1994.

Katona, George, *War Without Inflation: The Psychological Approach to Problems of War Economy*, New York, 1942.

Kaufman, Henry, *On Money and Markets: A Wall Street Memoir*, New York, 2000.

Kauonides, Lakis C., and Geoffrey E. Wood, *Debt and Deficits*, Aldershot, UK, 1992.

Kautsky, John H., *The Politics of Aristocratic Empires*, Chapel Hill, NC, 1982.

Kelly, J. M., *A Short History of Western Legal Theory*, Oxford, UK, 1992.

Kennedy, Paul, *The Rise and Fall of the Great Powers*, London, 1988.

Kent, Bruce, *The Spoils of War*, Oxford, UK, 1989.

Ker, Frederick I., and Wilfred H. Goodman, *Press Promotion of War Finance*, Toronto, 1946.

Kerr, E., *The Effects of Wars and Revolutions on Government Securities*, New York, 1917.

Keynes, J. M., *The Economic Consequences of the Peace*, London, 1919.

———, *A Revision of the Treaty*, London, 1922.

———, *A Tract on Monetary Reform*, London, 1923.

———, *The General Theory of Employment, Interest and Money*, London, 1936.

———, *How to Pay for the War*, London, 1940.

Kindelberger, Charles, *Manias, Panics and Crashes*, London, 1989.

———, "The Economic Crisis of 1619–1623," *Journal of Economic History*, 1991.

———, *A Financial History of Western Europe*, Oxford, UK, 1993.

King, Gregory, *Natural and Political Observations on England*, 1696, reprinted Baltimore, 1936.

Kirshner, Julius, "The Moral Theology of Public Finance: A Study and Edition of Nicholas de Anglia's Quaestio Disputata on the Public Debt of Venice," *Archivium Fratrum Praedicatorum*, 1970.

Kitchen, Martin, *Nazi Germany at War*, London, 1995.

Klug, Adam, *The German Buybacks, 1932–1939. A Cure for Overhang?* New Haven, CT, 1989.

Koenigsberger, Helmut, *The Government of Sicily Under Philip II of Spain*, London, 1951.

Kotlikoff, Lawrence, *Generational Accounting,* New York, 1992.

Krasilnokoff, Jens A., "Aegean Mercenaries in the Fourth to Second Centuries B.C.: A Study in Payment, Plunder and Logistics of Ancient Greek Armies," *Classica et Mediavalia,* 1992.

Krosigk, Graf Schwerin von, *Staatsbankrott: Finanzpolitik des Deutschen Reiches 1920–1945*, Göttingen, Germany, 1974.

Kushpeta, O., *The Banking and Credit System of the USSR,* Boston, 1978.

Labrousse, Ernst, *Les Prix du froment en France, 1726–1913,* Paris, 1970.

Ladurie, Le Roy, "Les Comptes fantastiques de Gregory King," *Annales*, 1968.

Lancel, Serge, *Carthage: A History,* Oxford, UK, 1992.

Landes, David, *Bankers and Pashas,* Cambridge, MA, 1958.

Lane, Frederick C., "Public Debt and Private Wealth: Particularly in Sixteenth-Century Venice," in: *Mélanges en honneur de Fernand Braudel,* Toulouse, France, 1973.

———, *Venice, A Maritime Republic,* Baltimore, 1973.

Lane, Frederick C., and Rheinhold C. Mueller, *Money and Banking in Medieval and Renaissance Venice,* Baltimore, 1985.

Lavoisier, Armand, *Oeuvres de Lavoisier,* ed. M. Dumas, Paris, 1864.

Law, John, *Oeuvres complètes,* ed. Paul Harsin, Paris, 1934.

Lawson, Henrietta M., *Jay Cooke, Private Banker,* Cambridge, MA, 1936.

Lawson, M. K., "Taxation in the Reigns of Aethelred II and Cnut," *English History Review,* 1989.

Lazaro, Josep Fontana, "Deuda publica, evolución de la hacienda y crecimiento: Algunas sugerencias para su estudio," in: *Historia de la hacienda en España (Siglos XIV–XX),* Madrid, 1991.

Liberty Loan Commission, *The Liberty Loan of 1917,* New York, 1917.

Lieberman, F., *The National Assembly in the Anglo-Saxon Period,* Halle, Germany, 1913.

Lindholm, Richard W., "German Finance in World War II," *American Economic Review,* 1947.

Lloyd George, David, *The Truth About Reparations and War Debts,* London, 1932.

Locke, John, *Some Considerations on the Lowering of Interest and Raising the Value of Money,* London, 1691.

———, *Two Treatises on Government,* London, 1694.

Lopez, R. E., ed., *The Dawn of Modern Banking,* New Haven, CT, 1979.

Lotz, Walter J. E., *Deutsche Staatsfinanzwirthschaft in Kriege,* Stuttgart, 1927.

Lüthy, Herbert, *La Banque protestante en France: De la révocation de l'Édit de Nantes à la Révolution,* Paris, 1959.

Lutz, Ralf Haswell, ed., *The Fall of the German Empire, 1914–1918,* New York, 1969.

Luzzatto, Gino, *Il Debito pubblico della Repubblica di Venezia,* Milan, 1963.

Lynch, John, *Bourbon Spain,* Oxford, UK, 1989.

Macaulay, T. B., *The History of England from the Accession of James II*, London, 1914.

Mackworth, Sir Humphrey, *Sir Humphrey Mackworth's Proposal: Being a New Scheme Offer'd for the Payment of the Publick Debts, for the Relief of the South Sea Company, and for the Easing the Nation of the Land and Malt Tax,* London, 1720.

Maddison, Angus, "A Comparison of Levels of GDP per Capita in Developed and Undeveloped Countries, 1700–1980," *Journal of Economic History,* 1983.

Mair, Lucy, *Primitive Government: A Study of Traditional Political Systems in Eastern Africa,* London, 1962.

Malamoud, Charles, *Debt and Debtors,* New Delhi, 1983.

Mallett, Sir Bernard, and C. Oswald George, *British Budgets: Second Series, 1913–14 to 1920–21,* London, 1929.

Malthus, Thomas, *Principles of Political Economy,* London, 1820.

Mandeville, Jon E., "Usurious Piety: The Cash Waqf Controversy in the Ottoman Empire," *International Journal of Middle East Studies,* 1979.

Marichal, Carlos, *Century of Debt Crisis in Latin America,* Princeton, NJ, 1989.

Marion, François, *Histoire financère de la France depuis 1715,* Paris, 1914.

Markovitch, T. J., *L'Industrie française de 1789 à 1964,* Paris, 1966.

Marks, L. F., "La crisi finanziaria a Firenze, 1494–1502," *Archivio Storico Italiano,* 1954.

———, *The Development of the Institutions of Public Finance in Florence During the Last Sixty Years of the Republic, 1470–1530,* Unpublished D.Phil. thesis, Oxford University, 1954.

Marongiu, Antonio, *Medieval Parliaments: A Comparative Study*, English transl., London, 1968.

Mathias, Peter, and Patrick O'Brien, "Taxation in Britain and France, 1715–1810," *Journal of European Economic History,* 1976.

Mauss, Marcel, *The Gift: Forms and Functions of Exchange in Archaic Societies,* transl. I. Cunnision, London, 1954.

McCoy, Drew, R., *The Elusive Republic: Political Economy in Jeffersonian America,* Chapel Hill, NC, 1981.

McCucker, J. J., *Money and Exchange in Europe and America, 1600–1775,* Chapel Hill, NC, 1978.

McCulloch, J. R., *Collected Works,* ed. Patrick O'Brien, London, 1995.

McEvedy, Colin, and Jones, Richard, *Atlas of World Population History,* London, 1978.

McGrane, R. C., *The Panic of 1837,* Chicago, 1924.

———, *Foreign Bondholders and American State Debts,* New York, 1935.

McIlwain, C. H., *The Growth of Political Thought in the West,* London, 1932.

Meiggs, Russell, *The Athenian Empire,* Oxford, UK, 1972.

A Member of the House of Commons., *Some Seasonable Considerations for Those Who Are Desirous, by Subscription, or Purchase, to Become Proprietors of South Sea Stock: With Remarks on the Surprising Method of Valuing South-Sea Stock, Publish'd in the Flying-Post of Saturday, April the 9th, 1720,* London, 1720.

Merk, Frederick, *Manifest Destiny and Mission in American History,* New York, 1963.

Merton, Robert, *Mass Persuasion: The Social Psychology of a War Bond Drive,* Boston, 1945.

Michelsen, A., P. N. Apostol, and M. B. Bernatsky, *Russian Public Finances During the War,* New Haven, CT, 1928.

Migeotte, Loepolde, *L'Emprunt public dans les Cités Grecques,* Quebec, 1984.

———, *Les Souscriptions publiques dans les cités Grecques,* Quebec, 1992.

Millar, James R., "History and Analysis of Soviet Bond Policy," *Soviet Studies,* 1975.

———, "Financing the Soviet War Effort in WW II," *Soviet Studies,* 1980.

Milward, Alan S., *War, Economy and Society 1939–1945,* London, 1977.

———, *Nazi Germany at War,* London, 1979.

———, *The Reconstruction of Western Europe 1954–51,* London, 1984.

Mirabeau, Honoré-Gabriel de Riquetti, *Oeuvres: Les discours*, Paris, 1921.

Miskimin, H., "The Enforcement of Gresham's Law," in: Anna Vannini Marx, ed., *Credito banche ed investimenti, Secoli XIII–XX,* Prato, 1985.

Missale, Alessandro, *Public Debt Management,* Oxford, UK, 1999.

Mitchell, B. R., *International Historical Statistics: Europe, 1750–1988,* Basingstoke, UK, 1992.

———, *International Historical Statistics: The Americas, 1750–1988,* Basingstoke, UK, 1993.

Mitchell, B. R., and Phyllis Deane, *Abstract of British Historical Statistics,* Cambridge, UK, 1962.

Mitchell, B. R., and H. G. Jones, *Second Abstract of British Historical Statistics,* Cambridge, UK, 1971.

Mitchell, Broadus, *The Price of Independence: A Realistic View of the American Revolution,* Oxford, UK, 1974.

Mitchell, W. C., *A History of the Greenbacks,* Chicago, 1903.

Molho, Anthony, *Florentine Public Finance, 1400–1433,* Cambridge, MA, 1975.

———, "Tre città-stato e il loro debito pubblico," in: *Italia 1350–1450: Tra crisi, trasformazione, sviluppo,* Pistoia, Italy, 1993.

———, *Marriage Alliance in Late Medieval Florence,* Cambridge, MA, 1994.

Montesquieu, Charles de Secondat, *De l'esprit des lois,* reprinted Paris, 1923.

Moreineau, Michel, "Budgets de l'état et gestion des finances royales en France au dix-huitième siècle," *Revue Historique,* 1980.

Morgan, E. V., *Studies in British Financial Policy, 1914–25,* London, 1952.

Moscow Financial Institute, *The Soviet Financial System,* Moscow, 1966.

Moulton, Harold G., *The New Philosophy of Public Debt,* Washington, DC, 1943.

Moulton, Harold G., and Cloena Lewis, *The French Debt Problem,* New York, 1926.

Moulton, Harold G., and Constantine E. McGuire, *Germay's Capacity to Pay: A Study of the Reparation Problem,* New York, 1923.

Moulton, Harold G., and Leo Paslovsky, *World War Debt Settlements,* London, 1927.

———, *World Debts and World Prosperity,* Washington, DC, 1932.

Mouré, Kenneth, *Managing the Franc Poincaré,* Cambridge, UK, 1993.

Mousnier, Roland, *La Vénalité des offices sous Henry IV et Louis XIII,* Rouen, France, 1946.

Mueller, Reinhold C., *Money and Banking in Medieval and Renaissance Venice,* Vol. II, *The Venetian Money Market: Banks, Panics, and the Public Debt, 1200–1500,* Baltimore, 1997.

Murphy, Antoine, *Richard Cantillon: Entrepreneur and Economist,* Oxford, UK, 1987.

———, *Lohn Law,* Oxford, UK, 1997.

Murphy, Henry C., *National Debt in War and Transition,* New York, 1950.

Myers, Henry A., *Medieval Kingship,* Chicago, 1982.

Nathan, Otto, *Nazi War Finance,* New York, 1944.

National Association of Manufacturers, *The Public Debt and What to Do About It,* New York, 1952.

Neal, Larry, "Power and Profit in Economic History," *Journal of Economic History,* 1977.

———, *The Rise of Financial Capitalism: International Capital Markets in the Age of Reason,* Cambridge, UK, 1990.

Necco, Achile, *Il Corso dei titoli di borsa in Italia dal 1861 al 1912,* Turin, Italy, 1915.

Nelson, Benjamin, *The Idea of Usury,* Chicago, 1969.

Nettels, Curtis, "The Economic Consequences of War," *Journal of Economic History,* 1943.

Nevin, Edward, *The Problem of the National Debt,* Cardiff, Wales, 1954.

Noonan, John T., Jr., *The Scholastic Analysis of Usury,* Cambridge, MA, 1957.

North, Douglass C., and Barry Weingast, "Constitutions and Commitment: The Evolution of Institutions Governing Public Choice in Seventeenth Century England," *Journal of Economic History,* 1989.

Noyes, Alexander D., *The War Period of American Finance, 1908–1925,* New York, 1926.

Oberholtzer, E. P., *Jay Cooke, Financier of the Civil War,* Philadelphia, 1907.

O'Brien, Patrick, "The Costs of British Imperialism," *Past and Present,* 1988.

———, "The Political Economy of British Imperialism," *Past and Present*, 1988.

O'Brien, Patrick, and Philip A. Hunt, "The Rise of a Fiscal State in England 1485–1815," *Historical Research,* 1993.

O'Brien, Patrick, and Caglar Keyder, *Economic Growth in Britain and France, 1780–1914,* London, 1978.

Oliver, James H., "The Ruling Power: A Study of the Roman Empire in the Second Century After Christ Through the Roman Oration of Aelius Aristides", *American Philosophical Society*, 1953.

Oppers, Stefan E., "The Interest Rate Effect of Dutch Money in Eighteenth Century Britain," *Journal of Economic History,* 1993.

Overy, R. J., *War and Economy in the Third Reich,* Oxford, UK, 1994.

Paine, Thomas, *The Decline and Fall of the English System of Finance,* Paris, 1796.

Pamuk, Sevket, "In the Absence of Domestic Currency: Debased European Coinage in the Seventeenth-Century Ottoman Empire," *Journal of Economic History,* 1997.

Parker, Geoffrey, *The Army of Flanders and the Spanish Road, 1567–1659,* Cambridge, UK, 1972.

———, "The Emergence of Modern Finance in Europe, 1530–1730," in: Carlo M. Cipolla, ed., *Fontana Economic History of Europe,* Vol. II, New York, 1974.

———. "Loan Hands," *Times Literary Supplement*, 23 May 1986.

Partner, Peter, "Papal Financial Policy in the Renaissance" *Past and Present,* 1980.

Patterson, Orlando, *Freedom in the Making of Western Culture,* London, 1991.

Patterson, William, *A Brief Account of the Intended Bank of England,* London, 1694.

Peacock, A. T., and J. Wiseman, *The Growth of Public Expenditure in United Kingdom,* Princeton, NJ, 1961.

Perkins, Howard Cecil, *Northern Editorials on Secession,* New York, 1942.

Pezzolo, L., *L'oro dello stato: Società finanza e fisco nella Repubblica veneta del secondo '500,* Venice, 1990.

Phillips, John A., *The Great Reform Bill and the Boroughs,* Oxford, UK, 1992.

Pigou, A. C., *The Economy and Finance of War,* London, 1916.

Pinaud, Pierre-François, "The Settlement of Public Debt from the Ancien Régime, 1790–1810," *French History,* 1991.

Pinto, Isaac, *Traité de la circulation et du crédit,* Amsterdam, 1771.

Platt, D.C.M., *Finance, Trade and Politics 1815–1914,* Oxford, UK, 1968.

———, *Foreign Finance in Continental Europe and the United States 1815–1870,* London, 1984.

Plebano, Achille, *Storia della finanza italiana nei primi quarant'anni dell'unificazione,* Palermo, Sicily, 1900.

Plumb, J. H., *The Growth of Political Stability in England 1675–1725,* London, 1967.

Polanyi, Karl, ed. *Trade and Market in the Early Empires,* Glencoe, IL, 1957.

Pole, J. R., *Political Representation in England and the Origins of the American Republic,* London, 1966.

Poliakov, Léon, *The Aryan Myth: A History of Racist and Nationalist Ideas in Europe,* London, 1971.

Porter, A. N., and R. F. Holland, eds., *Money, Finance and Empire, 1790–1960,* Totowa, NJ, 1985.

Poulson, Barry, *Economic History of the United States,* New York, 1981.

Prasad, Beni, *The State in Ancient India,* Allahabad, India, 1928.

Prichett, W. K., *The Greek State at War,* Berkeley, CA, 1991.

Pullan, Brian, *Rich and Poor in Renaissance Venice,* Oxford, UK, 1971.

Pütter, John Stephen, *An Historical Development of the Present Constitution of the Germanic Empire,* transl. Josiah Durnford, London, 1790.

Ramsay, David, *The History of the American Revolution*, Philadelphia, 1789.

Rasler, Karen A., and William R. Thomson, "Global Wars, Public Debts, and the Long Cycle," *World Politics,* 1983.

Ratchford, Benjamin, *American State Debts,* Durham, NC, 1941.

———, "History of the Federal Debt in the United States," *American Economic Review,* 1947.

Rattigan, W. H., *The Roman Law of Persons,* London, 1873.

Raudachuri, Tapan, "The Mughul Empire," in: *Cambridge Economic History of India,* Cambridge, UK, 1982.

Reich, Robert B., *The Work of Nations: Preparing Ourselves for 21st-Century Capitalism,* New York, 1991.

Répaci, Francesco A., *La finanza pubblica italiana nel secolo 1861–1960,* Bologna, Italy, 1962.

Reuter, Timothy, "Plunder and Tribute in the Carolingian Empire," *Royal Historical Society,* 1985.

Rich, John, and Graham Shipley, *War and Society in the Greek World,* London, 1993.

Richards, R. D., "The 'Stop of the Exchequer,' " *Economic History,* 1933.

Richardson, Dorsey, *Will They Pay? A Primer of the War Debts,* Philadelphia, 1933.

Richardson, James, ed., *Messages and Papers of the Presidents,* New York, 1897.

Riley, James C., "Dutch Investment in France, 1781–87," *Journal of Economic History,* 1973.

———, *International Government Finance and the Amsterdam Capital Market 1740–1815,* Cambridge, UK, 1980.

———, *The Seven Years' War and the Old Regime in France: The Economic and Financial Toll,* Princeton, NJ, 1986.

———, "French Finances, 1727–1768," *Journal of Modern History,* 1987.

Riley, James C., and John J. McKusker, "Money Supply, Economic Growth, and the Quantity Theory of Money: France, 1650–1788," *Explorations in Economic History,* 1983.

Robbins, Lord, *Against Inflation,* London, 1979.

Robinson, Maxine, *Islam and Capitalism,* 1966, transl. Brian Pearce, London, 1974.

Rolinck, Arthur J., François R. Velde and Warren E. Weber, "The Debasement Puzzle: An Essay in Medieval Monetary History," *Journal of Economic History,* 1996.

Roseveare, Henry, *The Financial Revolution, 1660–1760,* London, 1991.

Roustit, Yvan, "La Consolidation de la dette publique à Barcelona au milieu du XIVe siècle," *Estudios de la Storia Moderna,* 1954.

Rowe, J. Z., *The Public-Private Character of United States Central Banking,* New Brunswick, NJ, 1965.

Rowley, C. T., *et al.*, eds., *Deficits*, Oxford, UK, 1987.

Ruiz Martin, Felipe, *Las finanzas de la monarchia hispanica en tiempos de Felipe IV (1621–1665),* Madrid, 1990.

Sahlins, Marshall D., "Poor Man, Rich Man, Big-Man, Chief," *Comparative Studies in Society and Religion,* 1963.

Saint-Simon, Duc de, *Memoirs*, ed. W. H. Lewis, London, 1964.

Saletore, R. N., *Early Indian Economic History,* London, 1975.

Samuel, Lawrence R., *Pledging Allegiance: American Identity and the Bond Drive of World War II,* Washington, DC, 1997.

Samuelson, Robert J., "Clinton's Nemesis," *Newsweek*, 1 February 1993.

Sarkar, K. R., *Public Finance in Ancient India,* New Delhi, 1978.

Savage, J. D., *Balanced Budgets in American Politics,* Ithaca, NY, 1988.

Sayers, R. S., *Financial Policy 1939–45,* London, 1956.

Schama, Simon, *Citizens*, New York, 1989.

The Schemes of the South-Sea Company and of the Bank of England, As Propos'd to the Parliament for the Reducing of the National Debts, London, 1720.

Schnapper, Bernard, "Fixation du denier des rentes, et l'opinion parlementaire au XVIe siècle," *Revue d'histoire moderne,* 1957.

Schnerb, Robert, "De la constituente à Napoleon: Les vicissitudes de l'Impôt indirect," *Annales*, 1947.

Schreker, Ellen, *The Hired Money: The French Debt to the United States, 1917–1929,* New York, 1978.

Schremmer, D. E., "Taxation and Public Finance: Britain, France, and Germany," in: *Cambridge Economic History of Europe,* Vol. VIII, Cambridge, UK, 1989.

Schubert, Eric S., "Innovations, Debts, and Bubbles: International Integration of Financial Markets in Western Europe, 1688–1720," *Journal of Economic History,* 1988.

Schuker, Stephen A., *American Reparations to Germany, 1919–1933,* Princeton, NJ, 1988.

Schumpeter, A. J., *Ten Great Economists*, Oxford, UK, 1951.

Schumpeter, E., "English Prices and Public Finance, 1660–1822," *Review of Economic Statistic*, 1938.

Schweitzer, Mary M., "State Issued Currency and the Ratification of the U.S. Constitution," *Journal of Economic History,* 1989.

Scott, Peter, and Paul Johnson, *The Economic Consequences of Population Aging in Advanced Societies,* London, 1988.

Scott, W. R., *The Constitution and Finance of English, Scottish and Irish Joint-Stock Companies to 1720,* Cambridge, UK, 1911.

Seligman, Edwin, *Loans versus Taxes in War Finance,* New York, 1918.

Seligmann, Armand, *La Première Tentative d'emission fiduciaire en France: Élude sur les billets de monnaie du Trésor Royal à la fin du règne de Louis XIV (1701–1718),* Paris, 1925.

Sen, S. N., *Ancient Indian History and Civilization,* New Delhi, 1988.

Shakespeare, H. J., *The Royal Loans,* Shrewsbury, UK, 1986.

Sharkey, Robert P., *Money, Class, and Party,* Baltimore, 1959.

Sharpe, Kevin, *The Personal Rule of Charles I,* New Haven, CT, 1992.

Shatzmiller, Joseph, *Shylock Reconsidered: Jews, Moneylending, and Medieval Society,* Berkeley, CA, 1990.

Shelton, Judy, *The Coming Soviet Crash: Gorbachev's Desperate Pursuit of Credit in Western Financial Markets,* New York, 1989.

Sherman, Senator John, *Speeches and Reports of John Sherman,* New York, 1879.

Sherwig, J. M., *Guineas and Gunpowder,* Cambridge, MA, 1969.

Sieveking, Heinrich, *Studio sulle finanze Genovesi nel Medievo,* Genoa, 1906.

Simonsen, Jorgen Baek, *Studies in the Genesis and Early Development of Caliphal Taxation System,* Copenhagen, 1988.

Skidelsky, Robert, *John Maynard Keynes*, London, 1983–2000.

Skinner, Quentin, *The Foundations of Modern Political Thought,* Cambridge, UK, 1978.

Smith, Adam, *The Wealth of Nations,* London, 1776.

Smith, F. Fairer, *War Financing and Its Consequences,* London, 1936.

Smith, John Masson Jr., "Mongol and Nomadic Taxation," *Harvard Journal of Asiatic Studies,* 1970.

Sokolnikov, G.Y., *Soviet Policy in Public Finance,* Stanford, CA, 1931.

Soysal, Yasemin Nuhoglu, *Limits of Citizenship: Migrants and Postnational Membership in Europe,* Chicago, 1994.

Spooner, F. C., *The International Economy and Monetary Movements in France, 1493–1720,* Cambridge, MA, 1972.

Spufford, Peter, *Money and Its Uses in Medieval Europe,* Cambridge, UK, 1988.

Stabile, Donald, and Jeffrey Cantor, *The Public Debt of the United States: An Historical Perspective,* New York, 1991.

Stanuell, C. A., *British Consols and French Rentes,* London, 1909.

Stephens, J. N., *The Fall of the Florentine Republic, 1512–1530,* Oxford, UK, 1983.

Stern, Fritz, *Gold and Iron,* New York, 1977.

Stern, S., *Fourteen Years of European Investments 1914–1928,* New York, 1929.

Stevens, Robert Warren, *Vain Hopes, Grim Realities: The Economic Consequences of the Vietnam War,* New York, 1976.

Stevenson, D., *French War Aims Against Germany, 1914–1919,* Oxford, UK, 1982.

Stevenson, G. H., "The Imperial Administration," in: *Cambridge Ancient History,* Vol. X, Cambridge, UK, 1934.

Stone, Bailey, *The Parlement of Paris, 1774–1789,* Chapel Hill, NC, 1981.

Stourm, René, *Les Finances de l'ancien régime et de la Révolution,* Paris, 1885.

Strauss, André, "Trésor public et marché financier: Les emprunts d'etat par souscription publique (1878–1901), *Revue d'histoire moderne*, 1982.

Street, Henry, *Governmental Liability, A Comparative Study*, Cambridge, UK, 1953.

Studenski, Paul, and Hermann E. Krooss, *Financial History of the United States*, New York, 1963.

Stuijvenburg, J. H., "Prices and National Income in Holland 1620–1978," *Journal of European Economic History*, 1982.

Sussman, Nathan, "Debasements, Royal Revenues, and Inflation in France during the Hundred Years' War, 1415–22." *Journal of Economic History*, 1993.

Suter, Christian, *Debt Cycles in the World Economy*, Boulder, CO, 1992.

Swanson, Donald F., and Andrew P. Trout, "Alexander Hamilton, Conversion, and Debt Reduction," *Explorations in Economic History*, 1992.

Swart, K. W., *The Sale of Offices in the Seventeenth Century*, The Hague, 1949.

Sydenham, M. J., *The First French Republic, 1792–1804*, London, 1974.

Sylla, Richard, "William Duer and the Stock Market Crash of 1792," *Friends of Financial History*, 1992.

Tacitus, *Germania*, ed. J.G.C. Anderson, Oxford, UK, 1938.

Taylor, George, *Hamilton and the National Debt*, Boston, 1967.

Taylor, George V., "The Paris Bourse on the Eve of Revolution, 1781–89," *American History Review*, 1962.

Tennin, Peters, "Price Behavior in Ancient Babylon," *Explorations in Economic History*, 2002.

Temple, William, *Observations Upon the United Provinces*, 1672, ed. J. Clark, Cambridge, UK, 1932.

t'Hart, Marjolein, " 'The Devil or the Dutch': Holland's Impact on the Financial Revolution in England, 1643–1794, *Parliaments, Estates, and Representation*, 1991.

———, *The Making of a Bourgeois State: War Politics and Finance During the Dutch Revolution*, Manchester, UK, 1992.

t'Hart, Marjolein, J. Jonker, and van J. L. Zanden, eds., *A Financial History of the Netherlands*, Cambridge, UK, 1997.

Thayer, Theodore, "The Land Bank System in the American Colonies." *Journal of Economic History*, 1953.

Thompson, I.A.A., *War and Government in Habsburg Spain. 1560–1620*, London, 1976.

Toboso Sanchez, Pilar, *La deuda publica castellana durante el antigua regimen (juros) y su liquidacion en el siglo XIX*, Madrid, 1987.

Todd, Malcolm, *Everyday Life of the Barbarians*, New York, 1972.

———, *The Early Germans*, Oxford, UK, 1992.

Tracey, James, *A Financial Revolution in the Hapsburg Netherlands, 1515–1565*, Berkeley, CA, 1985.

———, *Holland Under Habsburg Rule, 1506–1566*, Berkeley, CA, 1990.

Trachtenberg, Marc, *Reparations in World Politics*, New York, 1980.

Treadgold, Warren T., *Byzantine State Finances in the Eighth and Ninth Centuries*, Boulder, CO, 1982.

Turner, Arthur, *The Cost of War: British Policy on French War Debts, 1918–1932*, Brighton, UK, 1998.

Twitchett, D. C., *Financial Administration under the T'ang Dynasty,* Cambridge, UK, 1953.

Twysden, Sir Roger, *Certaine Considerations Upon the Government of England,* ed. J. M. Kemble, 1849.

Ulloa, Modesto, *La Hacienda Real de Castilla en el reinado de Felipe II,* Madrid, 1986.

United Nations, *Report on Public Debt,* Lake Placid, NY, 1947.

———, *Statistical Yearbooks,* Lake Placid, NY, 1947–1950.

———, *Public Finance Information Papers, Italy,* Lake Placid, NY, 1950.

U.S. Bureau of the Census, *Historical Statistics of the United States: Colonial Times to 1957,* Washington, DC, 1960.

U.S. Congress Joint Committee on the Economic Report, *General Credit Control, Debt Management, and Economic Mobilization,* Washington, DC, 1951.

U.S. National Monetary Commission, *Banking and Currency Systems in England, France, Germany, Switzerland, Italy,* Washington, DC, 1910.

———, *The Credit of Nations,* Washington, DC, 1910.

———, *Banking Systems in Russia, Austro-Hungary, the Netherlands and Japan,* Washington, DC, 1911.

U.S. Treasury, *Fourth Liberty Loan: A Handbook for Speakers,* Washington, DC, 1918.

———, *Quarterly Bulletin,* 1970–2002.

Usher, A. P., "The Origins of Banking: The Primitive Bank of Deposit, 1200–1600," *Economic History Review,* 1934.

Valentino, André, *L'Emploi des fonds des Caisses d'Épargne Qrdinaire,* Paris, 1969.

van Caenegem, R. C., *An Historical Introduction to Private Law,* Cambridge, UK, 1988.

van der Wee, Herman, *The Growth of the Antwerp Market,* The Hague, 1963.

———, ed. *The Great Depression Revisited,* The Hague, 1972.

———, "Monetary, Credit and Banking Systems," in: *Cambridge Economic History of Europe,* Vol. V, Cambridge, UK, 1977.

van Kley, Dale, ed., *The French Idea of Freedom,* Stanford, CA, 1994.

Vauban, Sebastian le Prestre, *Le Dîme Royale,* Paris, 1707.

Velde, François R., and David R. Weir, "The Financial Market and Government Debt Policy in France, 1746–1793," *Journal of Economic History,* 1992.

Vernier, Richard, *Political Economy and Political Ideology: The Public Debt in Eighteenth-Century England and America,* unpublished D. Phil. thesis, Oxford, University 1993.

Veseth, Michael, *Mountains of Debt: Crisis and Change in Renaissance Florence, Victorian Britain and Postwar America,* Oxford, UK, 1990.

Villari, Rosario, *The Revolt of Naples,* Cambridge, UK, 1993.

Volpi, Franco, *Le Finanze dei Comuni e delle Province del Regno d'Italia 1860–1890,* Turin, Italy, 1962.

Voorhuis, Jerry, *Out of Debt, Out of Danger: Proposals for War Finance and Tomorrow's Money,* New York, 1943.

Vührer, A., *Histoire de la dette publique en France,* Paris, 1886.

Waley, Daniel, *The Italian City Republics,* London, 1978.

Waquet, Jean-Claude, "Who Profited from the Alienation of Public Revenues in Ancien Régime Societies?," *Journal of European Economic History,* 1982.

Warmington, B. H., *Carthage*, London, 1969.

Weill-Raynall, Etienne, *Les Réparations allemandes et la France*, Paris, 1947.

Weir, David R., "Tontines, Public Finance, and Revolution in France and England, 1688–1789," *Journal of Economic History*, 1989.

Weiss, Martin D., *The Great Money Panic*, Westport, CT, 1980.

Weiss, Roger W., "The Issue of Paper Money in the American Colonies, 1720–1774," *Journal of Economic History*, 1970.

Welch, David, *Germany, Propaganda and Total War. The Sins of Omission*, New Brunswick, NJ, 2000.

Wheeler, M., *The Indus Civilization*, Cambridge, UK, 1960.

Whitaker, T. K., *Financing by Credit Creation*, Dublin, 1947.

White, Eugene Nelson, "Was There a Solution to the Ancien Régime's Financial Dilemma?" *Journal of Economic History*, 1989.

Whittlesey, Charles R., *The Banking System and War Finance*, New York, 1943.

Wickham, Chris, *Land and Power: Studies in Italian and European Social History, 400–1200*, London, 1994.

Wilkeson, Samuel, *How Our National Debt May Be a National Blessing*, Philadelphia, 1865.

Wilkins, Myra, *The History of Foreign Investment in the United States to 1914*, Cambridge, MA., 1989.

Winckler, Max, *Foreign Bonds, An Autopsy*, Philadelphia, 1934.

Winter, J. M., ed., *War and Economic Development*, Cambridge, UK, 1975.

Witmer, Helen E., *Property Qualifications for Parliament*, New York, 1942.

Wolfe, Martin, *The Fiscal System of Renaissance France*, New York, 1972.

Wolozin, Harold, ed., *American Fiscal and Montary Policy, from the Pages of the New York Times*, New York, 1970.

Worden, Blair, *The Sound of Virtue: Philip Sidney's Arcadia and Elizabethan Politics*, New Haven, CT, 1996.

Wormell, Jeremy, *The Management of the National Debt of the United Kingdom, 1900–1932*, London, 2000.

Yang, Lien-Sheng, *Money and Credit in China: A Short History*, Cambridge, MA., 1952.

ACKNOWLEDGMENTS

This book is the product of nearly a decade of immersion in libraries, and I would like to acknowledge the help and kindness of many people who have assisted me over the years. Perhaps the most sustained contribution has been made by Jonathan Galassi at Farrar, Straus and Giroux. Without his encouragement and support, the book might never have been written. Another long-term debt of gratitude is owed to Jonathan Steinberg, who, as my tutor at Cambridge University many years ago, instilled in me a love of history that has never died, and who read and commented on most of the chapters of the book. Several other historians have read greater or lesser parts of the manuscript. Niall Ferguson waded his way through the entire first draft, and gave me not only suggestions and encouragement, but also access to his databases of nineteenth-century bond prices. Tony Honoré, Blair Worden, and Jeremy Wormell read different chapters of the book and offered many invaluable comments and corrections. The kind contribution of their time by these readers has done much to improve the book. Needless to say, they bear no responsibility for its defects. I would also like to thank Henry Kaufman for the instructive time that I spent talking to him about the world of postwar public finance, and Frank Dickens for providing the drawings necessary to re-create the cartoon that appears in the Epilogue. My thanks are owed, too, to the staffs of the Bodleian Library and of the many other libraries in which the book was researched for their assistance and courtesy over the years.

Among the many people at Farrar, Straus and Giroux who contributed to the original hardback edition, I would like to mention two in particular. Lauren Osborne read the entire manuscript and suggested numerous improvements to bring its rather unwieldy structure into focus. Thomas LeBien picked up the project with enthusiasm and understanding, and guided the book into production with meticulous care and attention. I would also like to thank Richard Baggaley and the others at Princeton University Press who have contributed to its publication in paperback.

Finally, a special debt of gratitude is owed to my wife and children, from whom I have received unfailing love and support, and whose patience with my periodic absences and my constant absentmindedness has not gone unappreciated, however much it may sometimes have seemed that I was too glued to my computer to notice. My friends and relations, too, have displayed an exemplary willingness to suspend disbelief in a project that must at times have appeared more mythical than real.

INDEX